THE GUINNESS WHO'S WHO OF

STAGE
MUSICALS

General Editor: Colin Larkin

GUINNESS PUBLISHING

Dedicated to Lionel Bart

FIRST PUBLISHED IN 1994 BY
GUINNESS PUBLISHING LTD
33 LONDON ROAD, ENFIELD, MIDDLESEX EN2 6DJ, ENGLAND

GUINNESS IS A REGISTERED TRADEMARK OF GUINNESS PUBLISHING LTD

BRITISH LIBRARY CATALOGUING-IN-PUBLICATION DATA
A CATALOGUE RECORD FOR THIS BOOK IS AVAILABLE FROM THE BRITISH LIBRARY

ISBN 0-85112-756-8

CONCEIVED, DESIGNED, EDITED AND PRODUCED BY
SQUARE ONE BOOKS LTD
IRON BRIDGE HOUSE, 3 BRIDGE APPROACH, CHALK FARM, LONDON NW1 8BD

EDITOR AND DESIGNER: COLIN LARKIN
EDITORIAL AND PRODUCTION: ALEX OGG, SUSAN PIPE AND JOHN MARTLAND
SPECIAL THANKS: DIANA NECHANICKY, TONY GALE, MARK COHEN, DAVID ROBERTS, SARAH SILVÉ
LOGO CONCEPT: DARREN PERRY

IMAGE SET BY L & S COMMUNICATIONS LTD

PRINTED AND BOUND IN GREAT BRITAIN BY THE BATH PRESS

EDITORS NOTE

The Guinness Who's Who Of Stage Musicals forms a part of the multi-volume Guinness Encyclopedia Of Popular Music. There are now 12 titles available in the series, with further volumes planned.

Already available:
The Guinness Who's Who Of Indie And New Wave Music.
The Guinness Who's Who Of Heavy Metal.
The Guinness Who's Who Of Fifties Music.
The Guinness Who's Who Of Sixties Music.
The Guinness Who's Who Of Seventies Music.
The Guinness Who's Who Of Jazz.
The Guinness Who's Who Of Country Music.
The Guinness Who's Who Of Blues.
The Guinness Who's Who Of Soul
The Guinness Who's Who Of Folk Music
The Guinness Who's Who Of Reggae.

Over the past 90 years musical theatre, or stage musicals as the genre is known in the UK, has developed into one of popular music's more spectacular forms. As the stage settings become more elaborate and automated, we question whether or not the art of the song written for the production has declined. In my conversations with a number of leading experts of musical theatre the overall opinion is that nowadays average songs are commonplace, good songs are plentiful but terrific songs are as rare to the stage musical of the 90's as a good song was to be found in an Elvis Presley movie of the 60s. The production has taken over from the music.
In this book we explore the early days of the musical such as simplistic operettas in the 20s and productions from the 30s such as The Belle Of New York on to more sophisticated American masterpieces which include Porgy

And Bess or Showboat. Ivor Novello and Noël Coward were pioneering quality productions with memorable shows such as Bitter Sweet, The Dancing Years and Perchance To Dream. The 'great' productions came fast and furious throughout the 40s and 50s when even the most casual observer could not fail to whistle or hum some of the unforgettable songs from Oklahoma!, Carousel, South Pacific, Guys And Dolls, The Pajama Game and countless others. During the 60s Britain fought the American dominance when Lionel Bart launched Oliver!, surely one of the greatest examples of perfect musical theatre.
In the last two decades despite the remarkable consistency of people like Stephen Sondheim and Jerry Herman in Amercia, the balance has changed with further British productions such as Jesus Christ Superstar, Cats, Evita and Les Misérables becoming massive box-office blockbusters. Andrew Lloyd Webber has emerged as the genre's most powerful personality. While many of us will continue to carp about the absent 'great song', the genre will continue to produce further impressive and 'even more spectacular than the last' stage musicals.

The following publications were used to check facts: American Song (The Complete Musical Theatre Companion), Ken Bloom. American Musical Theatre, Gerald Bordman. Gänzl's Book Of The Musical Theatre, Kurt Gänzl and Andrew Lamb. The British Musical Theatre (Volume II), Kurt Gänzl. Broadway Musicals Show By Show, Stanley Green. The World Of Musical Comedy, Stanley Green. Encylopedia Of The Musical, Stanley Green. Who's Who In The Theatre, Ian Herbert. Not Since Carrie: 40 Years Of Broadway Musical Flops, Ken Mandelbaum. Spread A Little

Happiness, Sheridan Morley. *London Musical Shows On Record 1889-1989*, Robert Seeley and Rex Bunnett. *Show Tunes 1905-1991*, Steven Suskin. *Theatre Week*. Both *Variety* and *The Stage And Television Today* continue to be a vital source of news and gossip.

Of all the books stemming from *The Guinness Encyclopedia Of Popular Music* this is the most home-grown. A vast amount of the research and writing was carried out in-house by John Martland. His enthusiasm, knowledge and consistency have made this volume such an impressive work. I also acknowledge the experience and talent of Ken Bloom, America's expert. From his New York base, Ken generously and unselfishly offered to proof read, and sadly for this edition, we did not have the time to utilize his red biro. His weekly radio programme on musical theatre is highly informed relaxed and entertaining and I look forward to his continuing advise and suggestions.

Tony Gale of Pictorial Press supplied all the photographs in this volume. Once again Susan Pipe co-ordinated the production with no fuss and ridiculously good temper.

The past year has been a particularly frenetic and difficult time and I have been fortunate to have had loyal friendship, love, help and support from the following: Brian Hogg, Johnny Black, Simon Barnett, John Reiss, Jason Bryant, Mark Cohen, John Orley, Ken Bolam, Len Harrow, Kip Trevor, Jane Stobart, Mustapha Sidki, David Larkin, Sabra Elliott, Carolyne Bowler, Tom, Dan, Carmen, Nana, Leone, Joanna and Diana.

Colin Larkin, March 1994

A

Abbott, George

b. George Francis Abbott, 25 June 1887, Forestville, New York, USA. An important director, author, and producer, whose distinguished career in the American theatre has lasted for over 50 years and gained him the title of Mr. Broadway. Abbott wrote his first play, a comedy-farce entitled *Perfectly Harmless*, while studying at the University of Rochester in 1910. Three years later he made his Broadway debut playing a drunken college boy *The Misleading Lady*. He continued to appear in productions such as *Lightnin'*, *Hell-Bent For Heaven*, and *Holy Terror* until 1925. In the same year he launched his writing career with *The Fall Guy*, and in 1926, with *Love 'Em And Leave 'Em*, he began to direct. Shortly after that, he became a producer for the first time with *Bless You Sister*. Since then, Abbott has served in a combination of all three of those capacities in well over 100 Broadway productions, including a good many musicals. In the 30s and 40s there were shows such as *Jumbo* (1935), *On Your Toes*, *The Boys From Syracuse*, *Too Many Girls*, *Pal Joey* (1940), *Best Foot Forward*, *Beat The Band*, *On The Town*, *Billion Dollar Baby*, *Barefoot Boy With Cheek*, *High Button Shoes*, *Look Ma, I'm Dancin'*, *Where's Charley?*, and *Touch And Go* (1949). Although he produced the smash hit *Call Me Madam*, *A Tree Grows In Brooklyn*, and a revival of *On Your Toes* in the early 50s, for the rest of the decade, and throughout the remainder of his career, Abbott gave up producing musicals in favour of directing, and writing the librettos. It was a time when the number of new musicals on Broadway was beginning to decline, but Abbott was involved with some of the most memorable - and one or two he would probably like to forget - including *Wonderful Town* (1953), *Me And Juliet*, *The Pajama Game*, *Damn Yankees*, *New Girl In Town*, *Once Upon A Mattress*, *Fiorello!*, *Tenderloin* (1960), *A Funny Thing Happened On The Way To The Forum*, *Fade Out-Fade In*, *Flora, The Red Menace*, *Anya*, *How Now, Dow Jones*, *The Education Of H*Y*M*A*N K*A*P*L*A*N*, *The Fig Leaves Are Falling* (1969), *The Pajama Game* (1973 revival), *Music Is*, *On Your Toes* (1983 revival), and *Damn Yankees* (1986 revival). George Abbott was 99 years old when he revised and directed that last show, and Broadway celebrated in style during the following year when he became an extremely spritely centenarian. He received a special Tony Award to add to his collection which includes six other Tonys (including one presented in 1976 for lifetime achievement), the Society of Stage Directors and Choreographers Award

of Merit (1965), and the 1959 Pulitzer Prize for Drama for *Fiorello!* Over the years, Abbott's contribution to the Broadway musical has been immense. He introduced the fast-paced, tightly integrated style which influenced so many actors, dancers, singers, and particularly fellow-directors such as Jerome Robbins and Bob Fosse. Another disciple is Hal Prince, who was arguably the leading director of musicals during the 80s. He swears that in 1993 he saw Abbott, at the age of 106, re-writing his 1955 hit show *Damn Yankees!*

Further reading: *Mister Abbott*, George Abbott.

Ace Of Clubs

A 'revue musical', with book, music and lyrics by Noël Coward, *Ace Of Clubs*, which opened at London's Cambridge Theatre on 7 July 1950, was set mainly in a Soho nightclub, and involved small-time gangsters and parcels of stolen jewels - a far cry from earlier Coward shows such as *Bitter Sweet* and *Tonight At 8:30*. His songs were still of the same high quality, though, and the score contained several amusing numbers such as 'Josephine', 'Three Juvenile Delinquents', the tongue-in-cheek, 'I Like America' ('New Jersey dames go up in flames if someone mentions bed/In Chicago, Illinois, any girl who meets a boy, giggles, and shoots him dead'), and a late night invitation from a lady cat to her mate, entitled 'Chase Me, Charlie' ('I'd like to wander for miles and miles/Wreathed in smiles/Out on the tiles with you'). As usual with Coward, there were ballads of yearning and regret, such as 'Why Does Love Get In The Way?', 'I'd Never, Never Know', 'Nothing Can Last Forever', and 'Sail Away', which Coward used as the title song of one of his last shows, in 1962. The main love interest was provided by Graham Payn, and Pat Kirkwood, who registered strongly with 'My Kind Of Man'. The cast also included Sylvia Cecil, Elwyn Brook-Jones, and future leading players such as June Whitfield, Vivien Merchant, and Jean Carson. On the first night, a section of the audience continually booed the production, and, although Coward still retained a loyal theatrical following in London, *Ace Of Clubs* closed in January 1951, after a run of 211 performances. Several of the songs, such as 'Josephine', 'Sail Away', and 'I Like America', were subsequently featured regularly by Coward in his cabaret act, which received a fillip following his performances in Las Vegas in 1955.

Adams, Lee

b. 14 August 1924, Mansfield, Ohio, USA. After studying at the Ohio State University and at Columbia University's Pulitzer School of Journalism in New York, Adams worked for a time in the newspaper and magazine business before meeting composer Charles Strouse in 1949. During the 50s the new team wrote material for a great many summer resort revues, and contributed to the New York production *Shoestring '57*. In 1960 they wrote the complete score for *Bye Bye Birdie* which ran for 607 performances and starred Dick Van Dyke and Chita Rivera. Two years later, their *All American* could only manage 80 performances, although it contained the lovely 'Once Upon A Time', which was introduced by Ray Bolger and Eileen Herlie. After collaborating with Jerry Herman on just one song - 'The Parade Passes By' - for his smash hit *Hello, Dolly!* (1964), Adams and Strouse had mixed fortunes during the next few years. *Golden Boy*, starring Sammy Davis Jnr. and Billy Daniels, ran for 569 performances, *It's a Bird, It's A Plane, It's Superman* could only manage 129, but *Applause* (1970), a vehicle for the Hollywood legend Lauren Bacall, gave the songwriters their second hit and stayed around for over two years. In the 70s and 80s, it was downhill all the way for Adams and Strouse, although the latter was successful with other collaborators. *I And Albert* was dismissed by London audiences after only three months, *A Broadway Musical* gave just one performance at the Lunt-Fontanne Theatre in New York, and an attempt to cash in on a previous success with *Bring Back Birdie* was given the bird and folded after four nights. Adams turned to Mitch Leigh, the composer of *Man Of La Mancha*, a show that had run for well over 2,000 performances in the 60s, but their attempt to musicalise a biography of the legendary producer Mike Todd, which they called *Mike*, closed during its pre-Broadway try-out. Not to be outdone, five years later they managed to get it into New York under the title of *Ain't Broadway Grand*. It certainly is, but the show only stayed there for 25 performances.

Adler, Richard

b. 3 August 1921, New York, USA. A composer, lyricist, and producer, who had two hit Broadway shows in the 50s but has been unable to come up with another one - so far. The son of a concert pianist, Adler was not attracted to classical music, and studied to be a writer at the University of North Carolina before spending three years in the US Navy. After his discharge he went into the advertising business, and composed the occasional song in his spare time. In the early 50s he met Jerry Ross (b. Jerold Rosenberg, 9 March 1926, The Bronx, New York, USA, d. 11 November 1955, New York, USA), and they began to write songs together. In 1953, contracted to Frank Loesser's publishing company, Frank Music, they had a hit with 'Rags To Riches' which became a US chart-topper for Tony Bennett. After contributing several numbers to the revue John Murray Anderson's Almanac, Adler and Ross wrote the complete score for *The Pajama Game* which opened on Broadway in May 1954, and ran for

1,063 performances. Several of the songs became popular outside the show, including 'Hernando's Hideaway', 'Hey There' (a US number 1 for Rosemary Clooney), and 'Small Talk'. Almost exactly one year later they were back again with the highly entertaining baseball musical *Damn Yankees*, which once again was full of lively and tuneful songs including 'Heart', which became successful for Eddie Fisher and the Four Aces, and 'Whatever Lola Wants', a chart hit for Sarah Vaughan and Dinah Shore. The show was settling in for a run of 1,019 performances when Ross died of leukaemia in November 1955. Three years later, 'Everybody Loves A Lover', another Adler-Ross song, which does not appear to have been in a show or film, became a hit for Doris Day. After Ross's death Adler turned his hand to producing, but without much success: *The Sin Of Pat Muldoon*, Richard Rodgers' *Rex*, and *Music Is* (for which Adler also wrote the music), were major disappointments. In the 60s he wrote both music and lyrics for *Kwamina*, and *A Mother's Kisses*, but neither took off. His score for *Kwamina*, a show whose theme is a plea for racial tolerance in Africa which starred his then wife Sally Ann Howes, and was regarded as a fine piece of work, can now be reassessed following the re-release of the Original Cast recording by Broadway Angel. Adler has also been actively writing for television commercials, and directing business conventions and political rallies.

After The Ball

One of Noël Coward's lesser-known efforts, *After The Ball* marked the first occasion on which he adapted an established work - Oscar Wilde's play, *Lady Windermere's Fan* - as the basis of one of his shows. The production opened at London's Globe Theatre on the 10 June 1954, with a cast that included the American actress, Mary Ellis, star of *Rose Marie*, *Glamorous Night* and *The Dancing Years*, Graham Payn, and Vanessa Lee and Peter Graves as Lord and Lady Windermere. A generally undistinguished score (for Coward) of some 20 songs had been truncated and revised prior to the West End opening, but still retained some exquisite moments, and included 'May I Have The Pleasure?', 'Mr Hopper's Chanty', 'I Knew that You Would Be My Love', 'I Feel So Terribly Alone', 'Sweet Day', 'Why Is It Always The Woman Who Pays?', 'Quartette', 'Something On A Tray', and 'Clear Bright Morning'. *After The Ball*, Noël Coward's penultimate London show, closed in November 1954 after a run of 188 performances. His final West End outing, *Sail Away*, was eight years ahead, and part of a remarkable renaissance which he enjoyed during the 60s.

Ain't Broadway Grand

'No, it ain't,' said one reviewer. The subject of his

disappointment had begun its life as *Mike*, five years before it was re-titled *Ain't Broadway Grand* for its New York opening at the Lunt-Fontanne Theatre in New York on 18 April 1993. The 'Mike' in question is Mike Todd, the dynamic film producer, who even had a complete wide-screen process, Todd-AO, named after him. In this current Broadway metamorphosis, set in 1948, Todd (Mike Burstyn) transforms an unsuccessful, high-brow musical satire of the US presidency called *Of The People*, into a smash-hit burlesque show. This considerable achievement requires the assistance of other famous names from the past, such as Joan Blondell (Maureen McNamara), Gypsy Rose Lee (Debbie Shapiro), and comedian Bobby Clark (Gerry Vichi). With a book by Broadway veterans Thomas Meehan (*Annie*) and Lee Adams (*Bye Bye Birdie*), and music and lyrics by Adams and Mitch Leigh (*Man Of La Mancha*), *Ain't Broadway Grand* attracted a barrage of criticism for a number of reasons, not least because of its 'indulging every Jewish stereotype', and a score that was so weak that the title number had to be reprised at least five times. The rest of the songs included 'The Theatre, The Theatre', 'Waiting In The Wings', 'Girls Ahoy!', 'A Big Job', 'The Man I Married', 'You're My Star', 'They'll Never Take Us Alive', and 'Time To Go'. That time came for *Ain't Broadway Grand* on 9 May, when it closed after just 25 performances.

Ain't Misbehavin'

An anthology celebrating the work of the great jazz pianist and entertainer, Thomas 'Fats' Waller, which included many of the songs he composed, and others that he recorded and are indelibly associated with him. *Ain't Misbehavin'* started out as a series of cabaret performances at the Manhattan Theatre Club, New York, in February 1978, before moving to the Longacre Theatre in May of that year. Conceived by Murray Horwitz and Richard Maltby Jnr., who also staged the show, *Ain't Misbehavin'* immediately captured the imagination of critics and public alike, and settled in for a long run. The musical supervision, orchestrations and arrangements were by Luther Henderson, who also played the piano for a cast of five: Nell Carter, Andre De Shields, Armelia McQueen, Ken Page, and Charlaine Woodard. During the show's spell on Broadway, Debbie Allen took over from Charlaine Woodard, in a production that reeked of the Harlem joints of the 30s, and accurately captured the sheer exuberance of Waller's style and humour through a selection of some 30 songs, which included 'Your Feet's Too Big', 'I'm Gonna Sit Right Down And Write Myself A Letter', 'When The Nylons Bloom Again', 'Keepin' Out Of Mischief Now', 'Yacht Club Swing', 'Honeysuckle Rose', and 'The Jitterbug Waltz'. After a run of 1,604 performances, the show was revived on Broadway 10

years later, complete with all five members of the original cast, and the fun started all over again.

Allegro

The third collaboration between Richard Rodgers and Oscar Hammerstein was completely out of character, coming as it did between two of their blockbusters, *Carousel* and *South Pacific*. Instead of adapting an established work as the basis of the show, Hammerstein's original book dealt with the corruption of a young doctor by a large Chicago hospital, complete with its wealthy, not necessarily unhealthy, patients. Married to his childhood sweetheart who is intent on the good life regardless of her husband's happiness or ethics, Joseph Taylor Jnr. (John Battles), eventually becomes disillusioned with his meaningless life, discovers his wife, Jennie (Roberta Jonay) is having an affair with one of the hospital's most important benefactors, turns down the offer of the hospital's top job, and goes back to his father's practice in the 'sticks', taking with him his new love (and a devoted admirer of his principles), Nurse Emily West (Lisa Kirk). A 'Greek chorus', which was placed at one side of the stage, spoke directly to the cast and to the audience, and provided a commentary on the proceedings. Rodgers and Hammerstein's score contrasted the romantically inclined 'A Fellow Needs A Girl', 'You Are Never Away', and 'So Far', with the affectionately reproachful 'The Gentleman Is A Dope', and the more robust 'Allegro', 'Money Isn't Everything', and 'Yatata, Yatata'. An ambitious, innovative work, with an unconventional set designed by Joe Mielziner, directed and choreographed by Agnes de Mille, *Allegro* ran for 315 performances on Broadway. Not many, when compared to some of the other Rodgers and Hammerstein productions, but it remains a show that is still regarded with affection and admiration, especially in London, where it has been revived twice in concert versions as part of the series of 'Lost Musicals' devised by Ian Marshall Fisher.

And So To Bed

This musical adaptation of J.B. Fagan's famous play about the English Elizabethan diarist, Samuel Pepys, opened in London in October 1951, and was the somewhat surprising brainchild of Leslie Henson, one of England's most celebrated theatrical clowns; it proved to be his last West End musical. Vivian Ellis contributed an intriguing 17th century-style score, which contained a mixture of musical influences, such as madrigal, jig, sarabande, and rigaudon, in a variety of numbers that included the charming 'Love Me Little, Love Me Long', and 'Gaze Not On The Swans', along with 'Amo, Amas', 'And So To Bed', 'Bartholemew Fair', 'Moppety Mo', and 'Beauty Retire'. Leslie Henson (complete with periwig) played Samuel Pepys, with Betty Paul as his wife. Paul had starred in one of Ellis's big 40s hits, *Bless The Bride*. The remainder of the cast included the American actress, Jessie Royce Landis, as Pepys's lover, Mistress Knight, and, fresh from his native Australia, Keith Michell as Charles II. Michell would later go on to another celebrated regal role as the star of the television series and film of *Henry VIII And His Six Wives*. *And So To Bed* was a popular show, and ran in the West End for 323 performances, closing in July 1952. In the following year, Leslie Henson toured with a revised version in which Mistress Knight and the King were played by the popular husband and wife singing duo, Anne Ziegler and Webster Booth.

Anderson, Leroy

b. 29 June 1908, Cambridge, Massachusetts, USA, d. 18 May 1975. Anderson studied at the New England Conservatory of Music and at Harvard University, where he was organist and choirmaster from 1929-1935. During most of this same period he was also orchestral director at the university. In 1935 he left the comparative security of academia to earn his living as a freelance musician. He composed and arranged music for the Boston 'Pops' Orchestra, then under the direction of Arthur Fiedler, and began to build a reputation as a composer of light orchestral works. One of his first successes, composed in 1939, was 'Jazz Pizzicato'. Anderson was in the US Army for four years from 1942, then returned to his career with a string of popular compositions, most of which he recorded with specially assembled orchestras. His best-known works include 'Fiddle-Faddle', 'Syncopated Clock', 'Sleigh Ride', 'Blue Tango', 'Belle Of The Ball', 'Musical Typewriter', 'Plink, Plank, Plunk', 'Serenata' and the tune that became his theme, 'Forgotten Dreams'. He died in May 1975.

Anderson, Maxwell

b. 15 December 1888, Atlantic, Pennsylvania, USA, d. 28 February 1959, Stamford, Connecticut, USA. A distinguished author and librettist, Anderson studied at Stanford and North Dakota Universities before working on newspapers in the late teens/early 20s. As a playwright his works for the theatre include *What Price Glory?*, *Mary Of Scotland*, *Both Your Houses* (Pulitzer Prize for Drama 1933), *Winterset*, *The Wingless Victory,* and *Key Largo*. He also wrote the book and lyrics for two Broadway musicals in collaboration with composer Kurt Weill. *Knickerbocker Holiday* (1938), contained the haunting 'September Song' and 'It Never Was You', and was filmed in 1944, while *Lost In the Stars* (1944) is perhaps best-remembered for its title song which is still being recorded in the 90s. Anderson also wrote for two films, *Never Steal Anything Small* ('It Takes Love To Make A Home' and the title song), and *Midnight Lace* ('What Does A Woman Do?').

Andrews, Julie

b. Julia Wells, 1 October 1935, Walton-On-Thames, Surrey, England. After singing lessons with Madam Lillian Stiles-Allan, which formed her precise vocal style and typically English delivery, she made her professional debut in her parent's variety act at the age of 10. Two years later she performed at the London Hippodrome in the Pat Kirkwood musical, *Starlight Roof*, and the following year appeared in the Royal Command Performance. On BBC radio, she was Archie Andrew's playmate in *Educating Archie*, while appearing on stage in the title role of *Humpty Dumpty* at the London Casino at the age of 13. Her big break came in 1954 when she played Polly Brown in the Broadway production of Sandy Wilson's *The Boy Friend*. Having insisted on only a one-year contract for the latter, she was available to star with Rex Harrison in one of Broadway's major musicals, Lerner & Loewe's *My Fair Lady*, later repeating her performance in London before returning to Broadway as Queen Guinevere, with Richard Burton as King Arthur, in *Camelot*. To her chagrin, she was not required for the movie versions of the last two shows but, instead, gained an Oscar for her performance as the 'flying nanny' in the title role of Disney's *Mary Poppins* in 1964. Since then, her career in film musicals has taken her from the blockbuster heights of *The Sound Of Music* to the critical depths of the Gertrude Lawrence bio-pic *Star*, with *Thoroughly Modern Millie*, and a transvestite role in *Victor/Victoria*, in-between. The latter film, and her straight roles in movies such as *10* and *S.O.B.*which were directed by her second husband Blake Edwards, have sometimes seemed a direct effort to counter her life-long cosy, old fashioned image. Nevertheless, she has been a major film star for over 25 years, and in 1989 was awarded BAFTA's Silver Mask in recognition of her outstanding contribution to the medium. She was not so successful on the small screen, and her 1992 ABC comedy series *Julie* received poor reviews. In the same year, she sang the role of Anna in a CD recording of *The King And I*, amid general amazement that she had never played the part on the stage; British actor Ben Kingsley was her regal partner in the studio. In 1993 Andrews returned to the New York stage for the first time since *Camelot* (1960), and attracted ecstacic reviews for her performance in the Off-Broadway Sondheim revue *Putting It Together*.
Albums: *My Fair Lady* (1956, Broadway Cast) *Camelot* (1961, Broadway Cast), with Carol Burnett *Julie And Carol At Carnegie Hall* (1962), *Mary Poppins* (1964, film soundtrack), *The Sound Of Music* (1965, film soundtrack), *A Christmas Treasure* (1968), *Love Me Tender* (1983), *The Secret Of Christmas* (1977),

Julie Andrews

Broadway's Fair (1984), *The Sound Of Christmas* (1987), *Julie Andrews And Carol Burnett At The Lincoln Center* (1989), *Love Julie* (1989), *The King And I* (1992, studio cast).

Further reading: *Life Story Of A Superstar*, John Cottrell. *Julie Andrews*, Robert Windeler.

Annie

The events surrounding the chequered history of the making of *Annie*, the fourth biggest Broadway hit musical of the 70s and its 90s sequel, *Annie Warbucks*, could probably form the basis of a dramatic production capable of winning a Pulitzer Prize. The lyricist and director, Martin Charnin (b. 24 November 1934, New York, USA), is credited with the idea of producing a musical show based on the famous US comic strip, *Little Orphan Annie*. That was in 1971, but it was to be over five years later, on the 21 April 1977, before *Annie* opened at the Alvin Theatre on Broadway. As his composer and librettist, Charnin recruited Charles Strouse (b. 7 June 1928, New York, USA) and Thomas Meehan. The basic concept of the show did not immediately appeal to producers or financiers, and so it was not until it was presented at the Goodspeed Opera House, Connecticut, in the summer of 1976 (at which point producer Mike Nicolls got on board) that the *Annie* bandwagon began to roll, and a Broadway opening became a feasible proposition. The story, set in 1933, concerns the orphan Annie (Andrea McCardle) and her dog Sandy. She is trying desperately to find her parents, so that she can escape the clutches of Miss Hannigan (Dorothy Loudon), the orphanage's hard-hearted matron. In line with the show's 'greasepaint sentimentality' and 'unabashed corniness', Annie is eventually adopted by the millionaire industrialist Oliver 'Daddy' Warbucks (Reid Shelton), partly through the good offices of his friend, President Roosevelt (Raymond Thorne), whom Annie serenades with the perhaps over-optimistic 'Tomorrow', a song that apparently helps the President work out his economic policy, and also ensures 'A New Deal For Christmas'. The other numbers, which contributed to an enormous Broadway hit, and a run of 2,377 performances, included 'I Don't Need Anything But You', 'I Think I'm Gonna Like It Here', 'It's A Hard-Knock Life', 'Little Girls', 'You're Never Fully Dressed Without A Smile', 'Easy Street', and 'Maybe'. It all ended happily, if a little confusingly: Annie can finally be adopted because her parents are 'no longer with us', and the conniving Miss Hannigan is arrested for fraud. The show won several Tony Awards, including best score and best musical. In 1978, the prominent UK television actor, Stratford Johns, played Daddy Warbucks in a successful London production, and there was a West End revival in 1982. In the same

year a film version of *Annie* was released, with Albert Finney as Warbucks, and Aileen Quinn as Annie.

In January 1990, a sequel to *Annie*, entitled *Annie 2: Miss Hannigan's Revenge*, opened at the Kennedy Center Opera House in Washington D.C. During the next three years, with the constant and passionate co-operation of producer Karen Walter Goodwin, Charnin, Strouse and Meehan undertook extensive re-writes, and, with a revised title, *Annie Warbucks*, spent some time in Chicago, and toured theatres in Texas, and west coast cities such as Los Angeles, Pasadena, and San Diego. A Broadway opening was set for December 1992, postponed until March, and then April. Finally, with new producers on board, the show was slimmed-down from a $5.5 million Broadway high-risk operation, to an adventurous $1 million production which opened - with its third Annie in three years - Off Broadway at the Variety Arts Theatre on 9 August 1993. (A weary Martin Charnin said: 'This is the ninth time I have put this mother into rehearsal.') On-stage, the time is Christmas morning, and the woman from the welfare, Commissioner Harriet Doyle (Arlene Robertson), is insisting that Daddy Warbucks (Harve Presnell) finds a wife within 60 days or it's back to the orphanage for Annie (Kathryn Zaremba). The ideal candidate seems to be Daddy's Chinese secretary, Grace (Marguerite MacIntyre) ('That's The Kind Of Woman'), but he thinks that she is far too young, and favours the more mature Sheila Kelly (Donna McKechnie) ('A Younger Man'), whom we all know, well before the predictable ending, does not even stand a chance. The rest of the score included 'Annie Ain't Just Annie Any More', 'The Other Woman', 'Above The Law', 'I Got Me', 'Changes', 'Love', the jivey 'All Dolled Up', a touching tale of unrequited love, 'It Would Have Been Wonderful', and 'I Always Knew' (which was 'Tomorrow' Mark II). The show will never be another *Annie*, but then, at least, as one critic pointed out, 'Charnin, Strouse, and Meehan can now get on with the rest of their lives.'

Annie Get Your Gun

When *Annie Get Your Gun* opened at the Imperial Theatre on 16 May 1946, it was to a changed Broadway. The old-fashioned style of musical comedy had been overtaken by the massive successes of *Oklahoma!* in 1943 and *Carousel* in 1945. Nevertheless, the producers of *Annie Get Your Gun* chose to follow older principals in their staging of the new show. With a score by veteran composer Irving Berlin and a book by Dorothy and Herbert Fields, the show had a formula plot which traced the burgeoning love affair between two sharpshooters, Annie Oakley and Frank Butler, who were real-life members of Buffalo Bill's Wild West Show. Rivals in the arena, the pair overcome numerous obstacles including

Annie Oakley (*Annie Get Your Gun*)

rescuing the show from bankruptcy. In the course of the show, Annie matures from an ungainly hillbilly into a self-assured showbiz superstar. Produced by the composers of *Oklahoma!* and *Carousel*, Richard Rodgers and Oscar Hammerstein II, *Annie Get Your Gun* starred Ethel Merman in the role of Annie and her powerful performance played a major part in the show's enormous success. Berlin's score is regarded as his masterpiece, and the cast, which included Ray Middleton as Butler, and Marty Ray as Buffalo Bill, had at their disposal many outstanding song such as 'Doin' What Comes Natur'lly', 'Anything You Can Do', 'The Girl That I Marry', 'You Can't Get A Man With A Gun', 'They Say It's Wonderful', 'I Got Lost In His Arms', 'I Got The Sun In The Morning', and a rousing number that has since become an unofficial anthem for the American musical theatre, 'There's No Business Like Show Business'. *Annie Get Your Gun* ran for 1,147 performances on Broadway and the 1947 London production starring Dolores Gray and Bill Johnson was an even greater success. Mary Martin starred in a revival which toured the USA in 1957, and Merman reprised her original role for a 1966 Broadway production which included a new Berlin song, 'An Old-Fashioned Wedding'. West End revivals included one in 1986 when pop singer Suzi Quatro played Annie, and another in 1992, with Kim Criswell. The somewhat disappointing 1950 screen version starred Betty Hutton and Howard Keel.

Anyone Can Whistle

A celebrated flop, all the more so because it was the second complete Broadway score to be written by Stephen Sondheim, following on from his smash-hit *A Funny Thing Happened On The Way To The Forum* (1962). *Anyone Can Whistle* opened at the Majestic Theatre on the 4 April 1964, and closed nine performances later. Sub-titled, 'A Wild New Musical', it had a book by Arthur Laurents, who also directed. Laurents had worked with Sondheim before on the librettos of the enormously successful *West Side Story* and *Gypsy*. This time his story wasn't nearly so clear-cut - in fact it was downright confused and eccentric. Cora (Angela Lansbury) is the mayoress of a small town whose corrupt council creates a phoney miracle - a non-stop flow of water from a rock - only to find that a group of inmates from the Cookie Jar, the local mental institution, mix with the visiting tourists, so that nobody knows which is which. Nurse Fay Apple (Lee Remick) becomes romantically attached to Dr. Hapgood (Harry Guardino), who turns out to be another 'cookie'. When Sondheim's score was detached from the weird goings-on in the theatre, and heard on the Original Cast album which was recorded on the day after the show closed, it proved to be one of his most appealing, and included songs such as 'A Parade In Town', 'Come Play Wiz

Me', 'Everbody Says Don't', 'I've Got You To Lean On', 'See What It Gets You', 'With So Little To Be Sure Of', and 'Anyone Can Whistle'. The vinyl album became a highly priced cult item until the advent of the CD.

Anything Goes

Regarded as the show that confirmed Ethel Merman as a Broadway star, *Anything Goes* was originally the brainchild of P.G. Wodehouse and Guy Bolton, but their book, which set the show around a shipwreck at sea, was hastily revised by Howard Lindsay and Russell Crouse prior to the show's Broadway opening on 21 November 1934, following the sinking of the S. S. Morrow Castle a few weeks earlier. However, Wodehouse's influence is apparent in the 'goofy shipboard plot of intersecting romances', involving a hard-bitten nightclub singer, Reno Sweeney (Ethel Merman), and her friend, Billy Crocker (William Gaxton) who stows away on the liner so that he can be near his latest love, the debutante, Hope Harcourt (Bettina Hall). Much of the comedy is provided by a 'toothy British milord', a 'bogus debutante', a 'boozy Manhattan tycoon', and the accident-prone Moonface Martin (Victor Moore), a small-time gangster masquerading as a minister of religion, who is intent on becoming America's Public Enemy No. 1, but cannot even make it into the Top 10. Cole Porter's outstanding score gave Merman four numbers which were to be forever associated with her: 'I Get A Kick Out Of You', 'Blow, Gabriel, Blow', one of Porter's wittiest 'catalogue' or 'list' songs, 'You're The Top' (a duet with Gaxton), and 'Anything Goes' ('If fast cars you like/If low bars you like/If old hymns you like/If bare limbs you like/If Mae West you like/Or me undressed you like/Why, nobody will oppose'). There was also a charming ballad, 'All Through The Night', which became a hit outside the show for Paul Whiteman. *Anything Goes* played 420 performances in New York, a substantial run for the 30s, and did well in London, too, where Reno Sweeny changed her name to Reno Lagrange because she was played by the French actress, Jeanne Aubert. In 1936, a film version starred Merman and Bing Crosby, and Crosby was present again, 20 years later, when Hollywood tried once more to capture the magic of the original show. Stage revivals abounded. The 1962 New York version was reasonably successful, while the 1969 London production, starring jazz singer Marion Montgomery, was a flop. The most satisfying revival was mounted in 1987 by the Lincoln Center Theatre, with a new book by Timothy Crouse and John Weidman, and a score that was augmented by several other classic Porter songs, such as 'It's De-Lovely', 'Easy To Love', and 'Friendship'. Directed by Jerry Zaks, and brilliantly choreographed by Michael Smuin, the new production starred Patti LuPone,

Lauren Bacall (*Applause*)

who excelled in the role of Reno, with Howard McGillin as Billy Crocker, *Anything Goes* won three Tony Awards including 'best revival', and ran until September 1989, a total of nearly 800 performances. McGillin reprised his role when the Lincoln Center production transferred to London, with Elaine Paige as Reno, and the popular British actor, Bernard Cribbins as Moonface. Paige, together with the lyricist Tim Rice, was instrumental in mounting the show in the West End. In the early 90s, over 50 years after Reno Sweeney changed her name and her nationality for the 1935 London production, a further (gender) change became necessary for Reno in the all-male, gay production of *Anything Goes*, which played several US venues before the performance rights were withdrawn.

Applause

Adapted by Betty Comden and Adolph Green from Mary Orr's story, *The Wisdom Of Eve*, and the highly acclaimed 1950 movie, *All About Eve*, *Applause* marked the Broadway musical debut of the celebrated film star, Lauren Bacall. Her performance as Margo Channing, the ghastly, ageing stage actress, who somehow allows her life and her lover, Bill Harrington (Len Cariou), to be taken over by an adoring young fan, Eve Harrington (Penny Fuller), won Bacall a great deal of applause from the critics and public alike, following its opening at New York's Palace Theatre on 30 March 1970. The score, by Charles Strouse and Lee Adams, was not generally considered to be one of their best, and included 'Who's That Girl?', 'Fasten Your Seatbelts', 'Think How It's Gonna Be', 'But Alive', 'One Of A Kind', 'Welcome To The Theatre', 'Backstage Babble', 'She's No Longer A Gypsy', 'The Best Night Of My Life', and 'Applause', a rousing production number somewhat akin to 'There's No Business Like Show Business'. The show won Tony Awards for best musical, and for its director and choreographer, Ron Field, and ran for 896 performances. During the run, Lauren Bacall was succeeded by two other highly popular movie actresses, Anne Baxter, who had played Eve Harrington in the movie, and Arlene Dahl. Bacall recreated her role in London in 1972, where *Applause* ran for nearly a year.

Apple Tree, The

An unconventional show, consisting of three one-act musical plays, *The Apple Tree* opened at the Shubert theatre in New York on the 18 October 1966. The cast included Barbara Harris, Larry Blyden, Carmen Alvarez, Robert Klein, Marc Jordan, and Alan Alda - several years before he made an enormous impact in the television series, *MASH*. In Act I of *The Apple Tree*, Alda played the part of Adam in an adaptation of Mark Twain's *The Diary Of Adam And Eve*. In Act II,

which was based on Frank R. Stockton's story, *The Lady Or The Tiger*, he had the role of the brave Captain Sanjar, who, after being caught in an ungentlemanly amorous situation with a Princess (Barbara Harris), is required to go through one of two doors - to greet the 'lady' or the 'tiger'. The third act was taken from Jules Feiffer's fantasy, *Passionella*, the tale of a poor little chimney sweep (Harris), who dreams she is a big movie star, and marries Flip (Alda), a hip-swivelling rock 'n' roll sensation in a spectacular sequence directed by Mike Nicholls making his Broadway musical debut. Jerry Bock and Sheldon Harnick wrote the score, and collaborated with Jerome Coopersmith on the book. The songs included 'The Apple Tree', 'Here In Eden'. 'Eve', 'Lullaby (Go to Sleep, Whatever You Are)', 'Beautiful, Beautiful World', 'Oh, To Be A Movie Star', 'Which Door?', 'Gorgeous', 'Fish', 'What Makes Me Love Him?', and 'I've Got What You Want'. Barbara Harris won the 1967 Tony Award for best actress, and *The Apple Tree* ran for over a year, a total of 463 performances

Arc de Triomphe

Ivor Novello and Mary Ellis, two of the West End's brightest stars of the 30s and 40s, were reunited in this show for the first time since *The Dancing Years* (1939). *Arc De Triomphe*, set in the early 1900s, opened at London's Phoenix Theatre on 9 November 1943. With Novello's book and music, and Christopher Hassall's lyrics, Ellis was cast as a French opera singer, Marie Forêt, whose progress through a tormented and dramatic plot, leading to her eventual elevation as a great prima donna, involved her in repelling the advances of the impresario, Adhémar Janze (Raymond Lovell), in favour of an on/off love affair with a struggling cabaret performer, Pierre Bachelet (Peter Graves), who was later killed in World War I. The climax of the piece was a one-act opera, *Joan Of Arc*, which gave Mary Ellis the opportunity to prove what a magnificent actress and singer she was. Elisabeth Welch, another favourite of Novello's, sang 'Dark Music', and the rest of the score, which was not considered by the critics to be out of Novello's top drawer, included 'Easy To Live With', 'The Shepherd's Song', 'Paris Reminds Me Of You', 'Waking Or Sleeping', 'Man Of My Heart', and 'France Will Rise Again', which received a rousing treatment from Ellis. Unable to acquire the Adelphi Theatre because a smash-hit revival of *The Dancing Years*, in which he himself was appearing, was still in residence, Novello opted to present *Arc de Triomphe* at the Phoenix, where the stage was really much too small, and the production suffered accordingly. London's wartime air raids did not help much either, and the show closed in May 1944 after a run of 222 performances.

Arcadians, The

There has probably never been a more appropriate sub-title for a show than the one accorded *The Arcadians*: 'A Fantastic Musical Play' sums it up perfectly. One reason for its durability and continued popularity may well be that audiences are constantly returning in the hope of furthering their understanding of the extremely complicated plot. On the other hand, they may well be luxuriating in the delightful and tuneful score, with music by Lionel Monkton and Howard Talbot, and lyrics by Arthur Wimperis. *The Arcadians* opened at the Shaftesbury Theatre in London on 28 April 1909, and the diabolical plot was the work of librettists Mark Ambient and Alexander M. Thompson. According to them the peaceful community of Arcady, which has been forgotten by Old Father Time, is shattered when an aeroplane, which they think is a serpent, lands in their midst. The pilot, James Smith (Dan Rolyat), who thinks he is in the Garden of Eden, tells a lie (lying is not tolerated in Arcady), so he is dropped into the Well of Truth and emerges as the shepherd, Simplicitas. He and the lovely Sombra (Florence Smithson) travel to London where, since his transformation, he is no longer recognized, so he opens a restaurant with his former business partner's wife. And that is only a very small part of the story. In Act 2 there is a scene at the Askwood race track in which the fashionable onlookers look through their binoculars at imaginary horses. A similar scene was created more than 40 years later by Alan Jay Lerner in *My Fair Lady*, although he did not arrange to bring the winning horse on stage, as producer Robert Courtneidge did for *The Arcadians*. The show had a truly memorable score, and was full of engaging songs such as 'The Pipes Of Pan', 'The Joy Of Life', and 'Already Is Ever Young', all sung by Florence Smithson; 'The Girl With The Brogue' (Phyllis Dare), 'Charming Weather' and 'Half Past Two' (Phyllis Dare and Harry Welchman), 'Somewhere' (Dan Rolyat), and 'My Motter', which is sung in typically gloomy fashion by Alfred Lister. He plays the jockey Peter Doody, who is attacked by his horse. Another important song, 'All Down Piccadilly', was added at a later date, and became an accepted part of the score. *The Arcadians* became all the rage in Edwardian London, and enjoyed an incredible run of 809 performances. Robert Courtneidge's daughter, Cicely Courtneidge, was in the cast for a time, and, some years later, starred with her husband, Jack Hulbert, in one of the many revivals of the show. An American production played at the Liberty Theatre in New York for 193 performances during the early part of 1910, and a silent film version was released in 1927. In 1993, a CD containing a comprehensive recording of the complete score, first issued in 1968, was released in the UK, along with several tracks which were actually made by members of the original cast.

Are You Lonesome Tonight?

Alan Bleasdale's 'allegory-biography' of Elvis Presley, directed by Roger Lefévre, opened on 13 August 1985 at London's Phoenix Theatre, with the sight of the King's coffin being placed into the back of a hearse, closely attended in death (as in life) by his manager, Colonel Tom Parker (Roger Booth), who was clutching a Presley doll. This was seen by some as an attempt by Bleasdale to symbolise the singer as a working-class hero who was shamelessly exploited during his life, and to 'redress the balance' following the 'muck-raking biographies' that appeared following Presley's death in 1977. The stage set, designed by Voytek, and built on three levels, was dominated by an enormous floral guitar and foil-wrapped Cadillac radiators. Upstairs, the young Presley (Simon Bowman), gave an electric performance, and 'scaled the pelvic heights of 'Jailhouse Rock' and 'Hound Dog'', while disaffected roadies and other former aides dished the dirt to the gentlemen of the press. Downstairs, Martin Shaw, complete with the purple jump-suit and protective shades, portrayed 'the bloated former idol, laden with obscene breakfasts', as a self-mocking, yet still sensually arrogant wreck. The show's highspots were inevitably the spectacular set-pieces featuring Presley's imperishable hits, such as 'Blue Suede Shoes', 'All Shook Up', 'One Night With You', and many more. *Are You Lonesome Tonight?* was voted the best musical of 1985 in the Evening Standard Drama Awards, and ran until July 1986, a total of 354 performances.

Arlen, Harold

b. Hyman Arluck, 15 February 1905, Buffalo, New York, USA, d. 23 April 1986. The son of a cantor, Arlen sang in his father's synagogue, but was soon playing ragtime piano in local bands and accompanying silent pictures. In the early 20s he played and arranged for the Buffalodians band, – then in 1925 shook off small-town connections when he took a job in New York City, arranging for Fletcher Henderson and working in radio and theatre, as a rehearsal pianist. Indeed, his first composition began as a rehearsal vamp and was developed into 'Get Happy', with lyrics by Ted Koehler. Arlen was soon composing songs regularly and in collaboration with Koehler wrote eight Cotton Club revues, one of which included a song, 'Stormy Weather', which Ethel Waters made into an American classic. In 1934 Arlen went to Hollywood to write songs, but continued composing for Broadway musicals. Apart from Koehler, his lyricists have included Dorothy Fields, Les Robin, Johnny Mercer, Yip Harburg and Ira Gershwin. Among the stage shows for which

Arlen wrote were *Earl Carroll Vanities* (which included 'I've Got The World On A String' and 'I Gotta Right To Sing The Blues'), *Rhythm Mania* ('The Devil And The Deep Blue Sea') and *St. Louis Woman* ('Come Rain Or Come Shine'). In Hollywood he worked on *Take A Chance* (1937), which included 'It's Only A Paper Moon', *Star-Spangled Rhythm* (1941, 'Hit The Road To Dreamland'), *The Sky's The Limit* (1943, 'One For My Baby' and 'My Shining Hour'). Among other great successes, mostly written for films but which have become an integral part of American music, are 'The Man That Got Away', 'Let's Fall In Love', 'Blues In The Night', 'That Old Black Magic', and a song written for (but almost cut from) the 1939 film *The Wizard Of Oz,* 'Over The Rainbow'. Arlen's songs have been recorded by countless singers and used frequently by jazz artists. He also made occasional records himself, singing with Duke Ellington and with Barbra Streisand. In 1993 a revue entitled *Sweet And Hot: The Songs Of Harold Arlen*, was circulating in the USA.

Selected albums: *Harold Sings Arlen (With Friend)* (1966), *Harold Arlen In Hollywood* (1979), *Harold Sings Arlen* (1983), *I Love To Sing* (1988).

As The Girls Go

A vehicle for the ex-vaudeville headliner, 60 years old Bobby Clark, who was making his last Broadway appearance in a musical, *As The Girls Go* opened at the Winter Garden Theatre on 13 November 1948. In William Roos's highly imaginative book, Waldo Wellington (Clark), is the husband of Lucille Thompson Wellington (Irene Rich), the first woman President of the United States. That makes Waldo the First Gentleman, which apparently gives him licence to constantly chase dozens of nearly naked girls while running through an extensive repertoire of pure hokum, with the accent on the clever manipulation of props, and other noisy, fast-moving pieces of business. Jimmy McHugh and Harold Adamson's score contained several good songs, such as 'You Say The Nicest Things, Baby' and 'I Got Lucky In The Rain', both of which proved to be appealing duets for Bill Callahan, who played the president's son, and his girl friend, Kathy Robinson (Betty Jane Watson). Watson was replaced during the show's run by Fran Warren, a popular vocalist who had several US hits, including 'A Sunday Kind Of Love'. The show's other songs included 'As The Girls Go', 'Father's Day', 'It's More Fun Than A Picnic', 'There's No Getting Away From You', the brash and progressive 'Rock, Rock, Rock', and Clark's amusing 'It Takes A Woman To Take A Man'. Ostensibly, the choreographer was Hermes Pan, designer of the dances for several Fred Astaire movies, but Buddy Clark no doubt inserted much mayhem of his own during the production

which ran for 420 performances.

As Thousands Cheer

Following a year after their previous collaboration on *Face The Music*, this innovative revue with some memorable music and lyrics by Irving Berlin and witty, satirical sketches by Moss Hart, opened on Broadway at the Music Box Theatre on 30 September 1933. The complete show was designed as a newspaper, with headlines, and sections devoted to features, news stories, comic strips, social affairs, theatre, and so on. The weather section gave Berlin the opportunity to introduce 'Heatwave', which was sung by Ethel Waters, and the agony column was handled by Harry Stockwell, dispensing advice for the 'Lonely Heart'. Clifton Webb and Marilyn Miller (making her last Broadway appearance before her death three years later), emerged from an old photograph, singing 'Easter Parade' in the spectacular rotrogravure sequence ('The photographers will snap us/And you'll find that you're in the rotrogravure'), and some of the most prominent household names of the day flitted through the newspaper's pages: Marilyn Miller portrayed Barbara Hutton and Joan Crawford; Helen Broderick masqueraded as Aimee Semple MacPherson, Louise (Mrs Edgar) Hoover, Queen Mary - and the Statue of Liberty; Clifton Webb somehow became John D. Rockefeller, Douglas Fairbanks Jnr., and Mahatma Gandhi; and Ethel Waters was a superb Joséphine Baker. Waters was involved in the only deliberately serious news item in an otherwise light-hearted periodical when she sang 'Supper Time', which was preceded by the headline: 'UNKNOWN NEGRO LYNCHED BY FRENZIED MOB'. The show's other numbers included 'Harlem On My Mind' (Waters), and 'How's Chances?', in which Clifton Webb (Prince Alexis Mdivani) serenaded the Woolworth hieress, Barbara Hutton (Marilyn Miller). The finale revealed one of Hart and Berlin's smartest ideas when the 'US Supreme Court' decreed that no musical show could finish with the conventional song reprises, thereby making way for a brand new number, 'Not For All The Rice In China'. *As Thousands Cheer* was a smash-hit - the Broadway show of the season that everyone wanted to see - and ran for 400 performances.

Ashman, Howard

b. 1951, Baltimore, Maryland, USA, d. 14 March 1991. A lyricist, librettist, playwright and director. After studying at Boston University and Indiana University, where he gained a master's degree in 1974, Ashman moved to New York and worked for publishers Grosset & Dunlap, while starting to write plays. One of his earliest works, *Dreamstuff*, a musical version of *The Tempest*, was staged at the WPA Theatre, New York, where Ashman served as artistic director from 1977-82. In 1979, the WPA presented a musical version of Kurt Vonnegut's *God Bless You, Mr Rosewater*, written by Ashman in collaboration with composer Alan Menken, which became a cult hit. In 1982, again at the WPA, they had even bigger success with *Little Shop Of Horrors*, the story of Audrey II, a man-eating plant. The show became the highest grossing and third-longest-running musical in off-Broadway history. It won the New York Drama Critics Award 1982-83, and the London Evening Standard Award for 'Best Musical'. As well as writing the book and lyrics, Ashman directed the stage show, and the 1961 film version, from which the song, 'Mean Green Mother From Outer Space', was nominated for an Academy Award. Disenchanted with Broadway following his flop show, *Smile*, with music by Marvin Hamlisch (1988), Ashman moved to Hollywood, and the animated features of Walt Disney. One of Ashman's own songs, with the ironic title: 'Once Upon A Time In New York', was sung by Huey Lewis in *Oliver & Company* (1988), and the following year he was back with Menken for *The Little Mermaid*. Two of their songs from the film, 'Kiss The Girl' and 'Under The Sea' were nominated for Academy Awards. The latter won, and Menken also received the Oscar for 'Best Score'. Two years later they did it again, with their music and lyrics for *Beauty And The Beast* (1991); 'Disney's latest animated triumph, boasts the most appealing musical comedy score in years, dammit'. Three songs from the film were nominated by the Academy, this time with the title number emerging as the winner, along with the score. Menken received an unprecedented five BMI awards for this work on the film. In Ashman's case his Academy Award was posthumous - he died of AIDS on 14 March 1991, in New York, USA. Menken signed a long-term contract with Disney, the first result of which was *Newsies*, a turn-of-the-century story, using real actors, with lyrics by Jack Feldman. Before Ashman died, he had been working with Menken on the songs for *Aladdin*, and one of them, 'Friend Like Me', was eventually nominated for an Academy Award. Menken completed work on the film with British lyricist, Tim Rice, and their 'Whole New World' won the Oscar, as did Menken's score. 'Whole New World' also won a Golden Globe award, and the version by Peabo Bryson and Regina Belle topped the US chart in 1993.

Aspects Of Love

It is an indication of Andrew Lloyd Webber's powerful influence on the British musical theatre during the 80s, that this show - his follow-up to the smash-hit, *The Phantom Of The Opera* - ran for over three years, and was still considered to be a failure. Prior to its opening at the Prince of Wales Theatre on 17 April 1989, the show had a £2 million box office

advance - and a widely publicised cast change. The film and television actor, Roger Moore, had been set make his West End debut as the French aristocrat, Charles Dillingham, but, after finding himself unable to cope with 'the technical side of the singing', he was replaced by the Australian actor, Kevin Colson. Based on a novel by David Garnett, *Aspects Of Love* was another 'sung-through' opera-style show, with the book and music by Lloyd Webber, and lyrics by Don Black and Charles Hart. The tale of romantic entanglements involved the young hero, Alex Dillingham (Michael Ball) and a flighty French actress Rose Vibert (Ann Crumb), whose lives are complicated by Alex's shady uncle, Charles (Kevin Colson), a bisexual Italian sculptress, Giulietta Trapani (Caron Skinns), and Jenny (Lottie Mayer), the teenage daughter of the French actress and the shady uncle. Colson and Mayer had one of the best numbers, the enchanting 'The First Man You Remember', but Michael Ball, the man with the 'stupendous tenor voice', sang the big hit, 'Love Changes Everything', which he took into the upper reaches of the UK chart. The show was a springboard to his own networked television show and concert tours. *Aspects Of Love*'s other musical selections included 'Parlez-Vous-Francais', 'Seeing Is Believing', 'A Memory Of Happy Moments', 'Everybody Loves A Hero', 'She'd Be Far Better Off With You', 'Other Pleasures', 'There Is More To Love', 'Falling', and 'Anything But Lonely'. The British critics reserved judgement on the show and it was ignored by the two main theatre awards bodies, SWET and the Laurence Olivier committee, although it did receive the Ivor Novello Award for best musical. The US critics had no such reservations - they savaged it following its Broadway opening at the Broadhurst Theatre April 1990, when Ball, Crumb, and Colson reprised their London roles. 'Annoyingly shallow', 'an endless stream of clichés and predictable rhythms', 'grotesque and overproduced' have all been culled from one typical review. The show was nominated for six Tony Awards - did not win any - and folded after a run of 377 performances, losing several million dollars, and proving to a lot relieved Americans show people that even the Lloyd Webber name did not guarantee a stay of several years. However, *Aspects Of Love* did undertake road tours of the USA and several other countries around the world. The London production closed in June 1992 following 1,325 performances. During its time in the West End, the leading roles were taken by artists such as Michael Praed, Claire Burt, and Sarah Brightman who played Rose for the last few weeks of the run. In 1992, a 'chamber version' of the show was presented in some parts of the USA, directed by Robin Phillips, whose concept differed widely from the original lavish staging by Trevor Nunn, and in 1993/4 the show returned to the West End for a limited run.

Assassins

Stephen Sondheim's eagerly awaited first musical of the 90s opened for a limited engagement of two months, Off Broadway at the 139-seater Playwrights Horizons, on 27 January 1991, and, even for him, it was an extraordinary piece of work. Directed by Jerry Zaks, with a book by John Weidman, it told the stories of nine of the 13 people who have tried - four of them successfully - to kill the President of the United States. It was a cabaret-style show with a fairground setting complete with fairy lights, a shooting gallery, and a row of booths from which the assassins emerged to play out their individual dramas. Sondheim complemented their contrasting revelations and motives with a score that followed the opening 'Hail To The Chief' (intriguingly played on a calliope), with what amounted to a potted history of American popular music with its collection of marches, Kentucky waltzes, folk songs, vaudeville, - all manner of pastiche - and some wicked, mocking parodies. The assembled killers' agreement that 'Everybody's Got The Right', was followed by 'Ballad Of Booth' (John Wilkes Booth was the first successful (Lincoln) assassin); 'How I Saved Roosevelt', 'Gun Song', 'The Ballad Of Czolgosz', 'Unworthy Of Your Love', 'The Ballad Of Guiteau' (a song-and-dance number on the steps of a scaffold), 'Another National Anthem', and a reprise of 'Everybody's Got The Right'. With an outstanding cast that included Terrence Mann (Leon Czolgosz), Greg Germann (John Hinckley), Jonathan Hadary (Charles Guiteau), Eddie Korbich (Guiseppe Zangara), Lee Wilkoff (Samuel Byck), Annie Golden (Lynette 'Squeaky' Fromme), Debra Monk (Sara Jane Moore), Victor Garber (John Wilkes Booth), and Jace Alexander (Lee Harvey Oswald), Assassins was described variously as 'an attack on the American Dream', 'Sondheim's angriest work since Sweeney Todd', 'a lethally brilliant musical', and 'an aimless project'. The New York run sold out immediately, as did the London production which was mounted at the newly refurbished Donmar Warehouse in October 1992. For London, Sondheim added a new number, 'Something Just Broke', for a scene late in the show that portrayed the reaction of some bystanders to President Kennedy's assassination, perpetrated by the latest in the line of what Assassins' librettist, John Weidman, called the 'peculiarly American people'.

Astaire, Fred

b. Frederick Austerlitz, 10 May 1899, Omaha, Nebraska, USA, d. 22 June 1987. By the age of seven Astaire was dancing in vaudeville with his sister, Adele (b. 18 September 1896, d. 25 January 1981).

The duo made their Broadway debut in 1917 and the following year were a huge success in The Passing Show Of 1918. During the 20s they continued to dance to great acclaim in New York and London, their shows including Lady, Be Good! (1924) and Funny Face (1927). They danced on into the 30s in The Band Wagon (1931). but with The Gay Divorce, (1932) their partnership came to an end. Adele married Charles Cavendish, the younger son of the Duke of Devonshire. The Astaires had dabbled with motion pictures, perhaps as early as 1915 (although their role in a Mary Pickford feature from this year is barely supported by the flickering remains), but a screen test for a film version of Funny Face had resulted in an offhand summary of Adele as 'lively' and the now infamous dismissal of Astaire: 'Can't act. Can't sing. Balding. Can dance a little.' Despite this negative view of his screen potential, Astaire, now in need of a new direction for his career, again tried Hollywood. He had a small part in Dancing Lady (1933) and was then teamed with Ginger Rogers for a small spot in Flying Down To Rio (1933). Their dance duet was a sensation and soon thereafter they were back on the screen, this time as headliners in The Gay Divorcee (1934). A string of highly successful films followed, among them Roberta and Top Hat (both 1935), Follow The Fleet and Swing Time (both 1936), Shall We Dance? (1937) and The Story Of Vernon And Irene Castle (1939). Astaire then made a succession of films with different dancing partners, including Paulette Goddard in Second Chorus (1940), Rita Hayworth in You'll Never Get Rich (1941) and You Were Never Lovelier (1942), and Lucille Bremer in Yolanda And The Thief (1945) and Ziegfeld Follies (1946). His singing co-leads included Bing Crosby in Holiday Inn (1942) and Blue Skies (1946) and Judy Garland in Ziegfeld Follies and Easter Parade (1948). He was reunited with Rogers in The Barkleys Of Broadway (1949) and danced with Vera Ellen, Betty Hutton, Jane Powell, Cyd Charisse, Leslie Caron, Audrey Hepburn and others throughout the rest of the 40s and on through the 50s. By the late 50s he was more interested in acting than dancing and singing and began a new stage in his film career with a straight role in On The Beach (1959). A brief return to a musical came with Finian's Rainbow (1968), but apart from hosting, with Gene Kelly, three compilation-films of musical clips, he had abandoned this side of his work. During the 50s, 60s and 70s he also appeared on US television, mostly in acting roles but occasionally, as with An Evening With Fred Astaire (1958), Another Evening With Fred Astaire (1959) and The Fred Astaire Show (1968), to sing and dance (in the three cases cited, with Barrie Chase). By the early 80s, for all practical purposes he had retired. Off-screen Astaire led a happy and usually quiet life. His first marriage lasted from 1933 to 1954, when his wife

Fred Astaire

died in her mid-40s; they had two children, Fred Jnr. and Phyllis Ava. He remarried in 1980, his second wife surviving his death on 22 June 1987. Astaire made his recording debut in 1923, singing with Adele, and in 1926 the couple recorded a selection of tunes by George Gershwin with the composer at the piano. He recorded steadily but infrequently during the 30s and 40s, and in 1952 made his first long playing record for Norman Granz, *The Astaire Story*, on which he was accompanied by jazz pianist Oscar Peterson. He continued to make records into the mid-70s, usually of songs from his films or television shows, while soundtrack albums and compilations from many of his earlier film appearances continued to be issued. As a singer, Astaire presented songs with no artifice and never did anything to dispel the impression that he was merely an amateur with few natural gifts. Yet for all this his interpretations of popular songs were frequently just what their composers and lyricists wanted, and many such writers commended him for the engaging manner in which he delivered their material. A key factor in their approval may well have lain in his decision, perhaps forced upon him by the limitations of his vocal range, to sing simply, directly and as written. Among the composers who rated him highly were masters of the Great American Popular Songbook such as Irving Berlin, Jerome Kern, Cole Porter, Gershwin, Harold Arlen, Johnny Mercer and Harry Warren.

As an actor, he was usually adequate and sometimes a little more so, but rarely immersed himself so completely in a role that he ceased to be himself and, indeed, did little to disprove the first part of his screen test summation. As a dancer, however, it is impossible to assess his contribution to stage, television and especially to musical films without superlatives. Like so many great artists, the ease with which Astaire danced made it seem as though anyone could do what he did. Indeed, this quality might well have been part of his popularity. He looked so ordinary that any male members of the audience, even those with two left feet, were convinced that given the opportunity they could do as well. In fact, the consummate ease of his screen dancing was the end result of countless hours of hard work, usually alone or with his longtime friend, colleague, co-choreographer and occasional stand-in, Hermes Pan. (Ginger Rogers, with whom Astaire had an uneasy off-screen relationship, recalled rehearsing one number until her feet bled.) For slow numbers he floated with an elegant grace and, when the tempo quickened, the elegance remained, as did the impression that he was forever dancing just a fraction above the ground. The sweatily energetic movements of many other screen dancers was, perhaps, more cinematic, but it was always something that Astaire would not have considered even for a moment. Alone, he created an entirely original form of screen dance and after his first films, all previous perceptions of dance were irrevocably altered. In the world of showbiz, where every artist is labelled 'great' and words like 'genius' have long ago ceased to have realistic currency, Fred Astaire truly was a great artist and a dancer of genius.

Selected albums: *The Astaire Story* (1952), *Three Evenings With Fred Astaire* (1958-60), *Another Evening With Fred Astaire* (1959), with Bing Crosby *A Couple Of Song And Dance Men* (1975), with Bing Crosby *How Lucky Can You Get!* (1993). Compilations: *Lady, Be Good!* (1924-33), *Starring Fred Astaire And Ginger Rogers* (1936-37), *Dancing, Swinging, Singing And Romancing* (1941-46), *Crazy Feet* (1983), *Fred Astaire Collection* (1985), *An Evening With* (1987), *Easy To Dance With* (1987), *Starring Fred Astaire* (1987), *Top Hat, White Tie And Tails* (1987), *Astairable Fred* (1988), *Cheek To Cheek* (1988), *Puttin' On The Ritz* (1988), *The Fred Astaire And Ginger Rogers Story* (1989), *The Cream Of* (1993).

At Home Abroad

Subtitled 'A Musical Holiday', this revue opened in New York at the Winter Garden Theatre on 19 September 1935. With music by Arthur Schwartz and lyrics by Howard Dietz, the setting was a world cruise, seen through the eyes of Otis and Henrietta Hatrick (Herb Williams and Vera Allen), which gave Beatrice Lillie, who played an alleged smuggler, the bride of an Alpine guide, and a ballet dancer, among other things, a good excuse to excel in 'Get Yourself A Geisha' ('Do you mind if we give you a tip on/The way you should really see a Nippon?') and 'Paree', along with her classic sketch set in a London department store in which she portrays a Mrs. Blogden-Blagg attempting to order 'two dozen double damask dinner napkins'. The other leading lady in the show was Ethel Waters, who adopted several roles, including a French lady, and a native of Harlem who lectured the natives in the Congo on her position as a 'Hottentot Potentate' ('The heathens live on a bed of roses now/And Cartier rings they're wearin' in their noses now'). Waters also sang 'Thief In The Night', 'Loadin' Time', and duetted on 'Got A Bran' New Suit' with the tap dancer, par excellence, Eleanor Powell, who was then on the brink of Hollywood stardom. In *At Home Abroad* Powell had three other numbers: 'That's Not Cricket', 'The Lady With The Tap', and 'What A Wonderful World', which she performed with Woods Miller, who also sang Schwartz and Dietz's most enduring song from the show, 'Love Is A Dancing Thing'. Comedians Eddie Foy Jnr. and Reginald Gardiner were in the cast, and the list of sketch writers included Dion Titheradge, who wrote the amusing lyric to Ivor Novello's 'And Her Mother

Ethel Waters (*At Home Abroad*)

Came Too' more than 10 years previously. The show, which ran for 198 performances, was the first Broadway musical to be directed by Vincente Minnelli, who went on to play a major part in the Hollywood musicals of the 50s.

At The Drop Of A Hat
(see **Flanders And Swann**)

Babes In Arms
Richard Rodgers and Lorenz Hart were right at the top of their form for this show which opened at the Shubert Theatre in New York on 14 April 1937. Their libretto dealt with the familiar story of a future Broadway hit show that starts out with one of a group of kids shouting: 'Hey, let's put it on in my father's barn!'. In *Babes In Arms* the kids' parents are vaudevillians who are away, working in touring productions, and their offsprings have to produce an original show or be sent to a work farm. Nobody in the cast was that well-known - not then - but that did not seem to bother audiences who were enchanted by Rodgers and Hart's outsanding score which contained some of the biggest hit songs in the history of American popular music, such as 'Where Or When', sung by the 16 years old Mitzi Green and Ray Heatherton, 'The Lady Is A Tramp' (Green), 'Johnny One Note' (Wynn Murray), 'I Wish I Were In Love Again' (Grace McDonald and Rolly Pickert), and 'My Funny Valentine' (Green). Alfred Drake, who later created the role of Curly in *Oklahoma!*, made his Broadway debut in *Babes In Arms*, singing the title song with Green and Heatherton; and Dan Dailey, destined to be one of Hollywood's favourite song-and-dance men, was in the chorus. Also featured were two more superior Hollywood hoofers, Harold and Fayard, The Nicholas Brothers. After transferring to the Majestic Theatre in October, the show continued for a run of 289 performances. The 1939 film version starred Judy Garland and Mickey Rooney.

Babes In Toyland
Victor Herbert returned to the Broadway musical stage for *Babes In Toyland* following a sabbatical as the director of the Pittsburgh Symphony Orchestra between 1901 and 1903. The show opened at the Majestic Theatre in New York on 13 October 1903, with Herbert collaborating again with Glen MacDonough, the librettist and lyricist with whom he had worked on *The Gold Bug* (1896). MacDonough's story told of the 'Babes', Jane (Mabel Barrison) and Alan (William Norris), who find themselves in Toyland following a shipwreck which has been engineered by their evil Uncle Barnaby (George Denham). During their exciting journey to the magical city they meet a host of nursery rhyme characters, such as Simple Simon, Bo Peep, Little Boy Blue, and many others, who help the Babes bring their wicked uncle to the Toyland court, where he gets his just deserts. The stage sets and special effects were spectacular as was Herbert and MacDonough's beguiling score, which included the lively 'March Of The Toys', along with 'Song Of The Poet', 'Go To Sleep, Slumber Deep', 'I Can't Do The Sum', 'Toyland', 'Never Mind, Bo-Peep', and 'Barney O'Flynn'. *Babes In Toyland* ran for 192 performances - a creditable performance at a time when Broadway was seeing an average of over 20 new musicals each season. Since then there have been three film versions: the well-received 1934 production starring Laurel and Hardy; a 1961 Disney adaptation, with Ray Bolger, Tommy Sands, Jack Donahue, and Annette Funicello; and the 1986 version with Drew Barrymore, which dumped most of the songs in favour of a new Leslie Bricusse score.

Baby
Baby opened at the Ethel Barrymore Theatre in New York, on 4 February 1983, and proved to be another of those musicals with a score that is considered to be outstanding, but the show itself fails to achieve its potential, and loses a lot of money. Sybille Pearson's book, based on a story by Susan Yankowitz, deals with three couples: a dean and his wife in their 40s with three children in college; an athletics coach and his wife in their 30s who are yearning for a child (Nick is 'shooting blanks', according to the doctor); and a pair of students who believe that becoming parents is 'a breeze'. As the show opens, all of the couples believe they are expecting babies. It transpires that Nick and his Pam are mistaken, and one of the highlights of the witty and sensitive score by lyricist Richard Maltby Jnr. (who also directed) and composer David Shire, is 'Romance', the song that accompanies their efforts to reverse that fact, at 11 pm precisely on certain days of the month. The score was not the show's problem: it included several emotional, amusing and pertinent numbers, such as 'And What If We Had Loved Like That?', 'Baby, Baby, Bay', 'What Could Be Better?', 'I Want It All', 'Fatherhood Blues', 'At Night She Comes Home To Me', and the ballad of affirmation, 'The Story Goes On'. One of reasons for the failure of *Baby* to attract

audiences in sufficient numbers to affray its costs, could well have been the word-of-mouth concerning a scene in which the progress of sperm and the development of a foetus was projected onto a large set of computer-operated curtains. Perhaps, even in the enlightened 80s, patrons of the musical theatre were not prepared for that. The cast of Liz Callaway, James Congdon, Catherine Cox, Beth Fowler, Todd Graff, and Martin Vidnoc, soldiered on for 241 performances in New York, and the show was premiered in the north of England in 1990, where two of its stars were American song-and-dance man, Tim Flavin, and the British actress, Dilys Watling.

Bad Boy Johnny And The Prophets Of Doom

'The most blasphemous show in town - and it's being performed in a house of God', wrote one critic after this rock musical materialized on 27 January 1994 at the Union Chapel, a Congregational church in the inner-London borough of Islington, following it's successful run in Australia. Over the past several years, UK audiences have become accustomed to some extremely weird Antipodean goings-on via imported television soaps such as *Neighbours* and *Home And Away*, but even those programmes have so far stayed clear of storylines involving 'a foul-mouthed harmonica-playing pope in dark glasses who dies of heart failure while being seduced by a naked nun (there is also a Virgin Mary stripper and a priest who urinates into the Communion Cup)'. Daniel Abineri, a veteran of *The Rocky Horror Show*, conceived, wrote, and directed this highly controversial production, and chose Mark Shaw, the regular frontman of an appropriately titled band Then Jericho, to play Big Bad Johnny, the first rock 'n' roll Pope. The permanently phlegmatic comedian Craig Ferguson is Father MacLean, the holy father's 'all-raping, all-pillaging' nemesis, and the lightly-clad Desire is portrayed by Eve Barker. The show closed after only 10 performances following protests from nuns, and others including Father Kit Cunningham of St. Ethelreda's Church, Holborn, London, who said the musical should be consigned to the dustbin. The author and critic Sheridan Morley commented: 'Suddenly there is a scary puritanism moving through. It's as if we've gone back to the 1950s.'

Bailey, Pearl

b. 29 March 1918, Newport News, Virginia, USA, d. 17 August 1990, Philadephia, Pennsylvania, USA. Pearlie Mae, as she was known, was an uninhibited performer, who mumbled her way through some songs and filled others with outrageous asides and sly innuendoes. She entered the world of entertainment as a dancer but later sang in vaudeville, graduating to the New York nightclub circuit in the early 40s. After working with the Noble Sissle Orchestra, she became band-vocalist with Cootie Williams with whom she recorded 'Tessa's Torch Song' previously sung by Dinah Shore in the movie *Up In Arms*. Bailey received strong critical acclaim after substituting for Rosetta Tharpe in a show, and was subsequently signed to star in the 1946 Harold Arlen/Johnny Mercer Broadway musical *St. Louis Woman*. A year later her slurred version of 'Tired' was the highlight of the movie *Variety Girl*. Subsequently her best films were *Carmen Jones* (1954), *St. Louis Blues* (1958) and *Porgy And Bess* (1959). During her stay with Columbia Records (1945-50) Bailey recorded a series of duets with Frank Sinatra, trumpeter Oran 'Hot Lips' Page and comedienne Moms Mabley. She also recorded some solo tracks with outstanding arrangers/conductors, Gil Evans and Tadd Dameron. Upon joining the Coral label in 1951, she employed Don Redman as her regular musical director, the association lasting for 10 years. In 1952, she had her biggest hit record 'Takes Two To Tango'. In that same year she married drummer Louie Bellson and he took over from Redman as her musical director in 1961. Although few of her records have sold in vast quantities, Bailey had always been a crowd-pulling, on-stage performer and, following her early stage triumph in *St. Louis Woman*, was later cast in other shows including *The House Of Flowers*, *Bless You All*, *Arms And The Girl* and an all-black cast version of *Hello, Dolly!*. She has also starred in several US television specials, playing down the double-entendre that caused one of her albums, *For Adults Only*, to be 'restricted from air-play'.

Selected albums: *Pearl Bailey A-Broad* (1957), *Gems* (1958), *For Adults Only* (1958), *Sings!* (1959), *St. Louis Blues* (1959), *Porgy & Bess & Others* (1959), *More Songs For Adults* (1960), *Songs Of Bad Old Days* (1960), *Naughty But Nice* (1961), *Songs She Loves By Arlen* (1962), *Come On Let's Play With Pearlie Mae* (1962), *Intoxicating* (1964), *Songs By Jimmy Van Heusen* (1964), *For Women Only* (1965), *Birth Of The Blues* (c.60s), *Cultered Pearl* (c.60s), *The Definitive* (c.60s), *For Adult Listening* (c.60s), *About Good Girls & Bad Boys* (c.60s), *C'est La Vie* (c.60s), *Risque World* (c.60s). Selected compilations: *The Best Of - The Roulette Years* (1991). Further reading: *The Raw Pearl*, Pearl Bailey.

Baker's Wife, The

With a book by Joseph Stein based on the 1938 movie, *La Femme de Boulanger* by Marcel Pagnol and Jean Giono, and a score by Stephen Schwartz, *The Baker's Wife* was supposed to be the major musical attraction of the 1976/7 Broadway season, but it did not get as far as New York. After opening in Los Angeles at the Dorothy Chandler Pavilion on 11 May 1976, it then toured for six months before closing in Washington, D.C. While the show was on the road the cast changed frequently, but Topol, the Israeli-

Pearl Bailey

born actor who had triumphed in *Fiddler On The Roof* more than 10 years earlier, stayed almost until the end, and Patti LuPone, star of another famous film adaptation, the 1993 musical, *Sunset Boulevard*, was at one time the leading lady. The simple plot involved a baker, who, after finding that a handsome chauffeur is driving his wife crazy, refuses to supply the town with any more bread until she comes to her senses and returns to him. Stephen Schwartz, whose run of hit shows had included *Godspell*, *Pippin*, and *The Magic Show*, provided the music and lyrics for several delightful songs, including 'Gifts Of Love', 'If I Have To Live Alone', 'Merci, Madame', 'Chanson', 'Where Is The Warmth?', 'Endless Delights', 'The Luckiest Man In The World', and 'Serenade'. Such was the quality and accessibility of the score that *The Baker's Wife* became a favourite subject for provincial theatre groups. On 27 November 1989, a re-worked production opened at the Phoenix Theatre in London. Directed by Trevor Nunn, whose 80s stage musical triumphs had included *Cats*, *Starlight Express*, and *Les Misérables*, the show starred Nunn's then-wife, Sharon Lee Hill, and Alun Armstrong, who was to have great success four years later in a London 'chamber' version of Stephen Sondheim's *Sweeney Todd*. Schwartz wrote several new numbers, such as 'Buzz-A-Buzz', 'Plain And Simple', and 'If It Wasn't For You', but *The Baker's Wife*'s folded after a disappointing run of only 56 performances.

Balalaika

A revised version of the 1933 musical play, *The Great Hussar*, with a book and lyrics by Eric Maschwitz, and music by George Posford and Bernard Grün, *Balalaika* opened at the Adelphi Theatre in London on 22 December 1936. The plot's initial locale is the exterior of the Balalaika Night Club in Montmartre just after World War I. An old man is singing a sad ballad ('Where Are The Snows?'), and the audience is soon transported back to the singer's homeland, the Russia of 1914, by way of the story of a lovely ballerina and singer, Lydia (Muriel Angelus), and her high-born lover, Peter (Roger Reville). With a series of lavish stage settings that rivalled even Ivor Novello's celebrated productions, the two young people survive the Revolution, foil an attempted assassination attempt on the Tsar, and finally melt into each others arms while in exile in Paris. The happy couple's principal duet was the delightful 'If The World Were Mine', and other highlights of the romantic and dramatic score included 'Red, Red Rose', 'Be A Casanova', 'Ballerina, Sad And Lonely', 'Nitchevo', 'In the Moonlight'/'Two Guitars', 'Vodka'/'Red Shirt', 'The Devil In Red', and, of course, 'At The Balalaika', which was sung in the show by the aristocratic Peter, accompanied by some Cossacks, but later achieved wider popularity, and

was recorded by such artists as Richard Tauber and Greta Keller. During its run *Balalaika* moved to different theatres within the West End, eventually closing in April 1938, after a run of 570 performances – a phenomenal performance for those days. Later in 1938 the show went on the road, and in the same year a Paris production was mounted with some additional songs by Robert Stolz. In 1939, *Balalaika* became the first British musical to be filmed in Hollywood, although, ironically, only the title song (with an amended lyric) survived from the original score. The rest of the songs were culled from various sources and composers. The film starred Nelson Eddy and the Hungarian soprano, Ilona Massey.

Ball, Michael

b. 27 July 1962, Stratford-Upon-Avon, England. After spending his early life in Plymouth, this popular singer studied at the Guildford School of Drama in Surrey before embarking on what has been, even by modern standards, a meteoric rise to fame. His first professional job was in the chorus of *Godspell* on a tour of Wales, after which he auditioned for a Manchester production of *The Pirates Of Penzance* - again for the chorus. Much to his surprise, he was given a leading role alongside Paul Nicholas and Bonnie Langford. In 1985, Ball created the role of Marius in the smash-hit musical *Les Misérables* at the Palace Theatre in London, and introduced one of the show's oustanding numbers, 'Empty Chairs At Empty Tables'. He subsequently took over the role of Raoul, opposite Sarah Brightman, in *The Phantom Of The Opera*, and then toured with her in the concert presentation of *The Music Of Andrew Lloyd Webber*. In 1989 his career really took off when he played Alex, a role that called for him to age from 17 to 40, in the same composer's *Aspects Of Love*. He was also in the 1990 Broadway production. Ball took the show's hit ballad, 'Love Changes Everything', to number 2 in the UK chart, and had modest success with one of the others, the poignant 'The First Man You Remember'. Further national recognition came his way when was contracted (for a reported £100,000) to sing all six of Britain's entries for the 1992 Eurovision Song Contest on the top-rated *Wogan* television show. He came second with the chosen song, 'One Step Out Of Time', which just entered the UK Top 20. In the same year he embarked on an extensive tour of the UK, playing many top venues such as the London Palladium and the Apollo, Hammersmith. He surprised many people by his lively stage presence and a well-planned programme which catered for most tastes, and included rock 'n' roll, Motown, standards such as 'Stormy Weather', 'You Made Me Love You', and 'New York, New York', and the inevitable show songs. 1993 saw more concerts, the release of his version of the title song from *Sunset Boulevard* (he was tipped for the lead at one time), and his participation in a new studio recording of *West Side Story*, with Barbara Bonney, La Verne Williams, and the Royal Philharmonic Orchestra. But the highlight of the year was his own six-part television series which gave him the opportunity to sing with some of the most illustrious names in music, including Cliff Richard, Dionne Warwick, Ray Charles, Monserrat Caballe, and Tammy Wynette.

Selected albums: *Always* (1993), *West Side Story* (1993), and Original Cast recordings.

Ballroom

This show brought the celebrated director/choreographer Michael Bennett back to Broadway for the first time since he contributed so much to *A Chorus Line* (1975), one of the biggest all-time hits of the musical theatre. *Ballroom* opened at the Majestic Theatre in New York, on 14 December 1978. The book was adapted by Jerome Kass from his own television movie, *Queen Of The Stardust Ballroom*, which had a music score by composer Billy Goldenberg, and lyrics by Alan and Marilyn Bergman. The trio remained on board for *Ballroom*, and added some new songs. Kass's story dealt with a lonely widow, Bea Asher (Dorothy Loudon), who meets and falls in love with Al Rossi (Vincent Gardenia) at the local dance hall, where middle-aged couples are still dancing 'in the old-fashioned way' (1978 was the year of *Saturday Night Fever*). As they become closer, Al reveals that he is (unhappily) married, and will never leave his wife, and Bea's decision to share him with someone else is spectacularly revealed in her show-stopping 'Fifty Percent'. Apart from that number and Loudon's 'A Terrific Band And A Real Nice Crowd', most of the songs, such as 'A Song for Dancin'', 'One By One', 'Dreams', 'Goodnight Is Not Goodbye', and 'More Of The Same', are performed by Nathan (Bernie Knee) and Marlene (Lynn Roberts), the vocalists at the Stardust Ballroom. Loudon and Roberts duet on 'Somebody Did All Right For Herself'/'Dreams', and Gardenia has only one chance to sing, in a duet with Loudon, entitled 'I Love To Dance'. Michael Bennett's dances ranged from foxtrots through waltzes, to 'The Hustle', which was even then three years out of date. Bea ends the bitter-sweet story, following her elevation to the Queen of the Stardust Ballroom with the heartfelt 'I Wish You A Waltz' (she died at the end of the television version), but 1978 Broadway audiences preferred the raunchy *The Best Little Whorehouse In Texas*, and the nostalgic *Eubie* to the schmaltz of *Ballroom*, which ran for just over three months.

Bamboula, The

A comparatively undistinguished piece, considering the quality of the creative collaborators: the book was by H.M. Vernon and Guy Bolton (of the Bolton-Kern-Wodehouse team); and the lyrics were written by the humorist Douglas Furber and Irving Caesar, whose *No, No, Nanette* ('Tea For Two', 'I Want To Be Happy') made its debut on Broadway in the same year. With a music score composed by Albert Sirmay and Harry Rosenthal, *The Bamboula* opened at His Majesty's Theatre in London on 24 March 1925, complete with a somewhat complicated Ruritania-style plot concerning the Prince of Corona, played by the comedian, W.H. Berry, who is mistaken for a youthful dance instructor, Jimmy Roberts (Harry Welchman), in his pursuit of the wealthy Donna Juanita da Costa (Dorothy Shale). The antics of all concerned bordered on farce, and the songs included 'Spring', 'Your Kiss Told Me', 'Sing A Song In The Rain', and 'After All These Years'. The West End run ended after 77 performances, but the show endured in subsequent provincial productions.

Band Wagon, The

Arthur Schwartz and Howard Dietz's finest revue - some say the best that Broadway has ever seen. A Max Gordon production, *The Band Wagon* opened at the New Amsterdam Theatre in New York on 3 June 1931. Unlike most of the other revues of the time on which numerous writers and composers laboured, this show reduced the collaborators to three: the playwright, humorist and drama critic, George S. Kaufman wrote the sketches with Howard Dietz, and Dietz (lyrics) and Schwartz (music) provided the songs. Heading the cast were Fred Astaire and his sister, Adele, who was making her final Broadway appearance before retiring to marry Lord Charles Cavendish. The critics were unanimous in their praise for a show in which 'each scene or episode serves to display a new angle of approach and craftsmanship'. Highlights included the opening 'It Had Better Be Good', 'New Sun In The Sky' (Astaire in white tie and tails, preening himself in front of a mirror); 'Hoops' (Fred and Adele as naughty Parisenne children), 'Where Can He Be?' (Helen Broderick), 'Dancing In The Dark' (sung by John Barker while ballerina Tilly Losch danced on an angled, illuminated mirrored floor), 'White Heat' and 'Sweet Music' (Fred and Adele Astaire), and the boisterous first act finale, 'I Love Louisa', in which the whole cast rode on a Bavarian-style merry-go-round mounted on the revolving stage. The show also featured the classic sketch, 'The Pride Of The Claghorns', a highly satirical view of Southern aristocratic values. Directed by Hassard Short, and choreographed by Albertina Rasch, *The Band Wagon* was one of those rare shows in which all the different elements - authors, artists, songs, sketches, dances, innovative lighting, and the rest - combined to create the perfect whole. It ran for

260 performances on Broadway. For the 1953 film version which teamed Fred Astaire with the top British song-and-dance man, Jack Buchanan, Schwartz and Dietz wrote 'That's Entertainment', and used several more songs taken from their other shows.

Bar Mitzvah Boy, The

Adapted by Jack Rosenthal from his original television play, *The Bar Mitzvah Boy* opened at Her Majesty's Theatre in London on 31 October 1978. The story of a young Jewish boy (Barry Angel) who finds himself unable to face his bar mitzvah ceremony, with all its significance of grown-up times ahead, did not transfer satisfactorily to the musical stage. Critics felt that the down-to-earth credibility of the original had been compromised, and that some of the characters, particularly the boy's father (Harry Towb) and mother (Joyce Blair), had become overly sweet and sentimental. The score, an Anglo-American affair, by the Broadway veteran composer, Jule Styne, and the British lyricist, Don Black, was not well received either, although there was some affection for a pretty love song, 'You Wouldn't Be You', and an amusing list song, sung by the children, 'Thou Shalt Not'. The other numbers included 'Why', 'This Time Tomorrow', 'The Sun Shines Out Of Your Eyes', 'I've Just Begun', and 'Where Is The Music Coming From?'. The show closed in January 1979 after only 77 performances. In 1987, the American Jewish Theatre presented *The Bar Mitzvah Boy* at the 92nd St. Y, Off Broadway, but without much success.

Barnum

The larger-than-life career of Phineas T. Barnum, the self-styled World's Greatest Showman, was tailor-made for a spectacular over-the-top musical and the lavish *Barnum* provided thrills and spills galore. It opened at the St. James Theatre in New York on 30 April 1980, starring Jim Dale, who gave a suitably flamboyant performance as Barnum, with Glenn Close as his wife Chary, and Marianne Tatum as Jenny Lind. Cy Coleman and Michael Stewart's score was full of entertaining numbers such as 'The Colours Of My Life', 'There Is A Sucker Born Ev'ry Minute', 'Come Follow the Band', 'Bigger Isn't Better', and 'One Brick At A Time'. The show won three Tony Awards, including one for Dale as best actor, and ran in New York for two years. The London production did even better, with another magnetic central performance, this time from Michael Crawford. When *Barnum* was revived in London in 1992 it again starred a British singer/actor, Paul Nicholas, in the role of the archetypal American showman.

Bart, Lionel

b. Lionel Begleiter, 1 August 1930, London, England. The comparative inactivity of Bart for many years has tended to cloud the fact that he is one of the major songwriters of 20th-century popular song. The former silk-screen printer was at the very hub of the rock 'n' roll and skiffle generation that came out of London's Soho in the mid-50s. As a member of the Cavemen with Tommy Steele he later became Steele's main source of non-American song material. In addition to writing the pioneering 'Rock With The Cavemen' he composed a series of glorious singalong numbers including 'A Handful Of Songs', 'Water Water' and the trite but delightfully innocent 'Little White Bull'. Much of Bart's work was steeped in the English music-hall tradition with a strong working class pride and it was no surprise that he soon graduated into writing songs for full-length stage shows. *Lock Up Your Daughters* and *Fings Ain't Wot They Used To Be* were two of his early successes, both appearing during 1959, the same year he wrote the classic 'Living Doll' for Cliff Richard. Bart was one of the first writers to introduce mild politics into his lyrics; beautifully transcribed with topical yet humourously ironic innocence, for example: 'They've changed our local Palais into a bowling alley and fings ain't wot they used to be.' As the 60s dawned Bart unconsciously embarked on a decade that saw him reach dizzy heights of success and made him one of the musical personalities of the decade. During the first quarter of the year he topped the charts with 'Do You Mind' for Anthony Newley; a brilliantly simple and catchy song complete with Bart's own finger-snapped accompaniment. The best was yet to come when that year he launched *Oliver!*, a musical based on Dickens' *Oliver Twist*. This became a phenomenal triumph, and remains one of the most successful musicals of all time. Bart's knack of simple melody combined with unforgettable lyrics produced a plethora of classics including the pleading 'Who Will Buy', the rousing 'Food Glorious Food' and the poignant 'As Long As He Needs Me' (also a major hit for Shirley Bassey, although she reputedly never liked the song). Bart was a pivotal figure throughout the swinging London scene of the 60s, although he maintains that the party actually started in the 50s. Lionel befriended Brian Epstein, the Beatles, the Rolling Stones, became an international star following *Oliver!'s* success as a film (winning six Oscars) and was romantically linked with Judy Garland and Alma Cogan. Following continued, although lesser success, with *Blitz!* and *Maggie May*, Lionel came down to reality when the London critics damned his 1965 musical *Twang*, based upon the life of Robin Hood. Bart's philanthropic nature made him a prime target for business sharks and he was wrested of much of his fortune by trusting too many people. By the end of the 60s the cracks were beginning to show; his dependence on drugs and alcohol increased and he watched many of his close friends die in tragic circumstances; Cogan with

Lionel Bart

cancer, Garland through drink and drugs and Epstein's supposed suicide. In 1969, *La Strada* only had a short run in New York before Lionel retreated into himself, and for many years kept a relatively low-profile, watching the 70s and 80s pass almost as a blur, only making contributions to *The Londoners* and *Costa Packet*. During this time the gutter press were eager for a kiss-and-tell story but Bart remained silent, a credible action considering the sums of money he was offered. During the late 80s Lionel finally beat his battle with booze and ended the decade a saner, wiser and healthier man. His renaissance started in 1989 when he was commissioned by a UK building society to write a television jingle. The composition became part of an award-winning advertisement, featuring a number of angelic children singing with Bart, filmed in pristine monochrome. The song 'Happy Endings' was a justifiable exhumation of a man who remains an immensely talented figure and whose work ranks with some of the greatest of the American 'musical comedy' songwriters. In the early 90s, his profile continued to be high, with revivals, by the talented National Youth Theatre, of *Oliver!*, *Maggie May* and *Blitz!;* the latter production commemorating the 50th anniversary of the real thing.

Batt, Mike

b. 6 February 1950. Beginning his career as an in-house music publisher and songwriter, Batt swiftly moved into production, working on albums by Hapshash And The Coloured Coat (which reputedly featured Brian Jones of the Rolling Stones) and the Groundhogs. It was not progressive rock however, as commercial ditties that best captured his talent, as evinced on numerous television advertisement jingles. By 1973, he discovered a new hit-making machine courtesy of the Wombles, a children's television programme that spawned a number of hit singles. He continued to produce for other artists, including the Kursaal Flyers, Steeleye Span and Linda Lewis. Like those 60s' producers, Andrew Loog Oldham and Larry Page, he also released some eponymous orchestral albums, including portraits of the Rolling Stones, Bob Dylan, Simon And Garfunkel, George Harrison, Elton John and Cat Stevens. Although Batt attempted to forge a career on his own as an artist, and hit number 4 with 'Summertime City' in 1975, his subsequent album forays failed to win mass appeal. Ultimately, it was as a songwriter that he took top honours, when Art Garfunkel took his 'Bright Eyes' to number 1 in 1979. Since then, Batt has continued to write for films and musicals, scoring again with David Essex's reading of *A Winter's Tale*. His ambitious stage musical *The Hunting Of The Snark* opened in London during 1991, and closed seven weeks later. It had been a favourite project of Batt's for several years. The 1986 concept album featured such diverse talents as Sir John Gielgud, Roger Daltrey, Julian Lennon, and Cliff Richard, accompanied by the London Symphony Orchestra.
Selected albums: *Schizophonic* (1979), *Tarot Suite* (1979), *Waves* (1980), *6 Days In Berlin* (1981), *Zero Zero* (1983), *Children Of The Sky* (1986), *The Hunting Of The Snark* (1986).

Mike Batt

Battling Butler

A musical farce by Stanley Brightman and Austin Melford, *Battling Butler* opened at the New Oxford Theatre in London on 8 December 1922. Jack Buchanan starred as Alfred Butler, a man who likes a good time away from his wife now and then. He pretends that he is the renowned boxer, Battling Butler, who occasionally has to spend a few weeks in isolation preparing for a fight. This enables Alfred to make his own social arrangements. Complications arise when Mrs Alfred Butler becomes suspicious, and Mrs Battling Butler takes a fancy to Alfred, who almost, but not quite, has to engage in a real bout of fisticuffs in an effort to conceal his guilty secret. The score, by composer Philip Braham and lyricist Douglas Furber, contained several engaging songs, including Alfred's plaintive 'Why Can't I?' ('Jonah got away with it/Why can't I?'), and 'It's A Far, Far Better Thing'; his duet with Mrs Battling Butler (Sylvia Leslie) entitled 'Dancing Honeymoon', and others, such as 'An Axe To Grind', 'Apples, Bananas And Pears', 'The Countryside', 'I Will Be Master', 'Mr Dumble', and 'Growing Up To Time'. The show, which marked Buchanan's first attempt at management, was a great success, and, after transferring to the Adelphi Theatre, closed in June 1923 after a run of 238 performances. It did even better in New York, when a radically revised version, without Buchanan, but with several new numbers by other composers, opened at the Selwyn Theatre in October 1923, and retained audiences' affections for 312 performances.

Beauty Prize, The

With a book and lyrics by George Grossmith and P.G. Wodehouse, and music by Jerome Kern, this show was a follow-up to the three collaborators' successful 1922 London musical, *The Cabaret Girl*. *The Beauty Prize* opened in the West End at the Winter Garden Theatre on 5 September 1923, but did not quite emulate the critical success of its predecessor, even though several artists who had appeared in *The Cabaret Girl*, including Dorothy Dickson, Heather Thatcher, and Grossmith himself, were in the cast. They were joined by the 'rubber-faced' comedian Leslie Henson who portrayed a Mr Odo Philpott - the first 'prize' in a beauty contest. The winner is Carol Stewart (Dorothy Dickson), and the duo's complicated escapades, which take them from Kensington to Florida, and several other places in-between, were eked out over three acts. The score included two amusing numbers, a duet for Grossmith and Dickson, 'You Can't Make Love By Wireless', and Henson's 'Non-stop Dancing Craze' ('Grandma's feet are getting tender/Father's burst his sock suspender'), along with others such 'It's A Long Long Day' (Grossmith), 'Honeymoon Isle' and 'Moon Love' (Dickson), 'Meet Me Down On Main Street' (Grossmith and Henson), and 'You'll Be Playing Mah-Jong', an allusion to one of the popular crazes of the day. The show had a reasonable run of 213 performances before its closure in March 1924.

Belle

One of the legendary flops of the London musical stage, *Belle* (or *The Ballad Of Doctor Crippen*), was adapted by the author Wolf Mankowitz from a play by Beverley Cross, and opened at The Strand Theatre, London, on 4 May 1961. It was more than 50 years before, in January 1910, that Doctor Hawley Harvey Crippen and his young mistress, Ethel le Neve, on the run from British police, were arrested on a ship off Canada after the captain had become suspicious and radioed Scotland Yard. The pair became known as the first criminal suspects to be 'caught by radio'. Back in London, the police found the remains of Crippen's wife, Cora Belle Elmore, buried under Crippen's cellar floor. She had once been a tawdry music hall singer, and it was in a music hall, and as a melodrama, that Mankowitz and Cross set the story of *Belle*. Jerry Desmonde, who had made his name as a brilliant straight man for Sid Field and Norman Wisdom, played George Lasher, the compère and chairman, who linked the different items with snippets of 'The Ballad Of Doctor Crippen'. The show's main characters, Crippen (George Benson), Ethel (Virginia Vernon), and Belle (Rose Hill), were joined by the entertainers, Jenny Pearl (Nicolette Roeg), who bore more than a passing resemblance to the great Vesta Tilley, and Mighty Mick (Davy Kaye) whose role could only be a tribute to another music hall legend, Little Tich. At the time Kaye was a noted comedy performer in London nightclubs. Monty Norman's score contained some 30 songs, including several entertaining pieces, mostly pastiche, such as 'Mister Lasher And The Mighty Mick', 'A Pint Of Wallop', 'Bird Of Paradise, 'Meet Me At The Strand', 'The Devil's Bandsmen', 'Waltzing With You', and 'Don't Ever Leave Me', but the show's hit number was 'The Dit-dit Song' ('His moniker was Marconi/He was such a clever sort of chap'), an amusing reference to the important role that radio played in the whole affair. The London critics savaged *Belle*, and the cartoonists had a field day, too. The show folded in June, after a run of only 44 performances.

Belle Of Mayfair, The

This musical comedy, which opened at the Vaudeville Theatre in London on 11 April 1906, was very similar in style and content to that of another Belle, *The Belle Of New York*, which was enormously popular at the turn of the century, and enjoyed several revivals in London through to the 40s. The two shows also had the same leading lady, the delightful Edna May, who was replaced during the run of *The Belle Of Mayfair* by Phyllis Dare. The rest of the cast included Farren Soutar, Murray Moncrieff, Louie Pounds, and Arthur Williams. The music was composed by Leslie Stuart, probably best known for his work on the early London smash-hit *Floradora*, and the book and lyrics were by Charles H. E. Brookfield and Cosmo Hamilton. Their score contained several pleasant songs such as 'Where You Go, Will I Go', 'Montezuma', and 'Come To St. George's'. The show had an excellent London run of 416 performances, but could only manage 140 in New York, even though it had a first rate American cast which included Irene Bentley, Christie MacDonald, and Bessie Clayton. Also added to the score was the popular 'Why Do They Call Me A Gibson Girl' (lyric: Leslie Stiles), which was sung by Camille Clifford.

Belle Of New York, The
As the 20th century dawned, London audiences were all still singing the praises and the songs from this show, which had opened at the Casino Theatre in New York on 28 September 1897. It only lasted for 56 performances on Broadway, but, when it arrived in London's West End in April of the following year, it immediately captured the imagination of the public, and surprised several important theatrical managers such as George Edwardes who had turned it down. On Broadway, Edna May created the role of Violet Gray, a Salvation Army girl who becomes the heir to a fortune belonging to Ichabod Bronson (Dan Daly). She has been chosen as the recipient of this windfall because Ichabod, although not averse to squiring the odd chorus girl himself, is a firm believer in organizations such as the Young Men's Rescue League and the Anti-Cigarette Society, and has found out that his playboy son, Harry (Harry Davenport), intends to marry the actress, Cora Angelique (Ada Dare). Violet, for her part, is intent on Harry getting the money - and her as well. Her saucy performance of 'At Ze Naughty Folies Bergére' does the trick - Ichabod cannot possibly leave his fortune to someone who behaves like that, and Harry's name goes back in the will. That story was the product of the vivid imagination of 'Hugh Morton' (Charles M.S. McLennen), who also wrote the lyrics for songs which had music by Gustave Kerker. These included 'They All Follow Me', 'Teach Me How To Kiss', 'The Purity Brigade', 'La Belle Parisienne', 'My Little Baby', 'On The Beach At Narragansett', And, of course, the lilting and lovely 'She Is The Belle Of New York', which was introduced by William Cameron in his somewhat bizarre role as Blinky Bill. Following the original 1898 West End production, in which the Broadway principles reprised their roles,

The Belle Of New York was revived nine times in London between 1901 and 1942, in various revised versions. The 1942 production starred Billy Danvers, Evelyn Laye, and Billy Tasker. The show proved to be extremely popular in Paris as well, and was presented there in 1903, 1916, and 1952. Broadway, too, enjoyed a retitled and revised version, *The Whirl Of New York*, in 1921, but only for 124 performances. The 1952 film version, with Fred Astaire and Vera Ellen, replaced the original songs with a score by Johnny Mercer and Harry Warren.

Bells Are Ringing
Despite its unlikely setting, a telephone answering service, the stage musical *Bells Are Ringing* benefited from a strong and original book, by Betty Comden and Adolph Green (they also wrote the lyrics) and some delightful tunes by Jule Styne. The show, which opened at the Shubert Theatre in New York on 29 November 1956, was created by Comden and Green for Judy Holliday with whom they had worked in the past. Holliday played the role of Ella Peterson, an employee of Susanswerphone, who becomes romantically involved with one of her unseen clients and also solves the problems of others. She won a Tony Award for her delicious performance, and another Tony went to Sydney Chaplin as best actor. Amongst the show's songs were two which have become standards, 'The Party's Over' and 'Just In Time', along with several other entertaining numbers such as 'Long Before I Knew You', 'Drop That Name', 'I'm Going Back', 'It's a Simple Little System', and 'Is It A Crime?'. *Bells Are Ringing* ran on Broadway for 924 performances, and a further 292 in London. A 1987 West End revival starred Lesley Mackie, and the Goodspeed Opera House in Connecticut mounted a production in 1990. Judy Holliday recreated her role for the 1960 screen version but the magic of the stage show was somehow mislaid in the transition.

Bennett, Michael
b. Michael DiFiglia, 8 April 1943, Buffalo, New York, USA, d. 2 July 1987, Tucson, Arizona, USA. A director, choreographer, and dancer, Bennett studied dance and choreography in his teens, and staged several shows at his local high school. After playing the role of Baby John in *West Side Story* on US and and European tours, he began his Broadway career as a dancer in early 60s musicals such as *Subways Are For Sleeping, Here's Love,* and *Bajour.* He made his debut as a choreographer in the 12-performance flop, *A Joyful Noise* (1966), which was followed a year later by another failure, *Henry And Sweet Henry.* His first hit came in 1968 with *Promises, Promises* when he created several original and lively dance sequences from Burt Bacharach and Hal David's highly contemporary

Judy Holliday (*Bells Are Ringing*)

score. During the next few years he choreographed the Katherine Hepburn vehicle *Coco* (1969), two Stephen Sondheim shows, *Company* (1970) and *Follies* (1971), along with *Seesaw* (1973), on which he was also the director and librettist. Then came *A Chorus Line* which opened in July 1975 and closed nearly 15 years later in April 1990. In 1994 it was still the longest running Broadway production, musical or otherwise. As its choreographer and director, Bennett devoted several years of his life to the show, auditioning, rehearsing, and directing productions throughout the world. He declined to spend any more time making a film version, and Richard Attenborough's 'uninspired' adaptation was released in 1985. Bennett's next musical was the short-lived *Ballroom* (1978), but he had one more major hit with *Dreamgirls* in 1981, which earned him his seventh and final Tony. In the early 80s he toyed with various projects including another musical, *Scandal*, but nothing materialised. In 1985 he signed as the director of *Chess*, the London musical by Tim Rice, and Bjorn Ulvaeus and Benny Andersson, two ex-members of the pop group Abba, but had to withdraw in January 1986 through illness. Later in the year he sold his New York property and moved to Tucson, Arizona, where he stayed until his death from AIDS in July 1987.
Further reading: *A Chorus Line And The Musicals Of Michael Bennett*, Ken Mandelbaum.

Bennett, Robert Russell

b. 15 June 1894, Kansas City, Missouri, USA, d.18 August 1981. A composer, arranger, conductor, and the leading orchestrator of Broadway musicals from the 20s through until 1960. At the age of 10 Bennett was giving piano recitals, and in his teens he studied harmony, counterpoint, and composition, and also played in dance halls and movie houses. While serving in the US Army during World War I he conducted and scored the music for various bands, and, on his release, got a job with the music publishers T.B. Harms & Company. From then on, for more than 30 years, he orchestrated over 300 scores for Broadway's leading composers, including *Rose-Marie, Showboat, Roberta, Very Warm For May, Of Thee I Sing, Girl Crazy, The Band Wagon, Porgy And Bess, Anything Goes, Carmen Jones, Bloomer Girl, Kiss Me, Kate, Finian's Rainbow, Lady In The Dark, Annie Get Your Gun, Bloomer Girl, Music In The Air, On A Clear Day You Can See Forever, Gay Divorce, Jumbo, Bells Are Ringing, Camelot, My Fair Lady*, and Richard Rodgers and Oscar Hammerstein II's blockbusters *Oklahoma!, Carousel, South Pacific*, and *The Sound Of Music*. Bennett also worked on some 30 films, and won an Oscar for his scoring of *Oklahoma!* in 1955. Three years later he had orchestrated Richard Rodgers' music for *Victory At Sea*, a Naval history of World War II presented on US television in 26 episodes. He also composed much serious music, including several operas, symphonies, and many other orchestral, solo and chamber pieces, but it is for his work for Broadway that he will be most remembered. Jerome Kern, Cole Porter, George Gershwin, Arthur Schwartz, Harold Arlen, Frederick Loewe, and the rest of the talented composers wrote the wonderful music, but the form in which it was heard in the theatre, the orchestral colourings, the empathy with the lyrics and the book, and the inspired selection of tempi - encapsulated in the memorable overtures to *My Fair Lady*, and *Oklahoma!* - all that and more depended on Robert Russell Bennett and the other highly skilled orchestral arrangers such as Phil Lang and Jonathan Tunick.
Further reading: *Instrumentally Speaking*, Robert Russell Bennett.

Berlin, Irving

b. Israel Baline, 11 May 1888, Temun, Siberia, Russia, d. 22 September 1989. Despite his foreign birth, Berlin became one of the most American of all songwriters. When he was four-years-old his family escaped a pogrom and travelled to the USA. His father was a cantor in his homeland, but in their new country had to earn his living as a meat inspector in New York City, singing in the synagogue only when the regular cantor was unavailable. An indifferent student, Berlin was happier singing, but in 1896, following the death of his father, he was obliged to work. At the age of 14 he began singing in saloons and on street corners. It was while engaged in this latter activity that he was 'discovered' and recommended to songwriter and publisher Harry Von Tilzer, who hired him to sing songs from the balcony of a 14th Street theatre. By 1906 Berlin had not advanced far, working as a singing waiter in Pelham's, a Chinatown restaurant frequented by New York's upper set, but he had taught himself to play piano and had started to write his own material. His first published song (lyrics only, music by Michael Nicholson) was 'Marie From Sunny Italy', from which he earned 37 cents and, apparently through a misprint on the sheet music, acquired the name by which he was thereafter known.
During the next few years he continued to write words and music, but also hung onto his work as a singing waiter. Several of the songs he wrote in these years were in Yiddish and were popular successes for artists such as Eddie Cantor and Fanny Brice. His first real songwriting success was 'My Wife's Gone To The Country' (1909, music by George Whiting), which was featured by Cantor. Like many other songwriters of the day, Berlin was fascinated by ragtime and tried his hand at several numbers, many of which had little to do with the reality of this

Irving Berlin

musical form except in their titling. In 1910, however, he had his first massive hit with such a song. 'Alexander's Ragtime Band', for which he wrote both words and music, made him a household name. Berlin capitalized upon the success of this song with 'Everybody's Doin' It' (1911), 'The International Rag' (1913) and others. In 1914, he scored a Broadway show, *Watch Your Step*, for dancers Vernon And Irene Castle, which included 'Play A Simple Melody', and followed it in 1915 with *Stop! Look! Listen!* which included 'I Love A Piano'. In addition to shows he wrote lasting popular pieces such as 'Woodman Spare That Tree' (1911), 'When The Midnight Choo Choo Leaves For Alabam' (1912), 'When I Lost You' (1913), his first major ballad, and the sentimental 'When I Leave The World Behind' (1915). During World War I Berlin was active in the theatre, writing an outstanding ballad in 'Kiss Me Again' and a handful of patriotic songs with only limited appeal. In 1918 he was drafted into the army and encouraged to write a show for the troops. For this hastily conceived and executed work he produced two memorable songs, 'Mandy' and 'Oh, How I Hate To Get Up In The Morning'. After the war came a steady stream of successful shows and popular songs, among the latter were 'A Pretty Girl Is Like A Melody' (1919), 'Say It With Music', 'All By Myself' (both 1921), 'All Alone' and 'What'll I Do' (both 1923). In 1925 he met, fell in love with, and a year later married Ellin Mackay, a member of New York's elite. One result of his meeting Mackay was a succession of fine ballads, including 'Remember' and 'Always' (both 1925). Although he was by now the biggest name in American songwriting, Berlin was always happy to contribute songs to the shows of others and in 1926 wrote 'Blue Skies' for *Betsy*, a show co-written by Richard Rodgers and Lorenz Hart. Among his songs of the late 20s were 'Shaking The Blues Away', 'The Song Is Ended' (1927), 'Marie' (1928), 'Let Me Sing - And I'm Happy' and 'Puttin' On The Ritz' (both 1930). In 1932, following a period of almost two years during which he appeared to have dried up, he recovered his confidence with 'Say It Isn't So' and 'Soft Lights And Sweet Music'. The following year he had a major Broadway success with *As Thousands Cheer*, a show which included 'Heat Wave' and the timeless 'Easter Parade'. During the 30s Hollywood was churning out numerous film musicals and, inevitably, Berlin was lured there to write scores for a succession of productions, some of which owe any subsequent fame to his contribution. Among the best of his films were *Top Hat* (1935), *Follow The Fleet* (1936) and *Carefree* (1938), all vehicles for newly-discovered hot properties, Fred Astaire and Ginger Rogers. Songs from these films included 'Cheek To Cheek', 'Isn't It A Lovely Day', 'Top Hat, White Tie And Tails',

'Let's Face The Music And Dance' and 'Change Partners'. *Alexander's Ragtime Band* (1938) was a feast for Berlin fans, with more than two dozen of his hit songs plus a new song, 'Now It Can Be Told'. Towards the end of the 30s, with rumblings of war coming from Europe, Berlin wrote a song especially for Kate Smith. This was 'God Bless America', a song which for a while was a serious contender as a national anthem.

As successful in films as he had been with stage musicals, Berlin again conquered Broadway, this time with *Louisiana Purchase* (1940), from which the hit song was 'Tomorrow Is A Lovely Day'. America's entry into the war roused Berlin's patriotism to new heights with a show, *This Is The Army* (1942), for which he wrote 'This Is The Army Mr. Jones' and 'I Left My Heart At The Stage Door Canteen'. A concurrent film project was *Holiday Inn*, which included two new classics, 'White Christmas' and 'Be Careful It's My Heart'. After the war Berlin, belying the fact that he had been writing hit songs for more than 30 years, struck a new lode of inspiration with *Annie Get Your Gun* (1946), brimming with hits, and after the less successful *Miss Liberty* (1949), found gold again with *Call Me Madam* (1950), which was followed by another downturn with *Mr President* (1962), his last Broadway musical. His post-war films included *Blue Skies* (1946), *Easter Parade* (1948) and *White Christmas* (1954), which mostly reprised old songs but included such new material as 'You Keep Coming Back Like A Song', 'A Couple Of Swells', 'It Only Happens When I Dance With You' and 'Count Your Blessing Instead Of Sheep'. By the 50s Berlin's musical inspiration had subsided and he wrote little more, although a 1966 song, 'An Old Fashioned Girl', was briefly popular. Despite, or perhaps because of, his foreign birth, Berlin was intensely American both in his personal patriotism and acute sense of what made American popular music distinctive. For the last 30 years of his long life, Berlin lived in semi-seclusion, ignoring media attempts to laud his achievements even at such significant milestones as his 100th birthday. He died in September 1989.

Further reading: *The Story Of Irving Berlin*, David Ewen. *Irving Berlin*, Michael Freedland. *Irving Berlin And Ragtime America*, I. Whitcomb, *As Thousands Cheer: The Life Of Irving Berlin*, L. Bergreen.

Bernadette

One of the most bizarre and spectacular failures in London musical theatre history. The show, which opened at the 2,000-seat Dominion Theatre in London on 21 June 1990, was based on the story of Bernadette Soubrious, a young peasant girl who had visions of the Virgin Mary at Lourdes in 1858. It was the brainchild of a piano-tuner and his wife, Gwyn and Maureen Hughes, who wrote the book, music and lyrics, and whose only previous contact with the world of show business had been when they wrote a song that was eliminated in a preliminary heat of the Eurovision Song Contest. From the start, *Bernadette* was dubbed 'The People's Musical'. Finance from conventional sources was scarce, and more than 2,500 readers of the *Daily Mirror* newspaper helped raise the £1.25 million needed to stage it. The largest investor, however, was the show's producer, William Z. Fonfé, an ex-chauffeur, who re-mortgaged his house so that he could inject some £500,000 in a project that he predicted would be 'the greatest musical since *West Side Story*'. The cast was led by 16-year-old Natalie Wright, who had been spotted in Andrew Lloyd Webber's *Aspects Of Love*. With an advance of £250,000, the show received an ecstatic first night reception, mainly because the audience consisted of hundreds of interested investors, who were easy to spot because they were dressed in anoraks, and sports - not dinner - jackets. The critics took a more jaundiced view: 'Pass the loaves and the fishes: they need a miracle'. . .'themeless songs to make laundry lists by'. . .'one-dimensional and confused'. . .'three thousand angels (investors), but not a prayer', were typical comments. To support their view, many of the reviewers quoted the song lyric: 'The seas may all run dry/but my love will never die.' In an effort to delay the inevitable, Natalie Wright released a record of the song, 'Who Are You', the Pope blessed the cast and the composers, and the 'angels' received requests for more money - to which they responded. It was all to no avail, *Bernadette* closed on July 14 after a run of only three weeks, with losses 'approaching £1.25 million', having been dubbed 'a miraculous failure'. The 'miracle', if there ever was one, would seem to be twofold: that a director of Ernest Maxin's standing (*Black And White Minstrel Show, Morecambe And Wise Show*) ever became involved; and that a group of amateurs thought they could mount a successful large-scale West End musical at a time when professionals were constantly failing to do so.

Bernstein, Leonard

b. Louis Bernstein, 25 August 1918, Lawrence, Massachusetts, USA, d. 14 October 1990, New York, USA. Bernstein was a major and charismatic figure in modern classical music, and the Broadway musical theatre. He was also a conductor, composer, pianist, author and lecturer. A son of immigrant Russian Jews, Bernstein started to play the piano at the age of 10. In his teens he showed an early interest in the theatre by organizing productions such as *The Mikado*, and an unconventional adaptation of *Carmen*, in which he played the title role. Determined to make a career in music, despite his father's insistence that 'music just keeps people awake at night', Bernstein eschewed the family beauty parlour business. He went

on to study firstly with Walter Piston and Edward Burlingaunt Hill at Harvard, then with Fritz Reiner, Isabella Vengerova and Randall Thompson at the Curtis Institute in Philadephia, and finally with Serge Koussevitzky at the Berkshire Music Institute at Tanglewood. Bernstein had gone to Harvard regarding himself as a pianist but became influenced by Dimitri Mitropoulos and Aaron Copland. They inspired him to write his first symphony, *Jeremiah*. By 1943 he was chosen by Artur Rodzinski to work as his assistant at the New York Philharmonic. On 14 November 1943, Bernstein deputized at the last minute for the ailing Bruno Walter, and conducted the New York Philharmonic in a concert which was broadcast live on network radio. The next day, for what would not be the last time, he made the front pages and became a celebrity over-night. In the same year he wrote the music for *Fancy Free*, a ballet, choreographed by Jerome Robbins, about three young sailors on 24 hours shore leave in New York City. It was so successful that they expanded it into a Broadway musical, with libretto and lyrics by Betty Comden and Adolph Green. Retitled *On The Town* and directed by George Abbott, it opened in 1944, with a youthful, vibrant score which included the anthem 'New York, New York', 'Lonely Town', 'I Get Carried Away' and 'Lucky To Be Me'. The 1949 film version, starring Frank Sinatra and Gene Kelly, and directed by Kelly and Stanley Donen, is often regarded as innovatory in its use of real New York locations, although Bernstein's score was somewhat truncated in the transfer. In 1950 Bernstein wrote both music and lyrics for a musical version of J. M. Barrie's *Peter Pan*, starring Jean Arthur and Boris Karloff. His next Broadway project, *Wonderful Town* (1953), adapted from the play, *My Sister Eileen*, by Joseph Fields and Jerome Chodorov, again had lyrics by Comden and Green, and starred Rosalind Russell, returning to Broadway after a distinguished career in Hollywood. Bernstein's spirited, contemporary score for which he won a Tony Award, included 'Conversation Piece', 'Conga', 'Swing', 'What A Waste', 'Ohio', 'A Quiet Girl' and 'A Little Bit Of Love'. The show had a successful revival in London in 1986, with Maureen Lipman in the starring role. *Candide* (1956) was one of Bernstein's most controversial works. Lillian Hellman's adaptation of the Voltaire classic, sometimes termed a 'comic operetta', ran for only 73 performances on Broadway. Bernstein's score was much admired though, and one of the most attractive numbers, 'Glitter And Be Gay', was sung with great effect by Barbara Cook, one year before her Broadway triumph in Meredith Willson's *The Music Man*. *Candide* has been revived continually since 1956, at least twice by producer Hal Prince. It was his greatly revised production, including additional lyrics by Stephen Sondheim and John

Latouche, to the originals by Richard Wilbur, which ran for 740 performances on Broadway in 1974. The Scottish Opera's production, directed by Jonathan Miller in 1988, is said to have met with the composer's approval, and Bernstein conducted a concert version of the score at London's Barbican Theatre in 1989, which proved his last appearance in the UK.

Bernstein's greatest triumph in the popular field came with *West Side Story* in 1957. This brilliant musical adaptation of Shakespeare's *Romeo And Juliet* was set in the New York streets and highlighted the violence of the rival gangs, the Jets and the Sharks. With a book by Arthur Laurents, lyrics by Sondheim in his first Broadway production, and directed by Jerome Robbins, Bernstein created one of the most dynamic and exciting shows in the history of the musical theatre. The songs included 'Jet Song', 'Something's Coming', 'Maria', 'Tonight', 'America', 'Cool', 'I Feel Pretty', 'Somewhere' and 'Gee, Officer Krupke!'. In 1961, the film version gained 10 Oscars, including 'Best Picture'. Bernstein's music was not eligible because it had not been written for the screen. In 1984, he conducted the complete score of *West Side Story* for the first time, in a recording for Deutsche Grammophon, with a cast of opera singers including Kiri Te Kanawa, José Carreras, Tatania Troyanos and Kurt Allman. Bernstein's last Broadway show, *1600 Pennsylvania Avenue* (1976) was an anti-climax. A story about American presidents, with book and lyrics by Alan Jay Lerner, it closed after only seven performances. Among Bernstein's many other works was the score for the Marlon Brando film, *On The Waterfront* (1954), for which he was nominated for an Oscar; a jazz piece, 'Prelude, Fugue and Riffs', premiered on US television by Benny Goodman in 1955; and 'My Twelve Tone Melody' written for Irving Berlin's 100th birthday in 1988. In his classical career, which ran parallel to his work in the popular field, he was highly accomplished, composing three symphonies, a full length opera, and several choral works. He was music director of the New York Philharmonic from 1958-69, conducted most of the world's premier orchestras, and recorded many of the major classical works. In the first week of October 1990, he announced his retirement from conducting because of ill health, and expressed an intention to concentrate on composing. He died one week later on 14 October 1990. In 1993, BBC Radio marked the 75th anniversary of his birth by devoting a complete day to programmes about his varied and distinguished career. A year later, *The Leonard Bernstein Revue: A Helluva Town*, played the Rainbow & Stars in New York.

Selected albums: *Bernstein Conducts Bernstein* (1984), *West Side Story* (1985), *Bernstein's America* (1988).

Further reading: *The Joy Of Music*, Leonard Bernstein. *Leonard Bernstein*, John Briggs. *Leonard Bernstein*, Peter Gadenwitz. *Leonard Bernstein*, Joan Peyser.

Leonard Bernstein (right)

Best Foot Forward

Sub-titled 'A Modern Musical Comedy', and set in Winsocki, a prep school in Pennsylvania, *Best Foot Forward* had a book by John Cecil Holm and a score by the new team of Hugh Martin and Ralph Blane. It opened at New York's Ethel Barrymore Theatre on 1 October 1941, and was directed by George Abbott, who also produced the show with Richard Rodgers (uncredited). The choreographer was Gene Kelly. The story deals with the bewildering complications that arise when Bud Hooper (Gil Stratton Jnr.) mischievously invites the glamorous movie star Gale Joy (Rosemary Lane) to the school prom. Sensing the possibility of a good publicity stunt, she accepts, but, following problems involving Bud's jealous girlfriend, Helen Schlesinger (Maureen Cannon), and a brawl during which she loses her dress as the students demand more than just autographs, she cannot wait to get back to Hollywood. The songs included 'Just A Little Joint With A Jukebox', 'What Do You Think I Am?', I Know You By Heart', 'Ev'ry Time', 'The Three B's', 'Shady Lady Bird', 'That's How I Love The Blues', and the lively 'Buckle Down, Winsocki', which achieved some popularity and became a hit outside the show for Al Jarrett And His Orchestra. *Best Foot Forward* ran on Broadway for 326 performances, and gave two future stars, Nancy Walker and June Allyson, their first real opportunity to shine. They also appeared in the 1943 film version, with Lucille Ball and William Gaxton. The 1963 stage show revival, which played Off Broadway at Stage 73, gave Liza Minnelli her first theatrical chance, just two years before she came to prominence in *Flora, The Red Menace*.

Best Little Whorehouse In Texas, The

The advance publicity for this musical with just about the most provocative title ever, ensured full houses when it opened Off Broadway at the Entermedia Theatre on 17 April 1978. New York audiences took to the show immediately, and it moved to Broadway's 46th Street Theatre two months later on 19 June. The book, by Peter Masterson and Larry L. King, was based on a magazine article by King which told of the last few days in the life of The Chicken Ranch, a long-serving Texan brothel that was having to close down after its activities had been exposed on an investigative television programme. Clint Allmon played Melvin P. Thorpe, the slick and slimy television front man, complete with bouffant blond wig, gaudy jacket, and a stars and stripes tie, while Carlin Glynn, as Miss Mona, the friendly establishment's 'hostess with the mostess', and Henderson Forsythe (Sheriff Ed Earl Dodd, her ex-lover), both won Tony Awards for their performances. Despite its title, the whole thing turned out to be a highly amusing, raunchy romp, with a few

sentimental moments too. The lively, atmospheric score, with its folksy, country quality, was by the former classical music student, Carol Hall, and included 'A Li'l Ole Bitty Pissant Country Place', 'Texas Has A Whorehouse In It', 'Girl, You're A Woman', 'Hard-Candy Christmas, 'Bus From Amarillo', 'TwentyFour Hours Of Lovin'', 'Good Old Girl', and 'Doatsy Me'. Several of the creative participants, including Masterson, King, and Hall, came from Texas, and it was Tommy Tune, another refugee from the 'lone star state', who provided the imaginative choreography. *The Best Little Whorehouse In Texas* surprised a lot of people, and ran on Broadway for 1,584 performances. The 1982 film version starred Dolly Parton and Burt Reynolds.

Better 'Ole, The

With a sub-title such as 'a fragment from France in two explosions, seven splinters and a gas attack', this show has to have been around during World War I. It did, in fact, open at the Oxford Theatre in London on 4 August 1917, with a book by Bruce Bairnsfather and Arthur Eliot, James Hurd's lyrics, and music composed by Herman Darewski. The show was set in the trenches of France, as seen through the eyes of Old Bill (Arthur Bourchier), and his soldier colleagues Alf (Sinclair Cotter) and Bert (Tom Wootwell). All three were characters that had been created by Bairnsworth in his widely enjoyed wartime cartoons. The show's title is taken from one of the drawings in which Old Bill is berating a fellow companion in his muddy pit with: 'If you know of a better 'ole then go to it!'. The show proved to be enormously popular both with the audience at home and those on leave from the war front. They left the theatre happily singing songs such as 'From Someone In France To Someone In Somerset', 'Tommy', 'She's My Gal', 'My Word! Ain't We Carrying On?', 'I'm Sick Of This 'Ere War', and 'Let's Dust Together'. One item, by the American songwriters Jimmy Monaco, James McCarthy and Howard Johnson, was interpolated into the score. It was called 'What Do You Want To Make Those Eyes At Me For', and its appeal endured to such an extent that it was sung by Betty Hutton in the 1945 film, *Incendiary Blonde*, and also entered the UK chart in versions by Emile Ford (1959) and Shakin' Stevens (1987). *The Better 'Ole* ran in London for an incredible 811 performances, and added another 353 in New York. The story was made into a silent film in 1918 under the title of *The Romance Of Old Bill*.

Betty

One of the early hits of World War I, *Betty* opened at Daly's Theatre in London on 24 April 1915. In an effort to vary the London musical theatre's normal fare of European operetta, the American librettist

Gladys B. Ungar was engaged to write the book with England's own Frederick Lonsdale. It dealt with the young, high-born, wild and irresponsible Gerald, the Earl of Beverly (Donald Calthrop), who, to spite his ducal father, marries Betty, a kitchen maid (Winifred Barnes). His action causes a good deal of trouble up at the 'big house', especially when the cad neglects the poor girl and carries on as before. Inevitably, with the help of severe paternal financial pressure, he learns the error of his ways, returns to Betty, and true love conquers in the end. Paul Rubens and Adrian Ross's score (with additional songs by Ernest Steffan and Merlin Morgan) contained several appealing ballads, including 'Can It Be Love?', 'The Duchess Of Dreams', 'Cinderella', 'If It Were True', 'It's A Beautiful Day Today', and a charming duet, 'Dance With Me', along with the amusing 'I Love The Girls', 'We Ought To Combine', and 'Opposite The Ducks'. *Betty* stayed in London for nearly a year, a total of 391 performances. A New York production opened in the autumn of 1916, but was not nearly so successful.

Beyond The Fringe

Born in 1960 as a late night 'fringe entertainment' at the Edinburgh Festival, this four-man satirical revue moved to the tiny Fortune Theatre in London on 10 May 1961. It was written and performed by the cast which consisted of four Oxbridge university graduates: Alan Bennett, Peter Cook, Jonathan Miller, and Dudley Moore. Unlike the smart and sophisticated revues such as *The Lyric Revue, Airs On A Shoestring*, and *Look Who's Here!*, which became so popular in the 50s, *Beyond The Fringe* was, in the words of the distinguished critic, Bernard Levin, 'so brilliant, adult, hard-boiled, accurate, merciless, witty, unexpected, alive, exhilarating, cleansing, right, true, and good that my first conscious thought as I stumbled, weak and sick with laughter, up the stairs at the end was one of gratitude.' Dudley Moore wrote the music for the 'series of unconnected skits' which included 'The Bollard', 'The Sadder And Wiser Beaver' (based on the press baron Lord Beaverbrook), 'Take A Pew', 'Aftermyth Of War', 'Sitting On A Bench' (a precurser to Cook and Moore's celebrated Derek and Clive characters), 'And The Same To You' (shades of David Lean's film, *The Bridge Over The River Kwai*), and 'The End Of The World', (a fashionably anti-nuclear piece). The production was highly acclaimed by public and press alike, including the London *Evening Standard* which gave the show its 1961 award for best musical. Bennett, Cook, Miller, and Moore left early in 1962, but the show continued with a second cast, eventually closing in March 1964 after 1,189 performances. The original quartet of performers went to Cape Town, Toronto, Washington, and Boston, before the Broadway premiere of *Beyond The Fringe* at the John Golden Theatre on 27 October 1962. This edition, which had been revised for American consumption, was widely applauded and the cast received a special Tony Award for 'their brilliance which has shattered all the old concepts of comedy'. Miller stayed with the show for about a year and the other three withdrew soon afterwards. As well as the New York run of 673 performances, another company toured the US for seven months. Alan Bennett and Jonathan Miller, the 'serious pair', have devoted much of the rest of their time to the theatre: Bennett as one of the UK's most celebrated playwrights, and Miller as a director of note for a variety of productions including opera. For more than a decade, Peter Cook and Dudley Moore were an enormously popular film and television comedy team, especially in the series, *Not Only . . . But Also*, before Moore combined a lucrative acting career in Hollywood with occasional flashes of brilliance as an accomplished jazz pianist. Cook has continued to be associated with satire via his association with the notorious *Private Eye* magazine, as well as being one of Britain's most familiar character actors and chat-show personalities. The Original Cast 'live' album of *Beyond The Fringe*, which charted in the UK and the USA, was re-released in 1993 in the Broadway Angel series.

Big Ben

This 'light opera' was Vivian Ellis's first post-war West End show, and reunited him with the author A.P. Herbert (b. 24 September 1890, Elstead, England, d. 11 November 1971), and the impresario C.B. Cochran. *Big Ben* opened at the Adelphi Theatre in London on 17 July 1946. Herbert was a noted crusader for justice, and a Member of Parliament from 1935-50, so it was hardly surprising that his somewhat unconventional story for *Big Ben* revolved around a shop girl, Grace Green (Gloria Lynne), who is elected to the House Of Commons. She is a Socialist, and her gentleman friend, the Hon. George Home (Eric Palmer), is a true-blue Conservative, but they are united in their opposition to a bill which would affect the drinking (of alcohol) habits of the community at large. Their unorthodox methods bring about their incarceration in a secure part of Westminster for a time, but the inevitable happy ending is never far away. Vivian Ellis wrote the words and music for what turned out to be one of his most agreeable scores. A fine cast which included Gabrielle Brune, David Davies, Eric Forte, Trefor Jones, and Yvonne Robinson, excelled in numbers such as 'London's Alight Again', 'Let Us Go Down The River', 'The Sun Is On The City', 'Who's The Lady?', 'Love Me Not', 'Do You Remember The Good Old Days?', 'London Town', and the rousing 'I Want To See The People Happy'. During the show's run of 172

Roger Miller (*Big River*)

performances, Carol Lynne was replaced in the leading role by one of Cochran's young 'discoveries', a future star of musical comedy and operetta, Lizbeth Webb; and Gabrielle Brune gave way to Noele Gordon, who eventually became a national figure in Britain through her involvement in the long-running television soap, *Crossroads*.

Big River

Notable for the Broadway debut of the country singer-songwriter Roger Miller. He provided both music and lyrics for this musical adaptation of Mark Twain's immortal book, *The Adventures Of Huckleberry Finn*. The show opened at the Eugene O'Neill Theatre in New York on 25 April 1985, and William Hautman's book was set mainly on the Missippi River, on which Huck (Daniel H. Jenkins) and the runaway slave Jim (Ron Richardson) make their bid for freedom. A fine supporting cast included John Short as Tom Sawyer, and Bob Gunton and René Auberjonois as King and Duke, a couple of con-men. Miller's songs, a mixture of bluegrass and and blues, with just a touch of gospel, were widely applauded. They included 'Muddy Water', 'You Ought To Be Here With Me', 'Guv'ment', 'Worlds Apart', 'River In The Rain', 'Leaving's Not The Only Way To Go', 'Waiting For The Light To Shine', and 'Worlds Apart'. To the surprise of many, *Big River* enjoyed a run of 1,005 performances, and, in a season almost bereft of new musicals, gained Tony Awards for best musical, score, book, featured actor (Ron Richardson), director (Des McAnuff), lighting (Richard Riddell), and scenic design (Heidi Landesman). The latter's atmospheric sets were one of the production's most attractive features.

Billy

The question was this: could a story that had already been the subject of a best-selling novel, and a successful film and play, go further and be turned into a hit musical show? The answer proved to be a most definite 'yes'. Keith Waterhouse's novel, *Billy Liar*, which had been adapted for the stage and screen by Waterhouse and Willis Hall, proved to be ideal material in the hands of librettists, Dick Clement and Ian La Frenais (*The Likely Lads*, *Porridge*, *Auf Wiedersehn, Pet*), and songwriters John Barry (music) and Don Black (lyrics). *Billy* opened at the Drury Lane Theatre in London on 1 May 1974. Michael Crawford, who had been acclaimed for his role in the film of *Hello, Dolly!* (1969), and would eventually attain superstardom in Andrew Lloyd Webber's *The Phantom Of The Opera* (1986), played the part of young Billy Fisher, the undertaker's clerk, who is forever dreaming of another life in the fantasy country of Ambrosia where he is the leader of his own private (female) army, far from reality and the drab environment of his native Yorkshire in the north of England. His long-suffering parents were played by Avis Bunnage and Brian Pringle, and his loyal girlfriends, the raunchy Rita, and the more refined Liz, by Elaine Paige and Diana Quick. Billy's flights of fancy were best reflected in the show's hit song, 'Some Of Us Belong To The Stars', 'The Lady From LA,' and the reflective 'I Missed The Last Rainbow', but Barry and Black distributed some fine, lively and pertinent numbers throughout the entire cast, including 'Happy To Be Themselves', 'It Were All Green Hills', 'Remembering', 'Any Minute Now', 'Is This Where I Wake Up?', 'Billy', 'The Witch', 'Aren't You Billy Fisher?', and 'Ambrosia'. *Billy* was the big hit London musical of 1974 and beyond, but audiences dwindled rapidly following Michael Crawford's departure. The multi-talented Roy Castle was in the leading role when the show closed after an impressive run of 904 performances. Plans for a major 1991 West End revival were aborted two weeks before it went into rehearsal, but, in the following year, the National Youth Theatre mounted a well-received production at The Edinburgh Festival Fringe, complete with two new songs. It starred the comedian, magician and television game show host, Andrew O'Connor, in the leading role.

Bing Boys Are Here, The

This was the first in a series of tremendously popular revues which played continuously at the Alhambra Theatre in London during the last two years of World War I. They all had scores by Nat D. Ayr (music) and Clifford Grey (lyrics), and the book for this initial show was written by George Grossmith Jnr. and Fred Thompson, and had additional songs by Eustace Ponsonby, Philip Braham, and Ivor Novello. It opened on 19 April 1916, and starred The Prime Minister of Mirth George Robey and Violet Loraine, who combined on the lovely ballad, 'If You Were The Only Girl In The World', which became one of the most cherished songs of the day. The score was chock full of other popular items such as 'Another Little Drink Wouldn't Do Us Any Harm', 'I Stopped, I Looked And I Listened', 'The Kipling Walk', 'The Kiss Trot', 'I Started My Day Over Again', 'Underneath The Stars', 'The Right Side Of Bond Street', 'Ragging The Dog', 'The Languid Melody', and 'Dear Old Shepherd's Bush'. Also in the cast were Gillie Potter, Maidie Andrews, Phyllis Monkman, Alfred Lester, Odette Myrtil, and Jack Morrison. *The Bing Boys Are Here* ran for 378 performances and was succeeded by *The Bing Boys Are There* which opened on 24 February 1917, again with a book by George Grossmith Jnr. and Fred Thompson, and additional songs by Eric Blore, Melville Gideon, Worton David, and Eustace Ponsonby. Robey was absent from this edition, but

Violet Loraine was back, and she sang the rousing hit, 'Let The Great Big World Keep Turning' as well as others such as 'So He Followed Me', and 'That Dear Old Home Of Mine' and 'Do You Like Me?' (both with Joseph Coyne). The rest of the score included 'The Bond Street Dress Parade', 'I'll Be Nice To You', 'Oh Yes! I Remember', 'Yula Hicki Wicki Yacki Dula', 'When You're Dancing With Me', 'That's What I Call Love', 'Who Taught You All Those Things You Taught Me?', and 'I Bring My Own Girls Along'. Also in the cast were Lorna and Toots Pound, Laddie Cliff, and Wilkie Baird. The exceptional success of both shows resulted in *The Bing Boys On Broadway,* which made its debut at the Alhambra on 16 February 1918. Robey returned for this final fling which ran for 562 performances, and so was still going strong well after the Armistice was signed in November of that year. Violet Loraine was there too, along with Lorna and Toots Pound, Clara Evelyn, Kitty Fielder, Dan Agar, and Arthur Finn. This time the book was provided by Fred Thompson and Harry M. Bernon, and, once again, Ayer and Grey came up with another massive hit song, 'First Love, Last Love, Best Love', as well as several other amusing and singable numbers such as 'Hello, New York', 'Take Me Back To Bingville', 'Indian Rag', 'Crinoline Days', 'Something Oriental', 'College Days', 'Day After Day', 'Shurr-up!', and 'Southern Home'. By the time it closed, the soldiers were returning home, but *The Bing Boys* series had served its purpose, and, together with *Chu Chin Chow, The Maid Of The Mountains,* and *'The Better 'Ole',* had provided invaluable entertainment through those dark years.

Bitter Sweet

Told in flashback, the stage musical *Bitter Sweet* is set in Vienna during the late 1800s, and recounts the story of Sari whose lover, Carl, is killed in a duel. Despite romantic events later in her life, she eventually marries a British Marquis, Sari remains emotionally faithful to her dead lover. *Bitter Sweet* was written by Noël Coward and opened in London in 1929 at His Majesty's Theatre where it ran for 18 months before transferring to the Lyceum. With book, music and lyrics by Coward, it was his first major musical triumph. Although it harked back to 19th-century Viennese operetta in its musical form, *Bitter Sweet* proved to be immensely popular and many of its songs have shown remarkable endurance, amongst them 'If Love Were All', 'Zigeuner' and the richly sentimental 'I'll See You Again'. The show starred Peggy Wood and George Metaxa and was later seen on Broadway. Subsequent revivals were rare, and the 1989 production at Sadlers Wells was said to be the first on the London stage for nearly 60 years. Two unsatisfactory film versions were made, in 1933 with Anna Neagle and Fernand Gravet, and 1940 with Jeanette MacDonald and Nelson Eddy.

Black, Don

b. 21 June 1938, Hackney, London, England. A prolific lyricist for film songs, stage musicals and Tin Pan Alley. One of five children, three boys and two girls, he worked part-time as an usher at the London Palladium before getting a job as an office boy and sometimes journalist with the *New Musical Express* in the early 50s. Then, after a brief sojourn as a stand-up comic in the dying days of the music halls, he gravitated towards London's Denmark Street, the centre of UK music publishing, where he worked as a song plugger for firms owned by Dave Toff and Joe 'Mr. Piano' Henderson. He met Matt Monro in 1960, when the singer was about to make his breakthrough with Cyril Ornadel and Norman Newell's 'Portrait Of My Love'. Encouraged by Monro, Black began to develop his talent for lyric writing. Together with another popular vocalist, Al Saxon, Black wrote 'April Fool', which Monro included on his *Love Is The Same Anywhere.* In 1964 Black collaborated with the German composer, Udo Jurgens, and together they turned Jurgens' Eurovision Song Contest entry, 'Warum Nur Warum', into 'Walk Away', which became a UK Top 5 hit for Monro. The singer also charted with 'For Mama', which Black wrote with Charles Aznavour. It was also popular for Connie Francis and Jerry Vale in the USA. In 1965 Black made his breakthrough into films with the lyric of the title number for *Thunderball,* the third James Bond movie. The song was popularized by Tom Jones, and it marked the beginning of a fruitful collaboration with composer John Barry. As well as providing Bond with two more themes, 'Diamonds Are Forever' (1971, Shirley Bassey), for which they received an Ivor Novello Award; and 'The Man With The Golden Gun' (1974, Lulu), the songwriters received a second 'Ivor', and an Academy Award, for their title song to *Born Free* in 1966. Black has been nominated on four other occasions: for 'True Grit' (with Elmer Bernstein, 1969), 'Ben' (Walter Scharf, a US number 1 for Michael Jackson in 1972, and a UK hit for Marti Webb in 1985), 'Wherever Love Takes Me', from *Gold* (Bernstein, 1972), and 'Come To Me', from *The Pink Panther Strikes Again* (Henry Mancini, 1976). It has been estimated that Black's lyrics have been heard in well over 100 movies, including *To Sir With Love* (title song, with Mark London, 1972, a US number 1 for Lulu), *Pretty Polly* (title song, Michel Legrand, 1967), *I'll Never Forget What's 'Is Name* ('One Day Soon', Francis Lai, 1968), *The Italian Job* ('On Days Like These', Quincy Jones, 1969), *Satan's Harvest* ('Two People', Denis King, 1969), *Hoffman* ('If There Ever Is A Next Time', Ron Grainer, 1970), *Mary Queen*

Of Scots ('Wish Was Then', John Barry, 1971), *Alice's Adventures In Wonderland* (several songs with Barry, 1972), *The Tamarind Seed* ('Play It Again', Barry, 1974), *The Dove* ('Sail The Summer Winds', Barry, 1974), and *The Wilby Conspiracy* ('All The Wishing In The World', Stanley Myers, 1975). In 1970, Matt Monro invited Don Black to become his manager, and he remained in that role until the singer died in 1985. Black considered Monro to be one of the finest interpreters of his lyrics, particularly with regard to 'If I Never Sing Another Song', which Black wrote with Udo Jurgens in 1977. The song became a favourite closing number for many artists, including Johnnie Ray and Eddie Fisher. In 1971, Black augmented his already heavy work load by becoming involved with stage musicals. His first score, written with composer Walter Scharf, was for *Maybe That's Your Problem*, which had a limited run (18 performances) at London's Roundhouse Theatre. The subject of the piece was premature ejaculation (Black says that his friend, Alan Jay Lerner, suggested that it should be called *Shortcomings*), but the critics called it 'a dismal piece'. However, one of the performers was Elaine Paige, just seven years before *Evita*. Paige was also in *Billy*, London's hit musical of 1974. Adapted from the straight play, *Billy Liar*, which was set in the north of England, Black and John Barry's score captured the 'feel' and the dialect of the original. The songs included 'Some Of Us Belong To The Stars', 'I Missed The Last Rainbow', 'Any Minute Now', and 'It Were All Green Fields When I Were A Lad', which was subsequently recorded by Stanley Holloway. The show, which ran for over 900 performances, made a star of Michael Crawford in his musical comedy debut. Black's collaborator on the score for his next show, *Barmitzvah Boy* (1978), was Jule Styne, the legendary composer of shows such as *Funny Girl* and *Gypsy*, amongst others. Although *Barmitzvah Boy* had a disappointingly short run, it did impress Andrew Lloyd Webber, who engaged Black to write the lyrics for his song cycle, *Tell Me On Sunday*, a television programme and album, which featured Marti Webb. Considered too short for theatrical presentation, on the recommendation of Cameron Mackintosh it was combined with Lloyd Webber's *Variations* to form *Song And Dance*, a two part 'theatrical concert'. In the first half, Webb, playing an English girl domiciled in the USA, 'wended her way through a succession of unsatisfactory love affairs' via songs such as 'Take That Look Off Your Face', which gave her a UK Top 5 hit and gained Black another Ivor Novello Award; 'Nothing Like You've Ever Known', 'Capped Teeth And Caesar Salad', and 'Tell Me On Sunday'. Wayne Sleep and his company of eight dancers performed the second half, to the music of *Variations*. The show ran in the West End for 781 performances before being

re-modelled and expanded for Broadway, where it starred Bernadette Peters, who received a Tony Award for her performance. Black teamed with Benny Andersson and Bjorn Ulvaeus, two former members of Abba, for the aptly title, *Abbacadabra*, a Christmas show which played to packed houses in 1983. Earlier that year, he had written the score for *Dear Anyone* with Geoff Stephens, a successful composer of pop hits such as 'Winchester Cathedral' 'You Won't Find Another Fool Like Me' and 'There's A Kind Of Hush'. The show first surfaced as a concept album in 1978, and one of its numbers, 'I'll Put You Together Again', became a Top 20 hit for the group, Hot Chocolate. The 1983 stage presentation did not last too long, and neither did *Budgie* (1988). Against a background of 'the sleezy subculture of London's Soho', the show starred Adam Faith and Anita Dobson. Black's lyrics combined with Mort Shuman's music for songs such as 'Why Not Me?', 'There Is Love And There Is Love', 'In One Of My Weaker Moments', and 'They're Naked And They Move', but to no avail - Don Black, as co-producer, presided over a £1,000,000 flop. Two years earlier, Anita Dobson had had a big UK hit with 'Anyone Can Fall In Love', when Black added a lyric to Simon May and Leslie Osborn's theme for *Eastenders*, one of Britain's top television soaps, and he collaborated with the composers again for 'Always There', a vocal version of their music for *Howard's Way*, which gave Marti Webb a UK hit. In 1989, Black resumed his partnership with Andrew Lloyd Webber for *Aspects Of Love*. Together with *Phantom Of The Opera* lyricist, Charles Hart, they fashioned a musical treatment of David Garnett's 1955 novel, which turned out to be more intimate than some of Lloyd Webber's other works, but still retained the operatic form. The show starred Michael Ball and Ann Crumb, and it nearly had a 'James Bond', when Roger Moore was originally cast as George Dillingham, but he withdrew before the show opened. Ball took the big ballad, 'Love Changes Everything', to number 2 in the UK, and the score also featured the 'subtle, aching melancholy' of 'The First Man You Remember'. *Aspects of Love* was not considered a hit by Lloyd Webber's standards - it ran for three years in the West End, and for one year on Broadway - and the London Cast recording topped the UK album chart. In the 90s, Don Black's activities remain numerous and diverse. In 1992, together with Chris Walker, he provided extra lyrics for the London stage production of *Radio Times*; wrote additional songs for a revival of *Billy* by the National Youth Music Theatre at the Edinburgh Festival; renewed his partnership with Geoff Stephens for a concept album of a 'revuesical' entitled *Off The Wall*, the story of 'six characters determined to end it all by throwing themselves off a ledge on the 34th storey of a London

highrise building'; wrote, with Lloyd Webber, the Barcelona Olympics anthem, 'Friends For Life' ('Amigos Para Siempre'), which was recorded by Sarah Brightman and Jose Carreras; and collaborated with David Dundas on 'Keep Your Dreams Alive', for the animated feature, *Freddie As F.R.O.7*. He spent a good deal of the year with Andrew Lloyd Webber and Christopher Hampton, writing a musical treatment of the Hollywood classic, *Sunset Boulevard*, which was set to open in London in June 1993. Black has held the positions of chairman and vice-president of the British Academy of Songwriters, Composers and Authors, and has, for the past few years, been the genial chairman of the voting panel for the Vivian Ellis Prize, a national competition to encourage new writers for the musical stage.
Selected album: *Matt Monro Sings Don Black* (1990).

Blackbirds Of 1928
The first and most successful of Lew Leslie's all-black revues opened at New York's Liberty Theatre on 9 May 1928. Leslie had mounted something similar in London two years before called simply *Blackbirds*, which by all accounts caused quite a stir in that conventional clime. It starred Florence Mills (who had come to prominence in *Shuffle Along* (1922)), Johnny Hudgins, and Lloyd Mitchell. The score for the 1926 *Blackbirds* was written by George W. Meyer, and included 'Silver Rose', 'Do The Black Bottom With Me', and 'On The Beach At Wika Kiki Blues'. Meyer also provided the songs for Leslie's 'racial reversal', *White Birds*, which starred Maurice Chevalier, and opened in London's West End in May 1927. *Blackbirds Of 1928* was a much grander affair, with an impressive cast which included Adelaide Hall, Aida Ward, Bill 'Bojangles' Robinson, and the 20 years old Elisabeth Welch. It marked the Broadway debut of songwriters Jimmy McHugh and Dorothy Fields, and introduced one of their biggest all-time hits, 'I Can't Give You Anything But Love', along with several other delightful numbers such as 'Dig-Diga-Doo', 'I Must Have That Man', 'Porgy', 'Doin' The New Low Down', 'Baby!', 'Bandanna Babies', 'Magnolia's Wedding Day', and 'Shuffle Your Feet And Just Roll Along'. Subsequent editions of *Blackbirds* on Broadway all contained some good things, but none of them recaptured the magic of 1928: the 1930 show starred Ethel Waters, Buck & Bubbles, Flournoy Miller, and the Berry Brothers, and featured Minto Cato singing Andy Razaf and Eubie Blakes's lovely ballad, 'Memories Of You'; Bill Robinson returned in the 1934 version in which Kathryn Perry introduced 'A Hundred Years From Today', a song that became a hit for Ethel Waters, and is usually associated with the trombonist and vocalist Jack Teagarden; and *Blackbirds Of 1939*, even with Lena Horne, and songs by such luminaries as George Gershwin, Johnny Mercer, Sammy Fain, Mitchell Parish, Rube Bloom, and others, still did not make it into a second week. Lew Leslie's London edition of *Blackbirds Of 1934* included the haunting 'Moonglow' by Eddie de Lange, Irving Mills, and Will Hudson, and the 1936 version of what are generally regarded now as the premier all-Negro revues, had songs by Mercer and Bloom, and gave West End audiences the opportunity to enjoy the acrobatic dancing of the Nicholas Brothers, who went on to star in many Hollywood musicals of the 40s.

Blaine, Vivian
b. Vivian Stapleton, 21 November 1921, Newark, New Jersey, USA. A vivacious actress and singer who created one of the American musical theatre's best-loved characters, Miss Adelaide, in Frank Loesser's *Guys And Dolls*. Blaine appeared on the stage of her local theatre, and later attended the American Academy of Dramatic Art. She subsequently toured in various musicals and in vaudeville before making her Broadway debut in *Guys And Dolls* in 1950. She gave a delightful performance as the dancegirl who has been waiting for 14 years in the hope that her fiancé, Nathan Detroit, will finally abandon his floating crap game and marry her. Her frustration boils over in 'Sue Me', and she is splendid in the ensemble numbers with the girls at the 'Hot Box', 'Take Back Your Mink' and 'A Bushel And A Peck', but the stand-out song is 'Adelaide's Lament' in which she shares the knowledge, just gleaned from a book, that there is a direct relationship between long engagements and ill health: 'The average unmarried female, basically insecure/Due to some long frustration may react/With psychosomatic symptoms, difficult to endure/Affecting the upper respiratory tract . . . In other words just from waiting around for that plain little band of gold/A person - can develop a cold.' In 1953 she repeated her success at the London Coliseum, and returned to Broadway five years later with *Say, Darling* in which she starred with Robert Morse, David Wayne, and Johnny Desmond. She subsequently toured extensively in a wide range of straight plays and musical revivals including *Zorba, Follies, Hello, Dolly!, Gypsy*, and *I Do! I Do!*. She succeeded Jane Russell in the role of Jo Anne in the Broadway production of *Company*, and has also performed in cabaret. In addition to her stage work, Blaine has appeared in several film musicals including *Jitterbugs, Something For The Boys, Nob Hill, State Fair* (1945), *Doll Face, If I'm Lucky, Three Little Girls In Blue, Skirts Ahoy*, and *Guys And Dolls* (1955). From then to the 80s her film work has mainly consisted of straight roles in features and on US television.
Selected albums: *Singing Selections From Pal Joey & Annie Get Your Gun* (50s), *Broadway's All Time Hits* (c.50s).

Blake, Eubie

b. James Hubert Blake, 7 February 1883, Baltimore, Maryland, USA, d. 12 February 1983. Eubie Blake grew up to the sounds of ragtime music, and before the turn of the century was playing piano in sporting houses and other similar establishments. Blake was a composer too, and in 1915 joined forces with Noble Sissle; they played in vaudeville as a double act and also wrote together extensively. In 1921 Sissle and Blake wrote the score for a Broadway show - a remarkable accomplishment for blacks at that time. *Shuffle Along*, which starred Flournoy Miller, Aubrey Lyles, Gertrude Saunders, and Sissle himself (with Blake on the piano), included several admirable songs, including 'Bandana Days', 'Gypsy Blues', 'Love Will Find A Way', 'Everything Reminds Me Of You', 'Shuffle Along', and 'If You've Never Been Vamped By A Brown Skin (You've Never Been Vamped At All)'. There was also one enormous hit, 'I'm Just Wild About Harry', which became popular at the time for artists such as Marion Harris, Ray Miller, and Paul Whiteman, amongst others, and gave a boost to Harry S. Truman's election campaign in 1948. Blake contributed to other Broadway musicals and revues such as *Elsie*, *Andre Charlot's Revue Of 1924*, and Lew Leslie's *Blackbird's Of 1930*. For the latter he and Razaf wrote 'Baby Mine', 'That Lindy Hop', 'My Handy Man Ain't Handy No More', and another substantial hit, the lovely reflective ballad 'Memories Of You'. After one more Broadway musical *Swing It* (1937), Blake reunited with Sissle for a while, and then spent much of World War II entertaining troops with the USO.

In the 50s Blake demonstrated and lectured on ragtime but his day seemed to be past. Then, in 1969, at the age of 86, Blake's fortunes were revived when John Hammond recorded the old man playing piano and talking about his life. The concurrent vogue for ragtime helped his comeback and the next years were filled with honours, recordings, concerts, festivals and television appearances; in 1978, his life and music were celebrated in a Broadway show, *Eubie*, which was also televised in the USA and later staged in London. In 1983 Blake contributed to the lists of favourite quotations when, on the occasion of his 100th birthday, he said: 'If I'd known I was going to live this long, I would've taken better care of myself.' He died five days later.

Selected albums: *The Wizard Of Ragtime* (1959), *The Eighty-six Years Of Eubie Blake* (1969), *At The Piano* (1974), *Eubie Blake In Concert* (1987). Compilation: *Eubie Blake, Blues And Rags: His Earliest Piano Rolls* (1917-21 recordings).

Further reading: *Reminiscing With Sissle And Blake*, Robert Kimball and William Bolcom.

Bless The Bride

An enormously successful and fondly remembered musical, this is the show that immediately comes to mind when the work of the British composer Vivian Ellis is discussed. *Bless The Bride* opened at London's Adelphi Theatre on 26 April 1947, and was still there over two years later. It proved to be the highlight of Ellis's occasional collaborations with the author A.P. Herbert, and the celebrated producer Charles B. Cochran. The female star of Herbert's story, which was set in the 1870s, was Cochran's 'pride and joy', Lizbeth Webb, in her first leading role. She played Lucy Veracity Willow, a young English girl who intends to marry the awfully reliable (and dull) Hon. Thomas Trout (Brian Reece). Leaving Thomas at the altar, she elopes with the dashing and debonair French actor Pierre Fontaine (Georges Guétary). During their subsequent adventures in France at the time of the Franco-Prussian war, they are separated for a time, but, reunited, they return to marry in England. Ellis's music and Herbert's lyrics were applauded from all sides. The lively and engaging score was full of good things, including three of Ellis's biggest hit songs, 'Ma Belle Margeurite' (Guétary), and two outstanding duets, 'This Is My Lovely Day' and 'I Was Never Kissed Before' (Guétry and Webb), along with others fine numbers such as 'Table For Two', 'Oh, What Will Mother Say?', 'Too Good To Be True', 'Silent Heart', 'Ducky', 'God Bless The Family', and 'Thomas T.', and 'Bless The Bride'. Brian Reece, who, at that point in his career, was about to become a national figure via the radio series *PC 49*, made the most of his comedy song, the prophetically titled 'My Big Moment'. *Bless The Bride* ran for 886 performances, despite opposition from 'new wave' American shows, such as *Oklahoma!* and *Annie Get Your Gun*, and probably would have continued for longer if Cochran had not decided to take it off to make room for his final collaboration with Ellis and Herbert (and his, Cochran's last West End production), *Tough At The Top*, which, in the event, only lasted for 154 performances. A major London revival of *Bless The Bride* was presented at Sadlers Wells in 1987, starring Jan Hartley as Lucy, Bernard Alane as Pierre, and the well-known television actor, Simon Williams, in the role of Thomas.

Blitz!

Lionel Bart was back at the top of his form with this follow-up to his smash-hit *Oliver!* (1960). For *Blitz!* which opened at the Adelphi Theatre in London on 8 May 1962, he not only wrote the book (with Joan Maitland), music, and lyrics, but directed the piece as well. Naturally enough, given the title and the author's Cockney heritage, it was set in the East End of London during the dark years of World War II, when all of Britain's big cities were under siege from

German bombers almost every night. The story concerns two families: one is Jewish - the other is not. Mrs Blitztein (Amanda Bayntun) has a pickled herring stall in Petticoat Lane's Sunday market, next to that of Alfred Locke (Bob Grant). Their dislike of each other is such, that messages have to be passed between them ('Tell Him-Tell Her') by Mrs Blitztein's daughter Carol (Grazina Frame), and Alfred's son Georgie (Graham James). Inevitably, the two young people fall in love, and express their feelings for each other in 'Opposites'. Meanwhile the small children are being moved out of the city to relative safety ('We're Going To The Country'), while Mrs Blitztein pours some of the scorn she normally reserves for Alfred into 'Who's This Geezer Hitler?' ('He's a nasty little basket with a black moustache/And we don't want him here'). Later, Carol is blinded in a air-raid, Georgie deserts from the Army, and there is a typical East End 'knees-up' wedding before a bomb destroys much of the immediate locality. Mrs Blitztein emerges from the rubble unscathed. Bart's rousing, and sometimes tender score, included 'Our Hotel', 'I Want To Whisper Something', 'Another Morning', 'Be What You Wanna Be', 'Petticoat Lane (On A Saturday Ain't So Nice)', 'Down The Lane', 'So Tell Me', 'Mums And Dads', and 'Is This Gonna Be A Wedding?'. Grazina Frame sang the haunting 'Far Away', which became a UK chart hit for Shirley Bassey, and the voice of Vera Lynn was heard on the 'radio' with 'The Day After Tomorrow'. The entire production was designed by Sean Kenny, whose huge mechanical sets, a mass of girders and metal platforms, was called by one critic 'the most remarkable spectacle to hit the London stage in my time.' The show was a tremendous success and ran for well over two years - a total of 568 performances. Nearly 30 years later, in September 1990, the National Youth Theatre of Great Britain staged a revival of *Blitz!* at London's Playhouse Theatre, and, in the following year, it was presented again, in the north of England. Also in 1991, the Original Cast album, which had featured in the UK charts in 1962, was re-released with three additional tracks.

Blood Brothers

Opening at the Lyric Theatre in London on 11 April 1983, the stage musical *Blood Brothers* was distinctly contemporary. It's tough and realistic setting, Liverpool in the depths of that city's despairing inner-urban collapse, mirrored the harshly unsentimental tale of brothers, separated as children, who grow up in very different and opposed social conditions. Despite being worlds apart in their social lives, they are drawn together and one eventually murders the other. At the end, a further tradition of the musical theatre was broken with both brothers lying dead. Written by Willy Russell, one of a handful of brilliant chroniclers of Liverpool's contemporary traumas and dramas, the show starred Barbara Dickson and what Sheridan Morley referred to as a 'hit-squad cast capable of slamming Russell's score out across the footlights'. Despite its grim atmosphere, the pungent reality of *Blood Brothers* helped make it a popular and critical success. Clive Hirschhorn, writing in the *Sunday Express*, called it 'a significant milestone in British musicals'. It was certainly that and remains a hard act to follow. Amongst Russell's songs were 'Marilyn Monroe', 'My Child', 'I'm Not Saying A Word', 'Light Romance' and 'Tell Me It's Not True'. The show earned a Laurence Olivier Award for best musical, and Dixon won for best actress. She was succeeded in the leading role of Mrs. Johnstone by Kiki Dee and, later Stephanie Lawrence. At first, for all its virtues, *Blood Brothers* proved difficult to export. Perhaps its greatest strength, its grittily uncompromising portrayal of the survival instinct that has helped make Liverpool such a unique city, is not only what makes it so good but also renders it difficult to transfer to stages in other countries. However, following a successful 1989 London revival, the show opened on Broadway in April 1993. Initial reaction was extremely cool until some members of the original cast were succeeded by more mature artists from the world of popular music, such as Petula Clark, and David Cassidy and his brother Shaun. Business then picked up considerably.

Bloomer Girl

Composer Harold Arlen's biggest Broadway success was way ahead of its time - in subject matter, at least. The book, by Sig Herzig and Fred Saidy, was based on a play by Dan and Lilith James, and dealt with the highly controversial subjects of civil liberties, women's rights - and the 'phasing-in' of ladies' bloomers during the American Civil War. Even before it opened at the Shubert Theatre in New York on 5 October 1944, rumours abounded that the show was attempting to 'cash in' on the success of *Oklahoma!* which had hit Broadway like a huge breath of fresh air during the previous season. There were similarities: they shared the same costume and set designers, the choreography for both shows was designed by Agnes de Mille (her Civil War ballet depicting the plight of women waiting for their men-folk to return from the conflict, was highly praised), and two of the principals from *Oklahoma!* (in which some garments that looked very much like bloomers were on display), Celeste Holm, who had played Ado Annie, and Joan McCracken (Sylvie), a former member of the American Ballet Company, were together again in *Bloomer Girl*. The setting is Cicero Falls, New York, in 1861, and Evelina Applegate (Celeste Holm), is so outraged when her domineering father - a manufacturer of hoop skirts - demands that she marry one of his salesman, that she joins her crusading aunt, Amelia 'Dolly' Bloomer (Margaret Douglass), in her fight for women's rights in general, and their freedom to wear comfortable clothing in particular. Evelina even converts a Southern slaveholder, Jefferson Calhoun (David Brooks), to her cause. They fall in love, and their duet, 'Right As The Rain', is one of the most appealing numbers in Harold Arlen and lyricist 'Yip' Harburg's score, which also included 'T'morra', T'morra'', 'It Was Good Enough For Grandma', 'Sunday In Cicero Falls', 'When The Boys Come Home', and 'Evelina'. There were also two songs that perfectly encapsulated one of the show's underlying themes, a desire for racial understanding: 'I Got A Song', and 'The Eagle And Me', which was performed by Dooley Wilson, who had made a big impression in the show, *Cabin In The Sky* (1940), and in the film, *Casablanca* (1942), in which he ostensibly sung 'As Time Goes By'. 'The Eagle And Me' subsequently became an important element in the repertoire of Lena Horne. *Bloomer Girl* enjoyed an impressive run of 654 performances, and was revived briefly in New York at the City Center in 1947. In 1992, a CD purporting to be the first *complete* Original Cast recording of *Bloomer Girl* since its first 78 issue, was released in MCA's Broadway Gold series.

Blossom Time

This was an American version of the Viennese operetta, *Das Dreimäderlhaus*, by A.M. Wilner and Heinz Reichert, adapted from the novel *Schwammerl*, by Dr. R.H. Bartsch, with music arranged by Heinrich Berté. It was based on the life and music of the composer Franz Schubert, and opened at the Ambassador Theatre in New York on 29 September 1921. For the US production, Schubert's music was arranged by the young Sigmund Romberg, and Dorothy Donnelly provided a revised book and lyrics. Her libretto was a tangled web of romantic intrigue in which Franz Schubert (Bertram Peacock) supposedly loses his inspiration, and his girl, Mitzi Krantz (Olga Cook), after his best friend, Baron Franz Von Schober (Howard Marsh), has serenaded her with Schubert's own songs. Marsh was widely applauded for his rendition of 'Serenade', and the complete score was a sheer delight, including as it did the wonderful 'Song Of Love', 'Three Little Maids', 'Peace To My Lonely Heart', 'This Is An Old Vienna Town', 'Tell Me Daisy', 'My Springtime Thou Art', and 'Let Me Awake'. After the remarkable New York run of 592 performances, several road companies toured the USA, and Broadway audiences enjoyed the show again in 1939 and 1943. In 1922, London audiences were offered a different version entitled *Lilac Time*. The musical adaptation was by Heinrich Berté and G.H. Clutsam, with a fresh book and lyrics by Adrian

Ross, and several appealing songs emerged such as 'Under The Lilac Bough', 'Three Little Girls', 'The Golden Song', 'My Sweetest Song Of All', 'Yours Is My Heart', and 'Just A Little Ring'. The cast included Dorothy Clayton, Courtice Pounds, and Clara Butterworth, and the show stayed at the Lyric theatre for well over a year. Several London revivals were presented through until the early 40s. Another production called *Blossom Time*, with a book by Rodney Ackland, and music and lyrics by G.H. Clutsam and Richard Tauber, 'based on the music of Franz Schubert', was presented in London in 1942. It was actually a vehicle for Richard Tauber, the Australian singer and composer who had been domiciled in England since 1938. He also starred in a film version of *Blossom Time* which was released in 1938. The show itself, in its many variations, remains a favourite of professional and amateur operatic societies throughout the world.

Blue For A Boy

With a book by Austin Melford, which was based on the German farce, *Hurrah! eine Junge!*, by Franz Arnold and Ernest Bach, *Blue For A Boy* opened at Her Majesty's Theatre in London on 30 November 1950. Sub-titled *What Shall We Do With The Body?*, it purported to be 'a musical romp' involving several well-known comedy performers such as the substantially built Fred Emney (complete with monocle and cigar), Richard Hearne (*not* in his usual character of Mr. Pastry), Bertha Belmore, and the show's author and director, Austin Melford. The plot was extremely complicated and involved step-sons, step-fathers, and step-mothers; female impersonations, and many of the various misconceptions and confused identities essential for a successful farce - and this one was very successful. The engaging songs by composer Harry Parr Davies and lyricist Harold Purcell, which were delivered with a great deal of verve and panache by the show's leading ladies, Hermene French and Eve Lister, included 'Lying Awake And Dreaming', 'At Last It Happened', and 'Blue For A Boy', which had a life outside of the show, particularly in a recording by Dick James and Pearl Carr. One critic described the production as 'sheer lunatic fun that keeps the theatre rocking', and it continued to do so for 664 performances.

Blue Paradise, The

Composer Sigmund Romberg's first successful musical production opened on 5 August 1915 at the Casino Theatre in New York. It was adapted from Ein Tag Im Paradies, a Viennese operetta by Edmund Eysler, and had lyrics by Herbert Reynolds. Edgar Smith's book tells the sad tale of the shy and gentle Mizzi, played by Vivenne Segal, who works at the Blue Paradise restaurant in Vienna. Her lover,

Rudolphe (Cecil Lean), leaves to seek his fortune in America, but when he returns several years later, she has changed beyond belief, and is now cynical and world-weary. Vivienne Segal was enchanting in her first Broadway book musical, and, together with Lean, introduced the show's big hit song, 'Auf Wiedersehn'. The number became widely popular, especially through a recording by Harry Macdonough and Olive Kline. The rest of Romberg's delightfully romantic score included 'One Step Into Love' 'My Model Girl (lyric: Harold Atteridge), and 'A Toast To A Woman's Eyes'. Several of Edmund Eysler's original songs were also retained. *The Blue Paradise* ran for a profitable 356 performances, and launched both Vivienne Segal and Sigmund Romberg on their memorable Broadway careers.

Blues In The Night

This celebratory revue of blues music first opened on 6 June 1982 Off Broadway at the Rialto Theatre where it starred Leslie Uggams and ran for 53 performances. Almost exactly five years later, a revised production which was conceived and directed by Sheldon Epps, was presented in June 1987 at the tiny Donmar Warehouse on the London Fringe. After an enthusiastic critical reception, it transferred to the Piccadilly Theatre in the West End on 23 September of the year. The show is set in a seedy hotel in Chicago in the 30s, and the residents consist of three women, the Lady from the Road (Carol Woods), the Woman of the World (Debby Bishop), the Girl with a Date (Maria Friedman), and a pianist, The Man in the Saloon, played by Peter Straker. The lovelorn ladies reflect on the vagaries of men through a long anthology of urban blues tunes and bluesy pop standards. Carol Woods gave a sensational performance, shimmying her way through raunchy numbers such as 'Kitchen Man' and 'Take Me For A Buggy Ride'. As the *Variety* critic noted, 'she is a buxom, big-voiced, emotionally generous, and physically articulate performer who embodies the gut-bucket spirit of early black vaudeville who stops the show twice, firstly with the blistering 'Lover Man', a searing expression of raw sexual need, and again with a sobbing and savage rendition of Bessie Smith's 'Wasted Life Blues'.' Some of the other songs in this feast for the blues connoisseurs and discerning pop fans, included 'Four Walls (And One Dirty Window) Blues', 'Stomping At The Savoy', 'New Orleans Hop Scop Blues', 'Taking A Chance On Love', 'Wild Women Don't Have The Blues', 'Lush Life', 'I'm Just A Lucky So-And So', 'Willow Weep For Me', 'Blues In The Night', 'Dirty No-Gooder's Blues', and 'Nobody Loves You When You're Down And Out'. After a London run lasting 11 months, Woods recreated her role for another Off Broadway production which made a brief appearance at the Minetta Lane Theatre in September 1988. Also in the cast were Brenda Pressley, Leilani Jones, and Lawrence Hamilton. In 1993, a new version directed by Clarke Peters and starring Patti Boulaye, toured the UK provinces.

Bock, Jerry

b. Jerrold Lewis Bock, 23 November 1928, New Haven, Connecticut, USA. Bock studied the piano from an early age and was soon able to play quite complicated compositions by ear. He wrote the music for various shows while studying at high school and the University of Wisconsin in the 40s, and subsequently worked on revues at summer camps and for television. In 1955 Bock and lyricist Larry Holofcener contributed some songs to the Broadway revue *Catch A Star*, and, a year later, with George Weiss, they provided the complete score for *Mr. Wonderful*, a musical vehicle for Sammy Davis Jnr., which ran for 383 performances. Bock and Holofcener's last assignment together was for the *Zeigfeld Follies* of 1956, which closed before it reached New York. Shortly afterwards, Bock met lyricist Sheldon Harnick (b. 30 April 1924, Chicago, Illinois, USA.), and they formed what is arguably the most important musicals partnership of the 60s. Harnick had been a danceband violinist before moving to New York in 1950 where he had several of his songs performed in revues such as *New Faces Of 1952* ('Boston Beguine') and *Shoestring Revue*. Bock and Harnick's first effort, *The Body Beautiful* (1958), was a failure, but *Fiorello!* (1959) ran for 795 performances. Next came the underrated *Tenderloin* (1960), a humorous exposé of vice in New York with some good songs including 'Little Old New York', 'The Picture Of Happiness', and 'How the Money Changes Hands'. In 1963 the team wrote several numbers for the critically acclaimed marionette show *Man In The Moon*, and, later in the same year, came up with what is considered to be their best score, for *She Loves Me*. With delightful songs such as 'Will He Like Me?, 'Ice Cream', 'A Trip To The Library', and 'She Loves Me', plus Broadway's favourite ingenue, Barbara Cook, it warranted a longer stay than just 302 performances. Bock and Harnick's next show clocked up more than 10 times that total in New York, and was a smash-hit around the world. *Fiddler On The Roof* (1964), starring Zero Mostel, became one of the most cherished of all Broadway musicals, and gave the world of popular music (and Jewish functions of all kinds) hit songs such as 'Matchmaker, Matchmaker', 'Sunrise, Sunset', and the immortal 'If I Was A Rich Man'. It proved impossible to follow, and for the remainder of the decade the composers worked on a variety of projects including a 'Sherlock Holmes' musical *Baker Street*; *The Apple Tree*, which was based on stories by Mark Twain and others, and ran for 463 performances; and *Her First Roman*, a rare musical adaptation of Bernard Shaw, for which they contributed a couple of songs. After *The Rothschilds* (1970), which had a strong Jewish theme and was similar in a way to *Fiddler On The Roof*, Bock and Harnick ended their partnership. Bock has been inactive for over 20 years, with no musical work at all forthcoming. In 1971, Harnick gave his 'observations on the fine art and craft of lyric writing' at a recital in the *Lyrics And Lyricists* series at the 92nd Street YM-YWHA in New York, and since then his projects have included *Pinocchio* (1973) with music by Mary Rodgers, *Rex* (1976) with music by Richard Rodgers, and an English translation of the *Umbrellas Of Cherbourg* with composer Michel Legrand for an 1979 Off Broadway production. In the 80s there was a projected musical *Dragons*, that does not seem to have materialised, and in the 90s Harnick collaborated with Joe Raposo on *A Wonderful Life*, and with Thomas Z. Shepard on *Love In Two Countries*, neither of which opened on Broadway immediately following their out-of-town tryouts.

Bolger, Ray

b. Raymond Wallace Bolger, 10 January 1904, Boston, Massachusetts, USA, d. 15 January 1987, Los Angeles, California, USA. An eccentric, rubber-legged dancer with a style and image that had to be seen to be believed. He started out as a comedian in 1922 with the Bob Ott Musical Repertory Company and four years later gained a small part in a Broadway show called *The Merry Whirl*. After a spell in vaudeville, he returned to Broadway in the late 20s and 30s in shows such as *Heads Up, George White's Scandals, Life Begins At 8:40*, and *On Your Toes* (1936). Bolger shot to stardom in the latter show in which he introduced the lovely 'There's A Small Hotel', and performed an hilarious eccentric dance in Richard Rodgers' famous 'Slaughter On Tenth Avenue' ballet. After leaving the show he moved to Hollywood and appeared in *The Great Ziegfeld, Rosalie, Sweethearts*, and one of the most memorable films of all-time, *The Wizard Of Oz* (1939), in which he played the Scarecrow in search of a brain. After returning to New York for the short-lived musical *Keep Off The Grass* (1940), he made one more film, *Sunny* (1941), before leaving for the South Pacific where he entertained troops with the USO during World War II. He was back on Broadway in 1942 for *By Jupiter*, and then the revue *Three To Make Ready* in which he stopped the show regularly with the charming 'That Old Soft Shoe', complete with straw hat and cane. Frank Loesser's *Where's Charley?* came along in 1948 and gave Bolger his greatest role; he introduced the gentle 'Once In Love With Amy', and it subsequently became his signature tune. During the 40s and 50s he made several more films including *Stage Door Canteen*,

Four Jacks And A Jill, The Harvey Girls, Look For The Silver Lining, Where's Charley?, and *April In Paris*. In 1962 and 1969 he appeared in two more stage musicals, *All American* and *Come Summer*, but mostly during the 60s and 70s he mixed feature films such as *Babes In Toyland, The Daydreamer, The Runner Stumbles*, and *Just You And Me Kid*, with television movies which included *The Entertainer, The Captains And The Kings*, and *Only Heaven Knows*. In 1984, in the MGM extravaganza *That's Entertainment*, he looked back affectionately on a career that had spanned well over half a century. Three years later he died of cancer at the age of 83.

Bolton, Guy

b. Guy Reginald Bolton, 23 November 1884, Broxbourne, England, d. 6 September 1979, London, England. An important librettist who was right there in the early part of the century when the real American musical was born. Bolton was the son of an American father and an English mother, and, after the family had moved to the USA, he began his adult life as an architect and wrote in his spare time. Early on he discovered that he worked best with others, and throughout his long and distinguished career his list of co-authors included George Grossmith, Clifford Grey, Philip Bartholmae, George Middleton, W. Somerset Maugham, and Eddie Davis. His two principal collaborators were Fred Thompson and P.G. Wodehouse, and, early on, Bolton teamed with Wodehouse and composer Jerome Kern for the famous Princess Theatre musicals which, with their smart and witty integrated books and lyrics, are considered to be a watershed in the evolution of the American musical. The best of these were *Oh, Boy!* (1917), *Leave It To Jane* (1917), and *Oh, Lady! Lady!!* (1918). From 1915 through until 1924, Bolton worked mostly with Kern and various lyricists on shows such as *90 In The Shade, Nobody Home, Very Good Eddie, Miss Springtime, Have A Heart, The Riviera Girl, Miss 1917, Oh, My Dear!, Sally, Tangerine, The Hotel Mouse, Daffy Dill, Sitting Pretty*, and *Primrose* (1924, London). By that time he had become the leading librettist around, and so was the logical choice to write the book (with Fred Thomson) for *Lady, Be Good!* (1924) the show which contained George and Ira Gershwin's first complete score. It turned out to a be joyous affair and was a big hit on Broadway and in London, and confirmed Fred Astaire and his sister Adele as musical comedy's premier dance team. During the next six years Bolton worked at a tremendous rate on shows such as *The Bamboula* (London), *Tip Toes, The Ramblers, Oh, Kay!, The Nightingale, Rio Rita, The Five O'clock Girl, She's My Baby, Rosalie, Blue Eyes* (London), *Polly, Top Speed, Simple Simon*, and *Girl Crazy*. The latter production, with its wonderful Gershwin score, was typical

Bolton - beautifully constructed, and full of fun and excruciating puns. However, just like the rest of his work, it was not going to win a Pulitzer Prize for drama, and that is the direction in which the Gershwins were heading. Their next show, *Of Thee I Sing*, had a book by George S. Kaufman which satirized America's social and political life and was quite different from the frothy confections that Bolton concocted. He seemed unable or unwilling to change his style, and, leaving Broadway to its own more serious devices, he moved to London, where, for the next decade, he collaborated mostly with Clifford Grey and Fred Thompson on a series of highly successful romps, many of which starred some of the London theatre's top talent such as Leslie Henson, Jack Buchanan, Elsie Randolph, Bobby Howes, and Evelyn Laye. They included *Song Of The Drum*, *Give Me A Ring*, *Seeing Stars*, *At The Silver Swan*, *Swing Along*, *This'll Make You Whistle*, *Going Places*, *Going Greek*, *Hide And Seek*, *The Fleet's Lit Up*, *Running Riot*, *Bobby Get Your Gun*, and *Magyar Melody* (1939). Bolton did not neglect Broadway entirely, and teamed up with his old chum P.G. Wodehouse in 1934 to write the book for the Cole Porter smash-hit *Anything Goes*, and returned to the US again during World War II to provide the librettos for *Walk With Music*, *Hold On To Your Hats*, *Jackpot*, and *Follow The Girls*. Just after the war, in 1947, he revised the book for a revival of the 1909/1910 hit, *The Chocolate Soldier*. In 1955, 50 years after his debut on Broadway with *90 In The Shade*, Old Father Time caught up with him. While the latest of his archaic efforts, *Ankles Aweigh*, was playing at the Mark Hellinger Theatre, just around the corner at the Royale, Sandy Wilson's *The Boy Friend* was spoofing exactly that kind of thing. It was time to call it a day, and Bolton wrote only one more book for Broadway when he adapted his and Marcelle Maurete's *Anastasia* for the 1967 musical production of *Anya*.

Further reading: *Bring On The Girls!*, Guy Bolton and P.G. Wodehouse. *Bolton And Wodehouse And Kern*, James H. Heineman.

Boublil, Alain

b. France. A librettist and lyricist, Boublil's first musical, the rock-opera *La Revolution Francaise* in 1973, marked the beginning of his collaboration with Claude-Michel Schönberg. Boublil co-produced the double-gold record album of the show which sold in excess of 350,000 copies. His original conception of the musical *Les Misérables* brought them together again in 1978, and, after two years of work, the show was produced at the Palais des Sports in Paris in September 1980. Three years later, Boublil was involved with two ex-members of Abba, Björn Ulvaeus and Benny Andersson, in a production of *Abbacadabra* at the Lyric Theatre, Hammersmith. In

1985, *Les Misérables* (with English lyrics by Herbert Kretzmer) began its London run, and, in January 1994, overtook *Jesus Christ Superstar* as the third longest-running London musical. After the show opened on Broadway in 1987, Boublil won two Tony Awards, and a Grammy for best Original Cast album. Boublil and Schönberg's latest blockbuster, *Miss Saigon*, hit the West End in 1989, and repeated its success in New York two years later. Impresario Cameron Mackintosh, who produced both hit shows, premiered two more of Boublil and Schönberg's compositions, 'Rhapsody For Piano And Orchestra' and 'Symphonic Suite', at London's Royal Albert Hall in 1992.

Boy Friend, The

Despite a quiet opening at London's Players' Theatre in April 1953, Sandy Wilson's stage musical *The Boy Friend* became a huge popular success after transferring to Wyndham's Theatre in the West End on 14 January 1954. An affectionate pastiche of the musical theatre of the 20s, the show starred Anthony Hayes, Hugh Paddick, Joan Sterndale Bennett, Larry Drew, John Rutland, and Anne Rogers, who came in 48 hours before it was due to open. Wilson wrote the book as well as the delightful score which included several memorable numbers such as 'It's Never Too Late To Fall In Love', 'Won't You Charleston With Me?', 'I Could Be Happy With You', 'Fancy Forgetting', 'The Boy Friend', 'Poor Little Pierrette', and the wistful 'Room In Bloomsbury'. While *The Boy Friend* settled in for a run of 2,084 performances in London, Julie Andrews made her Broadway debut in the US production which opened at the Royale Theatre on 30 September 1954 and ran for well over a year. A major New York revival was mounted in 1958, and London audiences enjoyed the show again in 1967 and 1984. At a photocall in 1993, Sandy Wilson, surrounded by a gaggle of potential flappers, announced that *The Boy Friend* would be back in the West End sometime in the following year. The 'disastrous' 1971 film version starred Twiggy and future Broadway star Tommy Tune, and was directed by Ken Russell.

Boys From Syracuse, The

Richard Rodgers and Lorenz Hart were in the autumn of their partnership (Rodgers and Oscar Hammerstein II's *Oklahoma!* was only five years away) when they wrote this appealing score for what is said to be the first musical based on a play by William Shakespeare. Librettist-director-producer George Abbott's adaptation of *The Comedy Of Errors* incorporated a variety of characters with names such as Antiphulus, Luce, Dromio, and Luciana, in a scenario that was based in Asia Minor. The story of mixed-up twins bordered on the farce: 'Did you bring your harp?'. 'No'. 'Good, then you can pick on me.' The cast included the well-known comedy performer Jimmy Savo, Teddy Hart (Lorenz Hart's brother who, rather conveniently, bore an uncanny resemblance to Savo), Eddie Albert, Wynn Murray, Ronald Graham, Muriel Angelus, Marcy Wescott, Betty Bruce, and Burl Ives (as Tailor's Apprentice). Rodgers and Hart's score contained three of their all-time standards: 'Sing For Your Supper', 'This Can't Be Love', and 'Falling In Love With Love', along with the lovely ballad 'You Have Cast Your Shadow On The Sea'. There were also a few point numbers such as 'What Can You Do With A Man?', 'Dear Old Syracuse', 'The Shortest Day Of The Year', 'Oh, Diogenes', and 'He And She'. The show, which began its run at the Alvin Theatre on 23 November 1938, ran for a somewhat disappointing 235 performances, but the 1963 Off Broadway revival stayed in New York for over twice as long. In November 1963 *The Boys From Syracuse* had its London premiere with a cast that included UK comedians Bob Monkhouse and Ronnie Corbett. Nearly 30 years later, in the summer of 1991, Londoners had another chance to savour the show's zany antics and melodic score when it played a limited season at the the Open Air Theatre in Regent's Park, and won a Laurence Olivier Award for best revival. The 1940 film version starred Allan Jones, Joe Penner, and Martha Raye. Other well-known musicals based on Shakespeare's works include *Kiss Me, Kate* (*The Taming Of The Shrew*) and *West Side Story* (*Romeo And Juliet*).

Brice, Fanny

b. 29 October 1891, New York City, New York, USA, d. 29 May 1951. In her early teens Brice appeared on the stage in both legitimate musical shows and in vaudeville. In 1910 she was booked into Florenz Ziegfeld's *Follies* and appeared in his shows regularly for the next dozen years, gradually rising to become one of Broadway's biggest stars. She also appeared in other Broadway shows including *Music Box Revue* (1928), in which she co-starred with Bobby Clark, and one, *Fanny*, written especially for her after she became a star. For the most part her act consisted of comic patter and novelty songs, many of which she sang in a Brooklyn dialect. Among her hits in this area of music was 'Second-Hand Rose'. Despite her plain features and gawky stage presence, or perhaps because of the affinity audiences felt with her for these characteristics, she later sang torch songs with great success. Among the songs in this style were 'When A Woman Loves A Man' and 'My Man', the song with which she was most closely linked. She made her first film appearance in 1928 in *Night Club* and *My Man*, but her real forte was the stage and after a half-dozen more films she gave up the cinema to concentrate on other areas of show business. Brice was also successful on radio, appearing in the title role of the popular series, Baby Snooks, which ran for six years from 1939. She died in 1951 but in 1964 her career and chequered private life (she was married to gambler Nicky Arnstein and showman Billy Rose) became the subject of a hit Broadway show. *Funny Girl*, written by Jule Styne and Bob Merrill and starring Barbra Streisand as Brice, ran for 1,348 performances and four years later provided the basis for a successful film and a 1978 sequel, *Funny Lady*.

Bricusse, Leslie

b. 29 January 1931, London, England. A composer, lyricist, librettist and screenwriter, Bricusse was influenced by the MGM musicals of the 40s, pariculary *Words And Music*, the Richard Rodgers and Lorenz Hart biopic. He originally intended to be a journalist, but, while studying at Cambridge University, started to write, direct and appear in the Cambridge footlights revues. In 1953, he wrote the music and lyrics (with Robin Beaumont) for *Lady At the Wheel*, a musical with the Monte Carlo rally as its setting, which included songs such as 'The Early Birdie', 'Pete Y'Know', 'Love Is' and a comedy tango, 'Siesta'. It was presented at the local Arts Theatre, and, five years later, had a limited run in the West End. Well before that, in 1954-5, Bricusse had appeared on the London stage himself, and with a theatrical legend, in *An Evening With Beatrice Lillie*. For a while during the 50s, he was under contract as a writer at Pinewood Film Studios, and, in 1954, wrote the screenplay, and the songs (with Beaumont), for *Charley Moon*, which starred Max Bygraves. The popular singer/comedian took one of the numbers, 'Out Of Town', into the UK Top 20, and it gained Bricusse his first Ivor Novello Award: he won several others, including one for 'My Kind Of Girl' (words and music by Bricusse), which was a UK Top 5 hit for Matt Monro in 1961. Bricusse also wrote a good deal of special material for Bygraves, including one of his 'catch-phrase' songs, 'A Good Idea - Son!'. Early in 1961, Bricusse went to New York to write for another Beatrice Lillie revue, taking Anthony Newley with him to develop ideas for a show of their own. The result, *Stop The World - I Want To Get Off*, written in around three weeks, opened in London's West End in July of that year, and stayed there until November 1962. It later ran for over 500 performances on Broadway, and was filmed in 1966. Book, music and lyrics were jointly credited to Bricusse and Newley - the latter starred as the central character, Littlechap, in London and New York. The score included several hit songs, including 'What Kind Of Fool Am I?', 'Once In A Lifetime' and 'Gonna Build A Mountain', as well as other, more specialized numbers, such as 'Lumbered', 'Typically

English' and 'Someone Nice Like You'. While Newley went off to appear in the off-beat, parochial movie, *The World Of Sammy Lee,* Bricusse collaborated with Cyril Ornadel on the score for the musical, *Pickwick* (1963), which starred the 'Goon with the golden voice', Harry Secombe, in the title role. His recording of the show's big ballad, 'If I Ruled The World', was a Top 20 hit in the UK, and, later, after the Broadway production had flopped, it became part of Tony Bennett's repertoire. Reunited in 1964, Bricusse and Newley's next major stage project, *The Roar Of The Greasepaint - The Smell Of The Crowd* (1965), was regarded as similar to their previous effort, a moral tale of a downtrodden little man, bucking the system. It toured (Bricusse: 'We managed to empty every provincial theatre in England'), but did not play the West End. Bricusse, and others, felt that comedian, Norman Wisdom, was miscast in the central role, and Newley took over for the Broadway run of 232 performances. Once again, though, the hit songs were there – in this case, 'Who Can I Turn To?' and 'A Wonderful Day Like Today', plus other items such as 'This Dream', 'The Beautiful Land', 'The Joker', 'Where Would You Be Without Me?', 'Nothing Can Stop Me Now' and 'Feeling Good'. The latter number was popularized in the USA by Joe Sherman, and received an impressive, extended treatment from Steve Winwood's UK rock group, Traffic, on their live *Last Exit* (1969). In 1964, Bricusse and Newley turned their attention to the big screen, providing the lyric to John Barry's music for the title song to the James Bond movie, *Goldfinger* (1964), which Shirley Bassey sang over the titles. Bricusse and Barry later wrote another Bond theme for *You Only Live Twice* (1968), popularized by Nancy Sinatra. In 1967, Bricusse wrote the screenplay and the complete song score for *Doctor Dolittle,* which starred Newley, along with Rex Harrison, who sang the Oscar-winning 'Talk To The Animals'. Considered an 'expensive dud', there was no mention of a *Doctor Dolittle II.* Far more to the public's taste was Roald Dahl's *Willy Wonka And The Chocolate Factory* (1971). Bricusse and Newley's score contained 'The Candy Man', a song which gave Sammy Davis Jnr. a US number 1 in the following year. Davis was one of the songwriting team's favourite people – Bricusse estimates that he recorded at least 60 of his songs, including a complete album of *Doctor Dolittle.* Davis also starred in a revival of *Stop The World - I Want To Get Off* during the 1978-79 Broadway season.

After writing several numbers for a 1971 US television adaptation of *Peter Pan,* which starred Danny Kaye and Mia Farrow, Bricusse and Newley returned to the stage with *The Good Old Bad Old Days.* Newley directed and starred in the show, which ran for 10 months in London, and included the jolly title song and several other appealing numbers, such as 'I Do Not Love You', 'It's A Musical World', 'The People Tree' and 'The Good Things In Life'. Since then, their back catalogue has been re-packaged in productions such as *The Travelling Music Show* (1978), with Bruce Forsyth; and *Once Upon A Song,* in which Newley occasionally appears when he is not singing for big dollars in Las Vegas. Also in 1978, Bricusse collaborated with composer Armando Trovajoli on *Beyond the Rainbow,* an English language version of the Italian musical *Aggiungi Una Posta Alla Tavola,* which ran for six months in London - a good deal longer than his own *Kings And Clowns.* He also wrote some new songs for a Chichester Festival Theatre production of his film score for *Goodbye, Mr Chips* (1982). By then, he was generally wearing his Hollywood hat, and had received Oscar nominations for his work on *Goodbye, Mr Chips* (1969, original song score, with John Willams), *Scrooge* (1970, original song score with Ian Fraser and Herbert W. Spencer, and his own song, 'Thank You Very Much'), *That's Life* (1986, 'Life In a Looking Glass', with Henry Mancin), *Home Alone* (1990, 'Somewhere In My Memory', with John Williams), and *Hook* (1991, 'When You're Alone', with John Williams). He won his second Academy Award in 1982, in collaboration with Henry Mancini, for the original song score to *Victor/Victoria.* Bricusse and Newley were inducted into the Songwriters' Hall Of Fame in 1989, a year that otherwise proved something of a disappointment for partners: an updated version of *Stop The World,* directed by, and starring Newley, staggered along for five weeks in London, and Bricusse's *Sherlock Holmes,* with Ron Moody and Liz Robertson, opened there as well, to disappointing reviews. The latter show re-surfaced in 1993, and toured the UK with Robert Powell in the title role, shortly after *Scrooge,* Bricusse's stage adaptation of his film score, had enjoyed a limited run at the Alexandra Theatre in Birmingham, England, with Newley in the title role. Also in 1993, Harry Secombe recreated his orginal role in *Pickwick* at Chichester and in the West End, and Broadway was buzzing with talk of possible stage productions of *Victor/Victoria,* and *Jekyll & Hyde,* a show that Bricusse wrote with Frank Wildhorn which was released on CD in 1990.

Brigadoon

Opening at the Ziegfeld Theatre in New York on 13 March 1947, the stage musical *Brigadoon* was the first major success of the songwriting team of Alan Jay Lerner and Frederick Loewe. Inspired by the writings of James Barrie, but very similar in plot to *Germelshausen,* a story by German writer William F. Gerstacker, *Brigadoon* is set in Scotland where two Americans come upon a quaint village. One of the visitors, Tommy Albright, falls in love with a local girl, Fiona MacLaren, only to discover that the village disappeared 200 hundred years ago and returns on just one day each century. When the village vanishes Tommy returns to the USA but his love for Fiona is such that he travels back to Scotland. There, the village is brought back to life just long enough for him to re-enter it before the mists close around it once again. Starring David Brooks and Marion Bell, the show had several delightful songs, such as 'The Heather On The Hill', 'From This Day On' 'I'll Go Home With Bonnie Jean', 'Waitin' For My Dearie', 'Come To Me, Bend To Me', 'There But For You Go I', and one hit, 'Almost Like Being In Love'. *Brigadoon* ran for almost 600 hundred performances and became the first musical ever to be chosen as Best Play by the New York Drama Critics Circle. Agnes De Mille won a Tony Award for her outstanding dance direction. The 1949 London production stayed at His Majesty's Theatre for 685 performances. *Brigadoon* was revived in New York in 1980, and again in 1986 when it was produced by the New York City Opera. West End audiences applauded the show once more in 1988 with Jacinta Mulcahy, Robert Meadmore, Lesley Mackie, and Robin Nedwell. It was filmed in 1954 with Gene Kelly and Cyd Charisse.

Brightman, Sarah

b. 14 August 1961, England. An actress and singer who first came to notice in 1978 when, with the dance group Hot Gossip, she made the UK Top 10 with the disco-pop single 'I Lost My Heart To a Starship Trouper'. It was all a far cry from her childhood ambition to become a ballet dancer. Three years later she won a part in Andrew Lloyd Webber's musical *Cats*, and was noticed again - this time by the composer himself - and they were married in 1984. The marriage lasted for six years, and, during that time, Sarah Brightman became established as one of the premier leading ladies of the musical theatre. After *Cats*, she appeared for a season at the Old Vic in Frank Dunlop's 1982 adaptation of *Masquerade*, and later in the year she was in Charles Strouse's short-lived musical *Nightingale*. All the while she was taking singing lessons, training her superb soprano voice so that she could undertake more demanding roles than those in conventional musical comedy. In 1984 she appeared in the television version of Lloyd Webber's *Song And Dance*, and also sang on the Top 30 album. A year later, she made her operatic debut in the role of Valencienne in *The Merry Widow* at Sadlers Wells, and gave several concerts of Lloyd Webber's *Requiem* in England and America, which resulted in another best-selling album. It also produced a Top 5 single, 'Pie Jesus', on which Brightman duetted with the 12-year-old Paul Miles-Kingston. In 1986 she scored a great personal triumph when she co-starred with Michael Crawford in *The Phantom Of The Opera*, and recreated her role two years later on Broadway. She had UK Top 10 hits with three songs from the show, 'The Phantom Of The Opera' (with Steve Harley), 'All I Ask Of You' (with Cliff Richard), and 'Wishing You Were Somehow Here Again'. In the late 80s and early 90s, she toured many parts of the world, including Japan and the UK, in a concert production of *The Music Of Andrew Lloyd Webber*. In December 1991, at the end of American leg of the tour, she took over the leading role of Rose in *Aspects Of Love* for the last few weeks of the Broadway run. She also joined the West End production for a time, but, while her presence was welcomed and her performance critically acclaimed, she was unable to prevent its closure in June 1992. In the same year Brightman was high in the UK chart again, this time duetting with opera singer José Carreras on the Olympic Anthem, 'Amigos Para Siempre (Friends For Life)', which was written, inevitably, by Andrew Lloyd Webber, with lyric by Don Black. In 1993 she made her debut in the straight theatre with appearances in *Trelawny Of The Wells* and *Relative Values*. Experienced West End observers expect Lloyd Webber to write a musical for her based on the life of Jessie Matthews, the graceful star of many 20s and 30s musicals, and to whom she bears an uncanny facial resemblance.

Selected albums: *Britten Folk Songs* (1988), with Peter Ustinov *Howard Blake: Granpa* (1988), *The Songs That Got Away* (1989), *As I Came Of Age* (1990), *Dive* (1993), and Original Cast recordings.

Broadway Angel

From the 50s onwards, Capitol Records recorded the Original Cast albums for a number of Broadway shows. Some of them, such as *Annie Get Your Gun*, *Kiss Me, Kate*, *The Music Man*, and *Funny Girl*, were enormous hits, whilst others, including *The Gay Life* and *Kwamina*, were most definitely not. In the early 90s, Broadway Angel began to re-release the material from the original vinyl albums on mid-price CDs, thereby enabling musicals fans to renew their worn-out, dog-eared copies of the originals, and also to discover, perhaps for the first time, that some of the shows that flopped contained some pretty good songs. As well as the productions listed above, early in 1994, the the label's Broadway Classics catalogue included *St. Louis Woman, Zorba, Follies, Can-Can, No Strings, The Boys From Syracuse* (25th anniversary revival cast), *The Unsinkable Molly Brown, Flahooley, Pal Joey, Plain and Fancy, A Funny Thing Happened On the Way To The Forum, Beyond The Fringe* (London and Broadway cast), *Top Banana, Little Mary Sunshine, Three Wishes For Jamie, By The Beautiful Sea, Cabin In The Sky, Tovarich, Fiorello, Tenderloin, Golden Boy, A Party With Betty Comden And Adolph Green*, and *Of Thee I Sing*.

In addition, the label had also released the Original Cast album of the current Broadway smash-hit, *Crazy For You*, and film soundtracks of *Oklahoma!*, *The King And I*, and *Carousel*. One of the other labels specializing in putting many glorious stage scores back into circulation is Sony Broadway.

Brown, Georgia
b. Lillie Klot, 21 October 1933, Whitechapel, London, England, d. 5 July 1992. Vocalist and actress Brown came from a poor working-class area of the east end and made her way to Broadway in true storybook fashion. Although jazz was her early influence (she adopted her name from 'Sweet Georgia Brown') the attraction of the British music hall tradition took over and from this she found great success for four decades. Her earliest stage show was with Brecht's *Threepenny Opera* in 1956. She was soon a major star being elevated to this position by the extraordinary success of Lionel Bart's *Oliver*. Her performance as Nancy remains her greatest, and her interpretation of 'As Long As He Needs Me' gave such drama and emotion to the song, that nobody has been able to equal (although Shirley Bassey had the hit record in 1960). She appeared in two more of Bart's productions, *Maggie May* and the film, *Lock Up Your Daughters* and continued to work with a lower profile on television, stage and in films. Her film credits included *A Study In Terror* (1965), *The Fixer* (1968) and *The Seven Per Cent Solution* (1976) in which she sang Stephen Sondheim's 'I Never Do Anything Twice'. After moving to the USA she performed in two shows on Broadway, *Carmelina* (1979) and *Roza* (1987). She returned to London to star in *42nd Street* and was a success in Steven Berkoff's *Greek*. Her most recent work was in her own show *Georgia Brown And Friends*, an apt title, as she had many friends and critical admirers and rarely received a bad review in her entire career.

Brynner, Yul
b. Youl Bryner, 11 July 1920, Sakhalin, Russia, d.10 October 1985, New York, USA. Sakhalin is a Siberian island north of Japan, and the date of Brynner's date of birth there is a matter for negotiation; it probably lies somewhere between 1915 and 1920. He spent his early childhood in Peking but was brought up in Paris where he sang in clubs before moving to America in 1941. There he worked in radio and toured as an actor until his Broadway debut with Mary Martin in the short-lived musical *Lute Song* in 1946. Two years later he reprised his role for London and subsequently worked as an actor and director in US television before creating one of the all-time great roles in Richard Rodgers and Oscar Hammerstein II's *The King And I* in 1951. He shaved his head for the character of the King of Siam, and the completely bald dome became his life-long trademark - although some said it limited his choice of future parts. His striking, sensual performance opposite the 'terribly English' Gertrude Lawrence earned him a Tony Award, and their duet, 'Shall We Dance?', remains one of the most memorable moments in the American musical theatre. Deborah Kerr, another delightful English actress, was his partner in the 1956 film version for which he won an Oscar. For most of the rest of his career he worked in films, and was highly acclaimed for his performances in many of them, particularly *Anastasia*, *The Brothers Karamazov*, *The Magnificent Seven*, *Taras Bulba*, and *Invitation To A Gunfighter*. In the early 60s he settled in Switzerland and spent a good deal of his time making documentary films about refugee children for the United Nations. He returned to America in 1972 and appeared with the English actress Samantha Eggar in the television series *Anna And The King Of Siam*. Five years later came a triumphant Broadway revival of *The King And I* which was also seen in London in 1979. He brought it back to New York again in 1985 even though he was suffering from lung cancer which entailed regular radiation treatment. It was the biggest hit of the season with Brynner's curtain calls lasting for so long that they became known as 'the third act'. In June 1985 he received a special Tony Award in recognition of his 4,525 performances in *The King And I*. He increased that figure by another 100 before he died at the Cornell Medical Centre in New York in October of that year.

Buchanan, Jack
b. 2 April 1890, Helensburgh, Strathclyde, Scotland, d. 20 October 1957, London, England. A major UK musical comedy, revue and film star, choreographer, director, producer and manager with a disarming, casual style, Buchanan's career spanned 40 years. He played in amateur dramatics and local music halls before moving to London to work as an understudy and chorus boy. Rejected for military service at the start of World War I because of poor health, he taught himself to dance, and played a leading role in the touring version of the West End hit musical comedy *Tonight's The Night* in 1915. His big break came two years later when he took over from Jack Hulbert in producer Andre Charlot's revue *Bubbly*, followed by another Charlot show, *A To Z*, in 1921. In the latter Buchanan sang one of his all-time hits 'And Her Mother Came Too', with Ivor Novello's music and a lyric by Dion Titheradge. Also in the cast were Beatrice Lillie and a young Gertrude Lawrence. After branching out into management with the musical farce *Battling Butler* at the New Oxford Theatre, Buchanan went to New York with Lillie and Lawrence to appear in *Andre Charlot's Revue Of 1924* at the Times Square Theater. Buchanan was a

Jack Buchanan with Daria Luna

substantial success on Broadway, and returned in 1926 with another Charlot revue in which he duetted with Lawrence on 'A Cup Of Coffee, A Sandwich, And You'. The recording reached number 5 in the chart and was his only US hit. Back in London in 1926 he was at his peak in Jerome Kern's *Sunny*. With Elsie Randolph as his regular leading lady, he appeared in dancing musicals such as *That's A Good Girl, Mr Whittington, This'll Make You Whistle*, and their last show together in 1943, *It's Time To Dance*. He also went back to New York for *Wake Up And Dream!* with Jessie Matthews, and *Between The Devil* with Evelyn Laye. Songs such as, 'Who', 'Goodnight Vienna', 'I Think I Can', 'There's Always Tomorrow', 'Fancy Our Meeting', 'Sweet So And So', 'Weep No More My Baby', 'By Myself' and 'I'm In A Dancing Mood', were delivered in a seemingly fragile, 'typically English' style. In his show *Stand Up And Sing* at the London Hippodrome in 1931, a very young Anna Neagle was discovered by film producer Herbert Wilcox who started her on the road to a long and distinguished film career by putting her into the Buchanan film *Goodnight Vienna*. Buchanan's own film career had started in 1925 with the silent, *Bulldog Drummond's Third Round*, and included a series of comedies, light dramas and farces such as *Yes, Mr Brown, Brewster's Millions* and *The Gang's All Here*. His first movie musical was *Paris*, with Corsican actress/singer Irene Bordoni, and he made several more including *Monte Carlo*, directed by Ernest Lubitsch, and co-starring Jeanette MacDonald, plus a few celluloid transfers of his hit stage productions. In 1953, the top UK and US song-and-dance men met in *The Band Wagon*. Buchanan and Fred Astaire's duet 'I Guess I'll Have To Change My Plan', and their clever version, with Nanette Fabray, of 'Triplets' fame, made this one of MGM's most acclaimed musical films, and the pinnacle of Buchanan's career.
Compilations: *That's A Good Girl* (1979), *The Golden Age Of Jack Buchanan* (1984), *Elegance* (1985), *This'll Make You Whistle* (1990).
Further reading: *Top Hat And Tails*, Michael Marshall.

Buddy

One of the most successful 'pop legend' musical biographies in recent years, this celebration of the brief life and times of Buddy Holly opened at the Victoria Palace Theatre in London on 12 October 1989. From a 'short' list of over 30 eager hopefuls, Paul Hipp was selected to portray the young rock 'n' roll singer-songwriter who made such an enormous impact in his brief spell at the top, before he perished in an air crash in 1959 at the age of 22, along with fellow artists Ritchie Valens and the Big Bopper. Paul Janes's book, which traces Holly's life from his hicksville roots and his first appearance with the Crickets at New York's Apollo theatre (whose management was expecting a black band), through the disputes with greedy managers and cynical record companies, and ending with the final concert at Clear Lake, Iowa, which took place just a few hours before the tragic accident. Long before that comes round, the audience has been letting rip and jiving in the aisles to such favourites as 'That'll Be The Day', 'Peggy Sue', and 'Oh Boy', and smooching, together with Buddy and his wife, to 'True Love Ways' and 'Raining In My Heart'. To the surprise of many, *Buddy* settled in for a long run, and touring companies also flourished. To mark the occasion of the show's 1,001 nights at the Victoria Palace three of the actors who had played the leading role, Paul Hipp, Billy Geraghty, and Chip Esten, appeared on the stage together, and, on 7 September 1993 the singer's 57th birthday, all tickets were sold at 50s prices: the best seats cost sixteen shillings (80 pence). *Buddy* opened on Broadway in November 1990, but was unable to sustain a run longer than 225 performances. Meanwhile, in London and several other locations, they continued to 'Rave On'.

Budgie

Even with big names in most departments, this show was one of the most spectacular flop musicals in London during the late 80s. It opened on 18 October 1988 at the Cambridge Theatre, with a starry cast that included Adam Faith, Anita Dobson, and John Turner. The book was by Keith Waterhouse and Willis Hall, authors of the 1974 smash-hit, *Billy*, and the music and lyrics were written by Mort Shuman, one half of the celebrated US songwriting team Doc Pomus and Shuman, and Britain's own Don Black. It was hoped that the teaming of Faith, who had played the leading role in the 70s television series on which the show was based, with Dobson, an accomplished actress who created the part of the barmaid Angie Watts in *Eastenders*, one of the UK's top small-screen soaps, would prove to be irresistible. The opposite proved to be true, and the 'over-romantized, sleazy' story of a small-time Cockney swindler and his reforming girlfriend, set in London's Soho district, was dismissed by the critics, and ignored by the public. Shuman and Black's score contained some mildly amusing numbers such as 'If You Want to See Palermo Again' and 'They're Naked And They Move', and the engaging ballad, 'There Is Love And There Is Love'. The remainder of the songs included 'In One Of My Weaker Moments', 'I'm Sure We Won't Fall Out Over This', 'Mary, Doris And Jane', 'Why Not Me?', 'Old Compton Street', and 'I Like That In A Man'. *Budgie* closed on 21 January 1989 after a run of only three months, with estimated losses in excess of over £1 million.

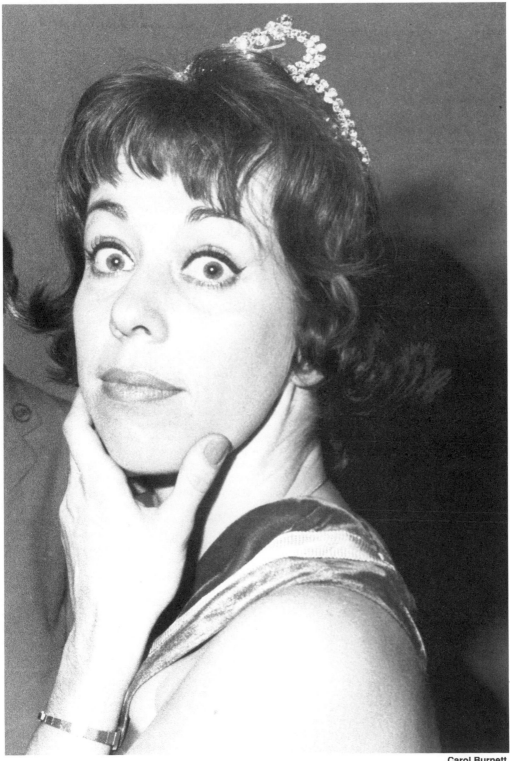

Carol Burnett

Burnett, Carol

b. 26 April 1933, San Antonio, Texas, USA. An actress, comedienne, and singer, Burnett was raised by her maternal grandmother in Los Angeles and studied theatre arts and English at the University of California. After graduating she worked in summer stock before moving to New York in 1954. Unable to find work as actress, she staged a show at the Rehearsal Club hotel in which she sang Eartha's Kitt's hit song 'Monotonous' from New Faces Of 1953. In 1957 she caused a stir at the Blue Angel nightclub with her rendition of 'I Made A Fool Of Myself Over John Foster Dulles'. This parody aimed at teenage rock 'n' roll groupies was written by Ken Welch, a songwriter and vocal coach whose material was ideally suited to her 'kooky' style. Years later he and his wife Mitzi wrote medleys for Burnett's television specials with Julie Andrews and others. In 1959 Burnett made an impressive Broadway debut as Princess Winnifred in Once Upon A Mattress, a successful musical based on the fairytale The Princess And The Pea. At around the same time she began appearing on The Garry Moore Show, and in the early 60s won an Emmy and several awards as favourite female performer on television. In 1962 she and Julie Andrews won more Emmys for the special Julie And Carol At Carnegie Hall. The two performers were teamed again in similar concerts at the Lincoln Centre (1971) and in Los Angeles (1989). Signed to CBS in 1962, Burnett's television career failed to take off during the next few years, and it was not until she returned to Broadway in the musical Fade Out-Fade In (1965) that her fortunes began to improve. Although the show itself - an affectionate look at the Hollywood of the 30s - was not well received, Burnett's 'genial comic impudence' and 'cheerful gaucherie' were singled out for praise, and her impression of Shirley Temple on 'You Musn't Be Discouraged' was hilarious. From 1967 CBS aired The Carol Burnett Show, a weekly prime-time variety show which featured a stellar lineup of guest stars and won 22 Emmys. In 1978, after appearing approximately 1,500 sketches, Burnett had had enough of the weekly grind and turned more to the theatre and feature films. In 1985 she was Carlotta Campion for two nights in the Stephen Sondheim tribute Follies In Concert, and gave marvellous renditions of the composer's 'survival anthem' 'I'm Still Here'. She returned to weekly television again in 1990 and chose an anthology format for her new series Carol And Company which added to her list of honours that already included People's Choice, Critics Circle, Photoplay, and Golden Globe Awards, along with her induction into the Television Academy Hall of Fame. In 1993 she starred in a new musical production From The Top, staged by the Long Beach Civic Light Opera. It was conceived and written by Ken Welch (of John Foster Dulles fame) and his wife Mitzi, and consisted of three one-act musicals. The first, My Walking Stick, is a back-stage vaudeville story set at the time of World War I, with songs by Irving Berlin; the second, called One Night In Marrakech, has words and music by Cole Porter; and the third and final piece, That Simpson Woman, is, naturally enough, an attempt to find a new angle on the famous Duke and Duchess of Windsor-in-exile saga, with a background of songs with lyrics by Ira Gershwin and music by a variety of composers.

Selected albums: Remembers How They Stopped The Show (1962), Let Me Entertain You (1964), Sings (1967).

Further reading: One More Time, Carol Burnett. Laughing Till It Hurts, J. Randy Taraborrelli.

Burrows, Abe

b. Abram Solman Borowitz, 18 December 1910, d. 17 May 1985, New York, USA. A distinguished director and librettist with many Broadway musicals and straight plays to his credit. Burrows studied to be a doctor and an accountant before eventually embarking on a career as a salesman. He was diverted from this course when he began to write radio comedy programmes such as Duffy's Tavern, and the late 40s hit Take Your Word. He also wrote and recorded a series of comedy songs, but his big break came when he collaborated with Jo Swerling on the witty book for Frank Loesser's Guys And Dolls, which is considered to be the quintessential Broadway musical. It gained Burrows the first of his many Tony Awards, and throughout the 50s he wrote or co-wrote the librettos for Make A Wish, Three Wishes For Jamie, Can-Can, Silk Stockings, Say, Darling, and First Impressions. In1961 he joined with Loesser again to create an hilarious skit on American big-business, How To Succeed In Business Without Even Trying, for which he he won another Tony, and a share in the Pulitzer Prize for Drama. Burrows also directed How To Succeed, as well as several other of the above shows including Three Wishes For Jamie, Can-Can, Say, Darling, and First Impressions. He also staged the Bert Lahr vehicle Two On The Aisle, Happy Hunting, and What Makes Sammy Run?, in which the popular singer Steve Lawrence made his 1964 Broadway debut. In later years, although Burrows was associated with some bizarre flops such as Breakfast At Tiffany's and a 1976 version of the classic Hellzapoppin'!, both of which failed to reach New York, he was frequently called upon (mostly uncredited) to successfully revise and revive other peoples' shows that were in trouble.

Further reading: Honest Abe, Abe Burrows.

By Jupiter

Richard Rodgers and Lorenz Hart's longest running original Broadway musical opened at the Shubert

Theatre on 2 June 1942. The two songwriters also wrote the book, which was based on Julian Thompson's play, *The Warrior's Husband*. *By Jupiter* is set in ancient Greece, and tells the amusing (and archaic) story of the Amazons, a breed of powerful, well-built, muscular women who dominate their own land and everyone who lives in it - male or female - until they are conquered - and absolutely captivated - by a tribe of marauding Greek warriors. Thereafter, the ladies are perfectly happy to forget about their previous superiority and assume a subordinate role. Ray Bolger, who had scored such a big success in Rodgers and Hart's *On Your Toes*, was the first choice for the part of Sapiens, the effeminate husband of the Amazonian chieftain, Queen Hippolyta (Benay Venuta). The leading female role of the Queen's sister, Antiope, was played by Constance Moore, whose passion for the leader of the invading army, Theseus (Ronald Graham), is what causes the Amazonian resistance to crumble in the first place. The score had several good moments, particularly the duet for Bolger and Venuta entitled 'Life With Father', although none of the songs really stood out and took off. The rest of the numbers included 'Nobody's Heart', 'Now That I've Got My Strength', 'Ev'rything I've Got', 'Jupiter Forbid', 'Careless Rhapsody', 'Here's A Hand', 'The Gateway To The Temple Of Minerva', and 'The Boy I Left Behind Me'. There was one beautiful ballad, 'Wait Till You See Her', sung by Ronald Graham, which did endure

through the years, although, ironically, it was removed for a time because the the show was too long, and only replaced shortly before the end of the run. After Ray Bolger departed to entertain US troops in the Far East, audiences dwindled rapidly, and *By Jupiter* closed after 427 performances. Only one Rodgers and Hart show - the 1952 revival of *Pal Joey* - stayed longer on Broadway. In 1963, *By Jupiter* was presented Off Broadway, where it ran for 118 performances.

Bye Bye Birdie

Generally regarded as the first Broadway musical to reflect the rock 'n' roll phenomenon of the 50s, *Bye Bye Birdie* opened in New York at the Martin Beck Theatre on 14 April 1960. Michael Stewart's book tells of Albert Peterson (Dick Van Dyke), a rock manager and promoter, whose only client, 'the hip-thrusting' Conrad Birdie (Dick Gautier) is about to be inducted into the US Army. Peterson and his long-suffering and loving secretary, Rose (Chita Rivera), decide to cook up one last publicity stunt: Birdie will travel to the small town of Sweet Apple, Ohio, where he will kiss Kim MacAfee (Susan Watson) the president of his fan club ('One Last Kiss'), and bid a temporary farewell to the nation - 'live' on the *Ed Sullivan Show* ('Elvis' allusions were everywhere). The sometimes hilarious events leading up to that historical moment, when he is knocked cold on prime-time television by Kim's jealous boyfriend,

Dick Van Dyke (*Bye Bye Birdie*)

Hugo (Michael J. Pollard), and the subsequent repercussions, involved Albert's overbearing mother, Mae (Kay Medford) and Kim's father, Mr MacAfee (Paul Lynde) who had always had a yen to be on the *Sullivan Show* ('Hymn To A Sunday Evening'). The rest of the score, by composer Charles Strouse and lyricist Lee Adams, was full of bright, lively, amusing, and sometimes satirical numbers. Three of them became familiar outside of the show: 'Put On a Happy Face', 'A Lot Of Livin' To Do', and the typical parents' plea for understanding, 'Kids' ('Why can't they be like we were, perfect in every way?'). The other songs included 'The Telephone Hour', 'An English Teacher', 'Honestly Sincere', 'One Boy', 'Baby, Talk To Me', 'Rosie', and the engaging ballad, 'How Lovely to Be A Woman'. *Bye Bye Birdie* won the Tony Award for best musical in 1961, and Tonys also went to librettist, Michael Stewart, and choreographer and director, Gower Champion, who won two. The show ran for 607 performances and significantly boosted the careers of Charles Strouse, Lee Adams, Gower Champion, and Chita Rivera. The latter reprised her role in the 1961 London production with Britain's own 'Birdie', Marty Wilde, which ran for 268 performances. Dick Van Dyke starred with Ann-Margret and Janet Leigh in the 1963 film version. A sequel, *Bring Back Birdie* opened on Broadway in 1981, but folded after four nights. In 1990, a 'classy revival' of the original *Bye Bye Birdie*, starring one of the American musical theatre's favourite sons, Tommy Tune, opened in St. Louis before embarking on a highly successful and record-breaking seven months nationwide tour.

C

Cabaret

Before arriving on Broadway as a musical comedy, *Cabaret* had enjoyed success in other forms. In 1935 Christopher Isherwood had published *Berlin Stories*, which told of the decadence of contemporary German society. The story was adapted for the stage by John Van Druten in 1951 under the title *I Am A Camera*, starring Julie Harris who also starred in the 1955 screen version. Van Druten's stage play was adapted as a musical by Joe Masteroff with music by John Kander and lyrics by Fred Ebb. *Cabaret* opened at the Broadhurst Theatre in New York on 20

November 1966 and was a great popular and critical success. It starred Jill Haworth as Sally Bowles, an amoral American nightclub singer living, working and loving, the latter somewhat indiscriminately, in Berlin. Joel Grey, as the egregious master of ceremonies at the Kit Kat Club where Sally works, gave the show's outstanding performance. Also in the cast was Lotte Lenya. The songs included 'Wilkommen', 'Tomorrow Belongs To Me', 'If You Could See Her Through My Eyes', 'Meeskite', 'Perfectly Marvelous', 'Don't Tell Mama', 'The Money Song', 'Married', 'What Would You Do?', and 'Cabaret'. Effectively evoking the contrasting social phenomena of cultural decay and the nascent National Socialist (Nazi) Party, the show combined high drama, realistic if unconventional morality, and strong characters with good songs. It ran for 1,165 performances, and won Tony Awards for best musical, supporting actor (Grey), supporting actress (Peg Murray), score, director (Harold Prince), choreographer (Ronald Field), scenic design (Boris Aronson) and costumes (Patricia Zipprodt). The 1968 London production bravely, and as it turned out successfully, starred classical actress Judi Dench as Sally Bowles. *Cabaret* was revived on Broadway in 1987 when Joel Grey recreated his original role, and in the West End in 1986 with ballet dancer Wayne Sleep as the Emcee. In 1993-4, the Donmar Warehouse on the London Fringe presented the show in the manner of a play with music, which prompted *Variety* to comment: 'In taking *Cabaret* away from Broadway, an essential verve that can only be defined as Broadway has been taken from *Cabaret*'. The 1972 film version starred Liza Minnelli as Sally with Grey reprising his role. Although effecting certain alterations to the plot, notably changing it from a loser's tale into a success story, the film version was highly successful and benefited from the performances of Grey and Minnelli, the latter having since become inseparable from the title song.

Cabaret Girl, The

With the cabaret-style of entertainment just catching on in England in the early 20s, this show, which opened at London's Winter Garden Theatre on 19 September 1922, could hardly have had a more appropriate title. It was an Anglo-American production, with the home-grown P.G. Wodehouse and George Grossmith providing the book and lyrics to music by 'the father of the American musical theatre', Jerome Kern. One of the show's stars, Dorothy Dickson, could claim to have a foot in both camps. She was born in Kansas City in the USA on 26 July 1896, but settled in London following her great success there in shows such as *Sally* (1921), which was also a Grossmith-Kern-Wodehouse affair. As with *Sally*, Dickson played the title role in *The*

Joel Grey (*Cabaret*)

Cabaret Girl. As Marilynn, an ordinary working girl, her efforts to win the affections of the high-born Jim Paradene (Geoffrey Gwyther), bring her into contact with Mr. Gripps (George Grossmith) and Mr. Gravvins (Norman Griffin), producers of the *All Night Follies*, who, knowing true love when they see it, attempt, in a sometimes misguided way, to bring the couple together. Despite animosity from his snooty aristocratic family, Marilynn gets her man - and a job at the cabaret. One critic suggested that 'Kern's melodies are touched with a certain dreamy and haunting wistfulness, even at their gayest . . . a refreshing holiday from jazz'. The show's two big numbers were 'Dancing Time', a duet for Marilynn and Gravvins, and 'Ka-Lu-A', which Kern borrowed from his recent show, *Good Morning, Dearie*, for Marilynn to sing at the end when she finally becomes a cabaret star. The rest of the score included 'Chopin Ad Lib', 'You Want The Best Seats, We Have 'Em', 'Mr. Gravinns-Mr. Gripps', 'First Rose Of Summer', 'Journey's End', 'Whoop-De-Oodle-Do', 'At The Ball', 'Shimmy With Me', 'Those Days Are Gone Forever', 'Looking all Over For You', and 'London, Dear Old London'. The talented comedienne, Heather Thatcher, another refugee from *Sally*, played the part of Little Ada, and performed the charming 'Nerves', with Gravvins and Gripps. Though not Kern at his very best, *A Cabaret Girl* was a bright and entertaining show, and ran for a creditable 361 performances.

Cabin In The Sky

A music fantasy based on the age-old theme of good and evil, with music by Vernon Duke and lyrics by John Latouche, *Cabin In The Sky* opened at the Martin Beck Theatre in New York on 25 October 1940. Lynn Root's book is set in the Negro South, where the devout Petunia (Ethel Waters) is making a deal with the Lord God regarding her good-for-nothing husband, 'Little Joe' (Dooley Wilson), who has been fatally injured in a street fight. Following her impassioned pleas, a life extension of six months is granted to enable Joe to mend his ways, and thereby give himself a chance of getting to Heaven. Complications arise when the Lord's General (Todd Duncan) and the boss man from 'down below', Lucifer Jnr. (Rex Ingram), vie for the soul of the unfortunate Joe, but, despite the occasional lapse (shooting Petunia, for instance), he is eventually forgiven by the Lord, and he and Petunia pass through the Pearly Gates together. Ethel Waters' performance in *Cabin In The Sky* is generally acknowledged to be her finest on Broadway (it was her only 'book' show, as opposed to revues), and she was applauded from all sides, especially for her joyous rendering of 'Taking A Chance On Love' (lyric with Ted Fetter), which brought the house down every

night. Duke and Latouche's score contained several other excellent numbers such as 'Do What You Wanna Do', 'Cabin In The Sky', 'Honey In The Honeycomb', 'Savannah', and 'Love Turned The Light Out'. The show, which was choreographed and directed by the innovative George Balanchine ran for 156 performances, and was revived briefly Off Broadway in 1964. Ethel Waters was also in the 1943 film version, along with an all-star cast that included Lena Horne, Eddie 'Rochester' Anderson, and Louis Armstrong.

Caesar, Irving

b. Isodore Caesar, 4 July 1895, New York City, New York, USA. After studying music while at school, Caesar worked in commerce for several years, mostly for the Ford Motor Company. Highly literate, and a graduate of several educational establishments for advanced students, he began writing lyrics for his own amusement. George Gershwin, a childhood friend, collaborated with him on some mildly successful songs written between 1916 and 1919. The pair then had a huge success with 'Swanee', a song that was taken up by Al Jolson. Caesar wrote many songs with a succession of collaborators during the 20s, among them 'Tea For Two' and 'I Want To Be Happy', both from *No, No Nanette* (1925, music by Vincent Youmans), 'Sometimes I'm Happy' from *Hit The Deck* (1927, Youmans again) and 'Crazy Rhythm' (1928, music by Joseph Meyer and Roger Wolfe Kahn). He also worked in Hollywood, writing lyrics for 'Count Your Blessings' (music by Gerald Marks), which was used in *Palooka* (1934), and 'Animal Crackers In My Soup' (music by Ray Henderson), which was sung by Shirley Temple in *Curly Top* (1935). In 1936 he co-wrote lyrics for 'Is It True What They Say About Dixie' with Sammy Lerner (music by Marks). Although he continued to write lyrics throughout most of his life, his best work was done before the outbreak of World War II. In his later years he often wrote to commissions from government departments on such subjects as safety and health.

Caesar's best-known number, 'Tea For Two', has been recorded by numerous artists in a wide variety of styles over the years, and became the title of a film starring Doris Day and Gordon MacRea in 1950. Over 40 years later, in July 1992, the song was the subject of a BBC radio programme in which Caesar related how it came to be written. The show also confirmed that he was still very much alive - and working - at the age of 97.

Cahn, Sammy

b. Samuel Cohen, 18 June 1913, New York, USA, d. 15 January 1993, Los Angeles, California, USA. The son of Jewish immigrant parents from Galicia, Poland,

Cahn grew up on Manhatten's Lower East Side. Encouraged by his mother, he learned to play the violin, joined a small orchestra that played at bar mitzvahs and other functions, and later worked as a violinist in Bowery burlesque houses. At the age of 16 he wrote his first lyric, 'Like Niagrara Falls, I'm Falling For You', and persuaded a fellow member of the orchestra, Saul Chaplin, to join him in a songwriting partnership. Their first published effort was 'Shake Your Head From Side To Side', and in the early 30s they wrote special material for vaudeville acts and bands. In 1935 they had their first big hit when the Jimmy Lunceford orchestra recorded their 'Rhythm Is Our Business'. The following year Andy Kirk topped the US Hit Parade with the duo's 'Until The Real Thing Comes Along', and Louis Armstrong featured their 'Shoe Shine Boy' in the Cotton Club Revue. In 1937 Cahn and Chaplin had their biggest success to date when they adapted the Yiddish folk song, 'Beir Mir Bist Du Schöen'. It became the top novelty song of the year and gave the Andrews Sisters their first million-seller. The team followed with 'Please Be Kind', a major seller for Bob Crosby, Red Norvo and Benny Goodman. During this time Cahn and Chaplin were also under contract to Warner Brothers, and soon after that commitment ended they decided to part company. In 1942, Cahn began his very productive partnership with Jule Styne, with their first chart success, 'I've Heard That Song Before'. Just as significant was Cahn's renewed association with Frank Sinatra, whom he had known when the singer was with Tommy Dorsey. Cahn and Styne wrote the score for the Sinatra films *Step Lively* (1944), ('Come Out Wherever You Are' and 'As Long As There's Music'); *Anchors Aweigh* (1945), ('I Fall In Love Too Easily', 'The Charm Of You', and 'What Makes The Sunset?') and *It Happened In Brooklyn* (1947), ('Time After Time', 'It's The Same Old Dream' and 'It's Gotta Come From The Heart'). Sinatra also popularized several other 40s Cahn/Styne songs, including 'I'll Walk Alone', 'Saturday Night Is The Loneliest Night In The Week', 'The Things We Did Last Summer', 'Five Minutes More', and the bleak, 'Guess I'll Hang My Tears Out To Dry', which appeared on his 1958 album, *Only The Lonely*. Some of their other hits included 'It's Been A Long, Long Time', associated with Harry James and his vocalist Kitty Kallen, 'Let It Snow! Let It Snow! Let It Snow!' (Vaughan Monroe), and 'There Goes That Song Again' (Kay Kyser and Russ Morgan). Cahn and Styne wrote the score for several other films including *Tonight And Every Night* (1945), two Danny Kaye vehicles, *Wonder Man* (1945) and *The Kid From Brooklyn* (1946), and *West Point Story* (1950). They also provided the songs for *Romance On The High Seas* (1948), the film in which Doris Day shot to international stardom, singing 'It's Magic' and 'Put 'Em In A Box, Tie 'Em With A Ribbon'. The two songwriters also wrote the Broadway show, *High Button Shoes* (1947), starring Phil Silvers (later Sgt. Bilko) and Nanette Fabray, which ran for 727 performances and introduced songs such as 'I Still Get Jealous', 'You're My Girl' and 'Papa, Won't You Dance With Me'. After *High Button Shoes* Cahn went to California, while Styne stayed in New York. Cahn collaborated with Nicholas Brodsky for a while in the early 50s, writing movie songs for Mario Lanza, including 'Be My Love', 'Wonder Why', 'Because You're Mine', 'Serenade' and 'My Destiny'. The collaboration also composed 'I'll Never Stop Loving You' for the Doris Day film, *Love Me Or Leave Me* (1955). Cahn and Styne re united briefly in 1954, ostensibly to write the score for the film, *Pink Tights*, to star Sinatra and Marilyn Monroe, but the project was shelved. Soon afterwards Cahn and Styne were asked to write the title song for the film, *Three Coins In The Fountain*. The result, a big hit for Sinatra and for the Four Aces, gained Cahn his first Academy Award. Cahn and Styne eventually worked with Monroe when they wrote the score for the comedy, *The Seven Year Itch* (1955). In the same year Cahn started his last major collaboration - with Jimmy Van Heusen and, some would say, with Frank Sinatra as well. They had immediate success with the title song of the Sinatra movie, *The Tender Trap* (1955), and won Academy Awards for songs in two of his movies, 'All The Way', from *The Joker Is Wild* (1957) and 'High Hopes', from *A Hole In The Head* (1959). A parody of 'High Hopes' was used as John F. Kennedy's presidential campaign song in 1960. Among the many other songs written especially for Sinatra were 'My Kind Of Town' (from *Robin And The Seven Hoods*)(1964) and the title songs for his best-selling albums, *Come Fly With Me, Only The Lonely, Come Dance With Me!, No One Cares, Ring-A-Ding-Ding!* and *September Of My Years*. Cahn and Van Heusen also produced his successful Timex television series during 1959-60. In the movies they won another Oscar for the song 'Call Me Irresponsible', (from *Papa's Delicate Condition*, 1963), Cahn's fourth Oscar from over 30 nominations, and contributed to many other films including 'The Second Time Around' (from *High Time*) and the title songs from *A Pocketful Of Miracles, Where Love Has Gone, Thoroughly Modern Millie* and *Star*. The songwriters also supplied the score for a television musical version of Thorton Wilder's play, *Our Town*, which introduced the songs, 'Love And Marriage' and 'The Impatient Years'. They also received critical approval for their score of the Broadway musical *Skyscraper* (1965), which included the songs, 'Everybody Has The Right To Be Wrong' and 'I'll Only Miss Her When I Think Of Her'. They also provided music and lyrics for the British musical *Walking Happy*, which opened on

Broadway in 1966. In 1969 Cahn dissolved his partnership with Van Heusen and collaborated once more with Jule Styne on the Broadway musical, *Look To The Lilies*. His other collaborators included Axel Stordahl and Paul Weston ('Day By Day' and 'I Should Care'), Gene DePaul ('Teach Me Tonight'), Arthur Schwartz ('Relax-Ay-Voo'), George Barrie ('All That Love To Waste'), and Vernon Duke ('That's What Makes Paris Paree', and 'I'm Gonna Ring The Bell Tonight'). In 1972 Cahn was inducted into the Songwriters Hall Of Fame after claiming throughout his lifetime that he only wrote songs so that he could demonstrate them. In the same year he mounted his 'one man show', *Words And Music*, on Broadway, and despite his voice being described by a New York critic as that of 'a vain duck with a hangover', the nostalgic mixture of his songs, sprinkled with amusing anecdotes of the way they came about, won rave notices and the Outer Circle Critics Award for the best new talent on Broadway. He repeated his triumph in England two years later, and then re-mounted the whole thing all over again in 1987. After over six decades of 'putting *that* word to *that* note', as he termed it, he died in January 1993. His books include a songbook, *Words And Music* and *The Songwriter's Rhyming Dictionary*.
Album: *I've Heard That Song Before* (1977).
Further reading: *I Should Care - The Sammy Cahn Story*, Sammy Cahn.

Call Me Madam

With advance ticket sales exceeding $1,000,000, the stage musical *Call Me Madam* was a guaranteed hit when it opened at the Imperial Theatre in New York on 12 October 1950. With a score by Irving Berlin, the book by Russell Crouse and Howard Lindsay was based loosely upon the life and career of Perle Mesta, a famous Washington, D.C. hostess who became the US Ambassador to Luxembourg. Ethel Merman played the dedicated diplomat Sally Adams, belting out her personal calling-card, 'The Hostess With The Mostes' On The Ball'. The remainder of a bunch of great numbers included 'The Best Thing For You', 'It's A Lovely Day Today', 'They Like Ike' (about US Army General Dwight D. Eisenhower, who attended the opening night), 'Marrying For Love', 'Can You Use Any Money Today?', and 'Something To Dance About'. There was also the delightful 'You're Just In Love', an engaging contrapuntal song with two melodies and two sets of lyrics and sung in the show by Merman and Russell Nype. The show won Tony Awards for best score, actress (Merman), and featured actor (Nype). It ran for almost 650 performances on Broadway and 485 in London, and was filmed in 1959 with Merman, George Sanders and Donald O'Connor.

Call Me Mister

A post-war revue in which most of the personnel, on and off-stage, were men and women who had served in the US armed forces or the USO. *Call Me Mister* opened at the National Theatre (now the Nederlander) in New York on 18 April 1946. The sketches, by Arnold Auerbach and Arnold B. Horwitt, and the songs, by Harold Rome, dealt with the problems of servicemen and women adjusting to civilian life after several years of war. Betty Garrett and Jules Munshin, both of whom were soon to join Frank Sinatra and Gene Kelly in a couple of Hollywood classics, *Take Me Out To The Ball Game* and *On The Town*, were two of the stars. Garrett had the show's big number, during which, as a USO hostess fed up to the teeth with a Latin diet of congas, sambas, and rhumbas, she implored: 'South America, Take It Away' ('That's enough, that's enough, take it back, my spines's out of whack/There's a strange click-clack in the back of my sacroiliac'). The song was recorded by many other artists, and became particularly successful for Bing Crosby with the Andrews Sisters, and Xavier Cugat. Lawrence Winters handled two of show's more serious moments well: when he sang 'The Face On The Dime', a genuine and moving tribute to President Roosevelt; and in the scene during which, after detailing his experiences in the army Transportation Corps with 'Red Ball Express', he, as a Negro, is unable to get a job as a civilian. Those two numbers also reminded audiences of Harold Rome's established credentials as a writer with a social conscience. The remainder of the score for *Call Me Mister*, however, was more light-hearted and slyly satirical, with only the occasional serious moment, and included such numbers as 'The Drugstore Song', 'Along With Me', 'Little Surplus Me', 'Call Me Mister', 'Going Home Train', 'Love Remains', 'Yuletide, Park Avenue', 'When We Meet Again', and 'Military Life (The Jerk Song)'. In fact, the only really serious aspect of the whole show was the degree of its success, which resulted in a run of 734 performances. The 1951 film version, with a story-line by Auerbach and Horwitt, starred Betty Grable, Dan Dailey, and Danny Thomas.

Camelot

Alan Jay Lerner and Frederick Loewe brought the stage musical *Camelot* into New York on 1 December 1960 despite the fact that their previous show, *My Fair Lady*, was still running. Inevitably compared and contrasted with that blockbuster, *Camelot* was generally held to be a much lesser show. Pre-opening events had also militated against success. Director Moss Hart suffered a heart attack, Loewe was hospitalized with bleeding ulcers, and technical problems beset out-of-town tryouts. Although there

Robert Goulet, Julie Andrews and Richard Burton (*Camelot*)

were good advance sales for Broadway, the critics greeted it lukewarmly. Nevertheless, *Camelot* built a good following with the public and ran for almost 900 performances. The show starred Julie Andrews as Queen Guinevere, Richard Burton as King Arthur, and Robert Goulet as Lancelot. Based upon T.H. White's *The Once And Future King*, a new version of the Arthurian legends, the score contained several good songs, including 'How To Handle A Woman', 'Follow Me', 'I Wonder What The King Is Doing Tonight', 'The Lusty Month Of May', 'C'est Moi', 'If Ever I Would Leave You' and the title number. During the show's run several cast changes were made, but of the originals Goulet was most striking, building a successful career upon this, his Broadway debut. The 1964 London production starred Laurence Harvey, later replaced by Paul Daneman, as the King. In 1993 the show was revived on Broadway following a long US tour. In this production Robert Goulet took the role of King Arthur, and received what were probably some of the worst reviews of his career so far. A moderately successful version of *Camelot* was filmed in 1967 with Richard Harris, Vanessa Redgrave and David Hemmings.

Can-Can

For *Can-Can*, his penultimate Broadway stage musical, which opened at the Shubert Theatre in New York on 7 May 1953, Cole Porter chose the setting of turn-of-the-century Paris. Abe Burrows' book was essentially a love story in which the participants get involved with an attempt by the city authorities to close down a Montmartre nightclub that features the outrageous can-can dance. As Judge Aristide Forestier (Peter Cookson) investigates allegations of impropriety at the nightclub operated by La Mome Pistache (Lilo). However, the real show-stopping star was Gwen Verdon as the dancer Claudine. With splendid choreography by Michael Kidd, *Can-Can* was a great success and ran for more than two years on Broadway. Verdon and Kidd both won Tony Awards, and there were fine all-round performances from the rest of the cast. However, the show's greatest strength lay in Porter's music and lyrics. The songs included 'It's All Right With Me', 'Allez-Vous-En', 'Come Along With Me', 'Maidens Typical of France', 'I Am In Love', Never Give Anything Away', 'Montmart'', 'Live And Let Live', and two major hits, 'C'est Magnifique' and Porter's eloquent hymn to the city he adored, 'I Love Paris'. In 1988, *Can-Can* was revived in Chicago with Chita Rivera, and in New York and London with Donna McKechnie. The outstanding Original Cast album was re-released on CD in 1993. A 1960 film version starred Frank Sinatra, Shirley MacLaine and Maurice Chevalier.

Candide

A famous flop when first presented at the Martin Beck Theatre in New York on 1 December 1956, *Candide* was later sympathetically revised and reached a much wider and appreciative audience. From the start, Leonard Berstein's music, and the lyrics, mostly by Richard Wilbur, have escaped much of the flak. It was the book by Lillian Hellman, based on Voltaire's novel, which attracted a good deal of criticism. The satirical story involves Candide (Robert Rounseville) and his adored Cunegonde (Barbara Cook), who are brain-washed by their philosophy professor Dr. Pangloss (Max Adrian) into believing that this is 'the best of all possible worlds'. After being confronted with real-life situations worldwide in Lisbon, Venice, Beunos Aires, Paris, and other exotic locations, the lovers come to terms with life as it is - imperfect, but perfectly acceptable. Barbara Cook was a joy, just a year before she captivated Broadway as Marion the librarian in *The Music Man*. The lush and melodic score, with its delightful touches of pastiche, included 'The Best Of All Possible Worlds', 'It Must Be So', 'Oh, Happy We', 'Glitter And Be Gay', 'You Were Dead, You Know', 'I Am Easily Assimilated', 'My Love', 'Ballad Of Eldorado', 'Bon Voyage', 'What's The Use?', and 'Make Our Garden Grow'. Extra lyrics were provided by Bernstein himself, Dorothy Parker, and John Latouche who died shortly before the show opened. Although critically well-received, *Candide* lasted for only 73 performances. It contrasted sharply in both content and box-office appeal with the 'darling' of that Broadway season - *My Fair Lady*. The 1974 production at the Broadway Theatre did much better. With a new book by Hugh Wheeler, some additional songs from Stephen Sondheim, and Hal Prince's innovative staging, *Candide* at last realised its potential and ran for 740 performances. In 1982 this 'comic operetta' as it was originally called, was taken into the repertoire of the New York City Opera. A 1959 London production with Denis Quilley and Mary Costa stayed at the Saville Theatre for under two months, and in 1988 *Candide* was presented by the Scottish Opera for a limited season at the Old Vic. In the following year Bernstein conducted the London Symphony Orchestra in a concert version of the show at the Barbican Theatre, and several members of that cast were on a two-CD recording of the score which was released in 1991.

Canterbury Tales

Originally the brainchild of Nevill Coghill, Professor of English Literature at Oxford University, who wrote an up-dated version of Chaucer's classic story for BBC Radio in the early 60s. With the aid of one of his ex-pupils, Martin Starkie, it was turned into a straight theatrical piece which was presented at the Oxford Playhouse in 1964. The recruitment of composers Richard Hill and John Hawkins, who had been working on a musical project of their own, entitled *Canterbury Pilgrims*, enabled Coghill and Starkie's *Canterbury Tales* to be expanded into a full-scale musical production which opened at London's Phoenix Theatre on 21 March 1968. The 'raciest, bawdiest, most good-hearted and good humoured show in London' appealed to the critics and public alike and settled in for a long run. The 'release of this pre-Puritan inheritance on stage' was due no doubt to the fact that, in the previous month, a bill had been passed in the House of Commons abolishing the theatrical censorship powers of the Lord Chamberlain. Significantly, the four Tales which the authors chose from Chaucer's originals, all dealt with the 60s generation's preoccupation with sex: there was at least one case of a kissed backside, a red-hot poker, a severe bout of bed-hopping, and several examples of cuckolding, leading up to the evening's optimistic and idealistic anthem, 'Love Will Conquer All'. The rest of the score with (Martin Starkie's lyrics) naturally enough echoed the shows main theme: 'I Have A Noble Cock' ('He crows at the break of day'), 'Darling, Let Me Teach You How to Kiss', 'Pilgrims' Riding Music', 'What Do Most Women Desire?', 'I Am For Ever Dated', 'Come On And Marry Me, Honey', and 'Fill Your Glass'. The first-rate cast included Wilfred Brambell (of BBC Television's *Steptoe And Son*) as the Steward, Kenneth J. Warren (the Miller), Jessie Evans (the Wife of Bath), Billy Boyle (the Clerk of Oxenford), Nicky Henson (the Squire), Gay Soper (Alison), and Pamela Charles (the Prioress). It was a rude, riotous romp, which went on to become one of London's most popular tourist attractions, although even its most ardent fans were probably surprised that *Canterbury Tales* sustained audiences' interest for a period of five years, closing in 1973 following a run of 2080 performances. A 1979 revival at the Shaftsbury Theatre failed to rekindle the show's original appeal. The novelty had worn off, and anyway, by then a very different kind of production, generally controlled by Andrew Lloyd Webber, was dominating the London musical theatre. As if to prove that parochial English humour does not travel well to America (and vice versa), a revised version, with Hermione Baddeley, played on Broadway in 1969, but lasted for only 121 performances, and New York sampled the show again in 1980, but to no avail. In 1991, *Canterbury Tales In Cabaret* was presented at the tiny Arts Theatre in London. The original show's co-author, Martin Starkie, directed and appeared in the piece.

Cantor, Eddie

b. Edward Israel Iskowitz, 31 January 1892, New York, USA, d. 10 October 1964, Hollywood, California, USA. An extremely popular comedian, singer and dancer. Highly animated in performance, jumping up and down, hands gesticulating, eyes popping and swivelling, giving rise to his nickname 'Banjo Eyes'. The son of Russian immigrants, Cantor was orphaned at an early age and reared by his grandmother. He sang on street corners before joining composer Gus Edwards' group of youngsters, and appearing in blackface for *Kid Cabaret* in 1912. George Jessel, another big star of the future, was in the same troupe. Cantor became a top performer in vaudeville before breaking into Broadway in Florenz Ziegfeld's *Midnight Frolics* (1916), leading to starring roles in the *Ziegfeld Follies* 1917-19. In the latter show, completely in character, he sang Irvin Berlin's saucy number, 'You'd Be Surprised', and it featured on what is considered to be the earliest 'original cast' album, on Smithsonian Records. After *Broadway Brevities* (1920) and *Make It Snappy* (1922), Cantor appeared in his two most successful Broadway shows. The first, *Kid Boots*, in 1923, ran for 479 performances, introduced two of his most popular songs, 'Alabamy Bound' and 'If You Knew Susie', and was filmed as a silent movie, three years later. The second, *Whoopee*, in 1928, teamed Cantor with a young Ruth Etting and was his biggest Broadway hit. The 1930 movie version only retained one song, 'Makin' Whoopee', from the original score, but it established Cantor as a Hollywood star, and was notable for the debut of dance-director Busby Berkeley and the use of two-colour technicolour. During the 30s and 40s, after reputedly losing heavily in the 1929 Wall Street Crash, he concentrated his efforts on films and radio. The extremely successful movies invariably featured him as the poor, timid little man, winning against all odds after wandering around some of Hollywood's most lavish settings, occasionally in blackface. They included *Glorifying The American Girl* (1929), *Palmy Days* (1931), *The Kid From Spain* (1932), *Roman Scandals* (1932), *Kid Millions* (1934), *Strike Me Pink* (1936), *Ali Baba Goes To Town* (1937), *40 Little Mothers* (1940), *Thank Your Lucky Stars* (1943), *Show Business* and *Hollywood Canteen* (both 1944). In the 30s he was reputed to be radio's highest-paid star via his *Chase & Sanborn* show with its famous theme, Richard Whiting's 'One Hour With You'. It is said that during this period Cantor had been responsible for helping Deanna Durbin, and later Dinah Shore and Eddie Fisher early in their careers. In 1941 Cantor made his last Broadway appearance in *Banjo Eyes* which ran for 126 performances and is remembered mainly for his version of 'We're Having A Baby'. After World War II he was on radio with his *Time To Smile* show and on early television in 1950 with the *Colgate Comedy Hour*. In the same year he played himself in the movie *The Story Of Will Rogers*. A heart attack in 1952 reduced his activities, eventually forcing him to retire,

Eddie Cantor

although he did appear in the occasional 'special'. He also dubbed the songs to the soundtrack of his bio-pic *The Eddie Cantor Story* in 1953, with Keefe Brasselle in the title role. The film contained some of the songs for which he was famous, such as 'Yes Sir, That's My Baby', 'How Ya Gonna Keep 'Em Down On The Farm', 'Oh, You Beautiful Doll', 'Margie', 'Ma (He's Making Eyes At Me)', and 'You Must Have Been A Beautiful Baby'. There were many others including 'My Baby Just Cares For Me', 'Everybody's Doing It', 'No, No Nora', Now's The Time To Fall In Love', 'Dinah', 'Keep Young And Beautiful' and 'Ida, Sweet As Apple Cider', which he always dedicated to his wife. He also wrote lyrics to some songs including 'Merrily We Roll Along' and 'There's Nothing Too Good For My Baby', and several books, including *Caught Short*, an account of his 1929 financial losses, and two volumes of his autobiography. He was awarded an Honorary Oscar in 1956, and died eight years later in Hollywood, California.

Selected compilations: *The Best Of Eddie Cantor* (1981), *Makin' Whoopee!* (1989).

Further reading: *Caught Short*, Eddie Cantor. *My Life Is In Your Hands*, Eddie Cantor. *Take My Life*, Eddie Cantor.

Card, The

Arnold Bennett's 1909 novel had already been the subject of a 1951 film, starring Alec Guinness, well before Cameron Mackintosh commissioned Keith Waterhouse and Willis Hall to adapt it for the musical stage in 1973. The show, which opened at the Queen's Theatre in London on 24 July of that year, was set in the Potteries area of Midlands England, and told the story of young, thrusting Denry Machin, a washerwoman's mischievous son who wangles his way to the position of Mayor of his town, diddling everyone who gets in his way. Jim Dale, the 50s pop star who became a respected actor, played the wheeler-dealer Denry, with Joan Hickson as his long-suffering mother, Eleanor Bron as the Countess who gives his career a leg-up, and John Savident as his first boss, the archetypical Potteries capitalist. In the roles of Denry's girlfriends were two future stars of the British musical theatre, Marti Webb and Millicent Martin. *The Card*'s score was written Tony Hatch and Jackie Trent whose catchy compositions during the 60s had provided many artists, notably Petula Clark, with massive world-wide hit records. None of the songs in this show attained chart status, but there were some attractive numbers. Webb had one of the best of them, a strong ballad entitled, 'I Could Be the One', and she joined Dale for the beguiling 'Opposite Your Smile' which Hatch and Trent recorded themselves, along with' Moving On'. The rest of the bright and lively score included 'That Once A Year Feeling', 'That's The Way The Money Grows', 'Nobody

Thought Of It', 'Nothing Succeeds Like Success', 'Come Along And Join Us', 'Lead Me', and 'Universal Kid Gloves'. The critics thought that Jim Dale, with his 'innocent cheerfulness', gave a 'virtuoso performance', and the show ran for 130 performances. Dale was soon to be based in America, where he created the title role of *Barnum* on Broadway in 1980. Hatch and Trent, too, soon left Britain to live in Australia, but when they returned in the early 90s, *The Card* was revised and revived. With some new songs, and additional lyrics by Anthony Drewe, the show toured UK provincial theatres in 1992 with the ex-children's television entertainer, Peter Duncan, in the lead, and John Savident playing his original part as Denry's role model.

Careless Rapture

Despite an uncertain start, the stage musical *Careless Rapture* proved to be a popular success for Ivor Novello. His previous show *Glamorous Night* had been a hit in 1935 but the management of London's Drury Lane Theatre took it off to make way for a previously arranged pantomime. With Novello and the management at loggerheads over this, he was invited to suggest a new production for the following year. Hastily writing an entirely new show, he offered them *Careless Rapture* but they turned it down. Before the end of 1936 however, the theatre was in difficulties and invited Novello to re-submit his musical. After ensuring he had an excellent deal, Novello presented and starred in the show opposite his regular leading lady, Olive Gilbert. *Careless Rapture*'s musical numbers, which included 'Why Is There Ever Goodbye?', 'Love Made The Song', and 'Wait for Me' showed signs of the haste in which they had been written and none had the endurance of much of his other music. Nevertheless, the show ran for 295 performances, long enough to restore the theatre's fortunes and helped consolidate Novello's place in the history of British musicals.

Carmen Jones

Although other musical shows had been adapted from operas, *Carmen Jones*, Oscar Hammerstein II's reworking of Georges Bizet's *Carmen* made few changes to either score or storyline. The setting was drastically altered, however, from Spain to America's deep south with a World War II parachute factory taking the place of the original's cigarette factory. Also dramatically affecting audience response was the fact that all the characters in *Carmen Jones* are black. Hammerstein's lyrics inventively update the original, changing the 'Seguidilla' to 'Dere's A Café On De Corner', the *Habañera* to 'Dat's Love', 'Stan' Up And Fight' in place of the 'Toreador's Song' and 'Dis Flower' for 'The Flower Song'. *Carmen Jones* is a tale of love and jealousy which ends when Joe, a military

Jackie Trent and Tony Hatch (*The Card*)

policeman guarding the factory, stabs Carmen Jones outside the arena where her new lover, prizefighter Husky Miller, is appearing. The resulting show, described by the producers as a musical play, was a powerful drama which lost none of the impact of Bizet's work, itself based upon a short novel by *Prosper Merimée*. For the original production, which opened at the Broadway Theatre in New York on 2 December 1943, two artists were cast in the demanding main roles, alternating between matinee and evening performances. Muriel Smith and Muriel Rahn played Carmen, with Napoleon Reed and Luther Saxon as Joe. *Carmen Jones* ran for just over 500 performances. The first-ever London production opened at the Old Vic in 1991 and ran for nearly two years. It won the Laurence Olivier, *Evening Standard*, and Critics' Circle awards for best musical, and its director, Simon Callow, also won an Olivier Award. The 1954 film version starred Dorothy Dandridge and Harry Belafonte, both of whose voices were dubbed (respectively by Marilyn Horne and La Vern Hutcherson).

Carnival

It's difficult to think of many Hollywood films that have been turned into successful musical shows, but *Carnival* is certainly one of them. It was based on *Lili* (1953), starring Leslie Caron, which had a screenplay by Helen Deutsch (based on a story by Paul Gallico), who also collaborated with composer Bronislau Kaper on the film's only song (as opposed to dance sequences), the enchanting 'Hi-Lili, Hi-Lo'. *Carnival* opened at the Imperial Theatre in New York on 13 April 1961, with a book by Michael Stewart, who had provided the plot for the smash-hit *Bye Bye Birdie* the year before, and a score by Bob Merrill, whose main claim to fame up until that time was as the writer of 50s novelty songs such as 'Feet Up (Pat Him On The Po-Po)' and '(How Much Is That) Doggie In The Window'. The majority of Merrill's numbers for *Carnival* were nothing like those. The show's theme, the gently lilting 'Love Makes The World Go 'Round', is established in the opening scene (there is no overture) in which exhausted members of a shabby French carnival troupe set up the tents and decorations for the next evening's performance. The song continues to insinuate throughout the story which tells of the young waif, Lili (Anna Maria Alberghetti), from the town of Mira, who joins the carnival and is captivated by Marco the Magnificent (James Mitchell), the narcissistic magician, until she realizes - just in time- that her heart really belongs to the lame puppeteer, Paul Berthalot (Jerry Orbach). The puppets were a delightful innovation, and they even had their own songs: 'Golden, Delicious Fish', 'The Rich', and the hilarious 'Yum-Ticky-Tum-Tum', as well as joining Lili in the charming 'Love

Makes The World Go 'Round'. The other songs, in a variety of styles and moods, included the rousing 'Grand Imperial Cirque De Paris', 'A Very Nice Man', 'Her Face', 'It Was Always You', 'Mira', 'She's My Love', 'I've Got to Find A Reason', 'Beautiful Candy', 'Everybody Likes You', and 'Humming'. A major contributor to the show's substantial success was its director and choreographer, Gower Champion, who, like Michael Stewart, had also worked on *Bye Bye Birdie*. Gower's imaginative staging and dance direction was acclaimed from all sides, and earned him two Tony Awards. Anna Maria Alberghetti also won a Tony for best actress. The show itself gained the New York Critics Circle Award for best musical. *Carnival* closed in 1963 after a run of 719 performances, and was revived briefly at New York's City Center five years later. A London production lasted only one month. In 1993, another revival, Off Broadway at the Theatre at St. Peter's Church, starred Emily Loesser, daughter of the legendary composer-lyricist Frank Loesser.

Carousel

Opening at the Majestic Theatre in New York on 19 April 1945, this show which had music by Richard Rodgers and a book and lyrics by Oscar Hammerstein II, came hard on the heels of the composers' huge success with *Oklahoma!*. Adapted from *Liliom*, a play by Ferenc Molnar, *Carousel* marked an important development in the fast-maturing American musical theatre. The story centres upon a love affair between Billy Bigelow, a self-confident fairground barker, and Julie Jordan, a shy young girl in a small New England town. The couple marry and when Billy learns that Julie is pregnant he tries to raise money by taking part in a robbery. To avoid capture Billy kills himself and is sent to Purgatory. Fifteen years later, Billy is allowed an opportunity to redeem himself and returns, unseen, to Earth to help his daughter through an emotional crisis. His sin purged, Billy can finally enter Heaven. The score is replete with fine music, from 'Carousel Waltz', played by the orchestra before curtain-rise, through 'If I Loved You', the dramatic 'Soliloquy', 'You're A Queer One, Julie Jordan', 'When The Children Are Asleep', 'A Real Nice Clambake' (written for *Oklahoma!*, as 'This Was A Real Nice Hayride' but dropped), 'Mister Snow', the reflective 'What's The Use Of Wond'rin'?', an exuberant 'June Is Bustin' Out All Over' to the climactic 'You'll Never Walk Alone'. The original cast included John Raitt as Billy and Jay Clayton as Julie. *Carousel* ran for 890 performances and was revived several times over the years. Raitt reprised his role in a 1965 version at the Lincoln Centre. The show opened in London in 1950 and ran for more than 550 performances. In 1992, an acclaimed production was mounted at the Royal National

Theatre, and later transferred to the Shaftesbury. It won Laurence Olivier Awards for best musical revival, actress (Joanna Riding), director (Nicholas Hyter), and supporting performance (Tarquin Olivier). The 1956 film version starred Gordon MacRae and Shirley Jones.

Carrie

There must have been worse shows than *Carrie* - a few even ran for less than *Carrie*'s tally of 16 previews and five performances - yet for some reason this show seems have been selected to represent the 'Broadway flops' - those often misguided, tasteless, and gloriously horrible and expensive short-lived productions, behind many of which have been some of the musical theatre's most illustrious names. It has even lent its name to a fascinating book: *Not Since Carrie: 40 Years Of Broadway Musical Flops*, by the American author and critic Ken Mandelbaum, which gives you an indication of just how bad it really was. The show was a Royal Shakespeare Company production, and started its life in Stratford-upon-Avon, England, in February 1988, with a three-week run before transferring directly to New York. Lawrence D. Cohen's book, which was adapted from a novel by Stephen King, tells of a repressed, sexually retarded young schoolgirl (Linzi Hateley), with telekinetic powers (her fingers 'spurt fire'), and a 'religious-nut mother' (Barbara Cook). The early part of the show deals with the girl's first menstruation, a 'nightmare passage to womanhood' (in UK theatrical circles the show was known as *Monthly: A Musical*). Much of what follows is unclear, but, in Act Two, several pigs are slaughtered, and then, in the finale, the mother and daughter appear to kill each other on a white staircase - there is a great deal of blood spilt in this show. The score, by Michael Gore (music) and Dean Pitchford (lyrics) (writers of the Academy Award-winning title song for the *Fame* movie), consists of a series of 'coarse semi-disco numbers interspersed with some soupy, soppy ballads', and included 'Dream On', 'Open Your Heart', 'Eve Was Weak', 'Don't Waste The Moon', 'Evening Prayers', 'Unsuspecting Hearts', 'Do Me A Favor', 'I Remember How Those Boys Could Dance', 'It Hurts To Be Strong', 'Unsuspecting Hearts', 'I'm Not Alone', 'Carrie', and, of course, 'Out For Blood'. Barbara Cook, Broadway's favourite ingénue of the 50s, who was in the middle of an 80s renaissance, soon realised how awful the whole thing was (she was nearly decapitated by a piece of scenery early on), and withdrew at the end of the Stratford run, which was not well received ('Is there a doctor in the house?') by the critics. Betty Buckley took her role for the Broadway opening on 12 May 1988 at the Virginia Theatre, where the auditorium had been completely painted black - in mourning, perhaps? Most of those concerned in one of the most celebrated disasters in contemporary musical theatre history came in for critical punishment, particularly the director Terry Hands, and choreographer Debbie Allen, who was best-known for her work on the television series, *Fame*. Linzi Hately, a 17-year old drama school graduate, escaped most of the flak, although her acting was compared unfavourably with that of Sissy Spacek in the 1976 film of *Carrie*. A London production is not planned for the near future.

Carroll, Earl

b. 16 September 1893, Pittsburgh, Pennsylvania, USA, d. 17 June 1948, Mount Carmel, Pennsylvania, USA. A producer, director, author, and songwriter. In the 20s and early 30s, Carroll's glamorous revues, 'Featuring The Most Beautiful Girls In The World', rivalled other similar -although perhaps more up-market - productions such as the *Ziegfeld Follies* and *George White's Scandals*. Carroll was selling programmes in theatres when he was 10 years old, before working his way around the world while still in his teens. From 1912-17 he was a staff writer with the Feist music publishing company, and also contributed material to Broadway shows such as *The Passing Show Of 1912*, the *Ziegfeld Follies Of 1913*, and *Pretty Miss Smith* (with composer Alfred Robyn) (1914). He wrote his first full scores for *So Long Letty* (1916) and *Canary Cottage* (1917). After serving as a pilot in World War II, Carroll worked with the composer Alfred Francis on *The Love Mill* (1918), and then moved into management and production to such an extent that, in 1922, he was able to build his own Earl Carroll Theatre in New York. Between 1923 and 1932 (plus an extra version in 1940), he staged a series of 'girlie' revues under the title of the *Earl Carroll Vanities*, with the exception of 1929 and 1935 when the shows were presented as the *Earl Carroll Sketchbook*. They all had decent runs, but there were notable editions in 1929, when the show ran for 440 performances, and featured songs mostly by E.Y. 'Yip' Harburg and Jay Gorney, such as 'Kinda Cute', 'Like Me Less, Love Me More', and 'Crashing The Golden Gate'; and in 1930, again with Harburg and Gorney's songs such as 'Ring Out The Blues' and 'I Came to Life'. In 1931, several of the numbers were written by Burton Lane and Harold Adamson, including 'Have A Heart', 'Goin' To Town', 'Love Come Into My Heart', and 'Heigh Ho, The Gang's All Here', plus interpolations from other songwriters such as Ray Noble, Reg Connelly and Jimmy Campbell with their 'Goodnight Sweetheart'; and in 1932, when the *Vanities* was staged by the young Vincente Minnelli, Lilian Shade introduced Harold Arlen and Ted Koehler's 'I Gotta Right To Sing The Blues', which Jack Teagarden adopted as his theme tune. 1931 was also the year that the new Earl Carroll

Theatre, 'the largest legitimate theatre in the world', opened on the site of the old one, with 3000 seats and a number of features that ranged from black velvet walls, to reconditioned air, to free soft drinks in the intermission. The naked girls and the onstage antics still had the critics fuming at what they considered to be 'a monstrosity of bad taste'. Many famous names appeared in Carroll's shows during the years, including Joe Cook, Sophie Tucker, W.C. Fields, Lilian Roth, Jack Benny, Helen Broderick, Jimmy Savo, Patsy Kelly, William Mahoney, Milton Berle, and one of Britain's brightest stars, Jessie Matthews, who, in the 1927 edition, suffered the indignity of having coins thrown onto the stage by a dissatisfied audience. Carroll was also involved in other Broadway and Off Broadway shows such as *Murder At The Vanities* (1933), and in several movies, *A Night At Earl Carroll's* (1940), *Earl Carroll's Vanities* (1945), and *Earl Carroll's Sketch Book* (1946). One of Broadway's most flamboyant showmen, Carroll died in an air crash in June 1948.

Cassidy, David

b. 12 April 1950, New York, New York, USA. The son of actor Jack Cassidy, David pursued a show-business career and received his big break after being cast in *The Partridge Family*. The television series was inspired by the life of another hit group, the Cowsills and it was not long before the Partridge Family began registering hits in their own right. Cassidy appeared as lead vocalist on their earnest 1970 US chart-topper, 'I Think I Love You'. Further hits followed and, in October 1971, Cassidy was launched as a solo artist. One month later he was number 1 in the US with a revival of the Association's 'Cherish'. Cassidy was classic teen-idol material but was ambivalent about the superficiality of his image and attempted to create a more adult sexual persona by appearing semi-naked in the pages of *Rolling Stone*. The publicity did not help his career at home, but by mid-1972 he was finding even greater success as a soloist in the UK, where teen-idols were suddenly in the ascendant. That year, he climbed to number 2 in Britain with 'Could It Be Forever' and enjoyed a solo chart-topper with a revival of the Young Rascals' 'How Can I Be Sure?' The more R&B-style 'Rock Me Baby' just failed to reach the Top 10 in the UK and peaked at number 38 in the USA. It was to be his last hit in his home country. By 1973, Cassidy was concentrating on the UK market and his efforts were rewarded with the Top 3 'I Am A Clown' and the double-sided 'Daydreamer'/'The Puppy Song' gave him his second UK number 1. His ability to raid old catalogues and recycle well-known songs to teenage audiences was reflected through further successful covers, including the Beatles' 'Please Please Me' and the Beach Boys' 'Darlin''. By the mid-70s, it was clear that his teen-

idol days were reaching their close, so he switched to serious acting, appearing in Tim Rice and Andrew Lloyd Webber's *Joseph And The Amazing Technicolor Dreamcoat*. In 1985, he made a surprise return to the UK Top 10 with the self-penned 'The Last Kiss', which featured backing vocals from George Michael. Two years later, he took over from Cliff Richard in the lead role of Dave Clark's musical *Time*. His teen-idol mantle was meanwhile passed on to his younger brother Shaun Cassidy. In 1993, the two brothers, along with veteran singer Petula Clark, boosted audiences considerably when they joined the Broadway production of Willy Russell's musical *Blood Brothers*.

Albums: *Cherish* (1972), *Could It Be Forever* (1972), *Rock Me Baby* (1972), *Dreams Are Nothin' More* (1973), *Cassidy Live* (1974), *The Higher They Climb* (1975), *Romance* (1985), *His Greatest Hits, Live* (1986). Compilation: *Greatest Hits* (1977).

Cat And The Fiddle, The

Although Jerome Kern's lyricist for this show, Otto Harbach, was steeped in the Viennese-style of music that had influenced the American musical theatre for so long in the early part of the 20th century, *The Cat And The Fiddle*, which opened at the Globe Theatre in New York on 15 October 1931, was a significant and successful attempt by the distinguished composer to up-date the long-standing, traditional form of operetta, and give it a more believable and accessible story-line. Harbach also wrote the book for the show which was sub-titled 'A Musical Love Story'. The setting is Brussels, where two students find that personally they are completely compatible - but musically they are worlds apart. The prize composition pupil at the local Conservatoire, Victor (Georges Metaxa) is more than aghast when he - mistakenly - thinks that a misguided impresario has introduced several examples of jazzy music, written by Shirley (Bettina Hall), into his score for a serious operetta, *The Passionate Pilgrim*. However, principles eventually dissolve into passion, and the inevitable happy ending ensues (*West Side Story* was over 25 years away). Two songs from the score, 'The Night Was Made for Love' and 'She Didn't Say 'Yes'' ('She loved to be *en rapport* with him/But not behind a bolted door with him'), were hits at the time for Leo Reisman And His Orchestra, and the latter song received an amusing reading, much later, from the husband-and-wife team of Steve Lawrence and Eydie Gorme. The rest of Kern and Harbach's ambitious and progressive score included 'I Watch The Love Parade', 'Poor Pierrot', 'Hh! Cha! Cha!', 'Try To Forget', 'The Breeze Kissed Your Hair', 'One Moment Alone', and 'A New Love Is Old'. *The Cat And The Fiddle* was a welcome hit in the dark days of the Depression, and ran for 395 performances, rather more than the 1932 London production at the Palace Theatre. The 1934 film version starred Jeanette MacDonald, Ramon Novarro, and Vivenne Segal. A recording of the complete score was never made available, but, in 1992, a CD was issued containing Kern's 'Entr'acte', an instrumental selection of songs from the score, and a lengthy two-part medley by the Light Opera Company, which included Peggy Wood's recordings of some of the show's most popular numbers.

Catch Of The Season, The

An early musical retelling of the Cinderella fable, *The Catch Of The Season* was presented by the renowned producer, Charles Frohman, and starred one of London's most familiar theatrical figures in the first part of the 20th century, Seymour Hicks, who also directed the piece. It opened at the Vaudeville Theatre in London on 9 September 1904, with Hicks as the Duke of St. Jermyns ('Prince Charming'), and Zena Dare as Angela Crystal ('Cinderella'). Hicks also collaborated on the book with Cosmo Hamilton, and the score was by Herbert E. Haines and Evelyn Baker (music) and Charles H. Taylor (lyrics). Their songs included 'My Rainbow', 'The Quaint Old Bird', 'Cigarette', 'My Singing Bird', 'Sombrero', 'Butterfly', 'Come Down From That Big Fir Tree', and 'A Wise Old Owl', amongst others. Intense interest in the show at the time was generated, not by the plot or music, but by 'its brazen introduction of the bare shoulders, padded hips, and upswept hairdos of the newly stylish Gibson Girl, inspired by the artist Charles Dana Gibson', and personified by Camille Clifford who played Sylvia Gibson in the show. Fashion shops of all descriptions were inundated with women demanding copies. Another, more pertinent point regarding this show is the degree of involvement of the young American composer, Jerome Kern. The London production of *The Catch Of The Season* had a song entitled, 'Molly O'Halloran', and so did the New York presentation which opened at Daly's Theatre on 28 August 1905. The American version of 'Molly O'Halloran', which is also known as 'Edna May's Irish Song' (May played the lead on Broadway), is definitely credited to Kern (both music and lyrics). He also interpolated several other songs (with various lyricists) into the US show, including 'Raining', 'Take Me On The Merry-Go-Round', and 'Won't You Kiss Me Before I Go?'. This all happened several years before he was engaged to write his first complete score. *The Catch Of The Season* had an extraordinary London run (for those days) of 621 performances, and played for 104 in New York.

Cats

Following the termination of his partnership with

Tim Rice which had resulted in such 70s hits as *Jesus Christ Superstar*, *Joseph And The Amazing Technicolor Dreamcoat*, and *Evita*, in 1980 the composer Andrew Lloyd Webber turned for the source of his next musical to a favourite collection of poems from his childhood, T.S. Eliot's *Old Possum's Book Of Practical Cats*, which was first published in 1939. After hearing some of his songs, the author's widow, Valerie Eliot, gave Lloyd Webber access to her late husband's letters and an unpublished poem about Grizabella the Glamour Cat, who became one of the show's leading characters, and introduced the hit song, 'Memory'. Together with producer Cameron Mackintosh, Lloyd Webber assembled a highly impressive creative team which included the RSC's Trevor Nunn (director), Gillian Lynne (associate director and choreographer), John Napier (designer), and John Hersey (lighting designer). Finance was not easy to come by - not many of the regular 'angels' (theatrical investors) fancied putting money into an English show about cats, but Lloyd Webber toured the television chat-show circuit and provided personal monetary guarantees so that *Cats* could open at London's New London Theatre on 11 May 1981. The show's action is played out on Napier's spectacular (permanent) set representing a gigantic rubbish dump, which, after dark, becomes alive with cats of all types, shapes and sizes. Soon, there are cats all over the place - in the aisles - everywhere, gathering for the Jellicle Ball during which one cat will be selected by the Jellicle leader and allotted an extra precious life. The main contenders in this 'match of the moggies' are Grizabella (Elaine Paige), Rum Tum Tugger) (Paul Nicholas), Asparagus (Stephen Tate), Mr Mistoffolees (Wayne Sleep), Deuteronomy and Bustopher Jones (Brian Blessed), Skimbleshanks (Kenn Wells), Griddlebone (Susan Jane Tanner), Rumpleteazer (Bonnie Langford), Mungojerrie (John Thornton), and Munkustrap (Jeff Shankley). Sarah Brightman, who, with the dance group Hot Gossip, had climbed high in the UK chart with 'I Lost My Heart To A Starship Trooper' in 1978, was in the chorus, and subsequently became Lloyd Webber's second wife. The opening night had to be postponed when the celebrated actress, Judi Dench, suffered a torn Achilles tendon, and Elaine Paige, who had made such an impact in *Evita*, took over the role of Grizabella. She is the one, the former Glamour Cat - turned dishevelled outcast, who, at the end of the evening, is chosen by Deutronomy to receive the prized additional life. Paige gave her big number, 'Memory', a highly dramatic reading, and her recorded version entered the UK Top 5. The song, with a tune from Lloyd Webber's trunk of unused items, had a lyric by Trevor Nunn which was based on Eliot's poem *Rhapsody On A Windy Night*. Because all the text in the show was taken from Eliot's writings, with a few minor revisions, the only other 'extra lyrics' credit was given to Richard Stilgoe. The remainder of the score included 'Prologue: Jellicle Songs For Jellicle Cats', 'The Naming Of The Cats', 'The Invitation To The Jellicle Ball', 'Moments Of Happiness', 'The Journey To The Heavyside Layer', 'The Ad-Dressing Of Cats', and several numbers in the names of the various characters, such as 'Old Gumbie Cat', 'Gus, Theatre Cat', and 'Growltiger's Last Stand'. Initial reviews were mixed, but word-of-mouth about Napier's environmental set and slinky black cat costumes, as well as Gillian Lynne's exciting and innovative choreography and the show's special effects, ensured full houses for a 'performance extravaganza that was then a radical departure from anything seen on the musical stage'. Napier and Lynne were both involved again in the Broadway production of Cats which opened at the Winter Garden Theatre on 7 October 1982, with Betty Buckley in the role of Grizabella. Since those days Cats has undertaken several US tours, and played in the major cities of Europe, Canada, Australia, Britain, and many other countries. Its awards have included: 1981 Evening Standard, Laurence Olivier, and Ivor Novello Awards for best musical; 1983 Tonys for best musical, book, score, director (Nunn), supporting actress (Buckley), costumes (Napier), lighting (Hersey), and Drama Desk Awards for music, costumes, lighting; 1989 Moliere Award for best musical. In 1992 Lloyd Webber's Really Useful Company announced that it was aware of 150 different recorded versions of 'Memory' (it even listed them), and in the same year the New York production of the show celebrated its 10th anniversary with the record-breaking run of 6,137 performances by A Chorus Line (the longest-running Broadway show of any kind, musical or otherwise) firmly in its sights. If Cats remains true to its billboard's boast of 'Now And Forever', it will pass that total in the summer of 1997. In London the show already holds the longevity prize for a musical, but will be hard-pushed to overtake the overall record of The Moustrap, which opened in 1952 - and is still going strong.

Cavalcade

A play with music, rather than a musical, Noël Coward's Cavalcade was nevertheless filled with songs. This patriotic epic, one of the most spectacular productions ever to be mounted on the English stage, opened at London's Drury Lane Theatre on 13 October 1931. Its cast of over 200 included Mary Clare, Edward Sinclair, John Mills, Irene Browne, Binnie Barnes, Una O'Connor, Arthur McCrae, and Moyra Nugent. The show depicted some of the important events of the first 30 years of the 20th century - the relief of Mafeking, the sinking of the Titanic, the funeral of Queen Victoria, World War I

- seen through the eyes of an English family. Although Coward himself did not appear in the piece, he recorded a medley of many of the popular songs of those days that permeated the action, such as 'Soldiers Of The Queen', 'Goodbye Dolly Gray', 'If You Were The Only Girl In The World', 'Take Me Back To Dear Old Blighty', and two numbers that he wrote especially for the show, 'Twentieth Century Blues', sung by Binnie Barnes, and 'Lover Of My Dreams' ('Mirabelle Waltz'), which was introduced by Stella Wilson. All of those, and Coward's version of the celebrated 'Toast From Cavalcade', which occurs towards the end of the show and was originally spoken by Mary Clare, were re-issued in 1992 on a 4-CD boxed set, Noël Coward: His HMV Recordings 1928-1953. The show ran for well over a year, and was revived, 50 years later in the 80s, at Farnham and Chichester in the UK, and in Canada. A 1933 film version made in Hollywood, starring Diana Wynyard and Clive Brook, won three Oscars, including best picture; and the popular 70s television series, Upstairs, Downstairs, was based on the show. Sheridan Morley, the author and critic and Coward's biographer, tells of the occasion when they were seated together at a 'fork luncheon' at the Savoy Hotel in London. Morley remarked that he (Coward) seemed to be the only person in the room in possession of a fork. Coward replied, 'But of course dear boy. You see, I wrote Cavalcade.'

Champion, Gower

b. 22 June 1920, Geneva, Illinois, USA, d. 25 August 1980, New York City, New York, USA. One of the most distinguished and influential directors and choreographers in the American musical theatre. Champion was brought up in Los Angeles and took dancing lessons from an early age. When he was 15, he and his friend, Jeanne Tyler, toured nightclubs as 'Gower and Jeanne America's youngest dance team'. After serving in the US Coast Guard during World War II, Champion found another dance partner, Marge Belcher, and they were married in 1947. In the 50s they appeared together on numerous television variety programmes and in their own situation comedy, The Marge And Gower Champion Show. They also made several film musicals including the autobiographical Everything I Have Is Yours, and their exuberant dancing to 'I Might Fall Back On You' and 'Life Upon The Wicked Stage' were two of the highlights of the 1951 remake of Show Boat, which starred Howard Keel and Kathryn Grayson. During the late 30s and 40s Champion worked on Broadway as a solo dancer and choreographer. In 1948 he began to direct as well, and won a Tony Award for his staging of the musical Lend An Ear, the show which introduced Carol Channing to New York theatre audiences. From then on he

Carol Channing

choreographed and directed a mixture of smash hits and dismal flops in a list which included *Three For Tonight, Bye By Birdie, Carnival, Hello, Dolly!, I Do! I Do!, The Happy Time, Sugar, Irene, Mack And Mabel* (1974), and *Rockabye Hamlet* (1976). They earned him another three Tonys and New York Critics and Donaldson Awards. After some years away from the Broadway he returned (uncredited) to 'doctor' *The Act* (1977), but could do nothing to prevent *A Broadway Musical* (1978) folding after only one night. He finished with a smash-hit though, when he choreographed and directed a 1980 stage adaptation of the movie classic *42nd Street*. During the show's tryout in Washington, Champion learnt that he had a rare form of blood cancer, and after the first curtain call on the New York opening night producer David Merrick told the cast and the audience that Gower Champion had died that afternoon.

Channing, Carol

b. 31 January 1921, Seattle, Washington, USA. An actress and singer with a style and appearance that are difficult to define. She has been variously as 'a blonde, wide-eyed, long-legged, husky voiced, scatty personality' - among other things. The daughter of a Christian Science teacher, Channing moved with her family to San Franciso at an early age, and later attended Bennington College in Vermont where she majored in drama and dance. In 1941 she appeared in Marc Blitzstein's labour opera, *No For An Answer*, but only for three Sunday nights. In the same year she served as an understudy in *Let's Face It* on Broadway, and had a small part in *Proof Through The Night* (1942). After playing nightclubs around New York, she returned to San Francisco in 1946 and won a part in the Hollywood revue *Lend An Ear*. Her performance in the Broadway version of the show led to her triumph as Lorelei Lee in *Gentlemen Prefer Blondes* in which she introduced several memorable numbers including 'A Little Girl From Little Rock' and 'Diamonds Are A Girl's Best Friend'. In 1954, she replaced Rosalind Russell in *Wonderful Town*, and, in the next year, had her first big flop with *The Vamp*. In the late 50s her nightclub act was so successful that it was turned into a one-woman revue entitled *Show Girl*, which played on Broadway in 1961. Three years later, she had her biggest success in *Hello, Dolly!*, as the matchmaker Dolly Levi, with a Jerry Herman score that included 'So Long, Dearie', 'Before The Parade Passes By', and the insinuating title song. She won a Tony Award for outstanding performance, but Barbra Streisand was preferred for the movie version. Channing's larger-than-life personality is perhaps more suited to the stage than film, although she was hilarious in *Thoroughly Modern Millie* (1967). Other film credits include *Paid In Full* (1950), *The First Travelling Saleslady, Skidoo*, and *Shinbone Alley* (voice

only). In 1974 she was back on Broadway in *Lorelei*, which, as the title suggests, was a compilation of the best scenes from *Gentlemen Prefer Blondes*. It lasted for 320 performances and had a reasonable life on the road. At that stage of her career, with good music suitable musical comedy roles hard to come by, Channing continued to work mostly on US television and in nightclubs, but in 1987 she co-starred with Mary Martin in James Kirkwood's aptly-named show *Legends!*. A year later she embarked on a concert tour of locations such as Kansas City and San Diego, accompanied at each stop by the local symphony orchestra. In 1990 she appeared at the Desert Inn, Las Vegas, and two years later she toured with Rita Moreno in *Two Ladies Of Broadway*.
Selected albums: *Carol Channing* (1964), *Carol Channing Entertains* (1965), and Original Cast and soundtrack recordings.

Charlie Girl

One of the biggest blockbusters in the history of the London musical theatre (pre-Andrew Lloyd Webber), *Charlie Girl* opened at the Adelphi Theatre on 15 December 1965. Initial reviews were of the 'it takes geniuses of inspired mediocrity to produce rubbish such as this' variety, but the public loved it from the start. As with that other enormously popular musical, *Me And My Girl*, whose long and glorious run was inconveniently interrupted (temporarily) by World War II, *Charlie Girl* utilises the age-old formula of mixing the English upper and lower classes, and allowing the latter to come off best. Hugh and Margaret Williams's book (with some humerous help from Ray Cooney) tells the sad tale of Lady Hadwell (Anna Neagle), who was on the stage as one of Cochran's Young Ladies before she married the late earl. It is not enough that she is beset by death duties, leaky roofs, and nosey tourists, but she also has a daughter Charlotte (Christine Holmes), who prefers to be known as Charlie and rides motorcycles. With this kind of laid-back attitude, Charlie is obviously destined to marry Lady Hadwell's Cockney *aide de camp*, Joe Studholme (60s pop star Joe Brown), who wants to be loved for himself alone, and not for his life-enhancing win on the football pools, the news of which has been brought to him by Nicholas Wainright (Derek Nimmo). Charlie's brief (innococent) affair with wealthy Jack Connor (Stuart Damon), the son of Kay Connor (Hy Hazell), Lady Hadwell's buddy from the Cochran days, is only a minor hitch before fireworks in the sky blaze out the message, 'Isn't It Flippin' Well Marvellous!' Adelphi audiences certainly thought so, and *Charlie Girl* ran there for nearly five and a half years, a total of 2202 performances, and won an Ivor Novello Award for best musical. The show's score, by David Heneker (*Half A Sixpence*) and John Taylor, showcased

Brown's charming, cheeky style in numbers such as 'My Favourite Occupation', 'Charlie Girl', 'I 'ates Money' (with Nimmo), 'Fish 'N' Chips', and 'You Never Know What You Can Do Until You Try' (with Neagle). Christine Holmes, had the delightful 'Bells Will Ring', 'I Love Him, I Love Him' and 'Like Love', while Hy Hazell excelled in 'Party Of A Lifetime', 'Let's Do A Deal' (with Neagle), and 'What Would I Get From Being Married?' Anna Neagle brought the house down regularly at the end of the first act with 'I Was Young'. During the run, this much-loved actress was created a Dame of the British Empire, and the cast borrowed the band parts from *South Pacific* which was at the Prince of Wales Theatre, and sang 'There Is Nothing Like A Dame' to her at the close of the evening's performance. She stayed with the show throughout, except for holidays, but Joe Brown was replaced by Gerry Marsden, without his Pacemakers (the role was 'tweaked' to explain his Liverpudlian accent). When the show closed in 1971 Neagle and Nimmo joined the successful Australian and New Zealand productions which included John Farnham, a British singer who was popular down-under. In 1986 a revised version of *Charlie Girl* was mounted at London's Victoria Palace, starring Paul Nicholas, Dora Bryan, Mark Wynter, Nicholas Parsons, and the dancing star of many MGM musical films, Cyd Charisse, but times had changed, and the production lasted for only six months.

Chess

As with two of his big hit shows of the 70s, *Jesus Christ Superstar* and *Evita* (both written with Andrew Lloyd Webber), Tim Rice opted to introduce this show by way of a studio concept album, which made the UK Top 10 in 1984. For *Chess*, Rice wrote the book and lyrics, and the composers were Bjorn Ulvaeus and Benny Andersen, two ex-members of the record-breaking Swedish pop group Abba. The album spawned two hit singles: Murray Head's 'disco-rap-style' 'One Night In Bangkok', which reputedly sold several million copies worldwide and did particularly well in the UK and the USA; and the atmospheric ballad 'I Know Him So Well', a UK number 1 for Elaine Paige with Barbara Dickson. The show itself opened at London's Prince Edward Theatre (replacing *Evita*) on 14 May 1986. Rice's book was generally considered at the time to be the weakest element in the show. It dealt with the familiar conflict between East and West - the Reds and the rest - but this time the different sides were personified by two chess grand masters, the USA world champion Frederick Trumper (Murray Head) and Anatoly Sergeievsky (Tommy Korgerg) from the USSR. After the prologue ('The Story Of Chess'), Frederick dumps the Russian challenger under the table in the middle of the World Championships

which are being held in a Tyrolean township, and eventually loses not only his crown, but his devoted 'second', Florence Vassy (Elaine Paige) to Anatoly, who defects in the best Nureyev tradition. During the dark intrigues that follow, Anatoly defends his title (with the help of a reformed Frederick) against another Russian challenger, and, reversing his original career move, bids a heartfelt farewell to Florence at the airport before flying off into the (red) sunset. The 'part opera - part chorale' score was generally well received for its 'witty, stylish lyrics and consistently listenable music' (although some called it sheer Euro-pop), not only for 'One Night In Bangkok' and 'I Know Him So Well', which were important elements within the context of the show, but for the touching ballad, 'Heaven Help My Heart', and other numbers such as 'Pity The Child' and 'Where I Want To Be', As befitted a musical of the 80s, *Chess* was full of 'technological glitz' and much of its £4 million budget was visible onstage in the form of an elaborate rolling and revolving hydraulic set, a vast bank of television monitors and various other high-tech gear. Despite the sniping of the critics, *Chess* ran in London until April 1989, a total of 1102 performances. The show's director, Trevor Nunn, who had taken over from the renowned American director-choreographer, Michael Bennett, when he became ill (he died from AIDS in 1987), also staged the 1988 Broadway version which was savaged by the critics and flopped, despite having been 'Americanized' and fitted with a new cast and book. *Chess* returned to the USA in 1990 for a 40 week tour, and then, two years later, the musical 'with more past lives than Shirley MacLaine', was reworked yet again for a limited run Off Broadway.

Chicago

Fred Ebb and Bob Fosse's book for this 'Musical Vaudeville', which opened on Broadway at the 46th Street Theatre on 3 June 1975, was based on a play by Maurine Dallas Watkins, and set in the Roaring 20s. A chorus girl, Roxie Hart (Gwen Verdon) has disposed of her unfaithful lover in an unlawful manner, but retains her freedom due to her talent for self-publicity and the skills of her disreputable, wheeler-dealer lawyer, the flash Billy Flynn (Jerry Orbach). She finds that she has some things in common with another hoofer (she killed the man in her life, too), Velma Kelly (Chita Rivera), so they decide to stop bumping people off and form a successful nightclub act. An unusual musical in some ways - it doesn't have a love story, and an M.C. introduces the numbers in true vaudeville style - the book takes a lot of sly digs at the shortcomings of the sometimes tawdry and corrupt American way of life in general, and its legal system in particular. The tongue-in-cheek score, by Fred Ebb and John

Kander, had more than a hint of pastiche, and included numbers such as 'Class', 'All I Care About', 'Roxie', 'I Can't Do It Alone,' 'Me And My Baby', 'My Own Best Friend', 'Mr. Cellophane', and 'Nowadays'. Two of the songs, 'All That Jazz' (Velma) and 'Razzle Dazzle' (Billy), had a life outside the show, and the latter received a lively reading from Bing Crosby on one of his last albums, *At My Time Of Life*. Gwen Verdon and Chita Rivera were both making their Broadway comebacks after an absence of some years, and their presence, together with that of Bob Fosse, ensured that the show was light on its feet and complete with an array of dances that were popular in those Prohibition times. The New York production ran for 898 performances, and the 1979 London version stayed in the West End for 18 months. Since then *Chicago* has proved to be a popular choice of provincial and stock companies in many parts of the world. In 1991 it was presented at the UK Leicester Haymarket Theatre, the springboard for many successful musicals, and, in the following year, the Long Beach Civic Light Opera Company's classy production starred Juliet Prowse and Kay Ballard. The story itself has been filmed twice, in 1927 under the title of *Chicago*, and again, in 1942, as *Roxie Hart*, starring Ginger Rogers, Adolphe Menjou, and George Montgomery.

Children Of Eden

'Excuse me, where's the nearest Exodus?', was one critic's morning-after reaction to this 'new biblical musical' which opened at London's Prince Edward Theatre on 8 January 1991. The staging was by John Caird, the co-director of *Les Misérables*, and his book, adapted from the Old Testament, told the familiar story from the Creation until just after the Flood. The music and lyrics were by Stephen Schwartz, whose *Godspell* had played 1,128 performances just along the road at Wyndhams Theatre 20 years earlier. The critics were quick to point out that God (Ken Page) and Eve (Shezwae Powell) were black, and they, along with Adam (Martin Smith) had somehow got kitted out in 'cute little costumes complete with shoes'; and that Cain's slaying of Abel was presented 'in the humdrum context of a family spat'. Schwartz's score of over 22 numbers, ranging 'from oratorio to gospel', included 'In Pursuit Of Excellence', 'In Whatever Time We Have', 'Let There Be', 'A World Without You', 'Children Of Eden', 'What Is He Waiting For?', and 'Ain't It Good'. Praise was reserved for John Napier's set and David Hersey's lighting, and especially for Richard Sharples' imaginative animal costumes and the actors' expressive use of them. This 'sentimental and silly' show ran for 10 weeks and reportedly lost its total investment of £2. 2 million.

Chinese Honeymoon, A

A run of 1000 performances does not seem such a remarkable feat in these days of Andrew Lloyd Webber's mega-hits, but in the early part of the 20th century, it was a remarkable achievement. This show, which opened at the Strand Theatre in London on 5 October 1901, was the first local production to pass the magic figure, and went on to add 75 more performances to the total. This musical comedy, with book and lyrics by George Dance and music by Howard Talbot, with additional songs by others, including Ivan Caryll, was set in the Chinese Kingdom of Ylang Ylang. Emperor Hang Chow has decreed that any member of the royal family who kisses another person has to marry them. Unbelievable complications ensue, involving the Lord Chancellor Chippee Choppy, a naval officer who leaves the service for the love of Fi Fi a hotel waitress, the English honeymooners Samuel Pineapple and his young ex-typist wife Marie, and a sweet singer named Soo Soo who is really a princess. Fortunately, the score was a good deal more straight-forward and harmonious and contained a number of jolly songs such as 'Martha Spank The Grand Pianner', 'I Want To Be A Lidy', 'The À La Girl', 'The Twiddly Bits', 'Sweet Little Sing-Sing', 'Roses Red And White', 'But Yesterday', 'A Paper Fan', 'Daisy With A Dimple On Her Chin', and 'A Chinese Honeymoon'. The cast included Lily Elsie, Marie Dainton, Louie Freear, and Lionel Rignold. The 1902 New York production ran for 376 performances, and there was a London revival in 1915.

Chocolate Soldier, The

Nearly 50 years before Alan Jay Lerner and Frederick Loewe created *My Fair Lady*, the ultimate musical adaptation of a George Bernard Shaw play, a Viennese operetta, *Der Tapfere Soldat*, which had been adapted from Shaw's *Arms And The Man*, was presented in Vienna in 1908. Re-named *The Chocolate Soldier*, with a book and lyrics by Stanislaus Stange who also directed the piece, and music by Oscar Strauss, the show moved to the Lyric Theatre in New York on 13 September 1909. In this satirical look at war and its consequences, Lt. Bumerli (J.E. Gardner), a Swiss soldier who is serving in the Serb army during its invasion of Bulgaria in 1885, is more fond of chocolate than he is of fighting. On the run from the enemy, he conceals himself, and his identity, in the home of the Bulgarian Colonel Popoff (William Pruette), and falls in love with the Colonel's daughter, Nadine (Ida Brooks Hunt). Despite opposition from her ex-boyfriend, the extremely brave Major Alexius Spiridoff (George Tallman), Bumerli's pacifism wins the day. These stories, of course, are made tolerable by the magnificent music that punctuates the sometimes overly dramatic scenes. *The Chocolate Soldier* contained several popular and enduring numbers, such as 'My Hero', 'Sympathy', 'Seek the Spy', 'Falling In Love', 'The Letter Song', 'Thank The Lord The War Is Over', 'Bulgarians', and 'The Chocolate Soldier'. The New York run of 296 performances was exceeded by the 1910 London production which lasted for exactly 500. Since then, the show has become a much-loved feature in the repertoires of light operatic companies around the world. The main professionals revivals have been on Broadway in 1921, 1930, 1931, and 1947 (a revised version by Guy Bolton); and London audiences were able to enjoy the show again in 1914, 1932, and 1940. The 1941 film of *The Chocolate Soldier*, with Nelson Eddy and Rise Stevens, used a different story based on Molnar's *The Guardsman*.

Chorus Line, A

The longest-running production (musical or non-musical) in the history of Broadway. Conceived, directed and co-choreographed (with Bob Avian) by Michael Bennett; with a book by James Kirkwood and Nicholas Dante, and a score by Marvin Hamlisch (music) and Edward Kleban (lyrics), the show began as a workshop production at producer Joseph Papp's New York Shakespeare Festival Public Theatre on the 21 May 1975. After a spell at the Newman Theatre in the same complex, *A Chorus Line* opened on Broadway at the Schubert Theatre on the 21 July 1975. Set in a bare Broadway theatre, the compelling story tells of a director, Zach (Robert LuPone), and his search for eight dancers from a group of 17 hopefuls which includes his former mistress, Cassie (Donna McKechnie). Assembled on a large, empty stage with just a mirror-covered rear wall, it was 'the quintessential Broadway show, summing up the heartbreak and frustrations of thousands of aspirant stars'. The production won the 1976 Pulitzer Prize for Drama, the New York Drama Critics Award for best musical, and Tony Awards for best musical, best musical actress (McKechnie), featured actor, musical, (Sammy Williams), featured actress, musical, (Carole Bishop); and for best director, book, score, lighting (Tharon Musser), and choreography. The songs included 'I Can Do That', 'What I Did For Love', 'Dance: Ten, Looks: Three', 'The Music And The Mirror', 'I Hope I Get It', and the spectacular finale, 'One'. *A Chorus Line* closed on Broadway on the 28 April 1990, following a run of 6,137 performances. After a six-minute standing ovation from the audience on the final evening, members of the 1975 cast joined the current performers on stage, and later, there was a public auction of souvenirs from the show, including some items from the wardrobe and even a sign from the lobby that stated: 'No Photos'. The total Broadway gross was estimated at over 140 million dollars. A London production opened in July 1976 and ran for nearly three years. Since then, productions have been licensed in countries such as Puerto Rico, Europe, South America, the Netherlands, Canada, and the Far East. A film version, directed by Richard Attenborough, was released in 1985.

Further reading: *A Chorus Line: The Complete Text*, Applause Books. *On The Line: The Creation Of A Chorus Line*, Baayork Lee, Thommie Walsh and Robert Viagas. *A Chorus Line And The Musicals Of Michael Bennett*, Ken Mandelbaum.

Chu Chin Chow

First staged at His Majesty's Theatre in London on 31 August 1916 when Britain was in the midst of World War I, *Chu Chin Chow* was one of the most successful of all British stage musicals, and ran for more than 2,200 performances. Written by Australian Oscar Asche, the show was set in an Arabian Nights fantasy land. Brimming with spectacular sets and 'lovely ladies', including Josie Collins, *Chu Chin Chow* became, in Sheridan Morley's words, the show for soldiers 'to see on one's last leave night . . . and as such it acquired sentimental and even patriotic qualities that were far more to do with the nature of the audience than with the actual score.' The score, with music by Frederic Norton, did, in fact, have some nice tunes, including 'The Robbers' Chorus' and 'Anytime's Kissing Time' but as Morley implies the music was almost incidental to the production's success. Revivals and transatlantic stagings failed, thus confirming *Chu Chin Chow*'s status as the right show for the times in which it emerged. A silent film version was released in 1923, followed by a talkie in 1934. The show was produced as an ice spectacular at the Empire Pool Wembley in 1953.

Cinderella

(see **Me And Juliet**)

City Of Angels

'The great American musical is back and showbusiness USA is breathing a little easier' is how one relieved critic put it after *City Of Angels* exploded into view at the Virginia Theatre in New York on 11 December 1989. Larry Gelbart's book, 'an hilarious Hollywood private-eye spoof', together with 'a 40s-era jazz-tinged score' by Cy Coleman (music) and David Zippel (lyrics), dazzled almost everyone, and was hailed as the most brilliantly inventive musical New York had seen for years. Gelbart's clever double-plot concerns the interlocking worlds of the screenwriter named Stine (Gregg Edelman) and the main character in the film he is writing, a tough private-eye named Stone (James Naughton), who is Stine's alter ego. Both Stone and Stine have a weakness for beautiful women, but Stine's main problem is the bully-boy film producer Buddy Fidler (Rene Auberjonois). Buddy's secretary, Donna, and Stone's secretary, Oolie, are both played by Randy Graff who has one of the show's big numbers, the bitter-sweet 'You Can Always Count On Me' ('I've been the "other woman" since my puberty began/I crashed the junior prom and met the only married man . . . One Joe who swore he's single got me sorta crocked, the beast/I woke up only slightly shocked that I'd defrocked a priest . . . But I've made a name with hotel detectives who break down doors/Guess who they expect to see/You can always count on me'. Another example of Zippel's witty lyrics comes in the double-entendres of 'The Tennis Song', in which Stone and his beautiful 'client', Alaura Kingsley, play around with lines such as, He: 'I bet you like to play rough'/She: 'I like to work up a sweat'/He: 'And you just can't get enough'/She: 'I'm good for more than one set'. The rest of the fine score included 'Double-Talk', 'What You Don't Know About Women', 'Ya Gotta Look Out For Yourself', 'With Every Breath I Take', 'Ev'rybody's Gotta Be Somewhere', 'Lost And Found', 'You're Nothing Without Me' - Stone and Stine tell each other, 'Stay With Me', and 'It Needs Work'. The show ran for over two years in New York, a total of 878 performances, and won three Outer Critics Circle Awards, eight Drama Desk Awards and Tonys for best musical, book, score, actor (Naughton), featured actress (Graff), and scenic design (Robin Wagner). Director Michael Blakemore repeated his brilliant staging for the London production which opened at the Prince of Wales Theatre in March 1993, but, in spite of ecstatic reviews and the Critics Circle London Theatre Award for Best Musical, it never caught on in the West End ('too sophisticated and tricky', some said), and stuttered along until November when it closed with losses estimated at £2.5 million.

Cochran, Charles B.

b. Charles Blake Cochran, 25 September 1872, Sussex, England, d. 31 January 1951, London, England. Britain's leading theatrical producer of musicals, revues, plays, operettas, and so much more during the 20s and 30s. A master showman, the like of which has never been seen before or since, he is said to have been annoyed when referred to as 'the English Ziegfeld', but then Florenz Ziegfeld did not present flea circuses, boxing matches, rodeos, or run the Royal Albert Hall. There were similarities though: both men specialised in lavish and spectacular theatrical extravaganzas, and, while the American had his lovely 'Ziegfeld Girls', the London stage was graced by 'Mr. Cochran's Young Ladies'. Many of these talented and delightful 'young things' went on

to become stars in their own right. Cochran is credited with discovering or significantly promoting Gertrude Lawrence, Tilly Losch, Jessie Matthews, Anna Neagle, Larry Adler, Evelyn Laye, John Mills, Alice Delysia, Hermione Baddeley, Elisabeth Welch, Binnie Hale, Beatrice Lillie, Pirandello, Douglas Byng, and numerous others. However, Cochran's most famous association was with the 'Master' himself, Noël Coward. After inviting Coward to write the words and music for the revue On With The Dance in 1925, during the next nine years Cochran produced some of the composer's most celebrated works, including This Year Of Grace, Bitter Sweet, Cavalcade, Private Lives, Cochran's 1931 Revue, Words And Music, and Conversation Piece. They parted in 1934 because Coward thought that the impresario had cheated him out of his fair share of royalties. From 1914 through to 1949, Cochran's London productions included Odds And Ends, More, Half-Past Eight, The Better 'Ole, As You Were, Afgar, London, Paris And New York, League Of Notions, Phi-Phi, Music Box Revue, Little Nellie Kelly, Cochran's Revue Of 1926, Blackbirds, One Dam Thing After Another, Castles In The Air, Wake Up And Dream, Ever Green, Cochran's 1931 Revue, Helen!, The Cat And The Fiddle, Music In The Air, Nymph Errant, Streamline, Anything Goes, Blackbirds Of 1936, Home And Beauty, Paganini, Happy Returns, Lights Up, Big Ben, Bless the Bride, and Tough At The Top. Early in 1951 Cochran was involved in a terrible accident at his London home. He scalded himself whilst taking a bath and was taken to the Westminster Hospital, but died 31 January.
Further reading: Secrets Of A Showman, I Had Almost Forgotten, Cock-A-Doodle-Doo, Showman Looks On, all by Charles B. Cochran. The Cochran Story, Charles Graves Allen. 'Cockie'-An Authoritative Life Of C.B. Cochran, Sam Heppner. Cochran, James Harding.

Cocoanuts, The

Irving Berlin meets the Marx Brothers does not sound like a particularly good idea for a musical, but the production which opened at New York's Lyric Theatre on 8 December 1925, amused and delighted audiences for nearly 400 performances. It was George S Kaufman's book which the Marx Brothers used (and sometimes modified) to create their usual brand of zany mayhem. The story concerns Henry W. Schlemmer (Groucho), a devious Florida hotel owner who deals in a little real estate on the side. He is aided, abetted, and sometimes hindered in his various shady transactions by two hotel guests, Silent Sam (Harpo), Willie The Wop (Chico), and the desk clerk Jameson (Zeppo). Complications arise when jewel thieves, posing as hotel residents, rob the wealthy Mrs Potter, played by Margaret Dumont (Groucho's regular 'stooge'), and try to 'frame' her future son-in-law. Berlin's score was largely unappreciated at the time, but in retrospect the lively, catchy songs such as 'The Monkey Doodle-Doo', 'A Little Bungalow', 'Lucky Boy', 'Florida By The Sea', and 'Why Am I A Hit With The Ladies?', were entirely right for this riotous romp. This was the second of the three Marx Brothers' Broadway musicals - the others were *I'll Say She Is* (1924) and *Animal Crackers* (1928). The Marx Brothers made their feature-film debut in the 1929 screen version of *The Cocoanuts*.

Cohan, George M.

b. George Michael Cohan, 3 July 1878, Providence, Rhode Island, USA, d. 5 November 1942, New York, USA. A legendary figure in the history of American popular entertainment: a performer, songwriter, playwright, director, producer, and a high-profile patriot. Cohan's paternal grandfather emigrated to America from County Cork, Ireland, and George was baptized in the family's Catholic faith. His parents were vaudevillians, and, from an early age, he and his sister, Josephine, joined them on stage as the Four Cohans. By the time he was eight, George had finished his conventional education, but already he was learning the skills that would make him one of the great show business all-rounders. He wrote sketches and dialogue for the family's headline act, and had his first song, 'Why Did Nellie Leave Home?', published when he was 16. Around this time, he also developed his curious dancing style, a straight-legged strut, with the body bent forward; and introduced his famous closing address to the audience: 'My mother thanks you, my father thanks you, my sister thanks you, and I thank you.' In 1899, Cohan married the singer and comedienne, Ethel Levey, who joined the Four Cohans, and they all appeared, two years later, in George's first Broadway musical comedy, *The Governor's Son*, for which, as with most of his future shows, he wrote the book, music and lyrics. However, neither that show, or the follow-up, *Running For Office* (1903), lasted for over 50 performances.

By 1904 Cohan was into his stride. In partnership with the producer, Sam H. Harris, he presented, starred in, directed, a series of (mostly) hit musical shows during the next 15 years. The first, *Little Johnny Jones*, was not successful initially, despite a score that included 'The Yankee Doodle Boy', 'Life's A Funny Proposition After All', and 'Give My Regards To Broadway', amongst others. Even so, the 'play with music' which told the story of an American jockey wrongfully accused of accepting a bribe to lose the English Derby race, is seen as a watershed in the history of the Broadway musical. With its brash, patriotic, flag-waving style, and a strong, believable plot, it marked the beginning of the indigenous American musical - a real alternative to the country's currently fashionable operettas which had originated in Europe. It was filmed as a silent in 1923, and again, in 1930. *Little Johnny Jones* was followed by *Forty-Five Minutes From Broadway*, which contained three enormously popular Cohan numbers: the title song, 'So Long Mary', and 'Mary's A Grand Old Name'. In *George Washington Jnr.* (1906), Cohan initiated one of his famous pieces of business, when he wrapped himself in the American flag during the song, 'You're A Grand Old Flag', which he had originally called 'You're A Grand Old Rag', until he was lobbied by various nationalistic societies. From then, until 1914, and the outbreak of World War I, Cohan's musical comedies were a regular feature of each New York season - he dominated the Broadway musical theatre. In 1907 there was *The Honeymooners*, a revised version of *Running For Office*, with a score that included 'I'm a Popular Man', If I'm Going to Die', and 'I'll Be There In The Public Square'. It was followed by others such as *The Talk Of New York* ('When We Are M-A-Double R-I-E-D', 'When A Fellow's On The Level With A Girl That's On The Square'), *Fifty Miles From Boston* ('Harrigan', 'A Small Town Girl'), *The Yankee Prince* ('Come On Down Town', 'I'm Awfully Strong For You'), *The Man Who Owns Broadway* ('There's Something About A Uniform'), *The Little Millionaire* ('Barnum Had The Right Idea', 'Any Place The Old Flag Flies'). In 1914, with the innovative *Hello Broadway!*, Cohan introduced the modern revue format to New York, later sustained by *The Cohan Revues* of 1916 and 1918. In 1917 he wrote 'Over There', generally considered to be the greatest of all war songs, for which he subsequently received the Congressional Medal. Two years later, he dissolved his partnership with Sam H. Harris and threatened to retire from show business following the strike of the Actors' Equity Association. As a producer as well as an actor, the dispute must have placed Cohan in something of a quandry, but he sided with the management against Equity, who won the bitter month-long dispute. In the process, Cohan lost many long-standing friends at a time when he was beginning to be regarded as old fashioned, in comparison with the more sophisticated writers and performers that were beginning to make their mark in the 20s. It was Cohan's last decade on Broadway as a writer and director of musical shows. These included *Little Nellie Kelly* (filmed in 1940, starring Judy Garland), *The Rise Of Rosie O'Reilly*, *The Merry Malones*, and *Billie* (1928). Ironically, nearly 10 years later, in 1937, Cohan made a triumphant return to the New York musical stage in George S. Kaufman and Moss Hart's political satire, *I'd Rather Be Right*, which had a score by Richard Rodgers and Lorenz Hart, two of the 'upstarts' who had made Cohan and his continual celebration of the American dream, seem 'corny'. In *I'd Rather Be Right*, Cohan played the role of the President of the USA, Franklin D.

Roosevelt, his first appearance in a musical that he hadn't written himself. Coincidentally, in Cohan's solitary appearance in a film musical, *The Phantom President* (1932), he played the part of a presidential candidate. His biggest impression on the cinema screen was made in 1942, when James Cagney portrayed him in the biopic, *Yankee Doodle Dandy*. Cagney's uncanny impersonation of Cohan - the arrogant, dynamic, charismatic performer, complete with that individual dancing style, reviving a clutch of imperishable songs, won him an Academy Award and the New York Drama Critics Award as 'Best Actor'. Cagney reprised his Cohan role in *The Seven Little Foys* (1955), when his bar-top dance with Bob Hope (as Eddie Foy), was the highlight of the picture. Other attempts to recapture, and cash in, on the Cohan larger-then-life image have included *George M!* (1968), a Broadway musical starring Joel Grey (fresh from his *Cabaret* triumph), which ran for over a year; and *Give My Regards To Broadway* another musical anthology which played some US east coast resorts in 1987.

In the latter years of his life, Cohan concerned himself solely with the straight theatre (apart from *I'd Rather Be Right*). His first break, at the age of 13, had been as a 'cocky, confident brat' in the play, *Peck's Bad Boy*, and, in parallel with his musical career, he had writtten some 40 plays, and presented and acted in his own, and other productions, including 13 Broadway credits. One of his critically acclaimed performances came in 1933, when he portrayed the kindly newspaper editor in Eugene O'Neill's comedy, *Ah, Wilderness!*, and his last stage appearance is said to have been in *Return Of The Vagabond* in 1940, two years before he died in November 1942. However, is it for his musical side, the songs - some 500 of them - and the 'naive, brash, optimistic, jaunty, and patriotic shows, and his participation in them, that caused him to be called 'the greatest single figure the American theatre has produced'. In the early part of the 20th century, one of the early New York theatres was named after him, and his statue overlooks Times Square, the heart of the territory over which he reigned for so long.

Further reading: *Twenty Years On Broadway*, George M. Cohan. *George M. Cohan: Prince Of The American Theatre*, Ward Morehouse. *George M. Cohan: The Man Who Owned Broadway*, John McCabe.

Coleman, Cy

b. Seymour Kaufman, 14 June 1929, New York, USA. Coleman was a pianist, singer, producer and a composer of popular songs, and scores for films and the Broadway stage. The youngest of the five sons of emigrants from Russia, Coleman was born and brought up in the Bronx, where his mother owned two tenement buildings. He began to pick out tunes on the piano when he was four-years-old, irritating his father, a carpenter, to such an extent that he nailed down the lid of the instrument. However, a local teacher was so impressed by Coleman's piano playing that she provided free lessons in classical music. Between the ages of six and nine, Coleman performed in New York at the Town Hall, Steinway Hall, and Carnegie Hall. While continuing his classical studies at the High School of Music and Art and the New York College of Music, from which he graduated in 1948, Coleman decided to change course and pursue a career in popular music. After a stint at Billy Reed's Little Club, he spent two years as a cocktail-lounge pianist at the plush Sherry Netherland Hotel in Manhattan, and played piano for several television programmes, including *The Kate Smith Show* and *A Date In Manhattan*. In 1950 he appeared with his trio, and singer Margaret Phelan, in the RKO short, *Package Of Rhythm*. During the early 50s, Coleman began to play in jazz clubs in New York and elsewhere, developing what he called a 'kind of bepoppy style'. By then he had been composing songs for several years. One of his earliest collaborators was Joseph Allen McCarthy, whose father, also named Joseph, wrote the lyrics for shows such as *Irene*, *Kid Boots* and *Rio Rita*. One of their first efforts, 'The Riviera', was included several years later on Johnny Mathis's *Live It Up*, while 'I'm Gonna Laugh You Right Out Of My Life' was recorded by singer-pianist Buddy Greco. Another, 'Why Try To Change Me Now?', received a memorable reading from Frank Sinatra in 1952. In the following year Coleman contributed 'Tin Pan Alley' to the Broadway show *John Murray Anderson's Almanac* and, around the same time, he wrote several songs for a Tallulah Bankhead vehicle *Ziegfeld Follies*, which never made it to Broadway. From the late 50s until 1962, Coleman had a 'stormy' working relationship with lyricist Carolyn Leigh. Together they wrote several popular numbers such as 'Witchcraft' (Frank Sinatra), 'The Best Is Yet To Come' (Mabel Mercer), 'A Moment Of Madness' (Sammy Davis Jnr.), 'When In Rome (I Do As The Romans Do)' (Vikki Carr/Barbra Streisand), 'You Fascinate Me So' (Mark Murphy), 'Playboy's Theme', 'The Rules Of The Road', 'It Amazes Me', 'I Walk A Little Faster' and 'Firefly'. The latter was written in 1958 for Coleman and Leigh's musical based on the memoirs of stripper, Gypsy Rose Leigh. The project was later abandoned, but the song became a hit for Tony Bennett, who was instrumental in bringing their work before the public, and included two of their songs in his famous Carnegie Hall concert in 1962. Two years before that, the team wrote the music and lyrics for the Broadway musical, *Wildcat*. The score included the show-stopper 'What Takes My Fancy', plus 'That's What I Want For Janie', 'Give A Little Whistle',

'You've Come Home', 'El Sombrero', and the march, 'Hey, Look Me Over'. The latter became a hit for Peggy Lee. Coleman and Lee later wrote 'Then Is Then And Now Is Now', together.

In 1962, Coleman and Leigh were back on Broadway with *Little Me*. *The Libretto*, by Neil Simon, was based on a successful novel by Patrick Dennis, and traced the life of Belle Poitrine. Sid Caesar played all seven of her lovers, from the 16-year-old Noble Eggleston to the geriatric skinflint Mr Pinchley. The score included 'Love You', 'Deep Down Inside', 'The Other Side Of The Tracks', 'Real Live Girl' and the show-stopper 'I've Got Your Number'. Despite a favourable reception from the critics, *Little Me* did not fulfil its potential, and folded after only 257 performances. In 1964, it was acclaimed in London, where comedian and song and dance man, Bruce Forsyth, played the lead, and a revised version was presented in the West End in 1984, starring the UK television comic, Russ Abbott. After *Little Me*, Coleman and Leigh went their separate ways, collaborating briefly again in 1964 for 'Pass Me By', which was sung by the British writer-performer, Digby Wolfe, over the opening titles of the Cary Grant movie, *Father Goose*. In the same year, Coleman wrote the catchy 'Take a Little Walk' with Buddy Greco, before teaming with the lyricist and librettist, Dorothy Fields. Fields was 25 years older than Coleman, with an impressive track record of standard songs for films and shows, written with composers such as Jimmy McHugh, Jerome Kern and Arthur Schwartz, plus the book for Irving Berlin's smash hit musical, *Annie Get Your Gun*.

In 1966 the new combination had their own Broadway hit with the score for *Sweet Charity*, a musical version of Federico Fellini's film, *Nights Of Cabiria*. The accent was very much on dancing in this 'sentimental story of a New York dancehall hostess, and her desperate search for love'. The Coleman-Fields score included 'Baby, Dream Your Dream', 'Big Spender', 'If My Friends Could See Me Now', 'There's Gotta Be Something Better Than This', 'Where Am I Going?' and 'I'm A Brass Band'. The show ran for 608 performances on Broadway, and for 14 months in London, where it starred Juliet Prowse. The lead in the 1969 movie version was taken by Shirley Maclaine, and it also featured Sammy Davis Jnr. as a hippie evangelist singing 'The Rhythm Of Life', and Stubby Kaye leading the ensemble in 'I Love To Cry At Weddings'. Coleman was nominated for an Academy Award for his musical score. After failing to get several other projects mounted, such as a biography of Eleanor Roosevelt and a stage adaptation of the 1939 James Stewart movie, *Mr. Deeds Goes To Washington*, Coleman and Fields were back on Broadway in 1973 with *Seesaw*, based on William Gibson's 50s comedy, *Two For The Seesaw*. The score

included 'Welcome To Holiday Inn', 'Poor Everybody Else' and the blockbusters 'It's Not Where You Start (It's Where You Finish)' and 'Nobody Does It Like Me'. The latter became successful outside the show as a cabaret number for artists such as Shirley Bassey and comedienne, Marti Caine. After Dorothy Fields' death in 1974, it was another three years before Coleman returned to Broadway with *I Love My Wife*, with book and lyrics by Michael Stewart. Adapted from Luis Rego's farce 'about two suburban couples and their bumbling attempt to engage in wife swapping', the production ran for 857 performances. It featured a small on-stage orchestra whose members sang, dressed in fancy clothes, and commented on the show's action. Coleman received the Drama Desk Award for a score which included 'Hey There, Good Times', 'Something Wonderful I Missed', 'Sexually Free', 'Lovers On Christmas Eve', 'Everybody Today Is Turning On' and the title song. Less than a year after the opening of *I Love My Wife*, Coleman contributed to *On The Twentieth Century*, which was based on a 30s play by Ben Hecht and Charles MacArthur, with lyrics and libretto by Betty Comden and Adolph Green. The production included the songs 'I Ride Again', 'Together', 'Never', 'She's A Nut' and 'Our Private World'. The show ran for over a year, and earned six Tony Awards, including best score of a musical. Coleman's next project, with lyricist Barbara Fried, was *Home Again*, which 'followed an Illinois family from the Depression to the Watergate scandal'. It closed in Toronto, during April 1979, two weeks before it was set to open on Broadway.

In complete contrast, *Barnum* (1980), a musical treatment of the life of showman P.T. Barnum, was a smash hit. Coleman's music and Michael Stewart's lyrics were 'catchy and clever, and occasionally very beautiful'. British actor, Jim Dale, received rave notices for his endearing performance in the title role, which called for him to sing and be a clown, ride a unicycle, and walk a tightrope. The part of his wife was played by Glenn Close, on the brink of her 80s movie stardom. The score included 'There's A Sucker Born Ev'ry Minute', 'One Brick At A Time', 'The Colours Of My Life' and 'Come Follow The Band'. *Barnum* ran for 854 performances and captured three Tonys and two Grammies for the Broadway Cast album. Its subsequent run of almost two years at the London Palladium was a triumph for Michael Crawford. During the early 80s Coleman mounted Broadway revivals of *Little Me* and *Sweet Charity* which gained four Tonys, including best revival of a play or musical. In 1988, Coleman wrote the music and lyrics, in collaboration with A.E. Hotchner, for *Let 'Em Rot*. It failed to reach New York, and when Coleman did return to Broadway in April 1989 with *Welcome To The Club*, that show was censured by the

critics, and only ran for a few performances. It proved to be a temporary setback, for in December of that year, Coleman had one of the biggest hits of his career with *The City Of Angels* utilizing David Zippel's lyrics, and a book by Larry Gelbart which 'both satirized and celebrated the film *noir* genre and the hard boiled detective fiction of the 1940s'. The 'smart, swingy, sexy and funny play', in which Coleman 'uses a scat singing quartet reminiscent of the Modernaires as a roving chorus', is like 'listening to *Your Hit Parade* of 1946, except that the composer's own Broadway personality remakes the past in his own effervescent, melodic style'. The show garnered six Tonys, three Outer Critics Circle Awards and eight Drama Desk Awards, among them those for best musical, best music and lyrics. The production included the songs 'With Every Breath I Take', 'The Tennis Song', 'What You Don't Know About Women', 'You're Nothing Without Me' and 'Double Talk'. *City Of Angels* was still running at the Virginia Theatre two years later. Meanwhile, Coleman had turned his attention to *The Will Rogers Follies: A Life In Revue*, which related 'the life story of America's favourite humorist in the style of a *Ziegfeld Follies*' (1991). With Keith Carradine in the title role, Peter Stone's book called for 'a mutt act, a world champion roper, four kids, 12 sisters, a ranchful of cowboys, Gregory Peck (his voice only), and girls wearing spangles, and, of course, girls wearing not much of anything at all', which was put together by director-choreographer Tommy Tune. For the lyrics to his pastiche melodies, Coleman turned again to Comden and Green for 'Never Met A Man I Didn't Like', 'Let's Go Flying', 'Will-O-Mania', 'It's A Boy!', 'The Powder Puff Ballet', 'Give A Man Enough Rope' and 'Marry Me Now/I Got You'. Despite initial notices citing 'lapses of taste' and 'a paltry case for a cultural icon', the show was still running eight months after its May opening, and gained Tony Awards for best musical and original score. In parallel with his Broadway career, Coleman wrote several film scores although they generally failed to match the critical acclaim of his stage work. His music for *Family Business* was termed by one critic as 'one of the most appalling music scores in recent memory'. Coleman's other film work included *Father Goose* (1964), *The Troublemaker* (1964), *The Art Of Love* (1965), *The Heartbreak Kid* (1972), *Blame It On Rio* (1984), *Garbo Talks* (1984) and *Power* (1986). He also worked in television, where he conceived and co-produced Shirley Maclaine's special *If They Could See Me Now* (1974), and produced her *Gypsy In My Soul* (1976), both Emmy-winning presentations. Coleman also performed with many symphony orchestras, including those of Milwaukee, Detroit, San Antonio, Indianapolis, and Fort Worth. Coleman was a director of ASCAP, and a governor of the Academy of Television Arts And Sciences, and the Dramatists Guild. He was also a member of the Songwriter's Hall of Fame, the Academy of Motion Picture Arts and Sciences, and the New York State Advisory Committee on Music. His honours included the La Guardia Award for Outstanding Achievement in Music and the Irvin Feld Humanitarian award from the National Conference of Christians and Jews.
Albums: *If My Friends Could See Me Now* (1966), the Cy Coleman Trio *Barnum* (1981), *Coming Home* (1988).

Comden, Betty

b. 3 May 1915, New York City, New York, USA. After graduating with a degree in science, Comden strove to find work as an actress. During this period, the late 30s, she met Adolph Green who was also seeking work in the theatre. Unsuccessful in their attempts to find acting jobs, Comden and Green formed their own troupe, together with another struggling actress, Judy Holliday. In the absence of suitable material, Comden and Green began creating their own and discovered an ability to write librettos and lyrics. At first their success was only limited, but in the early 40s they were invited by a mutual friend, Leonard Bernstein, to work on the book and lyrics of a musical he planned to adapt from his ballet score, *Fancy Free*. The show, retitled *On The Town* (1944), was a huge success and Comden and Green never looked back. This show was followed by *Billion Dollar Baby* (1945, music by Morton Gould) and an assignment in Hollywood for the musical films *Good News* (1947), *The Barkleys Of Broadway* (1949), *On The Town* and *Take Me Out To The Ball Game* (both 1949). In the early 50s Comden and Green were back on Broadway, collaborating with Bernstein again, on *Wonderful Town* (1953), and with Jule Styne on several occasions, most notably with *Bells Are Ringing* (1956) in which the leading role was played by their former associate Judy Holliday. Throughout the 50s Comden and Green worked steadily on Broadway and in Hollywood. Among their films were *Singing In The Rain* (1952), for which they wrote the screenplay, incorporating the songs of Herb Nacio Brown and *The Band Wagon* (1953), again contributing the screenplay which was peppered with the songs of Arthur Schwartz and Howard Dietz. For *It's Always Fair Weather* (1955) they wrote screenplay and lyrics (music by André Previn) and later in the 50s and into the 60s wrote screenplays for *Auntie Mame* (1958) and *Bells Are Ringing* (1960), among others. In the late 50s they also performed their own two-person stage show. After writing the libretto for *Applause* (1970) they rested on their remarkable laurels but continued to make sporadic returns to the musical stage with *On The Twentieth Century* (1978) and *A Doll's Life* (1982), and occasional revivals of their personal-appearance show both on the stage and on television.

Company

The first of what are sometimes called Stephen Sondheim's 'concept musicals', on which he collaborated with producer and director Harold Prince, opened at the Alvin Theatre in New York on 26 April 1970. The book, by George Furth, was based on five of his own one-act plays. It concerned Robert (Dean Jones), a bachelor who is extremely reluctant to change that status despite the well-intentioned and loving efforts of five married friends, although by the end of the piece he has begun to realise that a commitment to one woman - for better or worse - is what his life should be all about. This was a brilliant and revolutionary musical, with Sondheim using his words and music to comment on on the action as well as being part of it. In their own way, the songs were all memorable and apposite, and included 'Company', 'The Little Things You Do Together', 'Sorry-Grateful', 'You Could Drive A Person Crazy', 'Have I Got A Girl For You?', 'Someone Is Waiting', 'Another Hundred People', 'Getting Married Today', "Side By Side By Side', 'What Would We Do Without You?', 'Poor Baby', 'Tick, Tock', 'Barcelona', 'The Ladies Who Lunch', and 'Being Alive'. Just a few weeks into the run, Dean was succeeded by Lary Kert; the role of Robert had originally been intended for Anthony Perkins. The remainder of the fine cast included Barbara Barrie, George Coe, John Cunningham, Teri Ralston, Charles Kimbrough, Donna McKechnie, Charles Braswell, Susan Browning, Steve Elmore, Beth Howland, Pamela Myers, Merle Louis, and the incomparable Elaine Stritch. *Company* ran on Broadway for 690 performances and won Tony Awards for best musical, music and lyrics, book, and director. Scenic designer Boris Aronson also won for his innovative multi-level skeletel sets and effects. Several of the principals, including Kert, Ralston and Stritch, reprised their roles for the London production which ran for 344 performances. A fascinating videotape which was made of the original cast recording sessions revealed the agonies and the ecstasies involved in such a project, particularly Stritch's valiant attempts to lay down on tape the difficult 'The Ladies Who Lunch' in the early hours of the morning, when she probably would have just preferred to lay down. In 1992 the video was released by RCA under the title of *Original Cast Album: Company*, and, a year later, that same original cast (with the exception of Charles Braswell) assembled at the Vivian Beaumont Theatre in New York for two highly acclaimed concert versions of the show.

Connecticut Yankee, A

Richard Rodgers and Lorenz Hart's biggest Broadway hit of the 20s was adapted by Herbert Fields from Mark Twain's original story of *A Connecticut Yankee In King Arthur's Court*, and opened at the Vanderbilt Theatre on 3 November 1927. The scene is Hartford, Connecticut, and Martin (William Gaxford) has been given a suit of armour as a wedding present. It is a pity that he is not wearing it when his fiancé, Fay Morgan (Nana Bryant), crowns him with a champagne bottle for flirting with the attractive Alice Carter (Constance Carpenter) at his bachelor party. Out like a light, Martin dreams that he is back in the days of Camelot, and he and his friends are all members of the Round Table. Initially treated with suspicion, he ingratiates himself with King Arthur by introducing his own Industrial Revolution and supplying the Court with telephones, radios, and other modern devices. When he comes round he realises that he is about to marry the wrong girl, and decides to devote himself to Alice, the girl he really loves. Rodgers and Hart's score contained two of their big all-time hits, 'My Heart Stood Still' and 'Thou Swell', along with the amusing 'On A Desert Island With Thee' and 'I Feel At Home With You'. The show ran for 418 performances and found the songwriters at the height of their powers. Sadly, that was not the case when *A Connecticut Yankee* was revived on Broadway in 1943. With an updated book, in which just about everybody is dressed in naval uniform, and some new songs, the show ran for 135 performances but, five days after the opening, Hart died of pneumonia. One of the extra numbers, a 'list' song entitled 'To Keep My Love Alive', was sung by Vivienne Segal who gloried in one of Hart's most ingenious lyrics about a much-married lady who reveals her personal system of 'divorce': 'Sir Athelston indulged in fratricide/He killed his dad, and that was patricide/One night I stabbed him by my mattress-side/To keep my love alive.' There was nothing wrong with the score, so it was probably the 'nonsensical, lamentably incoherent' book which prevented the show being constantly revived. That was certainly the point made by UK critics when *A Connecticut Yankee* was presented at Regent's Park Open Air Theatre in 1993, 64 years after it flopped in London under the title of *A Yankee At The Court Of King Arthur*. The 1949 screen version, starring Bing Crosby and William Bendix, reverted to Mark Twain's original title, *A Connecticut Yankee At King Arthur's Court*.

Conversation Piece

Noël Coward wrote this 'romantic comedy with music' as a vehicle for the celebrated French actress, Yvonne Printemps. It opened at His Majesty's Theatre in London on 16 February 1934, and was, in fact, a costume operetta set in the upper crust Regency seaside town of Brighton, England, in 1811.

The impoverished nobleman, Paul, Duc de Chaucigny-Varennes (Noël Coward) and his ward, Melanie (Yvonne Printemps), have arrived in Brighton with the intention of finding a rich husband for the young lady. The first of several candidates is the Marquis of Sheere (Louis Hayward), and his father, the Duke of Beneden (Athol Stewart), is also a contender. For a while Paul seems to have captured the affections of the well-heeled Lady Julia Charteris, (Irene Browne) but, just before the curtain falls at the end of the final act, Paul and Melanie realise they are really meant for each other. Coward's score contained one of his best-loved songs, the lovely waltz, 'I'll Follow My Secret Heart', which he wrote for Yvonne Printemps, and she also sang the touching 'Nevermore'. The rest of the numbers included 'There's Always Something Fishy About The French', 'Regency Rakes', 'Dear Little Soldiers', 'The English Lesson', 'Brighton Parade', and 'Danser, Danser'. George Sanders, who was destined to play so many smooth and shady characters in a long career in films which began in 1936, was one of the 'Regency Rakes'. *Conversation Piece* had a disappointing run of only 177 performances. More had been expected of Coward, especially after the success of *Bitter Sweet* (1929) which was similar in style to this current show. Pierre Fresnay, who had helped Yvonne Printemps to learn enough English to tackle her role (much of the show's dialogue was in French), and who had substituted occasionally for Coward during the London run, played the lead when *Conversation Piece* played on Broadway for 55 performances. The original London cast recordings were issued on *Noël Coward: The Great Shows*, and when Coward made a new recording of the show in New York 17 years later, the part of the Marquis of Sheere was played by a young British actor who was just beginning to make an impact in films, Richard Burton.

Cook, Barbara

b. 25 October 1927, Atlanta, Georgia, USA. This singer's performance was neatly described by one critic as 'a style which marries a beautiful and undiminished soprano voice to nuance-rich phrasing and a skilled actress's emotional interpretation'. Cook's first professional engagement was at New York's Blue Angel club in 1950, where she sang mainly standards by the likes of George Gershwin, Jerome Kern and Rodgers And Hart. A year later she was starring on Broadway, as Sandy in the off-beat short-lived musical, *Flahooley*. In 1953, she played Ado Annie in a City Centre revival of *Oklahoma!*, followed by a national tour. The following year her performance as Carrie Pipperidge in another Richard Rodgers/Oscar Hammerstein II revival, *Carousel*, gained her the role of Hilda Miller in *Plain And Fancy* which ran for over 400 performances. In 1956, she

introduced Leonard Bernstein and Richard Wilbur's 'Glitter And Be Gay' in *Candide*, 'the season's most interesting failure' and, soon afterwards, played the lead in yet another New York revival of *Carousel*, with Howard Keel. The highlight of her early career came in 1957 when she appeared with Robert Preston in Meredith Willson's *The Music Man*, which ran for over 1,300 performances. In the role of Marion Paroo, the stern librarian, Cook excelled on numbers such as 'Till There Was You', 'Goodnight My Someone' and 'Will I Ever Tell You'. After gaining good reviews as a youthful Anna in *The King And I* at the City Centre, *The Gay Life* (1961) gave Cook her most dramatic role to date, with a superior Schwartz and Dietz score containing 'Something You Never Had Before', 'Is She Waiting There For You?' and 'Magic Moment'. Two years later, Cook appeared in *She Loves Me*. Bock and Harnick's score gave her the delightful 'Will He Like Me?', 'Dear Friend' and 'Ice Cream' among a double-album set. This was Cook's final major Broadway musical, although she did appear in the less successful *Something More!* (1964), and *The Grass Harp* (1971). She had been Broadway's favourite ingenue for 10 years and, for a while, continued to tour in well-received revivals such as *Showboat* (1966). She also appeared in several straight plays including *Any Wednesday* and *Little Murders*. In 1973 Cook starred in *The Gershwin Years*, celebrating the music of George Gershwin, and started playing clubs again, including the Brothers & Sisters in New York. In 1975, she made her concert debut *Barbara Cook At Carnegie Hall* and received a rapturous reception. The show was repeated in large cities throughout the USA. In 1976, she made her first visit to the UK, at the small Country Cousin club in London, where she had to compete with interference on the PA system from an adjoining taxi cab company. She was back at Carnegie Hall again in 1980 (*It's Better With A Band*), with a programme which included some more contemporary material, along with the show tunes, and an item co-written by her musical director, Wally Harper, called 'The Ingenue' ('The parts for boys you play against, they bring out all the clones to do/And movie roles you live to play, they give to Shirley Jones to do!'). In 1985 Cook's career received an enormous boost when she appeared in two performances of *Follies In Concert With The New York Philharmonic*, along with other Broadway luminaries such as Lee Remick, George Hearn, Elaine Stritch, and Carol Burnett. She scored a personal triumph, with Stephen Sondheim numbers 'Losing My Mind', 'The Girl Upstairs', 'Who's that Woman?' and 'Buddy's Eyes'. In September 1976 with her one-woman show, *Wait 'Til You See Her*, reached London's West End and was acclaimed by the critics and the public. In the following year, she was back on Broadway in *A*

Concert For The Theatre, and continued to play other US venues such as the Ballroom, New York. A hiccup occurred in the UK in 1988 when she withdrew from the Royal Shakespeare Company's touring production of the Broadway-bound musical, *Carrie*, but she continued to delight London audiences into the 90s. Besides her performances on original cast albums, she has also appeared on several Ben Bagley albums and a 1987 recording of *Carousel*, produced by Thomas Z. Shepherd. On the latter she was joined by Sarah Brightman and opera singers, Maureen Forrester, David Rendall and Samuel Ramey, all accompanied by the Royal Philharmonic Orchestra. Albums: *Barbara Cook At Carnegie Hall* (1976), *It's Better With A Band* (1986), *Barbara Cook Sings The Walt Disney Song Book* (1988), *As Of Today* (1989), *Close As Pages In A Book* (1993).

Cotton Club, The

This is one of several compilation shows which infiltrated London's West End in the early 90s. They generally took the form of tributes to famous composers such as Cole Porter (*A Swell Party*), Vivian Ellis (*Spread A Little Happiness*), and Duke Ellington (*Sophisticated Ladies*), although the catchment area could be extended to include composer/performers like Louis Jordan (*Five Guys Named Mo*), Buddy Holly (*Buddy*), a television producer, Jack Good (*Good Rockin' Tonite*), and a couple of Chicago gangsters from the world of television and films, *A Tribute To The Blues Brothers*. This particular production saluted an edifice, or rather what went on in that edifice. The Cotton Club, which opened at 644 Lenox Avenue in the Harlem district of New York in the early 20s, was operated by the Mafia. Throughout the 20s and 30s legendary performers such as Duke Ellington, Lena Horne, Cab Calloway, Jimmy Lunceford, Ethel Waters, Bill 'Bojangles' Robinson, the Nicholas Brothers, and many more, played, sang, and danced there - to strictly white audiences. This latest celebration of the area and the times (*Bubbling Brown Sugar* covered much the same ground in 1976) opened at London's Aldwych Theatre on 24 January 1992. In an attempt to link the numbers, it has a nominal book by Douglas Barron which involves four fictitious characters: Millie Gibson, whose career as a singing star is terminated by her drug addiction, and her niece, Dinah Andrews who takes over her spot a moment's notice and becomes a star; Jim Carlton, a fellow entertainer whose ambition is to get Millie to Paris; and the bandleader, Andy Chambers, who sings 'Minnie The Moocher' and so must represent Cab Calloway. Good singing performances were forthcoming from Debbie Bishop, Joanne Campbell, and Marilyn J. Johnson, and there was some outstanding tap dancing from Marcel Peneux. The choice of songs was sometimes suspect - 'That Old Black Magic' (1942) and 'I Got It Bad And That Ain't Good' (1941) were surely written too late for this shindig - but there is still a lot of mileage left in them and the other 20-odd numbers joyfully conjured up in this, the 'Feel Good Musical', which ran until June 1992.

Countess Maritza

Originally titled Gräfin Mariza (no 't') when it was first presented in Vienna 1924, this operetta, with lyrics and book by Harry B. Smith, is generally regarded as composer Emmerich Kálmán's masterpiece. Several of his previous works such as *The Gypsy Violinist* (1914), *The Csardas Princess* (1917), and *The Bajadere* (1922), had been produced in New York before *Countess Maritza* opened at the Shubert Theatre on 18 September 1926. The action takes place near the Hungarian border, on one of the many estates belonging to Countess Maritza (Yvonne d'Arle). The Countess, who is forever on her guard against fortune-hunters, falls in love with her land superintendent, unaware that he is the aristocratic Count Tassilo (Walter Woolf). Misunderstandings continue to prevail, but they are resolved when, about to leave, he reads the reference his employer has prepared for him - which turns out to be a proposal of marriage. Kálmán composed one of his loveliest melodies for Woolf to sing in 'Play Gypsies - Dance Gypsies', and the song was successful outside the show for the Polish born pianist-bandleader, Fred Rich And His Orchestra. The rest of Smith and Kálmán's sumptuous score included 'I'll Keep On Dreaming', 'The Call Of Love', and 'The One I'm Looking For'. The show had an impressive run of 321 performances. When it was presented in London in 1938 at the Palace Theatre, the title was changed to *Maritza*, but the 1983 West End production reverted to the original Broadway name. There have been three film versions, in 1925, 1932, and 1958.

Country Girl, A

A tremendously successful musical play, with a book by James T. Tanner, and a score by Lionel Monkton (music) and Adrian Ross (lyrics), with additional songs by Paul Rubens. *A Country Girl* opened at Daly's Theatre in London on 18 January 1902. The story concerns the trials and tribulations of Geoffrey Challoner (Hayden Coffin), who leaves England, and the ladies in his life, his true love Marjorie Joy (Lilian Eldée), and the village flirt Nan (Evie Greene), while he seeks his fortune overseas. On his return he brings with him The Rajah of Bhong (Rutland Barrington), and Princess Mehelaneh, who soon makes herself at home, and also makes Geoffrey a royal offer she feels that he can hardly refuse. However - good man - he turns her down, and decides to wed Marjorie, his 'little country girl'. Also in the cast were Huntley

Wright, Quinton Raikes, and Ethel Irving. The delightful score contained popular favourites such as the jaunty 'Yo-Ho, Little Girls, Yo-Ho', 'Molly The Marchioness', 'The Pink Hungarian Band', 'Not The Little Girl She Knew', 'Try Again, Johnny', 'Me And Mrs Brown', and 'Under The Deodar'. During the remarkable run of 729 performances, the score underwent drastic revisions, and even more so for the 1914 and 1931 revivals. *A Country Girl* was produced in New York in 1902 and 1911, and also played the L'Olympia in Paris in 1904.

Courtneidge, Cicely

b. Esmeralda Cicely Courtneidge, 1 April 1893, Sydney, Australia. Her father, actor/producer/writer Robert Courtneidge was appearing in the operetta *Esmeralda* when she was born, hence the name. Back in Britain she trained for the stage and at the age of 10 appeared as Fairy Peaseblossom in *Midsummer Night's Dream*, followed by her father's production of *The Arcadians* in 1909. She made her first records in 1911, singing selections from the show in which she was appearing, *(The) Mousme*. Courtneidge married musical comedy star Jack Hulbert in 1914, and while he was engaged in World War I she toured the music halls as a male impersonator and somewhat *risqué* comedienne. After appearing in several shows together Courtneidge and Hulbert made their first big impact as a team in the 1925 revue *By The Way*, with music by Vivian Ellis. It ran for over 300 performances before transferring to New York. *Lido Lady*, in 1926, with a Richard Rodgers/Lorenz Hart score, and *Clowns In Clover*, which opened in 1927 and ran for two years, confirmed their enormous popularity in London's West End. By now, Hulbert was also writing and producing. The team split up temporarily, and while he was appearing with Sophie Tucker in the musical play *Follow A Star*, Courtneidge was considered to be at her best in the Vivian Ellis revue *Folly To Be Wise*. For most of the 30s Courtneidge concentrated on making films such as *Ghost Train, Jack's The Boy, Aunt Sally, Soldiers Of The King, Me And Marlborough* and *Take My Tip*. She returned to the stage in 1937 in *Hide And Seek* and in the following year the Hulberts reunited for one of their biggest successes, *Under Your Hat*, yet again with music and lyrics by Vivian Ellis. It ran for over two years and was filmed in 1940. During World War II the team had substantial runs in *Full Swing* and their last show on the London stage together, *Something In The Air*, as well as undertaking extensive ENSA tours. After the war Courtneidge starred in *Your Excellency*, and *Under The Counter* in London and New York where it attracted extremely hostile reviews. In 1951 she undertook probably the best role of her career, playing Gay Davenport in the satirical backstage musical play, *Gay's The Word* by Ivor Novello and

Alan Melville. It gave her several good songs including 'Guards Are On Parade', 'It's Bound To Be Right On The Night', and 'Vitality', a number that epitomized her stage persona throughout her long career. The show ran at the Saville Theatre for 504 performances, and was Novello's last - he died three weeks after the opening. Courtneidge's final West End show was *High Spirits*, in 1963, a musical version of Noël Coward's 1941 play *Blithe Spirit*. Its songs did not suit her as well as others she had introduced over the years such as 'The King's Horses', 'Home', 'There's Something About A Soldier', 'We'll All Go Riding On A Rainbow' and 'I Was Anything But Sentimental'. During the 60s and 70s she toured in plays and revues including, with Hulbert, the semi-autobiographical *Once More With Music*. She also made several more films including a critically-acclaimed character part in Bryan Forbes's *The L-Shaped Room* (1963), and cameos in *Those Magnificent Men In Their Flying Machines* (1965), *The Wrong Box* (1966) and *Not Now Darling* (1972). The latter was released when she was aged 80. In the same year she was created a Dame of the British Empire. Cicely Courtneidge died on 26 April 1980, two years after Hulbert. In 1986, Courtneidge's history reached a new generation when her 'Take Me Back To Dear Old Blighty' was used as the opening for the Smiths' album *The Queen Is Dead*.

Further reading: *Cicely*, Cicely Courtneidge.

Coward, Noël

b. 16 December 1899, Teddington, Middlesex, England, d. 26 March 1973, Jamaica. Coward began his professional career as a child actor, appearing frequently on the stage. As a teenager he made his first film appearance in D. W. Griffiths's *Hearts Of The World* (1918), which was made in England and starred the Gish sisters, Dorothy and Lillian. By 1919 Coward was already writing plays and soon afterwards began his songwriting career. The revue, *London Calling!* (1923), included 'Parisian Pierrot', performed by Gertrude Lawrence, which became one of his most popular songs. In the same show Coward and Lawrence danced to 'You Were Meant For Me', for which special choreography was created by Fred Astaire. Although none was yet produced, Coward's stock of completed plays already included important works such as *The Vortex, Fallen Angels, Hay Fever* and *Easy Virtue*. When *The Vortex* opened in London in 1924, its frank approach to drug addiction created a sensation, which was repeated the following year when it opened on Broadway. Coward's songwriting progressed with 'Poor Little Rich Girl', composed for the revue, *On With The Dance*. In 1928 he had two productions playing in London's West End: *This Year Of Grace*, a sparkling revue for which he wrote script, music and lyrics, and *The Second Man*, in which he

Noël Coward

also starred. In the late 20s and early 30s Coward's output was remarkable in its quantity and high quality. His stage productions in this period included *Bitter Sweet*, from which came the song 'I'll See You Again', *Private Lives*, *Cavalcade*, which included 'Twentieth-Century Blues', *Words And Music*, with its hit song, 'Mad About The Boy', *Design For Living*, *Conversation Piece*, *Fumed Oak*, *Hands Across The Sea* and *Tonight At Eight-Thirty*. Apart from their intrinsic qualities, Coward's plays were significant in altering perceptions of how stage dialogue should be written and spoken in the English theatre with his more conversational approach replacing the previous declamatory style. The success of his stage work ensured that some of his material was brought to the screen. Amongst the films were *Cavalcade* (1933) and *Bitter Sweet* (1940). Towards the end of the 30s he wrote *Present Laughter* and *This Happy Breed*. During the early months of World War II, he wrote the play, *Blithe Spirit*, several songs including 'London Pride', and the screenplay and score for *In Which We Serve* (1942), which he also co-directed (with David Lean), in addition to taking the leading role. For his work on this film he received a special Academy Award. Coward's film commitments continued with screenplays for some of his earlier stage pieces including *Blithe Sprit*, *Brief Encounter* (both 1945), *The Astonished Heart* (1950) and *Tonight At Eight-Thirty* (1952). By the 50s, Coward's style of writing for the stage was seen as outmoded, but he regained a measure of his earlier West End success with *Relative Values* (1951) and with personal appearances at the Café De Paris, at which he sang his own songs to delighted audiences. In the 30s Coward had written his autobiography, *Present Indicative*, and had also written short stories and novels. In the 50s and early 60s he produced another autobiography, *Future Indefinite*, more novels and short stories and a volume of verse. Coward's spell at the Café De Paris had brought him to the attention of the American impresario Joe Glaser (who managed, among others, Louis Armstrong). Glaser was so impressed that he offered Coward an engagement at the Desert Inn, Las Vegas. To the surprise of many, Coward's Desert Inn performances were hugely successful, as was an album recorded live during his run, *Noël Coward At Las Vegas* (1955). Coward's triumph at Las Vegas led to a series of three television spectaculars for CBS. More stage productions followed in the 60s, among them *Nude With Violin* and *A Song At Twilight*. In his last years Coward appeared in numerous films, usually in cameo roles, often sending up his own image of the plummy-voiced, terribly nice, very English gentleman. One of the most gifted writers and entertainers the English theatre has produced, Coward was knighted in 1970 and in the same year was awarded a special Tony Award for distinguished achievement in the theatre. He was honoured with gala performances of his work in London and New York, the last of these being *Oh! Coward* early in 1973. Soon after this, Coward returned to his home in Jamaica, where he died in March 1973.

Albums: *Noël Coward At Las Vegas* (1955), *Noël Coward In New York* (1957), *The Masters' Voice: His HMV Recordings (1928-53)* (1993, 4-CD set).

Further reading: *Autobiography*, Noël Coward. *A Talent To Amuse*, Sheridan Morley. *The Life Of Noël Coward*, Cole Lesley. *The Lyrics Of Noël Coward*, Mandarin Books.

Cradle Will Rock, The

Sub-titled 'A Play In Music', this was one of the most unusual and controversial stage presentations in the pre-World War II era. The book, music, and lyrics were by Marc Blitzstein, who was a piano soloist with the Philadelphia Symphony Orchestra in his teens, and subsequently had been heavily influenced by Kurt Weill and Bertholt Brecht. *The Cradle Will Rock*, which dealt with a trades union's desperate attempt for recognition in a US steel town, was originally conceived for the Federal Theatre Project of the Works Progress Administration, with producer John Housman and director Orson Welles (three years before Citizen Kane). After failing to get on in Washington, the project was moved to New York, and scheduled for the Maxine Elliot Theatre on 16 June 1937. Under severe political pressure from a number of government departments, the Federal Theatre pulled out, and Welles and Housman diverted 800 people to the empty Venice (Jolsen) Theatre. Union rules prevented the actors performing on stage, so they gave their performances while seated in the auditorium, and the same rules meant Blitzstein had to provide a piano accompaniment in place of an orchestra. Still beset by all manner of problems, the show ran for 14 performances at the Venice, and gave a few weekend shows at the small Mercury Theatre, before its commercial opening on 3 January 1938 at the Windsor Theatre, where it stayed for 108 performances. The extreme left-wing story set in Steeltown, USA, in the which the young, idealistic union organizer, Larry Foreman (Howard de Silva) forces his unscrupulous boss, Mr. Mister (Will Geer), to recognize the union, also presented Blitzstein's positive attitude towards prostitution, and was punctuated with such numbers as 'The Freedom Of The Press', 'Joe Worker', 'Art For Art's Sake', 'Honolulu', 'Nickel Under Foot', 'The Cradle Will Rock', 'Drugstore Freedom', 'Croon-Spoon', and 'Doctor And Ella'. In revivals of the show, several well-known actors have played Foreman, including Alfred Drake (1947), Jerry Orbach (1964), and Randle Mell (1983).

Michael Crawford

Crawford, Michael

b. Michael Patrick Dumble-Smith, 19 January 1942, Salisbury, Wiltshire, England. An actor and singer who came to world-wide fame when he played the leading role in Andrew Lloyd Webber's hit musical, *The Phantom Of The Opera*, in 1986. His father was a fighter pilot during World War II and died six months before his son was born. Crawford sang in the school choir and later toured in the original productions of Benjamin Britten's *Let's Make An Opera* and *Noyes Fluddle*. While still a teenager he changed his name to Crawford (after seeing it on a biscuit box), and worked extensively in radio, and in films and television programmes for children. In the 60s he appeared in the late-night satirical BBC television series *Not So Much A Programme, More A Way Of Life*, and created the character of Byron, a 'rocker' who was thought to be typical of the swinging 60s. He also made a number of films including *The War Lover*, starring Steve McQueen, *Two Left Feet*, Richard Lester's *The Knack*, *A Funny Thing Happened On The Way To The Forum*, and *How I Won The War*, His London stage debut came in Neil Simon's *Come Blow Your Horn* (1962), which was followed by the off-beat comedy-drama *The Anniversary*. In 1967 he moved to New York and appeared in a pair of short plays written by Peter Shaffer entitled *White Lies* and *Black Comedy*. While in the latter piece, he was spotted by film director Gene Kelly who cast him as Cornelius Hackl in the screen version of *Hello, Dolly!* starring Barbra Streisand. It gained him an international following, but subsequent films such as *The Games*, *Hello, Goodbye*, and *Alice's Adventures In Wonderland*, were not so satisfying. In 1971 Crawford returned to the London stage in the long-running farce *No Sex, Please - We're British*, and, soon afterwards, was voted Funniest Man On Television for his performance as the accident-prone Frank Spencer in the situation comedy, *Some Mothers Do 'Ave 'Em*. In 1974 he starred in *Billy*, his first stage musical, and was voted Show Business Personality of the Year and received the Silver Heart Award from the Variety Club of Great Britain. In 1976 he appeared in the American two-hander comedy *Same Time, Next Year*, and, two years later, portrayed a mentally handicapped man who volunteers to be a guinea-pig for a medical experiment in *Flowers For Algernon*. After a further television series, *Chalk And Cheese*, Crawford was back on the London stage for the musical *Barnum*, in which he played the celebrated American showman P.T. Barnum, a role he prepared for by attending the New York Circus School for two months in order to acquire the necessary specialist skills. The show was a smash-hit and Crawford won an Olivier Award for his outstanding, charismatic performance. He stayed with *Barnum* in various places for several years, and, when

he returned with it to London at the Victoria Palace in 1985, it was estimated that more than 2.5 million people had seen the production. Around this time, Andrew Lloyd Webber heard him at singing practice and cast him in the leading role - opposite Sarah Brightman - in *The Phantom Of The Opera*. Following the show's opening night in October 1986 one critic was moved to write of him: 'It is surely one of the great performances, not only in a musical but on any stage in any year.' Two years later Broadway audiences felt the same, and he won the Tony Award for best actor in a musical. The show gave Crawford's singing career a tremendous boost (he had already made the UK Top 10 with one of the *Phantom*'s hit songs, 'The Music Of The Night'), and he embarked on extensive tours of several countries, including America, Australia, and the UK, with a concert production entitled *The Music Of Andrew Lloyd Webber*, supported by a 37-piece orchestra, soloists, and a back-up chorus. Recognition at home, where he is still unable to shake off the 'Frank Spencer' image, came in 1987 when he was awarded the OBE. In America he is billed as 'the matinee idol of the decade', and must have realised that he had hit the big-time when invited to duet with Barbra Streisand on 'The Music Of The Night' for her 1993 *Back To Broadway* album. The track was also included on his own release that year, *A Touch Of Music In The Night*, which turned out to be an intriguing mixture of standards ('Stormy Weather'), pop songs ('The Power Of Love'), and show tunes.
Selected albums: *Songs From The Stage And Screen* (1987), *With Love* (1989), *Performs Andrew Lloyd Webber* (1992), *A Touch Of Music In The Night* (1993), and Original Cast and soundtrack recordings.

Crazy For You

After losing a reported half a million dollars in Washington during its tryout in December 1991, *Crazy For You* exploded into the Shubert Theatre on 19 February 1992, sending shock waves along Broadway, the like of which had not been experienced for some considerable time. It was the kind of musical that America does best, and the perfect reposte to the imported British variety that had held sway on the 'great white way' for so long. The term, 'Loosely based on the 1930 musical *Girl Crazy*', meant that it contained a bunch of great songs by George and Ira Gershwin. A total of four numbers were retained from that production: 'I Got Rhythm', 'Could You Use Me?', 'Bidin' My Time', and the lovely 'But Not For Me'; and another 13 were culled from various other Gershwin shows. The story was changed, too: in Ken Ludwig's new book, which was adapted from the original by Guy Bolton and John McGowan, aspiring performer Bobby Child (Harry Groener), is sent by his wealthy mother (Jane

Connell) to foreclose on the old Gaiety theatre in Deadrock, Nevada. He falls for the theatre-owner's daughter, Polly (Jodi Benson), and, in an effort to impress her - and keep the Gaiety open - he imports most of the chorus girls from the fabulous *Zangler Follies*, and they put on a show - right there in the old barn . . . I mean, theatre. The lavish production, which was staged by Mike Ockrent, won the Tony Award for best musical, and other Tonys went to Broadway newcomer Susan Stroman for her superb choreography, and William Ivey Long for his 'sensational' costumes. While the Broadway production was settling in for a long run, a West End version, starring Ruthie Henshall and Kirby Ward, opened at the 1,600-seater Prince Edward Theatre on 3 March 1993. It gained Olivier Awards for Stroman and best musical, and was soon being cited as 'one of the biggest - if not *the* biggest - American musical in London history'.

Criswell, Kim

b. Hampton, Virginia, USA. An actress and singer who came to prominence in stage musicals during the 80s, with a style and voice reminiscent of the much-missed Ethel Merman. Criswell grew up in Chattanooga, Tennessee, where, so she says, the 'live' theare used to arrive in a bus and stay for just two nights. Her early influences were Julie Andrews, Barbra Streisand, and Judy Garland, and, like them, she started performing from an early age. After graduating from high school, she studied musical theatre at the University of Cincinnatti's College Conservatory of Music before moving to New York where she gained a featured part in a revival of *Annie Get Your Gun*. She made her Broadway musical debut in *The First* (1981), and then appeared in *Nine*, which was staged by Tommy Tune and had a cast of 21 women and only one male adult. Her other Broadway credits during the 80s included revivals of the *Three Musketeers* and *The Threepenny Opera* (re-titled as *3 Penny Opera*). In the latter show Criswell played Lucy, one of the leading roles in a production that was headed by the popular rock singer Sting. She has appeared as the featured soloist with several of America's leading symphony orchestras, and took part in concert stagings of Jerome Kern's *Sitting Pretty* at Carnegie Hall, and George and Ira Gershwin's *Girl Crazy* at the Lincoln Centre. She won the Helen Hayes award for her performance in *Side By Side By Sondheim*, and played the role of Grizabella (the feline who sings 'Memory') for six months in the Los Angeles production of Andrew Lloyd Webber's *Cats*. Between 1989 and 1991 Criswell starred in three London studio recordings of famous Broadway shows, *Anything Goes*, *Kiss Me Kate*, and *Annie Get Your Gun*, accompanied by a large orchestra directed by John McGlinn. He also conducted the London Sinfonietta

when Criswell joined Brent Barrett in *Cole Porter And The American Musical* at the Royal Festival Hall. In September 1991 she presented her one-woman show, *Doin' What Comes Naturally*, at the Shaw Theatre in London, and, just over a year later, co-starred with John Diedrich in a West End revival of *Annie Get Your Gun*. The show was acclaimed by the critics ('Criswell is the best Annie we have seen since Dolores Gray') but it folded after less than two months. In 1993 she he appeared in two very different kind of shows in the UK. The first, *Elegies For Angels, Punks And Raging Queens*, was a musical play that purported to tell the real-life stories of 33 individuals who have met their death through AIDS; while the other, a touring nostalgia show, *Hollywood And Broadway II*, with Bonnie Langford and Wayne Sleep, found her on more familiar ground. Her 1993 record releases were dissimilar, too: *The Lorelei* contained a mixture of well-known and neglected show tunes, while *Human Cry* turned out to be a pop album in a contemporary, and sometimes funky style. Selected albums: *Songs Of New York* (c.80s), *Fifty Million Frenchmen* (c.80s), *Anything Goes* (1989, Studio Cast), *Kiss Me, Kate* (1990, Studio Cast), *Annie Get Your Gun* (1991, Studio Cast), *The Lorelei* (1993), *Human Cry* (1993), and Original Cast recordings.

Crumit, Frank

b. 26 September 1889, Jackson, Ohio, USA, d. 7 September 1943, Longmeadow, Massachusetts, USA. Crumit's early career took a somewhat unusual route from the Culver Military Academy, Indiana, via the University of Ohio, into vaudeville as the One Man Glee Club. First recording in 1919 for the Columbia label , he later signed for Victor Records in 1924 and shortly after for Decca. Crumit played the ukulele, sang in a soft, warm voice, and was especially noted for his performance of novelty numbers, such as 'A Gay Caballero', 'Abdul Abulbul Amir' (and the follow-ups, 'The Return Of...' and 'The Grandson Of . . .'), 'The Prune Song', 'There's No One With Endurance Like The Man Who Sells Insurance', 'Connie's Got Connections In Connecticut', 'Nettie Is The Nit-Wit Of The Networks' and 'What Kind Of A Noise Annoys An Oyster?'. He is supposed to have written thousands of songs and adapted many others such as 'Frankie And Johnny' and 'Little Brown Jug' to suit his individual style. Crumit enjoyed great popularity throughout the 20s and 30s, appearing in several Broadway shows, including *Greenwich Village Follies*. He also appeared in *Tangerine* with his future wife, Julia Sanderson. They married in 1927 and retired from show business for two years. Following their comeback in 1929, they were extremely successful together on radio in the 30s as the Singing Sweethearts, and in 1939 began *The Battle Of The Sexes* game show which continued until

Crumit's death in 1943.

Albums: *Mountain Greenery* (1981), *Everybody's Best Friend* (1988), *Around The Corner* (1990)

D

Dale, Jim

b. Jim Smith, 15 August 1935, Kettering, Northamptonshire, England. Dale, a failed impressionist, who wanted to be an all-round entertainer, had a two-year gig with Carrol Levis' touring show as part of a comedy tumbling act. He then became a solo comedian and only turned to singing when he found people preferred his finale song to his tame comedy. He joined the BBC television series, *6.5 Special* in April 1957 and shortly after signed to Parlophone Records, where he was produced by George Martin. His only Top 20 hit came with his second single, a cover of Johnny Madara's 'Be My Girl', which reached number 2 in late 1957. He had three more UK Top 40 entries, the last being a version of the McGuire Sisters' US hit 'Sugartime' in 1958. In the 60s Dale pursued his acting career, and appeared in a string of successful *Carry On* films, and others, such as *Lock Up Your Daughters*. He made his West End debut in a musical, *The Wayward Way*, and appeared at the Edinburgh Festival in a pop version of *The Winter's Tale*. He also co-wrote the Seekers' smash hit, 'Georgy Girl', for which he was nominated for an Academy Award, and contributed to the music for movies such as *Shalako* and *Lola*. In the late 60s and early 70s, as member of the National Theatre Company, he appeared in several productions at the Old Vic and the Young Vic. He also made more films, including *Adolph Hitler - My Part In His Downfall* and *Digby, The Biggest Dog In The World*. In 1973, Dale played for six months at the Queen's Theatre, London in the musical, *The Card,* and around the same time, hosted the popular television show, *Sunday Night At The London Palladium*. In 1974 he went to the US with the National Theatre Company and created a stir with his performance as an 'ingratiating scamp' in the Moliére farce, *Scapino,* which brought him Drama Desk and Outer Critics Circle Awards, and a Tony nomination. During the late 70s, by now domiciled in the US, he appeared in stage productions of *Comedians* and *Privates On Parade*, as well as making several other

movies, three of them for the Disney Studio. In 1980 Dale found the ideal property for his talents in *Barnum,* a musical about the life of the US showman, which involved juggling, trampoline, and tightrope walking, among other skills. He won a Tony Award for his performance and stayed with the show for over a year, following ecstatic opening reviews. In the 80s he made more films, and appeared on the New York stage in productions as diverse as Peter Nichol's *Joe Egg* (1985), *Me And My Girl* (1987), and a revival of *Privates On Parade* (1989). In 1992 he returned to the UK, and his 60s roots, to play the title role in the film *Carry On Columbus*.

Selected album: *Jim!* (1958).

Dames At Sea

New York salutes Hollywood in this affectionate spoof of the Busby Berkeley-Harry Warren and Al Dubin-Dick Powell and Ruby Keeler-style film musicals of the 30s, which opened Off Broadway at the Bouwerie Theatre on 20 December 1968. This time, though, the setting is not 'by a waterfall', but the deck of a battleship where Ruby, the talented tap-dancer from the sticks (Bernadette Peters), climbs on board a youngster, but disembarks a star. The show is being being floated because its songwriter, Dick (David Christmas), happens to be a sailor, and is therefore able to offer an alternate venue when under the nicest kind of pressure from the leading lady, Mona (Tamara Long). Unfortunately for Mona, even a brief spell on the ocean wave does not agree with her - Ruby takes over, and she and Dick set off on life's long voyage together. George Haimsohn and Robin Miller wrote the book and lyrics, and the composer was Jim Wise. Their show's atmosphere and its songs reflected the good-natured send-up of the real thing (is 'Singapore Sue' any relation to 'Shanghai Lil'?), and included 'Choo-Choo Honeymoon', 'That Mister Of Mine', 'It's You', 'Good Times Are Here To Stay', 'Sailor Of My Dreams', and 'Star Tar'. It proved to be the first big break, not only for Mona, but also for Bernadette Peters who went on to become a major Broadway star, appearing in such shows as the failed, but fondly remembered, *Mack And Mabel*, and several Stephen Sondheim musicals. *Dames At Sea* sailed on for 575 performances - an impressive run for an Off Broadway show - and also played the Plaza 9 Musical Hall for a spell. It was revived again in New York in 1985.

Damn Yankees

Combining the improbable ingredients of a Faustian plot with a baseball setting, itself a notoriously jinx-ridden subject, the stage musical *Damn Yankees* was an unexpected hit following its opening on 5 May 1955. Written by Jerry Ross and Richard Adler, the show

Ray Walston (*Damn Yankees*)

starred the remarkable Gwen Verdon. The storyline of *Damn Yankees* follows hapless Senator Joe Boyd, a middle-aged baseball fan, who announces that he would willingly sell his soul to the Devil if only the team he supports could win the pennant. The Devil promptly appears and grants his wish although Joe believes he can outsmart 'Old Nick' if he can remain faithful to his wife. Rejuvenated, the Senator becomes Joe Hardy, a handsome young ballplayer, and is amorously entangled with Lola, the Devil's glamorous recreation of an ugly old hag. The Devil fails to make Joe unfaithful to his wife and eventually, after his team has won the pennant, Joe returns to plump middle-age and his dull and ordinary wife, while Lola reverts to being a hag. In addition to Verdon as Lola, the show starred Stephen Douglass as Joe and Ray Walston as 'Mr Applegate', the name by which the Devil was known for his earthly manifestations. Thanks to a powerful and sexy performance from Verdon and some of the music, notably 'Whatever Lola Wants', the show was a great success, running for over 1,000 performances.

Dance A Little Closer

Alan Jay Lerner's last Broadway show - a one-performace flop - had already been dubbed *Close A Little Faster* during previews, prior to the opening on the 11 May 1983 at New York's Minskoff Theatre. This music adaptation of Robert E. Sherwood's Pulitzer Prize-winning play, *Idiot's Delight*, had a book and lyrics by Lerner, who also directed. The composer, Charles Strouse, was adjudged to be the least guilty of the participating parties for his melodies to such numbers as 'Another Life', 'There's Never Been Anything Like Us', 'I Never Want To See You again', and the enchanting 'Dance A Little Closer', which is preserved in a recording by Liz Robertson, one of the show's stars, and Lerner's eighth wife. Len Cariou played Harry Aikens, a down at heel supper club entertainer who warms again to an old flame, Cynthia Brookfield-Bailey (Liz Robertson), when they are both holed up in an Austrian hotel on New Year's Eve, awaiting World War III. Cynthia was the mistress of a man who bore a remarkable resemblance to the American diplomat Henry Kissinger. There was an ice skating scene, too.

Dancin'

Bob Fosse had probably been waiting all his life for the opportunity to get rid of those tiresome librettos and get down to what the Broadway musical stage was all about for him - *Dancin'*. Over the years, this super-talented choreographer/director had created memorable dance sequences for such marvellous shows as *The Pajama Game, Damn Yankees, Bells Are Ringing, New Girl In Town, Redhead, How To Succeed In Business Without Really Trying, Little Me, Sweet Charity, Pippin*, and *Chicago*, amongst others, as well as performing a similar role for a string of Hollywood musicals. *Dancin'* opened at New York's Broadhurst Theatre on 27 March 1978, and stayed there for over four years, an incredible run totalling 1, 774 performances. The show had a team of 16 dancers who brilliantly executed Fosse's precision routines based on more than 20 carefully chosen musical numbers that ranged 'from Bach through John Philip Sousa and George M. Cohan to Johnny Mercer to Cat Stevens'. It soon became a popular foreign tourist attraction - you do not have to know the language to enjoy a show like this - and was a triumph for all concerned, especially Fosse, whose death in 1987 coincided with a (hopefully temporary) decline in the fortunes of the traditional Broadway musical in the face of the British invasion.

Dancing Years, The

With music and book by Ivor Novello, and lyrics by Christopher Hassall, *The Dancing Years* opened at the Drury Lane Theatre in London on 23 March 1939. It was a typical Novello story about a penniless composer who is in love with two women of entirely different social backgrounds - an innkeeper's daughter and an opera singer. The score contained several delightful songs, notably 'Waltz Of My Heart', 'Primrose', 'My Dearest Dear', and 'I Can Give You the Starlight'. In addition to Novello himself, the original cast included Mary Ellis, Roma Beaumont, Olive Gilbert, Peter Graves, and Anthony Nicholls. On September 1, with World War II looming, the London production closed. A year later, the show toured parts of the UK before returning to the West End at the Adelphi Theatre on 14 March 1942. It closed on 8 July 1944 after a run of 969 performances, making it the most popular London musical of the war years. There were two major revivals, in 1947 and 1968, and the show was presented as an ice spectacular at the Empire Pool Wembley in 1954. The ubiquitous British actor Dennis Price played the Ivor Novello role in the 1950 film version, and Anthony Valentine took the same part in a 1981 television production.

Daniels, Billy

b. 12 September 1915, Jacksonville, Florida, USA, d. 7 October 1988. He began his career as a singing waiter before working with dance bands and in vaudeville. In the late 30s he became popular in clubs and on radio. In 1943, during a club appearance, he performed 'That Old Black Magic', giving the song a highly dramatic, visually exciting treatment it had never had before, and from that time onwards the singer and the song were inseparable. At his best in a cabaret setting, Daniels was a natural for television and from 1950, in partnership with pianist Bennie

Payne, appeared regularly in the USA and UK. He made a few film appearances and was also in the television production of *Night Of The Quarter Moon*. P.J. Proby used much of Daniels' vocal technique with his epic ballads during the 60s. In 1975 he worked with Pearl Bailey in *Hello, Dolly!* and two years later starred in London in the UK version of *Bubbling Brown Sugar*. He also appeared with Sammy Davis Jnr. in the revival of *Golden Boy*. Offstage, Daniels frequently associated with underworld characters. He was stabbed in one incident and was once charged with a shooting. Late in his life he suffered ill-health and twice underwent heart by-pass surgery. He died in October 1988.

Selected albums: *Around That Time* (c.50s), *At The Stardust Las Vegas* (c.50s), *Love Songs For A Fool* (c.50s), *You Go to My Head* (1957), *The Masculine Touch* (1958), *At the Crescendo* (1959), *Dance To The Magic* (1959), *Bubbling Black Magic* (1978). Compilation: *The Magic Of Billy Daniels* (c.1976).

Davis, Sammy, Jnr.

b. 8 December 1925, Harlem, New York, USA, d. 16 May 1990, Los Angeles, California, USA. A dynamic and versatile all-round entertainer - a trouper in the old-fashioned tradition. The only son of two dancers in a black vaudeville troupe, called Will Mastin's Holiday In Dixieland, Davis Jnr. made his professional debut with the group at the age of three, as 'Silent Sam, The Dancing Midget'. While still young he was coached by the legendary tap-dancer, Bill 'Bojangles' Robinson. Davis left the group in 1943 to serve in the US Army, where he encountered severe racial prejudice for the first, but not the last, time. After the war he rejoined his father and adopted uncle in the Will Mastin Trio. By 1950 the Trio were headlining at venues such as the Capitol in New York and Ciro's in Hollywood with stars including Jack Benny and Bob Hope, but it was Davis who was receiving the standing ovations for his singing, dancing, drumming, comedy and apparently inexhaustible energy. In 1954 he signed for Decca Records, and released two albums, *Starring Sammy Davis Jr*, (number 1 in the US chart), featuring his impressions of stars such as Dean Martin and Jerry Lewis, Johnnie Ray and Jimmy Durante; and *Just For Lovers*. He also made the US singles chart with 'Hey There', from *The Pajama Game* and in the same year he lost his left eye in a road accident. When he returned to performing in January 1955 wearing an eyepatch he was greeted even more enthusiastically than before. During that year he continued to reach the US Top 20 with 'Something's Gotta Give', 'Love Me Or Leave Me' and 'That Old Black Magic'. In 1956 he made his Broadway debut in the musical *Mr Wonderful*, music and lyrics by Jerry Bock, Larry Holofiener and George Weiss. Also in the show were

the rest of the Will Mastin Trio, Sammy's uncle and Davis Snr. The show ran for nearly 400 performances and produced two hits, 'Too Close For Comfort', and the title song, which was very successful for Peggy Lee. Although generally regarded as the first popular American black performer to become acceptable to both black and white audiences, Davis attracted heavy criticism in 1956 over his conversion to Judaism, and later for his marriage to Swedish actress Mai Britt. He described himself as a 'one-eyed Jewish nigger'. Apart from a few brief appearances when he was very young, Davis started his film career in 1958 with *Anna Lucasta*, and was critically acclaimed in the following year for his performance as Sporting Life in *Porgy And Bess*. By this time Davis was a leading member of Frank Sinatra's 'inner circle', called variously, the 'Clan', or the 'Rat Pack'. He appeared with Sinatra in three movies, *Ocean's Eleven* (1960), *Sergeants 3* (1962), and *Robin And The Seven Hoods* (1964), but made, perhaps, a greater impact when he co-starred with another member of the 'Clan', Shirley MacLaine, in the Cy Coleman and Dorothy Fields' film musical, *Sweet Charity*. The 60s were good times for Davis, who was enormously popular on records and television, but especially 'live', at Las Vegas and in concert. In 1962 he made the US chart with the Anthony Newley/Leslie Bricusse number, 'What Kind Of Fool Am I?', and thereafter featured several of the their songs in his act. He sang Bricusse's nominated song, 'Talk To The Animals', at the 1967 Academy Awards ceremony, and collected the Oscar, on behalf of the songwriter, when it won. And in 1972, he had a million-selling hit record with the Newley/Bricusse song, 'The Candy Man', from the film, *Willy Wonka And The Chocolate Factory*. He appeared again on Broadway in 1964 in *Golden Boy*, Charles Strouse and Lee Adams' musical adaptation of Clifford Odet's 1937 drama of a young man torn between the boxing ring and his violin. Also in the cast was Billy Daniels. The show ran for 569 performances in New York, and went to London in 1968. During the 70s he worked less, suffering, it is said, as a result of previous alcohol and drug abuse. He entertained US troops in the Lebanon in 1983, and five years later undertook an arduous comeback tour of the USA and Canada with Sinatra and Dean Martin. In 1989 he travelled further, touring Europe with the show, *The Ultimate Event*, along with Liza Minnelli and Sinatra. While he was giving everything to career favourites such as 'Birth Of The Blues', 'Mr Bojangles' and 'Old Black Magic' he was already ill, although he did not let it show. After his death in 1990 it was revealed that his estate was almost worthless. In 1992, an all-star tribute, led by Liza Minnelli, was mounted at the Royal Albert Hall in London, the city that had always welcomed him. Proceeds from the concert went to the Royal

Sammy Davis Jnr.

Marsden Cancer Appeal.

Selected albums: *Starring Sammy Davis Jr* (1955), *Just For Lovers* (1955), *Mr. Wonderful* (1956, film soundtrack), *Here's Looking At You* (late 50s), with Carmen McRae *Boy Meets Girl* (late 50s), *It's All Over But The Swingin'* (late 50s), *Mood To Be Wooed* (late 50s), *All The Way And Then Some* (late 50s), *Sammy Davis Jr. At Town Hall* (1959), *Porgy And Bess* (1959), *Sammy Awards* (1960), *I Got A Right To Swing* (1960), *What Kind Of Fool Am I And Other Show-Stoppers* (1962), *Sammy Davis Jr. At The Cocoanut Grove* (1963), *As Long As She Needs Me* (1963), *Sammy Davis Jr. Salutes The Stars Of The London Palladium* (1964), *The Shelter Of Your Arms* (1964), with Count Basie *Our Shining Hour* (1965), *Sammy's Back On Broadway* (1965), *I've Gotta Be Me* (1969), *Sammy Davis Jr. Now* (1972), *Portrait Of Sammy Davis Jr.* (1972), *It's A Musical World* (1976), *The Song And Dance Man* (1977), *Sammy Davis Jr. In Person 1977* (1983), *Closest Of Friends* (1984). Compilations: *The Best Of Sammy Davis Jr.* (1982), *Collection* (1989), *The Great Sammy Davis Jr.* (1989), *Sammy Davis Jr Capitol Collectors Series* (1990).

Further reading: *Yes I Can*, Sammy Davis Jnr. *Why Me?*, Sammy Davis Jnr.

Day In Hollywood, A Night In The Ukraine, A

This innovative revue started its life at the tiny New End Theatre in Hampstead, England, in January 1979, before moving to the larger Mayfair Theatre in March for a run of 168 performances. Dick Vosburgh, an expatriate American author and journalist, wrote the book and lyrics, and the music was composed by Frank Lazarus. In the first half of the piece, Lazarus, and the cast which consisted of Paddie O'Neil, Sheila Steafel, John Bay, Maureen Scott, Jon Glover, and Alexandra Sebastian, ran through a series of sometimes hilarious sketches and songs culled from, and devoted to the golden era of America's west coast film capital. After the interval, the action switched to the Chekhov play, *The Bear* - which Vosburgh had adapted in the fashion of a Marx Brothers film comedy. Not surprisingly, the London critics loved it. The show must have come as welcome light relief after their recent 'glimpse of the future London musical' in the form of *Evita* at the Prince Edward Theatre. Ironically, it was *Evita* that triumphed over *A Day In Hollywood, A Night In The Ukraine* in several categories of the Tony Awards after Vosburgh's show had transferred to Broadway in 1980. However, the more intimate offering did win two of the Awards: featured actress (Priscilla Lopez) and outstanding choreography (Tommy Tune and Thommie Walsh). The New York production, with a revised book and three interpolated Jerry Herman songs, 'The Best In The World', 'Just Go The The Movies', and 'Nelson' ('Eddy', not 'Horatio'), was extremely well received

and ran for well over a year - a total of 588 performances.

De Mille, Agnes

b. 18 September 1905, New York City, New York, USA, d. 6 October 1993, Greenwich Village, New York, USA. An important and influential choreographer, director, and dancer, who 'helped transform the American musical theatre of the 40s and 50s'. After graduating with honours from the University of California, Agnes de Mille gave her first solo dance recital in 1928 at the Republic Theatre in New York. A year later she arranged the choreography for a revival of *The Black Crook* in Hoboken, New Jersey, and subsequently spent several years in London studying the ballet. In 1933 she arranged and staged the dances for Charles B. Cochran's production of *Nymph Errant* at the Adelphi Theatre in London, and later returned to America to work on shows such as *Hooray For What?* and *Swinging The Dream*, and the film, *Romeo And Juliet*. In 1939 she joined the Ballet Theatre in New York and choreographed productions such as *Black Ritual*, *Three Virgins And A Devil*, and Aaron Copland's *Rodeo*. Her work for the last-named, in which she herself danced the leading role, was highly acclaimed and led to her being hired for Richard Rodgers and Oscar Hammerstein II's first musical, *Oklahoma!* (1943). Her skilful blending of classical and modern dance which enhanced and developed the show's story, was highlighted by the 'Dream Ballet' sequence, a feature that became the benchmark for many a future musical. The list of her subsequent Broadway assignments, mainly as a choreographer, but occasionally as a director, included *One Touch Of Venus* (1943), *Bloomer Girl*, *Carousel*, *Brigadoon*, *Allegro*, *Gentlemen Prefer Blondes*, *Out Of This World* (1950), *Paint Your Wagon*, *The Girl In Pink Tights*, *Goldilocks*, *Juno*, *Kwamina*, *110 In the Shade*, and *Come Summer* (1969). Throughout her long and distinguished career Agnes de Mille received many awards, including two Tonys (for *Brigadoon* and *Kwamina*), and numerous other honours and citations. In her best work, her 'gift for narrative dance not only told stories, but each step and gesture came out of an individualized concept of each character's motivation. Her treatment of dancers as individual characters enabled the chorus dancers to become actors in the play'. As well as the Broadway shows, she maintained a full and satisfying career in ballet, performing directing and choreographing, and continued to work even after suffering a stroke in 1975 which left her partially paralysed. Her two final ballets were *The Informer* (1988) and *The Other* (1992).

Further reading: *Dance To The Piper. And Promenade Home. To A Young Dancer. Book Of The Dance. Speak To Me, Dance With Me*, all by Agnes de Mille.

De Sylva, Brown And Henderson
(see **Buddy De Sylva**; **Ray Henderson**)

De Sylva, Buddy
b. George G. De Sylva, 27 January 1895, New York City, New York, USA, d. 11 July 1950. Growing up in Los Angeles, De Sylva worked briefly in vaudeville while still a small child. In school and college he was active in theatrical pursuits, played in bands and wrote song lyrics. In his early 20s, De Sylva began a mutually profitable association with Al Jolson, who sang and recorded songs for which De Sylva wrote the lyrics. He collaborated with several composers including Jolson, George Gershwin, Rudolf Friml and Jerome Kern. His first hit was with Kern, 'Look For The Silver Lining', published in 1920. The following year Jolson introduced De Sylva's 'April Showers' (music by Louis Silvers) and in 1924, in his show, *Bombo*, Jolson sang 'California, Here I Come' (Jolson as co-lyricist, music by Joseph Meyer). Again with Jolson and Meyer, De Sylva wrote 'If You Knew Susie', and another popular success of the mid-20s was 'Keep Smiling At Trouble' (Jolson and Lewis E. Gensler). This same period saw De Sylva writing lyrics, often with other lyricists, to many of George Gershwin's compositions. These included 'I'll Build A Stairway To Paradise' (co-lyricist Ira Gershwin), 'Somebody Loves Me' (Ballard MacDonald), 'Why Do I Love You?' (Ira Gershwin) and 'Do It Again'. He also wrote lyrics to music by Victor Herbert, ('A Kiss In The Dark') and James F. Hanley, ('Just A Cottage Small By A Waterfall'). In 1925 De Sylva began his most fruitful association when he teamed up with composer Ray Henderson and lyricist Lew Brown. Their first success, again introduced by Jolson, was 'It All Depends On You'. Following this, and mostly written for the popular Broadway shows such as *Good News*, *Hold Everything*, *Follow Through*, *Flying High*, and some of the annual editions of *George White's Scandals*, came 'The Birth Of The Blues', 'Black Bottom', 'Life Is Just A Bowl Of Cherries', 'Good News', 'The Best Things In Life Are Free', 'The Varsity Drag', 'Luck In Love', 'Broadway', 'You're The Cream In My Coffee', 'Button Up Your Overcoat', 'My Lucky Star', 'Sonny Boy' (written for Jolson's 1928 early talkie, *The Singing Fool*), 'Aren't We All', 'An Old-fashioned Girl', 'My Sin' and 'If I Had A Talking Picture Of You.' The trio's involvement with talking pictures grew, as did the music publishing house they formed to market their own compositions and those of other songwriters. In 1931 De Sylva split from Brown and Henderson, opting to continue working in films while they wanted to concentrate on writing for the New York stage. The careers of the three songwriters was the subject of *The Best Things In Life Are Free*, a Hollywood bio-pic released in 1956. After the split,

De Sylva became involved in motion picture production, being successful with a string of musicals featuring child-star Shirley Temple. During the years he was involved in production he still wrote lyrics, but inevitably with much less frequency. At the end of the 30s, De Sylva, too, was in New York, where he engaged in theatrical production, enjoying considerable success with several hit musicals. In addition to producing, De Sylva also co-wrote the books for some of the shows, including Cole Porter's *Du Barry Was A Lady* (1939) and *Panama Hattie* (1940). In the early 40s De Sylva returned to film production in Hollywood. In 1942 he teamed up with Glen Wallichs and Johnny Mercer to found Capitol Records. He died, eight years later, in July 1950.

Dearest Enemy
Richard Rodgers and Lorenz Hart had interpolated songs into two Broadway shows, *Poor Little Ritz Girl* and *The Garrick Gaieties*, before writing the complete score for this, their first book musical. *Dearest Enemy* opened at New York's Knickerbocker Theatre on 18 September 1925, with a book by Herbert Fields which was set at the time of the American Revolution of the 18th century, and based on a supposedly true incident in which a Mrs. Robert Murray (Flavia Arcaro) delayed the British general, Sir William Howe (Harold Crane), by 'using her feminine charms', thereby enabling General Putnam's forces to join those of General Washington's on Harlem Heights. The other, more conventional love interest was provided by the English Captain Sir John Copeland (Charles Purcell) and an Irish-American girl, Betsy Burke (Helen Ford), who meet when her modesty is preserved only by a barrel (she has just emerged from a swimming pool), and later tell of their love for each other in the duet 'Here In My Arms'. That song, and the rest of the score, was a complete delight. Even this early in their partnership Hart was writing such literate, witty and relevant lyrics to Rodgers surprising and tender melodies. 'Here In My Arms' became popular in recordings by the orchestras of Jack Shilkret and Leo Reisman, and the rest of the score included 'Bye And Bye', 'Cheerio', 'War Is War', 'I Beg Your Pardon', 'The Hermits', 'Where The Hudson River Flows', 'I'd Like To Hide It', 'Sweet Peter', 'Old Enough To Love', and 'Here's A Kiss'. *Dearest Enemy* was staged by John Murray Anderson, one of Broadway's most innovative directors, and ran for 286 performances.

Dee, Kiki
b. Pauline Matthews, 6 March 1947, Bradford, England. Having begun her career in local dancebands, this popular vocalist made her recording debut in 1964 with the Mitch Murray-penned 'Early

Kiki Dee

Night'. Its somewhat perfunctory pop style was quickly replaced by a series of releases modelled on US producer Phil Spector before Kiki achieved notoriety for excellent interpretations of contemporary soul hits, including Tami Lynn's 'I'm Gonna Run Away From You' and Aretha Franklin's 'Running Out Of Fools'. Her skilled interpretations secured a recording deal with Tamla/Motown, the first white British act to be so honoured. However, although lauded artistically, Kiki was unable to attain due commercial success, and the despondent singer sought cabaret work in Europe and South Africa. Her career was revitalized in 1973 on signing up with Elton John's Rocket label. He produced her 'comeback' set, *Loving And Free*, which spawned a UK Top 20 entry in 'Amoureuse', while Kiki subsequently scored further chart success with 'I Got The Music In Me' (1974) and 'How Glad I Am' (1975) fronting the Kiki Dee Band - Jo Partridge (guitar), Bias Boshell (piano), Phil Curtis (bass) and Roger Pope (drums). Her duet with John, 'Don't Go Breaking My Heart', topped the UK and US charts in 1976, and despite further minor UK hits, the most notable of which was 'Star', which reached number 13 in 1981, this remains her best-known performance. She took a tentative step into acting by appearing in the London stage musical, *Pump Boys And Dinettes* in 1984. Kiki Dee's career underwent yet another regeneration in 1987 with *Angel Eyes*, which was co-produced by David A. Stewart of the Eurythmics. She has since appeared in Willy Russell's award-winning musical, *Blood Brothers* in London's West End, and was nominated for an Olivier Award for her performance in 1989.

Albums: *I'm Kiki Dee* (1968), *Great Expectations* (1971), *Loving And Free* (1973), *I've Got The Music In Me* (1974), *Kiki Dee* (1977), *Stay With Me* (1979), *Perfect Timing* (1982), *Angel Eyes* (1987). Compilations: *Patterns* (1974), *Kiki Dee's Greatest Hits* (1980).

Desert Song, The

Although damned by the critics when it opened at the Casino Theatre in New York on 30 November 1926, *The Desert Song* proved to be one of the most durable of American stage musical comedies. With music by Sigmund Romberg, and a book and lyrics by Otto Harbach, Oscar Hammerstein II, and Frank Mandel, the show was set in North Africa, where the French occupying forces are striving to capture the Red Shadow (Robert Halliday), leader of the Riffs, an outlaw band of Moroccan tribesmen. The famous renegade is in love with Margot (Vivienne Segal), but she is infatuated with the governor's son, Pierre. Captured by the Red Shadow, she eventually falls in love with him but then he is imprisoned by the governor's soldiers. All ends happily when the Red

Shadow is revealed to be Pierre in disguise. *The Desert Song* ran on Broadway for over 450 performances and was revived in 1946 and 1973. Amongst the show's songs are 'One Alone', 'The Riff Song', 'Romance', 'Margot', 'It', 'French Marching Song', 'Then You Will Know', 'Let Love Go', 'The Sabre Song', 'One Flower Grows Alone In Your Garden', and the title number. London audiences enjoyed *The Desert Song* for the first time in 1927, and on a further four subsequent occasions through until 1967. The latter production starred John Hanson who, from the late 50s, appeared in and managed a semi-permanent UK touring company which presented *The Desert Song* and other popular operettas. Film versions were released in 1929 (John Boles, Myrna Loy and Carlotta King), 1943 (Dennis Morgan and Irene Manning), and 1953 (Gordon MacRae and Kathryn Grayson).

Destry Rides Again

To most devotees of popular entertainment that title conjures up the celluloid image of Marlene Dietrich as the dance-hall girl known as Frenchy, driving the cowboys wild with her rendition of 'See What The Boys In the Back Room Will Have'. That was Hollywood in 1939, and 20 years later in New York, this stage version of Max Brand's satirical and entertaining impression of the American Wild West, opened on Broadway at the Imperial Theatre on 23 April 1959, and stayed there for over a year, a total of 472 performances. It came complete with a new book, by Leonard Gershe, and some fresh songs from the veteran composer-lyricist Harold Rome. The time is still the turn of the century, though, and Frenchy is continuing to sashay through the saloon, played this time by Dolores Gray, whose powerful vocal style could not be further away from Dietrich's sexy drawl. Andy Griffith is young Destry, the mild-mannered sheriff of Bottleneck, hired by the townspeople to get rid of Kent (Scott Brady) and his gang, who are terrorising the town. At first, Frenchy is one of Kent's crowd, but, after saving Destry's life, she defects to the side of law and order - with romantic consequences. Rome's score was not considered to be out of his top drawer - in any event, his subtle and sensitive style of writing rarely produced songs that became chart hits (apart from the out-of-character 'South America, Take It Away' (1946) - but it did contain some pleasing songs, including 'Anyone Would Love You', 'Ballad Of The Gun', 'I Know Your Kind', 'Every Once In A While', 'I Say Hello', 'That Ring On Your Finger', 'Once Knew A Fella', and 'Hoop De Dingle'. However, there was a good deal of approval - and a Tony Award - for choreographer and director Michael Kidd and his exciting dance sequences. He was back in New York after spending several years on the west coast working on classic film musicals such as

Barbara Dickson

The Band Wagon, Seven Brides For Seven Brothers, and *It's Always Fair Weather*. One of the outstanding dancers in *Destry Rides Again* was Swen Swenson, whose triumph in Cy Coleman and Carolyn Leigh's *Little Me* was just three years away.

Dickson, Barbara

b. 27 September 1947, Dunfermline, Fife, Scotland. Dickson earned her initial reputation during the 60s as part of Scotland's flourishing folk scene. An accomplished singer, she tackled traditional and contemporary material and enjoyed a fruitful partnership with Archie Fisher. In the 70s she encompassed a wider repertoire and became a popular MOR artist in the wake of her contributions to Willy Russell's *John, Paul, George, Ringo And Bert*, a successful London West End musical She enjoyed a UK Top 10 single in 1976 with 'Answer Me', while two later releases, 'Another Suitcase In The Hall' (1977) and 'January February' (1980), also broached the UK Top 20. In 1983, the Dickson/Russell combination scored again when she won a Laurence Olivier Award for her portrayal of Mrs Johnstone in his widely applauded musical *Blood Brothers*. Dickson maintained her popularity through assiduous television and concert appearances and in 1985 scored a number 1 hit with 'I Know Him So Well', a duet with Elaine Paige from the London musical, *Chess*. Its success confirmed Barbara Dickson as one of Britain's leading MOR attractions. In 1993, Dickson received renewed critical acclaim when she recreated her original role in the current West End revival of *Blood Brothers*.

Albums: with Archie Fisher *The Fate Of O'Charlie* (1969), *Thro' The Recent Years* (1969). Solo *From The Beggar's Mantle* (1972), *Answer Me* (1976), *Morning Comes Quickly* (1977), *Sweet Oasis* (1978), *The Barbara Dickson Album* (1980), *I Will Sing* (1981), *You Know It's Me* (1981), *Here We Go (Live On Tour)* (1982), *Barbara Dickson* (1982), *All For A Song* (1982), *Tell Me Its Not True* (1983, adapted from the musical *Blood Brothers*), *Heartbeats* (1984), *The Right Moment* (1986), *After Dark* (1987), *Coming Alive Again (Album)* (1989), with Elaine Page *Together* (1992), *Don't Think Twice It's Alright* (1993). Compilations: *The Barbara Dickson Songbook* (1985), *Gold* (1985), *The Very Best Of Barbara Dickson* (1986), *The Barbara Dickson Collection* (1987).

Dietz, Howard

b. 8 September 1896, New York City, New York, USA, d. 30 July 1983. Despite attending special schools for pupils of advanced intelligence, Dietz quit formal education while still in his teens. He studied journalism at Columbia University, where his classmates included two other future lyricists, Lorenz Hart and Oscar Hammerstein II. In 1917 he took a job in advertising, where his most lasting contribution to American popular visual culture was his design of a roaring lion logo for a tyro film producer named Samuel Goldwyn. Dietz had begun to dabble in lyric writing and after military service during World War I, he directed much of his energy into this activity. He worked on such Broadway productions as *Poppy* (1923) and *Dear Sir* (1924). Despite the latter having music by Jerome Kern, it was a flop; but Dietz persisted and soon afterwards was introduced to Arthur Schwartz, who suggested that they should work together. Dietz demurred, feeling that he was not up to Schwartz's standard. In any event, Dietz had been offered an important job with a new film production company that Samuel Goldwyn had formed, following a merger with Louis B. Mayer. Dietz became publicity and advertising director for Metro-Goldwyn-Mayer, later rising to vice-president. Soon after his appointment, Dietz met Schwartz again and thus began one of the great partnerships of American popular music.

Over the next dozen years Dietz and Schwartz wrote the scores for several Broadway musicals and revues, such as *The Little Show* (1929), *Grand Street Follies, Three's A Crowd, The Second Little Show, The Band Wagon, Flying Colors, Revenge With Music, At Home Abroad, Between The Devil*, and *Inside USA*. The shows contained a string of memorable songs, including 'I Guess I'll Have To Change My Plan', 'Something To Remember You By', 'The Moment I Saw You', 'I Love Louisa', 'New Sun In The Sky', 'Louisiana Hayride', 'A Shine On Your Shoes', 'Alone Together', 'You And The Night And The Music', 'If There Is Someone Lovelier Than You', 'Got A Bran' New Suit', 'Love Is A Dancing Thing', 'I See Your Face Before Me', 'Triplets', and 'Rhode Island Is Famous For You'. Their greatest song of this period, which Dietz used as the title of his 1974 autobiography, was 'Dancing In The Dark'. After 1936 Schwartz worked with other collaborators while Dietz concentrated on his work with MGM. In the early 40s Dietz returned to songwriting, this time with Vernon Duke, in a succession of stage productions, most of which were relative failures. Towards the end of the 40s he again teamed up with Schwartz on a stage show and on films, one of their new hits being 'That's Entertainment', written for the 1953 film *The Band Wagon*. Their renewed partnership was not as successful as that of the past, although the calibre of Dietz's writing always remained high. In the 50s he wrote the libretto and new English lyrics for the New York Metropolitan Opera productions of *Die Fledermaus* and *La Boheme*. In 1954 Dietz became seriously ill with Parkinson's disease and, although he lived for nearly 30 more years, his songwriting days were over.

Do I Hear A Waltz?

It has been called 'a creative match made in heaven', but for some of the participants it became a living hell. Put another way, the 'dream ticket' of Stephen Sondheim (lyrics), Richard Rodgers (music), and Arthur Laurents (book), became a kind of nightmare. Apparently, Sondheim was reluctant to commit himself to the project from the start, and in the event, he and Rodgers just did not get along. *Do I Hear A Waltz?* opened at the 46th Street Theatre in New York on 18 March 1965. It was based on Laurents' own play, *The Time Of The Cuckoo*, which had also been filmed in 1955 as *Summertime*, with Katherine Hepburn. The story concerns Leona Samish (Elizabeth Allen), 'a virginal spinster lady' who travels to Venice and falls in love with Renato Di Rossi (Sergio Franchi), who she subsequently discovers is a married man. Although, for the first time in her life 'she hears a waltz', she terminates the affair and returns from her holiday a sadder but wiser woman. Sondheim and Rodgers have both expressed their unhappiness and general dissatisfaction with each other, and with the piece, but their collaboration did result in a charming and interesting score. Several of the songs are well worthwhile, including a tourists' lament, 'What Do We Do? We Fly!' ('If it's white, it's sweet/If it's brown, it's meat/If it's grey, don't eat!'), 'Take The Moment', 'Moon In My Window', 'Someone Woke Up', 'Stay', 'Thinking', and the title song a typically lovely Rodgers waltz. Sondheim was forced to change the lyric to 'We're Gonna Be All Right', which was sung by a couple whose marriage was shaky, because it was considered 'not suitable for a Rodgers' musical'. The original surfaced during the 70s in the revue, *Side By Side By Sondheim*, and contained lines such as 'Sometimes she drinks in bed/Sometimes he's homosexual/But why be vicious?/They keep it out of sight/Just so we're gonna be all right'. *Do I Hear A Waltz* staggered along for only 220 performances, but is fondly remembered via its fine cast album. Revivals occasionally emerge particularly in Britain, where, in the early 90s, two concert versions and a production by the Guildhall School of Music were widely applauded.

Do Re Mi

Not remotely connected with the famous song of that title written in 1959 by Richard Rodgers and Oscar Hammerstein for their smash-hit musical, *The Sound Of Music*, this show, which opened a year later on 26 December 1960 at the St. James Theatre in New York, had a much more contemporary theme - and Phil Silvers. He had recently been 'demobilised' from the long-running television series in which he had starred as the conniving Sergeant Bilko, and was returning to the New York musical stage after an absence of nearly 10 years. Prospects looked good for *Do Re Mi* - the book was written by the celebrated author Garson Kanin, and Jule Styne (music), along with Betty Comden and Adolph Green (lyrics), provided the score. Nancy Walker, who had made such an impact on her Broadway debut in *High Button Shoes* nearly 20 years before, was Silvers' co-star in a story that concerned one of America's greatest gifts to the civilised world - jukeboxes. Hubie Cram (Phil Silvers) persuades some old slot machine hoodlums, Brains Berman, Fats O'Rear, and Skin Demopoulos, to come out of retirement and help him to make the big time. When their singer, Tilda Mullen (Nancy Dussault), is poached by rival businessman John Henry Wheeler (John Reardon), it sparks off a bitter jukebox war. In the end, Hubie decides it is better to have his wife, Kay (Nancy Walker), by the hearth (she leaves him for a time), than a jukebox in the Zen Pancake Parlour. Nancy Dussault and John Reardon had the show's big hit, 'Make Someone Happy', and they combined again on the unconventional 'Fireworks'. The rest of the delightful score included 'All You Need Is A Quarter', 'Cry Like The Wind', 'What's New At The Zoo?', 'The Late, Late Show', 'I Know About Love', 'Asking for You', 'All Of My Life', 'Adventure', and 'Ambition'. *Do Re Mi* ran for 400 performances on Broadway, but the London production, which starred Max Bygraves, Maggie Fitzgibbon, Jan Waters, and Steve Arlen, didn't appeal much to British audiences.

Donaldson, Walter

b. 15 February 1893, New York City, New York, USA, d. 15 July 1947. A self-taught pianist, despite his mother being a piano teacher, Donaldson began composing while still attending school. After leaving school he worked in various finance companies, but also held down jobs as a song plugger and piano demonstrator. He had his first small successes in 1915 with 'Back Home In Tennessee' (lyrics by William Jerome), 'You'd Never Know The Old Town Of Mine' (Howard Johnson) and other songs popularizing places and regions. Donaldson's first major success was 'The Daughter Of Rosie O'Grady' in 1918, just before he began a period entertaining at US army camps. After the war he had some minor successes with songs used in Broadway shows, the best known of which was 'How Ya Gonna Keep 'Em Down On The Farm' (Sam M. Lewis and Joe Young). It was another song, written by Donaldson with Lewis and Young, that established him as a major songwriter of the 20s. This was 'My Mammy', popularized by Al Jolson and which ever afterwards became synonymous with the blackface entertainer. Jolson also sang other Donaldson compositions, including 'My Buddy' and 'Carolina In The Morning' (both with Gus Kahn). With Kahn, Donaldson also wrote 'I'll See You In My Dreams', 'Yes Sir, That's

My Baby', 'I Wonder Where My Baby Is Tonight', 'That Certain Party', 'Makin' Whoopee' and 'Love Me Or Leave Me'. These last two songs came from the Broadway show, *Whoopee*, written by Donaldson and Kahn in 1928, where they were sung respectively by Eddie Cantor and Ruth Etting. When the Hollywood version of the show was filmed, in 1930, among additional songs Donaldson and Kahn wrote was 'My Baby Just Cares For Me'. Although his collaboration with Kahn was enormously successful, Donaldson sometimes worked with other lyricists, including George Whiting ('My Blue Heaven'), Howard Johnson ('Georgia'), Cliff Friend ('Let It Rain, Let It Pour') and Abe Lyman ('What Can I Say After I Say I'm Sorry'). On occasions he also wrote lyrics to his own music, notably on 'At Sundown', 'You're Driving Me Crazy' and 'Little White Lies'. In the 30s, Donaldson wrote many songs for films with such collaborators as Kahn and Howard Dietz, and he also worked with Johnny Mercer.

Donovan, Jason

b. Jason Sean Donovan, 1 June 1968, Malvern, Melbourne, Australia. Donovan appeared in the Australian television soap-opera, *Neighbours*, which, when shown on British television, commanded a considerable viewing audience of pre-pubescent/teenage girls who instantly took Jason's character, Scott Robinson, to their hearts. His co-star Kylie Minogue had already begun to forge a career in pop music when he also signed to the Stock, Aitken And Waterman label, PWL. In 1988 his first single, 'Nothing Can Divide Us Now' reached the UK Top 5. The follow-up was a collaboration with Kylie, 'Especially For You', which topped the UK charts in January the following year. Donovan consolidated his position as the Britain's top teen pin-up by scoring four more Top 10 hits, including 'Too Many Broken Hearts' (a number 1 hit), 'Sealed With A Kiss', 'Every Day (I Love You More)' and 'When You Come Back To Me'. His album, *Ten Good Reasons*, reached number 1 and became one of 1989's best-sellers. His success the following year was endorsed by Top 10 hits in 'Hang On To Your Love' and a re-make of the 1963 Cascades hit, 'Rhythm Of The Rain'. By this time Jason had left the cast of *Neighbours*. Although his acting talents were called upon for minor roles in film productions, it was not until 1991 that acting again showed off Jason's talents. His performances in the stage show of the Andrew Lloyd Webber/Tim Rice musical, *Joseph And The Amazing Technicolor Dreamcoat*, at the London Palladium, drew sell-out crowds and good reviews, taking many of his critics by surprise. A single from the show, 'Any Dream Will Do' reached number 1 in the UK chart, scotching any notion that Donovan was wavering as a hit-maker. The perception by many is of Jason simply

being a teen-idol, yet his obvious talent in acting and singing, and the extent of his loyal following, have echoes of previous teen-idols made good as all-round entertainers. In the spring of 1992, Donovan succeeded in having judgement in his favour in a libel action which he brought against *The Face* magazine. Later in the same year, his high-profile concert tour was greeted with a good deal of apathy and critical derision ('Jason's big rock dream turns sour'), and it was considered by many to be a retrograde career move when he returned to *Joseph* in the following year. For some time he alternated with other leading performers before taking over for the last few weeks before the show closed in February 1994.
Albums: *Ten Good Reasons* (1989), *Between The Lines* (1990), *Joseph And The Amazing Technicolor Dreamcoat* (1991, stageshow soundtrack), *All Around The World* (1993). Compilation: *Greatest Hits* (1991).

Dont Bother Me I Cant Cope

Conceived by director Vinnette Carroll at his Urban Arts Corps Theatre, this show, the title of which the authors are said to prefer without traditional punctuation, transferred to the Playhouse Theatre in New York on 19 April 1972. It was performed by an all-black cast, whose generally good-natured, self effacing exhortations regarding their proclaimed inferior position in the scheme of things - even in the modern world - was supplemented by music and lyrics by Micki Grant which ranged through a variety of musical styles including gospel, jazz, calypso, and downright joyful good-time music. The numbers included 'Dont Bother Me I Cant Cope', 'Good Vibrations' (not that one), 'Fighting For Pharoah', 'It Takes A Whole Lot Of Human Feeling', and 'Thank Heaven For You'. In the cast were Alex Bradford, Micki Grant, Hope Clarke, Bobby Hill, and Arnold Wilkerson. Opinions vary as to why this particular mixture of message and music took off, but it did, and in a big way - for nearly two and half years - a total of 1,065 performances. In 1976 Micki Grant, Hope Clarke, and Alex Bradford were the prime movers in another all-black production, *Your Arms Too Short To Box With God* (*sans* punctuation again), which was based on the Gospel according to St. Matthew, and provided the 'best singing and dancing on Broadway' for a time, and was revived twice in the early 80s. Delores Hall won a Tony Award for best featured actress. Another production with all-black entertainers and a book, music, and lyrics by Grant, entitled *It's So Nice To Be Civilized*, closed after one week in 1980.

Drake, Alfred

b. Alfredo Capurro, 7 October, 1914, New York City, New York, USA, d. 25 July 1992, New York, USA. An actor, singer, director, and author, Drake will always be associated with that magical moment when the curtain rose on *Oklahoma!* at the St. James Theatre in New York on 31 March 1943, and he made his entrance singing 'Oh, What A Beautiful Mornin''. The show marked a new and exciting beginning for the American musical theatre, and Drake reigned as its leading male star for more than a decade. After singing in the Glee Club at Brooklyn College, he made his stage debut in July 1935 at the Adelphi Theatre in New York in the chorus of *The Mikado*. A year later, he was in the chorus again, and also understudied one of the leading roles, in a City Centre revival of the *White Horse Inn*. In 1937 he introduced the title song in *Babes In Arms*, and was also featured in *Two Bouquets* (1938) with Patricia Morison, an actress who would later share in one of his greatest successes. From 1939-40 Drake also appeared in three Broadway revues, *One For The Money*, the *Straw Hat Revue* (with Danny Kaye), and *Two For The Show*, in which, together with Frances Comstock, he introduced the future standard, 'How High The Moon'. After his magnetic performance in *Oklahoma!*, Drake co-starred with Burl Ives in Walter Kerr's folk music tribute *Sing Out, Sweet Land* (1944), played Macheath in John Latouche and Duke Ellington's contemporary version of *The Beggar's Holiday* (1946), and took the role of Larry Foreman, the union organiser, in a revival of *The Cradle Will Rock* (1947). In 1948 he enjoyed what is often considered to be his greatest personal success in *Kiss, Me Kate*. Drake gave a marvellously witty and stylish performance in the role of Fred Graham, the egocentric thespian who is tormented on and off stage by his leading lady (Patricia Morison), who also happens to be his ex-wife, Lilli. His glorious lyric tenor voice delighted audiences on numbers such as 'Where Is the Life That Late I Led?', 'I've Come To Wive It Wealthily In Padua', and 'Were Thine That Special Face'. In 1951 he turned down the leading role in *The King And I*, but played it for a time in 1953 while Yul Brynner was on holiday. Two years later he completed a hat-trick of great roles when he played Hajj, the public poet in the musical version of *Kismet* (1955), for which he won New York Drama Critics, Donaldson, and Tony Awards. He reprised his role in the London production and for subsequent revivals. Along with the triumphs, Drake had his flop musicals too, as a performer, director and author. They included *The Liar* (1950), *Courtin' Time* (1951), *Lock Up Your Daughters* (1960), *Kean* (1961), and *Zenda* (1963). He made his final appearance in a Broadway musical in *Gigi* (1973), a lacklustre adaptation of the classic film which closed after three months. For most of his career he remained active in the straight, non-musical theatre, and was especially applauded for his Shakespearean roles which included Claudius to Richard Burton's Hamlet in John Gielgud's 1964 Broadway production. He bade

farewell to the Broadway stage in *The Skin Of Our Teeth* in 1975. Ironically, as is often the case with Hollywood, he was not required to recreate his major stage performances for the screen; Gordon MacRae and Howard Keel took care of those. Drake made only one film, a routine musical called *Tars And Spars* (1946). He appeared on plenty of television, though, and there still exists a 90-minute telecast of *Kiss, Me Kate* from 1958, in which he is said to be awesome. In 1990 Drake received his second Tony, a special award for lifetime achievement as perhaps 'the greatest singing actor the American musical theatre has ever produced'.

Dreamgirls

With a provocative book by Tom Eyen which tells of the peaks and troughs in the life of the Dreams, a black female singing group not a million miles away from the Supremes, *Dreamgirls* opened on Broadway at the Imperial Theatre on 20 December 1981 - and stayed for nearly four years. When it is apparent that they can make it right to the top, their manager, Curtis Taylor Jnr. (Ben Harney), tells the substantially built lead singer, Effie White (Jennifer Holliday), who has been his lover, to move over and to the rear, so that a more attractive girl can take the spotlight. The decision proves to be the right one for the group, and Effie eventually leaves and subsequently achieves her own, solo, stardom. Michael Bennett, the doyen of Broadway choreographers and directors, staged the show brilliantly, and there were some stunning moments, especially Effie's dramatic rendering of 'And I Am Telling You I'm Not Going'. That number, and the rest of the score, was the work of Henry Krieger and Tom Eyen, who succeeded in infusing the songs with a genuine Motown quality. They included 'When I First Saw You', 'I Am Changing', 'Fake Your Way To The Top', 'Cadillac Car', 'Hard To Say Goodbye, My Love', 'Dreamgirls', and 'Steppin' On The Bad Side'. *Dreamgirls* ran for 1,522 performances and dominated the Tony Awards cereremony, winning in six catagories: book, choreography (Bennett and Michael Peters), best actor (Harney), best actress (Holliday), featured actor (Cleavant Derricks), and lighting (Tharon Musser). In 1987, after an extensive road tour, a streamlined version of the show was welcomed back on Broadway for five months.

DuBarry Was A Lady

Cole Porter's third show with the dynamic Ethel Merman as his leading lady, and the third longest-running book musical of the 30s, opened at the 46th Street Theatre in New York on 6 December 1939. The book, by Herbert Fields and Buddy De Sylva, concerns Louis Blore (Bert Lahr), a washroom attendant at New York's Club Petite. Louis loves

May Daly (Ethel Merman), the star of the club's floorshow, and feels that a windfall of $75,000 from a win on the Irish Sweepstakes puts him in with a chance. He tries to improve his odds by preparing a potent potion for May's married boyfriend, Alex Barton (Ronald Graham), but accidentally drinks it himself and passes out. After waking from the trance, during which he imagines he is Louis XV and May is DuBarry, Louis realises that his place is really in the washroom, and leaves the field clear for Alex. The situation provides some marvellous opportunities for Lahr's inspired clowning and Raoul Péne duBois's spectacular settings and costumes. 'Do I Love You?', sung by Merman and Graham, was the only one of Porter's songs that became popular outside the show, but his score contained several other witty and memorable numbers such as two Merman and Lahr duets, 'Friendship' (She: 'If they ever hang you, pard, send a card.' He: 'If they ever cut your throat, write a note.' She: 'If they ever make a cannibal stew of you. Invite me too.' Both: 'It's friendship, friendship . . .') and 'But In The Morning, No!'. Merman also had several excellent solo opportunites with 'When Love Beckoned (In Fifty-Second Street)', 'Give Him The Oo-La-La', and 'Katie Went To Haiti'. Another interesting item was 'Well, Did You Evah?', sung in this show by Charles Walters and the future World War II 'pin-up girl', Betty Grable, and later revised for the 1956 film, *High Society*. *DuBarry Was A Lady*, the last Broadway musical of the decade, stayed on for 408 performances, and a London production, with Arthur Riscoe and Frances Day as Louis and May, ran for nearly six months. The 1943 film version starred Gene Kelly, Lucille Ball, Red Skelton, and Virginia O'Brien.

Dubin, Al

b. Alexander Dubin, 10 June 1891, Zurich, Switzerland, d. 11 February 1945. Brought by his parents to the USA when still a small child, Dubin grew up in Philadelphia. He wrote poetry and song lyrics while attending school, but his aspiration to become a professional songwriter was obstructed by parental hopes that he would follow in his father's footsteps as a surgeon. His education came to an abrupt halt in 1911 when he was expelled for neglecting his studies in favour of hanging out with musicians, gamblers and drunks, and he promptly headed for New York, and a career in music. A number of moderately successful songs were published in the years before World War I. During the war Dubin was gassed while serving in France, and soon afterwards he was back in New York writing songs. His work still met with only mild success until he had the idea of writing lyrics to several popular instrumentals, some of them from the classical field. The resulting songs included

'Humoresque' (music by Anton Dvorak) and 'Song Of India (Rimsky-Korsakov). More orthodoxically, he wrote lyrics for 'The Lonesomest Gal In Town' (Jimmy McHugh and Irving Mills). By the late 20s Dubin was in Hollywood where he was teamed with Joe Burke, with such popular results as 'Tip Toe Through The Tulips', 'Painting The Clouds With Sunshine', 'Sally', 'Love Will Find A Way' and 'Dancing With Tears In My Eyes'. In the early 30s, now collaborating with Harry Warren, Dubin began his most prolific and creative period. Among the many successes the duo enjoyed over a five-year period were 'You're Getting To Be A Habit With Me', 'Young And Healthy', 'We're In The Money', 'Shanghai Lil', 'Honeymoon Hotel', 'The Boulevard Of Broken Dreams', 'I'll String Along With You', 'I Only Have Eyes For You', 'Keep Young And Beautiful', Lulu's Back In Town', 'With Plenty Of Money And You', 'Confidentially', 'Lullaby Of Broadway', which won an Oscar, and 'Love Is Where You Find It' (co-lyricist with Johnny Mercer). Dubin's hits with other collaborators included 'Nobody Knows What A Red Headed Mama Can Do' (Sammy Fain and Irving Mills); 'Dancing With Tears In My Eyes', and 'For You' (Joe Burke) and 'South American Way' (Jimmy McHugh). Despite a lifestyle in which he indulged in excesses of eating, drinking, womanizing and drug-taking, Dubin wrote with enormous flair and speed. In addition to the foregoing collaborations with Warren, Dubin also wrote 'South American Way' (with McHugh), 'Indian Summer' (Victor Herbert), 'Along The Santa Fe Trail' (Will Grosz) and 'I Never Felt This Way Before' (Duke Ellington). By the end of the 30s, Dubin's lifestyle began to catch up with him and in the early 40s he suffered severe illness, the break-up of two marriages and a final collapse brought on by a drugs overdose. He died in February 1945.
Album: *42nd Street* (1981, US stageshow soundtrack).

Duke, Vernon

b. Vladimir Dukelsky, 10 October 1903, Parfianovka, Russia, d. 16 January 1969. Duke was a child prodigy; he was already composing music in the classical form. He studied extensively, mainly at Kiev and Odessa, but in the early 20s began experimenting with songs written in the style of such currently popular composers as Irving Berlin and George Gershwin. For these early efforts at popular song writing, he used pseudonyms, a practice he continued when, in 1921, he emigrated to the USA. For the next three decades he used his real name for his classical compositions and the name Vernon Duke for his popular songs. His first songs in the New World suffered through his lack of a thorough grasp of English and his adherence to the styles of other songwriters. By the mid-20s, Duke was in Paris, pursuing his classical studies and writing music for the piano and the ballet. In London in the late 20s, he wrote for the musical stage, mostly for revues and in the field of operetta. Back in the USA before the decade was out, he was hired to write incidental music for films but still hoped to find popular success. This began with 'I Am Only Human After All', with lyrics by E. 'Yip' Harburg and Ira Gershwin, which featured in *Garrick Gaieties Of 1930*. He continued to write for Broadway, with varying levels of success, and in the 1932 show, *Walk A Little Faster*, introduced his first standard, 'April In Paris' (with Harburg). For the 1934 show, *Thumbs Up*, Duke wrote his own lyric for another song destined to become a standard, 'Autumn In New York', and the same year wrote 'What Is There To Say?', and 'I Like The Likes Of You' for *Ziegfeld Follies*. For the *Ziegfeld Follies Of 1936* Duke composed 'I Can't Get Started', sung in the show by Bob Hope and Eve Arden. In 1940 he wrote the music for *Cabin In The Sky*, which opened on Broadway in October and featured an all-black cast. The show's songs included 'Taking A Chance On Love' (lyrics by John Latouche and Ted Fetter), introduced on the stage by Ethel Waters, and destined to become another standard. Duke's shows of the early 40s were not so well received and he followed his military service with a two-year sojourn in Paris. Back in the USA in the early 50s, Duke worked on a number of shows, but he was never able to recapture his earlier success. He continued to write classical music, including oratorios and ballets. He died in January 1969.

E

Earl Carroll's Vanities
(see **Carroll, Earl**)

Ebb, Fred
(see **Kander, John**)

Elegies For Angels, Punks And Raving Queens
After arousing a good deal of interest Off Broadway and on the London Fringe, this highly emotional play-with-music opened in June 1993 at the Criterion Theatre in the heart of the West End. It tells the tale from the point of view of some 30 individuals who died as a result of contracting AIDS from a wide variety of sources - such as 'a regular Joe who dropped into a brothel, to a granny who was given an infected blood transfusion'. The actors step forward one by one and tell their stories in verse and song. Kim Criswell, who gave a stunning performance in the 1992/3 London revival of *Annie Get Your Gun*, was the best-known name in a cast which also featured Kwama Kwei-Armah, Lily Savage, Trudie Styler, and comedian Simon Fanshawe. The score, with music by Janet Hood, and lyrics by the show's author, Bill Russell, was an intensely moving - and sometimes euphoric - blend of jazz, blues, and gospel. It could not run for long at a mainstream theatre, of course, even one as tiny as the Criterion, and, after a late-night show on 23 July to enable other West End actors to experience this thought-provoking piece, *Elegies* closed on the following night.

Ellis, Vivian
b. 29 October 1904, Hampstead, London, England. A highly respected composer, lyricist and author, chiefly celebrated for his fresh, witty and romantic music for revues and musicals in the UK during the period from the 20s through to the 50s. He also wrote the music for several films, including *Jack's The Boy*, starring Jack Hulbert and Cicely Courtneidge ('The Flies Crawled Up The Window'), *Piccadilly Incident* ('Piccadilly 1944'), *Public Nuisance No.1* ('Me And My Dog') and individual pieces such as 'Coronation Scot', which became the signature tune of the popular BBC radio series, *Paul Temple*, in the 40s, and emerged again in the 80s in a television commercial for British Rail. As an author, he published a number of novels, and a series of humorous books entitled *How To Make Your Fortune On The Stock Exchange* and *How To Enjoy Your Operation*, etc. Ellis's mother was an extremely talented violinist, and his grandmother, Julia Woolf, was the composer of a 1888 comic opera, *Carina*. His early ambition was to be a concert pianist, and he studied the piano with Dame Myra Hess and composition at the Royal Academy of Music, later giving a number of recitals. In his late teens, he developed an interest in light music and did the rounds of London's music publishers with some of his compositions, eventually getting a job as a reader and demonstrator with Francis, Day & Hunter. In the early 20s he composed the music for several numbers in revues such as *The Curate's Egg*, *The Little Revue*, and *The Punch Bowl*, and then, in 1924, wrote most of the songs (with lyrics by Graham John) for the successful Jack Hulbert and Cicely Courtneidge revue, *By The Way*. These included 'Three Little Hairs', 'By The Way', and 'Nothing Ever Happens To Me'. A year later, June (née Howard-Tripp) sang his 'Over My Shoulder' (lyric by Graham John) in *Mercenary Mary*, and she was one of several artists to

perform Ellis and John's hit 'Little Boy Blues' in another Hulbert and Courtneidge revue, *Clowns In Clover* (1927). In the late 20s, Ellis was represented by various compositions in several other West End shows, including *Kid Boots*, *Cochran's 1926 Revue*, *My Son John*, *Merely Molly*, *Palladium Pleasures*, *Blue Skies*, *The Girl Friend*, *Charlot Revue 1928*, *Vogue And Vanities*, *The House That Jack Built*, *A Yankee At King Arthur's Court*, and *Will O' The Whispers* (1928), in which 'I Never Dreamt' (words and music by Ellis), was sung by the popular American vocalist, 'Whispering' Jack Smith.

In 1929 Vivian Ellis moved on from the revue format and had his first musical comedy hit with *Mr Cinders*, which had a book and lyrics by Clifford Grey and Greatrex Newman, and additional music by Richard Myers. The show contained one of Ellis's most enduring numbers, 'Spread A Little Happiness', which was performed by Binnie Hale, and several other favourites, including 'Ev'ry Little Moment' (Binnie Hale and Bobby Howes), and Howes' comedy highspot, 'On the Amazon'. Despite initially cool reviews, the show was an enormous success, running for a total of 529 performances. Ellis himself was unable to attend the opening of the show - he was seriously ill in the South of France. On his return to Britain he collaborated with lyricist Desmond Carter for *Little Tommy Tucker* ('Let's Be Sentimental'), and again, for the wistful 'Wind In The Willows', which was featured in *Cochran's 1930 Revue* and became an extremely popular item in the repertoire of Leslie 'Hutch' Hutchinson. The show marked the beginning of an association with the impresario C.B. Cochran that was to prove one of the most important in Ellis's professional life.

In the early 30s Ellis experienced mixed fortunes. *Follow A Star* was a financial failure despite the presence in the cast of Jack Hulbert, and Sophie Tucker, who sang Ellis and Jack Yellen's powerful, bluesy 'If Your Kisses Can't Hold The Man You Love', which Tucker later used to close her cabaret act. *The Song Of The Drum* ('Within My Heart'), *Blue Roses* ('Dancing In My Sleep', 'If I Had Three Wishes', 'Where Have You Been Hiding?'), and *Out Of The Bottle* (music by Ellis and Oscar Levant), were disappointing too. *Stand Up And Sing*, starring Jack Buchanan and Elsie Randolph, was much more successful, and contained numbers by Ellis, Philip Charig and Douglas Furber, such as 'There's Always Tomorrow', 'It's Not You', and 'Night Time'. By 1934, Ellis was one of the leading figures in the British musical theatre. For the revue, *Streamline*, (1934), C.B. Cochran teamed him with the author, A.P. Herbert (b. 24 September 1890, Elstead, England, d. 11 November 1971), a collaboration that produced 'Other People's Babies' (sung by Norah Howard), among others, which provided a foretaste

of their fruitful partnership during the late 40s, and, briefly, in the 50s. In the meantime, Ellis turned once more to Desmond Carter for the lyrics to *Jill Darling* (1934), a charming musical comedy which starred Frances Day, one of Ellis's favourite leading ladies, and included 'Dancing With A Ghost', 'Nonny, Nonny, No', 'Pardon My English', 'Let's Lay Our Heads Together', 'A Flower For You', and another of the composer's all-time standards, 'I'm On A See-Saw', which was performed in vivacious fashion by Louise Browne and John Mills, who later became a celebrated dramatic actor. 'I'm On A See-Saw' was recorded by Fats Waller, in a typically ebullient version, and became successful in America for Ambrose and his orchestra - one of Ellis's rare transatlantic hits. In the late 30s, Ellis began to write more of his own lyrics for songs such as 'Drop In Next Time You're Passing' (*Going Places*), 'The Trees In Bloomsbury Square' and 'London In The Season' (*The Town Talks*), and the delightful 'She's My Lovely', sung by Bobby Howes in *Hide And Seek* (1937), and later adopted by bandleader Billy Ternent as his signature tune. In 1938, he had three hit shows running in the West End: *The Fleet's Lit Up* ('Little Miss Go-As-You-Please', 'Guess It Must Be The Spring', 'How Do You Do, Mr. Right?', 'Hide And Seek'), *Running Riot* ('Take Your Partners For The Waltz', 'When Love Knocks At My Door', 'Doing An Irish Jig'), and *Under Your Hat*, 'the funniest musical comedy for years', which ran for a total of 512 performances in London, and included Cecily Courtneidge's hilariously patriotic 'The Empire Depends On You', and other numbers such as 'Together Again', 'Keep It Under Your Hat', 'and 'If You Want To Dance'.

While those shows were running in London, Vivian Ellis lived for a time in Hollywood, where he wrote film songs for Deanna Durbin. He returned to Britain in the Spring of 1939, and subsequently joined the R.N.V.R. He reached the rank of Lieutenant-Commander, and spent most of World War II as a Command Entertainments Officer for E.N.S.A. After his release in 1945, Ellis resumed his collaboration with A.P. Herbert (book and lyrics) in C.B. Cochran's production of a 'light opera', entitled *Big Ben* (1946). Remembered particularly for introducing the 19 year old Lizbeth Webb to the London stage, the score included 'Let Us Go Down To The River', 'London Town', 'I Want To See The People Happy', 'Love Me Not', and 'Who's The Lady?', amongst others. One critic wrote that *Big Ben* lacked distinction, something that could never be said about Ellis and Herbert's next effort, *Bless The Bride* (1947), which was probably Vivian Ellis's biggest hit, and the climax of his career. Featuring hit songs such as the 'gaily traditional French pastiche', 'Ma Belle Marguerite', 'This Is My Lovely Day', and 'I Was Never Kissed

Before', *Bless The Bride* was essentially a romantic operetta set in Victorian England, and could hardly have been more different to the brash, young American import, *Oklahoma!*, which opened at a nearby London theatre in the same week. Nevertheless, with Georges Guétary and Lizbeth Webb in the leading roles, *Bless The Bride* settled into the Adelphi Theatre, and ran for 886 performances. One of the main reasons it closed in 1949 was that Cochran wanted to replace it with Ellis and Herbert's *Tough At The Top*, a decision that proved to be an expensive mistake - the new show ran for just over four months.

In the 50s, the US invasion of the British musical theatre that had begun with *Oklahoma!* in 1947, intensified. In the face of all that Americana, Vivian Ellis's first score of the decade couldn't have been more parochial. *And So To Bed* (1951) was a musical adaptation of J.B.Fagan's renowned play about the Elizabethan diarist, Samuel Pepys, for which Ellis was called upon to compose music in a variety of styles, such as madrigal, jig, and saraband. A rather unconventional choice for the leading role was 'rubber-faced' comic actor, Leslie Henson, whose idea the whole thing was, and the score included 'Gaze Not On The Swans', 'Moppety Mo', 'Love Me Little, Love Me Long', 'Amo, Amas', and 'Bartholomew Fair'. The show's musical director was Mantovani, later renowned for his 'cascading strings'. *And So To Bed* had a healthy run of 323 performances, and Ellis followed it, two years later, with a revue, *Over The Moon*, before renewing his partnership with A.P.Herbert for *The Water Gipsies* (1955). Ellis had written the melody for one song, 'Little Boat', in the film version of Herbert's 1930 novel, set on London's waterways, and now, over 20 years later, he contributed a complete musical score, which included Dora Bryan's amusing versions of 'Why Did You Call Me Lily?', 'You Never Know With Men', 'I Should Worry, and 'It Would Cramp My Style'. Her presence ensured the show's initial success, but when she became pregnant and had to leave, *The Water Gipsies* folded after a run of 239 performances. It was Vivian Ellis's last major musical production, and he has been quoted as saying that it may have been his best score. Of his other work around that time, his children's musical, *Listen To The Wind* (1954), contained several excellent songs, and he continued to contribute to productions such as *Half In Earnest*, *Four To The Bar*, *Six Of One*, *Mr Whatnot*, and *Chaganog* (1964).

In 1973 Vivian Ellis received the Ivor Novello Award for outstanding services to British music, and, 10 years later, he was presented with the Ivor Novello Lifetime Achievement Award and became the President of the Performing Right Society. In 1984, at the age of 80, he received the CBE, and, in the same year, the Vivian Ellis Prize, an annual award for the writers of new musicals, was instituted by the PRS. *Bless The Bride* was revived at London's Sadler's Wells Theatre in 1987, and Ellis's first musical comedy hit, *Mr Cinders*, also enjoyed a London revival in 1983, and again in 1993. The latter show was first produced in America in 1988, at the Goodspeed Opera House, and then, in 1992, it finally had its New York premiere at the Mazur Theatre. The show's hit song, 'Spread A Little Happiness', was sung in the 1982 film, *Brimstone And Treacle*, by Sting, the ex-lead singer with the UK band, Police; it gave him his first Top 20 chart entry, and his version was featured in an 80s television commercial for Lurpak butter. *Spread A Little Happiness* also became the title of a 'musical celebration of Vivian Ellis', devised by the author and critic, Sheridan Morley, and presented at the Whitehall Theatre, London in 1992. It meant that Vivian Ellis, a contemporary of Ivor Novello and Noël Coward, and one of the most important influences in the British musical theatre during the late 20s and 30s, still had his name up in lights more than 50 years later, alongside the present incumbents, such as Andrew Lloyd Webber.

Further reading: *Ellis In Wonderland*, Vivian Ellis. *I'm On A See-Saw*, Vivian Ellis.

Essex, David

b. David Albert Cook, 23 July 1947, London, England. Originally a drummer in the semi-professional Everons, Essex subsequently turned to singing during the mid-60s, and recorded a series of unsuccessful singles for a variety of labels. On the advice of his influential manager, Derek Bowman, he switched to acting and after a series of minor roles received his big break upon winning the lead part in the stage musical *Godspell*. This was followed by a more familiar role in the authentic 50s-inspired film *That'll Be The Day* and its sequel *Stardust*. The former reactivated Essex's recording career and the song he composed for the film, 'Rock On' was a transatlantic Top 10 hit. It was in Britain, however, that Essex enjoyed several years as a pin-up teen idol. During the mid-70s, he registered two UK number 1s, 'Gonna Make You A Star' and 'Hold Me Close', plus the Top 10 hits 'Lamplight', 'Stardust' and 'Rollin' Stone'. After parting with producer Jeff Wayne, Essex continued to chart, though with noticeably diminishing returns. As his teen appeal waned, his serious acting commitments increased, most notably with the role of Che Guevera in the production of *Evita*. The musical also provided another Top 5 hit with the acerbic 'Oh What A Circus'. His lead part in the film *Silver Dream Machine* resulted in a hit of the same title. Thereafter, Essex took on a straight non-singing part in *Childe Byron*. The Christmas hit, 'A Winter's Tale', kept his chart career alive, as did the

David Essex

equally successful 'Tahiti'. The latter anticipated one of his biggest projects to date, an elaborate musical *Mutiny* (based on *Mutiny On The Bounty*). In 1993, after neglecting his showbusiness career while he spent two a half years in the African region as an ambassador for Voluntary Service Overseas, Essex embarked on a UK concert tour, and issued *Cover Shot*, a collection of mostly 60s songs. In the same year he played the part of Tony Lumpkin in Oliver Goldsmith's comedy, *She Stoops To Conquer*, in London's West End. Despite pursuing two careers, Essex has managed to achieve consistent success on record, film and stage.

Albums: *Rock On* (1973), *David Essex* (1974), *All The Fun Of The Fair* (1975), *Out On The Street* (1976), *On Tour* (1976), *Gold And Ivory* (1977), *Hold Me Close* (1979), *Imperial Wizard* (1979), *The David Essex Album* (1979), *The David Essex Collection* (1980), *Be-Bop - The Future* (1981), *Silver Dream Racer* (1980), *Hot Love* (1980), *Stage Struck* (1982), *The Very Best Of David Essex* (1982), *Mutiny!* (1983), *The Whisper* (1983), *This One's For You* (1984), *Live At The Royal Albert Hall* (1984), *Centre Stage* (1987), *Touching The Ghost* (1989), *Spotlight On David Essex* (1993), *Cover Shot* (1993).

Etting, Ruth

b. 23 November 1907, David City, Nebraska, USA, d. 24 September 1978, Colorado Springs, USA. The famous torch singer sang on radio and in Chicago nightclubs before making her Broadway debut in *Ziegfeld Follies Of 1927* in which she made a tremendous impact with 'Shakin' The Blues Away'. In her next show, *Whoopee* (1928), she introduced 'Love Me Or Leave Me', which was subsequently always associated with her, and titled her 1955 film biography which starred Doris Day. After launching two more future standards, 'Get Happy' (*Nine-Fifteen Revue*) and 'Ten Cents A Dance' (*Simple Simon*), her sparkling rendition of an old Nora Bayes number, 'Shine On Harvest Moon', in *Ziegfeld Follies Of 1931*, made the song a hit all over again. By then she was one of America's brightest stars with her own radio shows and string of hit records. There were more than 60 of them between 1926 and 1937, including 'Lonesome And Sorry', 'Thinking Of You', 'The Song Is Ended', 'Back In Your Own Back Yard', 'Ramona', 'I'll Get By', 'Mean To Me', 'More Than You Know', 'Ain't Misbehavin'', 'Try A Little Tenderness', 'Love Is Like That', 'I'm Good For Nothing But Love', 'Guilty', 'Smoke Gets In Your Eyes', and 'Life Is A Song'. In the 30s she also made three films, *Roman Scandals*, *Hips Hips Hooray*, and *The Gift Of The Gab*, and in 1936 she appeared on the London stage in *Transatlantic Rhythm*. A year later she split from her husband and manager, Martin ('Moe The Gimp') Snyder, a Chicago 'hood' who had guided her career from the start. James Cagney played Snyder in *Love Me Or Leave Me*, and the story of his domination of Etting's life and his revenge wounding of her second husband - plus a great bunch of songs - made for an absorbing film. After Ruth Etting's career faded towards the end of the 30s, she entertained at intervals during World War II and enjoyed a brief comeback in the late 40s, when club patrons and radio listeners were reminded that she was one of the outstanding vocalists of her era.

Selected compilations: *On The Air* (1979), *Ten Cents A Dance* (1981), *America's Radio Sweetheart* (1989), *Ruth Etting* (several volumes, 1990).

Eurovision

This 'comedy of homosexual manners set against the backdrop of the Eurovision Song Contest', was written and directed by Tim Luscombe, and made its debut in 1992 at the Drill Hall in Bloomsbury, a fringe theatre devoted to lesbian and gay writing. While at the Drill Hall, the piece was brought to the attention of Andrew Lloyd Webber who presented it at his Sydmonton Festival in the summer of 1993, where it was extremely well received. He then decided to finance a London production which opened at the Vaudeville Theatre on 10 November 1993. It was immediately savaged by the critics who ridiculed the 'preposterous plot in which the ghosts of two gay lovers from ancient Rome materialise in the milieu of a thoroughly modern Eurovision Song Contest'. Anita Dobson, ex-*EastEnders* soap-star, played Katia Europa, 'who is suddenly possessed by something calling itself The Spirit of Europe', and she escaped more or less unscathed from the press hammering, as did James Dreyfuss (Gary) and Charles Edwards (Kevin) as the 'two gay young things'. There was one genuine Eurovision song, a former Greek entry entitled 'Bim-Bam-Bom!', and several original songs, including 'Grazie, Macedonia', by Jason Carr. The show's author, Tim Luscombe, was generally held responsible for the 'utter bilge', and he fought back, claiming that the critics seemed to be regarding the show as 'Ibsen' instead of a 'self-mocking entertainment' which had 700 people falling off their chairs every night'. It was all to no avail. Unlike Broadway, where a show can close after only one night, most West End cripples stagger on for a few weeks, but Andrew Lloyd Webber saw the writing on the wall, and pulled out the financial plug so that *Eurovision* disappeared down the drain after only a run of only three weeks with estimated losses of £275,000.

Ever Green

The renowned English impresario, C.B. Cochran, was taking a big risk in 1930 when he cast Jessie Matthews, one of the most popular stars of the

London stage, in *Ever Green*. A year before, another of the West End's favourite leading ladies, Evelyn Laye, had cited Mattthews as co-respondent in her petition for divorce from Sonnie Hale, and Jessie Matthews's co-star in *Ever Green* was to be that same Sonny Hale. Would the prim and proper English theatre-going public accept the situation? Well, they did, and the show proved to be the most successful of Matthews's career. Richard Rodgers and Lorenz Hart came up with a fine score, and it was their original idea that librettist Ben W. Levy used for his story of Harriet Green (Jessie Matthews), a young, somewhat pushy actress, who, to gain publicity for herself, purports to be a woman in her 60s whose looks have been preserved by the miracle of modern cosmetics. The problem is, that the man she loves, Tommy Thompson (Sonnie Hale), does not want to marry someone more than twice his age. As usual with a Cochran show there were some spectacular effects. One of the most delightful of these was the setting for the two stars' big number, 'Dancing On The Ceiling', when an enormous inverted chandelier was mounted on the revolving stage. The song had been cut from a previous Rodgers and Hart show, *Simple Simon*, and went on to become a much-admired standard, particularly in the version by Frank Sinatra on his *In The Wee Small Hours*. *Ever Green*'s pleasing score also contained 'If I Give In To You', 'In The Cool Of The Evening', 'Dear, Dear', and 'No Place Like Home', and the show ran for 254 performances. Jessie Matthews and Sonnie Hale married in 1931, and starred in the 1934 film version of *Evergreen* (one word), which had some different songs and a modified story-line.

Evita

In their preparation of the stage musical *Evita*, the composer and lyricist, Andrew Lloyd Webber and Tim Rice, developed a novel way of handling the intensely difficult problem of marketing a British musical show internationally. First, they produced an album of the show, ensured that it enjoyed maximum exposure, and only brought the show to the stage when they were assured of an audience. The story followed the unlikely, if real-life, drama of a woman of doubtful virtue who became the wife of a virulent fascist who rose to become his country's dictator. Despite the real-life Evita Peron's many shortcomings, she was greatly admired by many of her countrymen and women. Similarly, despite Rice's suitably acerbic lyrics, *Evita* became a paean of praise for a woman who had little to her credit other than the strength and determination to bring about her largely immoral ambitions. The stage version of *Evita*, which opened at the Prince Edward Theatre in London on 21 June 1978, starred Elaine Paige in the title role with Joss Ackland as Juan Peron and David

Essex as Che Guevara. Although most of the songs were 'show songs' in the sense that they really needed to appear in context to retain their validity, 'Don't Cry For Me Argentina', enjoyed considerable popularity, in particular in the original album version where it was sung by Julie Covington, and 'Oh, What A Circus' (David Essex) and 'Another Suitcase In Another Hall' (Barbara Dickson) both entered the UK charts. *Evita* ran for nearly eight years in London, and its success there was echoed in the USA where it became one of the earliest amongst a wave of British stage musicals that helped reverse the transatlantic tide, staying at the Broadway Theatre in New York for 1,567 performances. Since then it has been produced all round the world.

Expresso Bongo

Considered by many to be 'the most important and original British musical of its time', *Expresso Bongo* opened at the Saville Theatre on 23 April 1958. The book, by Wolf Mankowitz and Julian More, was taken from a newspaper piece by Mankowitz, and is said to have been based on the true-life story of the young ex-merchant seaman Thomas Hicks. He had been discovered in 1956, playing the guitar and singing in a Soho coffee-bar called the 2I's, by his future manager John Kennedy. He, and the agent Larry Parnes, changed Hicks's name to Tommy Steele, and moulded him into Britain's first rock 'n' roller. In this show, Herbert Rudge is also discovered at a trendy coffee-bar, but he is playing bongo drums, not guitar, hence his eventual stage name, Bongo Herbert. With the aid of a crafty agent, Johnnie (Paul Schofield), he quickly climbs the chart with 'Expresso Party', and then, just like Steele, shrewdly broadens his image, in Bongo's case with a magnificently ghastly hymn to his old mum, 'The Shrine On The Second Floor' ('There's a beautiful grey-haired Madonna/Who once taught me what life had in store'). The show was full of accurately drawn, colourful characters such as the stripper who wants to be a singer, Maisie King (Millicent Martin), a recording executive, Mr. Mayer (Meir Tzelniker), and a well-to-do, ageing actress, Dixie Collins (Hy Hazell), who gives Bongo a taste of the high-life, and arranges for him to be represented by an 'establishment' agent. Johnnie cannot compete, looks around for new talent, and decides to promote Maisie as a singer. The score, by David Heneker and Monty Norman (music) and Julian More, Monty Norman, and David Heneker (lyrics), was a match for the book. The songs were witty and satirical As well as Bongo's first chart hit and the 'mother' number, he sang the wry 'Don't You Sell Me Down The River'. Johnnie charted his ups and downs with 'I've Never Had It So Good' and 'The Gravy Train', while Maisie ground her hips (and a good deal more) to

'Spoil The Child'. She also had two poignant ballads, 'Seriously' and 'I Am'. Dixie reflected on her life in and out of the theatre with the touching 'Time', and joined Johnnie and Mr. Mayer for 'Nothing Is For Nothing'. Opinions as to the show's value were mixed, and along the lines of 'an adult approach' . . . 'wit, bite and topicality', . . . 'a raucous paeon of disgust aimed at the shoddy side of society'. It certainly was very different in style from that other British musical, Sandy Wilson's *Valmouth* (set in an English spa town inhabited by centenarians), which came into the Lyric when *Expresso Bongo* closed after a run of 316 performances. Even then the Tommy Steele connections continued: his brother, Colin Hicks, played the lead in the touring version of *Expresso Bongo*, and the show's co-composer and lyricist, David Heneker, wrote the score for Steele's smash-hit musical, *Half A Sixpence*, in 1963. The 1959 film of *Expresso Bongo* starred Laurence Harvey, Cliff Richard, Yolande Dolan and Sylvia Syms. Changes in the score resulted in the inclusion of 'A Voice In The Wilderness', written by Norrie Paramor and Bunny Lewis, which Richard took to number 2 in the UK chart.

F

Face The Music

Generally considered to be Irving Berlin's best score for some years, it came at a time when both he and America were recovering from the Depression, and the Prohibition bootleggers were about to be put out of business by the newly-elected President Roosevelt. *Face The Music* opened on Broadway at the New Amsterdam Theatre on 17 February 1932. The somewhat satirical book was the work of Moss Hart, who, in collaboration with the show's directors, Hassard Short and George S. Kaufman, fashioned a contemporary story of shady deals, in which Mrs. Martin Van Buren Meshbesher (Mary Boland), the wife of a police sergeant who, in the course of his duty, has accumulated a great deal of money from undisclosed sources. She panics, and tries to lose some of it by investing in a bizarre Broadway show. Unfortunately for her the show is a big success and makes even more money. As usual Berlin captured perfectly the mood and the period - the bitterness and cynicism that prevailed in America at that time: 'Let's

Have Another Cup Of Coffee' ('And let's have another piece of pie') was sung by the Rockefeller and Vanderbilt-types - the ex-swells (personified in the show by Katherine Carrington and J. Harold Murray) who are now eating at the Automat instead of the Astor. The song became widely popular through a recording by Fred Waring and his Pennsyvanians, and was sung lustily by Ethel Merman in the 1954 film, *There's No Business Like Show Business*. Carrington and Murray also had 'I Say It's Spinach', 'On A Roof In Manhattan', and the romantic and soothing 'Soft Lights And Sweet Music'. The latter song was also successful for Waring and his 'glee club'. *Face The Music* played for 165 performances and was revived briefly on Broadway in the following year.

Fain, Sammy

b. Samuel Feinberg, 17 June 1902, New York, USA, d. 6 December 1989, Los Angeles, California, USA. Fain was a prolific composer of Broadway shows and films for over 40 years, winning two Oscars, and nine nominations. Early in his career he worked for music publisher Jack Mills, and as a singer/pianist in vaudeville and radio. His first published song, with a lyric by Irving Mills and Al Dubin in 1925, was 'Nobody Knows What A Red-Haired Mamma Can Do', and was recorded, appropriately, by Sophie Tucker. In 1926 he met Irving Kahal (b. 5 March 1903, Houtzdale, Pennsylvania, USA), who was to be his main collaborator until Kahal's death in 1942. Almost immediately they had hits with 'Let A Smile Be Your Umbrella' and 'I Left My Sugar Standing In The Rain'. In 1929 their song, 'Wedding Bells Are Breaking Up That Old Gang Of Mine' was a hit for another singer/pianist, Gene Austin, and surfaced again 25 years later, sung by the Four Aces. Fain contributed songs to several early musical films including *The Big Pond* (1930) in which Maurice Chevalier introduced 'You Brought A New Kind Of Love To Me', the Marx Brothers' comedy, *Monkey Business* (1931) 'When I Take My Sugar to Tea', *Footlight Parade* (1933) 'By A Waterfall', *Goin' To Town* (1935) in which Mae West sang 'Now I'm A Lady' and 'He's A Bad, Bad Man But He's Good Enough For Me' and *Dames* (1934) which featured the song 'When You Were A Smile On Your Mother's Lips And A Twinkle In Your Daddy's Eye' - and in which Fain actually appeared as a songwriter. Fain's 30s Broadway credits included *Everybody's Welcome*, *Right This Way* (featuring 'I'll Be Seeing You' and 'I Can Dream Can't I'), *Hellzapoppin'* (reputedly the most popular musical of the 30s) and *George White's Scandals Of 1939* ('Are You Havin' Any Fun?' and 'Something I Dreamed Last Night'). During the 40s and 50s Fain collaborated with several lyricists including Lew Brown, Jack Yellen, Mitchell

Parish, Harold Adamson, E. Y. (Yip) Harburg, Bob Hilliard and Paul Francis Webster. In 1945 Fain worked with Ralph Freed, brother of the more famous lyricist and movie producer, Arthur Freed. Fain and Freed's 'The Worry Song' was interpolated into the Sammy Cahn/Jule Styne score for the Frank Sinatra/Gene Kelly movie *Anchors Aweigh* (1945), to accompany Kelly's famous dance sequence with the animated Jerry the mouse. Fain's greatest Hollywood success was in the 50s. He wrote the scores for two Disney classics: *Alice In Wonderland* (1951), 'I'm Late' with Bob Hilliard; and *Peter Pan* (1953), 'Your Mother And Mine' and 'Second Star To the Right' with Sammy Cahn. Also with Cahn, Fain wrote some songs for the *Three Sailors And a Girl* (1953) movie ('The Lately Song' and 'Show Me A Happy Woman And I'll Show You A Miserable Man'). In 1953 Fain, in collaboration with Paul Francis Webster, won his first Academy Award for the song, 'Secret Love', from their score for the Doris Day/Howard Keel movie, *Calamity Jane*. His second Oscar, the title song for the film, *Love Is A Many Splendored Thing* (1955), was also written in partnership with Webster, as were several other film title songs including 'A Certain Smile', 'April Love', and 'Tender Is The Night' which were all nominated for Academy Awards. Other Fain/Webster movie songs included 'There's A Rising Moon (For Every Falling Star)', from *Young At Heart* (1954) and 'A Very Precious Love', from *Marjorie Morningstar* (1958), both sung by Doris Day. Fain's last four Broadway musicals were *Flahooley* (1951) written with Harburg ('Here's To Your Illusions' and 'He's Only Wonderful'), *Ankles Aweigh* (1955) written with Dan Shapiro, *Christine* (1960), with Webster, and *Something More* (1964) with Alan and Marilyn Bergman. Fain continued to write films songs through to the 70s. He also made some vocal records, and had a US chart entry as early as 1926 with Al Dubin and Joe Burke's, 'Painting The Clouds With Sunshine'. He was voted into the Songwriters Hall Of Fame in 1971, and served on the board of directors of ASCAP from 1979 until his death from a heart attack on 6 December 1989. His main lyricist during the 50s, Paul Francis Webster (b. 20 December 1907, New York, USA), also wrote lyrics for other composers including Duke Ellington ('I Got It Bad And That Ain't Good'), Hoagy Carmichael ('Baltimore Oriole', 'Doctor, Lawyer, Or Indian Chief', and 'Memphis In June'), and for Dmitri Tiomkin film themes including *Rio Bravo* (1959), *The Alamo* (1960), *The Guns Of Navarone* (1961), *55 Days At Peking* (1963) and the title song for *Friendly Persuasion* (1956). Webster, partnered by Johnny Mandel, also won an Oscar in 1965 for the song, 'The Shadow Of Your Smile', from the film *The Sandpiper*.

Falsettoland
(see *March Of The Falsettos*)

Fanny
Based on the Frenchman Marcel Pagnol's film trilogy, *Marius*, *Fanny*, and *César*, which were made in the early 30s, this show marked the debut of one of Broadway's most important post-war producers, David Merrick. *Fanny* opened in New York at the Majestic Theatre on 4 November 1954, and stayed around for over two years. Joshua Logan, the show's director, co-wrote the book with the celebrated author and playwright, S. N. Behrman. Some critics felt that the librettists attempted too much - that it was not possible to do full justice to the complicated situations and personal relationships dealt with in the three books, in the space of one musical evening. Audiences were faced with the dramatic story of the young Marius (William Tabbert), who goes to sea against the wishes of his father, César (Ezio Pinza), leaving Fanny (Florence Henderson) to have his child. She marries the affluent sail-maker, Panisse (Walter Slezak), who brings up the boy, Césario, as his own. When Marius returns some years later, Césario wants to get to know his real father, but César insists that he stays with Panisse, and so Marius turns him away. Césario goes back to Panisse, who knowing that he is dying, pleads with Fanny to make a life together with Marius and the boy who means so much to them all. Harold Rome's music and lyrics, usually so full of social conscience and comment, echoes the intense emotional and sentimental feelings present in the story, with songs such as 'Restless Heart', 'Why Be Afraid To Dance?', 'Never Too Late For Love', 'To My Wife', 'I Like You', 'Love Is A Very Light Thing', 'Welcome Home', 'I Have To Tell You', and 'Be Kind To Your Parents'. The show's title song had some success in a recording by Eddie Fisher. Walter Slezak won the Tony Award for best actor, and *Fanny* ran for 888 performances on Broadway, and for more than 300 in London. In 1986, a revival was presented at the Goodspeed Opera House in Connecticut, USA. The 1960 film version - without the songs - was directed by Joshua Logan, and starred Leslie Caron, Maurice Chevalier, and Charles Boyer.

Fantasticks, The
Opening Off-Broadway at the Sullivan St. Playhouse on 3 May 1960, *The Fantasticks* became one of the longest-running theatrical presentations in American stage history. With music by Harvey Schmidt and a book and lyrics by Tom Jones, *The Fantasticks* is a simple love story in which a boy and a girl find true love with the slyly approving assistance of their parents. The best-known songs in the show were 'Soon It's Gonna Rain' and 'Try To Remember', along with others such as 'It Depends On What You

Pay', 'I Can See It', 'Plant A Radish', 'Much More', and 'Round And Round'. Among those who have appeared during its immensely long run are Jerry Orbach, Kenneth Nelson, David Cryer, Rita Gardner, Bruce Cryer, Eileen Fulton, and Bert Convy. Numerous other productions followed in towns and cities across the USA although a 1961 London production fared badly, some critics considering that the engaging intimacy of the original was lost in a regular-sized theatre. New York audiences, however, could not get enough of *The Fantasticks* and early in 1994 the show had comfortably passed a startling 14,000 performances.

Fiddler On The Roof

With music by Jerry Bock, lyrics by Sheldon Harnick and book by Joseph Stein, *Fiddler On The Roof* opened at the Imperial Theatre in New York on 22 September 1964. The story was based on tales by Sholom Aleichem which recounted episodes in the life of Tevye, a milkman living in a Jewish village in Czarist Russia. Set in the early years of the 20th Century, a time when Jewish orthodoxy, especially in matters of religion, language and custom, was under threat, *Fiddler On The Roof* was itself unorthodox. For one thing, religion was not traditional musical-comedy fare. Tevye's problems in coming to terms with change, his response to the wish of one of his

daughters to marry outside the faith, and the ever-threatening presence of anti-Semitism gave *Fiddler On The Roof* a depth and intensity more in keeping with straight drama than with song and dance. The show also had an unhappy ending, with Tevye and his wife and two of his daughters leaving for America, hoping but unsure that a married daughter will be able to follow with her husband and unable through tradition to bid farewell to another daughter who has married a gentile. Bock's music drew upon traditional folk forms and the libretto and lyrics used language replete with cultural references that gave audiences a strong sense of social awareness while simultaneously providing entertainment of the highest order. The show starred Zero Mostel as Tevye with Maria Karnilova as his wife, Golde, with other roles taken by Beatrice Arthur, as Yente the matchmaker, Joanna Merlin, Julia Migenes and Tanya Everett as the three older daughters, Austin Pendleton, Bert Convy and Michael Grainger. Amongst the songs were 'Matchmaker, Matchmaker', 'To Life', 'Sunrise, Sunset', 'Now I Have Everything', 'Do You Love Me?', 'Miracle Of Miracles' 'Tradition', and, unusually for any Broadway musical show, a song written especially with a particular performer in mind, 'If I Were A Rich Man', which was sung by Mostel. Indeed, although *Fiddler On The Roof* had many strengths, Mostel was the tower that ensured the

Topol (*Fiddler On The Roof*)

show's massive success. Nevertheless, the show continued to do good business after Mostel left at the end of the first year. His successors included Luther Adler, Herschel Bernardi and Jan Peerce. *Fiddler On The Roof*'s first Broadway run lasted for 3,242 performances and it was revived in 1976 with Mostel reprising the role of Tevye. The show won many awards including the New York Drama Critics' Circle Award as Best Musical, and Tony Awards for best musical, score, book, actor (Mostel), featured actress (Karnilova), choreographer (Jerome Robbins) and costumes (Patricia Zipprodt). The popular 'If I Were A Rich Man' also became a surprise UK Top 10 hit in a version by Topol, who played the role of Tevye in the London production which ran for over 2,000 performances, and in the 1971 film version.

Fields, Dorothy

b. 15 July 1905, Allenhurst, New Jersey, USA, d. 28 March 1974, New York, New York, USA. A librettist and lyricist; one of the few, and arguably the best and most successful female writers of 'standard' popular songs, and the first woman to be elected to the Songwriters Hall of Fame. The list of her distinguished collaborators includes Jerome Kern, Jimmy McHugh, Sigmund Romberg, Harry Warren, J. Fred Coots, Harold Arlen, Morton Gould, Oscar Levant, Arthur Schwartz, Albert Hague, Cy Coleman, and Fritz Kreisler. Dorothy Fields' parents were Lew and Rose, better known as the famous comedy team, Weber and Fields. She had one sister, and two brothers: Joseph, who became a Broadway playwright, and Herbert (b. 26 July 1898, d. 24 March 1958), a librettist, with whom she worked frequently. Shortly after she was born (while her parents were on holiday in New Jersey), Weber and Fields terminated their partnership, and Lew Fields became a Broadway producer and appeared in several of his own shows. It was because of her father's show business associations that Dorothy Fields, at the age of 15, took the lead in one of Richard Rodgers and Lorenz Hart's earliest musical shows, *You'd Be Surprised*, which played for one night at the Plaza Hotel Grand Ballroom in New York. After graduating from the Benjamin Franklin High School, Fields contributed poetry to several magazines, and worked with J Fred Coots (who went on to write the music for songs such as 'Love Letters In The Sand', 'Santa Claus Is Coming to Town', and 'You Go To My Head'), before being introduced to the composer Jimmy McHugh at Mills Brothers Music. With McHugh, she initially wrote sundry novelty numbers, and some songs for Cotton Club revues. The new team made their Broadway debut with the complete score for Lew Leslie's *Blackbirds Of 1928*, which starred Bill 'Bojangles' Robinson, Aida Ward and Adelaide Hall, and ran for over 500 performances.

The songs included 'Porgy', 'I Must Have That Man', 'Doin' The New Low Down', and future standards, 'I Can't Give You Anything But Love' and 'Diga Diga Doo'. In the same year, McHugh and Fields' next effort, *Hello Daddy*, proved to be a family affair, with Fields' brother Herbert as librettist, and her father as the producer and leading man, although the show's comedy hit number, 'In A Great Big Way', was sung by Billy Taylor. In 1930, another of Lew Leslie's lavish productions, *The International Revue*, contained two of McHugh and Fields' most enduring songs: 'On The Sunny Side Of The Street', which was introduced by Harry Richman, and 'Exactly Like You', a duet for Richman and Gertrude Lawrence.

After contributing 'Button Up Your Heart' and 'Blue Again' to the unsuccessful *Vanderbilt Revue* (1930), McHugh and Fields moved to Hollywood, and, during the next few years, wrote songs for movies such as *Love In The Rough* ('Go Home And Tell Your Mother', 'One More Waltz'), *Cuban Love Song* (title number), *Dancing Lady* ('My Dancing Lady'), *Hooray For Love* (title song, 'Livin' In A Great Big Way', 'I'm In Love All Over Again', 'You're An Angel'), and *The Nitwits* ('Music In My Heart'). *Every Night At Eight*, which starred Frances Langford, Harry Barris, Patsy Kelly, and Alice Faye, included two more McHugh and Fields all-time favourites: 'I'm In The Mood For Love' and 'I Feel A Song Coming On'; another, 'Don't Blame Me', was interpolated into the Broadway revue, *Clowns In Clover* (1933). Two years later, Dorothy Fields began to work with other composers, including Jerome Kern, with whom she collaborated on the score for the film, *Roberta*, which included 'Lovely To Look At', and 'I Won't Dance', a song that had been in Kern's locker for a couple of years, and which, for complex contractual reasons, is usually credited to five songwriters. The Kern/Fields partnership continued with *Swing Time*, the sixth Fred Astaire/Ginger Rogers screen musical. Often regarded as Kern's finest film score, the songs included 'Pick Yourself Up', 'Bojangles Of Harlem', 'Waltz In Swing Time', 'A Fine Romance' ('You're calmer than the seals in the Arctic Ocean/At least they flap their fins to express emotion'), and 'The Way You Look Tonight' ('With each word your tenderness grows/Tearing my fear apart/And that laugh that wrinkles your nose/Touches my foolish heart'), which gained Kern and Fields an Academy Award. During the remainder of the 30s, they worked together again on two Grace Moore vehicles, *I Dream Too Much* ('I'm The Echo', and the title song), *When You're In Love* ('Our Song', 'The Whistling Boy'); and others such as *One Night In The Tropics* ('Remind Me') and *Joy Of Living*, which starred Irene Dunne and Douglas Fairbanks Jnr., and included 'Just Let Me Look At You', 'What's Good About Good-Night?', and 'You Couldn't Be Cuter'

('My ma will show you an album of me that'll bore you to tears!/And you'll attract all the relatives we have dodged for years and years'). Dorothy Fields also wrote film songs with Oscar Levant ('Don't Mention Love To Me', 'Out Of Sight, Out Of Mind'), Max Steiner ('I Can't Waltz Alone'), and provided new lyrics to Fritz Kreisler's music in *The King Steps Out*. Before the end of the decade Fields was back on Broadway, working with the composer Arthur Schwartz on *Stars In Your Eyes*. Their score included 'This Is It', 'A Lady Needs A Change', 'Just A Little Bit More', 'I'll Pay The Check', and the show's highlight, 'It's All Yours', a duet by the stars, Ethel Merman and Jimmy Durante. In the early 40s, Dorothy Fields turned from writing lyrics and collaborated with her brother Herbert on the books for three highly successful Cole Porter musicals: *Let's Face It* (starring Danny Kaye), *Something for The Boys*, (Ethel Merman/Bill Johnson), and *Mexican Hayride* (Bobby Clark/June Havoc), each of which ran for well over a year. In 1945, the Fields partnership again served as librettists, and Dorothy wrote the lyrics, to Sigmund Romberg's music, for the smash-hit, *Up In Central Park*. Not surprisingly, with Romberg's participation, the score had operetta overtones, and included the robust 'The Big Back Yard', two charming ballads, 'April Snow' and 'Close As Pages In A Book', and a skating ballet in the manner of a Currier and Ives print. Towards the end of 1945, Dorothy Fields was set to collaborate again with Jerome Kern, on *Annie Get Your Gun*, a musical loosely based on the life of sharp-shooter, Annie Oakley. When Kern died in November of that year, Irving Berlin was brought in to write what is generally regarded as his greatest score, while Dorothy and Herbert Fields provided the highly entertaining book for a production which ran for 1,147 performances. In contrast, *Arms And The Girl* (1950) closed after only 134 shows, despite Rouben Mamoulian's involvement with Dorothy and Herbert Fields in a libretto which was based on the play, *The Pursuit Of Happiness*. The Dorothy Fields/Morton Gould score included Pearl Bailey's inimitable renderings of 'Nothin' For Nothin'' and 'There Must Be Somethin' Better Than Love'; a strange attempt at a tender love song called 'A Cow, And A Plough, And A Frau', and the double entendres of 'That's What I Told Him Last Night'. During the 50s, Dorothy Fields teamed again with Arthur Schwartz for two shows. The first, *A Tree Grows In Brooklyn*, was a critical success, but a commercial failure. Based on Dorothy Smith's best-selling novel, the witty and melodic score included 'If You Haven't Got A Sweetheart', 'I'll Buy You A Star', 'Make The Man Love Me', 'Look Who's Dancing', 'Mine Till Monday', 'I'm Like A New Broom', and 'Growing Pains'. Shirley Booth stopped the show each night with 'He Had Refinement', the story of Harry, her late spouse, who 'only used four-letter words that I didn't understand', and 'undressed with all the lights off until we was wed - a gentleman to his fingernails, was he!'. The show lasted for 270 performances, and so did the second Fields/Schwartz 50s collaboration, *By The Beautiful Sea* (1954), mainly due to the presence, once again, of Shirley Booth. The songs included 'Alone Too Long', 'Happy Habit', 'I'd Rather Wake Up By Myself', 'Hang Up!', 'More Love Than Your Love', 'By The Beautiful Sea', and 'Coney Island'. Far more successful, was *Redhead* (1959), which ran for 452 performances, and won the Tony Award for 'Best Musical'. Dorothy Fields and Albert Hague's score, which also won a Tony, included 'I Feel Merely Marvelous', 'I'm Back In Circulation', 'Just For Once', 'The Uncle Sam Rag', 'The Right Finger Of My Left Hand', 'Look Who's In Love', ''Erbie Fitch's Dilemma', and 'My Girl Is Just Enough Woman For Me'.

Dorothy Fields' last two Broadway scores were written with Cy Coleman, a composer who was 25 years her junior. The first, *Sweet Charity* (1966), a musical version of Federico Fellini's movie, *Nights Of Cabiria*, was conceived, directed and choreographed by Bob Fosse, and starred Gwen Verdon as the good-hearted hostess at the Fan-Dango ballroom, who almost - but not quite - realises her dream of being a conventional wife and mother. Fields and Coleman's score produced several popular numbers, including 'Big Spender' ('So let me get right to the point/I don't pop my cork for every guy I see!'), which quickly became associated with the UK singer Shirley Bassey, and 'Baby, Dream Your Dream', 'If My Friends Could See Me Now', 'I'm A Brass Band', 'Where Am I Going?', 'There's Gotta Be Something Better Than This', 'Too Many Tomorrows', and 'I Love To Cry At Weddings' ('I walk into a chapel and get happily hysterical'). Fields' Broadway swansong came in 1973, with *Seesaw*. Her lyrics for this musical adaptation of William Gibson's play, *Two For The Seesaw*, are regarded as somewhat tougher than much of her previous work, although they continued to have the colloquial edge and the contemporary, witty, 'street-wise' quality that had become her trademark. The songs included 'Seesaw', 'In Tune', 'Spanglish', 'We've Got It', 'Welcome To Holiday Inn', 'Poor Everybody Else', 'I'm Way Ahead', and the two best-known numbers, 'Nobody Does It Like Me' ('If there's a problem, I duck it/I don't solve it, I just muck it up!'), and Tommy Tune's show-stopper, 'It's Not Where You Start (It's Where You Finish)'. The latter song closed with. . . 'And you're gonna finish on top!'. Dorothy Fields did just that, 45 years after she had her first Broadway hit with 'I Can't Give You Anything But Love'. Shortly before her death in March 1974, she appeared in a programme in the

Lyrics And Lyricists series at the Kaufmann Concert Hall, New York, giving her 'observations on the fine art and craft of lyric writing', and performing several of her own numbers.

Selected albums: *The Dorothy Fields Songbook*, Sally Mayes (1992).

Fifty Million Frenchmen

That is an awful lot of people to see during 'A Musical Comedy Tour Of Paris' - the sub-title of Cole Porter's first big hit show, which opened at New York's Lyric Theatre on 27 November 1929. Following the critical reaction to his *See America First* ('See *See America First* - last!'), Porter switched his milieu to Europe, where he had spent several pleasurable years during the 20s, and found success with *Paris*, which ran for six months on Broadway from October 1928. This second theatrical excursion to the city he loved, had a book by Herbert Fields which once again turned on the familiar theme - a rich man's desire to to be loved for himself and not for his money. Peter Forbes (William Gaxton) is the tormented soul this time, and he bets a friend, Michael Cummins (Jack Thompson), that he will be engaged to an attractive tourist, Looloo Carroll (Genevieve Tobin), within a month - and without any resource to his financial resources. Taking a job as a guide, he conducts Looloo on 'a musical comedy guide of city', which provides Norman Bel Geddes with a marvellous opportunity to display his impressive settings, which include the Longchamps Racetrack, the Eiffel Tower, and the Café de la Paix. Porter's score was a joy, and contained one of his all-time standards, 'You Do Something To Me', as well as the humorous 'You've Got That Thing' ('You've got what Adam craved when he/With love for Eve was tortured/She only had an apple tree/But you, you've got an orchard'), 'Find Me A Primitive Man' ('I don't mean the kind that belongs to a club/But the kind that has a club that belongs to him'), 'The Tale Of An Oyster', 'I Worship You', 'I'm Unlucky At Gambling', and, of course, a couple of affectionate hymns to the city, 'You Don't Know Paree' and 'Paree, What Did You Do To Me?'. The show ran for 254 performances, and launched Porter - who was already 38 years old when it opened - on a glittering career that lasted for another 25 years on Broadway. William Gaxton and Helen Broderick recreated their roles in the 1931 film version of *Fifty Million Frenchmen*, but the Hollywood interpretation was not classed as a musical.

Fine And Dandy

A rather bizarre title for a show, considering that it opened in New York at the height of the Depression, on 23 September 1930. The production was a vehicle for the much-loved ex-vaudevillian, Joe Cook, an extremely versatile and zany comedian whose routines included a range of highly amusing, inventive stories (particularly the one about the 'Four Hawaiians'), and a consistently entertaining display of circus-style skills such as acrobatics, juggling, and balancing - not to mention a degree of proficiency on the ukelele and saxophone. In Donald Ogden Stewart's plot for *Fine And Dandy*, Cook played the role of Joe Squibb, who, like the funny-man himself, was was adept at keeping several balls in the air at once (metaphorically speaking). These consisted of his female boss, Mrs. Fordyce (Dora Maughan), his girlfriend, Nancy Ellis (Alice Boulden) - and his wife and children! The show's music and lyrics were by Kay Swift and Paul James (a pseudonym for Swift's husband, a banker named James P. Warburg). Kay Swift (b. 19 April 1897, New York, USA, d. 28 January 1993, Southington, Connecticut, USA) was one of the few female composers of popular songs to have a degree of success on Broadway. With her husband she had contributed 'Can't We Be Friends?' to *The Little Show* in 1929, and was a close personal and professional associate of George Gershwin. For *Fine And Dandy* she and Warburg wrote the jaunty title song which was sung by Cook and Boulden, along with 'Let's Go Eat Worms In The Garden' (Boulden and Joe Wagstaff), and 'Jig Hope', a number that was performed by Eleanor Powell who subsequently tap-danced her way through several entertaining Hollywood musicals, notably *Broadway Melody Of 1940* with Fred Astaire. The show's big romantic ballad, 'Can This Be Love?' (Boulden), became successful through a recording by the pianistic duo Victor Arden and Ohman's Orchestra. They also made the best-sellers with 'Fine And Dandy', as did another rather more famous band led by Tommy and Jimmy Dorsey. On the strength of initial revues such as 'pretty nearly everything you've yearned for in the way of 1930 entertainment', and Cook's renowned inspired clowning, *Fine And Dandy* ran at Erlanger's Theatre (later known as the St. James) for 255 performances. That production is not connected with the 1942 London revue of the same name, which starred Leslie Henson, Stanley Holloway, Dorothy Dickson, and Douglas Byng.

Fings Ain't Wot They Used T'Be

This show originally opened on 17 February 1959 at the Theatre Royal, Stratford East, London, home of the *avant garde* director Joan Littlewood and her 'repertory company'. During two separate runs there it was completely revised and remodelled, and transferred to the Garrick Theatre in the West End on 11 February 1960. Set in the drab and dreary world of London's Soho district, with its prostitutes, pimps, and small time criminals, Frank Norman's book (Norman was an ex-convict) told of Fred Cochran

(Glynn Edwards), one of life's losers, who runs a sleazy gambling club - a haven for the local low-life. He can only dream of owning a big-time venue, but a large win on the horses means that he can at least have his place decorated by the camp decorator Horace Seaton (Wallas Eaton). Unfortunately, the reopening night party is ruined when Fred is beaten up for not providing the police with their usual slice of payola. There is a good deal more trouble and strife before Fred ends up with a knees-up *al fresco* wedding to his girlfriend Lily Smith (Miriam Karlin). The local milieu is populated by a variety of characters such as the crooked copper Sergeant Collins (Tom Chatto), plus two more members of the constabulary, played by Yootha Joyce and George Sewell, a civilian crook, Redhot (Edward Carrick), Tosher, the area's premier ponce (James Booth), and several 'ladies of the night', including Rosie (Barbara Windsor) and Betty (Toni Palmer). Lionel Bart, who had provided just the lyrics for *Lock Up Your Daughters* at the Mermaid Theatre in 1959, now wrote both words and music for this exhilarating piece. His songs, which so accurately captured the show's spirit and atmosphere, included 'G'Night Dearie', 'Layin' Abaht', 'Where It's Hot', 'Contempery', 'Meatface', 'The Ceilin's Comin' Dahn', 'Where Do Little Birds Go?', 'The Student Ponce', 'Big Time', 'Polka Dots,' 'Cop A Bit Of Pride', and 'Cochran Will Return'. The popular comedian-singer Max Bygraves took a cleaned-up version of the title song into the UK Top 5, and the personality pianist Russ Conway also had a minor hit with the tune. The critics were not keen on the show, but audiences loved it, and *Fings Ain't Wot They Used T'Be* enjoyed a two-year run of 897 performances. This established Lionel Bart as a real force in the London musical theatre, and won the *Evening Standard Award* for best musical.

Finian's Rainbow

Conceived by E.Y. 'Yip' Harburg, *Finian's Rainbow* this stage musical opened on Broadway on 10 January 1947. With book by Harburg and Fred Saidy, music by Burton Lane and lyrics by Harburg, the show was a fantasy with a strong satirical core. Central to the story was Harburg's desire to express his views on racial bigotry and political persecution. At the time he was blacklisted in Hollywood and had returned to Broadway out of necessity. Set in the Deep South, in Rainbow Valley in the mythical state of Missitucky, the story tells of Og, a leprechaun, who arrives there in search of Finian who has stolen a pot of gold from Glocca Morra in Ireland. The leprechaun grants three wishes, one of which turns Billboard Rawkins, a land-grabbing racist white Senator, into a black evangelist, humanizing him in the process, another gives the power of speech to Susan, a mute, while the third helps the local sharecroppers recover their land

from Rawkins. Songs from the show included 'How Are Things In Glocca Morra?', 'When I'm Not Near The Girl I Love', 'If This Isn't Love', 'The Great Come-And-Get-It Day' and 'Look To The Rainbow'. *Finian's Rainbow* starred David Wayne as Og, Albert Sharp as Finian, Anita Alvarez as Susan, Ella Logan as Sharon, Finian's sister, and Donald Richards as Woody, Sharon's boyfriend. With good songs and performances allied to Michael Kidd's exhilarating choreography, the show was a critical and popular success running for 725 performances. The 1968 screen version, which replaced political and social satire with sentimental whimsy, starred Fred Astaire, Petula Clark and Tommy Steele.

Fiorello!

With a book by Jerome Weidman and George Abbott which was based on the true story of Fiorello LaGuardia, the aggressive, extrovert US Congressman and Mayor of New York, *Fiorello!* opened at the Broadhurst Theatre on Broadway on 23 November 1959. The show's story began shortly before World War I when LaGuardia was first a conscientious, reforming lawyer, and then a Congressman who became a sworn enemy of the corruption that was endemic in the social and political life of New York. It continued through his time as a pilot during World War I, his initial unsuccessful campaign against James J. Walker, right up to the eve of his election as the Mayor of New York in 1933. Along the way, his wife, Thea (Ellen Hanley) dies, and he eventually finds happiness with his secretary Marie Fischer (Patricia Wilson). The role of the rough, tough, ebullient LaGuardia, was played by Tom Bosley, making his Broadway debut. The actor was subsequently best-known for his work on television, as the indulgent father in the 50s spoof, *Happy Days*, and another long-running series, *Father Dowling Investigates*. *Fiorello!*'s score, by Jerry Bock (music) and Sheldon Harnick (lyrics), included 'On the Side Of The Angels', 'The Name's LaGuardia', 'Politics And Poker', 'I Love A Cop', ''Til Tomorrow', 'When Did I Fall In Love?', 'Gentleman Jimmy', 'The Very Next Man', 'Marie's Law', and 'The Bum Won'. One of the most amusing numbers was 'Little Tin Box'. Setting aside a small sum therein each week apparently enabled certain of the city's apparently less than well-off citizens to buy yachts and Rolls Royces, or as one of them put it, in court: 'I can see your Honour doesn't pull his punches/And it looks a trifle fishy, I'll admit/But for one whole week I went without my lunches/And it mounted up your honour, bit by bit.' Chorus: 'Up your Honour bit by bit . . .' In spite of a few critical carpings *Fiorello!* was a great success and ran for 795 performances. It won Tony Awards for best director (George Abbott) outright, tied with *The Sound Of Music* for best

Louis Jordan (*Five Guys Named Moe*)

musical, composer, and librettists, and was also voted best musical by the New York Drama Critics. Even more prestigiously, it became only the third musical (not counting *Oklahoma!*'s special award in 1944) to be awarded the Pulitzer Prize for Drama. The 1962 London production stayed at the Princes Theatre for 56 performances.

Firefly, The

Composer Rudolph Friml's first Broadway score and the beginning of his partnership with Otto Harbach who wrote the book and lyrics, and with whom he collaborated for 10 musicals. *The Firefly* opened at the Lyric theatre in New York on 2 December 1912, Friml got the job because Victor Herbert, the original choice of the composer could not get along with Emma Trentini who plays the role of Nina Corelli. As *The Firefly* begins, Geraldine Van Dare (Audrey Maple) is about to sail for Bermuda on her uncle's yacht in the company of her fiancé Jack Travers (Craig Campbell). To escape the clutches of her drunken father, Nina (Trentini), an Italian street singer who lives in New York, disguises herself as a boy and manoeuvres herself aboard. After the most elaborate and complicated plot schemes, and some expert tutorage from the musican Franz (Henry Vogel), she becomes Giannini, a famous prima donna, and, of course, marries Jack Travers. As usual with operetta, the score, and not the story, is the important item, and this score is regarded as one of the best of its kind. It included lovely songs such as 'When A Maid Comes Knocking At Your Door', 'Sympathy', 'Giannina Mia', 'Love Is Like A Firefly', 'In Sapphire Seas', and 'An American Beauty Rose'. The show ran for 120 performances - a decent total in the early part of the century - and was filmed in 1937. The Hollywood version had a different story which involved spies in Spain, and starred Jeanette MacDonald and Allan Jones, who sang the enormously popular 'The Donkey Serenade'.

Five Guys Named Moe

This show was playing a limited five-weeks engagement in October 1990 at the tiny Theatre Royal, Stratford East, in London when it was spotted by superstar impresario Cameron Mackintosh who was so impressed that he negotiated contracts on the spot, enabling the production to transfer to the Lyric Theatre in Shaftesbury Avenue in December of that year. The show, which was conceived and written by Clarke Peters, is a tribute to the jazz-bluesman Louis Jordan, who is sometimes cited as the 'musical father' of Chuck Berry and Bill Haley, and therefore, by inference, of rock 'n' roll itself. The story concerns a love-lorn central character, Nomax (Dig Wayne), drowning his sorrows in drink and listening to the blues on an old-fashioned radio. The apparatus explodes, and he is confronted by the five Moes - these sharp-suited, fast-talking characters from a Jordan song - who set about improving his attitude and putting him straight about women and love. The group consists of: Big Moe (Kenny Andrews), Little Moe (Paul J. Medford), No Moe (Peter Alex Newton), Eat Moe (Omar Okai), and Four-Eyed Moe (Clarke Peters). Nexus's education is delivered via song and dance routines, some of which he is allowed to participate in. At times during the show the story is temporarily dispensed with, and the audience is invited on stage, and led in a conga around the theatre and then through the exits during the interval. The 20 or so songs from the 40s and 50s, which were written by Jordan or are indelibly associated with him, are delivered joyously with lots of verve and attack. They include 'Saturday Night Fish Fry', 'Ain't Nobody Here But Us Chickens', 'Is You Is, Or Is You Ain't (Ma' Baby)', 'What's The Use Of Getting Sober?' ('When you're gonna get drunk again'), 'Look Out Sister', 'Brother Beware', 'Caldonia', 'It Must Be Jelly ('Cause Jam Don't Shake Like That)', and 'Dad Gum Your Hide, Boy'. *Five Guys Named Moe* won the 1991 Olivier Award for best entertainment and settled in for a long run. It celebrated its 1,000th performance in June 1993, proclaiming 'The Joint Never Stops Jumpin''. A Broadway production opened in April 1992, with Frank Rich, the most important critic in New York who has never been enamoured of Cameron Mackintosh's productions, describing the show derisively as 'a British tourist's view of a patch of black American pop music history'. However, it survived that initial onslaught and remained at the Eugene O'Neill Theatre for over a year, a total of 445 performances.

Flahooley

Four years after *Finian's Rainbow* its authors E.Y. 'Yip' Harburg and Fred Saidy came up with another piece of whimsy called *Flahooley* which opened on 14 May 1951 at the Broadhurst Theatre in New York, and, unlike that previous show, did not stay around for too long. The action takes place in Capsulanti, Indiana, USA at the business premises of B.G. Bigelo, Inc., manufactures of all manner of dolls, and specialists in novelty items such as exploding cigars and similar playthings. Sylvester (Jerome Courtland), one of the Company's puppet designers, is in love with Sandy (Barbara Cook), a fellow puppet operator. Sylvester has come up with a revolutionary new puppet, but, before he can unveil it, a mission from Arabia arrives at the factory with a problem. Their Aladdin's magic lamp no longer produces a genie; can B.G. Bigelow, Inc. repair it? They can. The new puppet is revealed, and named Flahooley: it chews gum, it reads comic books - and it laughs! B.G. Bigelow (Ernest Truex) is delighted, and puts it on the market, but disaster strikes. A competitor has already developed a cheaper version (industrial spies?), and Sylvester is dismayed – will he ever have enough money to marry Sandy? While the magic lamp is being mended, Flahooley's hand touches it, and the resulting genie, Abou Ben Atom (Irwin Corey), organizes the production of Flahooleys in such numbers that the market is saturated. The citizens of Capsulanti arrange a genie hunt, intending to burn every Flahooley they can find. The lamp is seized by Elsa Bulinger, the leader of the reactionary mob, but Abou escapes and decides to become a Santa Claus. Bigelow flies off on a magic carpet to marry Najla (Yma Sumac), one of the Arabian delegation. Harburg's books and lyrics always had a social and political edge, although they were never dull or boring, and, as this show was written at the height of the McCarthy witch-hunts in America, it was inevitable that the prevailing climate would be reflected in this work. All the usual targets such as politicians, big business - capitalism in general - were examined and satirized. The show's more conventional songs were written by Harburg and composer Sammy Fain (a prolific film composer, this was regarded as Fain's best score for the stage). Jerome Courtland and Barbara Cook, in her first Broadway role, introduced 'Here's To Your Illusions', 'Who Says There Ain't No Santa Claus?', 'The World Is Your Balloon', 'He's Only Wonderful', and Cook also had the tender 'Come Back, Little Genie'. Other Harburg-Fain numbers included 'The Springtime Cometh', 'You, Too, Can Be A Puppet', 'Jump, Little Chillun!', and 'Flahooley!'. The remainder of the songs - written especially for the four-octave range of Yma Sumac by Mosises Vivanco, were 'Birds/Enchantment', 'Najla's Lament', and Najla's Song Of Joy'. *Flahooley* was a charming piece, with an excellent cast - including the delightful Baird puppets - but it failed dismally, and closed after only 40 performances. A second version, entitled *Jollyanna*, with a cast that included Bobby Clark, Mitzi Gaynor, John Beal, and Biff McGuire, opened on 11 September 1952 at the Curran Theatre in San Francisco, but closed during the pre-Broadway tryout.

Flanders And Swann

The son of an actor father, and a mother who had been a concert-violinist before she married, Michael Flanders (b. 1 March 1922, London, England, d. 14 April 1975), was brought up in a musical household. He learned to play the clarinet and made his stage debut at the age of seven in a singing contest with *Uncle Mac's Minstrel Show*. At Westminster School in London, where Peter Ustinov was one of his classmates, he started to write and stage revues. His search for a pianist led him to Donald Swann, and

their first revue together was *Go To It*. At Oxford University in 1940 Flanders played in and directed several productions for the Dramatic Society and made his professional debut as Valentine in Shaw's *You Never Can Tell*, at the Oxford Playhouse. In 1943, while serving in the Royal Navy Volunteer Reserve, having survived the infamous convoys to Russia, he was struck down by poliomyelitis. Three years later he was discharged from hospital, in a wheelchair, and with a full beard which he retained for the rest of his life. Unable to resume a normal acting career, Flanders turned to writing and broadcasting. He contributed lyrics to several West End revues, in collaboration with Swann, including *Penny Plain* (1951), *Airs On A Shoestring* (1953) and *Fresh Airs* (1956). Flanders also appeared extensively on radio, and later, television, in programmes ranging from sports commentary to poetry readings, and including a spell of two years as chairman of *The Brains Trust*. His translation of Stravinsky's *Soldier's Tale* (with Kitty Black), became the standard English version, and his concert performance of it with Peter Ustinov and Sir Ralph Richardson was a surprise sell-out at the Royal Festival Hall in 1956. After successfully entertaining their friends at parties with their own songs, Flanders and Swann decided to perform professionally, so on New Years Eve 1956 they opened their own two-man show, *At The Drop Of A Hat*, at the intimate New Lindsey Theatre, Notting Hill, west London, moving three weeks later into the West End's Fortune Theatre. The show was a smash hit and ran for over three years. It is said that Princess Margaret attended a performance, and came back the following week with the Queen and the Duke of Edinburgh. With Flanders' urbane image contrasting with Swann's almost schoolboy enthusiasm, they introduced songs such as 'The Hippopotamus ('Mud, Mud, Glorious Mud')', 'Misalliance', 'A Gnu', and 'Madeira M'Dear?'. Two albums from the show were released; the earlier mono recording being preferable to the later stereo issue. In 1959 the show opened on Broadway, billed as 'An After-Dinner Farrago', and later toured the USA, Canada and the UK. In 1963 at the Haymarket Theatre, London, they presented a fully revised version entitled *At The Drop Of Another Hat*, which included songs such as 'The Gas-Man Cometh', 'First And Second Law' and 'Bedstead Men'. During 1964 and 1965 they toured Australia, New Zealand and Hong Kong, before returning to the West End in 1965, and yet again, to New York in the following year. Meanwhile, Flanders was still continuing with his other work, writing, broadcasting and theatrical speech recitals. He published *Creatures Great And Small*, a children's book of verses about animals and, together with Swann, released an album of animal songs entitled *The Bestiary Of Flanders And Swann*.

Michael Flanders

Flanders was awarded the OBE in 1964, and died in April 1975.

Albums: *At The Drop Of A Hat* (1957), *Bestiary Of Flanders And Swan* (1961), *At The Drop Of Another Hat* (1964), *A Review Of Revues* (1975), *Tried By Centre Court* (1977), *The Complete Flanders & Swann* (3 CD set 1991).

Flora, The Red Menace

A curious piece in some ways, this show is mainly notable for the first appearance on Broadway of the 19-years-old Liza Minnelli, although she had made her first New York stage appearance two years earlier, Off Broadway, in a revival of *Best Foot Forward*. The production also marked the Broadway debut of the composer John Kander and his lyricist Fred Ebb. Their subsequent enduring relationship with Minnelli would eventually reach its peak in 1972 with the film version of *Cabaret*. *Flora, The Red Menace* opened at New York's Alvin Theatre on 11 May 1965, with a book, by George Abbott and Robert Russell, which was based on Lester Atwell's novel, *Love Is Just Around The Corner*. It was set in the early 30s when America was deep in the Depression, and told of Flora (Liza Minnelli), a naive young girl, who, because of her affection for her boy friend, Harry Toukarian (Bob Dishy), joins the Communist Party. She never becomes a totally committed comrade - Charlotte (Cathryn Damon) is far more dedicated to the Red cause, and to Harry for a time - but he resists her advances, and he and Flora resume diplomatic (and affectionate) relations. The best thing about the whole production was the score. Minnelli had several outstanding numbers including the tender 'Dear Love', 'All I Need (Is One Good Break)', 'Knock Knock', and 'Sing Happy'. There was also 'Not Every Day Of The Week', 'Palamino Pal', 'Street Songs', and a few comedy items such as 'The Flame', 'Express Yourself', and 'Sign Here'. The show existed for 87 peformances mainly on the strength of Minnelli, who won the Tony Award for best actress. Somehow it seemed out of place in a Broadway season that included *Fiddler On The Roof*, *Do I Hear A Waltz?*, *I Had A Ball*, and *Golden Boy*. A revised version of *Flora, The Red Menace*, with a new book by Derek Thompson, was presented Off Broadway in 1987, and that version played the UK Cambridge Arts Theatre in 1992.

Floradora

This is the kind of show that was all the rage in London and New York as the 20th century dawned. It opened first at the Lyric Theatre in London on 11 November 1899. In Owen Hall's book, *Floradora* is an island in the Phillipines, and also the name of the perfume that is manufactured there by a rich American, Cyrus Gilfain (Charles E. Stevens). The

complicated romantic entanglements that take place on the island, and in a castle in Wales - of all places - involve Angela Gilfain (Kate Cutler), Lady Holyrood (Ada Reeve), Dolores (Evie Greene), Frank Abercoed (Melville Stewart), and Arthur Donegal (Edgar Stevens). A private investigator, Arthur Tweedlepunch (Willie Edouin), is instrumental in unravelling the whole thing and making sure that all the lovers find the right and proper partners. The show's score was a collaboration between the composer Leslie Stuart, who also wrote some of the lyrics along with Ernest Boyd-Jones and Paul Rubens. Extra lyrics were provided by Alfred Murray and Frank A. Clement. The production, which ran for an incredible (for the time) 455 performances, attracted a great deal of attention mainly because of its Floradora Girls, a dainty sextette of parasol-twirling young ladies, accompanied by an equal number of straw-hatted young gentlemen. Their speciality song, 'Tell Me Pretty Maiden' ('Are there any more at home like you?'), swept the country, and, when the show reached the USA in 1900, the same number became popular all over again through recordings by Byron G. Harlan, Joe Belmont and the Floradora Girls; and Harry Macdonough with Grace Spencer. *Floradora* did even better in New York than in London, and gave 553 performances at the New Casino Theatre. The show's score contained several other popular items which became the hits of the day on both sides of the Atlantic, including 'I Want to Be A Military Man', 'The Silver Star Of Love', 'When I Leave Town, 'The Shade Of The Palm', 'Tact', 'When You're A Millionaire', and 'The Island Of Love'. There were London revivals in 1915 and 1931, and New York audiences saw the show again in 1920 when it ran for 120 performances.

Flower Drum Song

Most of Richard Rodgers and Oscar Hammerstein's blockbuster musicals were adapted from existing works, and this show was based on a novel by Chin Y. Lee. It opened at the St. James Theatre in New York on 1 December 1958, and was the only Broadway show that Gene Kelly directed. Hammerstein's book, written in collaboration with Joseph Fields, is set in San Francisco's Chinatown, and deals in a warm-hearted way with the problems of the Chinese, the Chinese-Americans, and their Americanized children. The difficulties posed by the various generation-gaps and cultures are sympathetically presented in a story of mail-order brides, marriage contracts, and fiendishly clever plot lines, resulting in the inevitable wedding ceremony. Mei Li (Miyoshi Umeki) is the lady who was delivered via by the US Mail, but she is not the bride. Linda Low (Pat Suzuki) is the lucky married lady, and she has one of the show's most popular numbers, 'I

Enjoy Being A Girl', as well as the duet, 'Sunday', with her groom, Sammy Fong (Larry Blyden). The rest of Rodgers and Hammerstein's lovely score included 'You Are Beautiful', 'A Hundred Million Miracles', 'I Am Going To Like It Here', 'Like A God', 'Chop Suey', 'Don't Marry Me', 'Grant Avenue', 'Love Look Away', 'Gliding Through My Memories', and 'The Other Generation'. Juanita Hall played Madame Laing 'an enthusiastic candidate for American citizenship'. She also also starred in Rodgers and Hammerstein's film of South Pacific which was released in the same year as Flower Drum Song began its Broadway run of 600 performances. The popular vocalist Anita Ellis was also in the show's cast. She played a nightclub singer, and had the novelty number 'Fan Tan Fannie'. That scene, and the rest of the production, was choreographed by Carol Haney, who introduced 'Hernado's Hideaway' in The Pajama Game. The 1960 London production of Flower Drum Song had different principal cast members, but Miyoshi Umeki recreated her role for the 1961 film version, which also starred Nancy Kwan.

Flying Colors

The American Depression was on the point of closing when this revue opened at the Imperial Theatre in New York on 15 September 1932. With music by Arthur Schwartz and lyrics and sketches by Howard Dietz, who also directed, this was obviously from same line that had produced The Band Wagon, Three's A Crowd and The Little Show. The talented cast, an ideal mixture of actors, dancers, comedians, singers, (and one harmonica virtuoso) included Clifton Webb, Charles Butterworth, Tamara Geva, Patsy Kelly, Philip Loeb, Vilma and Buddy Ebsen, Larry Adler, Imogen Coca, and Monette Moore. All the songs were of high quality, but there were three special numbers, 'Alone Together', 'Louisiana Hayride', and the exuberant 'A Shine On Your Shoes', which were destined to endure. The rest of the score included 'Two-Faced Woman', 'A Rainy Day', 'Mother Told Me So', 'Fatal Fascination', 'Meine Klein Akrobat', and 'Smokin' Reefers'. This smart, witty show which dealt with the recent hard times in America, and looked forward to better days (and politicians), was produced by Max Gordon and choreographed by Albertina Rasch. Flying Colors stayed around for a decent run of 188 performances, and Buddy Ebsen, a talented hoofer at the time, went on much later to star in the legendary television series The Beverley Hillbillies.

Flying High

Soon after its opening at the Apollo Theatre in New York on 3 March 1930, the celebrated newspaper columnist Walter Winchell dubbed this show, 'The Lindbergh of musical comedies'. That was a reference to its theme which reflected the American public's fascination with the pioneering flights of the late 20s in general, and Charles Lindbergh's 1927 record solo flight to Paris in particular. The creative crew for this trip, composer Ray Henderson, and lyricists Buddy De Sylva and Lew Brown, who also wrote the book with John McGowan, had already had some mileage from other US fads and fancies in previous shows such as Good News! (football and dancing), Hold Everything! (boxing), and Follow Thru (golf). Apparently, the plot was not complete until the show went into rehearsal, but it eventually turned out to a story about an aeroplane mechanic, Rusty Krause (Bert Lahr), who carelessly takes to the air in a plane that was supposed to be piloted by Tod Addison (Oscar Shaw). Not only does he take off, but he stays up there long enough to create a world endurance record simply because he does not know how to get down again. Todd does get airborne himself, but is forced to make a parachute jump. In the interests of of the show's romantic scenario he lands on a New York roof belonging to the lovely Eileen Cassidy (Grace Brinkley). Kate Smith, the powerful singer, was also in the cast, and had a show-stopper with 'Red Hot Chicago'. The rest of the typically De Sylva ballad and Henderson score - lively and entertaining, with the occasional classy balled - included 'I'll Know Him', 'Thank Your Father', 'Good For You - Bad for Me', 'Without Love', 'Mrs. Krauses's Blue-Eyed Baby Boy', and 'Wasn't It Beautiful While It Lasted?' The show was a big hit and ran for 357 performances, mainly duet to Lahr's hilarious antics. He starred with Charlotte Greenwood and Pat O'Brien in the 1931 film version.

Follies

Sometimes regarded as one of Stephen Sondheim's 'more accessible' shows, Follies opened at the Winter Garden in New York on 4 April 1971. James Goldman's book set the action at a stage reunion of ex-performers who had once appeared in the legendary Weismann Follies (obviously an allusion to the Ziegfeld Follies). The basic story concerns two ex-showgirls from the Follies who have both married stage-door-Johnnies 30 years ago. Phyllis and Ben Stone (Alexis Smith and John McMartin) and Sally and Buddy Plummer (Dorothy Collins and Gene Nelson) come to the reunion and, by looking back over the years and confronting ghosts of their former selves, are able to make adjustments to their present unhappy lives. A great deal of Sondheim's score, which contained some 22 songs, was pastiche of the songwriting greats such as Irving Berlin, Jerome Kern, Sigmund Romberg, Cole Porter, and De Sylva, Brown And Henderson - including 'Losing My Mind', 'The Story Of Lucy And Jessie', 'One More

Kiss', 'Loveland', 'Beautiful Girls', and 'Broadway Baby', but there were several other fascinating and intriguing items such as 'Who's That Woman?' (often referred to as 'the mirror number'), 'Ah, Paris!', 'Could I Leave You?', 'Buddy's Eyes', 'The God-Why-Don't-You-Love-Me-Blues', 'Rain On the Roof', 'Too Many Mornings', 'You're Gonna Love Tomorrow', and the survival hymn for all the old troupers, 'I'm Still Here', which was sung by the 40s film star Yvonne De Carlo in the role of Carlotta Campion. *Follies* was a spectacular and glamorous production, and opinions vary widely as to why it was not successful. Sondheim himself is said to feel that there were too many pastiche numbers, while co-director and choreographer Michael Bennett blamed the book. In any event, the show ran for 522 performances, and collected the kudos with the New York Drama Critics Award for best musical, and Tonys for best score, director, choreographer, scenic design, costumes, lighting, and actress (Alexis Smith). *Follies In Concert* with the New York Philharmonic played two nights at the Lincoln Centre in New York in September 1985 with an all-star cast which included Barbara Cook, George Hearn, Elaine Stritch, Carol Burnett, Lee Remick, and Betty Comden and Adolph Green. The fully staged 1987 London production, which was streamlined and extensively re-written, starred Julia McKenzie, Diana Rigg, Lynda Baron, Dolores Gray, Daniel Massey and Adele Leigh, and ran for 18 months.

Follow A Star

Although the music and lyrics for this piece were by Vivan Ellis and Douglas Furber, this was by no means a typical Ellis show. The reason was the dominating presence in the cast of the American entertainer Sophie Tucker. It was Tucker's second appearance in the London theatre, (as opposed to music halls and clubs), and her first book musical (she had played in the revue *Round In 50* in 1922). This time she brought along her two regular songwriters, Jack Yellen and Ted Shapiro, just in case Ellis and Furber did not come up with her particular kind of goods. Ironically, and much to Ellis's delight, the hit of the show, and the number which became so popular that she had to close with it, was 'If Your Kisses Can't Hold The Man You Love', which had music by Ellis and a lyric by Yellen. *Follow A Star* opened at the Winter Garden Theatre in London on 17 September 1930, with a book by Furber and Dion Titheradge. It was directed and choreographed by Jack Hulbert who also played a leading role. Hulbert had appeared in so many successful shows with his wife Cicely Courtneidge, but this time she had temporarily deserted musical comedy for the revue *Folly to Be Wise*, and left Hulbert to deal with Tucker, whose role in the show was as a cabaret singer (Georgia

Madison) who is elevated to better things when she inherits a title and becomes Lady Bohun. Jack Hulbert played Bobby Hilary, the lover of Georgia's daughter, Merrie Boon (Betty Davies). Ellis's music was as charming and delightful as ever in songs such as 'Don't Wear Your Heart On Your Sleeve', 'The First Weekend In June', 'The English Gentlemen, and 'You Do The Singing'. Tucker's numbers included 'Follow A Star', 'I Can Never Think Of The Words', and 'That's Where The South Begins', but they were cut when she left the show early in December ('If Your Kisses Can't Hold The Man You Love' stayed in) to be replaced by Maisie Gay when it reopened later in the month. The revised production had a disappointing run, closing after only 118 performances, and losing a good deal of its investment.

Follow That Girl

A kind of hectic musical tour of London, this show was adapted by composer Julian Slade and Dorothy Reynolds from their 1952 production, *Christmas In King Street*. It opened at the Vaudeville Theatre in London on 17 March 1960. The light and frothy story concerned Victoria (Susan Hampshire), whose parents, Mr. and Mrs. Gilchrist (James Cairness and Patricia Routledge), want her to marry one of two rich businessmen, Wilberforce (Robert MacBaine) or Tancred (Philip Guard). She gives them the slip, and, after a long and hectic chase, is finally captured by a policeman, Tom (Peter Gilmore), who takes her into custody, and marries her. Slade and Reynolds's score is generally regarded as among their very best work. The songs included 'Tra La La', 'Follow That Girl', 'Life Must Go On', 'Waiting for Our Daughter', 'Shopping In Kensington', 'Solitary Stranger', 'Lovely Meeting You At Last', 'I'm Away', 'Where Shall I Find My Love?', 'Three Victorian Mermaids', 'One, Two, Three, One', 'Doh Ray Me', and 'Taken For A Ride'. Gilmore and Hampshire both went on to television super-stardom, he in *The Onedin Line*, and she in *The Forsyth Saga* and *The Pallisers*. Grazina Frame, who was also in the cast of *Follow That Girl*, had her moment of glory when she starred in Lionel Bart's *Blitz* in 1962. In spite of its fun story and quality score, *Follow That Girl* received mixed notices, but had a reasonable run of 211 performances. Hardly in the same league as the same authors' *Salad Days* (2,283), but then that sort of success usually only comes along once in a lifetime.

Follow The Girls

A big wartime hit on both sides of the Atlantic, first saw the light of day at the New Century Theatre in New York on 8 April 1944. Guy Bolton, together with Eddie Davis and Fred Thompson, wrote the book which concerns Bubbles LaMarr (Gertrude

Neilson in her only book musical), a burlesque stripper whose career takes off in a big way at the Spotlight Club, a sanctuary for servicemen in Long Island, USA. Her boyfriend, Goofy Gale (Jackie Gleason), cannot get in to see her because, physically speaking, the army just does not want him. As this is a Bolton book (he wrote the jolly Princess Theatre japes with P.G. Wodehouse), and Gleason is also involved, Goofy complicates the issue by stealing, not an admiral or a colonel's uniform, but one that is worn by a Wave. The show's setting gave ample opportunites for lots of singing and dancing, and some of the supporting characters had 'Damon Runyon'-type names such as Dinky Riley and Spud Doolittle. Neilson made a big impression every night with 'I Wanna Get Married', and the rest of the score included 'You're Perf', 'Twelve O'clock And All's Well', 'Follow The Girls', 'I'm Gonna Hang My Hat', 'Out for No Good', and 'Tomorrow Will Be Yesterday Tomorrow'. *Follow the Girls* ran for over two years, a total of 882 performances, in New York, and played 572 shows at His Majesty's Theatre in London, where the popular local comedian Arthur Askey starred as Goofy, with Evelyn Dall as Bubbles. Another member of the West End Cast was Wendy Toye, who also directed the piece. She went on to become one of the British theatre's most admired and respected directors.

Follow Thru

Opening at New York's 46th Street theatre on 9 January 1929, and sub-titled 'A Musical Slice Of Country Life', this was another in a series of sporty shows (*Good News!* and *Hold Everything!* were about football and boxing) that songwriters De Sylva, Brown And Henderson had such success with in the 20s. *Follow Thru*'s book, by De Sylva and Laurence Schwab, turned the spotlight on golf. The show was the first big break on Broadway for comedian Jack Haley, who made a career out of playing shy diffident characters who are usually pursued by pretty women. This time he is the object of affection for Angie Howard (Zelma O'Neal), and when they do get together they give the evening a big lift with their version of one of the composers' all-time standards, 'Button Up Your Overcoat' ('Eat an apple ev'ry day/Get to bed by three/Take good care of yourself/You belong to me.'). Meanwhile, back on the greens and in the locker-room, Lora Moore (Irene Delroy) and Ruth Van Horn (Madeline Cameron) are locked in combat - for the country club's women's championship, and the chance to go round the course forever with the handsome, good guy, with a low-handicap, Jerry Downs (John Barker). Lora comes out top in both events. Another winner here, who gave the show a big lift, was 19 years old tap-dancer Eleanor Powell in her first book

musical, following her Broadway debut in *The Optimists* revue in 1928. She went on to Hollywood fame in the 30s and 40s. De Sylva, Brown And Henderson's songs, which were so typical of the happy-go-lucky 20s period, included 'My Lucky Star', 'You Wouldn't Fool Me, Would You?', 'I Want To Be Bad', 'Then I'll Have Time For You', and, of course, the smash-hit 'Button Up Your Overcoat', which became all the rage through recordings by Helen Kane, Paul Whiteman, Fred Waring's Pennsylvanians, and Ruth Etting. The show sang and danced its happy way to an impressive 403 performances in New York, and the London edition, *Follow Through*, which starred Leslie Henson, Ivy Tresmond, and Elsie Randolph, added another 148. Jack Haley and Zelma O'Neal recreated their original roles for the 1930 film version.

Folly To Be Wise

This popular revue, devised by Jack Hulbert and Paul Murray, opened on 8 January 1931 at the Piccadilly Theatre in London. Hulbert did not appear in it himself - at the time he was in the Vivian Ellis musical comedy, *Follow A Star*. His wife, Cicely Courtneidge was present, though, and right at the top of her form. She was joined in the cast by Nelson Keys and Ivor McLaren, together with a couple of visitors from the USA, Mary Eaton and J. Albert Traherne. The music and lyrics were provided by a variety of songwriters, including Vivan Ellis, Noel Gay, Harry Graham, Bert Kalmar, Harry Ruby, Herman Hupfield, and Dion Titheradge. Probably the best-known song to emerge from the show, at least as far as British audiences are concerned, was 'All The King's Horses' (Noel Gay and Harry Graham), which was given the full Courtneidge treatment, and became extremely popular for artists such as Jack Hylton And His Orchestra, The New Mayfair Orchestra conducted by Ray Noble, The Big Four, and, much later, Dennis Lotis with the Ted Heath Orchestra. Some of the other numbers included 'Looking For A Sunbeam', 'Three Little Words' (Kalmar-Ruby), and 'Sing Something Simple' (Hupfield). The show ran for 257 performances, which, for this kind of production in the days of general economic unrest in Britain during the early 30s, was considered to be a more than satisfactory state of affairs.

Forbidden Broadway

An annual revue conceived by Gerard Alessandrini, who also writes his own, sometimes hilarious, lyrics to popular show tunes in an effort to lampoon everything and anyone who dares to appear on the New York and London musical stage. The show was first performed as a cabaret revue at Palsson's Supper Club in New York on 15 January 1982. It moved Off Broadway in the following year, and settled in the

125-seater Theatre East. Annual editions have followed. Alessandrini's early targets included *Annie* and *Evita* (Andrew Lloyd Webber and Tim Rice were like manna from heaven to this revue), along with Broadway icons such as Ethel Merman, Mary Martin, Stephen Sondheim, and Tommy Tune. Later, highlights included 'The Ladies Who Screech' by 'Elaine Stritch'; 'My Souvenir Things', sung by 'Cameron Mackintosh' as he flogs t-shirts and coffee mugs; 'I've Strained In Vain To Train Madonna's Brain' (a hint of My Fair Lady?); 'I Get A Kick Out Of Me' by 'Patti LuPone'; shades of On The Town, and a dig at the celebrated director-choreographer Jerome Robbins, in 'Jerome, Jerome, I'm A Hell Of A Guy'; 'Julie Andrews's' 'I Couldn't Hit That Note' (to the tune of 'I Could Have Danced All Night'); a chandelier and a helicopter, representing *The Phantom Of The Opera* and *Miss Saigon*, in the merry duet 'Anywhere You Can Fly, I Can Fly Higher' (from Irving Berlin's 'Anything You Can Do, I Can Do Better'); and another stab at Lloyd Webber in which a Michael Ball clone converts the powerful ballad, 'Love Changes Everything' (from *Aspects Of Love*) into 'I, I Sleep With Everyone'. Michael Crawford, Barbra Streisand, and Broadway revivals such as *The Most Happy Fella*, *Guys And Dolls*, and the more contemporary shows, especially *Les Miserables*, all get the treatment. The 1992 edition presented some of the 'Best' of the last decade, and in the following year the show was still going strong - blessed with four 'Carol Channings' (only two of which were female). In 1989, a slightly Anglicized version ran for a short time at London's Fortune Theatre, and a similar production, *Forbidden Pittsburgh*, which was not associated with Alessandrini, reigned in that city in the late 80s. Some of the extremely talented cast members in the original have included Brad Ellis, Roxie Lucas, Susanne Blakeslee, Jeff Lyons, Michael McGrath, Mary Denise Bentley, Toni DiBuono, Brad Oscar, Craig Wells, and Dorothy Kiara.

Forever Plaid

This 'Heavenly Musical Hit' was greeted with rave reviews from every quarter when it opened Off Broadway at Steve McGraw's on 20 May 1990. Written, directed and choreographed by Stuart Ross, it concerns the return to earth of four aspiring crooners, the members of a close-harmony group called Forever Plaid. The guys were on their way to collect four tartan tuxedos in time for their first big gig, when the vehicle in which they were travelling collided with a school bus full of Catholic teenagers on their way to see the Beatles' debut on the *Ed Sullivan Show*. No Catholic casualties, but the Plaids were killed instantly. That was back in 1964, but 26 years later (and several times a week subsequently), 'through the power of Harmony and the expanding

holes in the Ozone layer combined with the positions of the Planets and all that Astro-Technical stuff, the Plaids return to perform the show they never got to do in life'. The rejuvenated quartet consisted of Jinx (Stan Chandler), Smudge (David Engel), Sparky (Jason Graae), and Frankie (Guy Stroman). Together with a bass player and pianist, they pay a joyous tribute to the close-harmony groups of the 50s, such as the Four Lads, the Four Preps, and the Four Aces, via a string of potently nostalgic numbers such as 'Three Coins In The Fountain', 'Love Is A Many Splendoured Thing', 'Catch A Falling Star', 'Chain Gang', 'Magic Moments', 'Sixteen Tons', 'Heart And Soul', and some 20-odd more. Perry Como comes in for the treatment as well. There is also a witty and irreverent send-up of the Beatles (the indirect cause of the Plaids' premature retirement) in 'She Loves You - Yes Siree'. Showered with unanimously ecstatic reviews ('37 out 37') along the lines of 'A high octane tour-de-force' and 'Screamingly funny! Entirely enchanting, utterly entertaining, awesome!', *Forever Plaid* settled in for a long New York run, and, during the next three years, repeated its success in 23 US cities. In September 1993 the show opened in London complete with the original cast except for Sparky who was played by Larry Raben. At the West End Apollo Theatre one aspect of the audience participation consisted of a minute's silence, while one brave soul who went up on to the stage was rewarded with a pack of plaid dental floss.

Forty-Five Minutes From Broadway

You can get to New Rochelle, New York, in forty-five minutes from the 'great white way', and that's the location George M. Cohan had in mind when he wrote the music, book, and lyrics for this show which opened at the New Amsterdam Theatre on 1 January 1906. As the curtain rises, Tom Bennet (Donald Brian) is expecting to inherit a great deal of money from his recently deceased millionaire uncle, which will enable to marry the actress, Flora Dora Dean (Lois Ewell), and keep her in a style to which she is rapidly becoming accustomed. However, the important last will and testament is missing - until Tom's secretary, the cocky Kid Burns (Victor Moore), finds it, and discovers that all the money has been left to the millionaire's housekeeper, Mary Jane Jenkins (Fay Templeton). Mary and the Kid fall in love, but, when he shows her the will, she thinks he wants her for the money. Perish the thought: it has never crossed the Kid's mind, and he tells her so in no uncertain terms. He would never contemplate marrying someone with that much money - so Mary eventually tears up the will. Cohan's score contained three of his most successful songs: 'Mary's A Grand Old Name', 'So Long Mary', and the title number. There was also 'Gentlemen Of The Press' and 'I

Want to Be a Popular Millionaire'. Moore, who played Kid Burns in the show, played him again in the 1907 musical *Talk Of New York*, before going on to a long and successful Hollywood career. When *Forty-Five Minutes From Broadway* was revived in New York 1912 (at the Cohan Theatre), Cohan himself took the lead. The show's initial run of only 90 performances gives no indication as to how innovative and different Cohan's ideas were. When this show was presented, America was still on a diet of European operetta, none of which had the flair or showmanship that this multi-talented personality displayed.

Fosse, Bob

b. Robert Louis Fosse, 23 June 1927, Chicago, Illinois, USA, d. 23 September 1987, Washington DC, USA. A director, choreographer, dancer, and actor for films and stage, Fosse was renowned particularly for his innovative and spectacular staging, with the emphasis very firmly on the exhilarating dance sequences. He studied ballet, tap and acrobatic dance from an early age, and, while still a youngster, performed with a partner as the Riff Brothers in vaudeville and burlesque houses. After graduating from high school in 1945, he spent two years in the US Navy before moving to New York and studying acting at the American Theatre Wing. He then toured in the chorus of various productions before making his Broadway debut as a dancer in the revue *Dance Me A Song* (1950). He worked on television and in theatres and clubs for a time until Hollywood beckoned and he moved to the west coast to appear in three films, *Give A Girl A Break*, *The Affairs Of Dobie Gillis*, and *Kiss Me, Kate* (1953). On his return to New York, he got his big break when author and director George Abbott hired him as a choreographer for *The Pajama Game* (1954). The show was a massive hit, and Fosse was much in demand - for a time at least. He met Gwen Verdon while working on *Damn Yankees* in 1955, and they were married in 1960. He choreographed *Bells Are Ringing* in 1956, and worked with Verdon again on *New Girl In Town* a year later. From then on, with the exception of *How To Succeed In Business Without Really Trying* (1961), he directed his shows as well as staging the dancing. Fosse's dual role is considered by critics to be a major factor in the success of highly successful productions such as *Redhead* (1959), *Little Me* (1962), *Sweet Charity* (1966), *Pippin* (1972), *Chicago* (1975) and *Dancin'* (1978). All the time he was back and forth to Hollywood, working on films such as *My Sister Eileen* (1955), *The Pajama Game* (1957), and *Damn Yankees* (1958), all three of which were well-received. However, *Sweet Charity* (1968), which Fosse controlled completely in his role as director and choreographer, was hammered by many critics for Shirley MacLaine's over-the-top performance, and particularly for the director's self-indulgent cinematography with its looming closeups, zooms, blurred focus effects. Fosse was in the wilderness for some time, but all was forgiven four years later when *Cabaret*, starring Liza Minnelli and Joel Grey, won eight Academy Awards, one of which went to Fosse. It was a box-office smash, and Fosse also satisfied most of the purists by confining the dance sequences to appropriate locations such as beer garden and a nightclub, rather than flooding the streets of Berlin with terpsichorean tourists. In the early 70s Fosse was applauded for his direction of *Lenny*, a film biography of the comedian Lennie Bruce, which starred Dustin Hoffman. In the light of Fosse's recent heart problems, his record as a workaholic, and his life-long obsesssion with perfection, many observers thought that *All That Jazz* (1979) was intended to be Fosse's own film biography with it's ghoulish, self-indulgent examination of life and death. However, no one denied the brilliance of the dance routines or the outstanding performance of Roy Schneider in the leading role. In 1983 Fosse wrote and directed his last movie, *Star 80*, which also had a lurid, tragic theme. Three years later, he wrote, staged, and choreographed his final Broadway musical, *Big Deal* - which definitely was not. Neither was it a fitting end to a brilliant career in which Fosse had created some of the most imaginative and thrilling dance routines ever seen on Broadway or in Hollywood - and won eight Tony Awards in the process. In 1987 he revived one of his most successful shows, *Sweet Charity*, and died shortly before the curtain went up on the night of 23 September.

Four Musketeers, The

Over the years, Alexander Dumas's famous story of The Three Musketeers has turned up in many forms on stage, television, and at least five films. This comedy musical, which opened at the Theatre Royal, Drury Lane in London on 5 December 1967, gave the highly experienced English writer, Michael Pertwee, the opportunity to turn the legend upside down. In Pertwee's book, the dashing and fearless D'Artagnan (Harry Secombe), is turned into 'Neddy' D'Artagna - a country bumpkin, an accident-prone figure, whose bravest deeds are accomplished purely by chance. His compatriots, portrayed here as womanising sots, were obviously recruited from some of Britains' top low-brow comedy talent, and included Porthos (Jeremy Lloyd), Athos (Glyn Owen) Aramis (John Junkin), with Kenneth Connor as (King Louis XIII). In complete contrast, Elizabeth Larner, whose thrilling voice had last been heard in the West End when she played Guinevere in *Camelot* (1964), was this time cast as Milady. Obviously, the whole affair was an attempt to repeat the success of *Pickwick*, four years earlier, but Laurie Johnson and Herbert

Kretzmer's score did not provide Secombe with anything nearly as powerful as 'If I Ruled the World', although its pleasant score did contain songs such as 'A Little Bit Of Glory', 'Think Big', 'What Love Can Do', 'Masquerade', There Comes A Time', 'Nobody's Changing Places With Me', 'Strike While The Iron Is Hot', 'If You Are Looking For A Girl', 'Got A Lot Of Love To Give', 'Give Me A Man's Life', and 'There's A New Face In The Old Town'. The critics did not like it much, and despite a decent run of over a year, a total of 462 performances, *The Four Musketeers* is reported to have lost much of its investment. Herbert Kretzmer, the journalist and lyricist, had his greatest success 20 years later, with *Les Misérables*.

Free As Air

Julian Slade and Dorothy Reynolds's follow-up to their 1954 mega-hit *Salad Days*, opened at London's Savoy Theatre on 6 June 1957 - at a time when *Salad Days*, itself, had nearly another three years to run. This musical play was set on the island of Terhou, a location the authors had based on Sark, one of the Channel Islands situated off the north coast of France. A somewhat philosophical piece, it told the story of the beautiful and wealthy Geraldine Melford (Gillian Lewis), who escapes from the press (and a persistant and unwelcome lover), and settles on this isolated island where she finally finds true happiness with one of the residents, Albert Postumous (John Trevor). Along the way (and in line with the play's 'back-to-nature approach') she also foils the attempts of the sophisticated Jack Amersham (Gerald Harper) and the hard-nosed newspaper reporter (Josephine Tewson) to bring 'progress and civilization' to the island. Also in the cast were Michael Aldridge, who played the Lord Paul Postumous, Dorothy Reynolds, Patricia Bredin, and Leonard Rossiter, who became a household name in British television situation comedies such as *Rising Damp* and *The Fall And Rise Of Reginald Perrin*. As usual, Julian Slade and Dorothy Reynolds came up with a delightful and elegant score, the highlight of which was probably the charming 'Let The Grass Grow', sung by Michael Aldridge with two of the islanders, played by Roy Godfrey and Howard Goorney. The other songs included 'I'm Up Early', 'I've Got My Feet On The Ground', 'A Man From the Mainland', 'Nothing But Sea And Sky', 'Free As Air', 'The Girl From London', 'I'd Like To Be Like You', 'We're Holding Hands', and 'Terhou'. *Free As Air* closed on 7 June 1958 after a run of 417 performances, proving that there was still a place in the theatre for the home-grown product, despite the current popularity of imported American shows such as *My Fair Lady*, *Bells Are Ringing*, *Where's Charley?* - and in December 1958 - *West Side Story*.

Friml, Rudolph

b. 8 December 1879, Prague, Bohemia, d. 12 November 1972, Hollywood, California, USA. An important composer who helped to perpetuate the romantic operetta-style of musical which was so popular in America at the turn of the century. After studying at Prague University, Friml toured Europe and America as a concert pianist and settled in the US in 1906. As a composer his first opportunity came when he took over from Victor Herbert on the score for *The Firefly* (1912) from which came 'Gionnina Mia' and 'Sympathy'. His collaborator for that show was Otto Harbach, and the two men worked together on a further nine productions. Throughout his career Friml's other lyricists and librettists included P.G. Wodehouse, Herbert Reynolds, Harold Atteridge, Rida Johnson Young, Oscar Hammerstein II, Brian Hooker, Clifford Grey, Dailey Paskman, Edward Clark, Chisholm Cushing, and Rowland Leigh. He composed the music for some of the most popular songs of the time in a list of shows which includes *High Jinks* ('The Bubble'; 'Love's Own Kiss'; 'Not Now But Later'), *The Peasant Girl* ('Love Is Like A Butterfly'; 'Listen, Dear'; 'And The Dream Came True'), *Katinka* ('Allah's Holiday'; 'I Want to Marry A Male Quartet'; 'Katinka'), *You're In Love* ('I'm Only Dreaming'; 'You're In Love'), *Glorianna* ('My Climbing Rose'; 'Toodle-oo'), *Sometime* ('Sometime'; 'Keep On Smiling') *Tumble Inn* ('Snuggle And Dream'; 'I've Told My Love'), *The Little Whopper* ('You'll Dream And I'll Dream'; ''Round The Corner'), *June Love* ('June Love'; 'The Flapper And The Vamp'; 'Don't Keep Calling Me Dearie'), *Ziegfeld Follies Of 1921* ('Bring Back My Blushing Rose'; 'Every Time I Hear The Band Play'), *The Blue Kitten* ('When I Waltz With You'; 'Cutie'; 'Blue Kitten Blues'), *Cinders* ('Belle Of The Bronx'; 'I'm Simply Mad About The Boys'), *Rose-Marie* ('Rose-Marie'; 'Indian Love Call'; 'Totem Tom-Tom'; 'Song Of The Mounties'), *The Vagabond King* ('Only A Rose'; 'Song Of The Vagabonds'; 'Some Day'), *The Wild Rose* ('Brown Eyes'; 'One Golden Hour'), *No Foolin'* ('Wasn't It Nice?'; 'Florida, The Moon And You'), *The Three Musketeers* ('March Of The Musketeers'; 'Ma Belle'; 'Queen Of My Heart'; 'Heart Of Mine'), *The White Eagle* ('Gather The Rose'; 'Give Me One Hour'), *Luana* ('My Bird of Paradise'; 'Aloha'), and *Music Hath Charms* (1934) ('My Heart Is Yours'; 'Sweet Fool'). In the lavish 1935 film version of Friml's first show, *The Firefly*, Allan Jones had a big hit with 'The Donkey Serenade' which was adapted from Friml's composition 'Chansonette', a piece he had originally written for the *Ziegfeld Follies Of 1923*. Some of his other shows were filmed and he also wrote the music for the 1947 movie *Northwest Outpost*. Friml's last two shows, *Luana* and *Music Hath Charms*, only ran for some 20-

Rudolph Friml

odd performances each and he appeared unable or unwilling to adapt his music to the ever-growing American-style of musical comedy, although he remained active in his later years and appeared frequently on US television.

From A Jack To A King

With a title borrowed from Ned Miller's 1963 hit record, *From A Jack To A King* opened in London's West End on 20 July 1992 at the Ambassador's Theatre, following a run at the tiny Boulevard Theatre in Soho. Bob Carlton's rock 'n' roll musical spoof of Shakespeare's *Macbeth*, followed his tremendous success in 1989 with *Return To The Forbidden Planet*, a rock version of *The Tempest*. In this show, Eric Glamis (Matthew Devitt) is a stand-in drummer for the Coronets, a band run by Duke Box (Christian Roberts). He aspires to replace the megastar lead singer Terry King (an arrogant Elvis Presley impersonation by Robert Dallas). Goaded by his lover, Queenie (Allison Harding), Glasmis tinkers with the King's motorbike ('Is this a spanner I see before me?') with fatal results. He gets the gig, though, and experiences (temporary) glory, but subsequent disillusionment. Large extracts, and sometimes complete speeches and scenes, are extracted from, not only *Macbeth*, but other works by the Bard, such as *Hamlet* and *Romeo And Juliet*. These are absorbed into the story, which is punctuated with lots of classic songs such as 'Shakin' All Over', 'You've Lost That Lovin' Feelin', 'Keep On Running', 'Leader Of The Pack', 'Stepping Stone'. Unfortunately for Carlton, the show arrived in London at a time when audiences were already being saturated with the old songs in shows such as *Good Rockin' Tonite*, *Buddy*, *The Cotton Club*, *Five Guys Named Moe* - and his own *Return To The Forbidden Planet* - and this may well have been the reason why *From A Jack To A King* was unable to stay around for longer than 202 performances.

Funny Face

When producers Alex A. Aarons and Vincent Freedley built the Alvin Theatre in New York, they each gave the project just a small part of their names ('Al' and 'Vin'), but a great deal of their money. Some of that money had been earned from George and Ira Gershwin's shows such as *Oh, Kay!*, *Tip-Toes*, and *Lady, Be Good*, and now there was more to be made from *Funny Face*, the Gershwins' latest offering, and the first presentation at their new theatre on 2 November 1927. The show's title had originally been *Smarty*, but a change of name was only one of a series of measures that were taken when the production was clearly in trouble during its pre-Broadway tryout. Robert Benchley, the renowned American humorist, and co-writer of the book with Fred Thompson, was replaced by Paul Gerard Smith; several songs were dropped, and five more added; and Victor Moore, who, for 20 years, had been one of Broadway and Hollywood's much-loved bumbling clowns, joined the party. Moore plays one of the two comic burglars caught up in a story of mistakes and mayhem. Frankie Wynne (Adele Astaire) is the ward of the autocratic Jimmie Reeve (Fred Astaire). She persuades her aviator boyfriend, Peter Thurston (Allen Kearns), to retrieve an her incriminating diary that belongs to her, from Jimmie's wall safe, but the silly boy comes away with a bracelet instead. This act of carelessness on his part sets off a mad chase that takes the assembled cast to exotic locations such as Lake Wapatog, New Jersey, and then on to the Paymore Hotel and the Two-Million Dollar Pier, Atlantic City. Fred and his sister, Adele, were together again with another Gershwin score, following their great success in 1924 with *Lady, Be Good!*. The songs were right out of the composers' top drawer - one all-time standard, "S'Wonderful" - and other great numbers such as the lovely ballad, 'He Loves And She Loves', 'Let's Kiss And Make Up', 'Tell The Doc' (an hilarious lampoon of psychiatrists), 'High Hat' (along with the white tie and tails, it became Astaire's trademark in many Hollywood movies), 'My One And Only', the engaging 'Funny Face', and 'The Babbitt And The Bromide', which Astaire later sung with Gene Kelly when they met for the first time on film in *Ziegfeld Follies* (1945). *Funny Face* was a tremendous success, and ran for 250 performances in New York. It played for two weeks longer than that in London, where the Astaires were very popular, especially with British Royalty. They were joined in the West End production by Sydney Howard and Leslie Henson. The 1957 film version, which had a different story but retained some of the songs, and borrowed others from different Gershwin shows, starred Fred Astaire (Adele had retired long since) with Audrey Hepburn and Kay Thompson. The story was overhauled yet again in 1983, when a projected Broadway revival of *Funny Face* underwent such drastic changes, that, although, as with the film, it had some of the original numbers, it turned out to be essentially a quite different show, and the title was changed to *My One And Only*. It starred Twiggy and Tommy Tune, and ran for 767 performances.

Funny Girl

Although the stage musical *Funny Girl* had reached New York in mid-February 1964, it did not open at the Winter Garden until 26 March. The problems delaying the show, which included a weak book, were never fully corrected. Nevertheless, *Funny Girl* was a great success thanks in the main to a magnificent central performance by Barbra Streisand. Based on the life of Fanny Brice, a popular Broadway

Zero Mostel (*A Funny Thing Happened On The Way To The Forum*)

star of the 20s, *Funny Girl* traced the life of an awkward, far-from-pretty girl, who rose from her East Side of New York origins to become a Broadway superstar. Audiences could not help but relate the story's subject to the new star they saw on the stage. With music by Jule Styne and lyrics by Bob Merrill, the songs included 'I'm The Greatest Star', 'The Music That Makes Me Dance', 'If A Girl Isn't Pretty, 'I Want To Be Seen With You Tonight', 'You Are Woman', 'Sadie, Sadie', and two show-stoppers for Streisand in 'Don't Rain On My Parade' and 'People'. The latter number gave her a Top 10 US hit, and is forever identified with her. Playing opposite Streisand in the role of real-life gambler and con-man Nicky Arnstein, was Sydney Chaplin. *Funny Girl* ran for 1,348 performances and confirmed expectations that the recently-discovered Streisand was herself bound for superstardom. She reprised her role in the short-lived London production and in the 1968 film version, with Omar Sharif as Arnstein. Some songs originally made famous by the real Fanny Brice were included in the film which, despite being overlong, brought Streisand the Acadamy Award as Best Actress in her first screen appearance.

Funny Thing Happened On The Way To The Forum, A

Stephen Sondheim's third Broadway show, and the first for which he wrote the music as well as the lyrics. It opened at the Alvin Theatre in New York on 8 May 1962, and was still there over two years later. The book, by Burt Shevelove and Larry Gelbart, was freely adapted from all 21 of the comedies by the Roman playwright, Plautus. Set 'in a street in Rome, on a day in spring, two hundred years before the Christian era', the show has been described variously as 'a funny vaudeville farce . . . a bawdy farcical musical . . . an old-fashioned musical burlesque' . . . and 'a riot of risqué patter'. The Prologus (the slave Pseudolus, played by Zero Mostel) addresses the audience and welcomes them with 'Comedy Tonight'. There follows a joyous, fast-moving romp, involving an old man, Senex (David Burns) and his wife, Domina (Ruth Kobart); their son, Hero (Brian Davies), their slave, Hysterium (Jack Gilford); another old man, Erronius (Raymond Walburn), a buyer and seller of courtesans, Marcus Lycus (John Carradine), a warrior, Miles Gloriosus (Ronald Holgate), and a virgin, Philia (Preshy Marker). Mostel, in his role as Pseudolus, slave to Hero, updates the audience regularly when he is not trying to help the other characters out of various embarrassing situations. Sondheim punctuated the action with songs such as 'Everybody Ought To Have A Maid', 'Bring Me My Bride', 'That'll Show Him', 'Love I Hear', 'Lovely', 'Free', 'I'm Calm', 'Pretty Little Picture', and 'Impossible'. The show ran for 964 performances and

scooped the Tony Awards, winning for for best musical, book, actor (Mostel), supporting actor (David Burns), director (George Abbott), and producer (Harold Prince) The 1963 London production, which stayed at the Strand Theatre for 762 performances, starred Frankie Howerd as Pseudolus, and a band of renowned British low-farce comedians, including Kenneth Connor, 'Monsewer' Eddie Gray, Robertson Hare, and Jon Pertwee. Howerd reprised his role in the 1986 West End revival which was directed by Larry Gelbart. His co-librettist, Burt Shevelove, staged the show when Broadway audiences saw it for the second time in 1972. Phil Silvers, who had been the original choice for Pseudolus in 1962, appeared in the revival until he had a stroke, and it was forced to close. The production won Tony Awards for Silvers and supporting actor, Larry Blydon. When he recovered, Silvers took the show to the UK provinces at a time when his popularity rating was high due to reruns of the Sergeant Bilko television show. In 1991, in an effort to reduce costs but still revive some favourite Broadway musicals, a scaled-down production of *A Funny Thing Happened On The Way To The Forum* was presented at the Church of the Heavenly Rest by the New York Theatre Company. The 1966 film version starred Zero Mostel, Phil Silvers, Jack Gilford, and Buster Keaton.

Garrick Gaieties, The

Sub-titled 'A Bubbling Satirical Musical Revue Of Plays, Problems and Persons', the first of three editions of this satirical revue was presented by the Theatre Guild Junior Players' a group of young Theatre Guild actors, for two Sunday performances on 17 May 1925, in an effort to raise money for their new theatre on 52nd Street in New York. The production aroused such interest, that it began a commercial run at the Garrick Theatre on 8 June that year. It was an irreverent mix of sketches and songs which lampooned the musical theatre in general, and the Theatre Guild in particular (a kind of early *Forbidden Broadway*, perhaps?). The show gave the young songwriters Richard Rodgers and Lorenz Hart their first big Broadway opportunity, and they came through with several outstanding numbers such as

'April Fool', 'Sentimental Me', 'On With The Dance', 'Old Fashioned Girl (lyric by Edith Meiser), 'Do You Love Me? (I Wonder)', 'Black And Blue', and 'Manhattan', a song that was first popularized by Ben Selvin and Paul Whiteman, and eventually became a much-loved standard. That first show ran for 211 performances, and a second edition opened a year later, again at the Garrick Theatre, on 10 May 1926. Once more, the score was by Rodgers and Hart, and included 'Keys To Heaven', 'Back To Nature', 'Say It With Flowers', 'It May Rain', 'What's The Use Of Talking?', 'A Little Souvenir', and an operetta spoof 'The Rose Of Arizona'. The show's big hit was 'Mountain Greenery', which became such as success on record for Mel Tormé, and turned up in the 1948 Rodgers and Hart biopic *Words And Music*, where it was sung by Perry Como and Allyn McLerie. The third, and final version of the *The Garrick Gaieties* was presented at the Guild Theatre in 1930, with songs by a variety of composers and lyricists. Several of the numbers had music by Vernon Duke, including 'I Am Only Human After All' (lyric by Ira Gershwin and Harburg), 'Too, Too Divine' (E.Y. 'Yip' Harburg and Duke), and 'Ankle Up The Altar With Me (Harburg and Richard Myers). Also in the score was 'Triple Sec', a 'progressive opera' by the *avant garde* composer, Marc Blitzstein, and 'Out Of Breath And Scared To Death Of You' by Johnny Mercer and Everett Miller, which is said to be Mercer's first published song. Some of the cast who were in the first *Gaieties* and still there at the end, included Sterling Holloway, Edith Meiser, James Norris, Hidegarde Halliday, and Philip Loeb, who also directed. Lee Strasberg, who later opened the famous acting studio, was in one of the shows, as was Libby Holman. Two talented newcomers in the third show were Ray Heatherton and the actress-comedienne Imogen Coca, and the future Hollywood star, Rosalind Russell, made her Broadway debut when the 1930 edition returned briefly to Broadway in October of that same year.

Gay Divorce

Opening at New York's Ethel Barrymore Theatre on 29 November 1932, this show was Fred Astaire's first stage musical without his sister, Adele (she retired after *The Band Wagon* in 1931) - and Astaire's own final Broadway appearance before leaving for Hollywood to star in some 30 musical films. Music and lyrics were provided by Cole Porter, and the book was written by Kenneth Webb and Samuel Hoffenstein from Dwight Taylor's adaptation of an unproduced play, *An Adorable Adventure*, by J. Hartley Manners. It seems that Mimi Pratt (Claire Luce) wants to divorce her husband. Guy Holden (Fred Astaire), a British novelist who loves Mimi, is mistaken for Toneti (Erik Rhodes), the professional

co-respondent Mimi has hired in an effort to shake herself loose. That kind of story can use a great score, and Porter came up with one of his best. Comedienne Louella Gear had the amusing 'I Still Love The Red, White And Blue' and 'Mister And Missus Fitch'; Erik Rhodes sang 'How's Your Romance?' ('Does he or not love you an awful lot?/Cold, tepid, warm, or hot/How's your romance?'); Eric Blore, who played an immaculate waiter in the show (and later made a career in films, usually as a butler), enquired 'What Will Become Of Our England?' ('When the Prince of Wales finds a wife'); Astaire crooned the haunting 'After You, Who?' ('I could search years but who else could change my tears/Into laughter after you?') and joined Claire Luce in 'I've Got You On My Mind' ('You're not wild enough/You're not gay enough/You don't let me lead you astray enough') and one of Porter's most potent love songs, 'Night And Day'. The composer claimed the music for the latter number was inspired by a Mohammedan call to worship that he had heard in Morocco. Initially, the show had an indifferent response, but the exposure of some of the songs, especially 'Night And Day', soon boosted audiences. The number became a nation-wide hit through recordings by Astaire himself (With Leo Reisman's Orchestra), Eddy Duchin, Charlie Barnet, Frank Sinatra, and Bing Crosby. *Gay Divorce* played 248 performances on Broadway, and another 180 in London in 1933, where Astaire, Luce, Rhodes, and Blore recreated their roles. It was revived briefly Off Broadway in 1960. Over 30 years later, in 1993, the show was presented by John McGlinn at Carnegie Hall's Weill Recital Hall complete with the original orchestrations by Hans Spialek and Robert Russell Bennett. The 1934 film version, called *The Gay Divorcée*, starred Astaire and Ginger Rogers, but the only song retained from the original score was 'Night And Day'.

Gay, Noel

b. Richard Moxon Armitage, 3 March 1898, Wakefield, Yorkshire, England, d. 3 March 1954, London England. A prolific composer and lyricist, Gay was responsible for many of the most popular and memorable songs in the UK during the 30s and 40s. A child prodigy, he was educated at Wakefield Cathedral School, and often deputized for the Cathedral organist. In 1913 he moved to London to study at the Royal College of Music, and later became the director of music and organist at St Anne's Church in Soho. After four years studying for his MA and B.Mus. at Christ's Church College, Cambridge, he seemed destined for a career in a university or cathedral. While at Cambridge he became interested in the world of musical comedy, and started to write songs. After contributing to the revue, *Stop Press*, he was commissioned to write the complete score for the *Charlot Show Of 1926*. He was also the principal composer for *Clowns In Clover*, which starred Jack Hulbert and Cecily Courtneidge, and ran for over 500 performances. Around this time he took the name of Noel Gay for his popular work to avoid embarrassment to the church authorities. In 1930, Gay, with Harry Graham, wrote his most successful song to date, 'The King's Horses', which was sung in another Charlot revue, *Folly To Be Wise*. He then collaborated with lyricist Desmond Carter for the score of his first musical show, *Hold My Hand* (1931). Starring Jessie Matthews, Sonnie Hale and Stanley Lupino, the songs included 'Pied Piper', 'What's In A Kiss', 'Hold My Hand' and 'Turn On The Music'. During the 30s Gay wrote complete, or contributed to, scores for popular shows such as *She Couldn't Say No*, *That's A Pretty Thing*, *Jack O'Diamonds*, *Love Laughs!*, *O-Kay For Sound* (the first of the famous Crazy Gang Music Hall-type revues at the London Palladium, in which Bud Flanagan sang Gay's 'The Fleet's In Port Again'), *Wild Oats* and *Me And My Girl* (1937). The latter show, with a book and lyrics by L. Arthur Rose, and starring Lupino Lane in the central role of Bill Sibson, ran for over 1,600 performances and featured 'The Lambeth Walk', which became an enormously popular sequence dance craze - so popular, in fact, that when the show was filmed in 1939, it was titled *The Lambeth Walk*. In the same year, with Ralph Butler, Gay gave Bud Flanagan the big song, 'Run Rabbit Run', in another Crazy Gang revue, *The Little Dog Laughed*. During the 40s, Gay wrote for several shows with lyrics mostly by Frank Eyton, including *Lights Up* ('Let The People Sing'), 'Only A Glass Of Champagne' and 'You've Done Something To My Heart'); *Present Arms*; *La-Di-Di-Di-Da'*; *The Love Racket*; *Meet Me Victoria*; *Sweetheart Mine*; and *Bob's Your Uncle* (1948). His songs for films included 'All For A Shilling A Day' and 'There's Something About A Soldier' Sung by Courtneidge in *Me And Marlborough* (1935); 'Leaning On A Lamp Post' introduced by comedian George Formby in *Feather Your Nest*; 'Who's Been Polishing The Sun', sung by Jack Hulbert in *The Camels Are Coming*; 'I Don't Want To Go to Bed' (Lupino in *Sleepless Nights*); and 'All Over The Place' (*Sailors Three*). Gay also composed 'Tondeleyo', the first song to be synchronized into a British talking picture (*White Cargo*). His other songs included 'Round The Marble Arch', 'All For The Love Of A Lady', 'I Took My Harp To A Party' (a hit for Gracie Fields), 'Let's Have A Tiddley At The Milk Bar', 'Red, White And Blue', 'Love Makes The World Go Round', 'The Moon Remembered, But You Forgot', 'The Girl Who Loves A Soldier', 'The Birthday Of The Little Princess', 'Are We Downhearted? - No!', 'Hey Little Hen', 'Happy Days Happy Months', 'I'll Always Love You', 'Just A Little Fond Affection', 'When Alice Blue Gown Met Little Boy Blue', 'I Was Much Better Off In The Army' and 'My Thanks To You' (co-written with Norman Newell). His other collaborators included Archie Gottler, Clifford Grey, Dion Titheradge, Donavan Parsons and Ian Grant. In the early 50s, Gay wrote very little, just a few songs such as 'I Was Much Better Off In The Army' and 'You Smile At Everyone But Me'. He had been going deaf for some years, and had to wear a hearing aid. After his death in March 1954, his publishing company, Noel Gay Music, which he had formed in 1938, published one more song, 'Love Me Now'. His son, Richard Armitage (b. 12 August 1928, Wakefield, England, d. 17 November 1986), a successful impresario and agent, took over the company, and extended and developed the organization into one of the biggest television and representational agencies in Europe. His clients included David Frost, Rowan Atkinson, Esther Rantzen, Russ Conway, Russell Harty, Jonathan Miller, John Cleese, the King's Singers and many more. The publishing side had several hit copyrights, including the Scaffold's 'Thank U Very Much'. After mounting several minor productions, Armitage revived his father's most popular show, *Me And My Girl*, in London in February 1985. With the versatile actor, Robert Lindsay as Sibson, a revised book, and two other Gay hits, 'The Sun Has Got His Hat On' and 'Leaning On A Lamp Post' interpolated into the score, it was an immediate success, and closed in 1993 after a stay of eight years, shortly after *Radio Times*, another production featuring Noel Gay's music, had enjoyed a brief West End run. Opening on Broadway in 1986, *Me And My Girl* ran for over 1,500 performances, New York's biggest hit for years. Armitage died three months after the show's Broadway debut.

Gay's The Word

A light musical comedy which turned out to be the last production involving Ivor Novello, one of the London musical theatre's favourite sons; he died less than a month after *Gay's The Word* opened at the Saville Theatre on 16 February 1951. Novello provided the book and lyrics, and Alan Melville wrote the sharp, witty lyrics for a show that, in some ways lampooned the composer's previous extravagantly staged operetta-style shows. This was particularly evident in 'Ruritania', the opening number for the chorus, with lines such as 'Since *Oklahoma!*/We've been in a coma'. Jack Hulbert directed the piece, and his wife, Cicely Courtneidge took the lead as Gay Daventry, a 'star actress in charge of a drama school'. Her young pupils included the lovely Linda (Lizbeth Webb) with her boyfriend,

Peter Lynton (Thorley Walters). The school was located in an English seaside town with lots of sea and sand, plus plenty of rocky cliffs, which gave Courtneidge a chance to be 'bossy', and the author an ideal excuse for a sub-plot involving smugglers and their midnight shenanigans. Courtneidge was her usually ebullient self. Even at the age of 57 she had lost none of the energy and enthusiasm for which she was renowned. Novello and Melville summed it up perfectly in 'Vitality', which she delivered with such style, along with another song that, as a seasoned trouper, could well have been her life-long creed, 'It's Bound To Be Right On The Night' ('Over cold pork, pink blancmange and unripe Stilton/You've rather a nasty supper with Jack Hylton'). The rest of the score included 'Gaiety Glad', 'Bees Are Buzzin'', 'Finder, Please Return', 'On Such A Night As This', 'A Matter Of Minutes', and 'Guards On Parade'. It was fitting, considering Novello's previous contributions to the London theatre, that he should go out with a big hit; Gay's The Word ran for 504 performances. It proved to be Cicely Courtneidge's last musical comedy in the West End (she still did revues) until 1964, and her appearance as Mme. Arcati in High Spirits, a musical adaptatation of Noël Coward's Blithe Spirit.

Gentlemen Prefer Blondes

This show opened at the Ziegfeld Theatre in New York on 8 December 1949, but the story immediately transported audiences back to the roaring 20s. Working on the basis that 'there's gold in them thar tycoons', Lorelei Lee (Carol Channing), has got herself engaged to Gus Esmond (Jack McCauley), who has made a fortune out of buttons. At midnight, she bids him a tearful farewell on the dockside (He: 'I'll be in my room alone every post meridien/She: 'And I'll be with my diary and that book by Mr. Gideon') as she sails with her best chum, Dorothy Shaw (Yvonne Adair), on the Ile de France. When she hits Paris, her pursuit of a life-style to which she would dearly like to become accustomed, involves a zipper tycoon, Josephus Gage (George S Irving), and sundry other potential gold-mines, such as Sir Francis Beekman (Rex Evans), as she takes in most of the glamorous sights of the city. As befits 'A Little Girl From Little Rock', she eventually returns home to marry her Mr. Esmond, and Dorothy also finds her happiness in America, with Philadelphian Henry Spofford (Eric Brotherson). The book, by Anita Loos and Joseph Fields, from Anita Loos's novel was charming and funny. Channing had appeared on Broadway the year before in the revue, Lend Me An Ear, but Gentleman Prefer Blondes rocketed her to stardom in the space of just a few weeks. The score, by Jule Styne (music) and Leo Robin (lyrics), was full of good songs. As well as the tender 'Bye, Bye Baby' (with McCauley), 'It's Delightful Down In Chile' (with Evans), and two numbers with the ensemble, 'Homesick Blues' and 'Gentlemen Prefer Blondes', Channing also had 'I'm Just A Little Girl From Little Rock' and the marvellous 'Diamonds Are A Girl's Best Friend' ('He's your guy when stocks go high/But beware when they start to descend/It's then that those louses go back to their spouses/Diamonds are a girl's best friend'). The rest of the songs included 'I Love What I'm Doing', 'Just A Kiss Apart', 'You Say You Care', 'I'm A'Tingle, I'm Aglow', 'Mamie Is Mimi', and 'It's High Time'. The show was a great success and ran on Broadway for 740 performances. A film version of Gentlemen Prefer Blondes with extra songs by Hoagy Carmichael and Harold Adamson, and starring Marilyn Monroe and Jane Russell, was released in 1953, and there was a sequel, Gentlemen Marry Brunettes, two years later. For some reason, the show was not presented in London until 1962 when Dora Bryan played Lorelei during a run of 223 performances. In 1974, Carol Channing starred on Broadway in the musical, Lorelei, which was sub-titled 'Gentlemen Still Prefer Blondes', retained some of the best features of the 1949 original, and incorporated a prologue and an epilogue in which Lorelei appeared as an older woman. The revised book was by Kenny Solms and Gail Parent, and Jule Styne contributed some new songs with lyrics by Betty Comden and Adolph Green. The show enjoyed a run of 320 performances.

George M!

A celebratory musical about the life of the multi-talented George M. Cohan (singer-dancer-author-director, and more), detailing his early days in vaudeville, through his ups and downs, to his final Broadway triumph when he portrayed President Franklin D. Roosevelt in I'd Rather Be Right in 1937. With a book by Michael Stewart, and John and Fran Pascal, George M! opened at the Palace Theatre in New York on 10 April 1968. After his triumph as the MC in Cabaret two years earlier, Joel Grey strutted his stuff somewhat in the manner of Cohan, but did not go for a precise impersonation as James Cagney did in the 1942 film, Yankee Doodle Dandy. Most of the songs associated with the master showman - all the flag-waving favourites - were included, many of which he wrote himself, such as 'Yankee Doodle Dandy', 'So Long, Mary', 'Forty-Five Minutes From Broadway', 'Harrigan', 'Over There', 'Mary's A Grand Old Name', 'You're A Grand Old Flag', and 'Give My Regards To Broadway'. The show also featured the future Broadway star, Bernadette Peters, in the relatively minor role of Cohan's sister. She made a sufficiently strong impression to be awarded a Theatre World Citation for her performance. These compilation shows are not everyone's idea of what the musical theatre should be all about, but they can be entertaining, and this one, which ran for 427 performances - over a year - was cited by a US critic as 'The one flicker of light in a drab Broadway season.'

George White's Scandals
(see **White, George**)

Gershwin, George
b. 26 September 1898, New York City, New York, USA, d. 11 June 1937. Although a poor student, and happy to spend his days playing in the streets, Gershwin took up piano when the family bought an instrument for his older brother, Ira Gershwin. He quickly showed enormous enthusiasm for music, taking lessons and studying harmony and theory. His musical taste was eclectic; he listened to classical music and to the popular music of the day, in particular the music of black Americans which was then gaining a widespread appeal. He became a professional musician in 1912, playing piano at holiday resorts in upstate New York and then working as a song plugger. He continued with his studies and began to write music. His first songs were undistinguished, but attracted the attention of important figures such as Sophie Tucker, Harry Von Tilzer and Sigmund Romberg. Some of his early compositions were influenced by ragtime - 'Rialto Ripples' (1916, with Will Donaldson) was one such example - and he also continued to gain a reputation as a performer. In 1917 he was hired as rehearsal pianist for a Jerome Kern - Victor Herbert Broadway show. His compositions continued to appear, some with lyrics by his brother Ira and others by Irving Caesar. It was a 1919 collaboration with Caesar that gave Gershwin his first hit: 'Swanee' had originally been played by the popular Arthur Pryor band, but it was when Al Jolson sang it in *Sinbad* (1919) that it became a success. Also in 1919, Gershwin was commissioned to write the music for *George White's Scandals Of 1919*. The score included such milestones in American popular music as 'I'll Build A Stairway To Paradise' (lyrics by Buddy De Sylva and Ira Gershwin) and 'Somebody Loves Me' (lyrics by De Sylva and Ballard MacDonald). In the early 20s Gershwin continued to write successful songs, including 'Do It Again' (with De Sylva), 'Oh, Lady, Be Good', 'Fascinating Rhythm' and 'The Man I Love' (with Ira). This same period saw his first success in an area of music removed from the popular song and the Broadway stage. An unsuccessful song from George White's *Scandals Of 1922*, 'Blue Monday Blues' (unsuccessful because it was dropped as being too downbeat), had attracted the attention of Paul Whiteman, who commissioned George to write an extended piece that was to be classical in structure but which would use the jazz idiom. The result was 'Rhapsody In Blue', first performed by Whiteman, with the composer at the piano, in 1924. The joint successes of the Gershwin brothers continued into the late 20s with 'That Certain Feeling', 'Someone To Watch Over Me', 'Clap Yo' Hands', 'Fidgety Feet', 'Do, Do, Do', 'Maybe', ''Swonderful', 'How Long Has This Been Going On', 'I've Got A Crush On You' and 'Liza' (the last with lyrics by Ira and Gus Kahn).

Many of the foregoing songs first appeared in shows for which the Gershwin brothers wrote complete scores, among them *Oh, Kay!* (1926), *Funny Face* (1927, which starred Adele and Fred Astaire) and *Rosalie* (1928 which also had contributions from P.G. Wodehouse and Romberg). The Gershwins' celebrity was maintained in the early 30s with *Strike Up The Band* (1930) with its popular title song, and *Girl Crazy* (1930), which starred Ethel Merman whose big number was 'I Got Rhythm' and which had Ginger Rogers in the ingenue role, singing 'But Not For Me' and duetting on 'Embraceable You'. In the pit band for *Girl Crazy* were up-and-coming musicians such as Benny Goodman, Glenn Miller and Gene Krupa. *Of Thee I Sing* (1931) was another hit, but the next two Broadway shows were flops. After the success of 'Rhapsody In Blue' Gershwin had again written music in classical form with his 'Concert In F' (1925), a tone poem, 'An American In Paris' (1928) and his 'Second Rhapsody' (1930). In 1935 his folk opera *Porgy And Bess* opened in Boston, Massachusetts, and despite early critical disapproval and audience disinterest, it became one of his most performed works, with songs such as 'It Ain't Necessarily So', 'Bess, You Is My Woman Now', 'Loves You, Porgy', 'I Got Plenty Of Nuttin'' and 'Summertime'. Having seen the possible end of their success story on Broadway, the Gershwin brothers went to Hollywood in 1936, which they had visited a few years earlier with only modest results. Now they entered into a new phase of creativity, writing 'They All Laughed', 'Let's Call The Whole Thing Off' and 'They Can't Take That Away From Me' for *Shall We Dance* (1937), which starred Astaire and Rogers, and 'Nice Work If You Can Get It' and 'A Foggy Day' for *A Damsel In Distress* (1937), in which Astaire again starred. It was while he was working on the next film, *The Goldwyn Follies* (1938), that George Gershwin was taken ill. A brain tumour was discovered and he died in June 1937. Despite the severity of his illness, Gershwin's songs for the film, 'Love Walked In' and 'Love Is Here To Stay' were among his best work. Although his lifespan was relatively short, Gershwin's work was not merely extensive but was also imperishable and provides a substantial contribution to the Great American Song Book. Little of his work has dated and it is performed as much, if not more, in

Ira Gershwin

the 80s and 90s as it ever was in his lifetime. As with so many of his contemporaries, Gershwin's popular songs adapted to the latest musical developments, in particular incorporating concepts from the jazz world and, not surprisingly, his work is especially popular among jazz instrumentalists. It is, however, with singers that the full glory of Gershwin's music emerges and he remains a key and influential figure in the story of American popular song. In 1992 the musical, *Crazy For You*, opened on Broadway. It was 'very loosely based' on the Gershwins' 1930 show, *Girl Crazy*, with several additional numbers, and was still running in the summer of 1993. In the same year, a West End production opened to rave notices, and looked set for long residency.

Further reading: *Gershwin*, Edward Jablonski. *The Memory Of All That: The Life Of George Gershwin*, Joan Peyser.

Gershwin, Ira

b. 6 December 1896, New York City, New York, USA, d. 17 August 1983. Like his younger brother, George Gershwin, Ira was an indifferent student but became fascinated by popular music and in particular by the lyrics of songs. He began writing seriously in 1917 and had a number of minor successes, sometimes using the pseudonym 'Arthur Francis'. In the early 20s he was closely associated with his brother, collaborating on several Broadway shows and creating some of the perennial standards of American popular song. Despite the high level of productivity the brothers maintained, and which produced such hits as 'That Certain Feeling', 'Someone To Watch Over Me', 'Do, Do, Do', ''Swonderful', 'How Long Has This Been Going On', 'I've Got A Crush On You', 'I Got Rhythm', 'But Not For Me' and 'Embraceable You', Ira Gershwin found time to write lyrics for other composers. Among these other songs were 'Cheerful Little Earful' (with Billy Rose and Harry Warren), 'Let's Take A Walk Around The Park' (with Warren and Yip Harburg) and 'I Can't Get Started' (with Vernon Duke). In 1931, the brothers' collaboration on the Broadway show, *Of Thee I Sing*, resulted in an unprecedented honour when it became the first musical to be awarded a Pulitzer Prize. In the years immediately after his brother's tragically early death, Ira Gershwin wrote little but eventually resumed work, collaborating with Kurt Weill on 'My Ship', Jerome Kern on 'Long Ago And Far Away' and Harold Arlen on 'The Man That Got Away'. In 1959 he published a book, *Lyrics On Several Occasions*. He retired the following year, occasionally working on lyrics of past successes when they needed refining or updating for revivals of the most popular Gershwin shows. He died in August 1983. Ten years later some his most popular lyrics were still being heard in New York and London in productions of *Crazy for You*, a re-hash of the Gershwins' 1930 hit, *Girl Crazy*.

Further reading: *Lyrics On Several Occasions*, Ira Gershwin. *The Complete Lyrics Of Ira Gershwin*.

Girl Crazy

The American Depression was biting hard, but Broadway itself was remarkably buoyant when *Girl Crazy* opened at the Alvin Theatre on 14 October 1930. The show's producers, Alex A. Aarons and Vincent Freedley, wanted Bert Lahr as their chief laughter-maker, but they had rather carelessly loaned him out to George White for *Flying Home!*, and could not get him back in time. So they signed the singing comedy team of Willie and Eugene Howard instead, although only Willie appeared in the show. In Guy Bolton and John McGowan's's contemporary tale of cowboy life, Willie plays the role of Gieber Goldfarb, a taxi driver who is hired by a wealthy New Yorker to transport his philandering son, Danny Churchill (Allan Kearns), 3000 miles to Custerville, a town that has not had a female resident in 50 years. Danny soon changes that situation by turning the family lodge into Buzzards, a dude ranch with imported New York showgirls and a gambling saloon which is managed by Slick Fothergill (William Kent) and his wife Kate (Ethel Merman). Danny himself falls for the local postmistresss, Molly Gray (Ginger Rogers), and Goldfarb gives up driving taxis and becomes the town's sheriff (Custerville gets through two of those a week). It was the first time that Ethel Merman had been seen and heard (!) on Broadway, and she excelled with 'Boy! What Love Has Done To Me!', and the smoochy 'Sam And Delilah' which was followed almost immediately by the ebullient 'I Got Rhythm' - just three of the outstanding nuumbers in this marvellous score by George and Ira Gershwin. Naturally enough, Kearns and Rogers shared the big romantic ballad, 'Embraceable You' and the getting-to-know-you 'Could You Use Me?'. Rogers also had 'Cactus Time In Arizona' and the wistful 'But Not For Me'. The rest of the songs included 'The Lonesome Cowboy', 'Bronco Busters', Geiber's campaign song, 'Goldfarb! That's I'm!', 'Land Of The Gay Caballero', and 'Treat Me Rough'. Another of the show's most endearing numbers, 'Bidin' My Time', was sung at various moments throughout the show by a quartet of cowboys played by the Foursome. That sequence was recreated in the film, *The Glenn Miller Story*, when James Stewart, as Miller, was supposed to be playing in the pit orchestra for *Girl Crazy*. Unlike many of Hollyood's inaccurate representations of Broadway musicals, this one was true. Miller did play in the orchestra along, with Benny Goodman and Gene Krupa, in what was an augmented version of Red Nichols' dance band. Nichols also had big record hits with 'I Got Rhythm' and 'Embraceable You'. With those songs, a bright, colourful production, and its famous curtain line: 'Go on - marry him Molly. It's 11:15 now.', *Girl Crazy* seemed to be set for a long run, but when Willy Howard and Ethel Merman left for the 1931 edition of George White's Scandals, it closed after 272 performances. Three film adaptations were made: an early talkie version in 1932, the definitive version with Judy Garland and Mickey Rooney in 1943, and a 1965 re-hash, *When The Boys Meet The Girls*, starring Connie Francis, Harve Presnell, Herman's Hermits, Louis Armstrong, and Liberace. More than 60 years later, on 24 February 1992, a 'revamp' of the show, entitled *Crazy For You*, conceived by Mike Ockrent and Ken Ludwig, opened on Broadway and became a smash-hit, winning the Tony Award for best musical. It repeated its success in London during the following year. In 1991, a CD recording of *Girl Crazy* was released complete with the original orchestrations by Robert Russell Bennett, and starring Lorna Luft, David Carroll, Judy Blazer, and Frank Gorshin.

Girl Friend, The

One of Richard Rodgers and Lorenz Hart's earliest shows, *The Girl Friend* opened at the Vanderbilt Theatre in New York on 17 March 1926. After their success with *Dearest Enemy*, the young songwriters teamed again with librettist Herbert Fields for this story of a six-day cycle race in which the apparent long-shot for the title is nobbled by unscupulous punters, which was a vehicle for the husband and wife dance team Eva Puck and Sammy White. They introduced Rodgers and Hart's Charleston-styled title song ('Isn't she cute?/Isn't she sweet?/An eyeful you'd die full/Of pleasure to meet/In my funny fashion/I'm cursed with a passion/For the girl friend!'), and one of the composers' loveliest ballads, 'The Blue Room' ('We will thrive on/Keep alive on/Just nothing but kisses/With Mister and Missus/On little blue chairs'). Eva Puck also had the amusing 'The Damsel Who Done All The Dirt' ('The greatest of heroes/Would now rank as zeros/If not for the hem of a skirt'), and the rest of the score included 'Good Fellow Mine', 'Why Do I?', 'Hey, Hey', 'The Simple Life', 'Goodbye, Lenny', and 'Creole Crooning Song'. After initially poor audiences, the show picked up and ran for a creditable 301 performances. A different production with a new book, but still called *The Girl Friend*, opened in London on 8 September 1927. It contained several Rodgers and Hart numbers, including the title song, 'The Blue Room, 'What's The Use Of Talking?', and 'Mountain Greenery', and ran for 421 performances.

Girl From Utah, The

Even with its sub-title, 'The Acme Of Musical Comedy', this show would not be of any particular interest except that it contains a certain song. That song was not present when *The Girl From Utah* opened in London at the Adelphi Theatre on 18 October 1913 where it played for 195 performances. It was added, along with a few others, when the show was presented nearly a year later in New York. The score for the original West End production was written by Sidney Jones and Paul Robens (music) and Adrian Ross, Percy Greenbank, and Robens (lyrics). It included songs such as 'D'You Follow Me?', 'Una', 'Call Right Here', 'The Girl From Utah', 'Kissing Time', 'At The Bottom Of Brixton Hill', 'The Music Of Love', and 'When We Meet A Mormon'. The last two titles give a good clue as to the location and the subject of the piece. James T. Taylor's book was set in England, and dealt with Una Trance (Ina Claire), an American girl who flees to London in an attempt to avoid being added to a Mormon's wedding list - for wives. Although he pursues her to Europe, she is rescued from a meandering existence with the Mormon by a handsome local hoofer Sandy Blair (Joseph Coyne). When *The Girl From Utah* transferred to the Knickerbocker Theatre on Broadway in August 1914, producer Charles Frohman gave it the American touch, and commissioned some interpolations from an up-and-coming young composer named Jerome Kern, and here is where that special song comes in. Following its introduction in this show by David Brian (Sandy), 'They'll Never Believe Me', with a lyric by Herbert Reynolds, became one of the most enduring standards in the history of popular music. Aside from numerous recordings by some of the world's leading singers, it was featured in two London musicals, *Tonight's The Night* (1915) and *Oh! What A Lovely War* (1963, also the 1969 film), and in films such as the Jerome Kern biopic, *Till The Clouds Roll By* (1946, sung by Kathryn Grayson), and *That Midnight Kiss* (1949, Mario Lanza). Kern's other songs for the US version of *The Girl From Utah*, with lyrics by Harry B. Smith, were all of a very high standard, and included 'You Can Never Tell', 'Same Sort Of Girl', 'The Land Of Let's Pretend', 'Alice In Wonderland', 'We'll Take Care Of You' (The Little Refugees)', and the vivacious 'Why Don't They Dance The Polka?'. The rest of the New York cast included Julia Sanderson as Una and Joseph Cawthorn in the role of the Mormon. *The Girl From Utah*, which ran for 120 performances on Broadway, was an early example of the move, spearheaded by Kern, to create a modern American musical which would eventually replace the imported European operettas.

Glamorous Night

In *Glamorous Night*, his first great stage musical hit, Ivor Novello found a way of bringing to British

Jeremy Irons (*Godspell*)

audiences of the 30s a home-grown version of the highly-popular Viennese operettas of the late 19th Century. Filling the stage with beautifully-costumed elegant ladies and with some deliberately heart-tugging music, Novello concocted a fairy-tale world to which audiences flocked. The hugely improbable plot concerned the inventor of television who is paid handsomely by the head of radio to disappear and take his invention with him. He goes to the Ruritanian-style land of Krasnia, meets a gypsy princess who is about to marry the Krasnian king, saves her life, falls in love, is almost killed, then gives up his love for the greater good of Krasnia. Novello played the leading role of Anthony Allen opposite Mary Ellis as Militza Hajos. *Glamorous Night* opened in London at the Theatre Royal, Drury Lane on 2 May 1935, and Novello found himself with a show that looked as though it would run forever. In fact, the management of the theatre were forced to close it after only six months because of a prior commitment to stage a Christmas pantomime. However, after touring for a while, *Glamorous Night* reopened at the London Coliseum for a brief run in 1936. For all its short life, *Glamorous Night* set the pattern for Novello's future shows and he rarely varied this for the rest of his life. A 1937 film version starred Mary Ellis, Barry Mackay and Otto Kruger.

Godspell

One of the first of the rock-type religious musicals that began to emerge in the 70s, *Godspell* opened Off Broadway at the Cherry Lane Theatre in New York on 17 May 1971. It had a book, by John-Michael Tebelak, which was based on the Gospel according to St Matthew, and music and lyrics by newcomer Stephen Schwartz. The cast included Stephen Nathan (Jesus) and David Haskell (Judas), and the score contained songs such as 'All Good Gifts', 'Save The People', 'Prepare Ye The Way Of The Lord', 'Light Of The Best', and 'Day By Day', a number that epitomises this style of production, and which became an enormous US hit in a version by the Broadway original cast. After 2,124 performances, the show moved to a main house, the Broadhurst Theatre, for a further 527. The cast of the London production, which stayed at Wyndham's Theatre for nearly three years, included Julie Covington, David Essex, Marti Webb, and the future movie heartthrob Jeremy Irons. A 1993 revival at the Barbican Hall in London, which starred the actress and singer Gemma Craven, was not helped by the fact that 'Andy Crane, the blond and denimed childrens' television personality signed up to play Jesus, is strikingly uncharismatic and bland - this resurrection is not good news'.

Golden Boy

Frank Sinatra is said to have tried to discourage Sammy Davis, a fellow-member of the infamous 'Clan', from submitting himself to the discipline of an eight-shows-a-week stint in a Broadway musical. Davis, a major star in nightclubs and on records, made his debut on the 'great white way' in *Mr. Wonderful* in 1956, and, 12 years later, he ignored Sinatra's advice and opened in *Golden Boy* at the Majestic Theatre on 20 October 1964. Clifford Odets died a few months after he began to adapt his well-known play for this Broadway musical, and the work was finished by his friend, William Gibson. In a neat twist of both name and colour, the writers changed the name of the leading character, a boxer, from an Italian-American named Joe Bonaparte, to a Negro-American named Joe Wellington. Davis was impressive as the young fighter, who is determined to get out, get rich, and make it to the top. One of the oustanding features of the production was Donald McKayle's innovative and exciting choreography, particularly in the opening scene, which simulated a high-energy workout, and a marvellously conceived fight sequence. The score, by Charles Strouse (music) and Lee Adams (lyrics), received a mixed press. There was one show-stopper, 'Don't Forget 127th Street', in which Wellington berates his young fans, telling them to be proud of their Harlem roots. Davis also had a couple of telling ballads, 'Night Song' and 'I Want To Be With You', and the rest of the score included 'Workout', 'Everything's Great', 'Gimme Some', 'Lorna's Here', 'This Is The Life', 'While The City Sleeps', 'Golden Boy', 'Colourful', 'No More', and 'The Fight'. Also in the cast were Kenneth Tobey, who played Tom Moody, the fighter's manager; Paula Wayne in the role of Lorna Moon, a lady who shares her favours with both of them, and Billy Daniels as Eddie Satin. Davis was credited with being the main reason that *Golden Boy* played for well over a year in New York, a total of 569 performances, but West End audiences were not so impressed, and the London Palladium production folded after nearly four months. A 25th anniversary edition of the show, with a new book by Leslie Lee, reworked music and lyrics, and starring Obba Babatunde, played venues such as Miami's Coconut Grove Playhouse and the Candlewood Playhouse in New Fairfield, Connecticut, in the late 80s-early 90s.

Goldilocks

This show, which opened at the Lunt Fontanne Theatre in New York on 11 October 1958, afforded Broadway audiences their only opportunity to hear the music of Leroy Anderson, who was better known as a composer of of light, engaging, and some times humorous works, such as 'Blue Tango', 'Sleigh Ride', 'Forgotten Dreams', and 'The Typewriter'. Anderson's lyricists for *Goldilocks* were John Ford, and Walter and Jean Kerr. The husband-and-wife team also wrote the book, which was set in 1913, and was essentially a sometimes hilarious spoof on the silent-movie business. As the curtain rises, an actress Maggie Harris (Elaine Stritch, in one of her typically 'acerbic' roles), is about to give up the theatre and marry the millionaire George Randolph Brown (Russell Nype). Enter film producer-director Max Grady (Don Ameche) to remind her that she is, in fact, contracted to appear in his movie, *Frontier Woman*, which is about to begin shooting. Max tricks Maggie into filming enough footage for several movies, and, although they admit their feelings for each other, she fully intends to marry George. However, when the unexpected happens, and snow begins falls on the site of Max's latest movie - an Egyptian epic which is being shot in down-state California (in April) - she takes that as a sign that she should do something equally unconventional - so she marries Max instead. Jilted George has to make do with Lois (Pat Stanley), but both Stanley and Nype were consoled by receiving real-life Tony Awards for their performances. 'Never mind the story - the score's the thing,' has been said so many times, and this was yet another of them. The songs were indeed both charming and amusing. Stritch was beautifully served with 'Give The Little Lady', 'Whose Been Sitting In My Chair?', 'The Beast In You', 'I Never Know When', and 'Save A Kiss' (with Nype), and an 'abusive' duet with Ameche, 'No One'll Ever Love You' ('Like you do'). Ameche displayed an impressive singing voice in 'There Never Was A Woman', and the insistent, disbelieving 'I Can't Be In Love' (with the accent very much on the 'can't'), and the rest of the score included 'Lazy Moon', 'Lady In Waiting', 'Shall I Take My Heart And Go?' (Nype), 'Bad Companions', 'Two Years In The Making', and 'Heart Of Stone'. The Broadway veteran choreographer, Agnes de Mille, was acclaimed for her staging of both songs and dances, and she had a great time with the comic 'Pussy Foot'. It all added up to another of those fondly-remembered flops. A run of 161 performances equalled a reported finanancial loss in the region of $360,000 dollars - and an Original Cast album to treasure.

Good News!

The first, and probably the best of De Sylva, Brown And Henderson's 'fad' musicals which were so popular in the 20s, opened at the 46th Street Theatre in New York on 15 August 1927. College football was the craze in question this time, and, in the book by Laurence Schwab and De Sylva, Tom Marlow (John Price Jones) is in a quandary: he may not be allowed to continue to shine as the incandescent star of the Tait College football team if he fails his astronomy exam. What to do? Enter Connie Lane (Mary Lawlor), who is pretty, and pretty intelligent,

too. She guides Tom through the galaxies so that he can play in the big match. Naturally, because this is musical comedy, they find that they have other interests in common, one of which is singing the show's big love songs, 'Just Imagine', 'Lucky In Love', and 'The Best Things In Life Are Free', while the breezy title song, and what must surely rank as the Roaring 20s liveliest and most engaging Charleston-styled number, 'The Varsity Drag', is performed with great style and panache by Zelma O'Neil. The rest of the score included 'He's A Ladies Man' and 'A Girl Of The Pi Beta Phi'. *Good News!* was sub-titled 'The Collegiate Musical', and, just to emphasize the point, before the show started the George Olsen Orchestra, dressed in appropriate college uniforms, marched down the aisles of the auditorium shouting football slogans on their way to the orchestra pit. The high-spirited and exuberant production, which ran for 551 performances in New York, and a further 132 in London, was the epitome of that happy-go-lucky, razzle-dazzle era, with its flappers and bootleg gin, which would sadly plummet all too soon into the Depression. Some of the show's songs were destined to live on for many years, especially 'The Best Things In Life Are Free', which, although it was omitted from the 1930 film version of *Good News*, was included in the 1947 remake, and became the title of the 1956 De Sylva, Brown And Henderson biopic, starring Gordon MacRae, Ernest Borgnine, Dan Dailey, and Sheree North. In 1974, the show resurfaced on Broadway, starring Alice Faye and Gene Nelson - but did not stay around for long.

Good Rockin' Tonite

There was plenty of that when this show opened at the Strand Theatre in London on 28 January 1992. It was devised by Jack Good, the influential producer who gave British television its earliest - and many still say best - pop music programmes, such as *6.5 Special* and *Oh Boy!* Some of the early beneficiaries of his ingenuity were there on the show's opening night - rock 'n' roll survivors such as Cliff Richard, Lonnie Donegan, Joe Brown, Marty Wilde, and Jess Conrad. Brilliantly staged by Good and Ian Kellgran, the story, which was only loosely based on Good's life, was really an excuse to celebrate some 60 of those seminal numbers from the 50s and early 60s, in the onstage company of Tommy Steele (David Howarth), Gene Vincent (Michael Dimitri), Cliff Richard (Tim Whitnall), Eddie Cochrane, the Vernon Girls, and more. There was also an 'uncanny' impression of Billy Fury by Gavin Stanley, and a 'creepy' one of the agent Larry Parnes by David Howarth (again). Good himself, engagingly played by Philip Baird, 'stumbles amusingly through an obsessive relationship with music, and a stormy one with his wife (Anna-Juliana Claire) and the BBC's Head of Light Entertainment,

Robert Goulet

played hilariously by James Compton'. After the show transferred to the Prince Of Wales Theatre in July, the jiving in the aisles (literally) continued until November, when the show closed after a rock 'n' rolling 327 performances.

Goulet, Robert

b. Stanley Applebaum, 26 November 1933, Lawrence, Massachusetts, USA. An actor and singer, Goulet made his first professional engagement in 1951 with the Edmonton Summer Pops in 1951. He also played in *Thunder Rock* and *Visit To A Small Planet*. After appearing in Canadian productions of *South Pacific*, *Finian's Rainbow*, and *Gentlemen Prefer Blondes*, he moved to the US, and made his Broadway debut in 1960, when he played Sir Lancelot in the musical *Camelot*, introducing the poignant 'If Ever I Would Leave You'. He also began launching his singing career during this time, and appeared on the Ed Sullivan television variety programme as well as others of that kind. Goulet signed with Columbia Records in 1962 and had his first chart entry with 'What Kind Of Fool Am I?' from the musical *Stop The World - I Want To Get Off*. He won the Grammy Award for Best New Artist in 1962, and his greatest singles success came in 1965 with the operatic 'My Love Forgive Me (Amore, Scusami)'. By then he had already proven that his strength was in album sales, as was often the case with middle of the road performers at that time. His 1962 Columbia debut, *Always You*, had charted, but it was the following year's *Sincerely Yours...* and 1964's *My Love Forgive Me* that became Goulet's top-performing albums. In 1968 he returned to the Broadway musical theatre in *The Happy Time*, and won a Tony Award for his portrayal of the French-Canadian man-about-the-world Uncle Jacques. In the 70s and 80s he toured in several musical revivals and appeared extensively in concerts, cabaret (with his wife Carol Lawrence), and on his own television series. In 1993, after taking a new production of *Camelot* around the US (in which, more than 30 years on, he played King Arthur instead of Lancelot), Goulet brought the show to New York where it was greeted without enthusiasm.

Selected albums: *Always You* (1962), *Two Of Us* (1962), *Sincerely Yours...* (1963), *The Wonderful World Of Love* (1963), *Robert Goulet In Person* (1963), *Manhattan Tower/The Man Who Loves Manhattan* (1964), *Without You* (1964), *My Love Forgive Me* (1964), *Begin To Love* (1965), *Summer Sounds* (1965), *Robert Goulet On Broadway* (1965), *Traveling On* (1966), *I Remember You* (1966), *Robert Goulet On Broadway, Volume 2* (1967), *Woman, Woman* (1968), *Hollywood Mon Amour - Great Love Songs From The Movies* (1968), *Both Sides Now* (1969), *Souvenir D'Italie* (1969), *Greatest Hits* (1969), *I Wish You Love* (1970), *Close To You* (1992).

Grab Me A Gondola

In the 50s, many years before film actresses such as Barbra Streisand and Bette Midler had their own production companies, the major studios called their young ladies 'starlets', and required them to flaunt their assets at annual film festivals around the world. One of Britain's leading glamour girls was Diana Dors, and she and her mink bikini were a common sight at the cinematic celebrations which took place at various venues such as the Venice Film Festival. The lady, and the location, provided the inspiration for this highly successful musical which was written by Julian More, and opened at the Lyric theatre in London on 26 December 1956. Tom Wilson (Dennis Quilley) is a showbiz reporter, and has gone to Venice to interview Virginia Jones (Joan Heal), who is a very 'hot property'. Tom's girlfriend, Margaret Kyle (Jane Wenham), finds it difficult to believe that his interest in Virginia is exclusively professional, and is flattered when the unctuous Prince Luigi Bourbon Corielli (Guido Lorraine) suggests that they sip champagne together. However, Tom is just not the cheating kind, and anyway, Virginia needs the Prince to finance her Shakespearean ambitions ('Cravin' for Avon'), so everyone else is paired-off accordingly. Julian More, together with the composer, James Gilbert, contributed a delightful score, which included Heal's amusing introductory number, 'That's My Biography', and then she, and the rest of the cast, had a ball with numbers such as 'Plain In Love', 'The Motor Car Is Treacherous', 'Bid Him A Fond Goodbye', 'Star Quality', 'Man, Not A Mouse', 'Lonely In A Crowd', 'Jimmy's Bar', 'Chianti', 'What Are The Facts?', 'Rig 'O The Day', 'When I Find That Girl', and 'Rockin' At The Cannon Ball'. Heal, a veteran of the London revue scene, was outstanding, and, generally, the show had a first-rate cast. *Grab Me A Gondola* was light, bright, bubbly stuff - a perfect antedote to the current American musical invasion - an enormous hit which ran for 673 performances, and provided Julian More with his first West End success - *Expresso Bongo*, *Irma La Douce*, and *Songbook*, were all still a few years away.

Grand Hotel

With music and lyrics by Robert Wright and George Forrest (additional numbers by Maury Yeston) and a book by Luther Davis based on the novel by Vicki Baum and the classic 1932 film which starred Greta Garbo, John Barrymore, Joan Crawford and several other well-known Hollywood names, *Grand Hotel* opened at the Martin Beck Theatre in New York on 12 October 1989. Set in a ritzy Berlin hotel in 1928 when Germany was already on the brink of Nazism, the main characters in this heavily plotted story whirl through the revolving doors: there is Elizaveta Grushinskaya (Liliane Montevecchi) the aging

Dolores Gray

Russian ballerina, Felix von Gaigern (David Carroll) the impoverished romantic German nobleman, Otto Kringelein (Michael Jeter) a Jewish bookkeeper dying of cancer and blowing his life savings on a few days of high living, and Flaemmchen (Jane Krakowski) the pregnant typist who is desperate to make it in Hollywood. However the real star of the piece was Tommy Tune, whose fluid direction and razzle dazzle choreography made this the most visually exciting musical that Broadway had seen for many a year. The songs came in for some severe criticism, although there were several appealing numbers among the score which included 'As It Should Be', 'Some Have, Some Have Not', 'At The Grand Hotel', 'And Life Goes On', 'Fire And Ice', 'I Want To Go To Hollywood', 'Everybody's Doing It', 'Who Couldn't Dance With You?', 'Love Can't Happen', 'I Waltz Alone', 'Roses At The Station', 'Bolero' (brilliantly danced adagio-style by Yvonne Marceau and Pierre Dulaine) and 'How Can I Tell Her?'. One of the highspots towards the end of the piece (there was no interval) came when the bookkeeper Kringelein and the Baron Gaigern link arms and kick up their heels in the exuberant 'We'll Take A Glass Together'. After transferring to the Gershwin Theatre early in 1992 to make way for a revival of Guys And Dolls, Grand Hotel continued its run for 1,018 performances, before closing in May of that year. The show was showered with awards, including five Tonys, for costumes, lighting, and featured actor (Michael Jeter),. Most of the kudos went to Tommy Tune who won two Tonys, and several others, including a couple of Astaire awards for his brilliant direction and choreography. The London production of Grand Hotel opened at the refurbished 2,000-seater Dominion Theatre but, despite initially good reviews, never really took off and closed after three months with losses estimated at around £2 million. The original cast album was not issued until more than two and half years after the show opened. Most of the original principals recreated their roles but a notably exception was David Carroll who played the Baron. He died of AIDS in March 1992, and, as a tribute, the CD contains a live recording of his version of one of the show's most attractive ballads, 'Love Can't Happen'.

Gray, Dolores

b. 7 June 1924, Chicago, Illinois, USA. Gray first sang on radio with Milton Berle and Rudy Vallee. Making her Broadway debut in Cole Porter's Seven Lively Arts (1944), she went on to play in Are You With It and Sweet Bye And Bye in 1946, and was then chosen by Richard Rodgers and Oscar Hammerstein II for the lead in their London production of Annie Get Your Gun. That historic opening night, on her 21st birthday, she took London by storm with a performance that almost matched Ethel Merman's triumph in the role on Broadway (and with 1,304 performances in London, her run played longer than Merman's 1,147). She was back on Broadway in 1951 in Two On The Aisle, and followed this two years later with Carnival In Flanders, for which she won a coveted Tony Award. MGM signed her for It's Always Fair Weather (1955) in which she shared the spotlight with stars Gene Kelly and Cyd Charisse with her vibrant singing of 'Music Is Better Than Words' and 'Thanks A Lot But No Thanks'. She was rewarded with a starring role in Kismet, followed by The Opposite Sex in 1956, but because musicals were on the wane MGM had only the comedy Designing Woman to offer, and she returned to Broadway in Destry Rides Again. Gray worked steadily in television and clubs and made singles for Capitol showing that she was no mere stage belter but a sensitive interpreter of standards. Apart from the splendid Warm Brandy she has been heard only on soundtrack and original cast albums. After playing London in Gypsy in 1974 she returned in triumph in 1987 to bring welcome Broadway expertise to an all-British version of Stephen Sondheim's Follies.
Album: Warm Brandy.

Grease

After starting its life as a five hour amateur production in Chicago in 1971, Grease opened in New York, Off Broadway, at the Eden Theatre in February 1972. Following a surprisingly enthusiastic reaction there, it moved to the Broadhurst Theatre on Broadway on 7 June. The book, music and lyrics, by Jim Jacobs (b. 7 October 1942, Chicago, Illinois, USA) and Warren Casey (b. 2 April 1935, Yonkers, New York, USA, d. 8 November 1988), transported excited audiences (but not unimpressed theatre critics) back to the rock 'n' roll days of the 50s, when bored, sexually frustrated teenagers went around in gangs with names like 'Pink Ladies' and 'Burger Palace Boys'. At a reunion of the class of 1959, the assembled group relive the time when Danny Zuko (Barry Bostwick) and Sandy Dumbrowski (Carol Demas) met up again at Rydell High School after an innocent summer romance. At first they seemed to be incompatible - him with his tough, macho image - and her so prim and proper and virginal - quite unlike the seemingly hard-bitten Betty Rizzo (Adrienne Barbeau). However, by the end of the piece, it was Sandy (some years before the advent of women's lib) who changed her attitude and donned the leather jacket and tight pants - along with the rest of the uniform of a 'greaser''s steady girl friend. The satirical and highly entertaining score contained plenty of affectionate digs at the period ('Look at me, I'm Sandra Dee/Lousy with virginity'), and other numbers such as 'Summer Nights', 'Freddie, My Love', 'Beauty

School Dropout', 'We Go Together', 'Greased Lightnin'', 'There Are Worse Things That I Could Do', 'Mooning', and 'It's Raining On Prom Night'. *Grease* stayed on Broadway for 3,388 performances, closing in February 1980. The first London production, in 1973, ran for 236 performances, and starred the then unknown Richard Gere as Danny. Elaine Paige was also in the company as an understudy, and eventually took over the role of Sandy. The show was revived in the West End in 1979, and again, in 1993, when Paul Nicholas, who had succeeded Richard Gere in the original 1973 London production, collaborated with the impresario, Robert Stigwood, to present a radically revised version. It starred the Australian soap actor, Craig McLachlan and the popular US singer, Debbie Gibson, and incorporated several songs that were written by Barry Gibb, John Farrar, Louis St. Louis, and Scott Simon for the 1978 smash-hit *Grease* movie, such as 'Hopelessly Devoted To You', 'You're The One That I Want', 'Grease', and 'Sandy'. On-screen, Danny and Sandy were played by John Travolta and Olivia Newton-John.

Great Hussar, The
(see *Balalaika*)

Great Waltz, The
In a Broadway season that was dominated by the all-American, smart and sophisticated *Anything Goes*, one of the most spectacular and elaborate stage productions of the 30s, *The Great Waltz*, opened at New York's huge Center Theatre in the Rockefeller Centre on 22 September 1934. A gigantic undertaking - almost 200 performers appeared onstage, including an orchestra of some 50 musicians - the show was based on a London production of the operetta, *Waltzes In Vienna*, and had music and lyrics by Johann Strauss Jnr. and Desmond Carter. The book, by Moss Hart, details the struggles between the younger Strauss (Guy Robertson), and his father, Johann Strauss Snr. (H. Reeves-Smith), which eventually results in the latter relinquishing his position - and his baton - to his son. The score contained several attractive numbers such as 'Like A Star In The Sky', 'Danube So Blue', 'Love Will Find You', and 'While You Love Me'. Audience and critical reactions were mixed, but the show ran for a creditable 298 performances and was revived briefly in 1935. A different version of the *The Great Waltz* opened at London's Drury Lane Theatre in 1970. It had music by both Strauss Snr. and Jnr, with Robert Wright and George Forrest's lyrics, and a book by Jerome Chodorov which was based on a story by Moss Hart and Milton Lazarus. This production ran for more than 600 performances.

Green, Adolph
(see **Comden, Betty**)

Greenwich Village Follies
The first of these revues, which were similar, but less lavish than the Ziegfeld Follies, opened at the Greenwich Village Theatre on 15 July 1919. All of the eight editions, through to 1928, played on Broadway, and were presented by the Bohemians Inc. (Al Jones and Morris Green). Most of them were directed by John Murray Anderson who also contributed sketches and lyrics. The show's satirical targets included most aspects of the Greenwich Village district and its uninhibited, arty inhabitants. The first edition, which ran for 232 performances - the most successful of all - was subtitled 'A Revusical Comedy Of New York's Latin Quarter', and had songs by A. Baldwin Sloane, Arthur Swanstrom and John Murray Anderson which included 'My Marionette', 'I'm Ashamed To Look The Moon In The Face,' 'My Little Javanese', and 'Message Of the Cameo'. An additional number was Irving Berlin's 'I'll See You In C-U-B-A'. Subsequent editions continued to arrive with the occasional appealing song such as Dorothy Terris and Julian Robeldo's 'Three O'Clock In The Morning' (1921), 'Georgette' (1922) by Lew Brown and Ray Henderson (of De Sylva, Brown And Henderson), and Cole Porter's gorgeous 'I'm In Love Again' (1924), but, generally speaking, the music department was not this particular Follies' strongest point. However, a great many talented entertainers graced its various productions, including Bobby Edwards, Bessie McCoy, Cecil Cunningham, Ted Lewis And His Orchesra, James Watts, Rex Story, Grace La Rue, Benny Fields, Bobby Watson, Frank Crumit, Howard Marsh, Joe E. Brown, Sammy White and Eva Puck, Vincent Lopez And His Orchestra, Savoy And Brennan, and Florence Moore.

Greenwillow
A whimsical, fantasy piece, with music and lyrics by Frank Loesser, and a book by Loesser and Lesser Samuels, *Greenwillow* opened on Broadway at the Alvin Theatre on 8 March 1960. Based on B.J. Chute's novel, it was set in a mythical American village, and told the story of Gideon Briggs (Anthony Perkins) and his reluctance to marry his sweetheart, Dorrie (Ellen McCown), because he is afraid that he may have inherited the family trait - wanderlust - and so may up and leave her. Loesser's songs were tender and charming, and have continued to be admired. They included 'The Music Of Home', 'Summertime Love', 'A Day Borrowed From Heaven', 'Gideon Briggs, I Love You', 'Walking Away Whistling', and 'Faraway Boy'. Anthony Perkins, making his Broadway musical debut, had the reflective 'Never

Will I Marry', which attained some popularity. The whole affair was far removed from another of Perkin's projects in 1960, Alfred Hitcock's terrifying film, *Psycho*, in which he gave a performance that will always be remembered. The folksy, thoughful *Greenwillow* just did not appeal to New York theatre audiences at a time when the entertainment world in general was on the brink of the brash, swinging 60s, and it closed after only 95 performances. By then, Loesser was in the throes of a far different proposition, his 1961 blockbuster, *How To Succeed In Business Without Even Trying*, lasted for 1,417 performances.

Grenfell, Joyce

b. Joyce Irene Phipps, 10 February 1910, London, England, d. 30 November 1979, London, England. An actress, singer and author - a brilliant exponent of the monologue and witty song. The daughter of American parents - her mother's sister was Nancy Astor - Joyce Phipps used to describe herself as 'three fourths American'. She became interested in the theatre at an early age, and spent a term at RADA before marrying Reginald Grenfell in 1929. Subsequently, she worked for a time in commercial art, contributed to *Punch* and *Country Life*, and spent over three years as radio critic for the *Observer*. After impressing the humourist Steven Potter with her own charming recollection of a lecture that she had recently attended at a Women's Institute, she was engaged by the theatrical producer, Herbert Farjeon, for *The Little Revue* (1939). In the early 40s she appeared in other Farjeon revues, *Diversion*, *Diversion No. 2* and *Light And Shade*, and then, in 1944, toured extensively with ENSA, in the Near and Far East, and in India, entertaining the troops in British forces' hospitals, with comic monologues and songs. Two years later she was awarded the OBE. In *Sigh No More* (1945), at London's Piccadilly Theatre, Grenfell dressed as a schoolgirl for Noël Coward's witty 'That Is The End Of The News', and, in the same show, introduced 'Du Maurier', a song she had written with composer Richard Addinsell. They collaborated again on material for the revues, *Tuppence Coloured* (1947) and *Penny Plain* (1951), in which Grenfell also appeared. It was the beginning of a significant and enduring professional relationship. By the late 40s and early 50s, Grenfell was working more and more in radio - as a panellist on *We Beg To Differ*, and as the British host of *Transatlantic Quiz*. She made a couple of propaganda films during the war, but her movie career proper began in 1943 with a comedy, *The Demi-Paradise*, which starred Laurence Olivier and Margaret Rutherford. Grenfell appeared with Rutherford again, in *The Happiest Days Of Your Life* (1949), which also starred the lugubrious Alastair Sim. He and Grenfell managed to emerge unscathed from the *St. Trinians* film series. during the late 50s.

Grenfell's other film roles, some of them highly telling cameos, were in such as *Here Comes The Bride*, *The Galloping Major*, *Pickwick Papers*, *The Million Pound Note* and *The Americanization Of Emily*. It was on stage, though, that she really came into her own. In 1954 she wrote the book and lyrics, with Addinsell's music, for *Joyce Grenfell Requests The Pleasure*, which ran for nearly a year in London before transferring to Broadway in the following year. In America, Grenfell developed her one-woman show, toured US cities, and appeared on the *Ed Sullivan Show* several times in the late 50s. One Sullivan date saw her on the same bill with Elvis Presley ('a pasty-faced plump boy', as she recalled). She presented her solo effort in London for the first time in 1957, at the Lyric theatre, under the title of *Joyce Grenfell - A Miscellany*, and later took the show to Australia where it was called *Meet Joyce Grenfell*. Throughout the 60s she continued to tour extensively at home and abroad, and went back to Australia three times. In the early 70s she lost the sight of one eye and retired from the stage. During the next six years she published two volumes of autobiography, *Joyce Grenfell Requests The Pleasure* and *In Pleasant Places*, before cancer affected her other eye, too, and she died in 1979. Always an effective broadcaster, from 1966 she was an essential member of television's *Face The Music*, a general knowlege quiz about music, and had her own series on BBC2 for a time. As a performer she was unique, and impossible to pigeon-hole. The wonder is that, because of her 'terribly English' image, she was so popular around the world, particularly in America. With the gentle 'I'm Going To See You Today', which became her theme, the pomp of 'Stately As A Galleon', and many other favourites such as 'Maude', 'Nursery School', 'A Terrible Worrier', 'Time', 'Three Brothers', 'It's Almost Tomorrow', and two recorded duets with Norman Wisdom, 'Narcissus' and 'I Don't 'Arf Love You', she presented a refined, humorous, perceptive, yet never unkind view of society. One of her best remembered pieces is 'I Like Life', which accords with her own philosophy: 'I am not interested in the pursuit of happiness, but only in the discovery of joy'. Her companion on that journey, Reginald Grenfell, who edited some of her books, died in 1993. In 1988, the revue *Re: Joyce!*, 'a diverting and engaging mixture of anecdotal biography and quintessential sketch material', starring Maureen Lipman with Denis King, opened in London and continued to be presented at intervals into the 90s.

Selected albums: *Requests The Pleasure* (1955), *At Home* (1957), *The Collection* (1976), *The New Collection* (1978), *Joyce Grenfell Talking* (1981), *Keepsake* (1986), *Re: Joyce* (1988), *The Second Collection* (1988), *Songs And Monologues* (1991), *Requests The Plaeasure* (3-CD set, 1992). Maureen Lipman and Denis King *Re: Joyce!* (stage cast, 1989).

Joyce Grenfell

Further reading: *Darling Ma: Letters To Her Mother, 1932-1944*, Edited by James Roose-Evans. *George - Don't Do that...* (sketches and songs). *Stately As A Galleon* (sketches and songs). *Time Of My Life - Entertaining The Troops: Her Wartime Journals*, Joyce Grenfell. *Joyce Grenfell Requests The Pleasure*, Joyce Grenfell. *Joyce: By Herself And Her Friends*, Edited by Reggie Grenfell and Richard Garnett. *In Pleasant Places*, Joyce Grenfell.

Guys And Dolls

Opening at the 46th Street Theatre in New York on 24 November 1950, the stage musical *Guys And Dolls* was a predicted success. With a book by Abe Burrows and Jo Swerling, and music and lyrics by Frank Loesser, out-of-town tryouts were hugely successful and by the time of its opening night on Broadway the word was out that the show was a winner. Based upon the risque yarns of Damon Runyon, the dialogue and lyrics effectively captured the speech patterns of Runyon's larger-than-life characters and the music perfectly matched the show's mood. The story presents an account of a love affair between compulsive gambler Nathan Detroit and dancer Miss Adelaide, alongside of which develops another love story, this one between another gambler, Sky Masterson, and Miss Sarah Brown, a member of the 'Save A Soul Mission'. Other Runyonesque characters fill out the cast, notably Benny Southstreet, Big Jule, Harry the Horse, and Nicely-Nicely Johnson. During the course of the show true love eventually finds its way despite many obstacles, not least of which is police lieutenant Brannigan's desperate attempts to locate and close down Nathan's floating crap game, the oldest established in New York. By the end, Masterson is a reformed character and has married Sarah while Nathan and Miss Adelaide are about to marry after a 14-year long courtship. Loesser's songs included 'Fugue For Tinhorns', 'The Oldest Established' 'Take Back Your Mink', 'A Bushel And A Peck'. 'Adelaide's Lament', 'Marry The Man Today', 'Sue Me', 'If I Were A Bell', 'I've Never Been In Love Before', 'More I Cannot Wish You', and 'Luck Be A Lady'. Complementing the show's strong characterization and dramatic storyline, the producers cast actors rather than singers in the key roles, amongst them Sam Levene as Nathan, Vivian Blaine, who had worked in Hollywood musicals, as Miss Adelaide, Robert Alda as Sky, Isabel Bigley as Sarah, and Stubby Kaye as Nicely-Nicely who stopped the show every night with his exuberant singing of 'Sit Down, You're Rockin' The Boat'. Critics and public loved the show and it ran for some 1,200 performances, winning Tony Awards for best musical, actor (Alda), featured actress Bigley), director (George S. Kaufman), and choreographer (Michael Kidd). A London production

opened in 1953, and the show was revived in 1982 by the National Theatre, and again in 1985 with pop singer Lulu as Miss Adelaide. A major Broadway revival, starring Nathan Lane, Faith Prince, Peter Gallagher, and Josie de Guzman, opened in April 1992, and was widely acclaimed. It won Tonys for best revival, actress (Prince), and director (Jerry Zaks). The 1955 film version starred Marlon Brando as Sky (one of Sky's songs, 'My Time Of Day', was dropped because the actor was unable to sing it), with Jean Simmons as Sarah, Frank Sinatra as Nathan, and Vivian Blaine and Stubby Kaye reprising their roles.

Gypsy

With a book by Arthur Laurents, which was based on stripper Gypsy Rose Lee's autobiography, and music and lyrics by Jule Styne and Stephen Sondheim, this show opened at the Broadway Theatre in New York on 21 May 1959. Director and choreographer Jerome Robbins gave the production added strength and *Gypsy* looked good from the start, but the story's construction demanded a powerful lead in the role of Mamma Rose. She was the tough, ambitious mother of the two aspiring entertainers who grew up to be 'Louise' and 'June'; in real life Gypsy Rose Lee and her much more talented younger sister, screen actress June Havoc. In casting Ethel Merman the producers did not only get the best woman for the job, they also got an artist audiences would flock to see. The score is one of the most highly regarded in Broadway musical history, and included 'Let Me Entertain You', 'Together Wherever We Go', 'Small World', 'If Mamma Was Married', 'All I Need Is The Girl', 'You Gotta Have Gimmick', 'Mr. Goldstone', and Merman's blockbusters, 'Everything's Coming Up Roses' and 'Rose's Turn'. Other cast members included Sandra Church and Jack Klugman. The show ran for 702 performances, and was revived in 1974 with Angela Lansbury as Mamma Rose. This acclaimed production also played in London during 1973. The 1962 film version mysteriously miscast an over-demure Natalie Wood as Louise and an ultra-refined Rosalind Russell as Mamma Rose, a part that screamed out for a singer who could belt out a song as only Merman knew how. A new version of *Gypsy*, starring Bette Midler, was shown on US television in December 1993. It purported to be the first film of a complete musical to retain the complete text, with no material added or altered.

Hair

After an off-Broadway opening, the stage musical *Hair* came onto the Great White Way at the Biltmore Theatre on 29 April 1968. In jargon not yet in use, *Hair* was what might be described as 'alternative entertainment'. Amongst many things that made the show different was its forceful stand on matters like sex, politics, drugs, the draft and religion. It was the first musical of the hippie peace and love generation; many of the performers wore wigs as they had yet to grow their own hair. Strong language and nudity ensured a measure of shock value and doubtless helped fill seats with the prurient. Despite, or perhaps because of, its irreverence and decidedly contemporary attitude, *Hair* was received favourably by critics. The music was by Galt MacDermot with book and lyrics by Gerome Ragni and James Rado. Cast with mostly unknown young actors, *Hair* offered a joyous theatrical experience unlike that to which most Broadway regulars were accustomed. Amongst the cast were Lynn Kellogg, Melba Moore, Sally Eaton, Diane Keaton, and Lamont Washington. The songs included 'I Believe In Love', 'Hair', 'Hare Krishna', 'Walking In Space', 'Good Morning, Starshine'; other titles broke more new ground for establishment-Broadway: 'Prisoners In Niggertown', 'Hashish' and 'Sodomy'. Several artists had hits with songs from the show, notably the Fifth Dimension who topped the US chart with a medley which included 'Aquarius' and 'Let The Sunshine In'. The successfull 1968 London production had Paul Nicholas, Oliver Tobias and Marsha Hunt among the cast, (Alex Harvey was in the pit orchestra). A 1993 revival at London's Old Vic ('this show is about as topical as *The Pirates Of Penzance*') folded after two months. A film version of *Hair* appeared in 1979.

Half A Sixpence

The chirpy ex-merchant seaman Tommy Steele, moved impressively from rock 'n' roll stardom to musical comedy in this engaging adaptation of H.G. Wells's novel, *Kipps*, which opened at the Cambridge Theatre in London on 21 March 1963. Beverly Cross's book told of a young orphan, Arthur Kipps (Steele), who is an apprentice at Shalford's Drapery Emporium. When he inherits a large sum of money he abandons his childhood sweetheart, Ann (Marti Webb), in favour of Helen (Anna Barry), whom he feels is more in keeping with his newly acquired financial status and social-climbing ambitions.

Naturally, when he loses the cash he comes back down to earth, returns to Ann - and shrewdly turns down another fortune. David Heneker's score was a joy, and contained several lovely songs such as the apprentices' anthem to their boss, 'All In The Cause Of Economy', three gentle ballads 'Half A Sixpence', 'She's Too Far Above Me', and 'If The Rain's Got To Fall', and the rousing 'Money To Burn'. The show's musical highlight, 'Flash, Bang, Wallop!', was an ensemble piece during which Kipps and his bride are married, congratulated, and photographed. Steele was outstanding: - this was probably the best and most satisfying stage role of his long career - although no doubt he would argue with that. After a London run of 679 performances he took the show to Broadway in 1965 where it stayed at the Broadhurst Theatre for over a year. His co-stars in the 1967 film version were Julia Foster and Cyril Ritchard.

Hall, Adelaide

b. Adelaide Louisa Hall, 20 October 1901, Brooklyn, New York City, New York, USA, d. 7 November 1993, London, England. Though not a jazz singer, Hall has become one of the most famous vocalists in jazz history through her wordless vocals on such Duke Ellington recordings as 'Creole Love Call' and 'Blues I Love To Sing'. Other numbers with which she was indelibly associated, included 'Sophisticated Lady', 'Old Fashioned Love', 'Memories Of You', 'Solitude', 'Don't Get Around Much Anymore' and 'Don't Worry 'Bout Me'. Many of the songs she sang were written especially for her. Her fine soprano voice was developed by her father, a music professor. Like her friend, Lena Horne, her name will always be associated with Harlem's famous Cotton Club and the 'greats' who gathered there, such as Ellington, Fats Waller and composer Harold Arlen. Hall, a self-taught tap dancer, played in the Eubie Blake-Noble Sissle show In the early 20s and appeared in a series of revues including, *Shuffle Along*, *Chocolate Kiddies* and *Desires Of 1927*. She starred in Lew Leslie's *Blackbirds Of 1928*, in a cast which also included Bill 'Bojangles' Robinson, and Elisabeth Welch. The Dorothy Fields/Jimmy McHugh score introduced 'Diga Diga Doo', 'Doin' The New Low-Down', 'I Can't Give You Anything But Love' and a pre-Gershwin 'Porgy'. When the show transferred to the Moulin Rouge in Paris, Hall went with it, and stayed on to sing at the Lido. By this time she had married an English seaman, Bert Hicks. He opened a club for her, called La Grosse Pomme (The Big Apple), whose clientele included Django Reinhardt, Maurice Chevalier and Charles Boyer. In the early 30s she recorded with Duke Ellington and Willy Lewis in the USA, and was also accompanied by pianists Art Tatum and Joe Turner on a New York session which produced 'This Time It's Love'. During the rest of the decade she toured extensively in the USA and Europe, and by the late 30s had settled in Britain, where she lived for over 50 years. In 1938 Hall appeared at London's Theatre Royal, Drury Lane, in *The Sun Never Sets*, a musical in which she impressed audiences and critics with her version of Vivian Ellis's title song. In the same year she recorded four songs with Fats Waller in London: 'That Old Feeling', 'I Can't Give You Anything But Love', 'Smoke Dreams' and 'You Can't Have Your Cake And Eat It'. With her husband, she opened the Florida Club in Bruton Mews, but it was destroyed during a bombing raid in World War II. Later she joined an ENSA company and was one of the first artists into Germany after the liberation. After the war she worked consistently, singing in theatres throughout the country, on cruise liners, and on her own radio show, accompanied by the Joe Loss Orchestra. In 1951 she starred in the London version of Cole Porter's *Kiss Me Kate*, and, in the following year, sang 'A Touch Of Voodoo' and 'Kind To Animals' in Hugh Martin's hit musical, *Love From Judy*, at the Saville Theatre. In 1957 she was back on Broadway, with Lena Horne, in *Jamaica*, which ran for over 500 performances. In 1963, shortly after opening a new club, the Calypso, in London's Regent Street, Adelaide's husband Bert died. During the 60s and 70s, Hall was out of the limelight, but in the 80s, came a renaissance, partly sparked by the release of Francis Ford Coppola's film *The Cotton Club*. From then on she was in constant demand for cabaret at the Ritz Hotel, and other UK venues such as the Donmar Warehouse and the King's Head, Islington. In 1988, she presented her one-woman show at New York's Carnegie Hall, and three years later, was joined onstage at London's Queen Elizabeth Hall by artists such as Larry Adler, Ralph McTell and Roy Budd, in a concert to celebrate her 90th birthday.

Selected albums: *That Wonderful Adelaide Hall* (1969), *Hall Of Fame* (1970), *Hall Of Ellington* (1976), *There Goes That Song Again* (1980), *Hall Of Memories 1927-1939* (1990), *Crooning Blackbird* (1993).

Hamlisch, Marvin

b. 2 June 1944, New York City, New York, USA. Hamlisch was a pianist, arranger, and composer for Broadway musical shows and films. A child prodigy, he played the piano by ear at the age of five and when he was seven became the youngest student ever to be enrolled at the Juilliard School of Music. One of the first songs he wrote as a teenager was 'Travelin' Man', which was eventually recorded by his friend, Liza Minnelli on her first album, *Liza, Liza*. Through Minnelli, he was able to obtain work as a rehearsal pianist and assistant vocal arranger for some Broadway shows. Lesley Gore gave him his first song hit, in 1965, when she took his 'Sunshine, Lollipops And

Rainbows' (lyric by Howard Liebling) into the US Top 20. After majoring in music at Queen's College, Hamlisch wrote the theme music for Sam Spiegel's 1968 film, *The Swimmer*, starring Burt Lancaster. After that, he moved to Hollywood and wrote the music for two Woody Allen comedies, *Take The Money And Run* (1969) and *Bananas* (1971). He also scored two Jack Lemmon films *The April Fools* (1969) and *Save The Tiger* (1973), for which Lemmon won an Oscar. In 1971 his song 'Life Is What You Make It', with a lyric by Johnny Mercer, written for the Walter Matthau movie, *Kotch*, was nominated for an Academy Award.

Three years later, in April 1974, he collected an impressive total of three Oscars. For *The Way We Were*, he won Best Original Dramatic Score and Best Title Song in conjunction with lyricists Alan and Marilyn Bergman. His third Oscar was for his adaptation of Scott Joplin's music for *The Sting*. Hamlisch's piano recording of one of the film's main themes, 'The Entertainer', sold over a million copies. In July 1975, his first Broadway musical, *A Chorus Line*, opened at the Schubert Theatre. Conceived and directed by Michael Bennett, the songs included 'One', 'What I Did For Love', 'Nothing' and 'I Hope I Get It', with lyrics by the virtually unknown Edward Kleban, which suited perfectly the story of a group of dancers auditioning for an idiosyncratic director. The production was showered with awards: the Pullitzer Prize For Drama (1976); Tony Award for Best Musical; New York Drama Critics Circle Award for Best Musical; and several others including a Tony Award for the Hamlisch-Kleban score. The Original Cast album was estimated to have sold 1,250,000 copies by October 1983. *A Chorus Line* closed in March 1990 after an incredible run of 6,137 performances, making it Broadway's longest-running show. It was filmed in 1985, with a somewhat controversial choice of director in Richard Attenborough.

Hamlisch was back on Broadway in 1979 with *They're Playing Our Song*, which had a book by Neil Simon, and lyrics by Carole Bayer Sager. This two-hander, starring Robert Klein and Lucie Arnaz, about the stormy relationship between two songwriters, (with three singing alter egos each), is said to have been based on Hamlisch's and Sager's own liaison. The songs included 'Fallin'', 'If He Really Knew Me', 'They're Playing Our Song', 'When You're in My Arms 'and 'I Still Believe In Love'. The show played over 1,000 performances on Broadway and did well at London's Shaftesbury Theatre, where it starred Gemma Craven and Tom Conti. Hamlisch also provided the music (with lyrics by Christopher Adler) for a production of *Jean Seberg*, which enjoyed a brief run a London's National Theatre in 1983, and, three years later, was represented on Broadway again, with

Smile (lyrics by Howard Ashman), which closed after only 48 performances. Movie collaborations between Hamlisch and Carole Bayer Sager during the 70s included the Oscar-nominated 'Nobody Does It Better', from the James Bond feature, *The Spy Who Loved Me* (a US number 2 hit for Carly Simon), 'Better Than Ever' (from the Burt Reynolds' film, *Starting Over*), the theme from *Ice Castles*, 'Through The Eyes Of Love' (Academy Award nomination) and 'If You Remember Me' (from Franco Zeffirelli's *The Champ*). Hamlisch also wrote the scores for three Neil Simon film comedies, *Chapter Two* (1979), *Seems Like Old Times* (1980) and *I Ought To Be In Pictures* (1982); the 1981 US film version of *Pennies From Heaven*, (in collaboration with veteran bandleader Billy May); *The January Man*, a Kevin Kline thriller; and *Ordinary People*, the Academy Award-winning film for 1980. He received an ASCAP award for his score to *Three Men And A Baby*, one of 1987's top-grossing films, and gained Academy Award nominations for songs written with Alan and Marilyn Bergman, 'The Last Time I Felt Like This' from *Same Time Next Year* (1978), and 'The Girl Who Used To Be Me' from *Shirley Valentine* (1989). He was also nominated for his score for the Oscar-winning film *Sophie's Choice* (1982) and, with Edward Kleban, found himself on the short list again, with 'Surprise, Surprise', from the movie version of their Broadway show, *A Chorus Line*. Hamlisch's film scores in the early 90s included *Frankie And Johnny*, *The January Man*; and *Missing Pieces*, which contained the song 'High Energy', written with David Zippel. Hamlisch collaborated with Zippel again, on the score for Neil Simon's *The Goodbye Girl*, which, even with Bernadette Peters in the cast, could only manage a run of 188 performances in 1993. In the same year, Hamlisch conducted the London Symphony Orchestra at the Barbican Hall in the European premiere of his 25-minute work 'The Anatomy Of Peace'.

Albums: *The Sting* (1974, film soundtrack), *The Entertainer* (1974), *The Way We Were* (1974, film soundtrack), *A Chorus Line* (1975, Broadway Cast), *The Spy Who Loved Me* (1977, film soundtrack), *Ice Castles* (1979, film soundtrack), *They're Playing Our Song* (1979, Broadway Cast), *They're Playing Our Song* (1980, London Cast).

Further reading: *The Way I Was*, Marvin Hamlisch with Gerald Gardner.

Hammerstein, Oscar, II

b. 12 July 1895, New York City, New York, USA, d. 23 August 1960. Hammerstein was born into a family with long-standing theatrical associations. His father, William Hammerstein, was manager of New York's Victoria theatre, and an uncle, Arthur Hammerstein, was a Broadway producer. Most famous of all his ancestors was his grandfather, Oscar Hammerstein I, who had made a fortune in industry before becoming one of New York's leading theatrical impresarios and founder of the Manhattan Opera. Although he studied law, the young Oscar's background inevitably affected him and, while still at school he wrote for shows. He was doubtless also influenced by some of his fellow students, who included future songwriters Lorenz Hart and Howard Dietz. Oscar's show business career began when he was employed by his uncle as assistant stage manager and soon afterwards he wrote a stage play and then a musical together with Herbert Stothart, who later became General Music Director at MGM. Hammerstein then wrote *Tickle Me* (1920) in collaboration with Otto Harbach. Subsequently, Hammerstein and Harbach teamed up again as co-lyricists and co-librettists to write a show with Vincent Youmans and Stothart, the successful *Wildflower* (1923). They followed this by working with Rudolf Friml on *Rose-Marie* (1924), which proved to be a classic of American operetta. The hit songs of the show were 'Rose-Marie' and 'Indian Love Call'. Hammerstein's next partnership was with Jerome Kern, which resulted in *Sunny* (1925), with 'Sunny' and 'Who?' as the big hits.

The following year he worked with George Gershwin on *Song Of The Flame*, and the year after that with Harbach and Sigmund Romberg on *The Desert Song*, which produced lasting successes such as 'The Desert Song' ('Blue Heaven') and 'One Alone'. Hammerstein teamed up again with Kern in 1927 for *Show Boat*, writing lyrics for 'Why Do I Love You?', 'Can't Help Lovin' Dat Man', 'Only Make Believe' and 'Ol' Man River'. In 1928 he rejoined Harbach and Friml to gain further acclaim with *The New Moon*, which featured 'Lover Come Back To Me' and 'Softly As In A Morning Sunrise'. He continued to work with Kern, and during the next few years their shows were liberally scattered with songs which became standards, among them 'The Song Is You', 'I've Told Ev'ry Little Star', and 'All The Things You Are'.

In the early 30s Hammerstein was lured to Hollywood, where he met with only limited success. Although some of the films on which he worked were box-office failures, he nevertheless co-authored several timeless songs, including, 'When I Grow Too Old To Dream' (with Romberg) and 'I Won't Dance' (with Harbach and Kern), the latter for the 1935 Astaire-Rogers film, *Roberta*. Other songs written with Kern for films were 'Can I Forget You', 'The Folks Who Live On The Hill', 'I'll Take Romance' and 'The Last Time I Saw Paris', which won an Oscar in 1941. In the early 40s Hammerstein's career took a new direction and the ups and downs of the past were forgotten with a series of smash-hit Broadway shows, all written with a new partner. He had worked briefly with Richard Rodgers in 1928 and again in 1935, but now with Rodgers's regular collaborator, Lorenz Hart, silenced by alcoholism and despair, a new partnership was formed. The first production of Rodgers and Hammerstein was *Oklahoma!* (1943), which was followed by *Carousel* (1945), *Allegro* (1947), *South Pacific* (1949), *The King And I* (1951), *Me And Juliet* (1953), *Pipe Dream* (1955), *Flower Drum Song* (1958) and *The Sound Of Music* (1959). Collectively, these shows were among the most successful in the history of the American musical theatre, with *Oklahoma!* running for 2,212 performances and winning a Pulitzer Prize - as did *South Pacific*, which ran for 1,925 performances. In addition to their stage successes, Rodgers and Hammerstein wrote a film, *State Fair* (1945), which included the Oscar-winning song, 'It Might As Well Be Spring', and a television show, *Cinderella* (1957). A brief list of songs from their stage musicals includes such well-loved hits as 'Oh, What A Beautiful Morning', 'People Will Say We're In Love', 'The Surrey With The Fringe On Top', 'If I Loved You', 'You'll Never Walk Alone', 'Some Enchanted Evening', 'Younger Than Springtime', 'Bali Ha'i', 'Hello, Young Lovers', 'Shall We Dance?', 'No Other Love' and 'Climb Ev'ry Mountain'. In between *Oklahoma!* and *Carousel*, Hammerstein wrote a new libretto and new lyrics for Georges Bizet's opera, *Carmen*. The new show, *Carmen Jones*, opened on Broadway in 1943 and was a great success. The show was transferred to the screen in 1954 and, most recently, was revived in London's West End in 1991. One of Broadway's most successful lyricists, Hammerstein wrote with engaging simplicity, a trait which set him well apart from his predecessor, Hart. His remarkable contribution to America's theatrical tradition was profound and his irreproachable standards represented the culmination of the traditional, operetta-based style of musical comedy. In 1993, the 50th anniversary of Rodgers and Hammerstein's first collaboration on 'America's most loved musical', was celebrated by the publication of *OK! The Story Of Oklahoma!*, by Max Wilk. In addition, *A Grand Night For Singing*, a revue which was packed with their songs, played for a brief spell on Broadway.

Further reading: *Some Enchanted Evening: The Story Of Rodgers and Hammerstein*, J.D. Taylor. *The Rodgers And Hammerstein Story*, Stanley Green. *The Sound Of Their Music: The Story Of Rodgers And Hammerstein*, Frederick Nolan.

Hanson, John

b. John Stanley Watts, 31 August 1922, Oshawa, Ontario, Canada. A singer, actor, and producer. Hanson moved to the UK with his parents in 1925 and was brought up in Scotland. He sang as a boy soprano in his local choir and made several broadcasts in the early 30s. When he left school he became a production engineer before making his professional debut in 1946 at a concert in Birmingham. He made his name initially on radio programmes such as *Songs From The Shows*, accompanied by the orchestras of Geraldo and Mantovani, and Troise And His Mandoliers, and later became a regular on *Friday Night Is Music Night*, *Fred Hartleys' Hour*, and *Ray's A Laugh*. It was Mantovani who gave Hanson his first opportunity on television and he eventually had his own series *John Hanson Sings* which was introduced by 'A Song Of Romance', one of his own compositions. In 1957 he began to organize and appear in touring revivals of romantic musicals from the past. He played the Red Shadow in *The Desert Song*, and the role became indelibly associated with him. It was followed by *The Student Prince*, *The Vagabond King*, *Lilac Time*, *Rose Marie*, and *Maid Of The Mountains*. In Britain the beat boom was well under way, but Hanson - who by then was being termed 'the last of the matinee idols' - continued to bring a glorious taste of nostalgia to eager and appreciative audiences throughout the UK. In 1965 he took the leading role in *The World Of Ivor Novello* and a year later appeared in *When You're Young*, for which he wrote the book, music, and lyrics. In 1967 he made his West End debut in *The Desert Song* which was succeeded by *The Student Prince*. Both London productions transferred to Blackpool for summer seasons in 1969/70. In 1972 at the Prince of Wales Theatre he played John Carteret in *Smilin' Through*, his own musical adaptation of the film of the same name. Over the next few years he continued to tour in nostalgic productions such as *Lilac Time*, *Rose Marie*, *The Dancing Years*, and *Glamorous Night*. After producing and directing a farewell tour of *The Desert Song* in 1976/7, he devoted most of his time to concerts and summer seasons, and was still active until the mid-80s when he was forced to retire through ill health.

Selected albums: *The Student Prince-Vagabond King* (1961), *Lilac Time-Maid Of the Mountains* (1964), *In Musical Comedy* (1964), *Music Of Ivor Novello* (1965), *Songs Of Romance* (1965), with Vanessa Lee *This Is London* (1966), *Encores* (1966), *When You're Young* (1966), *Desert Song-New Moon* (1967), *Rodgers And Hammerstein Favourites* (1968), *My Songs Of Love For You* (1969), *Desert Song-Student Prince* (1970), *Great Songs From Great Films* (1970), *Smilin' Through* (1972), *Lilac Time-Maid Of The Mountain* (1973), *Sings Friml Favourites* (1973), *I'll Sing You A Thousand Love Songs* (1973), *The Dancing Years-White Horse Inn* (1975), *Sings 20 Showtime Greats* (1977). Compilations: *Showcase* (1968), *Sings Songs From His Shows* (1976), *Spotlight On John Hanson* (1977), *Favourites* (1984).

Further reading: *Me And My Red Shadow*, John Hanson.

Happy Time, The

Two years after their triumph on Broadway with *Cabaret*, John Kander and Fred Ebb returned with this very different show, which opened on 18 January 1968 at the Broadway Theatre in New York. N. Richard Nash's book, based on the novel by Robert L. Fontaine, told the warm and touching story of a French-Canadian family who find themselves in a state of flux. Jacques (Robert Goulet), an unattached, fancy-free magazine photographer, returns home for a while, and discovers that his nephew, Bibi Bonnard (Mike Rupert), is growing up fast and wants to leave his home and grandpére, (David Wayne), to get out and see the world with his uncle. In the end the boy is persuaded to stay, and Grandpa Bonnard also hangs on to the show's most convivial number, 'The Life Of The Party' ('If your festivities include a soirée/You ought to give it ease, the easiest way/Beside the caviar and chocolate soufflé/You better have me there, the life of the party'). The rest of this affectionately regarded score included 'A Certain Girl', 'The Happy Time', 'Please Stay', 'Tomorrow Morning', 'I Don't Remember You', 'Seeing Things', 'Without Me', 'St. Pierre', and '(Walking) Among My Yesterdays'. During the *The Happy Time*'s run of 286 performances, there was some difference of opinion as to choreographer-director Gower Champion's use of blown-up photographs and filmed sequences for some of the show's scenes. The Tony Awards committee was obviously impressed because they gave him two Awards, and Robert Goulet also received one for best actor.

Harbach, Otto

b. Otto Abels Hauerbach, 18 August 1873, Salt Lake City, Utah, USA, d. 24 January 1963, New York City, New York, USA. An important lyricist and librettist for more than 20 years, Harbach was one of the links between traditional operetta and America's indigenous musical comedy. After beginning his career as an academic, Harbach wrote for newspapers and advertising agencies in the early part of the century before collaborating with the composer Karl Hoschna on the score for the successful Broadway musical *The Three Twins* in 1908. One of the show's songs, 'Cuddle Up A Little Closer, Lovey Mine', became popular at the time for Ada Jones and Billy Murray. Harbach and Hoschna worked together on four more shows, *Madame Sherry* ('Every Little Movement'; 'The Smile She Means For Me'), *Dr. Deluxe*, *The Girl Of My Dreams*, and *The Fascinating Widow*. After Hoschna's death in 1911 Harbach collaborated with several notable composers including Oscar Hammerstein II, Rudolph Friml, Herbert Stothart, Louis Hirsch, Aladar Renyi, Alfred Newman, Vincent Youmans, William Daly, Sigmund Romberg, George Gershwin, and Jerome Kern. There are several all-time hits among his list of nearly 40 shows which included *The Firefly* ('Giannina Mia'; 'Sympathy'; 'Love Is Like A Firefly'), *High Jinks* ('Love's Own Kiss'; 'The Bubble'), *Katinka* ('My Paradise'), *You're In Love* ('I'm Only Dreaming'), *Going Up* ('Kiss Me; 'If You Look Into Her Eyes'; 'The Tickle Toe'), *Mary* ('The Love Nest'; 'Waiting'), *Tickle Me* ('If A Wish Could Make It So'), *Wildflower* ('Bambalina'; 'April Blossoms'), *Rose Marie* ('Rose Marie'; 'Indian Love Call'; 'Song Of The Mounties'), *No, No, Nanette* ('I've Confessed To The Breeze'; 'No, No, Nanette'), *Sunny* ('Who'; 'D'Ya Love Me?'), *The Desert Song* ('The Desert Song'; 'The Riff Song'; 'One Alone'), *The Wild Rose* ('Brown Eyes'), *Lucky* ('The Same Old Moon'), *The Cat And The Fiddle* ('The Night Was Made For Love'; 'She Didn't Say 'Yes''; 'Try To Forget'), and *Roberta* (1933) ('Smoke Gets In Your Eyes'; 'The Touch Of Your Hand'; 'Yesterdays'). Over the years, several of them such as *The Desert Song*, *The Cat And The Fiddle*, *Roberta*, *Rose Marie*, and *No, No, Nanette*, were turned into popular films. One of Harbach's earliest shows, *Madame Sherry*, was subsequently rewritten following its original run and several popular songs by other composers were added, such as 'Put Your Arms Around Me, Honey', 'Oh! You Beautiful Doll', 'Ciribiribin', and 'Walking the Dog'. This later version was revived at the Goodspeed Opera House, Connecticut, in 1992. The acclaimed production was adapted and directed by Martin Connor who re-staged it at London's Guildhall School of Music in 1993.

Harburg, E.Y. 'Yip'

b. Edgar Harburg, 8 April 1896, New York City, New York, USA, d. 5 March 1981, Los Angeles, California, USA. An important lyricist during the 30s and 40s, Harburg was born on New York's Lower East Side, the son of Jewish immigrant parents, and given the nickname 'Yipsel' (meaning 'squirrel'). At high school, he worked on the student newspaper with fellow pupil, Ira Gershwin, before they both attended the City College of New York, where Harburg began to write light verse. After graduating in 1918, he worked for a time as a journalist in South America, before returning to New York to run his own electrical supply business. Hit by the stock market crash of 1929, he resorted to versifying, and, with composers such as Jay Gorney, Vernon Duke and Lewis Gensler, contributed songs to several Broadway revues and musicals, including *Earl Carroll's Sketch Book*, *Earl Carroll's Vanities*, *Garrick Gaieties*, *Shoot The Works* and *Ballyhoo Of 1932*.

In 1932, in the midst of the Depression, Harburg and Gorney wrote the socially significant 'Brother, Can You Spare A Dime', for the revue *Americana* (or *New Americana*). It became extremely successful on records for Bing Crosby and Rudy Vallee. *Americana* also contained several other Harburg lyrics, including 'Satan's Li'l Lamb', which marked the beginning of his long and fruitful collaboration with the composer Harold Arlen. Another of their early songs, 'It's Only A Paper Moon' (1933), was written in association with Billy Rose. In collaboration with Vernon Duke, Harburg wrote another future standard, 'April In Paris', for the Beatrice Lillie stage musical, *Walk A Little Faster*; and 'I Like The Likes Of You' and 'What Is There To Say?' for the *Ziegfeld Follies Of 1934*. Also in 1934, together with Arlen and Ira Gershwin, he contributed the score to *Life Begins At 8.40*, which included 'You're A Builder-Upper', 'Fun To Be Fooled', 'What Can You Say In A Love Song' and 'Let's Take A Walk Around The Block'. After that, Harburg moved to Hollywood and worked with Arlen on three Warner Brothers movie musicals, *The Singing Kid*, starring Al Jolson ('You're The Cure For What Ails Me', 'I Love To Sing-A'), *Stage Struck* ('Fancy Meeting You', 'In Your Own Quiet Way'), and *Gold Diggers Of 1937* ('Let's Put Our Heads Together', 'Speaking Of The Weather').

Around this time, the two writers also produced one of their most memorable songs, 'When The World Was Young', which received a classic reading from Frank Sinatra nearly 20 years later on his *In The Wee Small Hours*. A brief spell in New York for Harburg resulted in the stage score (with Arlen) for *Hooray For What?* ('God's Country', 'Down With Love'), but both songwriters were back in Hollywood in 1939 to work on one of the most famous films in the history of the cinema. *The Wizard Of Oz*, starring Judy Garland and such beloved characters as the Tin Man, the Scarecrow, and the Cowardly Lion, was one of the first movies in which the songs were seamlessly integrated into the plot. Harburg is also said to have made a significant contribution to the screenplay, collecting and blending several different stories together. The film included numbers such as 'Ding Dong The Witch Is Dead', 'We're Off To See The Wizard', 'If I Only Had A Brain', 'Follow The Yellow Brick Road', and the immortal, yearning, 'Over The Rainbow', for which Harburg and Arlen won an Academy Award. It was all a far cry from their next movie project, *The Marx Brothers At The Circus*, which contained the amusing 'Lydia, The Tattooed Lady' ('When her robe is unfurled, she will show you the world/If you step up, and tell-her-where/For a dime you can see Kankakee or Paree/Or Washington crossing the Delaware'). During the 40s Harburg continued to write mostly for films. These included *Babes On Broadway* ('Chin Up, Cheerio,

Carry On'), *Ship Ahoy* (with Burton Lane), in which Frank Sinatra sang 'The Last Call For Love', 'Poor You' and 'Moonlight Bay' with the Tommy Dorsey Orchestra, *Cabin In The Sky* (with Arlen) ('Happiness Is Just A Thing Called Joe'), *Thousands Cheer* (with Earl Brent) ('Let There Be Music'), *Can't Help Singing* (with Jerome Kern), starring Deanna Durbin, with songs such as 'More And More', 'Swing Your Sweetheart', 'Cal-i-for-ni-ay', and *Hollywood Canteen* (1944) (with Burton Lane) ('You Can Always Tell A Yank').

Harburg teamed up with Lane again, in 1947, for the Broadway show, *Finian's Rainbow*. This time, as well as the lyrics, Harburg, with Fred Saidy, also wrote the book - a fantasy laced with social commentary, and a score which included numbers such as 'How Are Things In Glocca Morra?', 'If This Isn't Love', 'Look To The Rainbow', 'Old Devil Moon', 'When I'm Not Near The Girl I Love', 'Something Sort Of Grandish', 'Necessity', 'When The Idle Poor Become The Idle Rich', 'That Great Come-On-And-Get-It Day', and 'The Begat'. The show ran for over 700 performances on Broadway, but it was 1968 before Hollywood took a chance on the whimsical piece. The film version, directed by Francis Ford Coppola, starred Fred Astaire, Petula Clark, and Tommy Steele. Harburg had always been strongly political, and in the 40s and early 50s, the time of the McCarthy witch hunts, he became even more so. His work for the stage show, *Bloomer Girl*, (1944, with Arlen), which had a Civil War background, included 'The Eagle And Me', a passionate plea for racial equality and freedom; and *Flahooley* (1951) (with Sammy Fain), took as swipe at the incongruities of 'Big Business'. Its score included songs such as 'Here's To Your Ilusions', 'The Springtime Cometh', and 'He's Only Wonderful'. In *Jamaica* (which starred Lena Horne, and had another Harburg/Saidy libretto.), urban life was scrutinized. The Harburg/Arlen songs included 'Coconut Sweet', 'Take It Slow, Joe', 'Ain't It The Truth?', 'Push De Button' and 'Napoleon'. Harburg's last two Broadway shows, *The Happiest Girl The World* (1961) and *Darling Of The Day* (1968), did not survive for long.

After a period of nearly 20 years, Harburg was invited back to Hollywood in 1962 to write the songs, with Arlen, for the movie cartoon *Gay Purr-ee*. They included 'Little Drops Of Rain', 'Mewsette', and 'Paris Is A Lonely Town'. Also with Arlen, he wrote the title song for *I Could Go On Singing* (1963), Judy Garland's last film. Throughout his life Harburg received many awards and citations, including the Humanity in Arts Award from Wayne State University. He died in a car crash in Los Angeles, in March 1981. Four years later, a biographical revue, *Look To The Rainbow*, devised and directed by Canadian author and broadcaster Robert Cushman, and starring Broadway veteran Jack Gilford, played in London's West End.

Further reading: *Rhymes For The Irreverent*, E.Y. Harburg. *At This Point In Rhyme*, E.Y. Harburg. *The Making Of 'The Wizard Of Oz'*, Al Jean Harmetz. *Who Put The Rainbow In The Wizard Of Oz? Yip Harburg, Lyrisist*, Harold Meyerson and Ernie Harburg.

Harnick, Sheldon
(see **Bock, Jerry**)

Harrison, Rex
b. Reginald Carey Harrison, 5 March 1908, Huyton, England, d. 2 June 1990, Manhattan, New York, USA. A stylish and urbane actor, Harrison had a long and distinguished career in dramatic and light comedy roles both in the theatre and in films, but will probably be remembered by the public at large for his sublime portrayal of Professor Henry Higgins in one of the all-time great musicals, *My Fair Lady*. He made his stage debut in the provincial theatre in 1924, and six years later appeared in the West End and made his first film. From then on he skilfully mixed his stage commitments and movie work until 1956 when he spent two years on Broadway in *My Fair Lady*, a performance which earned him a Tony Award. He reprised the role-of-a-lifetime in London in 1958 and

won an Oscar for his part in the 1964 film version. His individual spoken-style of singing was tremendously effective on numbers such as 'The Rain In Spain', 'Why Can't The English?', 'I'm an Ordinary Man', and 'I've Grown Accustomed To Her Face'. In spite of his extraordinary success with the show he made no further stage musicals, and only one other film musical, *Doctor Dolittle* (1967), which proved to be a highly expensive disaster. His many career highlights included an Order of Merit from Italy for his portrayal of Pope Julius II in Carol Reed's film *The Agony And The Ecstasy*, and the knighthood he received from Queen Elizabeth II in honour of his stage career. Only a month before his death he was starring on Broadway opposite two other old stagers, Glynis Johns and Stewart Granger, in Somerset Maugham's *The Circle*. Noel Harrison, Rex Harrison's son from his second marriage to actress Lilli Palmer, was a familiar figure on the London cabaret scene in the 50s, but is probably best-known for his 1969 UK Top 10 single 'Windmills Of Your Mind', the theme from the Steve McQueen movie *The Thomas Crown Affair*, and for his appearances in the highly popular television series *The Man From UNCLE*. In the late 80s he toured in his new one-man show *Adieu Jacques*, based on the life and songs of the late Jacques Brel, and in 1994 he was set to achieve a lifetime ambition by appearing in the New York Gilbert And Sullivan

Rex Harrison (left)

Players production of *The Pirates Of Penzance*.
Selected album: *His Favourite Songs* (1979), and
Original Cast recordings.
Further reading: *Rex*, Rex Harrison. *A Damned
Serious Business: My Life In Comedy*, Rex Harrison. *A
Life Of Rex Harrison*, Alexander Walker.

Hart, Lorenz

b. 2 May 1895, New York City, USA, d. 22
November 1943. An outstanding student, Hart was
writing both poetry and prose in his mid-teens. In
1918 he met Richard Rodgers, with whom he
established an immediate rapport. They wrote
numerous songs together in their first year of
collaboration, among them some which were used in
current Broadway shows. Nevertheless their songs
were not widely known, at that time. The situation
changed in 1925 with 'Manhattan' and 'Sentimental
Me', both written for *The Garrick Gaieties*. They
followed this with their first complete Broadway
show, *Dearest Enemy* (1925), which included 'Here In
My Arms'. The following year brought *The Girl
Friend*, with hits in the title song and 'Blue Room'. In
1926 they wrote 'Mountain Greenery' and the same
year, for *Peggy-Ann*, 'A Tree In The Park'. In 1927
they wrote 'Thou Swell' for *A Connecticut Yankee*, a
show which also featured 'My Heart Stood Still', a
song written originally for an earlier show. In the late
20s and early 30s their shows met with only moderate
success, but the songs continued to flow - 'You Took
Advantage Of Me', 'With A Song In My Heart', 'A
Ship Without A Sail', 'Ten Cents A Dance' and
'Dancing On The Ceiling'. Rodgers and Hart
worked together in Hollywood for a while, their
songs including 'Isn't It Romantic', 'Love Me
Tonight', 'Lover' and 'It's Easy To Remember'. Back
on Broadway in 1935, they wrote *Jumbo*, which
included 'My Romance', 'Little Girl Blue' and 'The
Most Beautiful Girl In The World'. They followed
Jumbo with *On Your Toes* (1936) which included
'There's A Small Hotel', *Babes In Arms* (1937) which
introduced 'Where Or When', 'My Funny Valentine'
and 'The Lady Is A Tramp' and *I'd Rather Be Right*
(1937) with 'Have You Met Miss Jones?'. Their two
shows of 1938 were *I Married An Angel* and *The Boys
From Syracuse*, featuring, respectively, 'I Married An
Angel' and 'Spring Is Here' and 'Falling In Love With
Love' and 'This Can't Be Love'. Later song successes
for the duo were 'I Didn't Know What Time It Was',
from *Too Many Girls* (1939), 'It Never Entered My
Mind', from *Higher And Higher* (1940) and
'Bewitched, Bothered And Bewildered' and 'I Could
Write A Book' from *Pal Joey* (1940). Their last show
together was *By Jupiter* (1942) from which came
'Careless Rhapsody'. Hart was of a nervous and
unstable disposition, caused mainly by a troubled
personal life. He was perpetually disorganized,

fulfilling popular assumptions about songwriters by
scribbling ideas and sometimes complete lyrics on
scraps of paper which he stuffed into pockets and
forgot about until Rodgers, a thoroughly organized
man, urged him into action. Worried over his small
stature, his latent homosexuality and the problems of
meeting theatrical deadlines, Hart turned increasingly
to alcohol. He backed out of a show he and Rodgers
were to have written in 1942 and drifted into despair,
seeking solace in drink. He died in November 1943.
Of all the many gifted lyricists to appear in the USA
in the 20s and 30s, Hart was perhaps the most poetic.
His early studies and deep appreciation of language
gave him insight into words and their uses. Many of
his best lyrics stand apart from their musical context
and have a life of their own. His ear for rhymes, and
his ability to create vivid word pictures, contributed
towards some of the finest popular songs of all time.
Despite the difficulties and unhappiness he
experienced in his private life, his work is filled with
lightness, enduring charm and ready wit; qualities
which mark him as a true genius among songwriters.
Further reading: *The Complete Lyrics Of Lorenz Hart*,
eds. Dorothy Hart and Robert Kimball.

Hart, Moss

b. 24 October 1904, New York, USA, d. 20
December 1961, Palm Springs, California, USA. A
distinguished librettist, director, and playwright who
was particularly renowned for his work with George
S. Kaufman. Hart is supposed to have written the
book for the short-lived *Jonica* in 1930, but his first
definite Broadway musical credit came three years
later when he contributed the sketches to the Irving
Berlin revue *As Thousands Cheer*. Subsequent revues
for which he co-wrote sketches included *The Show Is
On*, *Seven Lively Arts*, and *Inside USA*. During the
remainder of the 30s Hart wrote the librettos for *The
Great Waltz* (adapted from the operetta *Waltzes Of
Vienna*), *Jubilee*, *I'd Rather Be Right* (with Kaufman),
and *Sing Out The News* (which he also co-produced
with Kaufman and Max Gordon). In 1941 he came
up with one of his wittiest and inventive books for
Lady In Dark which starred Gertrude Lawrence, and
gave Danny Kaye his first real chance on Broadway.
Thereafter, as far as the musical theatre was
concerned, apart from the occasion revue Hart
concentrated mostly on directing, and sometimes
producing, shows such as Irving Berlin's *Miss Liberty*,
and Alan Jay Lerner and Frederick Loewe's smash-hits
My Fair Lady and *Camelot*. He won a Tony Award
for his work on *My Fair Lady*. His considerable output
for the straight theatre included *Light Up the Sky*, *The
Climate Of Eden*, *Winged Victory*, and (with Kaufman)
Once In A Lifetime, *You Can't Take It With You* (for
which they both won the Pulitzer Prize) and *The Man
Who Came To Dinner*. Hart also wrote the screenplays

for two film musicals, *Hans Christian Andersen* (1952) and the 1954 remake of *A Star Is Born*, starring Judy Garland. His absorbing autobiography, *Act One*, was filmed in 1963 with George Hamilton as Hart and Jason Robards as Kaufman.

Further reading: *Act One*, Moss Hart.

Have A Heart

Appropriately sub-titled The-Up-To-The-Minute Musical Comedy, *Have A Heart* marked the beginning of a highly significant partnership. Jerome Kern (music), Guy Bolton (book), and P.G. Wodehouse (book and lyrics), invented their own kind of witty, tuneful, and contemporary musical, far removed from the imported European operetta which ruled in America at the time. The show opened at the Liberty Theatre in New York on 11 January 1917, and only lasted for 76 performances. It's demise was due, in part at least, to the departure of the star comedian, Billy B. Van, who had been hired by Henry W. Savage (an ogre of a producer) on the condition that Wodehouse and Bolton pay half of his salary for the first three months. At the end of the period, Savage fired him! In *Have A Heart*, Van plays an elevator boy who becomes involved with a couple who decide to be radical, and elope on the eve of their divorce. He scored a big hit with 'Napoleon', and there were several other amusing and tenderly romantic songs which complemented the plot perfectly and gave audiences a foretaste of the delights to come in future shows. These included 'You Said Something' and 'I Am All Alone' (lyrics by Kern and Wodehouse), 'They all Look Alike', 'Daisy', 'The Road That Lies Before', 'Honeymoon Inn', 'Bright Lights', and 'I'm Here, Little Girl, I'm Here'. *Have A Heart* was one of 25 new musicals to open on Broadway during the 1916/7 season. *Oh, Boy!*, the next Kern-Bolton-Wodehouse effort, and the first of their renowned Princess Theatre shows, opened in February 1917 and ran for 475 performances.

Hello, Dolly!

Opening at the St. James Theatre in New York on on 16 January 1964, the stage musical *Hello, Dolly!* swiftly became one of the most talked-about shows in the history of the American musical theatre. Michael Stewart's book was adapted from the Thornton Wilder play *The Matchmaker*, which itself was based on other sources. *Hello, Dolly!* recounts the tale of Dolly Gallagher Levi, a self-appointed matchmaker who seeks to inveigle into marriage a wealthy New York merchant, Horace Vandergelder. Sub-plots follow the love life of Vandergelder's clerk, Cornelius Hackl, and Mrs Molloy, the lady Vandergelder thinks Dolly is trying to match with him. With a fine score by Jerry Herman, choreography and direction by Gower Champion, and excellent central performances, the show survived near-disaster in out-of-town tryouts and by the time it reached New York was set to become a massive box-office hit. For its New York opening the show starred Carol Channing as Dolly, and she was succeeded during its 2,844-performance run by Phyllis Diller, Betty Grable, and Ethel Merman, amongst others, while various touring companies starred Channing, Grable, Raye, Dorothy Lamour, Mary Martin and Eve Arden. In the original cast, David Burns played Vandergelder, Eileen Brennan was Mrs Molloy with Charles Nelson Reilly as Cornelius. The songs included 'Dancing', 'Put On Your Sunday Clothes', 'Before The Parade Passes By', 'Elegance', 'It Takes A Woman', 'Ribbons Down My Back', and 'So Long, Dearie'. Numerous recordings were made of the rousing title number, with Louis Armstrong's version topping the US chart, and winning Grammy Awards as Best Song and Best Male Vocal. *Hello, Dolly* won Tony Awards for best musical, book, score, actress (Channing), director-choreographer, producer (David Merrick), musical director (Shepard Coleman), scenic design (Oliver Smith), and costumes (Freddy Wittop).The 1969 film version, which composer Herman regards as definitive, starred Barbra Streisand, Walter Matthau, Marianne McAndrew and Michael Crawford. Mary Martin took the lead in the 1965 London stage presentation, and an all-black production with Pearl Bailey and Billy Daniels played on Broadway in 1975. Three years later, another revival starred Carol Channing, giving audiences a second chance to see the outstanding interpreter of one of the great roles of the modern musical theatre in America. London audiences were also granted the same opportunity when Channing reprised her role in the West End in 1979.

Hellzapoppin

This highly successful revue vehicle for the old-time vaudeville comedy team of Olsen and Johnson (Ole Olsen and Chic Johnson) opened at New York's 46th Street Theatre, on 22 September 1928, and was quickly transferred to the Winter Garden Theatre when it became obvious to the producers (i.e. Olsen and Johnson) that they had a more than substantial hit on their hands. The dynamic duo were credited with the sketches, too, which involved Barto and Mann, the Radio Rogues, Hal Sherman, and Ray Kinney, but the songs were provided by others, and included the odd opus such as 'Fuddle Dee Duddle' and 'Time To Say Aloha' by Sammy Fain and Charles Tobias, 'Abe Lincoln' by Earl Robinson and Alfred Hayes, and an interesting item entitled 'Boomps-A-Daisy', which was written by Annette Mills, and, more than 50 years later, is still a party-dance favourite when the old, and the not-so-old folks, get together. As for *Hellzapoppin*, its nightly onstage party, with its unsophisticated and deliciously decadent humour, ran on and on for a record 1,404 performances, replacing *Pins And Needles* as the longest-running Broadway musical production. Olsen and Johnson, together with Martha Raye, starred in the 1941 film version. In 1976, an attempted revised revival, with music and lyrics by Cy Coleman, Carolyn Leigh, Hank Bebe, and Bill Heyer, and starring Jerry Lewis, Lynn Redgrave, Joey Faye, and Brandon Maggart, opened in Baltimore, Maryland, but closed during its pre-Broadway tryout.

Henderson, Ray

b. Raymond Brost, 16 December 1896, Buffalo, New York, USA, d. 31 December 1970. Born into a show business family, Henderson studied music but was a self-taught pianist. In 1918 he became a song promotor New York City and spent his free time writing songs. He met with no success until 1922, when he joined lyricist Lew Brown. They had a succession of popular hits with 'Georgette', 'Humming' and 'Annabelle' (all 1922). During the early and mid-20s Henderson worked with various other lyricists, his triumphs included 'That Old Gang Of Mine' (1923, with Billy Rose and Mort Dixon), 'Bye Bye Blackbird' (1926, with Dixon), 'Five Feet Two, Eyes Of Blue' and 'I'm Sitting On Top Of The World' (both 1925, with Sam M. Lewis and Joe Young). In 1925 he began an association with Buddy De Sylva with 'Alabamy Bound'. The same year Brown joined the team, and the three men quickly became one of the most formidable songwriting teams in the USA for their work on Broadway musicals such as *Good News, Hold Everthing, Follow Through, Flying High, George White's Scandals*. They wrote 'It All Depends On You', 'Lucky Day', 'Black Bottom', 'Broken-Hearted', 'The Birth Of The Blues', 'The Best Things In Life Are Free' (which became the title of a 1956 Hollywood biopic about the trio), 'The Varsity Drag', 'You're The Cream In My Coffee' and 'Good News'. In the late 20s De Sylva, Brown and Henderson went to Hollywood, where they wrote 'Sonny Boy' overnight for Al Jolson to sing in a film that was approaching completion. Although written as a spoof, Jolson sang it straight and it became one of his greatest hits. The team then wrote the score for *Sunny Side Up* (1929), which included the title song, 'If I Had A Talking Picture Of You' and 'I'm A Dreamer Aren't We All'. Other film songs include 'Button Up Your Overcoat' and 'I Want To Be Bad'. In 1931 the partnership was dissolved, with De Sylva becoming a successful film producer. Henderson and Brown remained collaborators for further hit songs such as 'Life Is Just A Bowl Of Cherries', 'My Song' and 'The Thrill Is Gone'. In the late 30s Henderson's other collaborators included Ted Koehler, Irving Caesar and Jack Yellen. Henderson retired in the late 40s, and worked sporadically on a never-completed opera. He died in 1970.

Henson, Leslie

b. 3 August 1891, Notting Hill, London, England, d. 2 December 1957, Harrow Weald, Middlesex, England. An actor, director, manager, and producer, Henson, with his bulging eyes, facial contortions ('which resembled a mandarin about to sneeze') and croaky voice, was one of the outstanding comedians in British musical comedy in the first half of the century. He attended drama school while in his teens, and toured with concert parties from around 1910. Four years later he went to New York and appeared on Broadway in the musical farce *Tonight's The Night*, and returned with it to the West End in 1915. In 1916 he scored a tremendous personal success in *Theodore And Company*, which was followed by satisfying runs in *Yes, Uncle!, Kissing Time, A Night Out, Sally, The Cabaret Girl, The Beauty Prize, Primrose, Tell Me More*, and *Kid Boots* (1926). Most of the shows were presented at the Winter Garden for one of London's leading producers, George Grossmith. From 1927 Henson also served as a manager, director and/or co-producer for a wide variety of shows, including those in which he appeared himself. Among the latter in the late 20s were *Lady Luck, Funny Face, Follow Through, Nice Goings On*, and *Lucky Break* (1934). In 1935 he and Firth Shephard took over control of the Gaiety Theatre and produced four of the comedian's biggest hit shows, *Seeing Stars, Swing Along, Going Greek*, and *Running Riot* (1938). Following the outbreak of World War II, Henson returned to the UK from a tour of South Africa and, together with Basil Deans, formed the British Forces entertainments unit ENSA (the troops called it 'Every Night Something Awful'), which set up its headquarters in the Drury Lane Theatre, recently vacated by Ivor Novello's musical, *The Dancing Years*. Throughout World War II Henson entertained troops in Europe, the Middle East, and Far East, returning to star in London revues such as *Up And Doing, Fine and Dandy*, and *Leslie Henson's Gaieties*. After the war, at the age of 57 he went back to musical comedy in the smash-hit *Bob's Your Uncle* (1948), and then appeared as Samuel Pepys, complete with full-bottomed wig, in *And So To Bed* (1951). His many and various theatrical roles left little time for films, but he did make a few, including *The Sport Of Kings* (1930), *A Warm Corner* (1934), *The Demi-Paradise* (1943), and *Home And Away* (1956).

Further reading: *My Laugh Story* and *Yours Faithfully*, both by Leslie Henson.

Herbert, Victor

b. 1 February 1859, Dublin, Eire, d. 26 May 1924,

Leslie Henson

New York, USA. An important composer during the transitional period in the early part of the century when the operetta form was overtaken by American musical comedy. Brought up in the south of England, Herbert studied classical music as a youngster. He played cello in various European symphony orchestras, all the while composing music for the concert platform. In 1885 he accepted a teaching post in Stuttgart where he married an opera singer. The following year he accompanied her on a visit to the USA where he also played, taught and studied. Among Herbert's compositions from his early days in the USA were 'An American Fantasy'. He then began writing operettas, and in 1898 one of the first of them, *The Fortune Teller*, became a great success in New York, establishing his reputation. Four years later Herbert became a US citizen. He continued writing classical music and operettas, and, over the next 20 years composed the music for some 30 Broadway shows, including *Boys In Toyland* (1903), *It Happened In Nordland* (1904), *Mlle. Modiste* (1906), *The Red Mill* (1906), *The Prima Donna* (1908), *Naughty Marietta* (1910), *Sweethearts* (1913), *Princess Pat* (1915), *Eileen* (1917), *The Velvet Lady* (1919), *Orange Blossoms* (1922), *The Dream Girl* (1924), and contributed to several editions of the *Ziegfeld Follies*. The shows contained some of the most memorable and popular songs of the day, including 'Gypsy Love', 'Tramp! Tramp! Tramp!', 'Every Day Is Ladies Day With Me', 'Eileen', 'Because You're You', 'Kiss In The Dark', 'Kiss Me Again', 'Italian Street Song', 'Neapolitan Love Song', 'Indian Summer', 'Romany Life', 'Ah, Sweet Mystery Of Life', 'Sweethearts', 'Moonbeams', 'Yesterthoughts', 'Thine Alone', and 'Rose Of The World'. His main lyricist collaborators included Rida Johnson Young, Henry Blossom, Buddy De Sylva, Harry B. Smith, Glen MacDonough, Gene Buck, and Robert Smith. Herbert also wrote musical scores for silent films (usually performed only in those motion picture theatres in main urban centres equipped to house a full orchestra) and grand operas. In February 1924 Herbert's 'A Suite For Serenades' was performed by Paul Whiteman's orchestra at a New York concert which also saw the first public performance of George Gershwin's 'Rhapsody In Blue'. Herbert's prolific output was achieved despite ill health but he suffered a fatal heart attack on 26 May 1924.

Herman, Jerry

b. 10 July 1933, New York City, New York, USA. Musically precocious, Herman was playing piano by the age of six under the tuition of his mother, a professional piano teacher. After high school, he studied design, but the sale of his first song persuaded him that this was where his true vocation lay. Redirecting his studies into the arts, he learned his

trade, and by the mid-50s was playing piano in New York clubs and writing material for several well-known entertainers. During the late 50s and early 60s he worked on a number of off-Broadway musical shows, sometimes writing book, lyrics and music. Some of these shows were successful, others less so, but his work was generally well received by audiences and critics. In 1964 his first major show opened on Broadway. *Hello, Dolly!* ran for 2,844 consecutive performances, a record up to that time, and gave a boost to the careers of many of the artists who appeared in the original run, in subsequent revivals, and in the 1969 film version. A little more than two years after *Hello, Dolly!* opened, Herman had another smash on his hands with *Mame*. With two such acclaimed shows behind him, Herman found it difficult to maintain such a high level for his next Broadway productions, although *Mack And Mabel* (1974) has gained justified retrospective admiration, particularly for such songs as 'I Won't Send You Roses'. In 1983, Herman's form returned with another triumph, *La Cage Aux Folles*. Although a generation removed from the past masters of the American musical theatre, Herman's style adheres closely to the earlier formulas and he brings to his best work a richness sadly lacking in that of many of his contemporaries.
Selected album: *An Evening With Jerry Herman* (1993).

High Button Shoes

Having established themselves as popular songwriters for Tin Pan Alley, and movies such as *Step Lively* and *Anchors Aweigh*, Sammy Cahn and Jule Styne turned to Broadway, and wrote the music and lyrics for this show which opened at the Century Theatre, on 9 October 1947. In Styne's case, it was be the beginning of a long and glorious stage career during which he composed the music for such legendary shows as *Gentlemen Prefer Blondes*, *Bells Are Ringing*, *Gypsy*, *Do Re Mi*, and *Funny Girl*. Stephen Longstreet based the book for *High Button Shoes* on his novel, *The Sisters Like Them Handsome*, and Phil Silvers, who had appeared on Broadway in *Yokel Boy* (1939), rocketed to stardom as Harrison Floy, a small-time con-man who sells off some of his neighbours' land which turns out to be a useless swamp. He escapes with the money, and throughout the rest of the story, loses it, wins it back, and then loses it again, in a series of hair-brained schemes. Silvers was ideally cast as the accident-prone loser, and the strong supporting cast included Nanette Fabray, Jack McCauley, Joey Faye, Helen Gallagher, and Donald Saddler. Cahn and Styne's score contained several numbers that became popular hits, such as 'I Still Get Jealous', which was recorded by the Three Suns, Harry James, and Gordon MacRae; 'Papa, Won't You Dance With Me?', Doris Day, Skitch Henderson; and 'You're My

Phil Silvers (left - *High Button Shoes*)

Girl', which Frank Sinatra took into the US Hit Parade. Sinatra also made an appealing recording of another song from the show, 'Can't You Just See Yourself?'. The rest of the score included 'There's Nothing Like A Model 'T'', 'Get Away For A Day In The Country', and 'On A Sunday By The Sea'. One of the most spectacular sequences in the show was the 'Bathing Beauty Ballet', which was choreographed by a young Jerome Robbins who went on to a glittering future on Broadway and in Hollywood. *High Button Shoes* ran for a more than decent 727 performances in New York, and for a further 291 in London.

High Spirits

Yes, it most definitely was, as the subtitle suggested, 'An Improbable Musical Comedy'. Any show in which a zany spiritualist - in this case, the infamous Mme. Arcati (Beatrice Lillie) - arranges for the spectre of a man's first wife Elvira (Tammy Grimes), to return to earth for one last lap of honour, is surely nearer to farce than *Fiddler On The Roof*. The latter show, along with *Funny Girl*, *Hello, Dolly!*, and *She Loves Me*, was the kind of opposition that *High Spirits* was up against during its Broadway run which began at the Alvin Theatre on 7 April 1964. The show was based on Noël Coward's 1941 play, *Blithe Spirit*, and Coward himself directed at first, but is said to have been replaced at a later stage by Gower Champion. It was

to be Coward's last connection with the New York musical theatre. The British actor, Edward Woodward, played Condomine, the poor unfortunate earthly soul whose second marriage to Ruth (Louise Troy), is terminated when she (Ruth) is accidentally killed by wife number 1 in the course of trying to take her husband back with her to the 'other side'. Woodward, one of the UK's most respected actors, and a more than competent singer, would eventually arbitrarily dispose of a few people himself on worldwide television as *The Terminator*, following on from his early small-screen break in *Callan*. The men responsible for adapting *Blithe Spirit* for the stage were Hugh Martin and Timothy Gray, and they also contributed the pretty, though unexciting score, which included 'Forever And A Day', 'Was She Prettier Than I?', 'The Bicycle Song', 'I Know Your Heart', 'If I Gave You', 'Something Tells Me', 'Go Into Your Trance', 'Where Is The Man That I Married?', 'Faster Than Sound', 'Home Sweet Heaven', 'Something Is Coming To Tea', and 'You'd Better Love Me', which attained some sort of popularity, and is probably better known as 'You'd Better Love Me (While You May)'. No showstoppers there, and the reason for the production's 375-run existence was no doubt due to the presence of the redoubtable and irrepressible Beatrice Lillie in what what was to be her final Broadway show.

Coincidentally, Cicely Courtneidge, who played the role of Mme. Arcati in the London production of *High Spirits*, was also saying goodbye to theatre audiences there, following a glorious career which began more than 50 years before with the Arcadians in 1909.

Hired Man, The

In Howard Goodall's marvellous adaptation of Melvyn Bragg's novel, *The Hired Man* brought to the musical stage a powerful story of mining and farming life around the Lake District in the early years of the century. Opening at the Astoria Theatre in London on 31 October 1984, and tracing one family's domestic tribulations against the disturbing background of World War I, pit disasters and the birth of trades unionism, the plot was strong meat. Appropriately, Goodall took his musical inspiration from a powerful English musical tradition. His absorption of the grandeur of the choral work of Edward Elgar gave the show an impressive undercurrent. Sweeping along plot and characterization, the music counterpointed major national and international events even as it highlighted such decidedly domestic affairs as work in the mines, and such day-to-day country life as experienced at the hiring fairs. Among the cast were Claire Burt, Paul Clarkson, Julia Hills, Gerald Doyle, and Richard Walsh. The songs included 'Song Of The Hired Men', 'Work Song', 'Men Of Stone (Union Song)', 'What A Fool I've Been', and 'When You Next See That Smile'. Despite high critical regard, the show, which was produced by Andrew Lloyd Webber, folded after 164 performances and lost money at the box-office.

Hit the Deck

Herbert Fields's book for this 'Nautical Musical Comedy' was based on the 1922 play, *Shore Leave*, by Hubert Osborne. With music by Vincent Youmans, and lyrics by Clifford Grey and Leo Robin, it began the 'stage phase' of its existence on 25 April 1927 at the Belasco theatre in New York, and stayed around for 352 performances. Field's story turned out to be yet another reworking of that familiar musical comedy saga of a boy (or girl) discovering that his (or her) beloved is blessed with a big bundle of cash. The marriage is always immediately called off - true happiness, they always agree, is based on love, and not lucre. Of course, they also invariably have second thoughts. Looloo Martin (Louise Groody) owns a coffee shop in Newport, Rhode Island, USA, and a lot of her customers are sailors. She is completely besotted by one of them, Bilge Smith (Charles King), and, in an effort to tie the marriage knot, is perfectly prepared to follow him to the ends of the earth - in Bilge's case that means China. Even out there, the sailor is reluctant to restrict himself to just one girl (Looloo) in one port (Rhode Island), particularly when he finds out that Looloo is wealthy. Matters are resolved when the lady agrees to assuage his pride and assign all the money to their first offspring. Youmans' songs with Grey and Robin included 'Join The Navy', 'Loo-Loo', 'Harbour Of My Heart', 'Why, Oh Why?', 'Lucky Bird', and 'Hallelujah!' which became something of a hit through recordings by Nat Shilkret, the Revelers, and Cass Hagen. Another of Youmans's numbers for the show, 'Sometimes I'm Happy' (with a lyric by Irving Caesar), also became popular at the time via Roger Wolfe Kahn, and a recording by two members of the original cast, Louise Groody and Charles King. The song, which was not all like the smart, sophisticated material that Cole Porter, for instance, was writing at the time, had a charming, artless lyric: 'Sometimes I'm happy, sometimes I'm blue/My disposition, depends on you/I'll never mind the rain from the sky/If I can see the sun in your eye'. It endured, and was included, along with 'Hallelujah', in the 1930 and 1955 screen versions of the show, but omitted from the 1936 film, *Follow The Fleet* (which was also based on the original concept), in favour of an Irving Berlin score. The 1927 London stage production, which starred Stanley Holloway and Ivy Tresmand, used more or less the same songs, and ran for 277 performances.

Hockridge, Edmund

b. 9 August 1923, Vancouver, British Columbia, Canada. Hockridge was one of the UK's premier musical comedy leading men, with rugged looks, a sure manner and a big, strong baritone voice. He first visited the UK in 1941 with the Royal Canadian Air Force, and helped set up the Allied Expeditionary Forces Network, which supplied entertainment and news for troops in Europe. He also sang on many of the broadcasts, several of them with fellow Canadian Robert Farnon who was leader of the Canadian Allied Expeditionary Force Band. After the war, he featured in his own coast-to-coast show for the CBC, playing leading roles in operas such as *La Bohème*, *Don Giovanni* and Gilbert And Sullivan operettas. After seeing some Broadway musical shows such as *Brigadoon* and *Carousel*, on a visit to New York, he decided that there was more future for him in that direction. That was certainly the case, for on his return to the UK in 1951, he replaced Stephen Douglass as Billy Bigelow in *Carousel* at the Drury Lane Theatre, London. When the run ended he replaced Jerry Wayne as Sky Masterson in *Guys And Dolls* at the Coliseum, and stayed at that theatre for two more shows, *Can-Can*, and *The Pajama Game*, in which he created for the London stage, the roles of Judge Aristide Forestier and Sid Sorokin. From the latter show he had one of his biggest record hits, 'Hey

Edmund Hockridge

There'. His other 50s singles included 'Young And Foolish', 'No Other Love', 'The Fountains Of Rome', 'Sixteen Tons', 'The Man From Laramie', 'A Woman In Love', 'More Than Ever' and 'Tonight'. Extremely popular in theatres and on television, he played a six-month season at the London Palladium, appeared in six Royal Command Performances, and was Canada's representative in the Westminster Abbey Choir at the Queen's Coronation in 1953. He headlined the cabaret on the liner QE2's maiden voyage, and toured Europe extensively, both in revivals of musicals, and his own one-man show, which contained over 30 songs.

In the early 80s he toured the UK with successful revivals of *The Sound Of Music* and *South Pacific*, before returning to Canada in 1984 for a concert tour with Robert Farnon and the Vancouver Symphony Orchestra. In 1986, 35 years after he strode onto the Drury Lane stage as young, arrogant Billy Bigelow, he played the part of senior citizen, Buffalo Bill, in a major London revival of *Annie Get Your Gun*, with pop star, Suzi Quatro, as Annie. In the early 90s, Hockridge toured with his show, *The Edmund Hockridge Family*, being joined onstage by his wife, Jackie, and their two sons, Murray and Stephen.

Albums: *Edmund Hockridge Sings* (1957), *In Romantic Mood* (1957), *Hooray For Love* (1958), *Hockridge Meets Hammond* (1975), *Make It Easy On Yourself* (1984), *Sings Hits From Various Musicals* (1985).

Hold Everything!

College football having proved to be a winning formula for De Sylva, Brown And Henderson in their *Good News!* (1927), two years later they placed their collective fingers firmly on the pulse of the New York theatre-going public, and deduced - quite rightly - that the noble art of boxing would be good for a few rounds as the subject matter for another amusing musical comedy. The result, *Hold Everything!*, opened at the Broadhurst Theatre on 10 October 1929, with a book by De Sylva and John McGowan in which 'Sonny Jim' Brooks (Jack Wilding), a welterweight contender, is temporarily estranged from his girlfriend, Sue Burke (Ona Munson), when she discovers that he is being coached in various aspects of his technique by the young and extremely sociable Norine Lloyd (Betty Compton). Sue may be down, but she is not out, and when she is bad-mouthed by his opponent, the reigning champ, 'Sonny Jim' bounces off the ropes, clinches the title, and signs her to a long-term contract. Much of the show's humour was provided by Victor Moore and Bert Lahr, who made a big impact in the role of Gink Schiner, a punch-drunk fighter who rather carelessly floors himself instead of his opponent. As usual, De Sylva, Brown And Henderson's lively, carefree songs fitted the action like a glove. They included 'To

Know You Is To Love You', 'Don't Hold Everything', 'Too Good To Be True', and one of the songwriters' all-time big ones, the zippy 'You're The Cream In My Coffee', which became popular for a great many artists and bands, particularly Ben Selvin, Ted Weems, and Ruth Etting. It all added up to a lot of fun, and America would soon be in need of a lot more of that particular commodity - the Wall Street Crash and the Depression were just around the corner. With the Roaring 20s rapidly running out of steam, *Hold Everything!* held on for 413 performances in New York, and added another 173 to that total in London. The 1930 film version, which starred Joe E. Brown, was considered to one of the best of the earlie talkie comedies.

Holman, Libby

b. Elsbeth Holzman, 23 May 1904, Cincinnati, Ohio, USA, d. 18 June 1971, Stamford, Connecticut, USA. Holman was regarded by some as the first great white torch singer, and by others as 'a dark purple menace', because of her tempestuous private life. She played minor roles in Broadway musicals such as Richard Rodgers and Lorenz Hart's *Garrick Gaieties* (1925), but became a featured star in *Merry-Go-Round* (1927), and *Rainbow* (1928), in which she gave a languorous performance of 'I Want A Man'. After making the US Top 10 in 1929 with 'Am I Blue?', she was acclaimed a major star following her performance in *The Little Show*, in which she sang 'Can't We Be Friends' and 'Moanin' Low'. Holman received rave reviews for her sultry renditions of 'Body And Soul' and 'Something To Remember Me By' in *Three's A Crowd* (1930). Her career declined following the shooting of her husband Zachary Smith Reynolds. She was accused of his murder but the case was declared *nolle prosequi*, and never came to court. A comeback was made on Broadway in *Revenge With Music* (1934), in which she introduced 'You And The Night And The Music', and later appeared in Cole Porter's *You Never Know* (1938). Sadly, she never achieved her former heights. During the early 40s she caused a furore by appearing as a double-act with black folk singer Josh White, playing clubs and concerts in an era when a black male and white female stage relationship was frowned upon by many bookers and critics. Holman continued touring during the 50s presenting a programme called *Blues, Ballads And Sin Songs*, but still controversy followed her when she befriended ill-fated screen idol, Montgomery Clift. Mainly inactive in her later years, Holman is said to have died of carbon monoxide poisoning in June 1971.

Compilations: *The Legendary Libby Holman* (1979), *Something To Remember Her By* (1979).

Further reading: *Libby*, Milt Machlin.

Hooray For What!

A toned-down political and anti-war musical satire, *Hooray For What!* opened at New York's Winter Garden Theatre on 1 December 1937, nearly two years before World War II itself opened – in Europe at least. The book by Howard Lindsay and Russel Crouse, told of Chuckles (Ed Wynn), a horticultural scientist who invents a gas that kills appleworms – unfortunately it also kill humans as well. The discovery sparks off a string of diplomatic and political incidents and high-level conferences, culminating in Chuckles's appearance at the Geneva Peace Convention. While he is there, agents from an 'unfriendly power' steal the formula with the aid of a mirror, and so get it backwards. The result is a harmess laughing gas, which enables the world to breath a sigh of relief. During the pre-Broadway tryout, the show's originally powerful messages were modified somewhat – Agnes de Mille's anti-war ballet was cut – but with E.Y. 'Yip' Harburg providing the lyrics to Harold Arlen's music, there was always going to be an irreverent, and more 'sideways' look at issues and songs. Not content with coming up with 'In The Shade Of The *New* Apple Tree' in place of the cosy 1905 number, 'In the Shade of The *Old* Apple Tree', he actually had the tongue-in-cheek effrontery to question the basic ingredient of popular music itself – love. His witty 'Down With Love' contained lines such as 'Down with songs that moan about night and day . . . give it back to the birds and bees – and the Viennese . . . down with songs romantic and stupid/Down with sighs, and down with Cupid/Brother, let's stuff that dove/Down with love'. The rest of the fine score included 'Moanin' In The Mornin'', 'I've Gone Romantic On You', 'Life's A Dance', and 'God's Country', which was featured in the 1939 Judy Garland-Mickey Rooney film, *Babes In Arms*, and also became a hit in 1950 for both Frank Sinatra and Vic Damone. *Hooray For What!* stayed around for 200 performances – a reasonable run – and besides Ed Wynn, with his zany, crazy antics, the cast included Jack Whiting, Paul Haakon, June Clyde, Vivian Vance (who went on to become an important member of the 50s hit television show, *I Love Lucy*), and singers Hugh Martin and Ralph Blane, who were to make an impact on Broadway with their own songs in the 1941 show, *Best Foot Forward*.

Horne, Lena

b. 30 June 1917, Brooklyn, New York, USA. A dynamic performer, of striking appearance and elegant style. The daughter of an actress and a hotel operator, she was brought up mainly by her paternal grandmother, Cora Calhoun Horne. She made her professional debut at the age of 16 as a singer in the chorus at Harlem's Cotton Club, learning from Duke Ellington, Cab Calloway, Billie Holiday and Harold Arlen, the composer of a future big hit, 'Stormy Weather'. From 1935-36 she was featured vocalist with the all-black Noble Sissle's Society Orchestra, (the same Noble Sissle who, with Eubie Blake wrote several hit songs including 'Shuffle Along' and 'I'm Just Wild About Harry') and later toured with the top swing band of Charlie Barnet, singing numbers such as 'Good For Nothin' Joe' and 'You're My Thrill'. Sometimes, when Barnet's Band played the southern towns, Horne had to stay in the band bus. She made her Broadway debut in 1934 as 'A Quadroon Girl' in *Dance With Your Gods*, and also appeared in Lew Leslie's *Blackbirds Of 1939*, in which she sang Mitchell Parish and Sammy Fain's, 'You're So Indifferent' – but only for the show's run of nine performances. After a spell at the Café Society Downtown in New York, she moved to Hollywood's Little Troc Club and was spotted by Roger Edens, musical supervisor for MGM Pictures, and former accompanist for Ethel Merman, who introduced her to producer, Arthur Freed. In her first film for MGM, *Panama Hatti* (1942), which starred Merman, Horne sang Cole Porter's 'Just One Of Those Things', and a rhumba number called 'The Sping'. To make her skin appear lighter on film, the studio used a special make-up called 'Light Egyptian'. Horne referred to herself as 'a sepia Hedy Lamarr'. Her next two films, *Cabin In The Sky* and *Stormy Weather* both 1943, are generally regarded as her best. In the remainder of her 40s and 50s movie musicals (which included *Thousands Cheer*, *Swing Fever*, *Broadway Rhythm*, *Two Girls And A Sailor*, *Ziegfeld Follies*, *Till The Clouds Roll By*, *Words And Music*, *Duchess Of Idaho* and *Meet Me In Las Vegas*); she merely performed guest shots which were easily removable, without spoiling the plot, for the benefit of southern-state distributors.

Her 40s record hits included her theme song, 'Stormy Weather' and two other Arlen songs, ''Deed I Do' and 'As Long As I Live'. She also recorded with several big swing era names such as Artie Shaw, Cab Calloway and Teddy Wilson. During World War II, she became the pin-up girl for many thousands of black GIs and refused to appear on US tours unless black soldiers were admitted to the audience. In 1947 she married pianist/arranger/conductor Lennie Hayton, who also became her manager and mentor until his death in 1971. For a time during the 50s Lena Horne was blacklisted, probably for her constant involvement with the Civil Rights movement, but particularly for her friendship with Communist sympizer Paul Robeson. Ironically she was at the peak of her powers at that time, and although she was unable to appear much on television and in films, she continued to make records and appear in nightclubs which were regarded as her special forte. Evidence of that was displayed on *Lena Horne At The Waldorf Astoria*. The material ranged from the sultry 'Mood

Lena Horne

Indigo', right through to the novelty 'New Fangled Tango' and *Lena At The Sands*, with its medleys of songs by Richard Rodgers/Oscar Hammerstein II, Jule Styne and 'Yip' Harburg. Other US Top 30 chart albums included *Give The Lady What She Wants* and *Porgy And Bess*, with Harry Belafonte. Horne also made the US Top 20 singles charts in 1955 with 'Love Me Or Leave Me', written by Gus Kahn and Walter Donaldson for Ruth Etting to sing in the 1928 Broadway Show, *Whoopee*.

In 1957 Horne had her first starring role on Broadway when she played Savannah, opposite Ricardo Montalban, in the Arlen/Harburg musical, *Jamaica*. In the 60s, besides the usual round of television shows and records, she appeared in a dramatic role, with Richard Widmark, in *Death Of A Gunfighter* (1969). After Hayton's death in 1971 she worked less, but did feature in *The Wiz*, an all-black film version of *The Wizard Of Oz*, starring Diana Ross and Michael Jackson, and in 1979 she received an honorary doctorate degree from Harvard University. In May 1981, she opened on Broadway in her own autobiographical show, *Lena Horne: The Lady And Her Music*. It ran at the Nederland Theatre to full houses for 14 months, a Broadway record for a one-woman show. Horne received several awards including a special Tony Award for 'Distinguished Achievement In The Theatre', a Drama Desk Award, New York Drama Critics' Special Award, New York City's Handel Medallion, Dance Theatre of Harlem's Emergence Award, two Grammy Awards and the NAACP Springarn Award. She took the show to London in 1984, where it was also acclaimed. In 1993, after not singing in public for several years, Lena Horne agreed to perform the songs of Billy Strayhorn at the US JVC Jazz Festival.

Selected albums: *Lena Horne At The Waldorf Astoria* (1957), *Give The Lady What She Wants* (1958), with Harry Belafonte *Porgy And Bess* (1959), *Lena At The Sands* (1961), *Lena On The Blue Side* (1962), *Lena...Lovely And Alive* (1963), *Lena Goes Latin* (1963), with Gabor Szabo *Lena And Gabor* (1970), *Lena* (1974), *Lena, A New Album* (1976), *The Twenty Golden Pieces Of Lena Horne* (1979), *Lena Horne And Pearl Bailey* (1979), *Lena Horne: The Lady And Her Music* (1981, stageshow soundtrack), *Lena Horne And Frank Sinatra* (1984), *A Song For You* (1992)

Further reading: *In Person*, Lena Horne. *Lena*, Lena Horne with Richard Schikel.

House Of Flowers

Truman Capote is said to have got the idea for this show while visiting Port-au-Prince in Haiti in the late 40s. In an event, he wrote the libretto, and collaborated with composer Harold Arlen on the lyrics for what was a short-lived, but fondly remembered production. It opened at New York's Alvin Theatre on 30 December 1954, and told of the trials and tribulations of two brothels on an unidentified West Indies island. Madame Fleur (Pearl Bailey) tends the House of Flowers, while Madame Tango (Juanita Hall) performs a similar service for a rival concern. One of Madame Fleur's young blooms, Ottilie (Diahann Carroll), turns down the opportunity of real career advancement in favour of an exclusive love contract with the young and innocent Royal (Rawn Spearman), and eventually, Madame Fleur corners the terra firma market franchise when Madame Tango's operation is floated (on a world cruise). However, it is the unusual, but somehow overwhelming score that makes this a memorable show. It contained the delightful calypso-styled 'Two Ladies In De Shade Of De Banana Tree', along with 'I Never Has Seen Snow', 'I'm Gonna Leave Off Wearin' My Shoes', 'Smellin' Of Vanilla', 'Has I Let You Down?', 'One Man Ain't Quite Enough', and 'A Sleepin' Bee' which was sung in the show by Ottilie and Royal, and received what was probably its definitive version from Barbra Streisand on her first album. There was another lovely ballad, 'Don't Like Goodbyes', which was given the smoothest treatment by Frank Sinatra on his *Close To You*. During the pre-Broadway tryout there were rumours of backstage battles involving several of the principals, and, indeed, some particularly volatile personalities and egos assembled for this production. Diahann Carroll and Truman Capote both made highly impressive Broadway debuts, and Pearl Bailey was her usual dominating self. Oliver Messel's pastel-coloured sets, which somehow gave the whole affair a kind of etheral quality, were singled out for special praise. *House Of Flowers* had a disappointing run of 165 performances, and a 1968 Off Broadway revival was brief and to the point.

How To Succeed In Business Without Really Trying

If *Guys And Dolls* is considered to be composer and lyricist Frank Loesser's masterpiece, then this show must be right up there in second place. After its world première at the Shubert Theatre in Philadelphia on 4 September 1961, it opened on Broadway at the 46th Street Theatre just over a month later on 14 October. The libretto, by Abe Burrows, Jack Weinstock, and Willie Gilbert, based on a book of the same title by Shepheard Mead, was 'a witty satire on the methods and mores of Big Business in general, and in particular, on the wiles and ways of Big Business in new glass-enclosed office buildings on Park Avenue'. The story concerns a young man, J. Pierpont Finch (Robert Morse), who climbs from his position as a window-washer to the position of Chairman of the Board of the World Wide Wickets Company, Inc. His rapid rise is not due to diligence or hard work.

He simply follows the rules in a book called *How To Succeed In Business Without Even Trying*, which he pauses to consult whenever he is faced with an obstacle to his success ('How To'). With its aid, he is able to defeat his main rival, Bud Frump (Charles Nelson Reilly), the boss's oily nephew, and avoid the usual traps such as the office wolf, the office party, the dangerous secretary, and the big boss himself, J.B. Biggley (Rudy Vallee). Finch's girlfriend and main supporter is the attractive secretary Rosemary Pilkington (Bonnie Harris), who makes it clear that she would be 'Happy To Keep His Dinner Warm', while he goes onward and upward. When stuck for a time in the mailroom ('Coffee Break'), he emphasises that he considers the best route to advancement is 'The Company Way', while always bearing in mind, of course, that 'A Secretary Is Not A Toy' - even if she is Biggley's mistress. Additionally, although he agrees with Rosemary and her best friend Smitty (Claudette Sutherland), that it has 'Been A Long Day', it does not prevent him from being slumped over his desk, looking as though he has been working all night, when Biggley calls into the office on a Sunday morning en route to his round of golf. With cries of 'Groundhog!', they unite in Biggley's hymn to his alma mata, 'Grand Old Ivy' (Rip the Chipmunks off the field!'). From then on, Finch's onward and upward progress is positively phenomenal, and his self-assurance is undisguised as he sings 'I Believe In You' to his reflection in the executive washroom mirror. There are still some awkward moments to survive, including a treasure hunt during which the company's offices are wrecked, but Finch surmounts them all to become the Chairman, to marry Rosemary, and to watch his ex-rival Frump washing the office windows while reading a book entitled *How To Succeed In Business Without Even Trying*. 'I Believe In You', sung as a love song and not a soliloquy, achieved some popularity outside the show, particularly in a recording by Peggy Lee. The rest of the outstanding score included 'Paris Original', 'Rosemary', 'Cinderella, Darling', 'Love From A Heart Of Gold', and 'Brotherhood Of Man'. Rudy Vallee, the enormously popular singing idol of the 30s, and Robert Morse, who had previously appeared on Broadway in *Say, Darling* and *Take Me Along*, were perfectly cast, and the show reunited Frank Loesser, Abe Burrows, and producers Cy Feuer and Ernest Martin, 11 years after their collective triumph with *Guys And Dolls*. It was to be Loesser's final Broadway score, and he could not have gone out on a higher note. The show ran in New York for 1,417 performances, and was showered with awards: the prestigious Pulitzer Prize for Drama (1962), the New York Drama Critics Award for best musical, and Tony Awards for best musical, actor (Morse), lyrics,

librettists, and director (Burrows). The London production, starring Warren Berlinger and Billy De Wolfe, ran at the Shaftesbury Theatre for well over a year, and Rudy Vallee and Robert Morse reprised their original performances in the 1967 film version.

Hulbert, Jack
b. 24 April 1892, Ely, England, d. 25 March 1978, London, England. A popular actor, singer, dancer, director, author choreographer, and producer, whose jaunty onstage image was of the 'terribly British, "I say, old chap"' variety. Hulbert began to develop his various skills in undergraduate productions while he was studying at Cambridge University. In 1913, while appearing in the *Pearl Girl* in the West End, he met Cicely Courtneidge, the daughter of producer Robert Courtneidge, and they were married in the following year. *The Pearl Girl* was the first of 13 musicals in which they appeared together. During the next few years Hulbert established himself in a mixture of musical comedies and revues such as *The Cinema Star*, *The Arcadians*, *The Light Blues* (for which he was also co-librettist), *See-Saw*, *Bubbly*, *Bran-Pie*, *A Little Dutch Girl*, *Ring Up*, *Pot Luck*, and *The Little Revue Starts At 9* (1923). From 1925 onwards he co-produced and/or directed (and sometimes choreographed) a range of productions, particularly those in which he also acted. These included *By The Way* (in London and New York), *Lido Lady*, *Clowns In Clover*, *The House That Jack Built*, *Follow A Star* (1930), *Under Your Hat*, *Full Swing*, and *Something In The Air* (1943). After World War II, with *Oklahoma!* and the other American blockbusters on the horizon, Hulbert's smart and sophisticated style of musical comedy was less in demand, although he directed Cicely Courtneidge in the highly successful *Gay's The Word* in 1951. Over the years he introduced several popular songs, including 'The Flies Crawled Up The Window', 'My Hat's On The Side Of My Head', 'She's Such A Comfort To Me', and 'I Was Anything But Sentimental', a duet with his wife from their film *Take My Tip* (1937). Hulbert made several other light comedy movies during the 30s, - he and Courtneidge were just as popular on the screen as on the stage - such as *Elstree Calling* (1930), *The Ghost Train*, *Jack's The Boy*, *Bulldog Jack*, *Paradise For Two*, and *Kate Plus Ten*. From then on there were only occasional releases which included *Under Your Hat* (1940), *Into The Blue* (1951) *Spider's Web* (1960), and *Not Now Darling* (1973).
Selected album: *The Golden Age Of Cicely Courtneidge And Jack Hulbert* (1984).
Further reading: *The Little Woman's Always Right*, Jack Hulbert.

110 In The Shade
If only this show had not opened in the same 1963

Broadway season as *Hello, Dolly!* and *Funny Girl*, things might have been different; it would probably have won some awards for a start. Even so, when it made its debut at the Broadhurst Theatre on 24 October, *110 In The Shade* met with almost universal acclaim. The odd man out was Walter Kerr, the critc of the New York Herald Tribune, who called the song 'Little Red Hat' 'dirty and salacious', but lines such as 'I find us a spot/Where no one is at/Then I reach across and grab her little red hat' seem innocent enough today. That number, and the rest of the score was written by Tom Jones and Harvey Schmidt, whose first collaboration in 1960 had resulted in *The Fantasticks*, the record-breaking Off Broadway production. N. Richard Nash's book was adapted from his own 1954 play, *The Rainmaker*, and it was only after seeing that on US television that Jones and Schmidt came up with the idea of this musical. A feature film version, with Burt Lancaster and Katherine Hepburn had been released in 1956. The story is set in a bleak town in the American Midwest, where a self-styled rainmaker, the handsome Bill Starbuck (Robert Horton), has arrived to cure the problem ('Rain Song'). Lizzie Curry (Inga Swenson) has a problem of her own - she cannot find a husband ('Love Don't Turn Away'). Her father and brothers try to fix her up with the town's sheriff, File (Stephen Douglas), a shy divorcee ('A Man And A Woman'), but she prefers the glamorous Starbuck. He indulges in all the rigmarole that is needed to bring the much-needed rain, but is eventually revealed to be a con-man on the run. Even so, Lizzie is about to run away with him ('Is It Really Me?') until File at last reveals his own love for her ('Wonderful Music'). She decides to accept him, and settle for the quiet life. At that moment, the heavens open . . . Jones and Schmidt's lovely, tuneful score, complemented perfectly the folksy, sentimental feeling of the piece. The rest of the songs included 'Gonna Be A Hot Day', 'Lizzie's Comin' Home', 'Poker Polka', 'Hungry Men', 'You're Not Foolin' Me', 'Raunchy', 'Old Maid', 'Everything Beautiful Happens At Night', 'Little Red Hat', 'Melisande', and 'Simple Little Things'. *110 In The Shade* had a decent run of 330 performances, and Inga Swenson's performance was oustanding. She was widely tipped to win a Tony Award, but *Hello, Dolly!* simply swept the board. In 1992 the show was revived by the New York City Opera, with Karen Ziémba as Lizzie. It was taped for transmission on the *Great Performances* television series.

Hunting Of The Snark, The

Prior to 24 October 1991, Mike Batt was best-known in Britain as the arranger and producer of a highly successful series of children's novelty records (on which he also sang) involving the Wombles, a mythical group of small, furry, friendly creatures, who apparently lived on Wimbledon Common in south east London. Soon after that date he became renowned as an obstinate entrepreneur who had poured several years of his life, and a good deal of his own money, into a spectacular flop musical, *The Hunting Of The Snark*. The project, which was based on Lewis Carroll's epic nonsense poem, first surfaced in 1987 as a concept album which was narrated by Sir John Geilgud and John Hurt, and performed by such luminaries as Roger Daltrey, Art Garfunkel, Julian Lennon, Cliff Richard, Deniece Williams *et al.* Four years later, a concert version was well-received at the State Theatre in Sydney, Australia, and the full West End production opened at the Prince Edward Theatre in October 1991. It was Mike Batt's baby all along; he wrote the book, music, and lyrics, staged the show with James Hayes, and was also credited with the design and the orchestrations. The story concerned the search for an 'improbable beast', and involved the Bellman (Philip Quast) and his crew which consisted of the Beaver (Veronica Hart), the Butcher (John Partridge), the Barrister (Allan Love), the Banker (David Firth), the Baker (Mark McGann), the Bandmaster (Jae Alexander), the Broker (Peter Leadbury), and the Bishop (Gary Martin). The disc jockey and television presenter, Kenny Everett, made his West End musical theatre debut as the Billiard Marker, and the role of the author-narrator was played by the film and television actor, David McCallum. Quast, McGann, John Partridge, and Veronica Hart, were all singled out by the critics for special praise. Most of the reputed £2.1 million investment was up there on the stage for all to see, in the shape of a 50 piece orchestra and the high-tech computerized scenic projections. The score, with its 'prosaic music and portenteous lyrics', contained some 26 numbers including 'Children Of The Sky', 'Hymn To The Snark', 'Who'll Join Me On This Escapade?', 'Nursery Pictures', 'The Pig Must Die', 'As Long As The Moon Can Shine', and the prophetically titled 'Dancing Towards Disaster'. Audiences stayed away in their thousands (the Prince Edward is a medium-sized house with a capacity of 1,666), and, throughout November, Batt refused to bring the curtain down despite heavy losses. It was rumoured that Andrew Lloyd Webber, Tim Rice, and Cameron Mackintosh were contributing to the diminishing kitty. Some people loved what they regarded as 'one of the most unusual and intriguing musicals to be seen in the West End', and an angry exchange of opposing views raged in the letters column of *The Stage* newspaper. Finally, on 14 December, Batt could take no more and closed the show after only seven weeks, incurring personal losses that were estimated to be in excess of £600,000.

Hylton, Jack

b. 2 July 1892, Lancashire, England, d. 29 January 1965, London, England Hylton was the leader of an oustanding showband, often called 'Britain's answer to Paul Whiteman' because their repertoire included popular songs, novelties, light classical pieces and a few 'hot' jazz numbers. Hylton sang as a boy soprano in his father's bar before turning to the piano and organ. After playing in a small band at the Queen's Hall Roof in London, he took over, enlarged the group, and started recording in 1921. Although broadcasting occasionally, Hylton concentrated on 'live' performances, and built his showband into a major stage attraction. During the late 20s he toured Europe extensively, while still recording prolifically under several other names such as the Kit-Cat Band, the Hyltonians and the Rhythmagicians. He sold over three million records in 1929 alone, sometimes using gimmicks like flying low over Blackpool in an aircraft, to publicize Joe Gilbert's novelty song, 'Me And Jane In A Plane'. During the 30s his band became the first to broadcast directly to America. Subsequently, he toured the USA using local musicians, while still remaining the premier European showband. Hylton also made two films, *She Shall Have Music* (1935) and *Band Waggon* (1940) the movie version of the highly popular radio programme featuring Arthur Askey and Richard Murdoch. The band broke up in 1940, when several of the members were drafted into the forces. Hylton had used some of the best musicians, such as Ted Heath, Eric Pogson, Jack Jackson, Lew Davis, arranger Billy Ternent, featured guest, jazzman Coleman Hawkins, and singers Jack Plant, Sam Browne and Peggy Dell. With his vast experience, Hylton then moved on to become an impresario, presenting countless West End productions such as *Annie Get Your Gun*, *Kiss Me Kate*, *Call Me Madam* and many more. One of his most endearing legacies was the legendary series of Crazy Gang shows at the Victoria Palace, London. Shortly after presenting *Camelot* at the Drury Lane theatre in 1964, Hylton became ill and died in a London hospital in January 1965.

Compilations: *Jack Hylton And His Orchestra* (1966), *Bands That Matter* (1970), *The Band That Jack Built* (1973), *Plays DeSylva, Brown & Henderson* (1974), *A Programme Light Orchestra Favour's* (1978), *From Berlin - 1927/31* (1979), *Jack's Back* (1982), *Breakaway* (1982), *Swing* (1983), *The Talk Of The Town* (1984), *The Golden Age Of Jack Hylton* (1984), *I'm In A Dancing Mood* (1986), *Song Of Happiness 1931-33* (1987), *This'll Make You Whistle* (1988).

I Can Get It For You Wholesale

Notable mainly for the Broadway debut of the 19-years-old Barbra Streisand, who, in her role as an overworked secretary, stopped the show nightly with 'Miss Marmelstein', this show opened at the Shubert Theatre in New York on 22 March 1962. The 'wholesale' aspect referred to librettist Jerome Weidman's story, based on his own book, which was set in the 30s Depression days of the 'dog-eat-dog' world of New York's rag trade. Harry Bogen (Elliot Gould) is the tough small-time businessman, who will stop at nothing to get to the top, even though his mother, (Lillian Roth) and his girlfriend, Ruthie Rivkin (Marilyn Cooper) plead with him to change his ways. Ruthie is replaced by the flashy nightclub singer, Martha Mills (Sheree North) and, in the end, Harry gets his just desserts. Streisand was low down in the billing, but she was given another effective number, 'What's Are They Doing To Us Now?', in a what was generally considered to be a lack-lustre Harold Rome score, which also included 'Have I Told You Lately?', 'Momma, Momma', 'The Sound Of Money', 'A Gift for Today', 'On My Way To Love', 'Too Soon', 'What's In It For Me?', and 'Who Knows'. Even during the show's run of 300 performances, the young, self-assured lady who married the leading man (Gould), was recording her break-through *The Barbra Streisand Album*, complete with its prophetic sleeve-note by no less a person than Harold Arlen, part of which ran: 'I advise you to watch Barbra Streisand's career. This young lady has a stunning future'. How right he was.

I Do! I Do!

This musical opened at the 46th Street Theatre in New York on 5 December 1966 with a cast consisting of just two people. However, they were two extraordinary people - each of them a theatrical legend. Robert Preston had burst onto the Broadway scene some nine years previously as the conniving Professor Harold Hill in *The Music Man*, and Mary Martin's glorious career in musicals such as *One Touch Of Venus*, *South Pacific*, *Peter Pan*, and *The Sound Of Music*, was destined to end with this unusual two-hander. Tom Jones's book, which was adapted from the 1951 play, *The Fourposter*, by Jan de Hartog, told of a couple's 50 years of marriage, from their wedding day at the turn of the century, through the good times and bad, the arrival of the children, his affair, and finally, their exit from the large house to make way for a young couple with, no doubt, the same kind of aspirations that she (Agnes) and he (Michael) had all those years ago. Tom Jones and Harvey Schmidt's score augmented the story with appropriate numbers such as 'I Love My Wife', 'My Cup Runneth Over', 'Love Isn't Everything', 'Nobody's Perfect', 'Together Forever', 'What Is A Woman?', 'The Honeymoon Is Over', 'Where Are The Snows?', 'When The Kids Get Married', 'Someone Needs Me', 'Roll Up the Ribbons', and the title song. Carol Lawrence and Gordon MacRae succeeded the two original stars during the New York production which ran for over a year, a total of 560 performances. Jones and Schmidt are familiar with long runs - their Off Broadway show, *The Fantasticks*, has reigned for over 30 years. The London production of *I Do! I Do!*, with Ian Carmichael and Ann Rogers, played for 166 performances in 1968, and a brief 1976 West End revival starred Rock Hudson and Juliet Prowse.

I Love My Wife

Wife-swapping in Trenton, New Jersey, USA (population a healthy 92,124), was the slightly old-fashioned subject of Michael Stewart's book for this show which opened at the Ethel Barrymore Theatre on Broadway on 17 April 1977. The two couples, initially intent on being 'Sexually Free', 'Lovers On A Christmas Eve', where 'Everybody Is Turning On' because they each feel there is 'Something Wonderful I've Missed', were Ileen Graff, Lenny Baker, Joanna Gleason, and James Naughton. Of course, being decent, upright citizens, they changed their minds at the last minute - one of the men takes an age to undress - and even then has to finish his dessert - with both husbands affirming: 'I Love My Wife'. Those songs, and the show's outstanding number, 'Hey There, Good Times', were the work of Cy Coleman (music) and Michael Stewart (lyrics). A small onstage orchestra dressed in various fancy clothing, comments on the action in the manner of a Greek chorus, a device that was also used by Richard Rodgers and Lorenz Hart in *Allegro*. *I Love My Wife* caught on, and had a good run of 872 performances. The London production, which opened in October 1977, also did well. It starred Richard Beckinsale, an extremely popular actor in British television comedy programmes such as *Porridge*, who died so tragically young.

I Married An Angel

Originally intended for Hollywood, this adaptation by Richard Rodgers and Lorenz Hart of an Hungarian play by John Vaszary, changed course and flew into New York, and landed at the Shubert Theatre on 11 May 1938. It turned out to be a satirical, comic-fantasy concerning a banker in Budapest, Count Willy

Palaffi (Dennis King), who breaks off his engagement to Audrey Christie (Ann Murphy), swearing that he will only ever marry an angel. Lo and behold, an apparition answering to the name of Angel (Vera Zorina), flies in through Willy's window. They are wed, but Angel's open and honest winning ways cause chaos and confusion until she is taken in hand by Willie's sister, Countess Palaffi (Vivienne Segal). Walter Slezak, the Austrian character actor, who later had a successful Hollywood career, played the financial backer who bailed Willie out when he was in trouble. Vivenne Segal was a revelation. For more than 20 years she had valiantly hung on to her honour in operettas such as *The Desert Song* and *The Yankee Princess*, and yet, here she was in *I Married An Angel*, shining in a sophisticated comedy role. King, too, who was a classically trained singer, came from a similar background, and the two combined on one of Rodgers and Hart's loveliest ballads, the bleak 'Spring Is Here' ('Stars appear!/Why doesn't the night invite me?/Maybe it's because nobody loves me/Spring is here. I hear!'). King, of course, sang the title song, which also endured in the repertoires of several quality vocalists. The ex-ballet dancer, Vera Zorina, was graceful and charming, but Audrey Christie had the show-stopper, 'At The Roxy Music Hall', a hilarious send-up of that vast, venerable institution: 'Where they change the lights a million times a minute/Where the stage goes up and down when they begin in it/It's a wonder Mrs. Roosevelt isn't in it.' . . . 'Where the acrobats are whirling on their digits/Where the balcony's so high you get the fidgets/Where the actors seem to be a lot of midgets/At the Roxy Music Hall'. The rest of the composers' songs in a high quality score included 'Did You Ever Get Stung?', 'I'll Tell The Man In The Street', 'How To Win Friends And Influence People', 'A Twinkle In Your Eye', 'I'm Ruined', and 'Angel Without Wings'. This was an unusual show in many ways, for instance, there was a full-scale ballet in each of the two acts, and some of the dialogue leading up to the songs was rhymed and sung. The production was also notable as the Broadway debut of director Joshua Logan, who was associated with subsequent Rodgers and Hart shows, and with Rodgers and Oscar Hammerstein's *South Pacific*. Miss Segal's impact, too, earned her the plum role of Vera Simpson in *Pal Joey* in 1940. *I Married An Angel* enjoyed a good run of 338 performances, which was followed by a satisfying road tour. The 1942 film version starred Jeanette MacDonald and Nelson Eddy.

I'd Rather Be Right

Even before it opened, this eagerly awaited show, which marked George M. Cohan's return to the Broadway musical stage after an absence of nearly 10 years, had more than the usual set of problems. The composer, Richard Rodgers, who wrote the score with lyricist Lorenz Hart, did not like Cohan (the loathing was mutual) - and he did not care much for the director George S. Kaufman (*he* did not like musicals) either, who co-authored the book with Moss Hart. Cohan, in turn, could not stand President Franklin D. Roosevelt, the somewhat controversial figure he had been chosen to play in his come-back vehicle. However, with the exception of Roosevelt, the rest of the combatants assembled on 2 November 1937 at the Alvin Theatre for the opening of what promised to be an historic event: it was the first time that a President had been portrayed in a book musical - as opposed to a revue - and a satirical one, at that. As the curtain rises, the setting is New York's Central Park on the 4th July. Peggy (Joy Hodges) and Phil (Austin Marshall) are in love, but feel that they ought to wait to get married until Phil gets an increase in salary - which his boss has refused to give him until Roosevelt balances the budget. Phil falls asleep, and in his dreams the two young people meet Roosevelt who promises to do what he can to help, but all his efforts, which include the introduction of hundred dollar postage stamps, and the hiring of pickpockets by the Treasury Department, come to nothing. Phil and Peggy decide to get married anyway. In spite of fears that the show might turn out to be an attack on the President, it was, in fact, a warm-hearted piece which poked fun at most of the prominent political figures of the day, with the notable exception of Eleanor Roosevelt (she was on holiday at the time). Initially, Cohan, who was appearing for the first time in a musical that he had not written himself, took some liberties with the material, particularly 'Off The Record', a song about Al Smith the Democratic candidate who had lost to Herbert Hoover in the 1928 election. In any event, Rodgers' music was not considered to be anywhere near his best, although Hart's lyrics were as sharp and witty as ever in songs such as 'We're Going To Balance The Budget', 'Sweet Sixty-Five', 'I'd Rather Be Right', 'Take And Take And Take', and the charming 'Have You Met Miss Jones?'. The latter number was the nearest the show came to having a love song, and it went on to become something of a minor standard. *I'd Rather Be Right* played for 290 performances in New York before undertaking a successful road tour.

I'm Getting My Act Together And Taking It On The Road

Produced by Joseph Papp at his New York Shakespeare Festival Public Theatre, the launchpad for several successfull musical productions through the years, including *A Chorus Line*, this show opened on 14 June 1978. Nancy Ford (music) and Gretchen Cryer (lyrics and libretto) were well-known in the US feminist movement, and their work consistently reflected their beliefs. In this piece, Ford plays a divorced 39 year old pop singer on the come-back trail, who, with the help of her manager, played by Joe Fabiani, discovers her true self, and becomes a completely liberated person through her songs. These included 'Happy Birthday', 'Dear Tom', 'Natural High', 'Old Friend', 'Miss America', and 'Strong Woman Number'. After six months, the show transferred to the Circle in the Square Theatre in Greenwich Village, and eventually ran for 1,165 performances. During that time, other well-known names such as Betty Buckley, Phillis Newman, Carol Hall, and Virginia Vestoff played the leading role. In 1981, a London production starring Ben Cross, Nicky Croydon, Diane Langton, Greg Martyn, and Megg Nichol, played briefly at the Apollo Theatre. How different it was from the current West End hit, Andrew Lloyd Webber's *Cats*.

Imagine

Devised by Keith Strachen and Ian Kellgren (who also directed) from an original idea by Bob Eaton, with additional material by Liam Lloyd, this tribute to John Lennon played the Liverpool Playhouse Theatre late in 1992. Mark McGann, who portrayed the late Beatle in the play, *Lennon*, in the early 80s, and on film in *John And Yoko - A Love Story*, once again gives a performance that 'nurtures the the shrewd, enquiring mind of John behind his eyes, and masters not only his native arrogance, his comic manner, bearing and stance, but his grim lips in repose'. In *Imagine*, the direct narrative is shared by Cynthia Lennon (Caroline Dennis), Yoko Ono (Ava de Souza), and composite characters such as an American fan (Francine Brody). Some 40 Beatles numbers are played and sung 'live' by McGann, along with Karl Lorne (Paul), Peter Ferris (George), and Paul Case (Ringo). Andy Walmsley's setting varies between a New York skyline and a section of the Cavern Club, and the evening provides 'moments of glorious affirmation as John Lennon's career describes its meteoric curve from rock musician to freaked-out martyr - with some marvellous songs along the way'.

In Dahomey

A significant production in the history of the musical theatre on both sides of the Atlantic. It is said to be the first full-length musical written and performed by black Americans to play a major Broadway theatre, and, perhaps rather less importantly, it introduced sophisticated New Yorkers to the current dance craze - a syncopated predecessor to ragtime - the cakewalk. In fact, one of the most popular moments in the show came when the audience was invited to judge a cakewalk competition by the level of its applause. *In Dahomey* opened on 18 February 1903 at the New York Theatre, with a book by Jesse A. Shipp which told of a gang of Boston con-men who plan to colonize Africa with the money they enveigle out of a geriatric millionaire. The popular ex-vaudeville team of Bert Williams and George. W. Walker supplied most of the comedy, and a lively score by Will Marion Cook (music) and Paul Lawrence Dubar (lyrics), included 'I'm A Jonah Now', 'I Want to Be A Real Lady', and 'On Emancipation Day'. *In Dahomey* only ran for 53 performances in New York, but, somewhat surprisingly, none of the expected racial tensions materialised, and the production was acclaimed for its verve and enthusiam. Those factors also took London by surprise. Audiences there were not used to that level of exuberance, but they liked it, and the show stayed at the Shaftesbury Theatre for 251 performances during 1903, with Williams and Walker in their original roles.

Inside U.S.A.

The last of the seven always entertaining revues with music and lyrics by Arthur Schwartz and Howard Dietz opened at the New Century Theatre in New York on 30 April 1948. The show, which was also produced by Schwartz, is said to have been 'suggested' by John Gunther's famous book, but that was not apparent in the sketches by Arnold Auberbach, Arnold B. Horwitt, and Moss Hart. The indomitable Beatrice Lillie skylarked around along with Jack Haley in a series of comical geographical situations in which they, as two Indians in Alberquerque, resolutely refuse the offer of the whole country ('We Won't Take It Back'), and become involved with members of a choral society who are intent on solving the problems of pollution in Pittsburgh. 'Haunted Heart' was the song that achieved some popularity outside the show in recordings by Perry Como and Jo Stafford, and another ballad, 'First Prize At The Fair', was also singled out for praise. The novelty show-stopper was a United States list song, 'Rhode Island Is Famous For You', which was performed in the show by Haley, and was fairly conventional early on: 'Old whiskey, comes from old Kentucky/Ain't the country lucky?/New Jersey gives us glue' . . . 'Grand Canyons, come from Colorada/Gold comes from Nevada/Divorces also do' . . . but then 'declined' into the amusingly excruciating: 'Pencils come from Pencilvania/Vests from Vest Virgina/And tents from Tentassee'. The composer himself gave the song a more than adequate reading nearly 30 years later on his *From The Pen Of Arthur Schwartz*. The show's other numbers were 'Blue Grass', 'My Gal Is Mine Once More', and 'At The Mardi Gras', and the chorus contained some famous names: Jack Cassidy, who went on to star in *Wish You Were Here* and *She Loves Me*, and become the father of pop star David Cassidy before marrying Shirley Jones; and Carl Reiner, who achieved fame in the 60s as the writer of television's *The Dick Van Dyke Show. Inside U.S.A.* enjoyed a run of 399 performances, and, shortly after it closed, Schwartz devised a television variety programme based on the idea, which used the same songs, and starred Peter Lind Hayes and Mary Healy.

Into The Woods

Once again Stephen Sondheim came up with something surprising and original for this show which made its debut at the Martin Beck Theatre in New York on 5 November 1987. He and director-librettist James Lapine transformed a series of nursery rhyme characters, Cinderella (Kim Crosby), Red Riding Hood (Danielle Ferland), Jack (Ben Wright) And The Beanstalk, and Rapunzel (Pamela Winslow) into what one critic called 'a symbolic world of adulthood and self-discovery'. The tales are linked by the Baker (Chip Zien) and his wife (Joanna Gleason), who desperately want a child. A nearby Witch (Bernadette Peters) offers to solve their sterility problem if the baker will deliver to her within three days: Cinderella's slipper, Red Riding Hood's cape, Jack's cow, and Rapunzel's hair. The Baker obliges, and his wife duly becomes pregnant. Thereafter, the story takes on Freudian overtones, and becomes a 'timely moral allegory for adults'. Red Riding Hood is swallowed by the wolf but later emerges unscathed; Rapunzel goes mad, Jack's mother and Red Riding Hood's grandmother die suddenly, and the witch is transformed into her younger self. Sondheim's score was regarded as 'melodic and lyrically rich', and included such numbers as the recurring 'Into The Woods', 'Any Moment', 'Children Will Listen', 'It Takes Two', 'I Know Things Now', 'Moments In The Woods', and 'No More'. Another song which attracted some attention was 'Agony', a duet for two princes (Robert Westenberg and Chuck Wagner) who decide that adultery is more fun than fidelity. *Into The Woods* ran for 764 performances, slightly over-par for Sondheim, and won Tony Awards for the score, book, and best actress (Joanna Gleason), despite *The Phantom Of The Opera* running off with most of them in that year. It also gained the New York Drama Critics Circle and Drama Desk Awards for best musical. The 1990 London production, which ran for five months, starred Julia McKenzie as the Witch, and gained Olivier Awards for the director (Richard Jones) and best actress (Imelda Staunton as the Baker's wife).

Irene

Yet another show based on the familiar 'Cinderella' rags-to-riches story, this is, nevertheless, one of America's most treasured musical productions. It opened at the Vanderbilt Theatre in New York on 18 November 1919. James Montgomery's book, based on his own play, Irene O'Dare, told of a poor young girl (Edith Day), who works for an upholsterer, who is sent by her employer to do some work for Donald Marshall (Walter Regan) at his grand home in Long Island. Impressed by the personable girl, Donald arranges a job for her at an establishment belonging to a male fashion designer, Mme. Lucy (Bobby Watson). She charms everyone, including the extra-snobbish J.P. Bowden (Arthur Burckly), who gives a her a party, and becomes stricken with love for her, until he discovers that she is from 'the other side of the tracks'. Donald, however, has no such prejudice, and, after the usual trouble with his high-falutin family, he and Irene eventually marry. The memorable score, by Harry Tierney (music), who was making his Broadway debut, and Joseph McCarthy (lyrics), produced one enormous hit, 'Alice Blue Gown', which was introduced by Edith Day, and later became popular through recordings by Day herself, and Frankie Masters, Ozzie Nelson, and Glenn Miller. There were some other good songs, too, such as 'Castle Of Dreams', 'The Talk Of The Town', 'Sky Rocket', 'To Be Worthy Of You', 'Irene', and the exuberant 'The Last Part Of Every Party'. During the show's run of 670 performances, a record for a Broadway musical, which it held for 18 years, Edith Day left to recreate her role in the London production which stayed at the Empire Theatre for almost a year. The show's incredible popularity continued via road companies which at one stage were estimated to be around 17 in number. In 1973, more than 50 years after it had first been produced, Irene was revived in New York with the popular film actress, Debbie Reynolds, making her Broadway debut. In the revised book by Joseph Stein, Hugh Wheeler, and Harry Rigby, Irene O'Day's days as a model were long gone, and she was now - of all things - a piano tuner. Several changes were made to the score, including the addition of some songs by Charles Gaynor, Fred Fisher, and Otis Clements; and two others, both with lyrics by Joseph McCarthy, 'You Made Me Love You' (music by Jimmy Monaco), and 'I'm Always Chasing Rainbows' (music by Harry Carroll), which was originally used in the show *Oh Look!* (1918). Once again, the show endeared itself to the public, and stayed around for 604 performances. Two films of *Irene* were made, a silent version in 1926, with Colleen Moore, and another, in 1940, starring Anna Neagle, Ray Milland, and Roland Young.

Irma La Douce

This show originally opened at the tiny Theatre Gramont in Paris on 12 November 1956, and gave the city a new star - young Colette Renard - in the leading role. The book and lyrics were written by the ex-taxi driver and novelist Alexandre Breffort, and

the music was provided by Marguerite Monnet, who had written several songs for Edith Piaf, including 'Poor People Of Paris', which became a big hit in France, and gave the personality pianist, Winifred Atwell, a UK number 1. Serious doubts were expressed as to whether this tender, typically French love story between a prostitute and her pimp, could weather the Channel crossing, and survive the trip to London's West End. In the event, it did so triumphantly. The production arrived at the Lyric Theatre, via the seaside town of Bournemouth, on 17 July 1958, with an English book and lyrics by three comparitive newcomers to the musical theatre, Julian More, David Heneker, and Monty Norman. Rather than 'Anglicize' the show completely, the writers inserted a glossary of terms in the theatre programme, a device which had also been found to be necessary in France. The list of 'translations' included, Milieu (underworld), Poule (tart), Mec (pimp), and Grisbi (money). The story is set in the the backstreets, off the Pigalle ('Valse Milieu'), with its small-time crooks ('Tres Tres Snob') and the poules, such as Irma-la-Douce (Elizabeth Seal). She falls in love with an impoverished law student, Nestor-le-Fripe (Keith Michell) ('The Bridge Of Caulaincourt'), and they live together ('Our Language Of Love') while Irma continues to work so that Nestor can continue his studies ('She's Got The Lot'). Nestor disguises himself as Monsieur Oscar, and becomes her sole client ('Dis-Donc'), but he soon becomes disenchanted with the double life ('The Wreck Of A Mec'), and dispenses with his altar ego ('That's A Crime'). He is found guilty of murder ('Le Grisbi Is Le Root Of Le Evil In Man') and sent to Devil's Island ('From A Prison Cell'), but he escapes ('There Is Only One Paris For That'), and returns to Irma just in time for the birth of their baby ('Christmas Child'). The production was a triumph all round, with a particularly strong supporting cast which included Clive Revill (Bob-le-Hontu), John East (Polyte-le-Mou), Julian Orchard (Police Inspector), and Gary Raymond (Frangipane). It ran for more than three and half years in London, a total of 1,512 performances, and the New York edition, in which several of the principals recreated their roles, played for over a year. Elizabeth Seal won the Tony Award for best actress, and Elliot Gould, who was on the brink of a successful film career at the time, played an Usher, a Priest, and a Warder. The 1963 film of *Irma La Douce* starred Shirley MacLaine and Jack Lemmon, but deleted all the songs, and used some of the music as background themes.

Iron Man, The

With the smash hit, razzle-dazzle production of the Who's *Tommy* doing 101.1% business on Broadway, its creator, Pete Townshend, turned his hand to this much smaller project which opened for a three month

Pete Townshend (*The Iron Man*)

season at the Young Vic in London on 25 November 1993. Together with the show's director David Thacker, he adapted Poet Laureate Ted Hughes' 1968 book of children's fairytales into a musical production 'which is pitched somewhere between a children's show with a strong ecological message and one of those hippy musicals which surfaced in the late 60s and early 70s'. On a set 'that makes the rubbish dump in *Cats* look like an assembly line in a Japanese car factory', there emerges from time to time a 12 feet-high figure with vast headlamps for eyes, spanners for hands, and huge cans for feet. In between all of that is another load of junk. Actually none of the critics went that far, but, with hardly any exceptions, they did not like the show much. One of the main quibbles was the 'watering down' of certain characters such as the Star Spirit (Josette Bushell-Mingo), who, in Hughes' book, is a giant male dragon, and in this production is 'prettified and turned into a female sex symbol'. As to the plot, for most of the time the huge metal giant, accompanied by the Spirit of the Iron Man (Trevor Michael Georges), eats every piece of metal he can find ('cannabalism', one reviewer called it) and threatens to dominate the earth until a young boy named Hogarth (Anthony Barclay), together with some of his friends, pacifies him by singing 'Let's Have A Ball-Bearing Ball'. Townshend's music was deemed to be a good deal stronger than his lyrics in a score which contained numbers such as 'Over The Top We Go', 'Man Makes Machines', 'Dig!', 'Every Young Kid Has To Train', 'When Eyes Meet In Silence', 'I Eat Heavy Metal', 'I Awake Deep In The Night', 'Fast Food', 'I'm Not Gonna Run Anymore', 'Was There Life Before This Love?', and a typical 60s 'flower-power' plea for love and understanding, 'What We Want Is A Brand New Year'. Not an auspicious event, but, following *Tommy*'s triumph, it may be wise not to bet against Townshend eventually getting it right.

It's A Bird, It's A Plane, It's Superman

A camp version of the famous comic strip, with a book by David Newman and Robert Benton, this show zoomed into the Alvin Theatre in New York on 29 May 1966, and zoomed out again just four months later. In the stage musical phase of his varied and interesting life - as opposed to the film or printed page - Clark Kent (Bob Holiday), the meek and mild newspaper reporter on the *Daily Planet*, is still prepared to strip off to reveal that famous suit complete with large letter 'S', at the merest hint of a national emergency. Surely Superman should have suspected foul play when the mad scientist, Dr. Sedgwick (Michael O'Sullivan), invites him to a dedication ceremony in his honour at the physics hall, while he (Sedgwick) sneaks away to blow up the Metropolis city hall? What a stroke of luck he is in

the power station to rescue Lois Lane (Patricia Marand), before streaking into the atmosphere to intercept a missile in mid-air that is destined for the city. Throw in an egotistical columnist, Max Mencken (Jack Cassidy), and an amusing score by Charles Strouse (music) and Lee Adams (lyrics), and somehow it is difficult to understand why the show did not run for more than 129 performances. One of the songs, 'You've Got Possibilities', received a much attention, and most of the other numbers were enjoyable, including 'It's Superman', 'We Don't Matter At All', 'The Woman For The Man', 'Ooh, Do You Love You!', 'What I've Always Wanted', 'You've Got What I Need', 'Pow! Bam! Zonk!', and 'It's Super Nice'. In the 80s there was the famous series of big block-buster movies, starring Christopher Reeve, and then, in 1992, the stage show resurfaced in a production by the Godspeed Opera House, Connecticut, USA. The roles of Superman/Clark Kent and Lois were played by Gary Jackson and Kay McClelland, Strouse and Adams contributed several new songs, including 'Thanks To You', 'Karabitz!', and 'It's Up To Me', but the best notices went to 'Flying By Foy', 'the world's largest flying effects company', whose aerial manoeuvring of Superman over the heads of the audience was, by all accounts, sensational.

Ives, Burl

b. Burl Icle Ivanhoe Ives, 14 June 1909, Hunt Township, Jasper County, Illinois, USA. One of the world's most celebrated singers of folk ballads, with a gentle, intimate style. Ives was also an actor on the stage and screen, an anthologist and editor of folk music. A son of tenant farmers in the 'Bible Belt' of Illinois, Ives was singing in public for money with his brothers and sisters when he was four years old. Many of the songs they sang originated in the British Isles, and were taught to them by their tobacco-chewing grandmother. After graduating from high school in 1927 Ives went to college intending to become a professional football coach. Instead, he left college early, in 1930, and hitch-hiked throughout the USA, Canada and Mexico, supporting himself by doing odd jobs and singing to his own banjo accompaniment, picking up songs everywhere he went. After staying for awhile in Terre Haute, Indiana, attending the State Teachers College, he moved to New York, and studied with vocal coach, Ekka Toedt, before enrolling for formal music training at New York University. Despite this classical education, he was determined to devote himself to folk songs. In 1938, he played character roles in several plays, and in the same year had a non-singing role on Broadway, in George Abbott's musical comedy, *The Boys From Syracuse*, followed by a four-month singing engagement at New York's Village Vanguard nightclub. He then toured with the Richard Rodgers/Lorenz Hart musical, *I Married An Angel*. In 1940 Ives performed on radio, singing his folk ballads to his own guitar accompaniment on programmes such as *Back Where I Come From*, and was soon given his own series entitled *Wayfaring Stranger*. The introductory, 'Poor Wayfaring Stranger', one of America's favourite folk songs, and by then already over 100 years old, became his long-time theme. Drafted into the US Army in 1942, Ives sang in Irving Berlin's military musical revue, *This Is The Army*, both on Broadway and on tour. In 1944, after medical discharge from the Forces, Ives played a long stint at New York's Cafe Society Uptown nightclub, and also appeared on Broadway with Alfred Drake in *Sing Out Sweet Land*, a 'Salute To American Folk And Popular Music'. For his performance, Ives received the Donaldson Award as Best Supporting Actor. During the following year, he made his concert bow at New York's Town Hall, and played a return engagement in 1946. Also in that year he made his first film, *Smoky*, with Fred McMurray and Anne Baxter, and appeared with Josh White in a full-length feature about folk music. Ives's other movies, in which he played characters ranging from villainous to warmly sympathetic, included *So Dear To My Heart* (1948), *East Of Eden* (1955) and *Cat On A Hot Tin Roof* (1958), in which he played Big Daddy, re-creating his highly acclaimed Broadway performance in the Tennessee Williams play; *Wind Across The Everglades* (1958), *Desire Under The Elms* (1958), *The Big Country* (1958), for which he received an Oscar as the Best Supporting Actor; and *Our Man In Havana* (1960). In 1954, Ives played the role of Cap'n Andy Hawkes in a revival of Jerome Kern and Oscar Hammerstein II's *Show Boat* at the New York City Center. In the 60s and 70s he appeared regularly on US television, sometimes in his dramatic series, such as *O K Crackerby* and *The Bold Ones*, and several music specials. In the 80s, he was still continuing to contribute character roles to feature films and television, and perform in concerts around the world. Back in 1948, his first chart record, 'Blue Tail Fly', teamed him with the Andrews Sisters. The song, written by Dan Emmett in 1846, had been in the Ives repertoire for some years. Other US Top 30 hits, through to the early 60s, included 'Lavender Blue (Dilly Dilly)', 'Riders In The Sky (Cowboy Legend)', 'On Top Of Old Smokey', 'The Wild Side Of Life', 'True Love Goes On And On', 'A Little Bitty Tear', 'Funny Way Of Laughin'' and 'Call Me Mr In-Between'. Many other songs were associated with him, such as 'Foggy Foggy Dew', 'Woolie Boogie Bee', 'Turtle Dove', 'Ten Thousand Miles', 'Big Rock Candy Mountain', 'I Know An Old Lady (Who Swallowed A Fly)', 'Aunt Rhody' and 'Ballad Of Davy Crockett'. Ives published several collections

of folk ballads and tales, including *America's Musical Heritage - Song Of America*, *Burl Ives Song Book*, *Tales Of America*, *Burl Ives Book Of Irish Songs*, and for children, *Sailing On A Very Fine Day*.

Albums: *The Wayfaring Stranger* (1959), *Burl Ives Sings Irving Berlin* (1961), *The Versatile Burl Ives!* (1962), *It's Just My Funny Way Of Laughin'* (1962), *Ballads And Folk Songs* (early 60s), *Walt Disney Presents Burl Ives - Animal Folk* (1964), *Times They Are A-Changin'* (late 60s), *Chim Chim Cheree* (1974), with the Korean Children Choir *Faith And Joy* (1974), *Bright And Beautiful* (1979), *Burl Ives Live In Europe* (1979), *How Great Thou Art* (1974), *Songs I Sang At Sunday School* (1974), *I Do Believe* (1974), *Junior Choice* (1974), *Payin' My Dues Again* (mid-70s), *Little White Duck* (1977), *Shall We Gather At River* (1978), *Talented Man* (1978), *Live In Europe* (1979), *Stepping In The Light* (1984), *Love And Joy* (1984), *The Very Best Of* (1993), *A Little Bitty Tear: The Nashville Years 1961-65* (1993), and the series *Historical America In Song*, for Encyclopedia Britannica.

Further reading: *The Wayfaring Stranger*, Burl Ives.

Jacques Brel Is Alive And Well And Living In Paris

This cabaret-style revue which celebrates the songs of the well-known Belgian composer, author, and performer, opened Off Broadway at the Village Gate on 22 January 1968, and ran for an incredible 1,847 performances. The show was conceived by Americans Mort Shuman and Eric Blau, who also wrote the lyrics and sundry other additional material. Jacques Brel's original critical and satirical approach to his life and work was impressively reflected in the upwards of 20 numbers that were used in the piece. These included some tender ballads, 'Marieke', 'Old Folks', and 'You're Not Alone', along with an impressive variety of other songs, such as the exuberant 'Carousel' and 'Brussels'. Shuman himself was in the cast of four, along with Shawn Elliot, Alice Whitfield, and Elly Stone, who got to sing most of the best songs, and received all the best notices. She also starred in the London production, along with Shuman, Elliot, and June Gable, but that folded after only 41 performances. Some 20 years later, Stone's connection with the show was renewed when she directed a revival which ran briefly at the Town Hall, New York in 1988. The performers then were Karen Akers, Shelle Ackerman, Kenny Morris, and Elmore James. By then the title was an anachronism - Jaques Brel had died in 1978. Even so, the piece has become a cult item over the years - a kind of tourist attraction - so it was fitting that, in 1993, a 25th anniversary production was mounted at its original birthplace, the Village Gate, directed of course, by Elly Stone.

Jamaica

Lena Horne, making her only appearance in a Broadway book musical, was the main attraction when this show opened at the Imperial Theatre in New York on 31 October 1957. Ironically, it is sometimes claimed that Harry Belafonte was first choice for the leading role until he became unwell (Horne herself says: 'There's always been talk of a slight resemblance!'). If that is so, the book, by E.Y. 'Yip' Harburg and Fred Saidly, obviously underwent some radical changes to enable Savannah (Lena Horne), to become the object of affection for Koli (Ricardo Montalban), a fisherman who lives on a mythical, magical tropical paradise known as Pigeon Island. Savannah is dissatisfied with that particular island, and would much prefer to move to another one where there is a bit more action - Manhattan, for instance. However, after briefly flirting with an example of the civilization from that area in the shape of Joe Nashua (Joe Adams), she thinks better of it, and decides to settle for what she has got. The show had a top-notch score by Harburg and composer Harold Arlen, which included the outstanding ballad, 'Cocoanut Sweet', along with 'I Don't Think I'll End It Today', 'Ain't It The Truth', 'Pretty To Walk With', 'Little Biscuit', 'Incompatibility', 'Take It Slow, Joe', 'Napoleon', an amusing 'list' song, and Savannah's hymn to Manhattan, 'Push De Button'. A few years later, another of the songs, 'What Good Does It Do?', received a sensitive reading from Tony Bennett on an album he recorded in concert at Carnegie Hall in New York. On the strength of Lena Horne's box-office appeal (she was at her peak around this time), the show ran for nearly a year and a half, a total of 559 performances.

Jeeves

This is the skeleton in the cupboard of Andrew Lloyd Webber, the most successful composer of stage musicals during the past 20 years. Most of the creative giants of Broadway and the West End have had their superflops - Alan Jay Lerner (Dance A Little Closer), Lionel Bart (Twang!!), and Stephen Sondheim (Anyone Can Whistle), to mention only a few - and this show proves that Lloyd Webber is no exception. It occurred at Her Majesty's Theatre in London on 22 April 1975, and was despatched, 38 performances

later, on 24 May. The composer had already tasted substantial success with Jesus Christ Superstar and Joseph And The Amazing Technicolor Dreamcoat, and another smash-hit, Evita, was only three years into the future. Tim Rice, his collaborator on all three of those productions, was unavailable for Jeeves (perhaps he was at a cricket match), so Lloyd Webber turned to the celebrated comedy playwright Alan Ayckbourn for what one critic claimed was 'like a dream of all the Wodehouse novels combined in the ultimate ghastly weekend'. Jeeves (Michael Aldridge) and Bertie Wooster (David Hemmings) were joined by the usual Drones Club crowd, a veritable gaggle of girlfriends, and various other comical characters. Members of the cast included Betty Marsden, Gordon Clyde, Christopher Good, John Turner, Bill Wallis, Angela Easterling, Graham Hamilton, and Gabrielle Drake. Critics felt that Lloyd Webber's music failed to capture the lively, happy-go-lucky flavour of the 20 and 30s period in a score which contained such songs as 'Code Of The Woosters', 'Banjo Boy', 'Female Of The Species', 'When Love Arrives', 'Half A Moment', 'Summer Day', and 'Jeeves Is Past Its Peak'. It must have seemed such a good idea at the time, but the 'straggling, heavy-handed affair' proved to be only a slight hiccup in the careers of both Andrew Lloyd Webber and Alan Ayckbourn.

Jelly's Last Jam

Although full to the brim with the music of the legendary pioneer jazz composer, pianist, and bandleader Jelly Roll Morton, this is an original book musical, and not just a run-down of a bunch of songs, most of which are over 60 years old. Jelly's Last Jam opened at the Virginia Theatre in New York on 26 April 1992. The book, by a newcomer to Broadway, George C. Wolfe who also directed the piece, opens with Morton (Gregory Hines) recently demised. Up (or down) there, in the anti-room in which the big decisions as to the eventual direction (eternity-wise) are made, the Chimney Man (Keith David), reviews the evidence as to Morton's earthly behaviour - from his early piano-playing days in Storyville brothels, through his self-appointed position as the 'inventor of jazz', to his controversial rejection of his African ancestry. Morton's own compositions are supplemented by some additional material from Luther Henderson, who also adapted and orchestrated the musical side of the whole production, and a set of sometimes saucy and sardonic lyrics by Susan Birkenhead. Naturally, with Hines on board, the tap dancing is sensational, but the entire cast, including Savion Glover as the young Morton, Stanley Wayne Mathis in the role of Jack the Bear, Morton's best friend, and Tonya Pinkins as his sexy girlfriend, were all outstanding. With the benefit of some memorable musical numbers such as 'Lovin' Is A Lowdown

Blues', 'Play The Music For Me', 'The Last Chance Blues', 'The Chicago Stomp', 'Dr. Jazz', and many more, *Jelly's Last Jam* sang and danced its way into 1993, but after May of that year, when Hines was replaced by Brian Mitchell, things were never quite the same, although the highly popular Ben Vereen took over the role of the Chimney Man around the same time. However, the show still ran for a year and a half, closing in September 1993. Considering that it opened in the same season as *Falsettos*, along with *Crazy For You* and a revival of *Guys And Dolls* which show-cased three of America's favourite composers, George and Ira Gershwin, *Jelly's Last Jam* did remarkably well in the kudos stakes. In the Drama Desk Awards, Gregory Hines tied with Nathan Lane (*Guys And Dolls*) for best actor, and won outright the awards for featured actress (Tonya Pinkins), lyrics, orchestrations-musical adaptations, and book. In the Tony department, awards went to Hines, Pinkins, and lighting designer Jules Fisher. US television viewers were given a rare opportunity to see the creators and performers discussing the show's roots and relevance, in *Jammin': Jelly Roll Morton On Broadway*, which was transmitted in November 1992.

Jesus Christ Superstar

Although originating in the UK, the first staging of *Jesus Christ Superstar* was on Broadway, where it opened at the Mark Hellinger Theatre on 17 October 1971. With a book by Tom O'Horgan, which was based on the New Testament, music by Andrew Lloyd Webber and lyrics by Tim Rice, the show was originally released as an album with a cast that included Murray Head, Yvonne Elliman, Ian Gillan and Mike d'Abo. Record sales were of the spectacular, gold disc variety, and helped counteract the generally unfavourable reviews from the New York critics. Nevertheless, one critic, Otis L. Guernsey Jnr, was far-sighted enough to observe that despite the show's 'indigestible stage imagery' and its 'questionable taste', it was also 'as unstoppable as a circus'. Criticism from religious leaders, who disliked the equating of Christ with a pop star on the decline, helped publicize the show and it ran for 720 performances at the Mark Hellinger Theatre. The London production, which made its debut at the Palace Theatre on 9 August 1972, marked the beginning of Lloyd Webber's unstoppable circus of lavishly-staged, thinly-plotted shows which continue into the 90s. Paul Nicholas was among a West End cast which sang songs such as 'Heaven On Their Minds', 'This Jesus Must Die', 'Gethsemane', 'Could We Start Again Please', and 'Everything's Alright'. Another of the numbers, a most appealing ballad, 'I Don't Know How To Love Him', became a hit for Yvonne Elliman and Helen Reddy. The show ran until August 1980, a total of 3,358 performances, and

reigned as the third-longest-running musical in the history of the London theatre (after *Cats* and *Starlight Express*) until it was overtaken by *Les Misérables* in January 1994. Over the years it enjoyed phenomenal success all over the world, and in 1992 a 20th anniversary concert production toured the UK, starring one of the original performers, Paul Nicholas. Also in that year, a highly distinctive Japanese-language version by the Shiki Theatrical Company of Tokyo ('a kubuki-style production') was presented at the Dominion Theatre. Critical comments ranged from 'A memorable evening' to 'Seeing this ghastly show once 20 years ago was bad enough, but here it is again, banal and garish as ever.'

Jill Darling

After touring the UK provinces under the title of *Jack And Jill*, the re-named and revised *Jill Darling* opened in the West End at the Saville Theatre on 19 December 1934. The composer Vivian Ellis had gone to extreme lengths to bring together his 'dream couple', Frances Day and Arthur Riscoe, in this musical comedy by Marriot Edgar. His story told of a young girl, Jill Sonning (Frances Day), who, for reasons that are not entirely clear, is masquerading as an Hungarian cabaret performer, while Arthur Riscoe has a double role - as Pendleton Brown, who is running for Parliament on an 'anti-booze' ticket, and Jack Crawford, who substitutes for Brown when he gets drunk. Vivian Ellis and Desmond Carter wrote a lovely score which gave the two leading players 'Let's Lay Our Heads Together' and 'I'd Do The Most Extraordinary Thing', and several other charming pieces such as 'Dancing With A Ghost' (Riscoe), along with 'I'm In Budapest' and 'Pardon My English' (Day). The second leads, Louise Brown and John Mills (later to become a celebrated straight actor), had the jolly 'Nonny, Nonny, No', as well as the surprise hit of the show, 'I'm On a See-Saw', which became successful for Ambrose And His Orchestra in America, and was subsequently recorded by Fats Waller in 1952. In a scene reminiscent of a 40s Hollywood movie, the show's backer, a young South African by the name of Jack Eggar, 'suggested' that there might part in *Jill Darling* for his wife, Teddi St. Dennis, and Ellis and Carter obligingly whipped up 'Bats In The Belfrey' for the lady to sing with the young Edward Molloy. The show was a great success, but, after Frances Day had to leave in the early summer of 1935 to fulfil a filming commitment (she was replaced by a *real* Hungarian), business fell off, and the production closed after a run of 242 performances. There was a revival at the Winter Garden Theatre in 1944, with Riscoe in his original role, and Carol Lynne as Jill, but it only lasted for for two months.

Jolson, Al

b. Asa Yoelson, c.1885, Snrednicke, Lithuania, d. 23
October 1950. Shortly before the turn of the century,
Jolson's father, Moses Yoelson, emigrated to the
USA. In a few years he was able to send for his wife
and four children, who joined him in Washington
DC. Moses Yoelson was cantor at a synagogue and
had hopes that his youngest son, Asa, would adopt
this profession. After the death of their mother, the
two sons, Asa and Hirsch, occasionally sang on street
corners for pennies. Following the example of his
brother, who had changed his name to Harry, Asa
became Al. When family disagreements arose after his
father remarried, Al went to New York where his
brother had gone to try his luck in show business. For
food-money, he sang at McGirk's, a saloon/restaurant
in New York's Bowery and later sang with military
bands during the time of the Spanish-American War.
Back in Washington, he attracted attention when, as a
member of the audience at the city's Bijou Theater,
he joined in the singing with entertainer Eddie
Leonard. The vaudevillian was so impressed he
offered the boy a job, singing from the balcony as part
of the act. Al refused but ran away to join a theatrical
troupe. This venture was short-lived and a week or so
later he was back home but had again altered the
spelling of his name, this time to Al Joelson. In the
audience, again at the Bijou, he sang during the stage
act of burlesque queen Aggie Beeler. Once more he
was made an offer and this time he did not refuse.
This job was also brief, because he was not content to
merely sing from the balcony and Beller would not
allow him to join her on the stage.

Joelson moved to New York and found work as a
singing waiter. He also appeared in the crowd scenes
of a play which survived for only three performances.
Calling himself Harry Joelson, he formed a double act
with Fred E. Moore but abandoned this when his
voice broke. Reverting to the name Al he now joined
his brother Harry and formed an act during which he
whistled songs until his voice matured. The brothers
teamed up with Joe Palmer to form the act Joelson,
Palmer and Joelson, but again changed the spelling to
shorten the space taken on playbills. In 1905 Harry
dropped out of the act and the following year Al
Jolson was on his own. In San Francisco he
established a reputation as an exciting entertainer and
coined the phrase which later became an integral part
of his performance: 'All right, all right, folks - you
ain't heard nothin' yet!' In 1908 Jolson was hired by
Lew Dockstader, leader of one of the country's two
most famous minstrel shows, and quickly became the
top attraction. Around this time he also formed a
lifelong association with Harry Akst, a song plugger
who later wrote songs including 'Dinah', 'Baby Face'
and 'Am I Blue?'. Akst was especially useful to Jolson
in finding songs suitable for his extrovert style. In

1911 Jolson opened at the Winter Garden in New
York City, where he was a huge success. That same
year he made his first records, reputedly having to be
strapped to a chair as his involuntary movements were
too much for the primitive recording equipment.
Also in 1911 he suggested that the Winter Garden
show be taken on tour, sets and full cast, orchestra
and all, something that had never been done before.
In 1912 he again did something new, putting on
Sunday shows at the Garden so that other show
business people could come and see him. Although he
sang in blackface for the regular shows, local bylaws
on religious observance meant that the Sunday shows
had to be put on without sets and make-up. He
devised an extended platform so that he could come
out in front of the proscenium arch, thus allowing
him to be closer to his audience with whom he was
already having a remarkable love affair.

Among his song successes at this time were 'The
Spaniard That Blighted My Life' and 'You Made Me
Love You'. One night, when the show at the Garden
was overrunning, he sent the rest of the cast off stage
and simply sang to the audience who loved it. From
then on, whenever he felt inclined, which was often,
he would ask the audience to choose if they wanted
to see the rest of the show or just listen to him.
Invariably, they chose him. Significantly enough, on
such occasions, the dismissed cast rarely went home,
happily sitting in the wings to watch him perform. By
1915 Jolson was being billed as 'America's Greatest
Entertainer' and even great rivals such as Eddie
Cantor and George Jessel had to agree with this title.
In 1916 Jolson made a silent film but found the
experiment an unsatisfactory experience. Jolson's
1918 Broadway show was *Sinbad* and his song
successes included 'Rockabye Your Baby With A
Dixie Melody', 'Swanee' and 'My Mammy'. In 1919
he again tried something unprecedented for a popular
entertainer, a concert at the Boston Opera House
where he was accompanied by the city's symphony
orchestra. Jolson's 1921 show was *Bombo* which
opened at a new theatre which bore his name,
Jolson's 59th Street Theater. The songs in the show
included 'My Mammy', 'April Showers', 'California
Here I Come' and 'Toot, Toot, Tootsie (Goo' Bye)'.
During the mid-20s Jolson tried some more new
departures; in 1925 he opened in *Big Boy*, which had
a real live horse in the cast, and in 1927 he performed
on the radio. Of even more lasting significance, in
1926 he returned to the film studios to participate in
an experimental film, a one-reel short entitled *April
Showers* in which he sang three songs, his voice
recorded on new equipment being tested by
Vitaphone, a company which had been acquired by
Warner Brothers. Although this brief film remained
only a curio, and was seen by few people, the system
stirred the imagination of Sam Warner, who believed

Al Jolson

that this might be what the company needed if it was to stave off imminent bankruptcy. They decided to incorporate sound into a film currently in pre-production. This was *The Jazz Singer* which, as a stage show, had run for three years with George Jessel in the lead. Jessel wanted more money than the Warners could afford and Eddie Cantor turned them down flat. They approached Jolson, cannily inviting him to put money into the project in return for a piece of the profits. *The Jazz Singer* (1927) was a silent film into which it was planned to interpolate a song or two but Jolson, being Jolson, did it his way, calling out to the orchestra leader, 'Wait a minute, wait a minute. You ain't heard nothin' yet!' before launching into 'Toot, Toot, Tootsie'. The results were sensational and the motion picture industry was revolutionized overnight. The Warner brothers were saved from bankruptcy and Jolson's piece of the action made him even richer than he already was. His follow-up film, *The Singing Fool*, (1928) included a song especially written for him by the team of De Sylva, Brown And Henderson. Although they treated the exercise as a joke, the results were a massive hit and Jolson's recording of 'Sonny Boy' became one of the first million sellers.

Although Jolson's films were popular and he was one of the highest paid performers in Hollywood, the cinema proved detrimental to his career. The cameras never fully captured the magic that had made him so successful on Broadway. Additionally, Jolson's love for working with a live audience was not satisfied by the film medium. His need to sing before a live audience was so overpowering that when his third wife, the dancer Ruby Keeler, opened on Broadway in *Show Girl*, he stood up in his seat and joined in with her big number, 'Liza'. He completely upstaged Keeler, who would later state that this was one of the things about him that she grew to hate the most. Jolson continued to make films, among them *Mammy* (1930) which included 'Let Me Sing And I'm Happy', and *Big Boy* (1930), generally cited as the film which came closest to capturing the essence of his live performances. Back on Broadway in 1931 with *The Wonder Bar*, Jolson was still popular and was certainly an extremely rich man, but he was no longer the massive success that he had been in the 20s. For a man who sang for many reasons, of which money was perhaps the least important, this was a very bad time. Fuelling his dissatisfaction was the fact that Keeler, whose film career he had actively encouraged and helped, was a bigger box-office attraction. Despite spreading a thin talent very wide, Keeler rose while Jolson fell. In 1932 he stopped making records and that year there were no shows or films, even though there were still offers. He made a film with Keeler, *Go Into Your Dance* (1935) in which he sang 'About A Quarter To Nine', and participated in an early television pilot. Not surprisingly for a man who had

tried many new ventures in show business, Jolson was impressed by the medium and confidently predicted its success, but his enthusiasm was not followed up by producers. He made more films in the late 30s, sometimes cameos, occasionally rating third billing but the great days appeared to be over. Even his return to Broadway, in 1940 in *Hold Onto Your Hats*, was fated to close when he was struck down with pneumonia. The same year Jolson's marriage to Keeler ended acrimoniously.

On 7 December 1941, within hours of learning of the Japanese attack on Pearl Harbor, Jolson volunteered to travel overseas to entertain troops. Appearing before audiences of young men, to whom he was at best only a name, Jolson found and captured a new audience. All the old magic worked and during the next few years he toured endlessly, putting on shows to audiences of thousands or singing songs to a couple of GIs on street corners. With Harry Akst as his accompanist, he visited Europe and the UK, Africa and the Near and Far East theatres of war. Eventually, tired and sick, he returned to the USA where doctors advised him not to resume his overseas travels. Jolson agreed but instead began a punishing round of hospital visits on the mainland. Taken ill again, he was operated on and a part of one lung was removed. The hospital visits had a happier ending when he met Erle Galbraith, a civilian X-ray technician on one of the army bases he visited, who became his fourth wife. The war over, Jolson made a cameo appearance in a film and also performed on a couple of records, but it appeared as though his career, temporarily buoyed by the war, was ended. However, a man named Sidney Skolsky had long wanted to make a film about Jolson's life and, although turned down flat by all the major studios, eventually was given the go-ahead by Harry Cohn, boss of the ailing independent Columbia Pictures, who happened to be a Jolson fan. After surmounting many difficulties, not least that Jolson, despite being over 60 years old, wanted to play himself on the screen, the film was made. Starring Larry Parks as Jolson and with a superb soundtrack on which Jolson sang all his old favourites in exciting new arrangements by Morris Stoloff, *The Jolson Story* (1946) was a hit. Apart from making a great deal of money for Columbia, who thus became the second film company Jolson had saved, it put the singer back in the public eye with a bang. He signed a deal with Decca for a series of records using the same Stoloff arrangements and orchestral accompaniment. All the old songs became hugely popular as did 'The Anniversary Song' which was written especially for a scene in the film in which his father and mother dance on their wedding anniversary (Hollywood having conveniently overlooked the fact that his real mother had died when he was a boy). The film and the records, particularly 'The Anniversary Song', were especially popular in the UK.

In the USA Jolson's star continued to rise and after a string of performances on radio, where he became a regular guest on Bing Crosby's show, he was given his own series, which ran for four years and helped encourage Columbia to create another Jolson precedent. This was to make a sequel to a bio-pic. *Jolson Sings Again* (1949) recaptured the spirit and energy of the first film and was another huge success. In 1950 Jolson was again talking to television executives and this time it appeared that something would come from the discussions. Before anything could be settled, however, the US Army became involved in the so-called 'police action' in Korea and Jolson immediately volunteered to entertain the troops. With Harry Akst again accompanying him, he visited front-line soldiers during a punishing tour. Exhausted, he returned to the USA where he was booked to appear on Crosby's radio show which was scheduled to be aired from San Francisco. On 23 October 1950, while playing cards with Akst and other long-time friends at the St. Francis hotel, he complained of chest pains and died shortly afterwards. Throughout the 20s and into the mid-30s, Jolson was the USA's outstanding entertainer and in 1925 his already hyperbolic billing was changed to 'The World's Greatest Entertainer'. Unfortunately, latterday audiences have only his films and records to go on. None of the films can be regarded as offering substantial evidence of his greatness. His best records are those made with Stoloff for the soundtrack of the biographical films, by which time his voice was deeper and, anyway, recordings cannot recapture the stage presence which allowed him to hold audiences in their seats for hours on end. Although it is easy to be carried away by the enthusiasm of others, it would appear to be entirely justified in Jolson's case. Unlike many other instances of fan worship clouding reality, even Jolson's rivals acknowledged that he was the best. In addition, most of those who knew him disliked him as a man, but this never diminished their adulation of him as an entertainer. On the night he died they turned out the lights on Broadway, and traffic in Times Square was halted. It is hard to think of any subsequent superstar who would be granted, or who has earned, such testimonials. There has been only a small handful of entertainers, in any medium, of which it can be truly said, we shall never see their like again. Al Jolson was one of that number.

Selected albums: *The Best Of Jolson* (1963), *Say It With Songs* (1965), *Immortal Al Jolson* (1975), *Jolson Sings Again* (1974), *You Ain't Heard Nothin' Yet* (1975), *20 Golden Greats* (1981), *20 More Golden Greats* (1981), *The Man And The Legend Vols 1 & 2* (1982), *The Man And The Legend Vol 3* (1983), *Al Jolson Collection Vols. 1 & 2* (1983), *The World's Greatest Entertainer* (1983), *Al Jolson Collection* (1985). Further reading: *Jolie: The Story Of Al Jolson*, Michael Freedland.

Joseph And The Amazing Technicolor Dreamcoat

Andrew Lloyd Webber's eventual domination of musical theatre throughout the world started with this show. It was intitially a 20-minute 'pop cantata' based on the biblical character of Joseph, which he wrote with Tim Rice for an end-of-term concert at Colet Court Boys' School in the City of London. That was in March 1968, and, during the next five years, it was gradually revised and expanded during performances in the UK at a variety of venues including the Central Hall Westminster, St. Paul's Cathedral, the Edinburgh Festival, the Haymarket Ice Rink, the Roundhouse, and the Young Vic. On 17 September 1973, a production opened at London's Albery Theatre, with Gary Bond as Joseph, and ran for 243 performances. Throughout the 70s, the show was often presented in and around London, generally with pop stars such as Paul Jones and Jess Conrad in the lead, and in 1976 it had its New York premiere at the Brooklyn Academy of Music. Five years later, in November 1981, *Joseph* opened on Broadway, and ran for 824 performances. However, it was not until Lloyd Webber decided to present it at the London Palludium in June 1991, that the piece was finally developed into its present two-hour, two-act form. A significant factor which contributed to its sensational reception in the 2,271-seater house, was the inspired casting of the teeny-boppers' idol Jason Donovan, ex-star of the popular Australian television soap, *Neighbours*. When Donovan went on holiday, Lloyd Webber did it again, and replaced him with Phillip Schofield, another highly popular television personality. He and Donovan proceeded to alternate during much of the run. While he was associated with the show, Donovan sued a fringe magazine, *The Face*, for allegedly inferring that he was homosexual. The High Court heard that the hit song from *Joseph*, 'Any Dream Will Do', which Donovan took the the top of the UK chart, was adapted by gays to become 'Any Queen Will Do'. The whole affair has travelled a long way from its inception in 1968. According to one critic, the simple story of Joseph, son of Jacob, and his brothers, which is narrated in this production by Linzi Hately, is 'a lurid, synthetic Joseph, accompanied by spoofs of sentimental American ballads, calypso, and Presley rock', with 'Joseph's prison cell filled with bopping lovelies', and 'an Elvis lookalike in Tutankhamun gear emerging from a vast sphinx, to sing at inordinate length', while 'Donovan, a macho Goldilocks, makes a climactic entrance in primeval batmobile with lion-heads and wings'. Nevertheless, the score which contained Lloyd Webber's tongue-in-cheek pastiches and some of Rice's deceptively ingenuous lyrics retained its appeal, with songs such as 'One More

Phillip Schofield and Jason Donovan (*Joseph And The Amazing Technicolor Dreamcoat*)

Angel To Heaven', 'Joseph's Coat', 'Go, Go, Go, Joseph', and 'Pharaoh's Story'. When it closed in January 1994, *Joseph* had become the longest-running show ever at the London Palladium. In the early 90s, Joseph fever spread quickly. Donny Osmond - who once, just like Joseph, was part of a brother act - played the lead in Canada, and a Broadway revival opened in November 1993.

Jubilee

The story goes that the celebrated composer Cole Porter took librettist Moss Hart and director Monty Woolley on a round-the-world cruise to think up ideas for this show. The jaunt lasted for about five months, but the resulting show was unable to stay around for that long. Perhaps the ship docked for a while in England, because the inspiration for the plot is said to have been the Silver Jubilee of Britain's King George V and Queen Mary. The result of the trio's deliberations commenced at the Imperial Theatre in New York on 12 October 1935, and posed the question as to what might happen to an imaginary (Anglicised) royal family, also about to celebrate their jubilee, who have been advised to take off their tiaras for a while, and go incognito to avoid the embarrassment of a left-wing coup. The King (Melville Cooper) and the Queen (Mary Boland), along with their children, welcome this break from conformity, and revel in their new-found freedom which gives the King an opportunity to perfect his rope tricks. In the course of their travels they meet up with several characters bearing a remarkable resemblance to celebrities of the day: there's Charles Rausmiller ('Johnny Weissmuller') played by Mark Plant, and Eric Dare ('Noël Coward') as portrayed by Derek Williams (the Queen has a crush on both of those); and Eve Standing ('Elsa Maxwell'), who was played to a 'T' by Mary Boley. Another famous real-life name in the cast was Montgomery Clift the future cult film actor. Aged only 15, he played the good Prince Peter, and on the first night of the show, out of town in Boston, he received a kidnap threat. It turned out to be from a woman whose son had failed the audition for his part. One more cast member of the Moss Hart's mythical royal family, over 50 years before she became a reality in England, was the prophetically named Princess Diana. However, Mary Boland was the box-office draw, and when she left after four months to resume her film career, her replacement, Laura Hope Crews, was unable to create sufficient impact to prevent the show closing after 169 performances. So, only a limited number of privileged theatre-goers were able to listen to that outstanding Cole Porter score which included 'Mr. And Mrs. Smith', 'Me And Marie', 'When Love Comes Your Way', 'A Picture Of Me Without You', 'The Kling-Kling Bird On The Divi-Divi Tree', and three of the composer's all-time standards, 'Why Shouldn't I?', 'Just One Of Those Things', and 'Begin The Beguine', which became such a big hit for Artie Shaw in 1938.

Jumbo

Beset by all kinds of troubles, and undecided for a time whether it was a musical or a circus (it was finally classed as the latter), Jumbo eventually lumbered into the newly renovated Hippodrome in New York, several weeks late, on 16 November 1935. The book, by Ben Hecht and Charles McArthur, told the story of the feuding male figureheads of two circus families who are brought to their senses by the love between the son of one, and the daughter of the other. The show was an extravagant spectacle, and an enormous undertaking, costing upwards of $300,000, with equestrian, acrobatic, and aerial dances, a cast of nearly a hundred, and almost as many animals. Gloria Grafton and Donald Novis played the young lovers, and they shared the three classic songs that emerged from Richard Rodgers and Lorenz Hart's lovely score, 'Little Girl Blue', 'My Romance' ('Wide awake, I can make my most fantastic dreams come true/My romance, doesn't need a thing but you'), and 'The Most Beautiful Girl In The World'. The other numbers included 'Over And Over Again' and 'The Circus Is On Parade', both of which were sung by Bob Lawrence and Henderson's Singing Razorbacks. The star of the show was one of the world's greatest clowns - in the widest sense - Jimmy Durante, who played the role of press agent Claudius B. Bowers and introduced the lively and amusing 'Laugh' and 'Women'. Paul Whiteman And His Orchestra were another big attraction in a magnificent spectacle that ran for just over seven months, 233 performances, but inevitably lost money for its flamboyant producer, Billy Rose. The 1962 film version, which is generally known as *Billy Roses's Jumbo*, had a modified storyline, and starred Durante, Doris Day, Stephen Boyd, and Martha Raye.

K

Kahn, Gus

b. 6 November 1886, Koblenz, Germany, d. 8 October 1941. Kahn was a prolific lyricist during the

20s and 30s, for Tin Pan Alley, stage and films. He was not particularly well-known by the public, but was highly regarded in the music business for his vivacious, colloquial lyrics. He was once voted by a 'trade' poll as the second most popular US songwriter after Irving Berlin. In 1891, he was brought by his immigrant parents to Chicago where the family settled. He started writing songs while at high school, but it was not until after he collaborated with his future wife, composer Grace LeBoy, that he had some success with 'I Wish I Had A Girl', in 1908. His first big hit came in 1915 with 'Memories', written with composer Egbert van Alstyne. In the following year, Kahn collaborated with him again, and Tony Jackson, for 'Pretty Baby', which became one of Kahn's biggest hits, and was featured in the bio-pics (Al) *Jolson Sings Again* (1949) and *The Eddie Cantor Story* (1953); two artists who benefited substantially from Kahn's output. 'Pretty Baby' was just one of a series of Kahn 'baby' songs which evoke the 'jazz age' of the 20s. These included 'Yes Sir, That's My Baby', 'There Ain't No Maybe In My Baby's Eyes', 'My Baby Just Cares for Me', 'I Wonder Where My Baby Is Tonight' and 'Sing Me A Baby Song', all written with composer Walter Donaldson, Khan's major collaborator. Donaldson, with his playboy image, was the antithesis of Kahn with his sober, family background. Other songs by the team included 'That Certain Party', 'Carolina In The Morning', 'My Buddy' and 'Beside A Babbling Brook'. Some of their best work was contained in the 1928 Broadway show *Whoopee*. Starring Ruth Etting and Eddie Cantor, it introduced 'I'm Bringing A Red Red Rose', 'Love Me Or Leave Me', 'My Baby Just Cares for Me' and 'Makin' Whoopee', the lyric of which is considered to be one of Kahn's best. The show later became an early sound movie in 1930.

In 1929, Kahn contributed to another Broadway musical, *Show Girl*. This time his collaborators were George and Ira Gershwin. The trio produced 'Liza', for the show's star, Ruby Keeler. It is said that, during at least one performance, Keeler's husband, Al Jolson, stood up in the audience and sang the song *to her*. In 1933, Kahn went to Hollywood to work on various movies ranging from the Marx Brothers' *A Day At The Races* ('All God's Chillun Got Rhythm'), to *Spring Parade*, starring Deanna Durbin, singing 'Waltzing In The Clouds'. In 1933, his first Hollywood project, with composer Vincent Youmans, was *Flying Down To Rio*, which featured the title song, and 'The Carioca'. It was also the first film to bring together Fred Astaire and Ginger Rogers. Unfortunately it was Youmans' last original film score before he died in 1946. For the next eight years Kahn's output for films was prolific. They included *Bottoms Up* ('Waiting At The Gate For Katy'), *Caravan* ('Ha-Cha-Cha' and 'Wine Song'),

Hollywood Party ('I've Had My Moments'), *Kid Millions* ('Okay Toots', 'When My Ship Comes In' and 'Your Head On My Shoulder'), *One Night Of Love*, *The Girl Friend*, *Love Me Forever*, *Thanks A Million* (with Dick Powell singing the title song), *San Francisco* (the title song sung by Jeanette MacDonald), *Rose Marie* ('Just For You' and 'Pardon Me, Madame'), *Three Smart Girls* (Deanna Durbin singing 'Someone To Care For Me'), *Everybody Sing* ('The One I Love'), *Girl Of The Golden West* ('Shadows On the Moon' and 'Who Are We To Say'), *Lillian Russell* (a bio-pic of the famous 1890s entertainer) and *Ziegfeld Girl* ('You Stepped Out Of A Dream', written with composer Nacio Herb Brown, and sung by Tony Martin). Kahn's last song, in 1941, realised a life-long ambition to write with Jerome Kern; their song was called 'Day Dreaming'.

Throughout his career Kahn had many different collaborators, including bandleader Isham Jones ('I'll See You In My Dreams', 'The One I Love Belongs To Somebody Else', 'Swingin' Down The Lane', and 'It Had To Be You'), Richard Whiting ('Ukulele Lady'), Whiting and Ray Egan ('Ain't We Got Fun'), Whiting and Harry Akst ('Guilty'), Ted Fio Rito ('I Never Knew', 'Charley My Boy' and 'Sometime'), Ernie Erdman, Elmer Schoebel and Billy Meyers ('Nobody's Sweetheart Now'), Erdman and Dan Russo ('Toot Toot Tootsie, Goodbye'), Wilbur Schwandt and Fabian Andre ('Dream A Little Dream Of Me' - a later hit for 'Mama' Cass Elliott), Charlie Rossoff ('When You And I Were Seventeen'), Carmen Lombardo and John Green ('Coquette'), Neil Moret ('Chloe'), Wayne King ('Goofus'), Matty Malneck and Fud Livingston ('I'm Through With Love'), Malneck and Frank Signorelli ('I'll Never Be The Same') and Victor Schertzinger ('One Night Of Love'). In the 1951 movie, *I'll See You In My Dreams*, based on his life, Kahn was portrayed by Danny Thomas, and his wife, Grace LeBoy by Doris Day. Gus Kahn had died 10 years earlier in October 1941, in Beverley Hills, California, USA.

Kalmar, Bert

b. 10 February 1884, New York City, New York, USA, d. 18 September 1947. Ill-educated and a runaway before he was in his teens, Kalmar's life was completely immersed in showbusiness. In the years before World War I he wrote lyrics for a number of songs with various composers, among them Harry Ruby. For the next few years each wrote with other collaborators, but by the beginning of the 20s they recognized the special qualities of their work together. Throughout the 20s they wrote for Broadway musicals such as *Ladies First*, *Broadway Brevities Of 1920*, *Ziegfeld Follies Of 1920*, *Midnight Rounders Of 1921*, *Greenwich Village Follies Of 1922*, *Helen Of Troy-New York*, *Puzzles Of 1925*, *The*

Ramblers, *Five O'Clock Girl*, *Lucky*, *Good Boy*, and *Animal Crackers*. The latter score was written for the Marx Brothers, and contained songs such as 'Who's Been Listening To My Heart?', 'Watching The Clouds Roll By', and 'Hooray For Captain Spaulding'. Other songs from those shows included 'Oh! What A Pal Was Mary', 'So Long, Oo-long', 'Who's Sorry Now?', 'Thinking Of You', 'The Same Old Moon', 'Dancing The Devil Away', 'Some Sweet Someone', and 'I Wanna Be Loved By You'. By the 30s Kalmar and Ruby were writing songs for films and one of their first, and the song by which they are best remembered, was 'Three Little Words'. It became the title of the songwriters' 1950 film biography when they were played by Fred Astaire and Red Skelton. Other songs from their Hollywood period were 'Just A Perfect Combination' and 'I Love You So Much'. Most of their songs were written for either stage or screen but among their great successes were 'Nevertheless' and 'A Kiss To Build A Dream On' - written for neither medium. (This last song did not become popular until the 50s after some rewriting by Oscar Hammerstein II.)

Kander, John

b. 18 March 1927, Kansas City, Missouri, USA. An important composer for the American musical theatre from the early 60s, Kander studied music as a child, continued at college and was determined to make his way in the musical theatre. He had some successes in the early 50s with various lyricists before meeting Fred Ebb in 1962. Ebb (b. 8 April 1932, New York, USA) had already dabbled with lyric writing, and had collaborated with Jerry Herman on some songs for the short-lived musical *From A To Z* (1960). Among Kander and Ebb's first efforts were 'My Coloring Book' and 'I Don't Care Much', both of which were recorded by Barbra Streisand. The new team made their Broadway debut in 1965 with the score for *Flora, The Red Menace*, which included an eye-catching, Tony Award-winning performance, by Liza Minnelli, who would subsequently perform much of their work, and become indelibly associated with them. Although *Flora* was unsuccessful, Kander and Ebb were invited to write the score for *Cabaret* (1966), which starred Joel Grey and Jill Haworth, and won seven Tony Awards including best score. They wrote two additional songs, 'Money, Money' and 'Mein Herr', for the 1972 film version in which Liza Minnelli gave a sensational performance and won an Oscar. The television special produced by Ebb for Minnelli, *Liza With A Z*, also won an Emmy award, with a Grammy later going to the recorded highlights album. Ebb's television work continued with the production of *Ol' Blue Eyes Is Back* (1972) for Frank Sinatra. Other Broadway shows followed, including *The Happy Time*, *Zorba*, *70, Girls, 70*, and *Chicago*, which opened in 1975 and ran for 923 performances.

John Kander and Fred Ebb with Liza Minnelli

In the same year, the duo wrote some songs for the film *Funny Lady*, which starred Barbra Streisand, and followed this with music for two Minnelli films, *A Matter Of Time* (1976) and *New York, New York* (1977). The theme from the latter became an enormous, enduring hit for Frank Sinatra in 1980. Back on Broadway, Kander and Ebb wrote scores for *The Act* (1977) with Minnelli, *Woman Of The Year* (1981), which starred Lauren Bacall, and *The Rink* (1984), yet another Minnelli vehicle. In 1991 they were inducted into the New York Theatre Hall of Fame, and a revue, *And The World Goes 'Round*, which utilised some 30 of their songs, opened Off Broadway and ran for nearly a year. In 1993 their spectacular musical *Kiss Of The Spider Woman*, starring Chita Rivera, won several Tony Awards in New York following its transfer from the West End. Apart from their work together, both Kander and Ebb have had successful independent careers. Kander has written music for film soundtracks, including *Kramer Vs. Kramer* (1980); Ebb has continued to produce and co-produce numerous television specials, including *Gypsy In My Soul* (1976) and *Baryshnikov On Broadway* (1980).

Kane, Helen

b. Helen Schroder, 4 August 1904, New York, USA, d. 26 September 1966. Kane is remembered these days as the singer portrayed by Debbie Reynolds in *Three Little Words*, the 1950 film biography of songwriters Bert Kalmar and Harry Ruby. Kane, (who dubbed the Reynolds vocal), was the baby-voiced singer who rose to fame on Broadway in the late 20s. She began her career in vaudeville and night clubs but was much-acclaimed for an appearance with Paul Ash And His Orchestra at New York's Paramount Theatre. She was then featured in such Broadway shows as *A Night In Spain* (1927) and *Good Boy* (1928) in which she sang 'I Wanna Be Loved By You', the 'Boop-Boop-A-Doop' hit that was re-created by Reynolds. After her Broadway success she moved to Hollywood in the late 20s, appearing in several films, including *Nothing But The Truth* (1929), featuring one of her biggest hits, 'Do Something', plus *Sweetie* (1929), *Pointed Heels* (1930), *Dangerous Nan McGrew* (1930), *Heads Up* (1930), and the all-star spectacular, *Paramount On Parade* (1930). Meanwhile, she continued to make hit records such as 'That's My Weakness Now', 'Get Out And Get Under The Moon', 'Me And The Man In The Moon' and 'Button Up Your Overcoat'. Often acknowledged to have been a major influence in the creation of Grim Natwick's cartoon character Betty Boop, Kane continued her career throughout the 30s playing mainly nightclubs. Kane was, for the most part, largely forgotten until the arrival of *Three Little Words*, at which point she became a minor celebrity amid a new generation. She died in September 1966.

Kaufman, George S.

b. 14 November 1889, Pittsburg, Pennsylvania, USA, d. 2 June 1961, New York, USA. For a man who was supposed to hate music with considerable fervour, George S. Kaufman made significant contributions as a librettist and director to a variety of productions in the American musical theatre from the 20s through to the 50s. Early in his career he worked as a newpaper columnist for several years in Washington and later in New York where he became one of the brightest young talents in the early 30s, many of whom, including Kaufman, Ring Lardner, Dorothy Parker, Alexander Woollcott, and Robert Benchley, were members of the Algonquin Hotel's Round Table set. After co-writing the book with Marc Connelly in 1923 for *Helen Of Troy, New York*, which had a score by Bert Kalmar and Harry Ruby, Kaufman contributed sketches or was the librettist or co-librettist on a number of other Broadway musical productions including *The Music Box Revue* (Third Edition), *Be Yourself!*, *The Cocoanuts*, *Animal Crackers*, *The Little Show*, *Strike Up The Band*, *Nine-Fifteen Revue*, and *The Band Wagon* (1931). By now an established figure, he also directed most of the subsequent productions on which he worked. In the 30s and 40s these included *Of Thee I Sing*, for which he won a Pulitzer Award, *Face The Music* (director only), *Let 'Em Eat Cake*, *I'd Rather Be Right*, *Sing Out The News*, *Seven Lively Arts*, *Hollywood Pinafore*, and *Park Avenue* (1946). In 1950 Kaufman earned a Tony Award for his direction of the brilliant *Guys And Dolls*, and, five years later, collaborated with his second wife, the actress Leueen MacGrath, on the book for the Cole Porter musical *Silk Stockings*. His work in the musical theatre was just a part of his wider output. He is credited with 45 plays written in conjunction with some 16 known collaborators who included Edna Furber, Ring Lardner, and his principal later collaborator Moss Hart. With Hart he wrote some of the American theatre's most enduring comedies - *Once In A Lifetime*, *You Can't Take It With You* (for which he won his second Pulitzer Prize), and *The Man Who Came To Dinner*.
Further reading: *George S. Kaufman: An Intimate Portrait*, Howard Teichmann. *George S. Kaufman And His Friends*, Scott Meredith.

Kaye, Danny

b. David Daniel Kominsky, 18 January 1913, Brooklyn, New York, USA, d. 3 March 1987, Los Angeles, California, USA. Kaye was an extraordinary entertainer and an apparently inexhaustible comedian, mimic and dancer who seemed to be able to twist his face and body into any shape he wanted. As a singer, he specialized in very fast double talk and tongue-twisters, but could present a gentle ballad equally well. He was also an indefatigable ambassador for numerous charities, especially the United Nations International Children's Emergency Fund (now UNICEF), for which he travelled and worked for many years. A son of Jewish immigrant parents from Russia, Kominsky originally wanted to join the medical profession, but dropped out of high school when he was 14 years old, and hitch-hiked to Florida with his friend, Louis Eilson, where they sang for money. On their return to New York, they formed an act called Red And Blackie, and performed at private functions. During the day, Kominski worked as a soda-jerk, and then as an automobile appraiser with an insurance company. The latter job was terminated after he made a mistake which is said to have cost the company some $40,000. Kominski and Eilson then obtained summer work as 'toomlers', creators of tumult or all-round entertainers, in the Borscht Circuit summer hotels and camps in the Catskill Mountains. After five years, Kominski was earning $1,000 per season.

In 1933, he joined David Harvey and Kathleen Young on the vaudeville circuit in their dancing act, the Three Terpsichoreans, and was billed for the first time as Danny Kaye. An early on-stage accident in which he split his trousers, elicited much laughter from the audience and was incorporated into the act. Signed by producer A.B. Marcus, the group toured the USA for five months in the revue, *La Vie Paree*, before sailing for the Orient in February 1934. It is often said that during this period of playing to non-English speaking audiences in Japan, China and Malaya, was when Kaye developed his face-making and pantomiming techniques, and his 'gibberish' singing with the occasional recognized word. Back in the USA in 1936, Kaye worked with comedian Nick Long Jnr. and toured with Abe Lyman's Band, before being booked by impresario Henry Sherek, to appear in cabaret at London's Dorchester Hotel. The engagement, in 1938, was not a success. Kaye commented: 'I was too loud for the joint'. (Ten years later in London, it would be an entirely different story.) While appearing in Max Liebman's *Sunday Night Varieties* in New York, Kaye met pianist-songwriter Sylvia Fine, who had been raised in the same Brooklyn neighbourhood, and majored in music at Brooklyn College. She became a powerful influence throughout his career, as his director, coach and critic. Working with Liebman's Saturday night revues at Camp Taimiment in the Pennsylvania Hills, during the summer of 1939, they started their collaboration, with Fine accompanying Kaye on the piano, and writing special material which included three of his most famous numbers, 'Stanislavsky', 'Pavlova' and the story of the unstable château designer, 'Anatole Of Paris'. The best of the material

was assembled in *The Straw Hat Revue* in which Kaye appeared with Imogene Coca, and opened on Broadway in September 1939. The show also featured a young dancer named Jerome Robbins. After Fine and Kaye were married in January 1940, Kaye appeared in a smash hit engagement at La Martinique nightclub in New York, which led to a part in *Lady In The Dark*, starring Gertrude Lawrence. On the first night, Kaye stopped the show with the Kurt Weill and Ira Gershwin tongue-twister 'Tchaikovsky', in which he reeled off the names of 50 real, or imagined, Russian composers in 38 seconds. After playing a return engagement at La Martinique, and a five-week stint at the Paramount Theatre, Kaye appeared again on Broadway, starring in the Cole Porter musical, *Let's Face It*, which opened in October 1941. Porter allowed Sylvia Fine and Max Liebman to interpolate some special material for Kaye, which included a 'jabberwocky of song, dance, illustration and double-talk' called 'Melody In 4F'. Kaye had to leave the show early in 1942, suffering from nervous exhaustion, but having recovered, he toured on behalf of the war effort and is said to have sold a million dollars worth of government bonds in six months. Rejected by the US Army because of a back ailment, he entertained troops with his two-hour shows in many theatres of operations including the South Pacific.

In 1944, Kaye made his feature film debut in *Up In Arms*, the first of a series of five pictures for Sam Goldwyn at MGM. His performance as a hypochondriac elevator boy, involving yet another memorable Fine-Liebman piece, 'Manic Depressive Pictures Presents: Lobby Number', moved one critic to hail his introduction as 'the most exciting since Garbo's'. Goldwyn was criticized, however for having Kaye's red hair dyed blonde. His remaining films for the studio included *Wonder Man*, in which he gave his impression of a sneezing Russian baritone with 'Orchi Tchornya'. This was the first of several films in which he played more than one character; *The Kid From Brooklyn* (1946), which featured 'Pavlova', *The Secret Life Of Walter Mitty* (1947), one of his best-remembered roles (six of them), and *A Song Is Born* (1948), one of his least remembered. In 1945, Kaye appeared for a year on his own CBS radio show with Harry James and Eve Arden, and during the following year the Kayes' daughter, Dena was born. When Kaye recorded the old standard, 'Dinah', he changed some of the 'i' sounds to 'e', so that the song ran: 'Denah, is there anyone fener? In the State of Carolena . . .' etc. His other hit songs included 'Tubby The Tuba', 'Minnie The Moocher', 'Ballin' The Jack', 'Bloop Bleep', 'Civilization' and 'The Woody Woodpecker Song', both with the Andrews Sisters; 'C'est Si Bon'; and 'Blackstrap Molasses', recorded with Jimmy Durante, Jane Wyman and

Danny Kaye

Groucho Marx. In 1948, Kaye returned to England, to appear at the London Palladium. His enormously successful record-breaking performances began an affectionate and enduring relationship with the British public. He is said to have received over 100,000 letters in a week. His shows were attended by the Royal Family; he met both Winston Churchill and George Bernard Shaw, and was cast in wax for London's Madame Tussauds Museum. He returned in 1949 for the first of several Royal Command Performances, and also toured provincial music halls throughout 1952. He endeared himself to the British by singing some of their parochial songs such as the novelty 'I've Got A Lovely Bunch Of Coconuts' and 'Maybe It's Because I'm A Londoner'. During one performance at the Palladium, when a member of the audience enquired after the state of Kaye's ribs, following a car accident, he ordered the lights to be lowered while he displayed the actual X-ray plates! Kaye went to Canada in 1950 and became the first solo performer to star at the Canadian National Exhibition, where he sold out the 24,000-seater stadium for each of his 14 performances.

He returned to his multiple roles in films such as *The Inspector General* (1949) and *On The Riviera* (1951), before embarking on the somewhat controversial,

Hans Christian Andersen (1952). After 16 different screenplays over a period of 15 years, and protests in the Danish press about the choice of Kaye to play their national hero, the film, with a final screenplay by Moss Hart, was the third biggest money-spinner in MGM's history. Frank Loesser's score produced several appealing songs, including 'No Two People', 'Anywhere I Wander', 'Inchworm', 'Thumbelina', 'The Ugly Duckling' and 'Wonderful Copenhagen', the latter reaching the UK Top 5. Kaye's other films during the 50s and early 60s included *Knock On Wood* (1954), said to be his favourite, in which he sang two more Fine numbers, the title song, and 'All About Me', *White Christmas* (1954), co-starring with Bing Crosby, Rosemary Clooney and Vera Ellen, *The Court Jester* (1956), *Me And The Colonel* (1958), *Merry Andrew* (1958), *The Five Pennies* (1959), a bio-pic of 20s cornet player Red Nichols (including a rousing version of 'When The Saints Go Marching In', with Louis Armstrong), *On The Double* (1961) and *The Man From The Diners' Club* (1963). After a break, he came back for *The Madwoman Of Challiot* (1969), and the following year, returned to Broadway in the role of Noah, in the Richard Rodgers and Martin Charnin musical, *Two By Two*. Shortly after the show opened, Kaye tore a ligament in his leg during a performance, and subsequently appeared on crutches or in a wheel chair, in which he tried to run down the other actors, adapting the show to his injury, much to the distaste of producer and composer, Richard Rodgers.

During the 70s and 80s, Kaye conducted classical orchestras and appeared on several television shows including *Peter Pan*, *Pinocchio* and *Danny Kaye's Look At The Metropolitan Opera*. He also played dramatic roles on television in *Skokie* and *The Twilight Zone*, but concentrated mainly on his charity work. He had started his association with UNICEF in the early 50s, and in 1955 made a 20-minute documentary, *Assignment Children*. He eventually became the organization's ambassador-at-large for 34 years, travelling worldwide on their behalf, and entering the *Guinness Book Of Records* by visiting 65 US and Canadian cities in five days, piloting himself in his own jet plane. During his career he received many awards including the French Legion d'Honneur, the Jean Hersholt Humanitarian Award, the Knight's Cross of the First Class of the Order of Danneborg, given by the Danish Government. Other awards included a special Academy Award in 1954, along with Tonys for his stage performances, plus Emmys for his successful 60s television series. He died in March 1987, following a heart attack.

Albums: *Hans Christian Andersen* (1953, film soundtrack), *Mommy, Gimme A Drink Of Water* (1958), with Louis Armstrong *The Five Pennies* (1959, film soundtrack), *For Children* (1974), with Ivor Moreton *Happy Fingers* (1977). Compilations: *The Best Of Danny Kaye* (1982), *The Very Best Of Danny Kaye - 20 Golden Greats* (1987).

Further reading: *The Danny Kaye Saga*, Kurt Singer.

Kaye, Stubby

b. 18 November 1918, New York City, New York, USA. An actor and singer who carved himself an instant slice of musical history by stopping the show as Nicely-Nicely Johnson in the original Broadway production of *Guys And Dolls* - and then doing it all over again three years later in London. Kaye got his first break when he came first on the Major Bowes Amateur Hour on US radio in 1939. During the late 30s and early 40s he toured as a comedian in vaudeville, and made his London debut in USO shows during World War II. His role in *Guys And Dolls* (1950) was not a leading one, but he was outstanding in numbers such as 'Fugue For Tinhorns', 'The Oldest Established', 'Guys And Dolls', and the rousing 'Sit Down You're Rockin' The Boat'. He had one more big success on Broadway in 1956 as Marryin' Sam in *Li'l Abner*, and subsequently toured in revivals, played nightclubs as a comedian, and appeared on the television series *Love And Marriage*

Stubby Kaye with the Goldwyn Girls

Howard Keel

and *My Sister Eileen*. Unlike many stage performers he moved easily into films, and appeared in a variety features including *Guys And Dolls*, *Li'l Abner*, *40 Pounds Of Trouble*, *Cat Ballou* (with Nat King Cole), *Sweet Charity*, *The Cockeyed Cowboys Of Calico County*, *The Dirtiest Girl I Ever Met*, *Six Pack Annie*, and *Who Framed Roger Rabbit?*. The ample figure and sunny disposition he displayed as Nicely-Nicely in 1953 endeared him to London audiences and he made frequent appearances in the UK, including one in the musical *Man Of Magic* in 1956. Eventually he settled in Britain and married Angela Bracewell who came to fame in the 50s in her role as the hostess of the audience participation game 'Beat The Clock' in the top rated television variety show *Sunday Night At The London Palladium*. After appearing in the West End in 1983 in the short-lived musical *Dear Anyone*, Kaye returned to Broadway two years later and won the only good notices in the musical *Grind*, a real disaster which was described by one critic as 'art slaughter'. He continued to work in the UK and in 1986 starred as Ring Lardner in the radio play *Some Like Them Cold*.
Selected album: *Music For Chubby Lovers* (1962), and Original Cast and film sountrack recordings.

Keel, Howard

b. Harold C. Leek, 13 April 1917, Gillespie, Illinois, USA. After starting his career as a singing waiter in Los Angeles, Keel became an 'in-house entertainer' for the huge Douglas aircraft manufacturing company. In 1945, he appeared in *Carousel* on the west coast and then travelled to the UK to appear in the London production of *Oklahoma!*. At this time he was known as Harold Keel, having reversed the spelling of his last name. Now, he changed his first name and after making a non-singing appearance in the film, *The Small Voice* (1948), he returned to the USA where he landed the role of Frank Butler in the film *Annie Get Your Gun* (1950). He continued to make films, mostly musicals, including *Show Boat* (1951), *Kiss Me Kate* and *Calamity Jane* (both 1953), *Rose Marie* and *Seven Brides For Seven Brothers* (both 1954) and *Kismet* (1955). By the 60s he was touring the US in revivals of popular shows, and appearing in non-musical low-budget western movies. In 1981 his acting career received a boost when he started to appear in the long-running television soap, *Dallas*. This revived interest in his singing, particularly in the UK, and in 1984 he recorded his first solo album. Although untrained, Keel's rich and powerful baritone voice and commanding stage and screen presence made him a good leading actor for musical comedies. In 1993, with his tongue firmly in his cheek, he announced his Farewell Tour of the UK.
Selected albums: *And I Love You So* (1984), *Reminiscing* (1985), *The Collection* (1989), *The Great*

MGM Stars (1991), *Close To My Heart* (1991), and the soundtrack albums from the above musicals.

Kern, Jerome

b. 27 January 1885, New York City, New York, USA, d. 11 November 1945. Taught piano by his mother, Kern proved to be a gifted musician with a remarkable ear. While still at junior school he was dabbling with composition and by his mid-teens was simultaneously studying classical music and writing songs in the popular vein. He became a song plugger in New York's Tin Pan Alley and occasionally accompanied leading entertainers of the day. Some of his early songs were picked up by producers of Broadway shows and were also used in London, a city Kern visited first in 1902-3 and thereafter held in great affection. During the next few years Kern became a familiar figure at theatres in London and New York, working on scores and acting as a rehearsal pianist. Throughout this period, Kern was learning his craft as a songwriter and in the 1914 Broadway show, *The Girl From Utah*, originally staged in London, his ability flowered with the song 'They Didn't Believe Me'. A string of musical shows followed, most enjoying only modest success but Kern's talent was growing and theatrical impresarios were fully aware of his potential. In 1917, *Oh, Boy!* opened. The score was by Kern with lyrics by P.G. Wodehouse, with whom Kern had already collaborated. The hit of this show was 'Till The Clouds Roll By'. The following year he wrote 'Bill' for *Oh, Lady! Lady!!*, but the song was dropped in deference to the wishes of the leading lady. During the early 20s Kern was perhaps the most prolific composer on Broadway, with numerous shows to his credit. Among the songs and shows were 'Look For The Silver Lining' from *Sally* (1920) and 'Who?' from *Sunny* (1925). The highlight of Kern's 20s musicals was *Show Boat* (1927), with lyrics by Oscar Hammerstein II. Apart from the earlier song, 'Bill', which he had written with Wodehouse, and which was revived for the new show, the Kern-Hammerstein partnership produced a succession of show-stopping songs: 'Ol' Man River', 'Make Believe', 'Why Do I Love You?', 'Can't Help Lovin' Dat Man' and 'It Still Suits Me'. Subsequent shows for Broadway did not match the enormous success of *Show Boat*, but fine songs were invariably found in every score, among them 'Smoke Gets In Your Eyes' from *Roberta* (1933). When this became a film in 1935, two new songs were added, 'Lovely To Look At' and 'I Won't Dance'. Even one of Kern's most unsuccessful shows, *Very Warm For May* (1939) contained the classic 'All The Things You Are'. From the late 30s Kern had begun to spend more time working on films than on stage productions and by the early 40s this was where most of his energies were

Jerome Kern

spent. Among his film songs were 'The Way You Look Tonight' (lyrics by Dorothy Fields), which won the Oscar for Best Song in 1936, 'A Fine Romance' (again, with Fields), 'Dearly Beloved' (Johnny Mercer), 'Long Ago And Far Away' (Ira Gershwin - an especially beautiful if rarely performed song), 'In Love In Vain' (Leo Robin) and 'The Last Time I Saw Paris' (Hammerstein), the latter won Kern another Oscar in 1940. Having conquered Broadway and Hollywood, Kern now turned to writing music for the concert platform, writing a classical suite based upon his music for *Show Boat* and a suite entitled 'Mark Twain: A Portrait For Orchestra'. He was discussing the possibility of a new Broadway show, *Annie Get Your Gun*, when he collapsed and died in November 1945. An outstanding songwriter with an ability to find beautiful lilting melodies with deceptive ease, Kern's work has remained popular with singers and jazz musicians. Half a century after his last great songs were written, his music remains fresh and undated. There are several compilations of Kern's music, performed by various artists currently available.

Kidd, Michael

b. Milton Greenwald, 12 August 1919, New York City, New York, USA. An important choreographer and director who pioneered a joyful and energetic style of dancing. Kidd was a soloist with the Ballet Theatre (later called the American Ballet Theatre) before making his Broadway debut as choreographer with *Finian's Rainbow* in 1947. He won a Tony Award for his work on that show, and earned four more during the 50s for *Guys And Dolls* (1950), *Can-Can* (1953), *Li'l Abner* (1956), and *Destry Rides Again* (1959). His other shows around that time were *Hold It*, *Love Life*, and *Arms And The Girl*. From *Li'l Abner* onwards he also directed, and sometimes produced, most of the shows on which he worked, but it was as a choreographer of apparently limitless invention that he dominated the Broadway musical during the 50s. In the 60s and early 70s he worked on productions such as *Wildcat*, *Subways Are For Sleeping*, *Here's Love*, *Ben Franklin In Paris*, *Skyscraper*, *Breakfast At Tiffany's* (which closed during previews), *The Rothschilds* (1970), *Cyrano*, and a revival of *Good News* (1974). Kidd also filled the big screen with his brilliant and exuberant dance sequences in classic Hollywood musicals such as *The Band Wagon*, *Seven Brides For Seven Brothers*, *It's Always Fair Weather*, and *Hello, Dolly!*. He also co-starred with Gene Kelly and Dan Dailey in *It's Always Fair Weather*, and appeared in several other films including *Movie Movie*, an affectionate parody of a typical 30s double-feature which went largely unappreciated in 1979.

Yul Brynner (*The King And I*)

King

'The road to opening night, now shifted to April 18, has been the bloodiest of any musical in recent memory. Writers, directors, a producer, and even a leading actor, have either walked out or been fired after rows over racial politics and money.' That was the kind of advance publicity that this show received prior to its first performance which eventually took place at the Piccadilly Theatre in London on 23 April 1990. The £2.5 million production, which was directed by Clarke Peters, and based on the life of the controversial civil rights leader, Martin Luther King Jnr., had a book by Lonnie Elder III, music by Richard Blackford, and lyrics by Maya Angelou and Alistair Beaton. Just prior to the opening, Angelou left in a huff, and demanded that her name be removed from the credits, but that was refused, and although Elder is credited with the final libretto, the completed work was the product of many hands. Apparently, one of Angelou's objections was that 'it takes a black man to write about a black man and there hasn't been a single black man in the writing of this show.' That was also the reported attitude of King's widow, Coretta Scott King, who initially withheld her approval from the project. Most critics savagely dismissed the book and the production in general as 'an insignificant little offering' . . . 'of such banality it is in itself a crime against humanity' . . . 'evoking a pocket history of bloody protest marches, political intrigue, factionalism, melodramatic Jim Crowism, and character defamation, but with little dramatic flair and less depth'. American opera singers Simon Estes (King) and Cynthia Haymon (Coretta) were absolved from the blame - in the singing department, at least. The score, 'a mix of jazz, gospel, and showbiz pizzazz', consisted of some 24 numbers, along the lines of 'Cotton's My Momma', 'Bus Boycott', 'Welcome To Atlanta', 'Equal Rights', 'No More Sorrow', 'The Price Of Freedom'. 'They're After You're Vote', 'Sacrifice', 'For I Am An American', 'Safe In Your Arms', and one inspired by King's immortal words, 'I Have A Dream' ('so did I,' said one cynic, 'but I fought against temptation and stayed awake.'). More money was ploughed in, but to no avail. Not many shows could withstand that sort of battering, and King closed after six weeks, with losses estimated at between £2.6 million and £3.3 million.

King And I, The

With music by Richard Rodgers and book and lyrics by Oscar Hammerstein II, The King And I opened at the St. James Theatre in New York on 29 March 1951. It starred Yul Brynner as the King of Siam and Gertrude Lawrence as Anna Leonowens, a schoolteacher hired to educate the royal children. Set in the 1860s, the story of The King And I was based on Anna Leonowens's book, The English Governess At The Siamese Court (Margaret Landon's novel, Anna And The King Of Siam, was also based upon the same source material). The project was Lawrence's brainchild and once she had set the wheels in motion and Rodgers and Hammerstein were hired to write it, the show was scheduled to become one of the great money spinners of Broadway. There is a strong storyline which contrasts an Oriental nation's attempts to advance towards the progressive ideologies of the west while still shackled to the concepts of a slave-owning, male-dominated society. With settings of Oriental opulence, a masterly score and superb central performances, The King And I was a great hit. Among the songs were 'I Whistle A Happy Tune', 'Hello, Young Lovers', 'Getting To Know You', 'Shall We Dance', 'I Have Dreamed', 'We Kiss In The Shadow' and 'Something Wonderful', which was sung by Dorothy Sarnoff as Lady Thiang. Additionally, there was the engaging 'March Of The Siamese Children' in which Rodgers effectively captured an Oriental flavour while using orthodox western musical forms. Fittingly, given her involvement in its creation, The King And I was a triumph for Lawrence. It was also her swan song; she died 18 months after the show's opening. For the 1956 screen version, Brynner reprised his bravura performance as the King, winning the Oscar as Best Actor, and Deborah Kerr appeared as Anna, her singing being dubbed by Marni Nixon. The King And I opened in London in 1953, starring Herbert Lom and Valerie Hobson and enjoyed revivals in the late 70s and mid-80s, the latter starring Brynner. In 1992, Julie Andrews, who many consider would have been the perfect Anna, sang the role for a studio cast CD, with British actor Ben Kingsley as the King. Over the years, the show has proved to be a convenient vehicle for artists from different branches of show business. In 1989 a Baltimore production starred Alan Jay Lerner's widow, Liz Robertson and the ballet superstar Rudolph Nureyev, and a 1991 London revival teamed the film and television performers Susan Hampshire and David Yip.

King's Rhapsody

With the stage musical King's Rhapsody, Ivor Novello maintained the successful formula of the Ruritanian-based fantasy that had stood him in such good stead for the past decade. Opening at the Palace Theatre in London on 15 September 1949, the production was replete with gypsy dances, unrequited love and hugely sentimental music, lyrics and concept. Critics were almost unanimous in their disdain, having gratefully adjusted to the new style of musical coming into London from the USA. However, by this stage of his career, Novello had built up a massive following and audiences flocked to see the show. The songs included 'A Violin Began To Play', 'Fly Home Little Heart' and 'Take Your Girl'. The cast was virtually a roll-call of Novello's private repertory company which included Olive Gilbert, Zena Dare, Phylis Dare and Vanessa Lee. *King's Rhapsody* was still playing to packed houses when Novello died suddenly on 5 March 1951. The show closed later in the year following a run of 881 performances. A 1955 film version starred Errol Flynn and Anna Neagle, and Vanessa Lee recreated her original role when the show was presented on BBC Television in 1957.

Kismet

This was by no means the first time George Forrest and Robert Wright had raided the world of classical music in an effort to come up with a hit Broadway musical. They had 'borrowed' elements of Greig for their highly successful *Song Of Norway* (1944), and for *Kismet* they turned to the work of Alexander Borodin. Forrest and Wright adapted the music and wrote the lyrics, and the book was by Charles Lederer and Luther Davis. When *Kismet* opened at the Ziegfeld Theatre in New York on 3 December 1953, it was met with a measure of indifference from the critics. However, by a fortuitous quirk of fate, there was a newspaper strike at the time and before the reviews were printed, the show was already a success. Audiences liked this lavish production, and *Kismet*, with its Arabian Nights setting, ran for 583 performances. Several of the songs became popular, including 'Stranger In Paradise', 'Baubles, Bangles And Beads', and 'And This Is My Beloved', but there were other attractive numbers too, such as 'Not Since Nineveh', 'Gesticulate', 'The Olive Tree' and 'Night Of My Nights'. Original cast members included Alfred Drake, Richard Kiley and Doretta Morrow. The show won Tony Awards for best musical, actor (Drake), and musical conductor (Louis Adrian). Drake and Morrow recreated their roles for the 1955 London production which ran for 648 performances. In the same year, a film version was released starring Howard Keel, Ann Blyth, Dolores Gray and Vic Damone. A 1978 version of the show, retitled *Timbuktu*, featured an all-black cast.

Kiss Me, Kate

Even before its 30 December 1948 opening at the New Century Theatre in New York, the word was out that the stage musical *Kiss Me, Kate* would be a hit. Whatever purists might think, it is hard to imagine any songwriter better suited than Cole Porter to blend words, wit and music with the work of Shakespeare. Using the device of a show-within-a-show, Bella and Sam Spewack's book deftly shifts back and forth between Shakespeare's Padua and present-day Baltimore, as a touring theatrical troupe put on performances of the Bard's work while simultaneously engaging in back-stage rivalries and love affairs. As the warring Fred and Lilli, who are

'acting' Petruchio and Kate in *The Taming Of The Shrew*, the show starred Alfred Drake and Patricia Morison. Despite their first-rate performances, however, the real stars of *Kiss Me, Kate* were Porter's songs which included 'So In Love', 'Always True To You In My Fashion', 'Wunderbar', 'I Hate Men', 'Another Openin', Another Show', 'Brush Up Your Shakespeare', 'We Open In Venice', 'Why Can't You Behave?', 'Were Thine That Special Face', 'Where Is The Life That Late I Led?' and 'Too Darn Hot'. *Kiss Me, Kate* ran for over 1,007 performances, and won a Tony Award for best musical. Patricia Morison recreated her role, opposite Bill Johnson, in the London production which stayed at the Coliseum for 501 performances. West End revivals were presented in 1970, with Emile Belcourt and Ann Howard, and in 1987 with Paul Jones, Nichola McAuliffe, Tim Flavin and Fiona Hendley. The 1953 film version, which captured much of the sparkle of the original (especially after its non-3-D reissue), starred Howard Keel and Kathryn Grayson as Fred and Lilli, and benefited from the vibrant dancing of Ann Miller. The film also included 'From This Moment On', a song not used in the stage version. *Kiss Me, Kate* was produced in several European and Far-Eastern countries and was revived in New York in 1956 and 1965 at the City Centre.

Kiss Of The Spider Woman

'And the curtain will shake, and the fire will hiss, here comes her kiss' - read the cobwebbed publicity handouts prior to the show's debut at London's Shaftesbury Theatre on 20 October 1992. Extensively revised following its New York/Purchase workshop in 1990, this production of *Kiss Of The Spider Woman* had received its world premiere in June 1992 in Toronto, Canada. Considered by many to be an unlikely - even unsuitable choice for a musical - it was adapted by Terrence McNally from Manuel Puig's 1976 novel, which was also made into an acclaimed film in 1984. The story concerns two cellmates in a prison somewhere in Latin America, the gay window dresser, Molina (Brent Carver), and the single-minded Marxist revolutionary, Valentin (Anthony Crivello). The two men are gradually drawn together and eventually become lovers. For some of the time, Molina lives in a fantasy world in which his childhood idol, film star, Aurora (Chita Rivera), frequently comes to life in a series of gaudy routines from her tacky 40s B-movies. Rivera is also the black-clad Spider Woman, the temptress who lures men to their death. In this way, the grim reality of the torture and persecution of life in the jail (almost too realistically created) is contrasted effectively with the unreal world outside. John Kander and Fred Ebb's score switched from 'serious' numbers such as 'The Day After That' and 'You Could Never Shame Me', to the spectacular 'Gimme Love', and more conventional and good-humoured songs which included the lovely 'Dear One', along with 'Dressing Them Up', 'Russian Movie', 'Morphine Tango', 'Gimme Love', and 'Only In The Movies'. Critical reaction was mixed, although both Brent Carver and Chita Rivera, making her first appearance in London for 30 years, were both highly acclaimed. Harold Prince's 'triumphant' direction and Jerome Sirlin's 'staggering scenic design, with the steel bars of the cells fading into fanciful projections of tropical jungles and glittering palaces of pleasure' were also applauded. Although it was voted best musical in the Evening Standard Drama Awards, *Kiss Of The Spider Woman* had a disappointingly short West End stay of nine months. In May 1993, a Broadway production, with Chita Rivera and Brent Carver, began its run at the Broadhurst Theatre, and scooped the Tony Awards, winning for best musical, score (tied with the Who's *Tommy*), book, actress (Chita Rivera), actor (Brent Carver), and featured actor (Anthony Crivello). It also gained the New York Critics' prize for best musical.

Kitt, Eartha

b. 26 January 1928, Columbia, South Carolina, USA. Raised in New York's Harlem, Kitt attended the High School for Performing Arts before joining Katharine Dunham's famed dancing troupe. At the end of a European tour Kitt decided to stay behind, taking up residence in Paris. Having added singing to her repertoire she was a success and on her return to New York appeared at several leading nightclubs. She appeared on Broadway in *New Faces Of 1952* introducing 'Monotonous', and was later seen more widely in the film version of the show. Her other Broadway shows around this time included *Mrs. Patterson* (1954) and *Shinbone Alley* (1957). She continued to work in cabaret, theatre and television, singing in her uniquely accented manner and slinkily draping herself across any available object, animate or otherwise. She made a few more films over the years, including playing leading roles in *St Louis Blues* (1958), with Nat 'King' Cole, and an all-black version of *Anna Lucasta* (1959), opposite Sammy Davis Jnr. Although her highly-mannered presentation of songs is best seen rather than merely heard, Kitt has made some songs virtually her own property, amongst them 'I Want To Be Evil', 'An Englishman Needs Time', 'Santa Baby', and 'I'm Just An Old-Fashioned Girl', a claim which is patently untrue. Her other record successes over the years have included 'Uska Dara - A Turkish Tale', 'C'est Si Bon', 'Somebody Bad Stole De Wedding Bell', 'Lovin' Spree', 'Under The Bridges Of Paris', 'Where Is My Man', 'I Love Men', and 'This Is My Life'. In 1978 Kitt appeared on Broadway with Gilbert Wright and Melba Moore in

Eartha Kitt

an all-black version of *Kismet* entitled *Timbuktu*. Her career has continued along similar lines on both sides of the Atlantic throughout the 80s and into the 90s although she was courted by a much younger audience (witness her collaboration on 'Cha Cha Heels' with Bronski Beat in 1989) who were suitably impressed by her irreverent coolness. In 1988 Kitt played the role of Carlotta Campion in the London production of *Follies* and sang Stephen Sondheim's legendary anthem to survival, 'I'm Still Here', which, appropriately, became the title of her second volume of autobiography. In the early 90s she performed her one-woman show in London and New York and appeared as a witch in the comedy/horror movie *Ernest Scared Stupid*. She also toured Britain with the Inkspots in the revue *A Night At The Cotton Club*.

Selected albums: *Down To Eartha* (1955), *Thursday's Child* (1956), *St. Lous Blues* (1958), *Revisited* (1961), *At The Plaza* (1965), *Bad But Beautiful* (1976), *At Her Very Best* (1982), *C'est Si Bon* (1983), *I Love Men* (1984), *Love For Sale* (1984), *The Romantic Eartha Kitt* (1984), *That Bad Eartha* (1985), *Eartha Kitt In Person At The Plaza* (1988), *I'm A Funny Dame* (1988), *My Way* (1988), *Primitive Man* (1989), *I'm Still Here* (1989), *Live In London* (1990), *Thinking Jazz* (1992). Compilations: *Diamond Series: Eartha Kitt* (1988), *Best Of Eartha Kitt* (1990).

Further reading: *Thursday's Child*, Eartha Kitt. *I'm Still Here*, Eartha Kitt.

Knickerbocker Holiday

Not a particularly successful show, but notable for the the participation of two much-admired American citizens, the distinguished character actor Walter Huston, and the celebrated playwright Maxwell Anderson; and the introduction of one the most cherished songs in the history of popular music, 'September Song'. *Knickerbocker Holiday* opened on 12 October 1938 at the Ethel Barrymore Theatre in New York, with a book by Anderson which was based on Washington Irving's *Knickerbocker History Of New York*. The show begins as Irving, played by Ray Middleton, is beginning to write his book, and then flashes back to New Amsterdam in 1647. The author himself is also transported back in time, and actually takes part in, and occasionally comments on certain aspects of the story that he is supposed to be writing. The piece, in which an all-powerful town council select the knife-sharpener Brom Breck (Richard Kollmar), as the candidate for their 'hanging day', only to see him reprieved by the incoming governor, Peter Stuyvesant (Walter Huston), was considered by many at the time to be a bitter attack on the US President, Franklin D. Roosevelt and his cabinet. *Knickerbocker Holiday* was the first production by the Playwrights Company, an organization which was made up of five distinguished (and sometimes,

disillusioned) American dramatists, which included Maxwell Anderson. The show's score, with Anderson's lyrics and music by Kurt Weill, was different in many respects from conventional Broadway show music. The songs were completely integrated into the plot, and included 'How Can You Tell An American?', 'Will You Remember Me?', 'The One Indispensable Man', ''You People Think About Love', 'There's Nowhere To Go But Up', 'Sitting In Jail', 'Our Ancient Liberties', 'No Ve Vould'nt Gonnto To Do It' (much of the dialogue is spoken in a strong Dutch accent), and a lovely ballad, 'It Never Was You'. Walter Huston sang the poignant 'September Song', and his recorded version became widely popular. The show itself was unable to sustain a long run, and closed after only 168 performances. After Huston's death in 1950, his version of 'September Song' was played in the film, *September Affair*, and was acclaimed all over again. It was also selected for the US National Academy of Recording Arts and Sciences (NARAS) Hall of Fame. In the 1944 film version of *Knickerbocker Holiday* the song was sung by Charles Coburn.

Kretzmer, Herbert

b. 5 October 1925, Kroonstad, South Africa. Kretzmer started in journalism and came to London in 1954, following a twin career as newspaperman (drama critic for *Daily Express*, television critic for *Daily Mail*) and lyricist. He wrote 'Can This Be Love?' with George Martin which was a UK Top 30 entry for Matt Monro and 'Goodness Gracious Me' and 'Bangers And Mash', both novelty hits for Peter Sellers and Sophia Loren. This led to further comedy duets including 'Kinky Boots', an *Avengers* spinoff for Patrick Macnee and Honor Blackman. His work for BBC television's *That Was The Week That Was* included the much-recorded 'In The Summer Of His Years', which was written, and performed by Millicent Martin, within hours of the assassination of President Kennedy. He wrote the London West End musicals *Our Man Critchton* (book and lyrics) and *The Four Musketeers* (lyrics) as well as the lyrics for Anthony Newley's cult musical film, *Can Heironymous Merkin Ever Forget Mercy Humppe And Find True Happiness?*. 'When You Gotta Go' has become a closing song for many cabaret singers, while 'On The Boards', performed in the film by Bruce Forsythe, is a skilfully-worded tribute to music hall. His English lyrics for Charles Aznavour's songs ('Yesterday When I Was Young', 'Happy Anniversary' and, for the ITV series 'The Seven Faces Of Woman', 'She') came to the attention of Cameron Mackintosh, who invited him to write an English version of the French musical based on Victor Hugo's novel, *Les Misérables*, extending the two-hour original into a three-hour show. The all-sung musical has been a West End success since 1985 and includes the witty and ingenious rhymes of 'Master Of The House' as well as the well-covered ballads, 'I Dreamed A Dream', 'On My Own' and 'Bring Him Home'. Kretzmer's lyrics have been translated into several languages to enable *Les Misérables* to be performed with enormous success throughout the world.

L

La Cage Aux Folles

After experiencing his biggest hits with the all-frills and femininity of *Hello, Dolly!* and *Mame*, composer and lyricist Jerry Herman gave Broadway a dose of effeminacy in 1983 with its first homosexual musical, *La Cage Aux Folles*. It opened at the Palace Theatre on 21 August with a book by Harvey Fierstein based on the play by Jean Poiret and the cult 1978 French–Italian movie, which itself was inspired by the real-life Les Allonges by the harbour in St. Tropez. The La Cage Aux Folles nightclub is owned by Georges (Gene Barry), whose cosy 20 years 'marriage' to his transvestite star Albin (George Hearn), is disturbed when Jean-Michel (John Weiner), Georges' son from his 'closet days', announces that he is to be married to the daughter of a family who would just not understand or appreciate his father's long-standing domestic relationship. Albin (stage name Zaza) has to fade into the background for a time, but returns to the scene masquerading as Georges' wife. Despite the show's highly contemporary theme, Herman's score was good old-fashioned musical comedy with a couple of beautifully poignant ballads, 'Song And The Sand' and 'Look Over There', the jaunty 'With You On My Arm', the defiant 'I Am What I Am', a rousing 'The Best Of Times', plus 'A Little More Mascara', 'Masculinity', and the hilarious tour of 'La Cage Aux Folles': 'It's slightly bawdy and a little bit 'new wave'/You may be dancing with a girl who needs a shave . . . Eccentric couples always punctuate the scene/A pair of eunuchs and a nun with a marine . . . All week long we're wondering who/Left a green Givenchy gown in the loo'. The show was a tremendous success, and stayed on Broadway for 1,176 performances and toured throughout the USA. Gene Barry, who has a reputation in America as a song-and-dance man but whose main success came in

Gene Barry (*La Cage Aux Folles*) with Kaye Stevens

television programmes such as *Burke's Law*, was a revelation. He was nominated for a Tony for best actor but the award went to George Hearn, and the show also won for best musical, score, book, director (Arthur Laurents), and costumes. Hearn recreated his role for the London production which also starred British actor Denis Quilley and ran for nine months.

Lady, Be Good!

Although he had already achieved international success, thanks to his popular songs and 'Rhapsody In Blue', George Gershwin was eager to continue to write for Broadway and his stage show, *Lady, Be Good!*, opened there on 1 December 1924. With a book by Guy Bolton and Fred Thompson and lyrics by Ira Gershwin, the show ran for 330 performances. *Lady, Be Good!* had several excellent production numbers and starred Adele and Fred Astaire. The plot, such as it was, centred upon a sister and brother dance team who, unavoidably 'resting' between jobs, survived by crashing parties as a pair of Spanish aristocrats. Amongst the show's songs were 'Oh, Lady, Be Good!', 'Little Jazz Bird' and 'Fascinating Rhythm'. Another song, 'The Man I Love', which had been written especially for Adele Astaire, was dropped during pre-Broadway tryouts but was rescued by Gershwin to gain a life of its own as one of the masterpieces of the Great American Song Book. The Astaires also starred in the show's 1926 London production. *Lady, Be Good!* was revived in London in the late 60s. A 1941 film entitled *Lady, Be Good!* , starring Ann Sothern and Robert Young, had a different storyline and many of the songs came from other sources.

Lady In The Dark

For his first Broadway book musical following his brother George's death in 1937, Ira Gershwin teamed with composer Kurt Weill for this show which arrived in New York at the Alvin Theatre on 23 January 1941. Moss Hart's book had started out as a straight play, *I Am Listening*, and when it became obvious that the piece would work better as a musical, Katherine Cornell, the original choice for leading lady, was replaced by Gertrude Lawrence. She played Liza Elliott, the editor of a highly successful fashion magazine who seeks psychiatric help in an effort to allay her feelings of insecurity, and to explain the extraordinary dreams that she is constantly experiencing. These generally concern four men: Kendall Nesbitt (Bert Lytell) her lover and professional patron; Randy Curtis, a Hollywood star played by Victor Mature, who was on the brink of a lucrative movie career himself, during which he became known as 'The Hunk'; Randall Paxton, the magazine's photographer (Danny Kaye making his Broadway musical comedy debut), and Charley

Johnson (Macdonald Carey), Liza's cantankerous advertising manager, and the man she eventually falls for. All the songs, except one, are presented in four dream sequences, linked together with Gershwin and Weill's beautifully ethereal ballad, 'My Ship', a song which subsequently received sensitive readings over the years from popular singers such as Tony Bennett and Buddy Greco. *Lady In The Dark* contained at least two more memorable songs, 'The Saga Of Jenny' and 'Tschaikowsky'. The former, performed in the Circus Dream by Gertrude Lawrence, stopped the show every night, and concerned a lady who, throughout her life, just could not make up her mind: 'Jenny made her mind up when she was twelve/That into foreign languages she would delve/But at seventeen to Vassar it was quite blow/That in twenty-seven languages she couldn't say no.' The number has been described as 'a sort of blues bordello', and, it is said, was written especially so that Lawrence could 'follow' the immense impact made by Danny Kaye with the tongue-twisting 'Tschaikowsky', in which he listed the names of 49 Russian composers in 39 seconds, the last few of which went thus: 'And Glazounoff and Caesar Cui, Kalinikoff, Rachmaninoff, Stravinsky and Gretchaninoff/I really have to stop, the subject has been dwelt upon enough!'. The remaining songs in what was a classy score included 'One Life To Live', 'Girl Of The Moment', 'This Is New', 'The Princess Of Pure Delight', and 'Tributes To Liza Elliott'. Following several cast changes in June 1941, *Lady In The Dark* completed a run of 467 performances, and then toured before returning to Broadway for another two and half months in 1943. A year later, a film version was released starring Ginger Rogers and Ray Milland, but minus several of the songs, and, 10 years after that, there was a US television production with Anne Sothern and Carleton Carpenter. The show endured in various other presentations, including a tour of the UK provinces in 1981, and an appearance at the Edinburgh Festival in 1988. In 1992, a CD was released of Gertrude Lawrence recreating her original role for a 1950 *Theatre Guild Of The Air* broadcast.

Lane, Burton

b. 2 February 1912, New York City, New York, USA. After studying piano as a child, Lane later played stringed instruments in school orchestras. Some early compositions written for the school band attracted attention, and while still in his early teens he was commissioned to write songs for a projected off-Broadway revue, which sadly never came to fruition. Now in his mid-teens, Lane joined the staff of the Remick Music Company where he was encouraged in his songwriting career by George Gershwin. In 1929, Lane began an association with Howard Dietz, writing additional material for a Broadway revue, *Three's A Crowd*. When the effects of the Depression

Lupino Lane

hit Broadway, Lane went to Hollywood where he worked on numerous musical films, often in collaboration with lyricist Harold Adamson. During the 30s Lane's screen songs included 'Heigh Ho, The Gang's All Here', 'You're My Thrill', 'Stop, You're Breaking My Heart', 'Says My Heart' and his first major hit, 'Everything I Have Is Yours'. Perhaps the most popular of his songs of this period were 'The Lady's In Love With You', from the film, *Some Like It Hot*, plus 'I Hear Music' and 'How About You?' (lyrics by Ralph Freed), sung by Judy Garland and Mickey Rooney in *Babes On Broadway* (1940).

In the 40s Lane returned to the Broadway stage with a succession of musicals which met with mixed response and included a number of good songs, but his first major success came in 1947 with *Finian's Rainbow*. With lyrics by Yip Harburg the show's songs included 'The Great Come-And-Get-It Day', 'Old Devil Moon', 'How Are Things In Glocca Morra?' and 'Look To The Rainbow'. Lane retained his links with Hollywood, writing scores and single songs, among the latter being 'Too Late Now' and 'How Could You Believe Me When I Said I Loved You When You Know I've Been A Liar All My Life?' (both with lyrics by Alan Jay Lerner). He continued to write throughout the 50s and into the 60s, even though the great days of the Hollywood musical were past and those of Broadway going through difficult times. In 1965, Lane and Lerner collaborated on *On A Clear Day You Can See Forever*, from which came 'Come Back To Me', and worked together again in 1978 on *Carmelina*. Despite some good songs, including 'One More Walk Around The Garden', this last show was a resounding flop. In 1979, Lane collaborated with Sammy Cahn on the score for an animated film version of *Heidi*, their songs including 'Can You Imagine?' and 'That's What Friends Are For'.

Lane, Lupino

b. Henry George Lupino, 16 June 1892, London, England, d. 10 November 1959, London, England. An actor, singer, dancer, choreographer, author, and director. Lane was born into a theatrical family which could trace its connections with the stage back to 1632 - one of his famous ancestors was the clown Grimaldi. At the age of four he was performing in theatres, and soon earned the nickname 'Nipper'. He developed his own individual style of extremely skilful, and sometimes dangerous comic acrobatic dancing, and appeared in many English and American two-reelers. However, his greatest impact was made in stage musicals where his trademark bowler hat and Cockney persona endeared him to audiences, especially those in London. From 1915 through to 1934 he appeared in the West End in musical productions such as *Watch Your Step*, *Follow The*

Crowd, *Extra Special*, *Afgar*, *League Of Notions*, *Puss-Puss* (1920), *Brighter London*, *Turned Up*, *Silver Wings* (1930), *The One Girl*, and *The Golden Toy*. In 1935, *Twenty To One*, a musical with a plot about horse racing, was Lane's first show as director and producer as well as actor. Two years later he had the biggest hit of his career with *Me And My Girl* (1937) in which he introduced the enormously popular 'Lambeth Walk'. In the 40s Lane continued on the London stage with *La-Di-Da-Di-Da*, *Meet Me Victoria*, and *Sweetheart Mine* (1946). Although he had enjoyed success in silent films during the 20s, he was unable to recreate his later stage appeal in talkies. However, he and Lillian Roth were acclaimed for their performances as second leads in *The Love Parade* (1929), which starred Maurice Chevalier and Jeanette MacDonald. Another well-known member of Lane's show business family was Stanley Lupino (b. 15 May 1894, London, England, d. 10 June 1942, London England), who was also an athletic dancer and a talented all-round performer. He appeared in London musical shows from 1913 until 1941, and introduced several amusing songs including Leslie Sarony's 'I Lift Up My Finger And I Say Tweet Tweet' in *Love Lies* (1929). Stanley Lupino was the father of the actress Ida Lupino, who went to Hollywood and starred in numerous films from the 30s through to the 80s, including *They Drive By Night*, *High Sierra*, and *Roadhouse*. Lupino Lane's only child, Lauri Lupino Lane, who appeared with his father in *Me And My Girl*, was a regular performer in UK variety theatres until television closed them down in the early 60s. He died at the age of 64 in 1986, and is reckoned to be the last in the line of the celebrated family of entertainers.

Further reading: *Born To Star - The Lupino Lane Story*, J.D. White. *From The Stocks To The Stars*, Stanley Lupino.

Lansbury, Angela

b. Angela Brigid Lansbury, 16 October 1925, London, England. An actress and singer who enjoyed a prolific career in Hollywood before blossoming into a star of Broadway musicals in the 60s. Angela Lansbury's grandfather was George Lansbury, the legendary social reformer, and leader of the British Labour Party for a time during the 30s. She was taken to America in 1942 by her widowed mother, a popular actress named Moyna MacGill. After attending drama school in New York, Lansbury received an Oscar nomination for her first film performance in *Gaslight* (1944). It was the beginning of a long career in Hollywood during which she appeared in several musicals including *The Harvey Girls* (1946), *Till The Clouds Roll By* (1947), *The Court Jester* (1956), *Blue Hawaii* (1961, as Elvis Presley's mother), and *Bedknobs And Broomsticks* (1971). For much of the time she played characters a good deal

Angela Lansbury with Richard Chamberlain

older than herself. From 1957 onwards, Lansbury played several straight roles on Broadway, but it was not until 1964 that she appeared in her first musical, *Anyone Can Whistle*, which had a score by Stephen Sondheim. It only ran for nine performances, but Lansbury's subsequent excursions into the musical theatre proved far more successful. She won wide acclaim, and Tony Awards, for her roles in *Mame* (1966), *Dear World* (1969), *Gypsy* (1974 revival), and *Sweeney Todd* (1979). She also took *Gypsy* to London in 1973. In the 80s, Lansbury began to work more in television and created the part of the writer-come-supersleuth, Jessica Fletcher, in the US series *Murder, She Wrote*. The programmes's long-term success resulted in her being rated as one of the highest-paid actresses in the world by the early 90s. In 1991 she received a Lifetime Achievement Award from the British Academy of Film and Television Arts (BAFTA), and, in the same, year, she lent her voice to Mrs Potts, the character that sang the Academy Award-winning title song in the highly acclaimed Walt Disney animated feature, *Beauty And The Beast*. In 1992, Angel Lansbury was back to her Cockney roots playing a charlady in the film *Mrs 'Arris Goes To Paris*.

Further reading: *Angela Lansbury - A Biography*, Margaret Wander Bonanno.

Laurence Olivier Awards

These awards are presented by the Society of West End Theatre in recognition of distinguished artistic achievement in West End Theatre. They were established in 1976 as the Society of West End Theatre Awards. Lord Olivier agreed to have his name associated with them in 1984 and they are now regarded as the highlight of the British theatrical year. The Awards are judged by three separate panels; for theatre, opera, and dance. The Theatre Panel comprises seven people chosen for their specialist knowledge and professional experience, plus six members of the theatre-going public. Anyone who applies to be included in the latter group should be prepared to see some 80 productions during the Awards year. The musical categories consist of: best director choreographer, actress, actor, supporting performance, revival, and the American Express Award for Best Musical. A musical production, or those associated with it, can also conceivably win in other sections such as best entertainment, costume design, lighting design, set design, outstanding achievement, and lifetime achievement. In 1993, the musicals prizes all went to the highly acclaimed British productions of the American shows *Carousel*, *Crazy For You*, and *Assassins*. The bronze Laurence Olivier Award itself was specially commissioned by the Society from the sculptor Harry Franchetti and represents the young Laurence Olivier as Henry V at the Old Vic in 1937.

Lawrence, Gertrude

b. Gertrud Alexandra Dagmar Lawrence Klasen, 4 July 1898, London, England, d. 6 September 1952. An actress/singer/dancer/comedienne, one of the most vivacious and elegant performers in the history

Gertrude Lawrence

of West End and Broadway theatre. Coming from a showbusiness family, her mother was an actress and her father a singer, Lawrence studied dancing under Madame Espinosa. She made her first proper stage appearance at the age of 12, as a child dancer in the pantomime *Babes In The Wood* at the south London, Brixton Theatre. In 1913, while studying acting and elocution under Italia Conte, where her cockney accent was obliterated, she met the 12-year-old Noël Coward who was to have such an important influence on her later career. After appearing in various provincial theatres in shows such as *Miss Lamb Of Canterbury* and *Miss Plaster Of Paris,* Lawrence made her West End debut in 1916 at the Vaudeville Theatre as principal dancer and understudy in Andre Charlot's revue, *Some*. In 1920, after taking a variety of roles in other revues such as *Cheep, Tabs* and *Buzz-Buzz*, she appeared as leading lady at Murray's Club, London's first cabaret entertainment. Later, she toured variety theatres with Walter Williams, before taking the lead, with Jack Buchanan, in *A-To-Z* (1921), followed by *De-De, Rats* and Noël Coward's *London's Calling* (1923), in which she introduced his bittersweet 'Parisian Pierrot'. She then co-starred on Broadway with Beatrice Lillie in the hit show, *Andre Charlot's Revue of 1924*, giving America its first taste of 'Limehouse Blues'.

In 1926, after more Charlot associations, including his *Revue Of 1926*, in which she sang 'A Cup of Coffee, A Sandwich And You', Lawrence became the first English actress to originate a role on Broadway before playing it in London, when she took the lead in her first 'book' musical, *Oh, Kay*, with a score by George and Ira Gershwin, which included 'Someone To Watch Over Me', 'Maybe', and 'Do-Do-Do'. After repeating her triumph in the West End, Lawrence appeared in several other musicals productions in the late 20s, although none were as lavish as the *International Revue* (1930) in New York, in which she sang Jimmy McHugh and Dorothy Fields's catchy 'Exactly Like You' with Harry Richman. In the same year she was back in London, co-starring with Coward in his sophisticated light comedy *Private Lives,* fondly remembered for lines such as 'Strange how potent cheap music is', and the waltz, 'Someday I'll Find You'. During the 30s Lawrence appeared in a number of successful straight plays, including *Can The Leopard?, Behold We Live, This Inconstancy, Heavy House, Susan And God* and *Skylark*. One musical highlight of the decade was *Nymph Errant* (1933), in which she sang the title song 'Experiment', 'How Could We Be Wrong?', 'It's Bad For Me' and one of Cole Porter's most amusing 'list songs', 'The Physician' ('He said my epidermis was darling/And found my blood as blue as could be/He went through wild ecstatics when I showed him my lymphatics/But he never said he loved me'). Another, *Tonight At 8.30*

(1936), saw her re-united with Coward in his series of one-act plays, two of which, *Shadowplay*, ('Then', 'Play Orchestra Play' and 'You Were There') and *Red Peppers* ('Has Anybody Seen Our Ship?' and 'Men About Town'), are particularly celebrated. That was the last time Lawrence was seen in a musical production in London. She and Coward took *Tonight At 8.30* to New York in 1936, and, five years later, Lawrence had her biggest Broadway success to date when she appeared in *Lady In The Dark*, with a score by Kurt Weill and Ira Gershwin, which gave her the droll 'Jenny' and the haunting 'My Ship'. For much of the 40s she toured countries such as Belgium, France, Holland and the Pacific Ocean Area, on behalf of the USO and ENSA, entertaining the Allied Troops. At the end of World War II, Lawrence began a three-year engagement as Eliza in a revival of *Pygmalion,* which played New York and toured the USA. She also appeared in various other straight plays in the UK and the USA, including *September Tide* (1949), and completed *The Glass Menagerie*, the last in a series of films she made, beginning with *The Battle Of Paris* (1929). In March 1951, she opened on Broadway in 'the most satisfying role of my career', Richard Rodgers and Oscar Hammerstein II's spectacular musical, *The King And I*, playing the part of the children's Governess, Anna for well over a year before being taken ill with a rare form of cancer. She died in September 1952, within a week of being admitted into hospital. Rodgers subscribed to the view, widely held throughout her lifetime, that Lawrence sang flat. 'Just the same', he said, 'whenever I think of Anna, I think of Gertie'.

In 1968, the movie, *Star!*, purported to relate her life story, starring Julie Andrews, and Daniel Massey as Noël Coward, it ran for almost three hours, ('cost $14 million and took four'), and was subsequently trimmed to two and re-titled *Those Where The Happy Times*. In the early 80s, Sheridan Morley, UK critic and author, devised the after-dinner entertainment, *Noel And Gertie,* which, revised and expanded, toured abroad and played in the West End in 1989, with Patricia Hodge as Gertie, and in 1991-92 with Susan Hampshire.

Selected albums: *Noël And Gertie* (1955), *The Incomparable Gertrude Lawrence* (1964).

Further reading: *Gertrude Lawrence: A Bright Particular Star*, Sheridan Morley.

Laye, Evelyn

b. Elsie Evelyn Lay, 10 July 1900, London, England. An actress and singer - one of the most celebrated leading ladies of the English musical stage. Her father was the actor and composer Gilbert Laye (he added the 'e' on to the family name for stage appearances) and her mother the actress Evelyn Stewart. Known as 'Boo' from when she was a baby, Evelyn Laye was constantly performing as a child, and made her professional stage debut at the age of 15 as a Chinese servant in a production entitled *Mr. Wu*. After appearing in *The Beauty Spot*, *Going Up*, and *The Kiss Call*, she had her first West End success in 1920 with *The Shop Girl*, in which she was backed by a chorus of real guardsmen as she sang 'The Guards' Parade'. In the early 20s she delighted London audiences in shows such as *Phi-Phi*, and *The Merry Widow. Madame Pompadour* (1923), her first show for C.B. Cochran, was a significant landmark in her career, and was followed by more good roles in stylish productions such as *Cleopatra*, *Betty In Mayfair*, *Merely Molly*, and *Blue Eyes*. By 1929, when Evelyn Laye introduced Drury Lane audiences to 'Lover, Come Back To Me' in Sigmund Romberg's musical *The New Moon*, she had become the brightest star on the London theatre scene; Cochran called her 'the fairest prima donna this side of heaven'. Around this time she was separated from her husband, the comedian Sonny Hale, and he later married one of her main 'rivals', the enchanting Jessie Matthews. She turned down the leading role in the London production of Noël Coward's *Bitter Sweet*, but triumphed in the 1929 Broadway production, and later succeeded Peggy Wood in the West End version. Her success on Broadway resulted in a trip to Hollywood and appearances in *One Heavenly Night* with John Boles, and *The Night Is Young*, in which she co-starred with Ramon Novarra and sang Sigmund Romberg and Oscar Hammerstein II's enduring 'When I Grow Too Old To Dream'. While in America she married the British actor, Frank Lawton, and they were together until he died in 1969. On her return to England she made more films, including *Princess Charming*, *Waltz Time*, and *Evensong* (1934). The latter is regarded as perhaps her most accomplished screen appearance. During the remainder of the 30s, Evelyn Laye was a 'ravishing' Helen of Troy in *Helen!*, appeared with the embryonic John Mills in *Give Me A Ring,* co-starred with the far more mature Viennese tenor Richard Tauber in *Paganini*, and returned to Broadway in 1937 with Jack Buchanan and Adele Dixon for *Between The Devil*. The show made history when it was presented for one night at the National Theatre in New York on the occasion of President Roosevelt's birthday, thereby becoming the first American Command Performance. In 1940 she sang 'You've Done Something To My Heart', 'Only A Glass Of Champagne', and 'Let The People Sing' in Ronald Jean's revue, *Lights Up*. During the remainder of World War II she appeared in the 1942 revival of *The Belle Of New York* and another Romberg-Hammerstein show, *Sunny River*. She also served as Entertainments Director for the Royal Navy, and led the first-ever concert party for the troops based in the remote Scapa Flow in the Orkneys. In 1945 Evelyn Laye returned to the London stage in *Three Waltzes*. Immediately after the war, when suitable parts in the musical theatre were few and far between, she played straight roles in plays throughout the UK and on a 1951 tour of Australia, but made a triumphant comeback to the London musical stage in *Wedding In Paris* in 1954. More straight plays followed before she starred in the musical, *Strike A Light* (1966), and replaced Anna Neagle for a time in the long-running *Charley Girl*. In her last musical (to date), *Phil The Fluter* (1969), she reflected on a better, more civilised age, in the memorable 'They Don't Make Them Like That Any More', a number that was so perfectly suited to her. In 1971 she appeared with Michael Crawford in the comedy, *No Sex, Please - We're British*, and two years later was awarded the CBE. During the rest of the 70s and 80s she made several more films, including *Say Hello To Yesterday*, with Jean Simmons and *Never Never Land* with Petula Clark, and did a good deal of television work. In 1992, at the age of 92, she toured parts of the UK with the nostalgia show, *Glamorous Nights At Drury Lane*, and received standing ovations. In July of that year, in *A Glamorous Night With Evelyn Laye At The London Palladium*, the elite of British show-business gathered to pay tribute and nod in assent as she sang 'They Don't Make Them Like That Any More'.

Selected albums: *Golden Age Of Evelyn Laye* (1985), *When I Grow Too Old To Dream* (1991).

Further reading: *Boo To My Friends*, Evelyn Laye.

Leave It To Jane

One of the five engaging and tuneful musicals that the team of Jerome Kern (music), Guy Bolton (book), and P.G. Wodehouse (book and lyrics) turned out in 1917, this particular production could not get into their favourite 499-seater Princess Theatre, situated on the corner of Broadway and 48th Street, because their *Oh, Boy!*, was still playing to packed houses for an incredible (in those days) 467 performances. So, *Leave It Jane* made its debut at the Longacre Theatre on 28 August 1917. Based on George Ade's play, *The College Widow*, and set in the football-mad Atwater College, the story concerns Jane Witherspoon (Edith Hallor), the college widow and the daughter of President Witherspoon, an extremely capable lady, who deals briskly with any problems that may arise. One such is when the highly talented and extremely supple Billy Bolton (Robert Pitkin), announces his intention to transfer his footballing talents to Atwater's deadly rivals, Bingham. Jane hits on the idea of Billy playing for Atwater under an assumed name, and, inevitably, she eventually changes hers to Bolton. The breezy, optimistic score included 'The Crickets Are Calling', 'I'm Going To Find A Girl', 'It's A Great Big Land', 'Just You Watch My Step', 'A Peach Of A Life', 'Poor Prune', 'Sir Galahad', 'The Siren's

Song', 'The Sun Shines Brighter', 'There It Is Again', 'Wait Till Tomorrow', 'What I'm Longing To Say', and 'Why?'. The novelty number that usually stopped the show was a highly amusing mock-Egyptian piece called 'Cleopattera', which was sung by Georgia O'Ramey, and had a typical Wodehouse lyric. He had the knack of noticing and using the current fad phrases, like 'ginks' and 'Oh, you kid!': 'She gave those poor Egyptian ginks/Something else to watch beside the Sphinx' . . . 'They'd take her hand and squeeze it, and murmer, "Oh, you kid!"/But you bet they never started to feed, till Cleopattera did'. That song, and 'Leave It To Jane', were sung by June Allyson in the Jerome Kern biopic, *Till The Clouds Roll By* (1946). *Leave It To Jane* ran for 167 performances in 1917, and was revived, over 40 years later in May 1959, when it remained Off Broadway at the Sheridan Square Playhouse for over two years, a remarkable 928 performances.

Leave It To Me!

Just a year after his riding accident, during which both his legs were very badly injured, Cole Porter came up with a terrific score for this funny and satirical show which opened at the Imperial Theatre in New York on 9 November 1938. With a book by Bella and Samuel Spewak which was based on their play, *Clear All Wires*, it heralded the Broadway debut of Mary Martin, who went on to become one of the American musical theatre's cherished leading ladies. Her big moment came as she sat on a trunk at a Siberian railway station clad in furs which she slowly and deliberately removed during Porter's wonderful 'My Heart Belongs To Daddy' ('So I want to warn you, laddie/Tho' I simply hate to be frank/That I can't be mean to Daddy/Cause my Da-da-da, daddy might spank.'). Closely in attendance were five male dancers, and the one visible over Martin's right shoulder in the publicity shots is Gene Kelly. After the show had been running for three months she received feature billing. Her saucy first impression is interesting because, it is said, that in subsequent shows she was extremely reluctant to be involved with material that was anywhere 'near the knuckle'. The Spewaks' story for *Leave It To Me!* told of the meek and mild Alonzo P. Goodhue (Victor Moore), whose wife, played by Sophie Tucker, raised such a big bundle of cash for President Roosevelt's re-election campaign, that Alonzo is made the American ambassador to the Soviet Union. This is precisely what he does not want, and he sets out make a real hash of things so that he will be recalled. Unfortunately for him, everything he touches turns out right - until he gets together with foreign correspondent Buckley Joyce Thomas (William Gaxton) to inaugurate a plan that will guarantee world peace. This, of course, is in nobody's interest,

and he is immediately removed, and returned to the USA. Gaxton and Tamara, who played his girlfriend, Colette, combined in two romantic duets, 'From Now On' and 'Far, Far Away', and she sang one of Porter's most potent love songs, 'Get Out Of Town'. The composer gave Sophie Tucker, appearing in her only Broadway book musical, one of her early 'advice to young ladies' numbers with the clever 'Most Gentlemen Don't Like Love' ('They just like to kick it around'. . . 'So just remember when you get that glance/A romp and a quickie/Is all little Dickie/Means/When he mentions romance.'), and she and the chorus also had 'Tomorrow'. There was lots of larking about in Red Square, and other appropriate locations, particularly by funny-men Gaxton and Moore who teamed in several other Broadway musicals. After its initial run of 291 performances, *Leave It To Me!* returned to New York for another two weeks in September 1939 when Mary Martin was succeeded by Mildred Fenton. During the subsequent tour, the character of Stalin was removed from the piece following the Russian dictator's signing of non-aggression pact with Hitler. Many years later, the show still retained some interest, and it was revived as recently as 1991 at the Arts Theatre in Cambridge, England.

Leigh, Carolyn

b. 21 August 1926, New York, USA, d. 19 November 1983, New York City, New York, USA. Carolyn Leigh was the lyricist with whom Cy Coleman was most identified. She began writing verse and doggerel when she was only nine-years-old and, after graduating from high school, studied at Queens College and New York University. She began her career by writing announcements for radio station WQXR and working as a copywriter for an advertising agency. By the time she was 25 years old Leigh is reputed to have written about 200 songs, although none had been published. In 1951, she wrote 'I'm Waiting Just For You', which were minor hits for Lucky Millinder, Rosemary Clooney, and later, Pat Boone. Her first success came in 1954 when Frank Sinatra took her 'Young At Heart', written with Johnny Richards, to number 2 in the US, and included it in the film of the same title, in which he starred with Doris Day. This led to Leigh being offered the chance to write the songs, with composer Mark 'Moose' Charlap, for the Broadway show *Peter Pan*. Their score included 'I'm Flying', 'I've Gotta Crow' and 'I Won't Grow Up'. Her collaboration with Coleman ran from the late 50s to 1962, which by all reports was a 'stormy' relationship. After the success of *Little Me* on Broadway the duo had an 'on-off' working relationship. In 1967, they wrote 'A Doodlin' Song', which was recorded by Peggy Lee. In the same year, Leigh teamed with composer Elmer

Bernstein to write the score for *How Now, Dow Jones*. The songs included 'Live A Little', 'Walk Away', 'He's Here!' and 'Step To The Rear'. Leigh was nominated for a Tony Award for her lyrics. During the latter years of her career she continued to write occasionally for the stage, television and films. She wrote the lyrics for the Bicentennial show *Something To Do* and for the television special, *Heidi*. Her other songs included 'How Little It Matters' (written with Phillip Springer), 'Stowaway' (with Jerry Livingston), 'Stay With Me', 'Love Is A Melody (Short And Sweet)', 'Disenchanted Castle', 'On Second Thought', 'In The Barrio', 'Westport' and 'Bouncing Back For More'. Her other collaborators included Morton Gould, Lee Pockriss and Marvin Hamlisch. She was working on a musical adaptation of *Smiles* with Hamlisch when she died from a heart attack in 1983.

Lend An Ear

Notable mainly for the Broadway debut of Carol Channing, the blonde comedienne with a the wide-eyed look and a voice that no-one has ever described satisfactorily, this revue opened at the National Theatre in New York on 16 December 1948, after stop-overs during the previous few years in Pittsburgh and Los Angeles. *Lend An Ear* was also the first Broadway musical to be directed and choreographed by the former dancer, Gower Champion, and Charles Gaynor, another new boy in the 'back-stage' department, contributed the witty music, lyrics, and sketches. Gaynor went through the card, pointing-up and lampooning a variety of targets, but some of the funniest moments came when he concentrated on a pair of celebrities who lived their lives according to the columnists, the effect on society by the growing influence of psychoanalysts, an opera company that just reads the librettos because it cannot afford an orchestra, and a wicked 20s spoof concerning a theatrical touring company that has sent out several versions of *The Gladioli Girl* over the years, none of which has returned. The songs, too, were affectionate parodies of the kind from days gone by, and included 'Give Your Heart A Chance To Sing', 'Doin' The Old Yahoo Step', 'Molly O'Reilly', 'Who Hit Me?', 'In Our Teeny Weeny Little Nest', 'Where Is The She For Me?'. The lively, young and talented cast consisted of William Eythe, Yvonne Adair, Jennie Lou Law, Gloria Hamilton, Bob Scheerer, and Gene Nelson, the song-and-dance man who had had begun his film career in 1947, and will be affectionately remembered for his performances in musicals such as *Lullaby Of Broadway*, *Tea For Two*, and especially *Oklahoma!*. In some ways, a suprising and gratifying production for its time, *Lend An Ear* enjoyed a good run of 460 performances.

Leonardo

Early in 1993, residents of the UK could have been forgiven for consulting their calendars to see if the date was April 1 after reading reports that the Republic of Nauro, a small island in the Pacific (population 8,000), was financing a West End musical show with the proceeds from its major export - bird droppings (they are high in phosphates). *LEONARDO - THE MUSICAL - A PORTRAIT OF LOVE*, which opened at the Strand Theatre in London on 3 June 1993, was the brainchild of Duke Minks, an advisor to the Nauruan government, and a former road manager with the 60s pop group, Unit 4 + 2, which had a UK number 1 in 1965 with 'Concrete And Clay'. Tommy Mueller, the co-writer of 'Concrete And Clay', is credited with *Leonardo*'s music and lyrics, along with Greg Moeller, Russell Dunlop, and Minks, who also produced the piece. John Kane's book ('half fact-half guesswork') begins and ends with the hero, Leonardo da Vinci (Paul Collis), on his deathbed - his masterpiece, the Mona Lisa, by his side. In Kane's scenario, Leonardo is commissioned by nobleman Francesco Del Giocondo (James Barron) to paint a portrait of his fiancé, Lisa (Jane Arden), but the artist falls in love with his model, and makes her pregnant. She cannot marry him, but must pretend that the child is Del Giocondo's or he will have them both killed. Eventually, she returns to the by now successful Leonardo, and begs his forgiveness, but he is accidentally killed by her husband in a jealous rage. Kane also hints at a homosexual relationship between the painter and his devoted friend, Melzi (Hal Fowler). Some 20 musical numbers accompanied this sad tale, and they included 'Who The Hell Are You?', 'Firenza Mia', 'Part Of Your Life', 'Just A Dream Away', 'Her Heart Beats', 'Endless As My Love', 'Just One More Time', 'Goodbye And No One Said A Word', 'Forever Child', 'Portrait Of Love', and 'She Lives With Me'. The President of Nauru hosted a first night party while the critics polished their prose: 'A great deal of risible tosh' . . . 'Only six months to Christmas and the first turkey has arrived', were typical tabloid comments. In addition, bearing in mind the source of the show's reported £2 million investment, there was a good deal of talk about fertiliser, and 'dropping us all in it'. *Leonardo* folded on 10 July after a run of just over four weeks. From his house in Cannes, Duke Minks, the instigator of it all, was quoted as saying: 'Leonardo died in Italy in 1519, and again in the Strand in 1993.'

Lerner, Alan Jay

b. 31 August 1918, New York, USA, d. 14 February 1988, Florida, USA. A lyricist and librettist; one of the most eminent and literate personalities in the history of the Broadway musical theater. Lerner played the piano as a child, and studied at the Juilliard School of Music, the Bedales public school in England, and Harvard University where he took a Bachelor of Science degree in the late 30s. After working as a journalist and radio scriptwriter, he met composer Frederick Loewe at the Lamb's Club in 1942. Loewe was educated at the Military Academy and at Stern's Conservatory in Berlin. He made his concert debut as a pianist at the age of 13, and, two years later, composed 'Katrina', a song which became popular throughout Europe. After moving to the USA in 1924, he did ranch work in the west, played the piano in beer halls and silent movie houses, and was a bantam-weight boxer for a time. Before he met Lerner, Loewe had also been involved in some unsuccessful musical shows. The new team's first efforts, *What's Up?* and *The Day Before Spring* (1945) ('A Jug Of Wine', 'I Love You This Morning'), did not exactly set Broadway on fire, but, two years later, they had their first hit with *Brigadoon*. Lerner's whimsical fantasy about a Scottish village which only comes to life every 100 years, contained numbers such as 'Waitin' For My Dearie', 'I'll Go Home To Bonnie Jean', 'The Heather On The Hill', 'Come To Me, Bend To Me', 'From This Day On', and the future standard, 'Almost Like Being In Love'. A film version was made in 1954, starring Gene Kelly, Cyd Charisse and Van Johnson.

After *Brigadoon*, Lerner collaborated with Kurt Weill on the vaudeville-style *Love Life* (1948), and then spent some time in Hollywood writing the songs, with Burton Lane, for *Royal Wedding* (1951). Among them was one of the longest-ever titles: 'How Could You Believe Me When I Said I Loved You (When You Know I've Been A Liar All My Life?)', expertly manipulated by Fred Astaire. Another of the numbers, 'Too Late Now', sung by Jane Powell, was nominated for an Academy Award. In the same year, Lerner picked up an Oscar for his story and screenplay for George and Ira Gershwins' musical film, *An American In Paris* (1951). Also in 1951, Lerner re-united with Loewe for the 'Gold Rush' Musical, *Paint Your Wagon*. The colourful score included 'They Call The Wind Maria', 'I Talk To The Trees', 'I Still See Elisa', 'I'm On My Way' and 'Wand'rin' Star', which, in the 1969 movie, received a lugubrious reading from Lee Marvin. Precisely the opposite sentiments prevailed in *My Fair Lady* (1956), Lerner's adaptation of *Pygmalion*, by Bernard Shaw, which starred Rex Harrison as the irascible Higgins, and Julie Andrews as Eliza ('I'm a good girl, I am'). Sometimes called 'the most perfect musical', Lerner and Loewe's memorable score included 'Why Can't The English?', 'Wouldn't It Be Loverly?', 'The Rain In Spain', 'I Could Have Danced All Night', 'On The Street Where You Live', 'Show Me', 'Get Me To The Church On Time', 'A Hymn To Him', 'Without You' and 'I've Grown Accustomed To Her Face'. 'Come To The Ball', originally written for the show, but discarded before the opening, was, subsequently, often performed, particularly by Lerner himself. After a run of 2,717 performances on Broadway, and 2,281 in London, the show was filmed in 1964, when Andrews was replaced by Audrey Hepburn (dubbed by Marni Nixon). The Broadway Cast album went to number 1 in the US charts, sold over five million copies, and stayed in the Top 40 for 311 weeks, still a record in the late 80s. In 1958 Lerner was back in Hollywood, with a somewhat reluctant Loewe, for one of the last original screen Musicals, the charming *Gigi*. Lerner's stylish treatment of Colette's turn-of-the-century novella, directed by Vincente Minnelli, starred Maurice Chevalier, Leslie Caron, Louis Jordan and Hermione Gingold, and a delightful score which included 'The Night They Invented Champagne', 'Say A Prayer For Me Tonight', 'I'm Glad I'm Not Young Anymore', 'Thank Heaven For Little Girls', 'Waltz At Maxim's', 'She Is Not Thinking Of Me' and the touching, 'I Remember It Well', memorably performed by Chevalier and Gingold. Lerner won one of the film's nine Oscars for his screenplay, and another, with Loewe, for the title song.

Two years later Lerner and Loewe returned to Broadway with *Camelot*, a musical version of the Arthurian legend, based on T.H. White's *The Once And Future King*. With Julie Andrews, Richard Burton and Robert Goulet, plus a fine score which included 'C'Est Moi', 'The Lusty Month Of May', 'If Ever I Would Leave You', 'Follow Me', 'How To Handle A Woman' and the title song; the show was on Broadway for two years. During that time it became indelibly connected with the Kennedy presidency . . . 'for one brief shining moment, that was known as Camelot' . . . The 1967 movie version was poorly received. In the early 60s, partly because of the composer's ill health, Lerner and Loewe ended their partnership, coming together again briefly in 1973 to write some new songs for a stage presentation of *Gigi*, and, a year later, for the score to the film *The Little Prince*. Lerner's subsequent collaborators included Burton Lane for *On A Clear Day You Can See Forever* (1965) ('Come Back To Me', 'On The S.S. Bernard Cohn', and others). Lerner won a Grammy Award for the title song, and maintained that it was his most oft-recorded number. He wrote with Lane again in 1979 for *Carmelina*. In the interim teamed-up with André Previn for *Coco* (1969), which had a respectable run of 332 performances, mainly due to its star, Katherine Hepburn; and Leonard Bernstein for *1600 Pennsylvania Avenue* (1976). Lerner's last Musical, *Dance A Little Closer* (1983), which starred his eighth wife, English actress Liz Robertson, closed after one performance. They had met in 1979 when he directed her, as Eliza, in a major

London revival of *My Fair Lady*.

Just before he died of lung cancer on 14 June 1986, he was still working on various projects including a musical treatment of the 30s film comedy *My Man Godfrey*, in collaboration with pianist-singer Gerard Kenny, and *Yerma*, based on the play by Federico Garcia Lorca. Frederick Loewe, who shared in Lerner's triumphs, and had been semi-retired since the 60s, died in February 1988, in Palm Springs, Florida, USA. In 1993, New Yorkers celebrated the 75th anniversary of Lerner's birth, and a remarkable and fruitful partnership, with *The Night They Invented Champagne: The Lerner And Loewe Revue*, which played a season at the Rainbow and Stars.

Further reading: *The Musical Theatre: A Celebration*, Alan Jay Lerner. *The Street Where I Live: The Story Of My Fair Lady, Gigi And Camelot*, Alan Jay Lerner. *A Hymn To Him: The Lyrics Of Alan Jay Lerner*.

Les Misérables

Opening in Paris in 1980, in the seemingly unlikely setting of a sports arena, *Les Misérables* brought light to the darkness of the European musical theatre. Taking as its improbable text, Victor Hugo's grim novel of one man's determined survival in the face of another's vengeful persecution, *Les Misérables* became a musical jewel. With music by Claude-Michel Schönberg, who also wrote the book with Alain Boublil, and lyrics by Herbert Kretzmer adapted into English from the French text by Boublil and Jean-Marc Natel, the show was originally staged at the Barbican in London on 30 September 1985 by Trevor Nunn and John Caird of the Royal Shakespeare Company. It subsequently transferred to the Palace Theatre and, after initially mixed reviews, settled in for a long run. Set in nineteenth-century France, the show was an impressive drama of political and social comment brimming with stirring music all impressively staged. The dramatic and memorable score included numbers such as 'I Dreamed A Dream', 'On My Own', 'Who Am I?', 'Come To Me', 'Do You Hear The People Sing?', 'Drink With Me To Days Gone By', and the grieving 'Empty Chairs At Empty Tables'. Starring Patti LuPone, Colm Wilkinson and Alun Armstrong, *Les Misérables* became the musical highlight of London's West End and ran on into the 90s as vivid proof that audiences were not deterred by musical shows with depth and that the musical theatre need not depend upon escapism for its continued existence. In February 1994, it overtook *Jesus Christ Superstar* as the third-longest-running musical (after *Cats* and *Starlight Express*) in the history of the London musical theatre. The American production, which opened at the Broadway Theatre in New York on 12 March 1987, soon became one of the hottest tickets in town, and won Tony Awards for best musical, score, book, featured actress (Frances Ruffelle), directors (Nunn and Caird), scenic design (John Napier), costumes (Andreane Neofitou), and lighting (David Hersey).

Further reading: *The Complete Book Of Les Misérables*, Edward Behr.

Let's Face It!

Danny Kaye confirmed the star qualities he had shown earlier in the year in *Lady In The Dark* when he played his first leading role on Broadway in this show which opened at the Imperial Theatre in New York on 29 October 1941. In *Lady In The Dark*, Kaye had been called upon to sing a song, listing 49 Russian composers, in 39 seconds; in *Let's Face It!*, he stopped the show with 'Melody In 4-F', which encapsulated a rookie soldier's first few weeks in the army - this time in 90 seconds. That particular piece of special material was written by Kaye's wife, Sylvia Fine and Max Liebman. Herbert and Dorothy Fields's book, which was based on the 1925 hit comedy, *The Cradle Snatchers*, deals with three wives who suspect that their husbands' sporting activities may be of the indoor, rather the outdoor variety, so they enlist the help of three soldiers from the local army camp to assist them in their own night-time manoeuvres. Howver, serious complications arise when the husbands return - with the girlfriends of the soldiers on their arms. With Kaye in the cast, were Eve Arden, Benny Baker, Edith Meiser, Vivan Vance, Mary Jane Walsh, and, in a minor role, Nanette Fabray, who later had success in other Broadway musicals such as *High Button Shoes*, and in several films, particularly The *Band Wagon* (1953) with Fred Astaire and Jack Buchanan. Cole Porter's score was smart and witty as usual, and included 'Ace In The Hole', 'Farming', 'Ev'rything I Love', 'A Little Rhumba Numba', 'A Lady Needs A Rest', and 'I Hate You Darling'. The composer's riposte to Kaye's 'Melody In 4-F' that he (Porter) allowed to be interpolated from another source, was another equally vocally taxing piece which Kaye shared with Eve Arden: 'Let's Not Talk About Love' ('Why not discuss, my dee-arie, the life of Wallace Bee-ery/Or bring a jeroboam on, and write a drunken poem on/Astrology, mythology, geology, philology/Pathology, psychology, electro-physiology/Spermology, phrenology/I owe you an apology/But let's not talk about love.'). During the show's New York run of 547 performances, Danny Kaye was succeeded by José Ferrer, and, when *Let's Face it* began its 10 months stay at the London Hippodrome, it starred Bobby Howes, Joyce Barbour, Jack Stamford, and Pat Kirkwood. The 1943 film version had Bob Hope, Betty Hutton, and Eve Arden.

Li'l Abner

The wonderful world of Dogpatch, a rural

community somewhere in the south of the USA, came to The St. James Theatre on Broadway in November, 1956 when librettists Norman Panama and Melvin Frank adapted Al Capp's famous comic strip, *Li'l Abner*, for the musical stage. All the familiar characters made the trip, including Daisy Mae (Edith Adams) who is still trying to catch Abner Yokum (Peter Palmer) in the annual Sadie Hawkins' Day Chase (if you catch 'em, Marryin' Sam [Stubby Kaye] will do the rest). Then there is Appassionata von Climax (Tina Louise) - she's after Li'l Abner as well - Earthquake McGoon (Bern Hoffman - *he's* after Ellie Mae, General Bullmoose (Howard St. John), Mammy Yokum (Charlotte Rae), Stupefyin' Jones (Julie Newmar), Romeo Scragg (Mark Breaux), Clem Scragg (James Hurst), Moonbeam McSwine (Carmen Alvarez), and many more. All of them are shocked when they hear that the US Goverment has such a low opinion of Dogpatch that they want to test an atom bomb there. Fortune smiles on the town and its amiable inhabitants when they discover that, back in Abraham Lincoln's time, the town was designated a national shrine. The lively and exhilarating score, by Johnny Mercer and Gene De Paul, was full of good things, including what could be said to be the community's theme song, 'Progress Is The Root Of All Evil', along with 'Past My Prime', 'Put 'Em Back', 'Oh Happy Day', 'Unnecessary Town', the rousing 'The Country's In The Very Best Of Hands', and a hymn to the founder of Dogpatch, the incompetent 'Jubilation T. Cornpone', which was sung by Stubby Kaye who was oustanding throughout, as usual. There was also the tender ballad, 'Love In A Home', and 'Namely You', which achieved some popularity through recordings by Lawrence Welk and Carmen McRae. Another of the songs, 'If I Had My Druthers', was included by Johnny Mercer on *Two Of A Kind*, an album he made with Bobby Darin in 1961. Michael Kidd won a Tony Award for his spirited choreography (just two years after his tremendous work in Hollywood on *Seven Brides For Seven Brothers*) and *Li'l Abner* enjoyed a run of 693 performances. The 1959 film version starred Peter Palmer, Leslie Parrish, Stubby Kaye, and some of the other actors from the show.

Lieberson, Goddard

b. 5 April 1911, Hanley, Staffordshire, England, d. 29 May 1977, New York City, New York, USA. A record company executive, composer, author, and musician. Lieberson was four years old when his family moved to Seattle, Washington. After graduating from the local university, he studied at the Eastman School of Music in New York, and originally intended to make a career as a composer. Financial reality intervened, and, in 1939, he became the assistant director of the Masterworks division of Columbia Records, part of the CBS group. During the 40s he recorded plays, operas, and other classical works, whilst at the same time rising to the position of executive vice-president of Columbia. In the late 40s, he was influential in the decision to select the 33 1/3 speed as the standard for the new long-playing record. The development also contributed directly towards his greatest success as a pioneering producer of original cast recordings of hit Broadway shows. He began in 1949 with *South Pacific*, for which he won the first of seven Gold Discs. The other award winners were *Flower Drum Song*, *Camelot*, *West Side Story*, *Mame*, *The Sound Of Music*, and *My Fair Lady*. He was so impressed by the score for the latter show that he persuaded CBS to become the sole investor – and, with sales of over six million units, they made a fortune. His 'amazing ear, his enthusiasm for theatre music, and his respect for the work he was doing' made him a legendary figure in the industry. Lieberson also recorded many shows when they had closed after only a few performances, convinced quite rightly in most cases, that the scores were worth preserving. He was responsible for recording the vast majority of the shows which are currently being re-released in CD form on the Sony Broadway label. During a long and distinguished career, Lieberson is credited with having signed many important artists, including Simon And Garfunkel and Bob Dylan. He rose to be the president of Columbia Records (1955-56), of the CBS/Columbia Group (1966-71 and 1973-75), but he will be remembered mainly for his sensitive and brilliant work in preserving so much wonderful Broadway music. His final recordings, in the early 70s, were *A Little Night Music*, *Billy*, and the record-breaking *A Chorus Line* (1975).

Life Begins At 8:40

One of the outstanding revues of the 30s, *Life Begins At 8:40* opened at the Winter Garden Theatre in New York on 27 August 1934. There was high quality throughout, in every department. The backstage team included directors Philip Loeb and John Murray Anderson who was renowned for his work on several editions of the Greenwich Village Follies, and his own John Murray Anderson's Almanac, and much else; the sketches were mainly written by David Freedman, and the songs were provided by the classy trio of Harold Arlen (music) with Ira Gershwin and E.Y. 'Yip' Harburg (lyrics). They included 'Let's Take A Walk Around The Block', 'What Can You Say In A Love Song?', 'Things', 'Fun To Be Fooled', 'Shoein' the Mare', 'I Couldn't Hold My Man', and 'You're A Builder-Upper', which had some success via recordings by Leo Reisman (with composer Harold Arlen), Henry King, and Glen Gray. Two of America's funniest song-and-dance men, Bert Lahr and Ray Bolger, led the cast, which also included Luella Gear, Frances Williams, Dixie Dunbar, Earl Oxford, and Brian Donlevy, the Irish-American actor who went on to become one of Hollywood's top tough guys. The combination of good songs and a series of sometimes hilarious sketches ensured a a decent run of 237 performances.

Lilac Time
(see **Blossom Time**)

Lisbon Story, The
One of the most popular West End musicals during World War II, *The Lisbon Story* opened at the London Hippodrome on 17 June 1943. Fifty years on, it is still recalled fondly because of the inclusion of the jaunty 'Pedro The Fisherman', which almost immediately became an enormous hit. The song was part of a score written by composer Harry Parr-Davis and lyricist Harry Purcell, who also provided a book in which wartime drama was mixed with sentimental music and lavish dance sequences in a spectacular and entertaining fashion. The story concerns a Parisian prima ballerina, Gabrielle Gerard (Patricia Burke), who colludes with the Nazis in an effort to secure the release of an important French scientist. When her deceit is discovered, she is executed. Albert Lieven played her German go-between, Carl von Shriner, and the cast also included Arséne Kiriloff, Zulia, Noele Gordon, Jack Livesey, Margaret McGrath, Reginald Long, and Joseph Dollinger. There were two major dance scenes and a lovely operetta sequence. The score contained several attractive numbers, including the waltz, 'Someday We Shall Meet Again', 'Never Say Goodbye', 'For The First Time (I've Fallen In Love)', 'Follow The Drum', 'Happy Days', and 'A Serenade For Sale', but it was 'Pedro The Fisherman', which was sung in the show by Vincent Tildsley's Master Singers, in sailor rig, that audiences were whistling when they left the theatre. Patricia Burke made a successful recording of the song, as did the distinguished tenor, Richard Tauber, who appeared with her in the 1946 film of *The Lisbon Story*. Probably the version that endured the most, and which received consistent exposure on BBC Radio's *Family Favourites* programme, was that by Gracie Fields.

Little Johnny Jones
George M. Cohan's first Broadway hit, and the beginning of his long association with producer Sam H. Harris. The show opened at the Liberty Theatre in New York on 7 November 1904, and, as was to become the norm throughout his career, Cohan provided the book, music and lyrics, as well directing and appearing in the piece. He is said to have got the idea for the plot from a newspaper account about an American jockey, Tod Sloane, who rode in the English Derby race in 1903. In Cohan's version, Johnny Jones refuses to be bribed to throw the race, but he loses anyway. When he arrives at Southampton docks to board a ship for his return to America, he is besieged by an angry crowd. Eventually they disperse and he is left alone waiting for a signal from his friend on the ship, now some way out at sea, to indicate that his innocence has been proved. The moment when the rocket soars into the sky and Jones goes into an exhuberant rendering of 'Give My Regards To Broadway', is one of the most memorable sequences in musical comedy history. It was recreated superbly by James Cagney when he starred in the George M. Cohan biopic, *Yankee Doodle Dandy*, in 1942. The latter film got it's title from 'The Yankee Doodle Boy', which Cohan introduced in *Little Johnny Jones*, along with other numbers such as 'Life's A Funny Proposition After All', 'If Mr. Boston Lawson Got His Way', and 'I'm Might Glad I'm Living And That's All'. Cohan's wife, Ethel Levy, had a leading role, and so did his mother and father, Helen and Jerry Cohan. Also in the cast was Donald Brian, the actor, singer, and dancer who was to appear in Cohan's next Broadway musical, *Forty-Five Minutes From Broadway*, before going on to star in other important shows such as *The Merry Widow* and *The Girl From Utah*, in which he introduced Jerome Kern and Herbert Reynolds' lovely song, 'They Didn't Believe Me'. Although Cohan is often criticized for his sentimental, flag-waving approach, *Little Johnny Jones*, with its strong score and solid, believable book is considered to a be significant landmark in development of the indigenous American musical. It ran for only 52 performances in its first outing on Broadway, but Cohan brought it back twice during 1905, and toured it extensively. The 1930 film version starred Alice Day and Eddie Buzzell. A 1981 revival of the show which began its life at the Goodspeed Opera House, Connecticut, amended the original plot and introduced some other Cohan songs. After using several actors in the lead role during its pre-Broadway tour, Donny Osmond, a former member of the Osmond Brothers, was chosen to play the part at the Alvin Theatre in New York - but for the one-night run only.

Little Mary Sunshine
On first sight a show with a title like that, and characters with names such as Mme. Ernestine Von Liebedich and General Oscar Fairfax, plus songs with titles like 'Do You Ever Dream Of Vienna?', the casual observer could be forgiven for thinking that this is an operetta. It is the date that gives the game away: *Little Mary Sunshine* opened Off Broadway (another clue) at the Orpheum Theatre on 19

November 1959. With rock 'n' roll already into its stride, there was not much of an audience in those days for genuinely new operetta, and, sure enough, this show turned out to be an elaborate spoof of the real thing. Sub titled A New Musical About An Old Operetta, *Little Mary Sunshine* unmercifully sends up prime examples of the genre such as *Rose Marie* and *Naughty Marietta*. Set in the upper reaches of the Colorado Rockies, Rick Besoyan's book tells the hot-blooded story of Mary Potts (Eileen Brennan), the hostess of the local hostelry, who makes it quite clear to the Rangers' Captain Big Jim Warrington (William Graham), that there is always plenty of room at her inn, for him. However, Big Jim is more interested in capturing the despicable Indian, Yellow Feather (Ray James), who has indicated on more than one occasion that he would like to get Mary into his wigwam. Fortunately for our heroine, she and Big Jim give out with the 'Colorado Love Call', which proves to have more of a deterrent effect on amorous, ambitious Indians than a whole company of cavalry. The sub-plot involves another young loving couple Nancy Twinkle (Elmarie Wendel) and Corporal Billy Jester (John McMartin), who promise to be true to each other 'Once In A Blue Moon'. The remainder of Rick Besoyan's score was in that same mocking vein, and included 'Look For Sky Of Blue', 'Playing Croquet', 'Tell A Handsome Stranger', 'Every Little

Nothing', 'Naughty Naughty, Nancy', and 'Such A Merry Party', and 'In Izzenschnooken On The Lovely Ezzenzook Zee', which is 'authentically' rendered by a visiting opera star of yesterday (or the day before), Mme. Ernestine Von Liebedich (Elizabeth Parrish). It all must have touched the right nerve, because *Little Mary Sunshine* became one of the longest-running Off Broadway musicals ever, during its run of 1,143 performances. Londoners did not seem to see the joke, and, despite the presence in the cast of comedy stalwarts such as Patricia Routledge and Bernard Cribbins, the show folded there after five weeks.

Little Me

Conceived as a vehicle for one of US television's favourite performers, Sid Caesar, the versatile comedian needed all his skills and ingenuity to cope with a scenario that called upon him to play seven different characters. The leading female role, on the other hand, is shared by two different actresses. *Little Me* opened at the Lunt-Fontanne Theatre in New York on 17 November 1962. Neil Simon's book, which was based on the play by Patrick Dennis, opens with the older Belle Poitrine (Nancy Andrews), 'queen of the silver screen', dictating her memoirs ('The Truth'). The young, ambitious Belle Schlumpfort (Virginia Martin) then relives the scenes

Sid Caesar (*Little Me*)

Glynis Johns (*A Little Night Music*)

as they actually occurred, and in each one she is accompanied by a male admirer played by Caesar. These range from her first love, the snobby 16-years-old Noble Eggleston, from whom she gets a taste for the high-life ('Rich Kids Rag') and yearns to be 'On The Other Side Of The Tracks', to the geriatric banker Amos Pinchley, who is surely a good person 'Deep Down Inside', the 'great French entertainer', Val du Val, ('Boom-Boom'), her temporary husband, Fred Poitrine a World War I sad soldier who yearns for a 'Real Live Girl', a dominating film director, ('Poor Little Hollywood Star'), and Prince Cherney 'the expiring regent of Rosenzweig' ('Goodbye'). George Musgrove, a childhood admire of Belle's, and now a big-time gambler, comes back into her life at one point and tries to seduce her with the sensuous 'I've Got Your Number'. This was the only major male role not played by Sid Caesar. At the end, the two Belles get together to try and make sense of it all and unite in 'Little Me'. The older Belle is then left alone, seated in her Beverly Hill mansion, realising that she has achieved her aims of 'wealth, culture and social position' - but not, unfortunately, Noble Eggleston. Cy Coleman and Carolyn Leigh's score was, in turn, witty and tender, especially in numbers such as 'Real Live Girl' ('Speaking of miracles, this must be it/Just when I started to learn how to knit/I'm all in stitches from finding what riches a waltz, can reveal/With a real, live girl'), and 'The Other Side Of The Tracks', which became popular through a recording by Tony Bennett. Bob Fosse won a Tony Award for the choreography, and the Broadway run of only 257 performances was followed by a much better reception in London, where the show stayed at the Cambridge Theatre for 10 months. It proved to be a personal triumph for Bruce Forsyth, the young comedian and television compere. In 1982, a Broadway revival, starring James Coco and Victor Garber, lasted for only a month, but, two years later, London audiences approved of the show again, with Russ Abbott, Lynda Baron, and Sheila White.

Little Night Music, A

Based upon an Ingmar Bergman film, A Little Night Music opened at the Shubert Theatre in New York on 25 February 1973. Set in Sweden at the turn of the century, the story follows the love lives of Frederick Egerman and Desiree, his former mistress, Egerman's new young wife and his son, and Desiree's other lover and his wife. With a strong cast which included Len Cariou, Glynis Johns and Hermione Gingold, the show was elegantly staged and filled with delightful, waltz-time tunes by Stephen Sondheim. The songs included 'Liaisons', 'The Miller's Son', 'Night Waltz', 'Every Day A Little Death', 'Remember?', 'It Would Have Been Wonderful', 'You Must Meet My Wife', and 'The Glamorous Life', but the hit of the show,

sung by Johns, was 'Send In The Clowns'. A Little Night Music ran for 601 performances and won Tony Awards for best musical, score, book (Hugh Wheeler), actress (Johns), supporting actress (Patricia Elliot), and costumes (Florence Klotz). The show was staged in London in 1975 with a production generally held to be superior to the New York version. Gingold reprised her role as the aged dowager who manipulates happy endings for the various love affairs, and continued to play the part in Los Angeles (1991) and the UK provinces (1992). A 1989 West End production starred Susan Hampshire, Lila Kedrova, Peter McEnery, Eric Flynn, and Dorothy Tutin. Although dozens of famous singers have recorded 'Send In The Clowns', (notably Judy Collins), few have ever managed to match the deeply moving interpretation brought to it by Johns in the original production. A 1978 film version, which starred Elizabeth Taylor, fortunately vanished from public gaze before it could do lasting harm to Sondheim's reputation.

Little Shop Of Horrors

After making its debut at the tiny WPA Theatre in New York, Little Shop Of Horrors moved to the Orpheum Theatre on the Lower East Side on 27 July 1982. The book, by Howard Ashman, was based on Charles Griffith's screenplay for the 1960 spoof of the horror movie genre, which had become a cult classic. Hardly the usual Broadway - or Off-Broadway - fare, the grisly tale tells of Seymour Krelbourn (Lee Wilkof), an assistant at Mushnick's florist shop on Skid Row, who decides to boost sales by producing a strange houseplant. He names it Audrey II, because of his love for sales assistant Audrey (Ellen Green), and finds that it grow faster if it is fed with a few drops of blood - and subsequently, human flesh. Things rapidly get out of hand as the monster - and the business - thrives, eventually devouring just about everything and everyone in sight. The amusing and imaginative score by Ashman and composer Alan Menken had some 'good rock in the Phil Spector Wall of Sound idiom', and included 'Grow For Me', 'Suddenly Seymour', 'Skid Row', 'Somewhere That's Green', and 'Little Shop Of Horrors'. The show's bizarre humour caught on in a big way, as Audrey II and Little Shop Of Horrors became a sort of phenomenon. It continued to amaze and delight Off Broadway audiences for 2,209 performances, and was awarded the New York Drama Critics Circle Award for best musical. The 1984 London production, which ran for over a year, also received the Evening Standard prize for outstanding musical. Ellen Green reprised her role in London, and for the 1986 film version which also starred Rick Moranis, Vincent Gardenia and Steve Martin.

Little Show, The

Composer Arthur Schwartz and lyricist Howard Dietz, one of the top Broadway songwriting teams of the 30s, got together for the first time to write several songs for this smart, classy revue which opened at the Music Box Theatre on 30 April 1929. Dietz also wrote most of the sketches, along with George S. Kaufman and others. He and Schwartz contributed 'I've Made A Habit Of You', 'Hammacher-Schlemmer, I Love You', and 'I Guess I'll Have To Change My Plan', ('I should have realized there'd be another man/Why did I buy those blue pajamas/Before the big affair began?'), which, for obvious reasons became known as 'The Blue Pajama Song', and, while never becoming a big hit, was one of the songwriters' hardy standards. It was very effectively sung by a couple of song-and-dance-men, Fred Astaire and Jack Buchanan in the film of The Band Wagon in 1953. It was introduced in The Little Show by Clifton Webb, who finally became recognized as a star in this revue, as did the resident funny man, 'dead-pan' Fred Allen. The third leading player, Libby Holman, had 'Can't We Be Friends?' (written by Kay Swift and Paul James - a pseudonym for her husband, James Warburg), which was quite a jolly little song for many years until Frank Sinatra turned it into a lonely ballad on his In The Wee Small Hours. Holman also sang the show's big hit, 'Moanin' Low', which had music and lyric by Ralph Rainger and Dietz. One of the other songs, 'A Little Hut In Hoboken', was one of a the few numbers written by Herman Hupfield in his career; two years later he produced another, 'As Time Goes By', which was later immortalised in the film, Casablanca. The Little Show ran for 321 performances. Without Holman, Webb, and Allen neither of the sequels did well. The Second Little Show (1929), again had some songs by Schwartz and Dietz ('You're The Sunshine', 'What A Case I've Got On You', and 'Lucky Seven') and one by Hupfield ('Sing Something Simple'), but only ran for 63 performances; and The Third Little Show (1930), starred Beatrice Lillie who introduced Noël Coward's 'Mad Dogs And Englishmen' to the American public. The show also contained another rare Hupfield number, 'When Yuba Plays The Rhumba On His Tuba', and stayed at Music Box Theatre for four months.

Lloyd Webber, Andrew

b. 22 March 1948, London, England. The Sir Arthur Sullivan of the rock age was born to a Royal College of Music professor and a piano teacher. His inbred musical strength manifested itself in a command of piano, violin and French horn by the time he graduated from Magdalen College, Oxford where he penned The Likes Of Us with lyricist (and law student) Tim Rice. As well as his liking for such modern composers as Hindemith, Ligeti and Penderecki, this first musical also betrayed a captivation with pop music that surfaced even more when he and Rice collaborated in 1967 on Joseph And The Amazing Technicolor Dreamcoat, a liberal adaptation of the scriptures. Mixing elements of psychedelia, country and French chanson, it was first performed at a London school in 1968 before reaching a more adult audience, via fringe events, the West End theatre (staring Paul Jones, Jess Conrad and Maynard Williams), an album and, in 1972, national television.

In the early 70s, Lloyd Webber strayed from the stage, writing the music scores for two British films, Gumshoe and The Odessa File. His next major project with Rice was the audacious Jesus Christ Superstar which provoked much protest from religious groups. Such fuss assisted million-plus sales of its double album which earned a Grammy Award. Among the studio cast were guest vocalists Michael d'Abo, Yvonne Elliman, Ian Gillan and Paul Raven (later Gary Glitter), accompanied by a symphony orchestra under the baton of André Previn - as well as members of Quatermass and the Grease Band. Issued well before its New York opening in 1971, the tunes were already familiar to an audience that took to their seats night after night as the show ran and ran. It attracted seven Tony Awards, including best score and best musical. The show also spawned a less than successful film version in 1976.

After the failure of Jeeves in 1974 (with Alan Ayckbourn replacing Rice) Lloyd Webber returned to form with Evita, an approximate biography of Eva Peron, self-styled 'political leader' of Argentina. It was preceded by high chart placings for its album's much-covered singles, most notably Julie Covington's 'Don't Cry For Me Argentina' and 'Oh! What A Circus' from David Essex. Evita was still on Broadway in 1981 when Cats, based on T.S. Eliot's Old Possum's Book Of Practical Cats, emerged as Lloyd Webber's most commercially satisfying work so far. It was also the composer's second musical without Rice, and included what is arguably his best-known song, 'Memory', with words by Eliot and the show's director, Trevor Nunn. Elaine Paige, previously the star of Evita, and substituting for the injured Judi Dench in the feline role of Grizabella, took the song into the UK Top 10. Subsequently, it became popular for Barbra Streisand, amongst others. With Song And Dance (1982), which consisted of an earlier piece Tell Me On Sunday (lyrics by Don Black) and Variations, composed on a theme by Paganini for his cellist brother, Julian, Lloyd Webber became the only theatrical composer to have three works performed simultaneously in both the West End and Broadway. Two items from Song And Dance, 'Take That Look Off Your Face' and 'Tell Me On Sunday' became hit singles for one of its stars, Marti Webb. Underwritten

Andrew Lloyd Webber with Sarah Brightman

by his Really Useful conglomerate, it was joined two years later by *Starlight Express* (lyrics by Richard Stilgoe), a train epic with music which was nicknamed 'Squeals On Wheels' because the cast dashed around on roller skates pretending to be locomotives. Diversifying into production, Lloyd Webber presented the 1983 comedy *Daisy Pulls It Off*, followed by *The Hired Man*, *Lend Me A Tenor* and Richard Rodgers and Lorenz Hart's *On Your Toes* at London's Palace Theatre - of which he had become the new owner.

Like Sullivan before him, Lloyd Webber indulged more personal if lucrative artistic whims in such as *Requeim*, written for his father, which, along with *Variations*, became a best-selling album. A later set, *Premiere Collection*, went triple platinum. A spin-off from *Requiem*, 'Pie Jesu' (1985), was a hit single for Paul Miles-Kinston and Sarah Brightman, the composer's second wife. She made the UK Top 10 again the following year, duetting with Steve Harley on the title theme from Lloyd Webber's *The Phantom Of The Opera* (adapted from the Gaston Lerous novel), and later with Cliff Richard with 'All I Ask Of You'. The original 'Phantom', Michael Crawford, had great success with his recording of 'The Music Of The Night'. Controversy followed with Lloyd Webber's battle to ensure that Brightman re-created

her role in the Broadway version in 1988. His US investors capitulated, reasoning that future Lloyd Webber creations were guaranteed box office smashes before their very conception. Ironically, *Aspects Of Love* (lyrics by Charles Hart and Stilgoe), also starring Brightman (by now Lloyd Webber's ex-wife), was rated as one of the failures (it did not recoup its investment) of the 1990/1 Broadway season, although it ran for over 300 performances. In London, the show, which closed in 1992 after a three year run, launched the career of Michael Ball, who had a UK number 2 with its big number, 'Love Changes Everything'. In April 1992, Lloyd Webber intervened in the Tate Gallery's attempt to purchase a Canaletto painting. Anxious, that it should remain in Britain, he bought the picture for £10 million. He was reported to have commented: 'I'll have to write another musical before I do this again'. So he did. *Sunset Boulevard*, a stage production of Billy Wilder's 1950 Hollywood classic, with Lloyd Webber's music, a book and lyrics by Don Black and Christopher Hampton, and starring Patti LuPone as Norma Desmond, opened in London on 12 July 1993 and had its American premier in Los Angeles five months later. By then, Lloyd Webber's name had topped the list of the 100 Most Powerful People In The American Theatre compiled by *Theatre Week* magazine. His knighthood was awarded for his services to the theatre, not only in the US and UK, but throughout the world - at any one time there are dozens of his productions touring, and resident in main cities. In 1992, *Cats*, complete with its billing, 'Now And Forever', celebrated 10 years on Broadway, and, together with *Starlight Express* and *Jesus Christ Superstar*, gave Lloyd Webber the three longest-running musicals in British theatre history for a time, before the latter show was overtaken by *Les Misérables* in January 1994. *Jesus Christ Superstar* celebrated its 20th anniversary in 1992 with a UK concert tour. Other Lloyd Webber highlights of that year included a series of concerts entitled *The Music Of Andrew Lloyd Webber* (special guest star Michael Crawford); a smash hit revival of *Joseph And The Amazing Technicolor Dreamcoat* at the London Palladium; and the recording, by Sarah Brightman and José Carreras, of his Barcelona Olympic Games anthem 'Friends For Life' ('Amigos Para Siempre'). Further reading: *Andrew Lloyd Webber*, G. McKnight. *Fanfare: The Unauthorized Biography Of Andrew Lloyd Webber*, J. Mantle. *Andrew Lloyd Webber: His Life And Works*, M. Walsh.

Lock Up Your Daughters

This show, which was the first to be presented at the new Mermaid Theatre in the City of London on 28 May 1959, was appropriately enough the brainchild of the Mermaid's founder, Bernard (later, Sir Bernard) Miles. His adaptation of Henry Fielding's *Rape Upon Rape*, was an extremely bawdy tale in which a gentle maiden, Hilaret (Stephanie Voss), and her would-be rapist, Ramble (Frederick Jaeger), appear before the lecherous Justice Squeezum (Richard Wordsworth). Squeezum's efforts to inflict his own individual brand of custodial sentence on Hilaret lead to highly complicated manoeuvres which involve the far-from-innocent Mrs Squeezum (Hy Hazel), and result in the Justice himself going to prison. The object of his affections is then reunited with her true love, Captain Constant (Terence Cooper). The score, by two young newcomers, composer Laurie Johnson and lyricist Lionel Bart (Bart's *Fings Ain't Wot They Used T'Be* was just starting out at Stratford) complemented perfectly the lusty outrages of the story, in songs such as 'Lock Up Your Daughters' ('Here come a rake!'), 'When Does The Ravishing Begin?', 'Red Wine And A Wench', and 'I'll Be There'. Hilaret *almost* seduces Squeezum 'On A Sunny Sunday Morning', and the other delights included 'Lovely Lover', 'Kind Fate', 'A Proper Man', 'It Must Be True', ''Tis Plain To See', and 'Mr. Jones'. The show ran for 330 performances, and subsequently had its US premiere in New Haven in April 1960. *Lock Up Your Daughters* returned to the Mermaid two years later before transferring to the Her Majesty's theatre in the West

End for a stay of some 16 months, and called in at the Mermaid again in 1969 for just a brief stay. Another American production, with 50s film star, Carleton Carpenter as Squeezum, was presented at the Goodspeed Opera House in 1982.

Loesser, Frank

b. Henry Frank Loesser, 29 June 1910, New York City, New York, USA, 28 July 1969. Loesser was a leading songwriter for the stage and films, from the 30s until the 60s. Initially, he wrote only lyrics, but later provided the music and lyrics, and sometimes co-produced through his Frank Productions. Born into a musical family, (his father was a music teacher, and his brother a music critic and pianist), Loesser declined a formal musical education, and trained himself. During the Depression years of the early 30s, following a brief spell at City College, New York, Loesser worked in a variety of jobs including city editor for a local newspaper, a jewellery salesman, and a waiter. His first published song, written with William Schuman in 1931, was 'In Love With a Memory Of You'. Loesser also wrote for vaudeville performers and played piano in nightclubs around New York's 52nd Street. In 1936, he contributed some lyrics to *The Illustrators Show*, with music by Irving Actman, including 'Bang-The Bell Rang!' and 'If You Didn't Love Me'; but the show closed after only five Broadway performances.
In 1937, Loesser went to Hollywood and spent the next few years writing lyrics for movies such as *Cocoanut Grove* ('Says My Heart'), *College Swing* ('Moments Like This' and 'How'dja Like To Make Love To Me?'), *Sing You Sinners* (Bing Crosby singing 'Small Fry'), *Thanks For The Memory* (Bob Hope and Shirley Ross singing 'Two Sleepy People'), *Hurricane* (Dorothy Lamour singing 'Moon Over Manakoora'), *Man About Town* ('Fidgity Joe' and 'Strange Enchantment'), *Some Like It Hot* (1939 film starring Bob Hope and Shirley Ross singing 'The Lady's In Love With You'), *Destry Rides Again* (Marlene Dietrich with a memorable version of 'See What The Boys In The Backroom Will Have'), *Dancing On A Dime* ('I Hear Music'), *Las Vegas Nights* ('Dolores'), *Kiss The Boys Goodbye* ('I'll Never Let A Day Pass By', 'Sand In My Shoes' and the title song), *Sweater Girl* ('I Don't Want To Walk Without You' and 'I Said No'), *Forest Rangers* ('Jingle Jangle Jingle'), *Happy-Go-Lucky* ('Let's Get Lost' and ''Murder' She Says'), *Seven Days Leave* ('Can't Get Out Of This Mood') and *Thank Your Lucky Stars* (Bette Davis singing one of Loesser's most amusing lyrics, which included the couplet: 'I either get a fossil, or an adolescent pup/I either have to hold him off, or have to hold him up!'). These songs were written in collaboration with composers: Burton Lane, Hoagy Carmichael, Alfred Newman, Matty Malneck,

Frederick Hollander, Louis Alter, Victor Schertzinger, Jule Styne, Joseph Lilley, Jimmy McHugh and Arthur Schwartz.

The first song for which Loesser wrote both music and lyrics is said to be 'Praise The Lord And Pass The Ammunition', and when he left Hollywood for military service during World War II he added some more service songs to his catalogue, including 'First Class Private Mary Brown', 'The Ballad Of Rodger Young', 'What Do You Do In The Infantry?' and 'Salute To The Army Service Forces'. He also continued to write for films such as *Christmas Holiday* (1944), 'Spring Will Be A Little Late This Year') and *The Perils Of Pauline* (1947), the bio-pic of silent movie-queen Pearl White, with Loesser's songs, 'Poppa Don't Preach To Me' and 'I Wish I Didn't Love You So', which was nominated for an Academy Award. Loesser finally received his Oscar in 1949 for 'Baby It's Cold Outside', from the Esther Williams/Red Skelton movie, *Neptune's Daughter*. In 1948, Loesser wrote 'On A Slow Boat To China', which became a hit for several US artists including Kay Kyser, Freddy Martin, Eddy Howard and Benny Goodman. In the same year he again turned his attention to the Broadway stage, writing the score for a musical adaptation of Brandon Thomas's classic English farce, *Charley's Aunt*. *Where's Charley?*, starring Ray Bolger, included the songs, 'My Darling, My Darling', 'Once In Love With Amy', 'The New Ashmoleon Marching Society And Student Conservatory Band' and 'Make A Miracle'. The show ran for a creditable 792 performances.

Far more successful, two years later, was *Guys And Dolls*, a musical setting of a Damon Runyan fable, starring Robert Alda, Vivian Blaine, Sam Levene, Isabel Bigley and Stubby Kaye. It ran for 1,200 performances, and is considered to be Loesser's masterpiece. As with *Where's Charley?*, he was now writing both music and lyrics, and the show is such a legend that it is worth listing all the principal songs; they were 'Fugue For Tinhorns', 'The Oldest Established', 'I'll Know', 'A Bushel And A Peck', 'Adelaide's Lament', 'Guys And Dolls', 'If I Were A Bell', 'My Time Of Day', 'I've Never Been In Love Before', 'Take Back Your Mink', 'More I Cannot Wish You', 'Luck Be A Lady', 'Sue Me', 'Sit Down, You're Rockin' The Boat' and 'Marry The Man Today'. The original cast album is still available in the 90s, and among the other associated issues were an all-black cast album, released on the Motown label, and *Guys And Dolls: The Kirby Stone Four*. A film adaptation of *Guys And Dolls* was released in 1955, starring Frank Sinatra, Marlon Brando, Jean Simmons, and Vivian Blaine. The movie version left out some of the original songs, and replaced them with 'A Woman In Love' and 'Adelaide'. In 1952, *Where's Charley?* was released on film, and the same year saw a

movie of the *Hans Christian Andersen* fairy tale, starring Danny Kaye in the title role, and a Loesser score which included 'Wonderful Copenhagen', 'No Two People', 'Anywhere I Wander', 'Inchworm' and 'Thumbelina'. The latter song was nominated for an Oscar, but was beaten by Dmitri Tiomkin and Ned Washington's 'High Noon'.

Loesser's next Broadway project was *The Most Happy Fella*, for which he also wrote the libretto. The show was adapted from the original story, *They Knew What They Wanted*, by Sidney Howard, which told the tale of an elderly Italian winegrower living in California, who falls in love at first sight with a waitress. Loesser created what has been called 'one of the most ambitiously operatic works ever written for the Broadway musical theatre'. Arias such as 'Rosabella' and 'My Heart Is So Full Of You' are contrasted with more familiar Broadway fare such as 'Standing On the Corner', 'Big D' and 'Happy To Make Your Acquaintance'. The show ran for 676 performances, far more than Loesser's 1960 production of the folksy *Greenwillow*, which closed after 95. It starred Anthony Perkins in his first musical, and contained a religious hymn, the baptism of a cow, and wistful ballads such as 'Faraway Boy' and 'Walking Away Whistling', along with 'Never Will I Marry' and 'Summertime Love', both sung by Perkins. A 3-album set, was issued, containing the complete score. In terms of the number of performances, (1,417), Loesser's last Broadway show, which opened in 1961, was his most successful. *How To Succeed In Business Without Really Trying* was a satire on big business which starred Robert Morse as the aspiring executive, J. Pierpont Finch, and Rudy Vallée as his stuffy boss, J.B. Biggley. The songs which, most critics agreed, fitted the plot completely, included 'The Company Way', 'A Secretary Is Not A Toy', 'Grand Old Ivy', 'Been A Long Day', 'I Believe In You' and 'Brotherhood Of Man'. The show became one of the select band of American musicals to be awarded a Pulitzer Prize; a film version was released in 1967. Loesser died of lung cancer on 28 July 1969, with cigarettes by his side. A life-long smoker, with a contentious, volatile temperament, he is regarded as one of the most original, innovative men of the musical theatre. In 1992, a major revival of *Guys And Dolls* was mounted on Broadway.

Further reading: *A Most Remarkable Fella*, Susan Loesser.

Loewe, Frederick

b. 10 June 1901, Vienna, Austria, d. 14 February 1988. Born into a musical family, (his father was a professional singer) Loewe studied piano as a child, appearing with the Berlin Symphony Orchestra in 1917. In 1924, he visited the USA, but failed to make an impact upon the local classical music scene.

Instead, he eked out a living playing piano in restaurants and bars, then roamed throughout the USA, tackling a variety of jobs, including prospecting and cowpunching. As a young teenager he had written songs and he resumed this activity in New York in the early 30s. His style was closely related to that popular in his birthplace and proved generally unsuccessful in his new homeland. In 1942, he formed a musical partnership with Alan Jay Lerner with whom he wrote songs for a succession of shows with results which varied between flops and modest successes. In 1947, the collaborators had their first major hit with *Brigadoon*, from which came 'The Heather On The Hill', 'From This Day On' and 'Almost Like Being In Love'. The association was renewed in 1951 with *Paint Your Wagon* with such songs as 'They Call The Wind Maria', 'I Talk To The Trees' and 'Wand'rin' Star'. In 1956, the team had their major success with *My Fair Lady*, which ran on Broadway for 2,717 performances. The score included such lasting favourites as 'On The Street Where You Live', 'Get Me To The Church On Time', 'With A Little Bit Of Luck', 'Wouldn't It Be Loverly?', 'The Rain In Spain', 'Why Can't The English?', 'I'm An Ordinary Man' and 'I Could Have Danced All Night'. After the huge success of *My Fair Lady* the team was invited to write a musical film and while Lerner was keen, Loewe was reluctant. In the end he agreed and the result, *Gigi* (1958) was one of the final flourishes of the old-style Hollywood musical. Among the songs from the film were 'Thank Heaven For Little Girls', 'I'm Glad I'm Not Young Anymore', 'I Remember It Well' and the title song. After being hospitalized with heart trouble, Loewe returned to his collaboration with Lerner in a new Broadway show, *Camelot*, which opened in 1960. Although the show's preproduction was marred with problems, the result was another success with such outstanding songs as 'If Ever I Would Leave You' and 'How To Handle A Woman'. This show proved to be the last important collaboration for Loewe and Lerner. They teamed up again in 1973 with a stage production of *Gigi* and the following year made their swan song with *The Little Prince*. Loewe died in February 1988.

London Calling!

The name 'Noël Coward' went up in West End lights for the first time when this André Charlot revue opened at the Duke of York's Theatre on 4 September 1923. Coward also co-wrote the book, with Ronald Jeans, and the music and lyrics with Philip Braham. Also in the cast was Coward's favourite leading lady, Gertrude Lawrence, along with Maisie Gay, Eileen Molyneux, and comedian Tubby Edlin. Fred Astaire, who was appearing with his sister Adele in *Stop Flirting* at the Shaftesbury Theatre,

arranged some of the dances. The songs included 'What Love Means To Girls Like Me', 'Carrie', 'Life In The Old Girl Yet', 'Sentiment', and 'Other Girls'. Gertrude Lawrence introduced one of Coward's most enduring numbers, 'Parisian Pierrot', and together they sang 'You Were Meant For Me', another future standard, written by Arthur Freed and Nacio Herb Brown. The show was a great success until Charlot decided to transfer Gertrude Lawrence and several other members of the company to the Broadway production of *André Charlot's London Revue Of 1924* which opened in January. Joyce Barbour replaced Lawrence, but *London Calling!* eventually ran out of steam.

Looking Through A Glass Onion

Subtitled 'John Lennon In Word And Music', this one-man show consisted of 'a series of wry monologues spliced with the singer's songs, which attempted to unearth the man beneath the mythology'. It was written by the Australian-based, British-born actor John Waters, and toured successfully for two years in Australia before opening at the 600-seater newly-refurbished subterranean Criterion Theatre in London on 18 October 1993. Waters himself starred in the piece, backed by a band which included Stewart D'Arrietta on keyboards and Hamish Stewart on drums. The title image, from the song 'Glass Onion', 'seems to promise a peeling away of the layers of a crystal ball', but what actually transpires is as non-chronological narrative framework around the songs, beginning at the end with Lennon at the door of his New York apartment block watching an autograph hound coming towards him. Waters' 'exaggerated Liverpudlian twang' in the spoken passages, supplemented by a 'good bluesy voice' for the classic Beatles and later, subtler songs, brought him some critical appreciation, but the concept as a whole was generally considered to be 'charmless and depressing - a fraction of the real thing'. Reportedly capitalised at £160,000 and expected to make a profit after three months, closure on 1 January 1994 presumably resulted in a small loss.

Lost In The Stars

Following their collaboration on *Knickerbocker Holiday* in 1938, composer Kurt Weill and librettist and lyricist Maxwell Anderson renewed their association more than a decade later for this show which opened at the Music Box Theatre in New York on 30 October 1949. It was a musical adaptation of Alan Paton's novel, *Cry, The Beloved Country*, which was set in apartheid South Africa, and told the powerful story of a black Anglican minister, Stephen Kumalo (Todd Duncan), whose son, Absalom (Julian Mayfield), is sentenced to hang after accidentally killing a young white man - a liberal - during an attempted robbery in Johannesburg. A few minutes before Absalom is due to die, the victim's father, James Jarvis (Leslie Banks), who is a supporter of apartheid, calls at Stephen Kumalo's house, and the two men unite in their grief. The music score reflected the show's brooding, tragic mood, and included "Thousands Of Miles', 'Cry, The Beloved Country', 'The Hills Of Ixipo', 'Train To Johannesburg', 'Stay Well', 'The Little Gray House', 'Trouble Man', 'Big Mole', 'A Bird Of Passage', 'The Wild Justice, 'Who Will Buy', and the haunting ballad, 'Lost In The Stars', which was sung in the piece by Todd Duncan, and has been recorded many times over the years by artists such as Tony Bennett, Vic Damone, Dick Haymes, Frank Sinatra, Lotte Lenya, and Singers Unlimited. It was to be Kurt Weill's last Broadway show - he died during the run of 273 performances, on 3 April 1950. Eight years later, *Lost In The Stars* entered the repertory of the New York City Opera, and, in 1972, it returned to Broadway for a month, starring Brock Peters as Stephen Kumalo. He also appeared in the 1974 film version, along with Melba Moore, Raymond St. Jacques, Clifton Davis, and Paula Kelly. The Long Wharf Theatre, New Haven, Connecticut, presented a 'chamber version' of the show in 1986, and the work received its UK professional premiere in a production by the New Sussex Opera at the Gardner Centre, Brighton, in 1991. Three years later, a new musical adaptation of Alan Paton's novel, by Frank Galati, was presented by the Goodman Theatre in Chicago. It used the book's title, *Cry, The Beloved Country*, and re-arranged the original score to such an extent that the Kurt Weill Foundation demanded that an apology be included in the showbill. Also in 1993, a 'fine new recording' of the score was issued, with a cast which included Arthur Woodley, Gregory Hopkins, Cynthia Clarey, Reginald Pindell, and Carol Woods, who had impressed in recent years in *Blues In The Night* and *The Goodbye Girl*.

Louisiana Purchase

This show, which made its debut at the Imperial Theatre in New York on 28 May 1940, was Irving Berlin's first Broadway score since his successful revue, *As Thousands Cheer*, which had brightened up America's gradual emergence from the Depression in 1933. In the intervening years, the prolific songwriter had scored several Hollywood films, including the classic Fred Astaire-Ginger Rogers musicals, *Top Hat*, *Follow The Fleet*, and *Carefree*. Morrie Riskin's humorous and satirical book was based on a story by B.G. 'Buddy' De Sylva, and was said to have been influenced by a recent political scandal involving Huey Long, a well-known Louisiana politician. The upstanding and incorruptible Senator Oliver P. Loganberry (Victor Moore), travels to New Orleans in an effort to disentangle the somewhat unconventional business methods practised by the Louisiana Purchase Company. The firm's lawyer, Jim Taylor (William Gaxton), tries to deflect the heat by putting the Senator in a series of compromising situations with the titillating trio of Marina Van Linden (Vera Zorina), Mme. Boredelaise (Irene Bordoni), and Beatrice (Carol Bruce). Happily, Loganberry emerges with his honour intact. As usual, Berlin's score complemented the story perfectly. Two of the numbers, 'It's A Lovely Day Tomorrow', sung by Bordini, and 'You're Lonely And I'm Lonely', which served as a duet for Moore and Zorina, became quite popular - the latter for Tommy Dorsey's Orchestra, with a vocal by the young Frank Sinatra. Carol Bruce made a memorable musical comedy debut, and sang the chirpy title song. The rest of the score included 'Outside Of That I Love You', 'Latins Know How', 'The Lord Done Fixed Up My Soul', 'Fools Fall In Love', 'What Chance Have I?', and 'You Can't Brush Me Off'. Chorus members, Hugh Martin and Ralph Blane, later went on to write the scores for *Best Foot Forward* on Broadway, and *Meet Me In St. Louis* in Hollywood. The presence of the familiar team of Gaxton and Moore ensured that *Louisiana Purchase* had a lot of laughs, and a successful run of 444 performances.

Love Life

A most unusual show, with music by Kurt Weill, and a book and lyrics by Alan Jay Lerner, *Love Life* opened at the 46th Street Theatre in New York on 7 October 1948 - just 18 months after *Brigadoon*, the author's first big Broadway success with Frederick Loewe. Contrasting sharply with *Kiss Me, Kate*, and *South Pacific*, which both made their debut in the same season, this unconventional show deals with a fantasy situation in which a married couple, Sam and Susan Cooper (Nanette Fabray and Ray Middleton) with their two children, reflect on their lives from the year 1791 until the present day - initially a happy, satisfying relationship, which declines into a pointless cynical arrangement - but without the protagonists aging at all. The individual scenes are linked by vaudeville acts, and no attempt is made to integrate the songs into the plot, such as it is - rather, they provide a commentary on the action that is taking place on the stage. Fabray had 'Green-Up Time' and 'Here I'll Stay' (which became a hit for Jo Stafford), and she won the 1949 Tony Award for best actress in a musical. The rest of the score included 'Progress', 'Economics', 'Mr. Right', and 'I Remember It Well', a title that Lerner remembered well enough to use it again in the Oscar-winning film, *Gigi*, in 1958. Considering the style and tone of the piece, a run of 252 performances seems to have been a reasonable outcome.

Patti LuPone

Lupino, Stanley
(see **Lane, Lupino**)

LuPone, Patti
b. 21 April 1949, Northport, New York, USA. An actress and singer who left several well-known Hollywood and Broadway stars feeling bitterly disappointed and distraught when she won the role of Norma Desmond in Andrew Lloyd Webber's 1993 London production of *Sunset Boulevard*. LuPone made her stage debut, tap dancing, at the age of four, and later took dancing classes with Martha Graham. She trained for the stage at the Juilliard School where she met the actor Kevin Kline. A six-year personal relationship was supplemented by a joint association with John Housman's Actor's Company, which gave them both invaluable experience in the straight theatre, and resulted in their appearance together – as the bride and bridegroom – in a short-lived Broadway musical, *The Robber Bridegroom* (1975). After several other flops, including *The Baker's Wife* (1976) and *Working* (78), LuPone won Tony and Drama Desk Awards for her performance in the leading role of *Evita* (1979) on Broadway, and stayed with the show 'until the strain of being obnoxious and dying from cancer every night got too much'. She returned to serious theatre in the provinces and had an occasionally effective part in films such as *1941* and *Witness*. In 1985 LuPone moved to London and appeared firstly in *The Cradle Will Rock*. In the same year, she became the first American actress and singer to gain a principal role with the Royal Shakespeare Company, in the the hit musical, *Les Misérable*. The names of both shows appeared on her 1985 Olivier Award. In complete contrast to those two roles, in 1986 she played Lady Bird Johnson in a US mini-series based on the ex-President's life, and, a year later, was back on Broadway in an acclaimed revival of *Anything Goes*. In the late 80s and early 90s LuPone had a major role in the popular US situation comedy, *Life Goes On*, and experienced some difficulty breaking free from her contract when the call came from Lloyd Webber. She first played Norma Desmond at the composer's Sydmonton Festival in the summer of 1992. Declining the use of the book on stage, she learnt the part and gave what was regarded as a 'sensational' performance. Soon afterwards it became obvious that she had stolen the role-of-a-lifetime from 'under the noses' of bigger names such as Meryl Streep, Angela Lansbury, Liza Minnelli, and Julie Andrews. *Sunset Boulevard* opened in the West End in July 1993, and LuPone was also contracted for the 1994 Broadway production.
Selected album: *Patti LuPone Live* (1993, 2-CD), and Original Cast recordings.

Lynne, Gillian
b. 1929, Bromley, Kent, England. An internationally acclaimed director and choreographer with over 40 London and Broadway shows to her credit. Gillian Lynne was originally a dancer and made her stage debut with the Sadlers Wells Ballet in 1944, remaining with the company for seven years, during which time she played several leading roles. During the 50s she danced many times at the London Palladium, and played Claudine in *Can-Can* at the Coliseum. In 1960 she appeared in John Cranko's *New Cranks* at the Lyric, Hammersmith, and choreographed her first ballet, *Owl And The Pussycat*, for the Western Theatre Ballet. Since that time Lynne has worked as a choreographer and/or director on musical productions such as *The Roar Of The Greasepaint - The Smell Of The Crowd*, *The Match Girls*, *Pickwick*, *How Now Dow Jones*, *Tonight At Eight*, *Songbook*, *Tomfoolery*, *Once Upon A Time*, *My Fair Lady*, *Cabaret*, *Cats*, and *The Phantom Of The Opera*. Her work on *Cats* earned her an Olivier Award, and the Austrian Government's Order of Merit for a production of the show which was presented in Vienna and subsequently played in East Berlin and Moscow. Her Paris production won the prestigious Moliére Award. She has also worked extensively for the Royal Shakespeare Company, the Royal Opera House, Covent Garden, and on more than 10 films including *Half A Sixpence*, *Man Of La Mancha*, and *Yentl*. Her television credits include *The Muppet Show* series, her own creation, *The Fool On The Hill*, which was based on the Beatles' music, and her BAFTA award-winning ballet *A Simple Man*. In 1993, as well as supervising and working on other productions world-wide, she re-staged and choreographed a UK revival of *Pickwick*, starring Harry Secombe.

McCarthy, Joseph
b. 27 September 1885, Somerville, Massachusetts, USA, d. 18 December 1943, New York, USA. McCarthy sang in cafes and worked for music publishers before writing songs such as 'That Dreamy Italian Waltz', 'That's How I Need You' and 'I Miss You Most Of All'. In 1913, with Jimmy Monaco, he produced one of popular music's all-time standards, 'You Made Me Love You', memorably sung and

recorded by hundreds of artists, including Al Jolson, Harry James, Judy Garland and Grace La Rue. Three years later, again with Monaco, and Howard Johnson, McCarthy wrote 'What Do You Want To Make Those Eyes At Me For?', which Betty Hutton sang in the 1945 movie *Incendiary Blonde*, the bio-pic of nightclub queen Texas Guinan. The song resurfaced in the UK in 1959, as a number 1 for Emile Ford And The Checkmates, and again in 1987, when it was a hit for rock 'n' roll revivalist, Shakin' Stevens. McCarthy collaborated largely with Harry Tierney contributing to *The Ziegfeld Follies Of 1919*. In the same year, Tierney and McCarthy wrote the songs for the hugely successful *Irene*, which was later filmed in 1940, starring Anna Neagle and Ray Milland, and was successfully revived at the Minskoff Theatre in 1973, with Debbie Reynolds as Irene. In 1920, Tierney and McCarthy added several songs to the European score of Charles Cuvillier's *Afagar* when it was staged on Broadway, starring the toast of London and Paris, Alice Delysia. After contributing to the revues - *The Broadway Whirl*, *Up She Goes* and *Glory* - the team wrote the score for Ziegfeld's 1923 hit, *Kid Boots*. After a brief break, McCarthy was back with Tierney in 1927 for the double event of the theatrical year. The show was the operetta, *Rio Rita*, the season's biggest musical hit. The score included 'The Rangers' Song', 'If You're In Love, You'll Waltz', 'You're Always In My Arms', 'Following The Sun Around', 'The Kinkajou' and the main duet, 'Rio Rita', sung by the show's stars, Ethelind Terry and J. Harold Murray. It ran for nearly 500 performances and was twice filmed: in 1929 and again in 1942. Tierney and McCarthy's last Broadway show together was *Cross My Heart* in 1928, which ran for only eight weeks. McCarthy's 1918 song, 'I'm Always Chasing Rainbows', written with composer Harry Carroll, was successful then for Charles Harrison, Harry Fox and Sam Ash, and was popular again in the 40s, after Judy Garland sang it so well in MGM's *Ziegfeld Girl* in 1941 - at the time McCarthy was winding up his career. His other songs included 'They Go Wild, Simply Wild, Over Me' (a hit for Marion Harris), 'Through', 'Ireland Must Be Heaven For My Mother Came From There', Night Time In Italy', 'I'm In The Market For You', 'Underneath The Arches' and 'Ten Pins In The Sky' (from the Judy Garland film, *Listen Darling*). In 1940, he wrote the songs for *Billy Rose's Aquacade* water carnival, including 'You Think Of Everything' and 'When The Spirit Moves Me'. McCarthy died three years later in 1943.

MacDermot, Galt

b. 18 December 1928, Montreal, Canada. Nostalgia reared its grey and grizzly head at the Palace Theatre in New York when *George M!*, a celebration of the life and works of George M. Cohan, opened on 10 April 1968. Just under three weeks later, audiences at the nearby Biltmore Theatre came face to face (and other parts of the anatomy) with what many theatregoers felt was the 'grim reality' of the present and future, in the full-frontal shape of *Hair*, the 'American Tribal Rock Musical'. Galt MacDermot wrote the music for what was not so much a show as a social phenomenon, and the book and lyrics were by Gerome Ragni and James Rado. The trio won Grammy Awards for the cast album which spent over a year in the US chart and spawned several hit singles, the most succesful of which was probably the Fifth Dimension's 'Aquarius/Let The Sunshine In'. During the 1970s, MacDermot's compositions featured in a variety of productions, including *Isabel's A Jezebel* (1970, London), *Two Gentlemen Of Verona* (Tony Award), *Dude*, *Via Galactica*, *Take This Bread*, an oritorio, *Vieux Carré*, *I Took Panama*, and *The Sun Always Shines On The Cool* (1979). In 1984, his musical, *The Human Comedy*, lasted for less than two weeks on Broadway, and was revived by the West Coast Ensemble in Hollwood as part of their 1993 season. For some considerable time during the late 80s MacDermot collaborated with the West Indian poet and playwright Derek Walcott on the score for *Steel*, which eventually had its world premiere at Cambridge, Massachusetts, in May 1991. His music for the show was a cosmopolitan mixture of calypso, blues, gospel, and ballads. A reminder, perhaps, of his early days - even before *Hair* - when his instrumental composition, 'African Waltz', won two Grammys and an Ivor Novello Award, and became a UK hit in 1961 for British jazzman Johnny Dankworth. Selected abums: *Disin-Hair-ited* (c.70s), *Haircuts* (c.70s).

McHugh, Jimmy

b. James Francis McHugh, 10 July 1894, Boston, Massachusetts, USA, d. 23 May 1969, Beverly Hills, California, USA. McHugh was a prolific composer for films and the Broadway stage. He was educated at St. John's Preparatory School and Holy Cross College, where he received an honours degree in music. After receiving professional tuition he worked as a rehearsal pianist at the Boston Opera House, and later as a song-plugger for the Boston office of Irving Berlin Music. After moving to New York, he wrote for Harlem's Cotton Club revues, and had hits with 'When My Sugar Walks Down The Street' (with lyrics by Irving Mills and Gene Austin, which was a record hit for Austin and popular 20s vocalist Aileen Stanley), and 'I Can't Believe That You're In Love With Me' (with lyrics by Clarence Gaskill). His first Broadway success was the score for the all-black revue, *Blackbirds Of 1928*, in collaboration with Dorothy Fields, who became his first main lyricist. The show's songs included 'I Can't Give You

Anything But Love', 'Diga Diga Doo', 'I Must Have That Man', 'Doin' The New Low-Down' and 'Porgy'. The original stars, Adelaide Hall and Bill 'Bojangles' Robinson were joined by the Mills Brothers, Ethel Waters, and the orchestras of Cab Calloway, Duke Ellington, and Don Redman on a rare reissue album. The McHugh/Fields team wrote the songs for two more Broadway shows, *Hello Daddy* (1929) featuring 'In A Great Big Way' and 'Let's Sit And Talk About You', and *International Revue* (1930), starring Gertrude Lawrence and Harry Richman, and featuring two important McHugh songs, 'On The Sunny Side Of The Street' and 'Exactly Like You'. McHugh and Fields also wrote songs for the Chicago revue, *Clowns In Clover*, which introduced 'Don't Blame Me'. During the 30s and 40s McHugh is reputed to have written songs for over 50 films, initially with Fields, and including the title song from *Cuban Love Song*; the title song from *Dinner At Eight*, starring Fred Astaire, Joan Crawford, and Clark Gable; the title song and 'You Say The Darndest Thing', from *Singin' The Blues*; 'Lost In A Fog' from *Have A Heart*; 'I'm In The Mood For Love' and 'I Feel A Song Coming On', from *Every Night At Eight*, starring Alice Faye; The title song from *Dancing Lady*; and two songs, 'Lovely To Look At' and 'I Won't Dance', for the film of the Broadway hit, *Roberta*, on which McHugh and Fields collaborated with Jerome Kern. After Fields, McHugh's other main collaborator was Harold Adamson. Together they wrote 'There's Something In The Air', from *Banjo On My Knee*; the title song and 'My Fine Feathered Friend', from *You're A Sweetheart*, starring Alice Faye and George Murphy; 'My Own', from *That Certain Age*; 'A Serenade To The Stars' and 'I Love To Whistle', from *Mad About Music*, starring Deanna Durbin; 'How Blue The Night', from *Four Jills In A Jeep*, starring Dick Haymes, Alice Faye, and Betty Grable; and eight songs for an early Frank Sinatra film, *Higher And Higher*, including 'The Music Stopped', 'I Couldn't Sleep A Wink Last Night', 'A Lovely Way To Spend An Evening' and 'I Saw You First'; 'Have I Told You Lately That I Love You' and 'A Lovely Night To Go Dreaming', from *Calendar Girl*; 'Red Hot And Beautiful' and 'Hushabye Island', from *Smash Up*; and 'In The Middle Of Nowhere' and 'I Get The Neck Of The Chicken', from *Something For The Boys*. Two other well-known McHugh/Adamson songs were 'Coming In On A Wing And A Prayer', and 'Love Me As Though There Were No Tomorrow'. In 1939, McHugh collaborated with Al Dubin for the song, 'South American Way'. It featured in the Broadway show, *Streets Of Paris*, and the movie, *Down Argentine Way*. In both show and film, it was given the full treatment by Carmen Miranda. In 1940, McHugh again wrote with Dubin, and Howard Dietz, for the show *Keep*

Off the Grass, which included the songs 'Clear Out Of This World' and 'A Latin Tune, A Manhattan Moon, And You'. Other popular McHugh songs include 'I'm Shooting High', 'Let's Get Lost', I'd Know You Anywhere', 'You've Got Me This Way', 'Sing A Tropical Song', "Murder' She Says', 'Say A Prayer For The Boys Over There', 'Can't Get Out Of This Mood', 'In A Moment Of Madness', 'Blue Again', 'Goodbye Blues', 'I've Just Found Out About Love And I Like It', 'Warm and Willing', 'The Star You Wished Upon Last Night', 'Where The Hot Wind Blows' and 'Massachusetts'. McHugh's collaborators during his long career included Ted Koehler, Frank Loesser, Johnny Mercer, Herb Magidson, Ralph Freed, Ned Washington and Arnold Johnson. During World War II, McHugh wrote several US government commissioned 'War Savings Bond' songs such as 'Buy, Buy, Buy A Bond' and 'We've Got Another Bond to Buy'. For his work during the war he was awarded the Presidential Certificate Of Merit. He continued writing well into the 50s, and in 1955 had a hit with 'Too Young To Go Steady', recorded by Patti Page and Nat 'King' Cole. Jimmy McHugh died in May 1969.

Mack And Mabel

High up on the list of fondly remembered flops - but mainly through the medium of the superb Original Cast recording - this show ran on Broadway for only two months. It opened at the Majestic Theatre in New York on 6 October 1974, with what must have seemed a stellar cast. It had David Merrick, the premiere producer of musicals throughout the 60s, director and choreographer Gower Champion, a book by Michael Stewart, a score by Jerry Herman (*Mame* and *Hello, Dolly!*), and, best of all, two outstanding performers, Robert Preston and Bernadette Peters, supported by Lisa Kirk and James Mitchell - and it still failed. The story is told in flashback: one of the great comedy silent movie innovators, Mack Sennett (Preston), remembers the early days and his first studio in Brooklyn ('Movies Were Movies'). He takes a sandwich delivery girl, Mabel Normand (Bernadette Peters), and puts her into pictures, but neither their private or professional relationship is satisfactory ('I Won't Send Roses'), and when Mabel gets the offer of a serious part, she walks out on him. The story ends in 1938, with Sennett leaving the movie business for ever. As well as Preston's 'Movies Are Movies' and 'I Won't Send Roses', (which is reprised as 'Who Needs Roses?' by Peters), the delightful and lively score included 'Look What Happened To Mabel', 'Big Time', 'I Wanna Make The World Laugh', 'Wherever He Ain't', 'Hundreds Of Girls', 'When Mabel Comes Into The Room', 'My Heart Leaps Up', 'Time Heals Everthing', 'Tap Your Troubles Away', and 'I

Promise You A Happy Ending'. In spite of receiving several Tony nominations (none, ironically for Herman), it just did not catch on and closed after 65 performances, losing an estimated $800,000. Two years later a new production, with a revised book, toured with David Cryer, Lucie Arnez, and Tommy Tune, and, since that time, there have been several US provincial presentations, including one at the Paper Mill Playhouse in 1988, with Lee Horsley as Sennett and Janet Metz as Mabel. In the UK, interest was aroused in the show when its overture was used by Torvill and Dean, in their successful bid for a gold medal in the Olympic Ice Dancing Championship in 1984. A BBC Radio 2 disc jockey, David Jacobs, began playing tracks from the album, and 'I Won't Send Roses', in particular, became one of the station's easy-listening favourites. Since then there have been frequent calls for a proper professional production, but, although both amateur versions and a one-night concert presentation have attracted a good deal of attention, Britain has yet to see the real thing.

McKenzie, Julia

b. 17 February 1941, Enfield, Middlesex, England. An actress, singer, and director. McKenzie started to perform at an early age, and attended the Sylvia Spriggs Dancing School. She was about to begin training to be a French teacher when she was offered a scholarship to study opera. After spending four years at the Guildhall School Of Music, she performed in provincial theatres and toured in operettas and musical comedies for a good number of years before coming to prominence in 1969 in the London production of *Mame*, which starred Ginger Rogers. In the early 70s she had her first introduction to Stephen Sondheim's work, with which she later became indelibly associated, when she took over one of the leading roles in *Company*. She also replaced Patricia Routledge in *Cowardy Custard* and, in 1974, appeared in *Cole*, another of the Mermaid Theatre's excellent anthology productions. McKenzie's biggest break came two years later with yet another celebratory revue - *Side By Side By Sondheim* - in which she co-starred with Millicent Martin, David Kernan, and Ned Sherrin. A surprise hit in London, the show was also well-received in New York where it ran for 384 performances. During the 80s, McKenzie gave a 'dazzling performance' as Lily Garland in *On The Twentieth Century*, won Variety Club and Olivier Awards for her portrayal of Miss Adelaide in *Guys And Dolls* at the National Theatre, and resumed her association with Sondheim in *Follies* and *Into The Woods*. The 90s could well be another Sondheim decade for McKenzie. In 1993 she played Mrs. Lovett at the Royal National Theatre in their highly acclaimed production of *Sweeney Todd*, and directed the New York premiere of *Putting It Together*, a revue

based on the composer's songs. The show tempted Julie Andrews back to the New York musical stage for the first time since *Camelot* (1960). Julia McKenzie has also worked extensively in the straight theatre and on television where she was voted 'Favourite Comedy Performer' three times in the 80s for her appearances in sitcoms such as *Maggie And Her*, *Fresh Fields*, and *French Fields*.

Selected album: *Show Stoppers* (1993), and Original Cast recordings.

Mackintosh, Cameron

b. 17 October 1946, Enfield, England. 'The Czar of theatrical producers' - that is what the American magazine *Theatre Week* called him in 1993. In the same issue they also rated him number 3 in their list of the 100 Most Powerful People in American Theatre. The son of a Maltese-born mother and a Scottish father, Mackintosh attended a small public school in Bath and became obsessed by the musical theatre at the age of eight after being taken to see a production of Julian Slade's *Salad Days* at Bristol Old Vic in 1954. After leaving school, where he was known as Darryl F. Mackintosh, he attended the Central School for Speech and Drama for a year before becoming an assistant stage manager at the Theatre Royal, Drury Lane when *Camelot* was running. His first forays into producing came with some budget-priced touring shows before he moved into the West End in 1969 with a revival of *Anything Goes*. It proved to be a disaster and was withdrawn after 27 performances. *Trelawny* (1972) and *The Card* (1973) fared better, and, after a number of provincial productions of varying degrees of profitability, Mackintosh's breakthrough finally came in 1976 with *Side By Side By Sondheim*. During the next few years he mounted successful revivals of *Oliver!*, *My Fair Lady*, and *Oklahoma!*, before his meeting with Andrew Lloyd Webber resulted in *Cats* in 1981. The show transformed the lives of both men, and became the prototype for future productions that overthrew the old style of musical and provided a simple and vivid theatrical experience which did not rely on big name stars, and was easily exportable. In the 80s Mackintosh went from strength to strength with *Song And Dance*, *Les Misérables*, *The Phantom Of The Opera*, and *Miss Saigon* (1989). In 1990 the latter show provided an example of just how powerful Mackintosh had become when American Equity initially objected to the casting of Jonathan Pryce in the Broadway version 'because it would be an affront to the Asian community'. After the producer threatened to withdraw the show altogether - and one or two others as well - capitulation was more or less immediate. The incident did nothing to improve the producer's ruthless (he prefers 'relentless') reputation with the New York theatre community, many of whom object to his dictatorial attitude and 'flashy' marketing methods. For some reason he deliberately did not use those ploys when his London hit, *Five Guys Named Moe*, transferred to Broadway, and that may well be one of the reasons for its relatively poor showing. In 1992 Mackintosh was involved with a rare flop which some say marked the beginning of his decline. *Moby Dick* ('a damp squib . . . garbage') is reported to have cost him £1 million and a great deal of pride during its 15-week run, and he hinted at the time that he may be past his peak. However, the highly impressive monetary facts continued to emerge: a personal salary of over £8 million in 1991, the 39th richest man in Britain, and the acquisition of a substantial stake in two West End theatres, the Prince of Wales and the Prince Edward. His love of musicals - that is all he produces - has caused Mackintosh to divert some of his reported £300 million wealth to a number of extremely worthy causes. As well as numerous donations to small theatrical projects, he provided £2 million to endow Oxford University's first professorship in drama and musical theatre, and his £1 million gift to the Royal National Theatre has enabled it to mount highly acclaimed revivals of *Carousel* and *Sweeney Todd*, the first two in a series of five classic musicals. It is not all philanthropy: Mackintosh is reported to retain the rights to the productions when they are eventually produced in the commercial sector. A knighthood is inevitable, but until then his kudos have included the 1991 *Observer* Award for Outstanding Achievement and the prestigeous Richard Rodgers Award for Excellence in Musical Theatre (1992). Previous recipients have been Harold Prince, Julie Andrews and Mary Martin. In 1993, for the benefit of an awe-struck journalist, he attempted to remember all the musicals he had running in various parts of the world. They included six *Cats*, 20 *Phantom Of The Opera*, 12 *Les Misérables*, seven *Miss Saigon*, four *Five Guys Named Moe*, two *Follies* . . . etcetera, etcetera, as Yul Brynner used to say.

Madame Sherry

With music by Hugo Felix and a book by Maurice Ordonneau, this 'Musical Vaudeville' or 'French Vaudeville', was presented in Paris and Berlin in 1902, and in London a year later. By the time it opened at the New Amersterdam Theatre in New York on 30 August 1910, it had been radically reworked, and had music by Karl Hoschna and a book and lyrics by Otto Harbach. The complicated story involves Edward Sherry (Jack Gardner), whose wealthy uncle Theophilus (Ralph Herz), sets him up in his own Sherry School of Aesthetic Dancing. Edward succeeds in convincing his uncle that his houskeeper, Catherine (Elizabeth Murray), is his wife and two of the dancing pupils are his children. At the

time, Edward loves Lulu (Frances Demarest), one of his terpsichorean teachers, but, by the end of the piece he has transferred his affections to Yvonne (Lina Abarbanell), who, fresh from the convent school, accedes to the title of Madame Sherry. Hoschna and Harbach's score contained 'Every Little Movement' ('Has a meaning of its own'), which became an enormous hit and a firm favourite in vaudeville and music halls through the years. The Dorsey Brothers Orchestra had some success with it, and the number was also featured in several 40s film musicals such as *Presenting Lily Mars* (Judy Garland), *Shine On Harvest Moon*, and *The Jolson Story*. The rest of the composers' score included 'The Smile She Means For You, 'I Want To Play House With You', and 'The Birth Of Passion'. Another song, 'Put You Arms Around Me Honey', which was written by Albert Von Tilzer and Junie McCree, and interpolated into the show, became extremely popular. It also turned up in several movie musicals including two Betty Grable vehicles, *Coney Island* and *Mother Wore Tights*. Lina Abarbanell was the main star of the piece, but comedienne Elizabeth Murray also made a strong impression, and helped the show enjoy a run of 231 performances. She went on to further success in *High Jinks*, *Watch Your Step*, and *Sidewalks Of New York*.

Maggie May

Lionel Bart, who liked to have a hand in most aspects of his shows, concentrated on writing just the music and lyrics for this one which opened at the Adelphi Theatre in London on 22 September 1964. His librettist was the Liverpudlian playwright Alun Owen, an appropriate choice considering that the story was set in and around the Liverpool Docks. Bart's project was inspired by the traditional ballad about a local prostitute, which was sung by the sailors and dockworkers in the area. In Owen's dramatic book dealing with trades union ethics and disputes, the streetwalker, Margaret Mary Duffy (Rachel Roberts), loses her childhood sweetheart, Patrick Casey (Kenneth Haigh), after he dies trying to prevent a shipload of arms going to South America. As in previous shows such as *Fings Ain't Wot They Used T'Be*, *Blitz!*, and *Oliver!*, Bart's score caught the mood and the style of the piece perfectly. The songs ranged from attractive ballads such as 'It's Yourself', 'The Land Of Promises', 'Lullaby', 'I Love A Man', and 'The Ballad Of The Liver Bird', to the more lively 'I Told You So', 'Dey Don't Do Dat T'day', 'Leave Her, Johnny, Leave Her', 'Shine, You Swine', 'We Don't All Wear D'same Size Boots', 'Maggie, Maggie May', and 'It's Yourself'. The critics were divided, but the public took to the show, partly perhaps because anything to do with Liverpool was of interest while the Beatles, and several other local groups, were constantly storming the pop charts. *Maggie May* had a highly respectable run of 501 performances, and also introduced a future star to the West End in the shape of Julia McKenzie who took over from Rachel Roberts occasionally. Part of Bart's score reached a wider audience when Judy Garland recorded four of the songs from the show, 'Maggie May', 'There's Only One Union', 'Land Of Promise', and 'It's Yourself', on an EP record. In 1992, nearly 30 years later, the National Youth Theatre of Great Britain mounted an acclaimed production of *Maggie May* at London's Royalty Theatre. It was a welcome feature of Lionel Bart's UK renaissance.

Magic Show, The

Proof of the unpredictablity of musical theatre audiences, this show, which was merely a series of spectacular set-piece magical illusions linked by a flimsy plot, opened at the Cort Theatre in New York on 28 May 1974, and closed over four and half years later after an incredible 1,920 performances. Stephen Schwartz, who can usually be relied upon to conjure up something out of the ordinary himself, wrote the music and lyrics, and the book was the work of Bob Randall. The latter dealt with the sad tale of a New Jersey nightspot, The Passaic Top Hat, which is saved from debt and the road to the depths of degradation, by the arrival of a magic act. Doug Henning was the wizard who made everything well, and he really was the star of the show, with a supporting cast made up of Dale Soules, David Ogden Stiers, and Anita Morris. The songs included 'Up To His Old Tricks', 'Lion Tamer', 'Style', 'West End Avenue', and 'The Goldfarb Variations'. 'Goldfarb' is a familiar name in musical comedy history. George and Ira Gershwin immortalised the taxi driver-turned sheriff in *Girl Crazy* (1930), with their song, 'Goldfarb! That's I'm!'.

Maid Of The Mountains, The

A favourite with amateur operatic societies throughout the world, this show was first presented in London at Daly's Theatre on 10 February 1917. The score was mainly by Harold Fraser-Simpson and James Tate (music) and Harry Graham (lyrics), with additional songs by F. Clifford Harris, James W. Tate, and (Arthur) 'Valentine'. Frederick Lonsdale's book was set in the high mountains of 'brigand land', and concerned the lovely Teresa (José Collins) who is arrested by General Malona (Mark Lester), the Governor of Santo, and is promised her freedom if her lover, the outlaw Baldasarre (Arthur Wontner), is captured. Complications arise when Teresa learns that Baldasarre has eyes for another, and in a fit of pique, she exposes him. Whereupon he is captured, and incarcerated on Devil's Island. All ends well when Teresa engineers his release, and they board a small boat and sail to the mainland - and into the sunset. The enchanting score included memorable songs such

as Fraser-Simpson and Graham's 'Love Will Find A Way'and 'Live For Today', along with the engaging 'A Bachelor Gay', 'My Life Is Love', and 'A Paradise For Two' by Tate, Harris, and Valentine. the show was an enormous success and ran for a record 1,352 performances - even longer than the other big London hit of World War I, *Chu Chin Chow*. It made a star of the fiery José Collins, who had already enjoyed a prosperous Broadway career before she appeared in *The Maid Of The Mountains*, but is always remembered for introducing 'Love Will Find A Way'. Perhaps if she had recreated her role in New York, the 1918 production of *The Maid Of The Mountains* would have stayed at the Casino Theatre more than 37 performances. In the event Collins did appear in the 1921 London revival, the first of several that were produced through until 1942. Thirty years after that, a revised version, with additional songs by Harry Parr-Davies, Harold Purcell, Rudolf Friml, and Brian Hooker, and starring Lynne Kennington, Gordon Clyde, Neville Jason, Jimmy Thompson, and Janet Mahoney, was presented at London's Palace Theatre. Compared to contemporary musicals such as *Jesus Christ Superstar* it was considered to be out of place and somewhat old-fashioned. The original concept was captured in the 1932 film with Nancy Brown and Harry Welchman.

Make Me An Offer

One of that band of typically English musicals that were around in the late 50s, which included *Fings Ain't Wot They Used T'Be* and *Expresso Bongo*. The creative team behind the latter came together again for this show which began its life at the innovative Theatre Royal, Stratford East, before opening in the West End at the New Theatre on 16 December 1959. The book was adapted by Wolf Mankowitz from his own slim 1952 novel and the 1959 film starring Peter Finch and Adrienne Corri, and was set in the world of small-time antique dealers based around London's Portobello Road market. Charlie (Daniel Massey), an expert in Wedgewood china, longs to own a beautiful piece for himself. His chance comes when he is involved with an auction (a particularly effective scene) for a complete (fake) Wedgewood room - and he ends up with a valuable (genuine) vase. Charlie's main rival dealer in the saga is the stunning Redhead (Dilys Laye), and his wife, Sally, was played by Diana Coupland. Some 20 songs, by David Heneker and Monty Norman, were skilfully incorporated into the plot, pointing up the various characters and situations as they occurred. They consisted of a blend of amusing and sentimental items, such as 'Make Me An Offer', Redhead's proposal that Charlie gallantly turns down; 'The Pram Song', 'I Want A Lock-Up', 'Portobello Road', 'Business Is Business', 'Whatever You Believe', 'It's Sort Of Romantic', 'If I Was A

Man', 'Dog Eat Dog', 'All Big Fleas', and 'Love Him'. *Make Me An Offer* had decent run of 267 performances, and won the 1959 *Evening Standard* Award for best musical.

Make Mine Manhattan

Sid Caesar, a comedian who specialized in subjects satirical, was on the brink of television super-stardom when he appeared with a clutch of fellow clowns, including Joshua Shelley and David Burns, in this show which opened at the Broadhurst Theatre in New York on 15 January 1948. It was Caesar's debut on Broadway, and in a format - the revue - that was on its last legs. The music was by Richard Lewine, with lyrics and sketches by Arnold B. Horwitt, and it went for all the usual New York targets in a pleasant and amusing way. The songs included 'Saturday Night In Central Park', 'Subway Song', 'Phil The Fiddler', 'Gentleman Friend', 'My Brudder And Me', and 'I Fell In Love With You'. It is ironic that a fairly simple, lightweight production such as this should run for 429 performances, when Caesar's triumphant return to Broadway 14 years later in *Little Me* could only manage 257.

Mame

Opening at the Winter Garden Theatre in New York on 24 May 1966 to excellent reviews, the stage show *Mame* was another hit for composer and lyricist Jerry Herman. Robert E. Lee and Jerome Lawrence's book was based on the play *Auntie Mame*, which was in turn adapted from Patrick Dennis's novel. Mame (Angela Lansbury) is an eccentric lady of indeterminate years but with a decidedly youthful approach to life, and her efforts to impart the elements of her lifestyle and philosophy to her young nephew, Patrick Dennis (Frank Michaels) and her Texan husband, Beauregard Burnside (Charles Braswell), made for a delightful show. There were some memorable songs in a score which included 'Open A New Window', 'The Man In The Moon', 'It's Today', 'We Need A Little Christmas', 'That's How Young I Feel', 'My Best Girl', and the poignant 'If He Walked Into My Life', which later received sympathetic readings from Matt Monro and Scott Walker. The enormously likeable title number was a US hit for Herb Alpert, and Herman won a Grammy for the Original Cast album. Another outstanding number in the show was the amusingly bitchy 'Bosom Buddies', sung by Mame and her lifelong 'chum', Vera Charles (Beatrice Arthur), in which they swopped compliments such as 'If I say that your tongue is vicious, if I call you uncouth/It's simply that who else but a bosom buddy will sit down and tell you the truth?'. *Mame* ran for 1,508 performances on Broadway and won Tony Awards for best actress (Lansbury), and featured actor and actress (Michaels

and Arthur). The 1969 London production starred the former Hollywood superstar Ginger Rogers. Touring versions of the show have proved convenient vehicles for several other 'maturing' ladies of the stage and screen, including Janis Paige, Jane Morgan, Ann Miller, Rosalind Russell (who had starred in the long-running *Auntie Mame* and its film version), Dolores Gray, Greer Garson, Eve Arden and Sylvia Sidney. Angela Lansbury reprised her role for the short-lived 1983 Broadway revival. A 1974 film version starred Lucille Ball and Robert Preston.

Man Of La Mancha

Staged at the ANTA Washington Square Theater, and hence just a little off-Broadway, *Man Of La Mancha* opened on 22 November 1965. Dale Wasserman's book combined elements of Miguel de Cervantes's classic novel, *Don Quixote*, with the troubled life of the author. Wasserman had earlier written a straight dramatic play which was televised in 1959, and was persuaded by producer-director Albert Marre to adapt it into a musical version. With music by Mitch Leigh and lyrics by Joe Darion, the show opened to good reviews and quickly built a following at the comparatively small ANTA Theater. Starring Richard Kiley as Cervantes/Quixote and Joan Diener as Aldonza, the story interweaved episodes in the life of Cervantes, who endured slavery and imprisonment, often for debt, before achieving success with the publication of his masterpiece. It proved to be an unexpected hit and won Tony Awards for best musical, actor (Kiley), score, director (Marre), and scenic design (Howard Bay). The careful integration of songs and lyrics into the development of the plot made it difficult for most of them to gain life outside the show, but there were several admirable numbers, including 'I'm Only Thinking Of Him', 'The Dubbing', 'Little Bird, Little Bird', 'What Do You Want From Me?', and 'I Really Like Him'. Another of the songs, 'The Impossible Dream', did achieve some measure of popularity especially in a recording by Jack Jones. It endured, and became a UK hit in 1992 for the local eccentric band Carter USM. *Man Of La Mancha* stayed at the ANTA theatre until March 1968 when it transferred to the larger Martin Beck Theatre where it continued its run for a total of 2,328 performances. The London production opened in March 1968 with Joan Diener and Keith Michell; Richard Kiley took over the lead in 1969. A 1992 Broadway revival, which starred Raul Julia and pop singer Sheena Easton, folded after 108 performances. Peter O'Toole appeared in the 'plodding, abysmal' film version in 1972.

March Of The Falsettos

The second in a series of musicals with music and lyrics by William Finn, all of which began Off

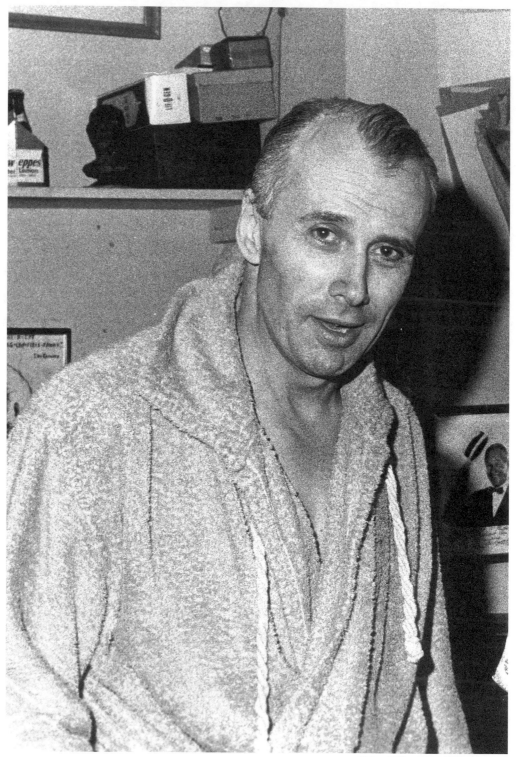

Richard Kiley (*Man Of La Mancha*)

Broadway at the experimental and innovative centre, Playwrights Horizons. The first of what is sometimes called 'The Marvin Trilogy', *In Trousers*, played for 16 performances from 26 March 1985 at the Promenade Theatre in New York, and has rarely been presented since. The third, and last, in the trilogy is entitled *Falsettoland*, and that piece is sometimes combined with *March Of The Falsettos* under the title of *Falsettos*. *March Of The Falsettos*, a piece which William Finn himself has called 'a passionate work about being scared to death of love', gave a total of 298 performances at Playwrights Horizons and the West Side Arts Centre from April 1981. It was set in 1979, and told of a Jewish father, Marvin (Michael Rupert), who discovers that he is homosexual, and leaves his wife, Trina (Alison Fraser) and young son, Jason (James Kushner), to go and live with his male lover, Whizzer Brown (Stephen Bogardus). In a neat twist, Marvin's wife marries his psychiatrist, Mendel (Chip Zien), and he is left alone. What has been called 'the most powerful and emotional score of the 80s, (there is no spoken dialogue) included 'Four Jews In A Room Bitching', 'This Had Better Stop', 'The Games I Play', 'The Chess Game, 'I Never Wanted To Love You', 'Trina's Song', 'This Had Better Come To A Stop', 'Love Is Blind', 'My Father's A Homo', and 'The Thrill Of First Love'.

Falsettoland, which opened in 1990, begins two years after *March Of The Falsettos*. Rupert, Bogardus and Zien recreated their original roles, and added to the cast was a doctor, Charlotte (Heather MacRae), and her lesbian lover, Cordelia (Janet Metz). After the excruciatingly difficult adjustments that all the characters had been forced to make in the previous show, the early mood in *Falsettoland* is one of 'whimsical goofiness', but that changes swiftly when Whizzer is diagnosed as having a deadly disease soon to be identified as AIDS. The family gather round his bedside, and the show culminates in young Jason's bar mitzvah in Whizzer's hospital room. The songs included 'Falsettoland', 'Year Of The Child', 'The Baseball Game', 'Everyone Hates His Parents', 'What More Can I Say?', 'Something Bad Is Happening', 'Days Like This', 'Unlikely Lovers,' 'You Gotta Die Sometime', and 'What Would I Do?'. Opinions as to the two shows' merit and value varied widely. To many, *March Of The Falsettos* was 'not just a musical about gay life in modern times, but a masterly feat of comic storytelling and a visionary musical theatre work', while others dismissed both *March Of The Falsettos* and *Falsettoland* as 'overrated Off Broadway cult items'. *Falsettoland* won Tony Awards for best book (Finn and James Lapine, who also directed) and score, and ran for a total of 245 performances. After over a decade on the fringe, Finn and Lapine's audacious and original concept finally graduated to Broadway in April 1992, when *March Of The Falsettos*

and *Falsettoland* were presented under the title of *Falsettos* at the John Golden Theatre for nearly 500 performances, and was rewarded with Tony Awards for book and score. A London production of *March Of The Falsettos*, with Simon Green, Paddy Navin, Barry James, Martin Smith, and Damien Walker, played 29 performances at the Albery Theatre in 1987.

Marlene, Das Musical

Originally titled *Sag Mir Wo Die Blumen Sind* (Where Have All The Flowers Gone?), this musical is based on British author Laurence Roman's biography of the legendary entertainer Marlene Dietrich. It opened at the small (785-seater) Theatre am Kurfürstendamm, Berlin, Germany, on 7 April 1993, almost a year after her death. Somewhat optimistically, in the light of subsequent events, the show's producer, Friedrich Kurz, booked the theatre, where Dietrich herself had performed in 1928, until the year 2000. Reportedly capitalized at between £1.5-2 million and directed by Terry Hands, formerly Artistic Director of the Royal Shakespeare Company, the production 'fast-frames 40 years of Dietrich's life, interspersed with a contemporary sub-plot about a troupe of drama students planning a tribute to her'. Along with the 'clumsy political allegories', there is a scene in which Dietrich romps in bed with her husband and his mistress, and, towards the end, Edith Piaf, played by a man wearing a white wedding dress, is brought on in a wheel chair. The 'charming, slightly plump' Jutta Habicht plays Dietrich in a cast of six which is accompanied by seven musicians. Most of the 20 songs are by Frederick Hollander, and include his bitter-sweet 'Falling In Love Again' from the memorable Dietrich film, *The Blue Angel*. Two months after the show opened it was retitled *Marlene, Das Musical* and drastically revised so that it became a more straight forward chronological life story, while still retaining plenty of sex and innuendo. More songs were added, but the enormous helium-filled Dietrich model which almost seemed to fill the stage was now missing. In any event, the changes were to no avail, and the show, which it was hoped would go some way towards re-estabishing Marlene Dietrich's reputation in a city that once reviled her, closed on 30 June 1993.

Martin, Mary

b. Mary Virginia Martin, 1 December 1913, Weatherford, Texas, USA, d. 3 November 1990, Rancho Mirage, California, USA. A legendary star of the Broadway musical theatre during the 40s and 50s, and one of its most charming, vivacious and best-loved performers. Her father was a lawyer, and her mother a violin teacher. She took dancing and singing lessons from an early age, married at 16, and

Mary Martin (*South Pacific*)

eventually ran a dancing school herself before moving to Hollywood where she auditioned constantly at the film studios, and worked in nightclubs and on radio. After being spotted by the producer Lawrence Schwab, her first big break came on Broadway in 1938 when she won a secondary role in the Cole Porter musical *Leave It To Me*. Almost every night she stopped the show with her 'sensational' rendering of 'My Heart Belongs To Daddy' while performing a mock striptease perched on top of a large cabin trunk at a 'Siberian' railway station. On the strength of her performance in that show she was signed to Paramount, and made 10 films over a period of four years, beginning with *The Great Victor Herbert* in 1939. Although her delightfuly warm personality and theatrical star quality, were not so effective on film, she did have her moments, particularly in *Rhythm On The River* (with Bing Crosby and Oscar Levant) and *Birth Of The Blues*, in which she joined Crosby and Jack Teagarden for 'The Waiter, And The Porter And The Upstairs Maid'. She also sang the title song in *Kiss The Boys Goodbye*, which became a big hit for Tommy Dorsey, and duetted with Dick Powell on 'Hit The Road To Dreamland' in *Star Spangled Rhythm*. While on the west coast, she married for the second time, to a Paramount executive Richard Halliday, who became her manager. In 1943 she returned to the stage, and, after failing to reach Broadway with *Dancing In The Streets*, scored a great success with *One Touch Of Venus* which ran for 567 performances. The role of a glamorous statue that comes to life and falls in love with a human had originally been intended for Marlene Dietrich, but it fell to Martin to introduce the haunting 'Speak Low,' and the show established her as a true star. She followed it with *Lute Song*, the show which introduced Yul Brynner to Broadway, before returning to Hollywood to reprise 'My Heart Belongs To Daddy' for the Cole Porter biopic *Night And Day*. A trip to London in 1947 for an appearance in Noël Coward's *Pacific 1860*, proved an unsatisfactory experience, and Martin returned to the USA to play the lead in a touring version of *Annie Get Your Gun*. Richard Rodgers and Oscar Hammerstein's smash hit *South Pacific* was next, and Martin's memorable performance, funny and poignant in turns, won her a Tony Award. Starred with opera singer Ezio Pinza, she introduced several of the composers' most endearing numbers, including 'I'm Gonna Wash That Man Right Out Of My Hair' (sung while she shampooed her hair on stage), 'A Wonderful Guy', 'A Cockeyed Optimist', and the hilarious 'Honeybun'. *South Pacific* ran for 1,925 performances in New York, and Martin recreated her role for the 1951 London production at Drury Lane where she was equally well received. During the rest of the 50s Mary Martin appeared in several straight plays, two highly regarded

television spectaculars - one with Ethel Merman (which included a 35-song medley), and the other with Noël Coward - as well as starring on Broadway with Cyril Ritchard in a musical version of *Peter Pan* (1954) which was taped and shown repeatedly on US television. In November 1959 Martin opened the Lunt-Fontanne Theatre in New York in what was to prove yet another blockbuster hit. Rodgers and Hammerstein's musical, *The Sound Of Music*, immediately produced reactions ranging for raves to revulsion, but it gave Martin another Tony Award and the chance to display her homespun charm with songs such as 'My Favourite Things' and 'Do-Re-Mi'. From the 'hills that were alive with music', Mary Martin plummeted to the depths in *Jennie* (1963), her first real flop. Thereafter, she and her husband spent more time at their home in Brazil, but in 1965 she was persuaded to embark on a world tour in *Hello, Dolly!* which included a visit to Vietnam, and a five-month stay in London. Her final appearance in a Broadway musical was in 1966 with Robert Preston in the two-hander *I Do! I Do!* which ran for 560 performances. In the 70s she did more straight theatre and won a Peabody Award for the television film *Valentine*. After her husband's death in 1973, Martin moved to Palm Springs to be near her friend Janet Gaynor, but returned to New York in 1977 to star with Ethel Merman in a benefit performance of *Together Again*. In the early 80s, Martin and Janet Gaynor were severely injured in an horrific taxicab crash in San Franciso which took the life of her longtime aide Ben Washer. Martin recovered to receive the applause of her peers in *Our Heart Belongs To Mary*, and to make her final US stage appearance in 1986 with Carol Channing in a national tour of James Kirkwood's comedy *Legends*. For much of the time she had to wear a shortwave radio device to prompt her when she forgot her lines. Mary Martin made her final appearance on the London stage in the 1980 Royal Variety Performance when she performed a delightful version of 'Honeybun', and then had to suffer the embarrassment of watching her son from her first marriage, Larry Hagman (the notorious J.R. Ewing from the television soap *Dallas*), forget his lines in front of a celebrity audience.

Selected albums: *Mary Martin Sings-Richard Rodgers Plays* (1958), *Sings For You* (c.50s), with Ethel Merman *Duet From Ford 50th Anniversary Telecast* (c.50s), and Broadway Cast recordings.

Further reading: *My Heart Belongs*, Mary Martin.

Matador

This show, which was 'inspired' by the life of the Spanish bullfighter El Cordobes, first surfaced in the form of a concept album recorded by Tom Jones in 1987. One of the tracks, 'A Boy From Nowhere', climbed to number 2 in the UK singles chart, and

Jessie Matthews

Jones was originally set to play the leading role in the stage production. Things did not work out that way, and when *Matador* opened at the Queens theatre in London on 16 April 1991, the central character of Domingo Hernandez was played by the young unknown John Barrowman, with Nicky Henson as his crafty manager. In an attempt to give the production some glamour, the actress Stephanie Powers, well-known in England for her appearances with Robert Wagner in the television series *Hart To Hart*, was brought in the play the part of an American film star, Laura-Jane Wilding. The character was thought to be based on Ava Gardner with whom El Cordobes is said to have had an affair. The score was by Michael Leander and Edward Seago, who had written hits for Gary Glitter, Engelbert Humperdinck and Cliff Richard, and the book, by Peter Dukes, was based on Leander and Seago's original storyline. Domingo's rise from the obscure village of Andalucia to the top of the bullfighting world despite a background of illiteracy, is thrillingly staged against a background of spectacular sets, but it is the dancing - particularly the flamenco dancing choreographed by Rafael Aguilar - which is the outstanding feature of the whole production. The score, which contained nothing else as memorable as 'A Boy From Nowhere', also included 'Panama Hat', 'No Way Out Of This Town', 'I Was Born To Be Me', 'I'll Take You Out To Dinner', 'Paseo And Corrida', 'To Be a Matador', 'Children Of The Sun', 'I'll Dress You In Mourning', and 'I'm You, You Are Me'. Critical reaction was mixed ('Risibly awful . . . a load of bull' was the worst), but the show never captured an audience and closed after three months with losses 'approaching £1 million'.

Matthews, Jessie

b. 11 March 1907, London, England, d. 19 August 1981. A member of a large and poor family, Matthews became a professional dancer at the age of 10. After a few years in the chorus of several shows in London's West End, she achieved recognition with a series of ingenue roles and some bit parts in films. By the late 20s she had become one of London's most popular stars. At the height of her career, in such shows as the 1930 London production of *Ever Green*, by Richard Rodgers and Lorenz Hart, Matthews was the epitome of the English musical comedy star: her delicate build and translucent beauty fully matched songs such as that show's ethereal 'Dancing On The Ceiling'. Her film work also grew and she made several movies in the UK and in Hollywood, usually second-rate musicals in which she shone effortlessly. Despite an appearance in the 1934 film version of her stage hit, slightly retitled as *Evergreen*, few of Matthews' film vehicles were worthy of her talent. An outstanding dancer, the poor quality of her films

militated against her continuing for long and by the 40s, her career was all but over. Her last appearance on a London stage in this part of her career was in the 1942 production of *Wild Rose*. After many years away from the public eye, spent mostly in Australia, Matthews returned to star in a daily BBC radio serial, playing the lead in *Mrs Dale's Diary*. Another London stage appearance followed with *The Water Babies* in 1973.
Further reading: *Over My Shoulder: An Autobiography*, Jessie Matthews and Muriel Byers London.

Maytime

With his score for this highly popular operetta, which was based on a German production, *Wie Einst In Mai*, Sigmund Romberg finally stepped out of Victor Herbert's shadow, and established himself as the leading composer of these gloriously musical, sentimental sagas. Rida Johnson Young wrote the book and lyrics, and the show's role-reversal story was set in New York, where well-off Ottilie Van Zandt (Peggy Wood) is prevented by her father, Matthew Van Zandt (William Norris), from marrying her true love, Richard Wayne (Charles Purcell), because, quite frankly, he comes from 'the other side of the tracks'. They go on to each marry their respective partners, although they meet socially and affirm their love for each other. When Ottilie's husband dies, she is left destitute, and her house and all her belongings are auctioned. Richard buys the house, and many years pass before their grandchildren encounter each other, and presumably find happiness together. The grandchildren were also played by Peggy Wood and Charles Purcell. The sweeping, romantic score included 'The Road To Paradise', 'Jump Jim Crow', 'In Our Little Home Sweet Home', 'Only One Girl For Me', and 'Will You Remember?', a lovely song which achieved wider recognition. One of the other numbers, 'Dancing Will Keep You Young', had music by Romberg and a lyric by Cyrus Wood. An enormously popular show - America's biggest hit of World War I - which all the soldiers aimed to see before they departed for the conflict. Its run of 492 performances was, for the time, astounding. The 1937 film of *Maytime*, which starred Jeanette MacDonald and Nelson Eddy, changed the story and discarded all the songs except for 'Will You Remember?'. The song was sung superbly by Jane Powell and Vic Damone in the 1954 Sigmund Romberg biopic, *Deep In My Heart*.

Me And Juliet

Perhaps because it emerged into the bright lights of Broadway in the same season as hits such as *Wish You Were Here*, *Wonderful Town*, and *Can-Can*, Richard Rodgers and Oscar Hammerstein's *Me And Juliet* was regarded by critics and public alike to be well below their par. Certainly, after blockbusters such as *Oklahoma!*, *Carousel*, and *The King And I*, a run of 358 performances was not remarkable by their standards. Unlike those three shows, *Me And Juliet* was not adapted from an existing work, but had an original book by Hammerstein. It opened at the Majestic Theatre in New York on 28 May 1953. The setting is a theatre, onstage and off, where a musical entitled *Me And Juliet* is playing. Jeannie (Isabel Bigley), a singer in the chorus, is being pleasantly pursued by Larry (Bill Hayes), the assistant stage manager, until electrician Bob (Mark Dawson), a nasty hard-drinking character, tries to muscle in on the romance to such an extent that he tries to murder her. The traditional 'fun-romance' situation that usually crops up in these kind of shows, in this case involves a dancer, Betty (Joan McCracken) and the stage manager, Mac (Ray Walston). The latter artist proved to be a memorable Luther Blissett in the film of Rodgers and Hammerstein's *South Pacific*, and he also gave a 'devil' of a good performance in *Damn Yankees* on both stage and screen. The score for *Me And Juliet* was light, and contained none of the composers' 'deeply meaningful songs' (such as 'You'll Never Walk Alone', 'Carefully Taught', etc.), but there were some pleasant songs, including 'Keep It Gay', 'It's Me', 'The Big Black Giant', 'A Very Special Day', 'I'm Your Girl', and 'Do I Love You Because You're Beautiful' and 'Marriage-Type Love', both of which achieved some modest popularity. Rodgers had used the melody of one of the other numbers, 'No Other Love', before, as part of the background score for the television documentary series, *Victory At Sea* (1952). The song became a big hit for Perry Como in America, and a UK number 1 for Ronnie Hilton. Rodgers remembered the song again, in 1957, and interpolated it into a US television version of *Cinderella*, which starred Julie Andrews. It was also present when *Cinderella* was adapted for the stage, and played the London Coliseum as a Christmas-time entertainment in 1958, with a cast that included Tommy Steele, Bruce Trent, Yana, Jimmy Edwards, Betty Marsden, and Kenneth Williams. Exactly 35 years after that, *Cinderalla* was staged in America by the New York City Opera.

Me And My Girl

With music by Noel Gay, and a book and lyrics by Douglas Furber and L Arthur Rose, *Me And My Girl* opened in at the Victoria Palace in London on 16 December 1937. The immensely popular Lupino Lane starred as Bill Snibson, a Cockney barrow-boy who becomes involved with the 'toffs', but stays true to Sally (Teddy St. Dennis), a girl from his own background. *Me And My Girl* was the first West End production to be televised live from a theatre, and after excerpts were transmitted by the BBC, audiences

flocked to see the show with its cheerful music and happy-go-lucky air. The show ran at the Victoria Palace until June 1940, a total of 1,646 performances, and, after a break, and a spell at the London Coliseum, it returned to the Palace for a further nine months in 1945/6. By that time everybody, it seemed, was doing 'The Lambeth Walk' and singing along with Bill and Sally to 'Me And My Girl'. There was yet another short-lived production at the Winter Garden in 1949/50. At this stage, Lupino Lane had played the lead in all of them. In February 1985, a revised version of the show, written by the humorist Stephen Fry, opened at the Adelphi Theatre in London. It was produced by Richard Armitage, Noel Gay's son, and starred the popular straight actor Robert Lindsay, and future Oscar-winner Emma Thompson. Also in the cast were veteran performers Frank Thornton and Ursula Smith, representing the 'toffs', who duetted the amusingly nostalgic 'If Only You Had Cared For Me'. Two other Noel Gay hits, ' Leaning On a Lamp Post' and 'The Sun Has Got His Hat On', were interpolated into the score, and coach parties galore continued to pour into the Adelphi for an incredible eight years. Along the way the show won Laurence Olivier Awards for best musical and actor, Robert Lindsay, who reprised his role for the 1986 Broadway production. New York audiences loved it too, and the show earned Tony Awards for Lindsay, best actress (Maryann Plunkett), and choreographer Gillian Gregory. Many years before all that, in 1939, a film version was released, starring Lupino Lane, of course.

Menken, Alan

(see **Ashman, Howard**)

Mercer, Johnny

b. John Herndon Mercer, 18 November 1909, Savannah, Georgia, USA, d. 25 June 1976, Los Angeles, California, USA. A lyricist, composer and singer, Mercer was an important link with the first generation of composers of indigenous American popular music such as Jerome Kern and Harry Warren, through to post-World War II writers like Henry Mancini. Along the way, he collaborated with several others, including Harold Arlen, Hoagy Carmichael, Gene DePaul, Rube Bloom, Richard Whiting, Victor Schertzinger, Gordon Jenkins, Jimmy Van Heusen, Duke Ellington, Billy Strayhorn, Matty Malneck, Arthur Schwartz and more. Most of the time, Mercer wrote the most literate and witty lyrics, but occasionally the melody as well.

He moved to New York in the late 20s and worked in a variety of jobs before placing one of his first songs, 'Out Of Breath And Scared To Death Of You', (written with Everett Miller), in the *Garrick Gaieties Of 1930*. During the 30s, Mercer contributed the lyrics to several movie songs, including 'If You Were Mine' from *To Beat The Band*, a record hit for Billie Holiday with Teddy Wilson, 'I'm An Old Cowhand' (words and music) (*Rhythm On The Range*), 'Too Marvellous For Words' (co-written with Richard Whiting for *Ready, Willing And Able*), 'Have You Got Any Castles, Baby?' (*Varsity Show*), 'Hooray For Hollywood' (*Hollywood Hotel*), 'Jeepers Creepers' (*Going Places*) and 'Love Is Where You Find It' (*Garden Of The Moon*).

Mercer's other songs during the decade included 'Fare-Thee-Well To Harlem', 'Moon Country', 'When A Woman Loves A Man' (with Gordon Jenkins and Bernard Hanighan), 'P.S. I Love You', 'Goody Goody', 'You Must Have Been A Beautiful Baby', 'And The Angels Sing', 'Cuckoo In The Clock', 'Day In - Day Out' and 'I Thought About You'. In the latter part of the decade, he appeared frequently on radio, as MC and singer with Paul Whiteman, with Benny Goodman and Bob Crosby. With his southern drawl and warm, good-natured style, he was a natural for the medium, and, in the early 40s, had his own show, *Johnny Mercer's Music Shop*. During this period, Mercer became a director of the songwriter's copyright organization, ASCAP. Also, in 1942, he combined with songwriter-turned-film-producer, Buddy DeSylva, and businessman, Glen Wallich, to form Capitol Records, which was, in its original form, dedicated to musical excellence, a policy which reflected Mercer's approach to all his work.

He had previously had record hits with other writers' songs, such as 'Mr Gallagher And Mr Sheen' and 'Small Fry', along with his own 'Mr. Meadowlark' (a duet with Bing Crosby), and 'Strip Polka'. For Capitol, he continued to register in the US Hit Parade with popular favourites such as 'Personality', 'Candy'; and some of his own numbers such as 'G.I. Jive', 'Ac-Cent-Tchu-Ate The Positive', 'Glow Worm'; and 'On The Atchison, Topeka, And The Santa Fe', which was also sung by Judy Garland in the film, *The Harvey Girls* (1946), and gained Mercer his first Academy Award.

His other 40s song successes, many of them from movies, included 'The Waiter And The Porter And The Upstairs Maid' (from *Birth Of The Blues*); 'Blues In The Night' and 'This Time's The Dream's On Me' (*Blues In The Night*); 'Tangerine', 'I Remember You' and 'Arthur Murray Taught Me Dancing In A Hurry' (*The Fleet's In*), 'Dearly Beloved' and 'I'm Old Fashioned' (*You Were Never Lovelier*) (Kern); 'Hit The Road To Dreamland' and 'That Old Black Magic', Billy Daniels' 'Identity Song' (*Star Spangled Rhythm*), 'My Shining Hour' (*The Sky's The Limit*) and 'Come Rain Or Come Shine', 'Legalize My Name' and 'Any Place I Hang My Hat Is Home', from the stage show *St. Louis Woman* (Arlen).

Two particularly attractive compositions were 'Fools Rush In' (with Rube Bloom), which was a big hit for Glenn Miller and the movie title song 'Laura', with Mercer's lyric complementing a haunting tune by David Raksin. Mercer's collaboration with Hoagy Carmichael produced some of his most memorable songs, such as 'Lazybones', 'The Old Music Master', 'Skylark', 'How Little We Know' and the Oscar-winning 'In The Cool, Cool, Cool Of The Evening', sung by Bing Crosby and Jane Wyman in the film *Here Comes The Groom* (1951). In the same year, Mercer provided both the music and lyrics for the Broadway show, *Top Banana*, a 'burlesque musical' starring Phil Silvers and a host of mature funnymen. The entertaining score included the witty 'A Word A Day'.

The 50s were extremely productive years for Mercer, with songs such as 'Here's To My Lady', 'I Wanna Be Around' (later successful for Tony Bennett), and yet more movie songs, including 'I Want To Be A Dancing Man', 'The Bachelor Dinner Song' and 'Seeing's Believing', sung by Fred Astaire in *The Belle Of New York*; 'I Like Men' (covered by Peggy Lee), 'I Got Out Of Bed On The Right Side' and 'Ain't Nature Grand' from *Dangerous When Wet;* and 'Something's Gotta Give' and 'Sluefoot' (words and music by Mercer) from another Fred Astaire film, *Daddy Longlegs*. Mercer also provided additional lyrics to 'When The World Was Young' ('Ah, The Apple Trees'), 'Midnight Sun', 'Early Autumn' and 'Autumn Leaves'. The highlight of the decade was, perhaps, *Seven Brides For Seven Brothers* (1954). Starring Howard Keel and Jane Powell, Mercer and Gene DePaul's 'pip of a score' included 'Spring, Spring, Spring', 'Bless Your Beautiful Hide', 'Sobbin' Women', 'When You're In Love', and 'Goin' Courtin', amongst others. Two years later Mercer and DePaul got together again for the stage show, *Li'l Abner*, starring Stubby Kaye, and including such songs as 'Namely You', 'Jubilation T. Cornpone' and 'The Country's In The Very Best Of Hands'. It ran on Broadway for nearly 700 performances and was filmed in 1959.

The early 60s brought Mercer two further Academy Awards; one for 'Moon River' from *Breakfast At Tiffany's* (1961), and the other, the title song to *The Days Of Wine And Roses* (1962). 'Moon River' was the song in which Mercer first coined the now-famous phrase, 'my huckleberry friend'. Danny Williams took the former song to the UK number slot in 1961, while namesake Andy Williams and Mercer's co-composer Henry Mancini both scored US Top 40 hits with the latter in 1963. Mancini also wrote other movie songs with Mercer, such as 'Charade', 'The Sweetheart Tree' (from *The Great Race*) and 'Whistling Away The Dark' (*Darling Lili*). In the early 70s, Mercer spent a good deal of time in

Britain, and, in 1974, wrote the score, with André Previn, for the West End musical, *The Good Companions*. He died, two years later, on 25 June 1976, in Los Angeles, California, USA.

Several of his 1,000-plus songs became an integral part of many a singer's repertoire. In 1992, Frank Sinatra was still using 'One For My Baby' (music by Harold Arlen), 'the greatest saloon song ever written', as a moving set-piece in his concert performances. 'Dream' (words and music by Mercer), closed Sinatra's radio and television shows for many years, and the singer also made impressive recordings of lesser-known Mercer items, such as 'Talk To Me, Baby' and 'The Summer Wind'. Memories of his rapport with Bing Crosby in their early days were revived in 1961, when Mercer recorded *Two Of A Kind* with Bobby Darin, full of spontaneous asides, and featuring Mercer numbers such as 'Bob White' and 'If I Had My Druthers', plus other humorous oldies, like 'Who Takes Care Of The Caretaker's Daughter' and 'My Cutie's Due At Two-To-Two Today'. Further recordings include: *Audio Scrap Book* (1964-74), *Johnny Mercer Sings Johnny Mercer, Ac-Cent-Tchu-Ate The Positive, Johnny Mercer's Music Shop* and *My Huckleberry Friend*. Several artists, such as Marlene VerPlanck and Susannah McCorkle, have devoted complete albums to his work. In 1992 Capitol Records celebrated its 50th anniversary by issuing *Two Marvellous For Words: Capitol Sings Johnny Mercer*, which included some of the label's most eminent artists singing their co-founder's popular song lyrics.

Further reading: *Our Huckleberry Friend: The Life, Times And Song Lyrics Of Johnny Mercer*, B. Back and G. Mercer. *Johnny Mercer In Song By Song*, C. Brahms and N. Sherrin.

Merman, Ethel

b. Ethel Agnes Zimmermann, 16 January 1909, Astoria, New York, USA, d. 15 February 1984, New York, USA. Merman was one of the most celebrated ladies of the Broadway musical stage. A dynamic entertainer, with a loud, brash, theatrical singing style, flawless diction, and extravagant manner she usually played a gutsy lady with a heart of gold. Merman worked as a secretary, then sang in nightclubs, gradually working up to the best spots. Noticed by producer Vinton Freedly while singing at the Brooklyn Paramount, she was signed for George and Ira Gershwin's Broadway show, *Girl Crazy* (1930), and was a great success, stopping the show with her version of 'I Got Rhythm', a song which became one of her life-long themes. She was equally successful in George White's *Scandals* (1931), in which she co-starred with Rudy Vallee, and sang 'My Song' and 'Life Is Just A Bowl Of Cherries', and *Take A Chance* (1932), when her two big numbers were 'Eadie Was A Lady' and 'Rise 'N' Shine'. In 1934, Merman starred in *Anything Goes*, the first of five Cole Porter musical shows. It was one of his best, full of song hits such as 'I Get A Kick Out Of You', 'All through The Night', 'You're The Top' (one of Porter's accomplished 'list' songs), 'Anything Goes' and 'Blow, Gabriel, Blow'. Merman also appeared in the 1936 film version of the show with Bing Crosby. The other Porter shows in which she appeared were *Red Hot And Blue!* (1936), co-starring Jimmy Durante and Bob Hope, with the songs, 'Down In The Depths (On The Ninetieth Floor)', 'It's De-Lovely' and 'Ridin' High'; *DuBarry Was A Lady* (1939), with 'But In The Morning, No!', 'Do I Love You?', 'Give Him The Oo-La-La', 'Katie Went To Haiti' and 'Friendship'; *Panama Hattie* (1940), featuring 'I've Still Got My Health', 'Let's Be Buddies', 'Make It Another Old-Fashioned, Please' and 'I'm Throwing A Ball Tonight'; *Something For The Boys* (1943) featuring 'Hey, Good Lookin', 'He's A Right Guy', 'Could It Be You' and 'The Leader Of A Big Time Band'. Merman's longest-running musical was Irving Berlin's *Annie Get Your Gun* (1946), which ran for 1,147 performances. As the sharp-shooting Annie Oakley, she introduced such Berlin classics as 'They Say It's Wonderful', 'Doin' What Comes Naturally', 'I Got The Sun In The Morning', 'You Can't Get A Man With A Gun', and the song which was to become another of her anthems, 'There's No Business Like Show Business'. Merman's next Broadway show, *Call Me Madam* again had an Irving Berlin score. This time, as Sally Adams, ambassador to the mythical country of Lichtenburg, she triumphed again with numbers such as 'Marrying For Love', 'You're Just In Love', 'The Best Thing For You', 'Can You Use Any Money Today?', and as 'The Hostess With The Mostest': 'On The Ball'.

She also starred in the 1953 film version of the show, with George Sanders, Donald O'Connor, and Vera Ellen. Often called the climax to Merman's career, *Gypsy* (1959), with a score by Jule Styne and Stephen Sondheim, saw her cast as the domineering mother of stripper, Gypsy Rose Lee, and Merman gave the kind of performance for which she had never before been asked. Her songs included 'Some People', 'Small World', 'You'll Never Get Away From Me', 'Together', 'Rose's Turn', and her triumphant hymn, 'Everthing's Coming Up Roses'. Such was her command of this role that the choice of Rosalind Russell for the film version was greeted with incredulity in some circles. Apart from a brief revival of *Annie Get Your Gun* (1966), and a spell as a replacement in *Hello, Dolly!*, (she had turned down the role when the show was originally cast), *Gypsy* was Merman's last Broadway appearance. Although the stage was her *metier*, she made several Hollywood films including *We're Not Dressing* (1934), *Kid Millions* and *Strike Me Pink* (both 1935 with Eddie Cantor)

Ethel Merman with Jimmy McHugh

Alexander's Ragtime Band (1938), with Tyrone Power, Alice Faye, and Don Ameche; and *There's No Business Like Show Business* (1954), in which she starred with Dan Dailey, Donald O'Connor and Marilyn Monroe. There were also non-singing roles in comedy films such as *It's A Mad, Mad, Mad, Mad World* (1963), *The Art Of Love* (1965) and *Airplane!* (1980). Merman appeared regularly on television from the 50s through to the 70s in specials and guest spots, and in cabaret. In 1953 she teamed up with another Broadway legend, Mary Martin, for the historic Ford 50th Anniversary Show, highlights of which were issued on a Decca album. On the same label was her *Musical Autobiography* (2-album set). Besides the many hits from her shows, her record successes included, 'How Deep Is The Ocean', 'Move It Over', 'Dearie'/'I Said My Pajamas (And Put On My Prayers)' and 'If I Knew You Were Coming I'd've Baked A Cake', all three duets with Ray Bolger. After a distinguished career, lasting over 50 years, Merman's final major appearance was at a Carnegie Hall benefit concert in 1982. She died in 1984. The following year a biographical tribute show, *Call Me Miss Birdseye*, starring Libby Morris, was mounted at the Donmar Warehouse Theatre in London.

Selected albums: *Merman Sings Merman* (1973), *Annie Get Your Gun* (1974), *Ethel's Ridin' High* (1975). Compilations: *Ethel Was A Lady* (1984), *The World Is Your Ballon* (1987), *Ethel Merman* (1988).

Further reading: *Who Could Ask For Anything More?* (US) *Don't Call Me Madam* (UK), Ethel Merman. *Merman*, Ethel Merman.

Merrill, Bob

b. H. Robert Merrill Levan, 17 May 1921, Atlantic City, New Jersey, USA. After working at a number of jobs in various parts of the USA, Merrill began singing in clubs and on the stage. He was also an effective mimic. After military service during World War II, he worked in Hollywood as a dialogue director and also made a handful of appearances as an actor. It was while working on a film that he was asked by comedienne Dorothy Shay to write some songs for her forthcoming album. Merrill did as she suggested, and the financial rewards this brought encouraged him to pursue songwriting as a career. Among the early songs he wrote were 'Lover's Gold' (music by Morty Nevins), 'Fool's Paradise' and 'The Chicken Song' (with Terry Shand). In 1950 Merrill had his first hit with 'If I Knew You Were Coming I'd've Baked A Cake' (Al Hoffman and Clem Watts). In the early 50s Merrill's successes included 'Sparrow In The Treetop', 'Truly, Truly Fair' and 'How Much Is That Doggie In The Window?'. Other 50s songs were 'Let Me In', 'Red Feathers' 'Walkin' To Missouri', 'Mambo Italiano', 'Where Will The Dimple Be?' and 'A Sweet Old-Fashioned Girl'.

Despite the success of these songs, Merrill wanted to write more serious music and, in 1956, he composed the score for the musical version of Eugene O'Neill's novel, *Anna Christie*, which opened on Broadway in May 1957 under the title, *New Girl In Town*. Merrill followed this with another O'Neill story, *Ah, Wilderness!*, which came to the stage as *Take Me Along*. Both shows had moderate success, each exceeding 400 performances, but his next show was his best. *Carnival* opened on 13 April 1961, and ran for 719 performances. Starring Anna Maria Alberghetti, the show included songs such as 'Love Makes The World Go Round', 'Yes, My Heart' and 'Her Face'. In 1964 he collaborated with composer Jule Styne on *Funny Girl* which proved to be an enormous hit, but, despite several attempts, his theatrical career declined thereafter. In 1972 Merrill wrote the lyrics for another Styne show, *Sugar*, which was based on the highly successful Billy Wilder film *Some Like It Hot*. Despite mixed reviews, it ran for 505 performances, and, retitled *Some Like it Hot*, became a short-lived vehicle for the popular UK entertainer Tommy Steele in 1992. Merrill teamed with Styne once again in 1993 (under the pseudonym of Paul Stryker) to provide extra lyrics for *The Red Shoes* which lasted for just three days. In contrast, however, a new career as a screenwriter blossomed and, in addition, he has taught at the University of California in Los Angeles.

Merrily We Roll Along

Two of the musical theatre's current heavyweights went into the Broadway ring during the the 1981/2 season. The result of the contest gave theatre-goers on both sides of the Atlantic a foretaste of the significant shift in the balance of power that was about to take place during the next 10 years: the English champion, Andrew Lloyd Webber, with *Joseph And The Amazing Technicolor Dreamcoat* scored 747 performances; and the native New Yorker, Stephen Sondheim, with *Merrily We Roll Along*, only 16 performances. Prior to the latter show's debut at the Alvin Theatre on 16 November 1981, the smart money was on a Sondheim show that eschewed the usual brittle exposition of contemporary life, in favour of a more traditional style musical entertainment - musical comedy - and that is what Sondheim eventually claimed it to be. George Furth's book was based on the 1934 play by George S. Kaufman and Moss Hart. The story, which is told in flashback, tells of a successful composer, Franklin Shepard (as a young man - Jim Walton; aged 43 - Geoffrey Horne), a lyricist, Charles Kringas (Lonny Price), and a mutual friend of the pair, Mary Flynn (Ann Morrison). Shepard is the central character, and the details of his wasted life - the betrayal of his wife and friends in the pursuit of money and glory over a period of some 20 years – are revealed before the final scene, in which – because in this piece the end is the beginning – the friends are meeting in 1957 for the first time. Sondheim constructed the score in what he called 'modular blocks' – the release of one song would be the verse of another, and the chorus of that one could serve as the release of the next, and so on. Some of the songs, such as 'Opening Doors', 'The Hills Of Tomorrow', and 'Good Thing Going'. were based on the same tune – it was Sondheim at his most inventive, and, at least, the composer was nominated for a Tony Award. The rest of the numbers included 'Not A Day Goes By', 'Franklin Shepard Inc.', 'Bobby And Jackie And Jack', 'Like It Was', 'It's A Hit', 'Now You Know', 'Meet The Blob', and 'Merrily We Roll Along'. Most aspects of the production came in for severe criticism: Eugene Lees's sparse sets, Larry Fuller's choreography, and a cast that was considered by many to be far too young and inexperienced. The celebrated partnership between Sondheim and director and producer Hal Prince came – perhaps temporarily to an end – with this show. As with most, if not all, Sondheim shows, this one continued to live on far beyond its two-weeks run in New York, via the excellent Original Cast album, and various provincial productions. One such, was mounted by the Leicester Haymarket Theatre in England, in 1992, the starting-off point for many fine original musicals and revivals. This one starred Michael Cantwell, Maria Friedman, Evan Pappas, Gareth Snook, and Jacqueline Dankworth, the daughter of jazz musicians John Dankworth and Cleo Laine.

Merry Widow, The

A perfect example of the kind of Viennese operetta that was so popular in the early part of the 20th century before it was overtaken by the more contemporary shows of Jerome Kern and the other pioneers of musical comedy. With it's superb score by Franz Lehár, *The Merry Widow* was first offered to the public at the Theatre an der Wien in Vienna, on 30 December 1905, under the title of *Die Lustige Witwe*. The book, by Victor Leon and Leo Stein, was based on Henri Meilhac's play *L'Attaché d'Ambassade*. Eighteen months later, on 8 June 1907, when it was presented by George Edwardes at Daly's Theatre in London, the show had a new book by Basil Hood (who declined to be credited), and English lyrics by Adrian Ross. The classic story concerns the arrival in France of Sonia Sadoya (Lily Elsie), a wealthy widow from Marsovia, who is hunting for a husband. If she marries a Frenchman, her millions will be lost for ever to the impoverished principality, and Ambassador Baron Popoff (George Graves) will be out of a job. Prince Danilo (Joseph Coyne), a secretary to the legation, is instructed to make sure that a Franco-Marsovian union does not take place, preferably by marrying the lady himself. The joyous and memorable score contained several enduring favourites such as 'Maxim's', 'I Love You So' (also know as the 'Merry Widow Waltz'), 'Love In My Heart Awakening', 'Vilia', 'Women', 'Home', 'A Dutiful Wife', 'The Girls At Maxim's, and 'Silly, Silly Cavalier'. Enthusiastic audiences, with the ladies dressed in their 'Merry Widow' attire, flocked to the theatre for 778 performances – it was a tremendous success. The 1907 New York production, with Ethel Jackson, ran for a year, and was followed by several Broadway revivals through to the 40s. West End audiences, too, saw the show on many occasions, including 1958 (with June Bronhill), 1969 (with Lizbeth Webb), and 1985 (Helen Kuchareck). All the revivals to date have had revised books and scores. Many other professional and amateur productions are taking place constantly throughout the world, one of the most recent being that mounted by the Paper Mill Playhouse, New Jersey, USA, in 1991. Three film versions have been released: in 1925 (silent), in 1934 with Jeanette Macdonald and Maurice Chevalier, and a 1952 remake with Fernando Lamas and Lana Turner.

Mexican Hayride

A Mike Todd production – a Cole Porter score – this show was one of the most lavish and successful of the World War II period. It opened at the Winter Garden Theatre in New York on 28 January 1944, and was still around well over a year later. The book, by Herbert and Dorothy Fields, follows Joe Bascom (Bobby Clark), an ex-numbers racketeer from the USA who is on the run in Mexico from the police – and various ladies – through a series of hilarious adventures and disguises. Porter's Latin-styled score was full of good things such as 'I Love You', which was sung in the show by Wilbur Evans, and later became a US number 1 record for Bing Crosby. The other lively and attractive numbers included 'Sing To Me, Guitar', 'Abracadabra', 'Carlotta', 'There Must Be Someone For Me', 'Girls', and 'Count Your Blessings'. Bobby Clark was the man they all came to see, and he was at the top of his form. The veteran comedian had spent around 17 years in vaudeville in partnership with Paul McCullough before he broke through on Broadway in 1922. June Havoc, sister of the legendary Gypsy Rose Lee, was also in the cast of *Mexican Hayride*, along with George Givot, Luba Malina, Corinna Mura, Edith Meiser, Bill Callahan, Paul Haakon, and Candy Jones. The 1948 film version starred Abbott And Costello, but Porter's songs were dropped so the film was not classed as a musical.

Meyer, Joseph

b. 12 March 1894, Modesto, California, USA, d. 22

June 1987, New York, USA. Meyer was a composer of popular songs, from the early 20s through the 40s. He studied the violin in Paris, and served as a cafe violinist when he returned to the USA in 1908. After military service in World War I, he spent some time in the shipping business before taking up songwriting. In 1922, with Harry Ruby, he wrote 'My Honey's Lovin' Arms', which became a hit for Benny Goodman, Isham Jones and the California Ramblers, and was successfully revived on Barbra Streisand's debut album in 1963. During the 20s and 30s, Meyer contributed songs to several stage shows, including *Battling Butler* ('You're So Sweet' and 'As We Leave The Years Behind') and *Big Boy* (starring Al Jolson singing 'California, Here I Come'). Another song from *Big Boy*, 'If You Knew Susie', was recorded by Eddie Cantor. Meyer also contributed to *Gay Paree* ('Bamboo Babies'), *Andre Charlote's Revue Of 1925* ('A Cup Of Coffee, A Sandwich, And You'), *Sweetheart Time* ('Who Loves You As I Do?'), *Just Fancy* ('You Came Along'), *Here's Howe* ('Crazy Rhythm' and 'Imagination'), *Lady Fingers* ('There's Something In That', 'An Open Book' and 'I Love You More Then Yesterday'), *Wake Up And Dream*, *Jonica*, *Shoot The Works* ('Chirp, Chirp'), the *Ziegfeld Follies Of 1934* and *New Faces Of 1936* ('It's High Time I Got The Low-Down On You'). His film songs included 'I Love You, I Hate You' (*Dancing Sweeties*), 'Can It Be Possible?' (*The Life Of The Party*), 'Oh, I Didn't Know', 'It's An Old Southern Custom', 'It's Time To Say Goodnight', 'I Got Shoes, I Got Shoesies' and 'According To The Moonlight' (George White's 1935 *Scandals*). His other popular numbers included 'Clap Hands, Here Comes Charley' (the signature tune of pianist, Charlie Kunz), 'Sweet So And So', 'Just A Little Closer', 'How Long Will It Last?' (used in the 1931 Joan Crawford-Clark Gable drama *Possessed*), 'Isn't It Heavenly?', 'I Wish I Were Twins', 'And Then They Called It Love', 'Hurry Home', 'Love Lies', 'Let's Give Love A Chance', 'Passe', 'But I Did', 'Fancy Our Meeting', 'I've Got A Heart Filled With Love', 'There's No Fool Like An Old Fool', 'Idle Gossip' and 'Watching The Clock'. His collaborators included Billy Moll, Billy Rose, Al Dubin, Jack Yellen, Cliff Friend, Buddy De Sylva, Herb Magidson, Al Jolson, Phil Charig, Irving Caesar, Carl Sigman, Frank Loesser, Eddie De Lange, and Douglas Furber. Meyer died, after a long illness, in June 1987, at the age of 93.

Milk And Honey

Jerry Herman's first Broadway score, and reputedly the first Broadway musical ever to have an Israeli setting - *Fiddler On The Roof* came along three years after *Milk And Honey* opened on Broadway at the Martin Beck Theatre on 10 October 1961. Don Appel's book deals mainly with the romantic relationship between Phil (Robert Weede) and Ruth (Mimi Benzell), two middle-aged American tourists in Israel. At the end of the piece, their on-off affair is still unresolved, mainly due to Ruth's not unreasonable misgivings concerning Phil's wife. Molly Picon played another American tourist - but one with a mission - a widow in determined pursuit of a new husband in the shape of Mr. Horowitz (Juki Arkin). Picon, a veteran of the Yiddish theatre, also starred in the film of *Fiddler On The Roof*. Other members of the cast included Tommy Rall and Lanna Saunders. Herman's score was acclaimed as 'melodically inventive', and particular praise was reserved for Phil and Ruth's touching 'Shalom'. However, the rest of the songs, such as 'There's No Reason In The World', 'That Was Yesterday', 'Let's Not Waste A Moment', 'Like A Young Man', 'As Simple As That', 'Chin Up, Ladies', and 'Independence Day Hora', were extremely impressive, and lingered in the memory. *Milk And Honey* ran for 543 performances - without making a profit. Still, the money would soon be rolling in for Herman: his first smash-hit, *Hello Dolly*, was set to make its elegant entrance on Broadway in 1964.

Minnelli, Liza

b. Liza May Minnelli, 12 March 1946, Hollywood, California, USA. An extremely vivacious and animated actress, singer and dancer, in films, concerts, musical shows and television. She was named Liza after the Gershwin song, and May after the mother of her film-director father, Vincente Minnelli. Liza's mother was show-business legend Judy Garland. On the subject of her first name, Miss Minnelli is musically quite precise: 'It's Liza with an 'z', not Lisa with a 's'/'Cos Liza with a 'z' goes zzz, not sss'. She spent a good deal of her childhood in Hollywood, where her playmates included Mia Farrow. At the age of two-and-a-half, she made her screen premiere in the closing sequence of *In The Good Old Summer Time*, as the daughter of the musical film's stars, Garland and Van Johnson. When she was seven, she danced on the stage of the Palace Theatre, New York, while her mother sang 'Swanee'. In 1962, after initially showing no interest in a show-business career, Minnelli served as an apprentice in revivals of the musicals, *Take Me Along* and *The Flower Drum Song*, and later played Anne Frank in a stock production. By the following year she was accomplished enough to win a Promising Personality Award for her third lead performance in an Off-Broadway revival of the 1941 Blane/Martin Musical, *Best Foot Forward*, and later toured in road productions of *Carnival*, *The Pajama Game*, and *The Fantasticks*. She also made her first album, *Liza! Liza!* which sold over 500,000 copies after it was released in 1964. In November of that year, Minnelli appeared with Judy Garland at the

Liza Minnelli

London Palladium. Comparatively unknown in the UK, she startled the audience with dynamic performances of songs such as 'The Travellin' Life' and 'Gypsy In My Soul'; - almost 'stealing' the show from the more experienced artist. Her first Broadway show, and an early association with songwriters John Kander and Fred Ebb, came with *Flora And The Red Menace* (1965), for which she was given a Tony Award, though the show closed after only 87 performances. In 1966, she made her New York cabaret debut at the Plaza Hotel to enthusiastic reviews and, in 1967, married Australian singer/songwriter, Peter Allen. Her film career started in 1968, with a supporting role in Albert Finney's first directorial effort, *Charlie Bubbles*, and in 1969, she was nominated for an Academy Award for her performance as Pookie Adams in the film of John Nichols' novel, *The Sterile Cuckoo*. She took time off from making her third film, *Tell Me That You Love Me, Junie Moon*, to attend the funeral of her mother, who died in 1969. In the following year she and Peter Allen announced their separation.

In 1972, Liza Minnelli became a superstar. The film of Kander and Ebb's Broadway hit, *Cabaret*, won nine Oscars, including Best Film and, for her role as Sally Bowles, Minnelli was named Best Actress and appeared on the front covers of *Newsweek* and *Time* magazines in the same week. She also won an Emmy for her television Special, *Liza With A Z*, directed by Bob Fosse. Her concerts were sell-outs; when she played the Olympia, Paris, they dubbed her 'la petite Piaf Americano'. In 1973, she met producer/director Jack Haley Jnr. while contributing to his film project, *That's Entertainment*. Haley's father had played the Tin Man in Judy Garland's most famous picture, *The Wizard Of Oz*. Haley Jnr and Minnelli married in 1974, and in the same year she broke Broadway records and won a special Tony Award for a three-week series of one-woman shows at the Winter Garden. Her next two movies, *Lucky Lady* and *A Matter Of Time* received lukewarm reviews, but she made up for these in 1977, with her next film project, *New York, New York*. Co-starring with Robert DeNiro, and directed by Martin Scorsese, Minnelli's dramatic performance as a young band singer in the period after World War II was a personal triumph. This was the last film she made until *Arthur* (1981), in which she played a supporting role to Dudley Moore. The musical theme for *Arthur*, 'Best You Can Do', was co-written by her ex-husband, Peter Allen. A renewed association with Kander and Ebb for the Broadway musical, *The Act* (1977), was dismissed by some critics as being little more than a series of production numbers displaying the talents of Liza Minnelli. She won another Tony Award, but collapsed from exhaustion during the show's run. In 1979, she was divorced from Jack Haley Jnr., and

married Italian sculptor, Mark Gero. Rumours were appearing in the press which speculated about her drug and alcohol problems, and for a couple of years she was virtually retired. In 1984, she was nominated for yet another Tony for her performance on Broadway in *The Rink*, with Chita Rivera, but dropped out of the show to seek treatment for drug and alcohol abuse at the Betty Ford Clinic in California. She started her comeback in 1985, and the following year, on her 40th birthday, opened to a sold-out London Palladium, the first time she had played the theatre since that memorable occasion in 1964; she received the same kind of reception that her mother did then. In the same year, back in the USA, Minnelli won the Golden Globe Award as Best Actress in *A Time To Live*, a television adaptation of the true story, *Intensive Care*, by Mary-Lou Weisman. During the late 80s, she joined Frank Sinatra and Sammy Davis Jnr. for a world tour, dubbed *The Ultimate Event!*, and in 1989 collaborated with the UK pop group, the Pet Shop Boys, on the album, *Results*. A single from the album, Stephen Sondheim's composition, 'Losing My Mind', gave Liza Minnelli her first chart entry, reaching the UK Top 10. She also appeared with Dudley Moore in *Arthur 2: On The Rocks*, and co-starred with Julie Walters in the film version of the successful British comedy musical, *Stepping Out* (1990). Minnelli's career in film and music has enabled her to transcend the title, 'Judy Garland's daughter'.

Albums: *Best Foot Forward* (1963, stageshow soundtrack), *Liza! Liza!* (1964), *It Amazes Me* (1965), *The Dangerous Christmas Of Red Riding Hood* (1965, film soundtrack), with Judy Garland *'Live' At The London Palladium* (1965), *Flora The Red Menace* (1965, film soundtrack), *There Is A Time* (1966), *New Feelin'* (1970), *Cabaret* (1972, film soundtrack), *Liza With A 'Z'* (1972, television soundtrack), *Liza Minnelli The Singer* (1973), *Live At The Winter Garden* (1974), *Lucky Lady* (1976), *Tropical Nights* (1977), *Live! - At Carnegie Hall* (1988), *Results* (1989), *Live From Radio City Music Hall* (1992).

Further reading: *Liza*, James Robert Parish.

Miss Hook Of Holland

One of the most popular London musicals in the early part of the century, this show was sub-titled a 'Dutch musical incident in two acts', when it opened at the Prince of Wales Theatre in London on 31 January 1907. The score was the work of Paul Rubens who had enjoyed great success five years earlier with *A Country Girl*. Rubens collaborated with Austen Hurgon on the book which concerns Mr. Hook (G.P. Huntley), a liqueur distiller in Amsterdam. His daughter, Sally (Isabel Jay) boosts the company's sales by inventing a liqueur made of 61 different ingredients, which she calls Cream In The Sky.

However, the important recipe is stolen and passed from hand to hand during a romantic, but sometimes bewildering plot, before it is returned to Hook's safe. None of the songs endured, but there were several pleasant numbers including 'Little Miss Wooden Shoes', 'The Sleepy Canal', 'A Little Pink Petty From Peter', 'Tra-La-La', 'The House That Hook Built', and 'Cream Of The Sky'. An excellent London run of 462 performances was followed by a further 119 at the Criterion Theatre in New York in 1907. In the same year the show was presented in Vienna, and there were London revivals in 1914 and 1932.

Miss Liberty

Three years after his biggest success with *Annie Get Your Gun* in 1946, Irving Berlin came up with the score for this show, which, on the face of it, had all the right credentials: a book by Pulitzer Prize-winning playwright Robert E. Sherwood, choreography by Jerome Robbins, direction by Moss Hart, and, of course, music and lyrics by Berlin himself. It opened at the Imperial Theatre in New York on 15 July 1949, with Sherwood's cosy, patriotic story set in New York and Paris in 1885. The plot tells of how Horace Miller (Eddie Albert), an inept newpaper photographer, travels to France to find the model who posed for the Statue Of Liberty. He returns with the wrong one, and all sorts of complications have to be overcome before everyone gathers at the statue's dedication ceremony to sing 'Give Me Your Tired, Your Poor', Berlin's musical adaptation of the poem by Emma Lazarus. Monique Dupont, played by the accomplished ballerina, Allyn McLerie, was the lady that Horace fell for in Paris and took back with him to America, only to find that, waiting for him there was his girlfriend, Maisie Dell (Mary McCarty). Berlin's score contained two songs that became popular: 'Let's Take An Old Fashioned Walk' was a big hit for Perry Como, and for Doris Day with Frank Sinatra; and both Como and Jo Stafford took 'Just One Way To Say I Love You' into the US Hit Parade. The rest of the numbers included 'Little Fish In A Big Pond', 'I'd Like My Picture Took', 'Homework', 'Falling Out Of Love Can Be Fun', 'Paris Wakes Up And Smiles', 'Only For Americans', and 'You Can Have Him', an untypical ballad containing 'truth and sarcasm, and dedicated to the 'other woman'' - ('You can have him/I don't want him/He's not worth fighting for/Besides, there's plenty more where he came from'), which received a sophisticated reading on the abum, *The Nancy Wilson Show!* (1965). Despite its virtues, and its patriotic theme, *Miss Liberty* did not start any parades, and closed after 308 performances.

Miss Saigon

A re-working of Puccini's enduring *Madame Butterfly*

as a Vietnam war tale, set in Saigon during the last days of the American presence there in 1975. The music was by Claude-Michel Schonberg, with lyrics by Richard Maltby Jnr. and Alain Boublil (adapted from the original French lyrics by Boublil) with additional material by Maltby. *Miss Saigon* opened at the Drury Lane Theatre in London on 20 September 1989. The dramatic story concerns a young marine, Chris (Simon Bowman), who falls in love with a would-be prostitute Kim (Lea Salonga), but, partly owing to the chaotic troop evacuation, returns to America without her. As with Puccini the wartime liaison ends in tragedy, with the soldier returning to Saigon only to find the girl has commited suicide. The show was hailed as being 'savagely objective . . . a critical shot at the destabilizing and corrupting American role in Vietnam . . . more than a mature musical, a tough popular opera, clear-headed but romantic, warm as well as sordid and brutal'. Jonathan Pryce played the central role of the Engineer, the cynical and ruthless owner of the sleazy Dreamland Bar, and he has the show's big number, 'The American Dream', a savage attack on US commercialism. The remainder of a score containing some 24 songs, with lyrics that are 'sharp, hard-hitting, elegantly but bitterly sardonic', included 'The Heat Is On In Saigon', 'The Movie On My Mind', 'Why God, Why?', 'The Last Night Of The World', 'You Will Not Touch Him', 'I'd Give My Life For You', 'Sun And Moon', 'Now That I've Seen Her', and 'The Sacred Bird'. Jonathan Pryce and Lea Salonga both won Olivier Awards for their outstanding performances, and *Miss Saigon* was widely acclaimed, and settled in for a long stay. The Broadway transfer was in doubt for some time when American Equity banned Pryce from reprising his role because 'it would be an affront to the Asian community'. When producer Cameron Mackintosh reportedly threatened to cancel the production, they relented, and, after opening in April 1991, the show recouped its $10.9 million investment in 39 weeks. Tony Awards went to Pryce, Salonga, and featured actor (Hinton Battle). Since then, *Miss Saigon* has been sucessfully presented in many parts of the world, including Toronto, where a new 2000-seater theatre, the Prince of Wales, was built especially to house the Canadian production.

Mlle. Modiste

Composer Victor Herbert's first collaboration with librettist and lyricst Henry Blossom was a tremendous success. - in the long term. After its debut at the Knickerbocker Theatre in New York on 25 December 1905, it ran for 202 performances. That was a decent enough run in those days anyway, and it gained in popularity over the years mainly due to the its star, the lovely Fritzi Scheff, and her close

Jonathan Pryce (*Miss Saigon*)

identification with the operetta during its many tours and subsequent Broadway revivals. Scheff played the role of Fifi, who works in a hat shop owned by Mme. Cecil (Josephine Bartlett). She is in love with Captain Etienne de Bouvray (Walter Percival), but their romance is disapproved of by her employer, and the gentleman's uncle, Compte. de St. Mar (William Pruett). Josephine would also like to sing on the stage, and she confides her ambitions to a visiting American, the wealthy Hiram Bent (Claude Gillingwater). He is so taken by her charm and manner, that he offers to pay for an extensive course of singing lessons. Inevitably, when the dissenters hear her beautiful voice, they protest no more, and the marriage is allowed to take place. Fritzi Scheff, who had been with the Metropolitan Opera before she made her Broadway debut in the title role of Babette in 1903, introduced 'Kiss Me Again', one of the most cherished ballads in the history of operetta, and she also excelled on the delightful 'If I Were On The Stage' and 'The Mascot Of The Troops'. Pruett had the resolute 'I Want What I Want When I Want It', and Percival sang the engaging 'The Time, The Place And The Girl'. The rest of the score included 'Love Me, Love My Dog', 'When The Cat's Away', and 'The Nightingale And The Star'. Fritzi Scheff, who was born in Vienna in 1879, made her last Broadway appearance as Mlle. Modiste in 1929 when she was 50 years old. She died in New York on 8 April 1954.

Moby Dick

'A Whale Of A Tale' according to the publicity hand-outs - but 'a whale of a mistake', according to the critics. They harpooned the show right at the start, and even with the financial clout of Cameron Mackintosh could not mend the wounds. *Moby Dick* was tried out at the tiny Old Fire Station in Oxford in the autumn of 1991, before opening at London's Piccadilly Theatre on 17 March 1992. In Robert Longden's book, sixth-form members of a girls' school bearing a remarkable resemblance to the infamous St. Trinian's, stage a production of Herman Melville's classic story in the school swimming pool. As one critic noted: 'The degree of camp, of music-hall smut and anachronism is extreme.' Cabaret singer Tony Monopoly plays Miss Dorothy Hymen, the establishment's headmistress, who in turn plays Captain Ahab (with a cricket pad where his peg leg should be) in the musical production of *Moby Dick*. When Ahab's ship sets sail, the schoolgirls, who are supposed to be sailors, appear scantily clad in gymslips and sexy stockings, and utter ancient jokes such as 'three years at sea and no sign of Dick'. Director and librettist Longden also wrote the lyrics, and the music was composed by Hereward Kaye. Their score, which contained more than 20 numbers - but no items that stood out - included 'Hymn', 'Forbidden Seas',

'Primitive', 'Love Will Always', 'Mr. Starbuck', 'Building America', 'Save The Whale', and 'Heave'. In the face of a vicious critical reaction and dwindling audiences, Mackintosh remained committed to the production until he was forced to close after a run of 15 weeks. He sanctioned the release of a double-CD which contained a recording of the show made over the sound system as a souvenir for the cast, and indicated that *Moby* was not sunk for ever. In 1993, a production was mounted by a theatre company in Boston, Massachussetts, and in the same year, a scaled-down, revised version, entitled *Moby!,* was presented in the city of Exeter, England.

Monsieur Beaucaire

A romantic operetta with music and lyrics by André Messager and Adrian Ross, and a book by Frederick Lonsdale, which was based on the novel by Brook Tarkington. Set in the stylish city of Bath, England, in the early 18th century, when it was ruled by the so-called King of Bath, Richard 'Beau' Nash, the familiar plot concerned yet another nobleman disguised as a commoner. In this instance, the Duc d'Orléans (Marion Green), son of the King of France, is masquerading as the barber Monsieur Beaucaire. In spite of stern opposition from the Duke of Winterset (Robert Parker) (a bounder who cheats at cards), the ducal barber wins the heart of Lady Mary Carlisle (Maggie Teyte), and eventually accedes to the throne of France. After opening at the Prince's Theatre in London on 19 April 1919, the show transferred to the Palace Theatre in July, and ran for 221 performances. The gay and lively score included songs such as 'Honour And Love', That's A Woman's Way', 'Honour And Love', 'Lightly, Lightly', 'Say No More', 'Gold And Blue And White', 'Red Rose', 'The Honours Of War', 'Going To The Ball', and 'I Love You A Little'. Maggie Teyte, who had sung in leading operatic roles before turning to the musical stage, was outstanding. *Monsieur Beaucaire* was presented on Broadway in December 1991, and was produced in Paris in 1925, 1929, 1935, and 1954. A London revival played Daly's Theatre in 1931. The 1946 film version starred Bob Hope and Joan Caulfield.

More, Julian

b. 1929, England. More was a librettist and lyricist for some of the most successful British hit musical shows of the late 50s. He became interested in the theatre while at Cambridge University, and was involved as a performer and writer in undergraduate revues, and contributed the occasional item to the Watergate Theatre. In 1953 he wrote some material for the London West End revue, *Airs On A Shoestring*, which starred Max Adrian, Moyra Fraser and Betty Marsden. Two years later, he collaborated with composer James

Gilbert for the Windsor Theatre production of a 'revusical', *The World's The Limit*, and, in the following year, they had a smash hit with *Grab Me A Gondola*. Set at the Venice Film Festival, with the character of the film star heroine 'moulded' on Britain's Diana Dors, the show starred Joan Heal, Denis Quilley and June Wenham. It featured numbers such as 'That's My Biography', 'Cravin' For The Avon', 'A Man, Not a Mouse' and 'New To Me'. Even more successful was *Irma La Douce* (1958) for which More, with Monty Norman and David Heneker, provided the English book and lyrics translation to Marguerite Monnet's music. The story included such songs as 'Our Language Of Love' and 'Dis-Donc', and ran for 1,512 performance in London, and over 500 in New York. The More-Heneker-Norman team combined with Wolfe Mankowitz later in 1958 for the startling *Expresso Bongo*. The 'most important British musical for years' starred Paul Schofield, Hy Hazell and James Kenny, and ran for nine months. The score, which included 'The Shrine On The Second Floor' and 'I've Never Had It So Good', virtually disappeared from the innovative 1960 film version starring Cliff Richard and Laurence Harvey. Ironically, the lead in the road version was taken by Colin Hicks, the brother of Tommy Steele. London's theatrical scene was changing and More was unable to match previous achievements. Throughout the 60s and 70s his offerings included *The Golden Touch* (with Gilbert); *The Art Of Living* (his last collaboration with both Norman and Heneker); *The Perils Of Scobie Prilt* (with Norman); *The Man From The West* (with David Russell); *Quick, Quick, Slow* (Norman); *Good Time Johnny* (Gilbert); *R Loves J* (with Alexander Ferris) and *Bordello* (with Americans Al Frisch and Bernard Spiro). In 1979 he was back with Monty Norman for *Songbook*, 'a burlesque tale' of the work of the prolific songwriter, Mooney Shapiro. Subsequently, More settled in France, with homes in Paris and Provence, and became a successful writer of travel books, emerging occasionally to write the book and lyrics to Gilbert Becaud's music for the Broadway show, *Roza* (1987), 'a maudlin and awkwardly constructed story and inferior songs'. He also adapted Abe Burrow's original book for a London revival of Cole Porter's *Can-Can* (1988).

Morgan, Helen

b. Helen Riggins 2 August 1900, Danville, Illinois, USA, d. 8 October 1941. After working at a number of unskilled jobs, Morgan began singing in small Chicago clubs. She graduated to revue, appearing in New York in *Americana* where she was spotted by Florenz Ziegfeld, who signed her to play the role of Julie in his 1932 revival of Jerome Kern's *Show Boat*. Morgan had appeared as Julie in a 1929 film version

of *Show Boat* but it was her appearance on Broadway in the role that made her a star. Her performance of 'Bill' was a show-stopper. In fact, the composer had written the song some years before but had refrained from including it in earlier shows until he found someone capable of the right interpretation. When he heard Morgan sing it he knew that, at last, the song could be used. Morgan also staked a claim to a song by George and Ira Gershwin; her interpretation of 'The Man I Love' helped her gain the accolade of being not merely one of the first but also the best of the 'torch singers'. Morgan appeared on Broadway in the 1931 *Ziegfeld Follies* and in *George White's Scandals Of 1936*. She was also in the 1936 screen remake of *Show Boat* but by the late 30s her career was in disarray and she was heavily dependent upon alcohol. As owner of a number of Prohibition-era speakeasies she had ready access to liquor and her health rapidly deteriorated until she died of cirrhosis of the liver. Her life story was traced in a 1957 screen biography, *The Helen Morgan Story*.
Further reading: *Helen Morgan, Her Life And Legend*, G. Maxwell.

Most Happy Fella, The

Any show that opened in the same season as *My Fair Lady* was bound to be somewhat overshadowed by Alan Jay Lerner and Frederick Loewe's masterpiece, which was so obviously going to be a smash hit. However, *The Most Happy Fella* was, in some ways, a more ambitious work than its female counterpart, and enjoyed a satisfactory run of 676 performances on Broadway. The show opened on 3 May 1956 at the Imperial Theatre, and immediately confused many of the critics: was it an opera? A play with music, perhaps?. Frank Loesser, who wrote the music, lyrics, and libretto, settled on 'an extended musical comedy'. His adaptation of Sidney Howard's 1924 Pulitzer Prize-winning play, *They Knew What They Wanted*, was set in Napa Valley, California, and tells of an Italian vintner, Tony (Robert Weede, a former opera singer making his Broadway debut), who is maturing rather more quickly that grapes in his vineyard. He longs for a wife, and proposes by post to Rosabella (Jo Sullivan, who later became Loesser's wife), a waitress he has noticed in a San Francisco restaurant. To increase his chances of success, he includes a photograph of his handsome young foreman, Joey (Art Lund), and she comes hurrying on down to meet him. Even though he has deceived her, she still marries Tony - but tarries with Joey. When she discovers that she is to have Joe's baby she is determined to leave, but Tony forgives her and adopts the child as his own. With spoken dialogue at a minimum, *The Most Happy Fella* is a virtually sung-through show, and Loesser's score has moments of high emotion in songs such as 'Somebody

Somewhere', My Heart Is Full Of You', and 'Joey, Joey'. Rosabella's friend, Cleo (Susan Johnson), who follows her out from San Francisco gets pretty friendly herself with one of the ranch hands, Herman (Shorty Long), and leads the company in a hymn to Dallas, the rousing 'Big 'D'. The show's big hit song was 'Standing On The Corner', which became popular in the US for Dean Martin, and the Four Lads who repeated their success in the UK, in competition with the vocal-instrumental trio, the King Brothers. Another of the show's lighter numbers, 'Happy To Make Your Acquaintance', also entered the UK chart in a version by Sammy Davis Jnr. and Carmen McRae. The rest of Loesser's highly distinguished score, which contained well over 30 songs in a wide variety of musical styles such as arias and choral pieces, included 'Ooh! My Feet', 'Mama, Mama', 'Warm All Over', 'I Like Everybody', 'Song Of A Summer Night', 'Sposalizio', 'How Beautiful The Days', 'Rosabella', 'The Most Happy Fella', and 'Abbondanza'. *The Most Happy Fella* was not everybody's idea of what a Broadway musical should be, but, during a 20 month stay on Broadway, it won the New York Drama Critics Award for best musical, and also for ran for 288 performances at the London Coliseum. Lund reprised his role in the West End, during which time he became quite a favourite of audiences there, and returned with Richard Rogers' *No Strings* in 1963. *The Most Happy Fella* was revived on Broadway in 1979, and was presented by the New York City Opera in 1991, with Giorgio Tozzi in the lead. In the following year, the show was back on Broadway again, via the Goodspeed Opera House and Los Angeles, this time with just a two-piano orchestration which Loesser had commissioned some years before. Although critically acclaimed, the production ran for only 229 performances and lost most of its $1.4 million investment. It was nominated for four Tony Awards, but won just one - Scott Warra for best featured actor - being pipped at the post for 'best revival' by *Guys And Dolls* - another Frank Loesser show. The Original Cast album was recorded in 'real time', in two long takes - just as it was performed in the theatre, and, even with part-retakes, was completed in one day, in comparison with the 1956 three-album set which took a week to record. In 1993, a concert performance of the complete score became 'the first of its kind to be broadcast on BBC radio in England'.

Mr. Cinders

English composer Vivian Ellis's first hit came in 1929 with this show which opened on 11 February at the Adelphi Theatre in London. Ellis's co-composer was Richard Myers, and the book and lyrics were by Greatrex Newman and Clifford Grey, with additional lyrics by Vivian Ellis and Leo Robin. As the title suggests, the book is a gender-reversal of the well-worn Cinderella story with Bobby Howes as Jim Lancaster whose father has married again, thereby providing Jim with two ugly step-brothers. Binnie Hale is the rich girl masquerading as a parlour maid who becomes his 'fairy godmother', and sings the show's big hit song, 'Spread A Little Happiness' while 'dressed as a parlourmaid, high-kicking around the stage with a feather duster'. The rest of the songs in a delightful and engaging score included 'On the Amazon', 'I'm A One-Man Girl', 'Ev'ry Little Moment', 'I've Got You', 'I Could Be True To Two', and 'I Want The World To Know'. Basil Howes, Jack Melford, and Lorna Lubbard were also in the cast, and Mr. Cinders was a tremendous hit right away. After five months at the Adelphi, the show transferred to the London Pavilion in March 1929, and continued to run for 529 performances. A film version with Kenneth and George Western (the Western Brothers), Clifford Mollison and Zelma O'Neal, was released in 1934. A major London revival opened in the West End in 1983 and stayed for two performances short of the original. It's star, Denis Lawson, won an Olivier Award for best actor. Probably sparked by the 1992 Vivian Ellis biographical revue, *Spread A Little Happiness*, London audiences saw *Mr. Cinders* again during the following year, but only briefly. All the revivals 'borrowed' the occasional Ellis song from his other shows. This was also the case when *Mr. Cinders* was produced in 1988 at the Goodspeed Opera House Connecticut, USA. The piece was finally given its New York premiere at the Mazur Theatre in 1992. The song, 'Spread A Little Happiness', has endured, and surfaces frequently. Sting, the ex-lead singer with the band, Police, sang it in the 1982 film, *Brimstone And Treacle*, and it became his first solo chart hit in the UK, and it was also used during the 80s in a television commercial for margarine.

Music Box Revue

Irving Berlin and producer Sam H. Harris built their brand new Music Box Theatre on New York's West 45th Street as a showcase for Berlin's prolific output of songs. The composer had contributed many of his early songs, such as 'A Pretty Girl Is Like A Melody' and 'You'd Be Surprised', Florenz Ziegfeld's elegant productions, and this lavish revue, a stylish mixture of comedy and songs, was the first of four annual editions to play at his own cosy 1,010-seater Music Box. It opened on 22 September 1921, with a cast that included William Collier, Wilda Bennett, Paul Frawley, Ivy Sawyer, Joseph Santley, Sam Bernard, and the Brox Sisters. Berlin himself, made a brief appearance in a scene with Miriam Hopkins, an actress who went on to a successful Hollywood career in the 30s, in films such as *Dr Jekyll And Mr Hyde*,

Trouble In Paradise, and *Becky Sharp*. 'Say It With Music' was the show's outstanding number, sung by Bennett and Frawley, and it became a recurring theme during the rest of the series. The other songs included 'Everybody Step', 'The Schoolhouse Blues', 'In A Cozy Kitchenette Apartment', 'My Little Book Of Poetry', 'They Call It Dancing', and 'The Legend Of The Pearls'. Hassard Short, who was just starting out on a career during which he would be acclaimed for his imaginative design and staging, was responsible for this show, and the next two, giving way to John Murray Anderson for the final edition. Short's innovative work was recognized as a major factor in the *Music Box Revue*'s impressive run of 440 performances. The 1922 show marked the Broadway debut of several future Broadway favourites, including the actor and singer William Gaxton, who later made a habit of appearing in musicals with one of America's most cherished clowns, Victor Moore, and the comedy team of ex-vaudevillians Bobby Clark and Paul McCullough. Comedienne Charlotte Greenwood, another artist who subsequently spent much of her time in Hollyood and will be remembered particularly for her portrayal of Aunt Eller in the film of *Oklahoma!*, was also in the cast, along with Grace LaRue, Margaret and Dorothy McCarthy, and the Fairbanks Twins. The songs included 'I'm Looking For A Daddy Long Legs', 'Crinoline Days', 'Will She Come From The East?', 'Pack Up Your Sins And Go To The Devil', and 'Lady Of The Evening', and ran for 330 performances. *The Music Box Revue of 1923* - Mark III - had some sketches by George S. Kaufman and Robert Benchley, who also personally introduced his famous 'Treasurer's Report'. The rest of the cast included Frank Tinney, Joseph Santley, and Ivy Sawyer. Grace Moore, who sang with the Meropolitan Opera in the late 20s, had the charming 'Tell Me A Bedtime Story', and 'The Waltz Of Long Ago', and she duettted with John Steel on 'An Orange Grove In California' and the plaintive 'What'll I Do?'. The latter song, one of Berlin's all-time standards, was interpolated during the run of the show. Audiences for these revues were gradually declining - the 1923 version ran for 273 performances, and the final, 1924 edition, only lasted for 184. For that one, Moore was back again, as were Clarke and McCullough, along with Claire Luce, Carl Randall, and Ula Sharon. The star was funny girl Fanny Brice, who sang 'Don't Send Me Back To Petrograd' and 'I Want To Be A Ballet Dancer'. Moore had the lovely 'Tell Her In Springtime' and 'Rockabye My Baby', and, with Oscar Shaw, she also introduced the wistful 'All Alone'. The 1923 edition also played at the Palace Theatre in London, where it starred Jessie Matthews, Fred Duprez, and Joseph Santley. This series of shows served as a launching pad

for Irving Berlin's long and illustrious career which peaked with *Annie Get Your Gun* in 1946, but endured for much longer than that.

Music In The Air

This delightful musical comedy, with just a hint of operetta, and a score by Jerome Kern and Oscar Hammerstein, opened at the Alvin Theatre in New York on 8 November 1932. With America staggering to its feet following the terrible Depression, Hammerstein chose to set the story in modern-day Bavaria. Music teacher Dr. Walter Lessing (Al Shean) travels from his home in Edenhorf to the the big city of Munich, in an effort to impress an old colleague with his new composition, 'I've Told Ev'ry Little Star'. He is accompanied by his daughter, Sieglinde (Katherine Carrington), who loves to perform her father's compositions, and her friend, Karl (Walter Slezak). They are all introduced to the fiery actress and singer, Frieda Hatzfeld (Natalie Hall), who is rehearsing a musical show which has been written by her long-time lover, Bruno Mahler (Tullio Carminati). When Frieda flounces out just before the opening night, Bruno, who is quite partial to the young Sieglinde tells her to 'go out there and come back a star'. Unfortunately, the young girl is totally lacking in star quality, and she and her father realise this, and decide to return to their quiet life in the country. The score is regarded as one of Kern's finest, with the songs skifully and sympathetically integrated into the plot. They included 'The Song Is You', 'There's A Hill Beyond A Hill', 'One More Dance', 'In Egern On The Tegern Sea', 'And Love Was Born', 'I'm Alone', 'I Am So Eager', 'We Belong Together', 'When Spring Is In The Air', and, of course, 'I've Told Ev'ry Little Star', which was introduced by Walter Slezak. *Music In The Air*'s Broadway run of 342 performances was followed by a further 275 in London, where Mary Ellis took the role of Frieda. The show returned to New York, with a revised book, for a brief spell in 1951. The 1934 film version starred Gloria Swanson, John Boles and Al Shean.

Music Man, The

This musical came to the Majestic Theatre in New York on 19 December 1957 after a difficult pre-opening history. With book, music and lyrics by Meredith Willson, the show had undergone several rewrites but the author's persistence paid off and on opening night the audience was caught up in the revivalist enthusiasm of the show's characters. The story concerns Harold Hill, an itinerant con-man who persuades the citizens of River City, Iowa, that what they need is a boys' band. He will teach them to play - and even supply the instruments. Naturally, not even a penny whistle materialises. *The Music Man* was filled with engaging old-fashioned charm with songs ranging from the soulful 'Goodnight, My Someone' and 'Till There Was You' to the rousing 'Seventy-Six Trombones', by way of 'Marian The Librarian', 'Shipoopi', 'My White Knight', 'The Sadder-But-Wiser Girl', 'Pick-A-Little, Talk-A-Little', 'Gary, Indiana', 'Wells Fargo Wagon', 'Sincere' ('How can there be any sin in sincere?/Where is the good in goodbye'), 'Piano Lesson' and 'Lida Rose'/'Will I Ever Tell You'. In casting film actor Robert Preston, who had never before danced or sung, in the central role of Harold Hill, the producers took a big chance because many of Willson's songs were far more complex than they appeared on the surface. As it turned out, it was inspired casting, with Preston ably charming his way through a minefield of counter melodies, rhythmic dialogue and strutting dance routines to earn rapturous applause and critical praise. He had a *tour de force* with 'Trouble', a grim warning regarding the moral danger of introducing a pool table into the community ('That game with the fifteen numbered balls is the Devil's tool'). Co-starring with Preston was Barbara Cook as Marian Paroo; other cast members included David Burns, Iggie Wolfington, Helen Raymond, Pert Kelton, and The Buffalo Bills. The show enjoyed success, and won Tony Awards for best musical, actor (Preston), featured actress (Cook), featured actor (Burns), and musical director (Herbert Green). Several companies toured the US, and the show was also staged in Europe; the 1961 London production, which ran for 395 performances, starred Hollywood heartthrob Van Johnson. Revivals were presented on Broadway in 1965, 1980, and 1993. A film version was released in 1962 with Shirley Jones as Marian and, thankfully, Robert Preston, thus allowing millions to appreciate the exuberance of his magnificent, larger-than-life performance as Professor Harold Hill.

Mutiny!

It started with a concept album, this musical adaptation of the classic novel *Mutiny On The Bounty* – a marketing play which had been used successfully by several authors and composers in the 70s, notably Andrew Lloyd Webber and Tim Rice. This time it was the British actor and singer David Essex who was behind the release of the 1983 recording of *Mutiny!*, which spawned his Top 10 hit 'Tahiti'. Essex wrote the music and collaborated with librettist Richard Crane on the lyrics for the stage production which eventually sailed into the Piccadilly Theatre in London on 18 July 1985. The distinguished actor Frank Finlay played Captain Bligh, with Essex as Fletcher Christian, but the main character was a fully rigged HMS Bounty which was mounted on an hydraulic system and spectacularly recreated the high seas by rocking and rolling the entire stage to and fro.

The score turned out to be 'a sequence of pastiche modal folk songs, shanties, ominous marches, and one effectively syncopated hornpipe', and included 'New World', 'Friends', 'Failed Cape Horn', 'Saucy Sal', 'Will You Come Back?', 'Falling Angels Riding', 'I'll Go No More A-Roving', and, of course, 'Tahiti'. In 80s West End terms, first night reviews such as 'Bounty in blunderland . . . caught in the doldrums . . . a very leaky showboat' should have heralded the end of the voyage, but *Mutiny!* rode the storm for a considerable time. Just as it was about to be recast with the American pop singer David Cassidy taking over from Essex, the show floundered and closed in September 1986 after a run of 526 performances without recovering its investment.

My Fair Lady

One of the most successful shows in the history of the American musical theatre, *My Fair Lady* opened to rave reviews at the Mark Hellinger Theatre in New York on 15 March 1956. The book, by Alan Jay Lerner, was based on George Bernard Shaw's play *Pygmalion*, and told of Professor Henry Higgins (Rex Harrison) attempts to transform a Cockney flower girl, Eliza Doolittle (Julie Andrews), into a society lady simply by teaching her to speak correctly. In the course of the story Higgins and Eliza fall in love and all ends happily, if a little differently from the way Shaw ended his play. Alan J. Lerner and Frederick Loewe's score was full of marvellous songs which included 'Wouldn't It Be Loverly?', 'I Could Have Danced All Night', 'On The Street Where You Live', 'Get Me To The Church On Time', 'With A Little Bit Of Luck', 'Show Me', 'I'm An Ordinary Man', 'Without You', 'Just You Wait', 'A Hymn To Him', 'Why Can't The English?' 'Ascot Gavotte', and 'I've Grown Accustomed To Her Face'. Harrison and Andrews were both superb. Their delight and joy when they realise that Eliza has finally 'got it' and celebrate their triumph with 'The Rain In Spain', remains a memorable and endearing moment. A strong supporting cast included Stanley Holloway (Alfred P. Doolitle, Eliza's father), Robert Coote (Colonel Pickering), Michael King (Freddy Eynsford-Hill), and Cathleen Nesbitt (Mrs. Higgins). *My Fair Lady* ran on Broadway for six-and-a-half years, a total of 2,717 performances, and won Tony Awards for best musical, actor (Harrison), director (Moss Hart), musical director (Franz Allers); and Oliver Smith (scenic design) and Cecil Beaton (costumes), both of whom made outstanding contributions to the lavish and spectacular production. Numerous road companies toured the show across the USA and it was subsequently presented in more than 20 other countries. Four of the principals, Harrison, Andrews, Holloway and Coote, recreated their roles for the London production which stayed at the Drury Lane

Twiggy (*My One And Only*)

Theatre for five and a half years. The Broadway cast album spent over 300 weeks in the US chart, many of them at number 1. The 1981 US revival with the 73-year-old Harrison and Catherine Nesbitt, who by then was 92, toured the US before spending some time in New York. By all accounts it attempted to stay true to the original version, which is more than can be said for some of the later efforts. The 1991 UK provincial production, with a cast headed by Edward Fox, was described by its director Simon Callow, as 'a politically correct' version, and the 1993 Broadway revival directed by Howard Davies, with Richard Chamberlain as Higgins and Stanley Holloway's son, Julian, as Doolittle, was 'stripped almost entirely of its romanticism and honed to a provocative post-modern edge', according to *Variety*. The famous 'Ascot Gavotte' scene 'is recreated as a living Magritte canvas, the actors in colourful finery descending from the flies to hover above the action against a field of brilliant blue'. The 1964 film version was reasonably faithful to the original stage show though, and starred Harrison, Holloway, and – somewhat controversially – Audrey Hepburn as Eliza. The American musical historian David Even suggested that one way or another *My Fair Lady* has generated approximately $800 million.

My One And Only

This show was similar in many ways to *Crazy For You*, which came along nine years later. Both productions were based on vintage shows with scores by George and Ira Gershwin: in *Crazy For You*, the producers went back to *Girl Crazy* (1930), and for *My One And Only*, which opened at the St. James Theatre in New York on 1 May 1983, librettists Peter Stone and Timothy S. Mayer reached back even further, and used the 1927 Fred Astaire hit, *Funny Face*, as their role model. Tommy Tune, Broadway's 80s equivalent of Astaire, was in this show, and also shared the choreography chores with Thommie Walsh, so the accent was very definitely on the dance. Tune's co-star was Twiggy, the English 60s fashion model, who had appeared in Ken Russell's film of *The Boy Friend* in 1971. Tune and Charles 'Honi' Coles stopped the show each night with their terpsichorean treatment of the title song, and some other numbers were retained from the original *Funny Face*, including 'He Loves And She Loves', ''S Wonderful', and 'Funny Face'. The rest of the score was culled from other Gershwin shows including 'I Can't Be Bothered Now', 'How Long Has This Been Going On?', and 'Nice Work If You Can Get It'. The story, such as it was, is Twiggy as a record-breaking swimmer and Tune as an intrepid pilot, get mixed up with some Prohibition-busting bootleggers in the late 20s world of Charles Lindbergh and non-stop flights to various capital cities of the world.

Tommy Tune won the 1983 Tony for best actor, and shared the prize for choreography with Thommie Walsh. The elegant tap dancer, Charles 'Honi' Coles, an ex-vaudevillian who dropped out of the performing business for a while in the 60s and 70s, made a triumphant Broadway comeback in this show at the age of 73, and won the Tony for best supporting actor in a musical. He died in 1992, shortly after receiving the National Medal of the Arts from President Bush. *My One And Only* continued to sing and dance to that gorgeous Gershwin music for a total of 767 performances.

Mystery Of Edwin Drood, The

In this innovative musical which was 'suggested by the unfinished novel of the same name by Charles Dickens', a newcomer to Broadway, the author and songwriter Rupert Holmes, invited the audience themselves to vote for what they thought should be the outcome at the end of the evening – and it proved to be a popular notion. The show opened at the Imperial Theatre in New York on 2 December 1985, and the story was told as if it was being performed as a play within a play at a London music hall in the late 19th century. The traditional figure of the emporium's Chairman was played by George Rose, and the rest of the cast was led by Betty Buckley, who played Drood, Cleo Laine as Princess Puffer the keeper of an infamous opium den, and Howard McGillan. Holmes's imaginative and relevant songs included 'Perfect Strangers', 'The Wages Of Sin', 'Moonfall', 'Don't Quit While You're Ahead', 'Both Sides Of The Coin', 'Ceylon', 'Off To The Races', and 'No Good Can Come From Bad'. The show had an excellent run of 608 performances, and, in a very poor season for new musicals, scooped the Tony Awards, winning for best musical, book, score, actor (Rose), and director (Wilford Leach). The short-lived London production starred Julia Hills, the pop singer Lulu, and Ernie Wise, the surviving partner of one Britian's best-loved comedy double acts, Morecambe And Wise.

Naughty Marietta

A comic operetta with music by Victor Herbert and a book and lyrics by Rida Johnson Young. It opened on 7 November 1910 at the New York theatre with a story set in New Orleans in 1870, where Naples-born Marietta d'Altena (Emma Trentini) has travelled in search of a husband. She finds the man of her dreams (in more ways than one) when the upstanding Captain Dick Warrington (Orville Harrold) finds that he too has been dreaming of the same song, 'Ah! Sweet Mystery Of Life'. It was only one of several numbers that endured from the attractive and tuneful score. The remainder included 'Tramp! Tramp! Tramp!', 'I'm Falling In Love With Someone', ''Neath The Southern Moon', 'Italian Street Song', 'Naughty Marietta', and 'Live For Today'. Even with the magnificent Trentini, *Naughty Marietta* folded after only 136 performances, but was revived on Broadway in 1912. Since then it has been frequently performed throughout the world, and is a part of the repertoire of the New York City Opera. The 1935 film version starred Jeanette MacDonald and Nelson Eddy.

New Girl In Town

Bob Merrill, previously known for writing novelty songs such as 'Sparrow In The Treetop', 'Feet Up (Pat Him On the Po-Po)', 'If I Knew You Were Comin' I'd've Baked A Cake', and '(How Much Is That) Doggie In The Window?', some of which became hits for Guy Mitchell, made his Broadway debut with this show which opened at the 46th Street Theatre in New York on 14 May 1957. George Abbott's book, which was based on Eugene O'Neill's 1921 play, *Anna Christie*, was set in New York at the turn of the century and told of a prostitute, Anna (Gwen Verdon), who returns to live with to her bargee father (Chris Christopherson) for a while. He is unaware of her occupation, but is soon put wise by his unsavoury lady friend, Marthy (Thelma Ritter). Matt Burke (George Wallace), a sailor with whom Anna falls in love, leaves her for a time when he, too, discovers her lifestyle, but he eventually returns in the hope that they can make a more conventional life together. The lively score included 'It's Good To Be Alive', 'Sunshine Girl', 'Did You Close Your Eyes?', 'If That Was Love', 'You're My Friend Ain'tcha?', 'Look At 'Er', 'At the Check Apron Ball', 'Roll Yer Socks Up', and 'There Ain't No Flies On Me'. The engaging and reflective 'Flings' ('Are meant to be flung' . . . 'As a girl, you start seethin'/Over guys just finished teethin'/Now if they're alive and breathin'/That's enough!') was given an amusing treatment on record from Carol Burnett and Martha Raye. When she starred in this piece, Gwen Verdon, one of the American musical theatre's favourite gypsies (dancers), was in the middle of a purple patch with shows such as *Can-Can*, *Damn Yankees*, and *Redhead* - with *Sweet Charity* and *Chicago* in the future. She shared the 1958 Tony Award for best actress with Thelma Ritter. *New Girl In Town* ran for

431 performances - an encouraging start for Merrill - who followed it in 1959 with *Take Me Along*, another adaptation of an O'Neill play, *Ah, Wilderness*.

New Moon, The

After a poor out-of-town tryout, *The New Moon* underwent drastic revisions before opening at the Imperial Theatre in New York on 19 September 1928. The story traced the adventures of Robert Mission, a French aristocrat in New Orleans in the late 18th Century. With music by Sigmund Romberg lyrics by Oscar Hammerstein II, and a book by Hammerstein, Frank Mandel and Lawrence Schwab, the lavish and spectacular production was a great success and ran for 509 performances. Amongst the songs were 'Lover, Come Back To Me', 'One Kiss', 'Softly, As In A Morning Sunrise', 'Wanting You', 'Love Is Quite A Simple Thing', and 'Stouthearted Men'. The two lovers, Robert and Marianne, were played by Robert Halliday and Evelyn Herbert. The 1929 London production, starring Evelyn Laye and Howett Worster, ran for 148 performances. *The New Moon* was revived in New York in 1942, 1944 and 1986. A film version, which changed the plot but retained most of the music, was released in 1930 with Grace Moore and Lawrence Tibbett, and the popular singing duo of Jeanette MacDonald and Nelson Eddy were in the 1940 remake.

New Yorkers, The

This early Cole Porter show is probably best remembered for the inclusion of the notorious 'Love For Sale'. With a lyric containing such lines as 'Appetizing young love for sale.' . . . 'If you want to buy my wares/Follow me and climb the stairs.', this 'threnody in which a frightened vocalist, Miss Kathryn Crawford, impersonates a lily of the gutters, vending her charms in trembling accents, accompanied by a trio of melancholy female crooners', was banned for some years by radio stations on both sides of the Atlantic. Sub-titled 'A Sociological Musical Satire', *The New Yorkers* opened at the Broadway Theatre on 8 December 1930. Herbert Fields's book, based on an idea of cartoonist Peter Arno's, propelled characters, swanky and seedy, around various Manhattan locations, both up-town and down. High society lady, Alice (Hope Williams), loves bootlegger and hoodlum, Al (Charles King), and they have 'Where Have You Been' and one of the score's best numbers, the supremely optimistic 'Let's Fly Away' ('And find a land that's so provincial/We'll never hear what Walter Winchell/Might be forced to say.'). The cast also included Frances Williams, who sang 'The Great Indoors' and 'Take Me Back To Manhattan'; and Barrie Oliver and Ann Pennington, who joined Frances Williams and Charles King for the witty 'I'm Getting Myself Ready For You'. The

Anthony Newley

much-loved clown, Jimmy Durante, together with his vaudeville partners, Eddie Jackson and Lou Clayton, played three hoods. Durante stopped the show most nights with one of his own songs, an item called 'Wood', during which he littered the stage with a wide range of wood products. The clean-cut vocal instrumental group, Fred Waring And His Pennsylvanians, who had been discovered by the show's producer, Ray Goetz, while playing in Los Angeles, also used some of their own material, but, musically, the show belonged to Porter. Shortly after it opened, he interpolated a hymn to the 'Big Apple', 'I Happen To Like New York' ('I like the sight and the sound and even the stink of it.'), which was sung by Oscar 'Rags' Ragland. *The New Yorkers* ran for 168 performances, and despite being banned from airplay, 'Love For Sale' was a hit for Libby Holman, Fred Waring, and later, Hal Kemp. It also became widely-heard in a version by Ella Fitzgerald on one of her *Cole Porter Songbooks*.

Newley, Anthony

b. 24 September 1931, London, England. After attending the Italia Conti Stage School Newley worked as a child actor in several films, including *The Little Ballerina*, *Vice Versa*, and in 1948 played the Artful Dodger in David Lean's successful version of *Oliver Twist*. He made his London theatrical debut in John Cranko's revue, *Cranks* in 1955, and had character parts in well over 20 films before he was cast as rock 'n' roll star Jeep Jackson in *Idle On Parade* in 1959. Newley's four-track vocal EP, and his version of the film's hit ballad, Jerry Lordan's 'I've Waited So Long', started a three-year UK chart run which included 'Personality', 'If She Should Come To You', 'And The Heavens Cried', the novelty numbers 'Pop Goes The Weasel' and 'Strawberry Fair' and two UK number 1 hits, 'Why' and Lionel Bart's, 'Do You Mind'. Newley also made the album charts in 1960 with his set of old standards, *Love Is A Now And Then Thing*. He made later appearances in the charts with *Tony* (1961), and the comedy album *Fool Britannia* (1963), on which he was joined by his wife, Joan Collins and Peter Sellers. In 1961 Newley collaborated with Leslie Bricusse (b. 29 January 1931, London) on the off-beat stage musical, *Stop The World - I Want To Get Off*. Newley also directed, and played Littlechap, the small man who fights the system. The show, which stayed in the West End for 16 months, ran for over 500 performances on Broadway, and was filmed in 1966. It produced several hit songs, including 'What Kind Of Fool Am I?', 'Once In A Lifetime' and 'Gonna Build A Mountain'.

In 1964 Bricusse and Newley wrote the lyric to John Barry's music for Shirley Bassey to sing over the titles of the James Bond movie, *Goldfinger*. The team's next musical show in 1965, *The Roar Of The Greasepaint -*

The Smell Of The Crowd, with comedian Norman Wisdom in the lead, toured the north of England but did not make the West End. When it went to Broadway Newley took over (co-starring with Cyril Ritchard), but was not able to match the success of *Stop The World,* despite a score containing such numbers as 'Who Can I Turn To?', 'A Wonderful Day Like Today', 'The Joker', 'Look At That Face' and 'This Dream'. In 1967 Newley appeared with Rex Harrison and Richard Attenborough in the film musical *Doctor Dolittle*, with script and songs by Bricusse. Despite winning an Oscar for 'Talk To The Animals', the film was considered an expensive flop, as was Newley's own movie project in 1969, a pseudo-autobiographical sex-fantasy entitled *Can Heironymus Merkin Ever Forget Mercy Humppe And Find True Happiness?* Far more successful, in 1971, was *Willy Wonka And The Chocolate Factory*, a Roald Dahl story with music and lyrics by Bricusse and Newley. Sammy Davis Jnr. had a million-selling record with one of the songs, 'The Candy Man'. They also wrote several songs for the 1971 NBC television musical adaptation of *Peter Pan*, starring Mia Farrow and Danny Kaye. Bricusse and Newley's last authentic stage musical, *The Good Old Bad Old Days*, opened in London in 1972 and had a decent run of 309 performances. Newley sang some of the songs, including 'The People Tree', on his own *Ain't It Funny*. In his cabaret act he continually bemoans the fact that he has not had a hit with one of his own songs. A major 1989 London revival of *Stop The World - I Want To Get Off,* directed by Newley, and in which he also appeared, closed after five weeks, and, in the same year, he was inducted into the Songwriters' Hall Of Fame, along with Leslie Bricusse. In 1991, Newley appeared on UK television with his ex-wife, Joan Collins, in Noël Coward's *Private Lives*, which included the famous 'Red Peppers' segment. In the following year, having lived in California for some years, Newley announced that he was returning to Britain, and bought a house there to share with his 90 year old mother. In the same year, he also appeared in England, at the Alexandra Theatre, Birmingham, in a successful limited run of the musical, *Scrooge*, which Bricusse adapted for the stage from the 1970 film.

Albums: *Love Is A Now And Then Thing* (1960), *Tony* (1961), *Stop The World - I Want To Get Off* (1962, London Cast), with Peter Sellers and Joan Collins *Fool Britannia* (1963), *The Roar Of The Greasepaint - The Smell Of The Crowd* (1965, Broadway Cast). Compilations: *The Romantic World Of Anthony Newley* (1970), *The Lonely World Of Anthony Newley* (1972), *The Singer And His Songs* (1978), *Anthony Newley: Mr. Personality* (1985), *Greatest Hits* (1991).

Paul Nicholas

Nicholas, Paul

b. 3 December 1945. Actor/singer Nicholas served a musical apprenticeship as pianist with Screaming Lord Sutch And The Savages. Then known as Paul Dean, he embarked on a singing career in 1964, but later changed his name to Oscar when this venture proved unsuccessful. Despite access to exclusive songs by Pete Townshend ('Join My Gang') and David Bowie ('Over The Wall We Go' - a comment on a contemporary rash of prison outbreaks), this second appellation brought no commercial comfort. However, it was during this period that the artist began his long association with manager Robert Stigwood, and he developed a career in pop musicals, appearing in some of the best onstage productions of the era. His debut in the love/rock musical *Hair* was followed by *Jesus Christ Superstar*. He appeared in Ken Russell's *Lisztomania* and had a major role in the film *Stardust*, starring David Essex. During the 80s his stage appearances have included *Cats* and the less-than-triumphant *Pirates*. Prior to that Nicholas finally achieved pop single success with several disco-style numbers for his mentor's RSO label. 'Dancing With The Captain' and 'Grandma's Party' reached the UK Top 10 in 1976, but his musical career increasingly took a subordinate role to thespian ambitions. Nicholas has since become a highly popular actor on television, performing light comedy and dramatic roles with confidence.

Albums: *Paul Nicholas* (1977), *Just Good Friends* (1986), *That's Entertainment* (1993).

Nick And Nora

This show was based on Dashiell Hammett's witty 30s comedy-drama movie, *The Thin Man*, which starred William Powell and Myrna Loy, and spawned several sequels. Its transfer from Hollywood to Broadway provided yet another insight into the agonizing trials and tribulations endured by the creators - and, some would say, the audiences - concerned with a contemporary musical production. After several postponements, the show actually started its previews at the Marquis Theatre in New York on 8 October 1991. These continued for 71 performances - an unprecedented nine weeks - while the highly experienced team of Arthur Laurents (director and librettist), Charles Strouse (music) and Richard Maltby Jnr., strove to get the show ready. After numerous changes to the cast, score and book, *Nick And Nora* finally faced the critics on December 8. The story, still set in the film world of the 30s, has Nora Charles (Joanna Gleason) doing a favour for her old girlfriend, the actress Tracy Gardner (Christine Baranski), by trying to find the murderer of studio book keeper, Lorraine Bixby (Faith Prince). Eventually, she gives way to husband Nick (Barry Bostwick), who comes out of retirement to solve the case himself. Not a show to appeal to feminists. There were high hopes for the score. Richard Maltby Jnr. was co-lyricist on *Miss Saigon*, and his collaborations with David Shire including *Baby* and *Starting Here, Starting Now*, had been duly noted. Charles Strouse had composed the music for several big Broadway hits, but his record revealed six flops in a row since *Annie* in 1977. Their songs met with a mixed reception. They included 'Is There Anything Better Than Dancing?', 'Everybody Wants To Do A Musical', 'Swell', 'Not Me', 'As Long As You're Happy', 'Look Whose Alone Now', and 'Let's Go Home', which some unkind critics took literally. The number that attracted the most attention was 'Men', which was sung by Faith Prince, and that too, with its lyric, 'I was nuts . . . dropped my pants like a putz', was regarded as 'astonishingly coarse' by one critic, and 'absolute dynamite' by another. There was an air of doom surrounding the production, anyway, and it folded after only nine performances (not forgetting the 71 previews) with estimated losses in excess of $2.5 million.

Nine

This musical adaptation of Federico Fellini's 1963 movie, *Eight And A Half*, had a book by Arthur Kopit, and music and lyrics by the Broadway newcomer, Maurey Yeston. It opened on 9 May 1982 at the 46th Street Theatre in New York. The story follows film director Guido Contini (Raul Julia) to Europe in his quest to recharge his physical and emotional batteries, and revitalize his personal life and career. This applies particularly to his continually changing relationships with the women in his life, such as his wife (Karen Akers), his first love, Saraghina (Kathi Moss), his mother (Taina Elg), his close friend and professional colleague, Liliane LaFleur (Liliane Montevecchi), his latest discovery, (Shelley Burch), and his current mistress, Carla (Anita Morris). Yeston's innovative and tuneful score was greeted with enthusiasm, and contained songs such as 'Be Italian', 'My Husband Makes Movies', 'Only With You', 'Be On Your Own', 'Folies Bergéres', 'A Call From The Vatican', 'Nine', 'Unusual Way', 'Simple', 'Getting Tall', and 'The Grand Canal'. Tommy Tune and Thommie Walsh were responsible for the choreography and reprised their collaboration a year later for *My One And Only*. Tune also directed the piece, and his extraordinary staging of a production which only included one adult male, four boys, and 21 women, was generally acclaimed. He won a Tony Award for his work, and *Nine* gained further Tonys for best musical, score, and featured actress (Liliane Montevecchi). The show surprised many critics, and ran for 732 performances. Productions were mounted in other countries, including Australia, where it starred John Diedrich. A concert version was presented at London's Festival Hall in 1992, with Liliane Montevecchi and Jonathan Price, the versatile actor who came to prominence as the engineer in *Miss Saigon*. The resulting two-CD set featured Ann Crumb, Elaine Paige, and a chorus of over 100, and is regarded as the most complete recorded version of Yeston's score.

No, No, Nanette

Unusually for a Broadway musical, *No, No Nanette* was far more popular when it was revived than when it was first staged. With music by Vincent Youmans, lyrics by Irving Caesar and Otto Harbach, and a book by Harbach and Frank Mandel, the show included several admirable songs, including 'You Can Dance With Any Girl At All', 'Too Many Rings Around Rosie', 'The Call Of The Sea', 'Peach On the Beach', 'Take A Little One-Step', and two that became classics, 'I Want To Be Happy' and 'Tea For Two'. *No, No, Nanette* opened at the Palace Theatre in London on 11 March 1925, with Binnie Hale and George Grossmith in the leading roles, and ran for 665 performances. The New York production, which made its debut at the Globe Theatre on 16 September of 1925, starred Ona Munsen, Donald Brian, Cecil Lean, and Jack McCauley. Although the show epitomised the happy-go-lucky all-singing, all-dancing atmosphere of the 20s, it closed after a disappointing run of 321 performances. Nearly half a century later, a strong cast which included Ruby Keeler, Helen Gallagher and Bobby Van, appeared in the 1971 New York revival which stayed around for over two years, and won Tony Awards for best actress (Gallagher), supporting actress (Patsy Kelly), choreographer (Donald Saddler), and costumes (Raoul du Bois). Touring companies proliferated, and there was another major production at Drury Lane in London with Anna Neagle, Anne Rogers, Tony Britton, and Thora Hird. There have been two film versions: in 1930 with Alexander Gray and Bernice Claire, and in 1940 with Anna Neagle and Victor Mature.
Further reading: *The Making Of No, No, Nanette*, Don Dunn.

No Strings

When Oscar Hammerstein died in 1960, composer Richard Rodgers lost the second of only two lyricists with whom he had worked throughout his illustrious career - the first, of course, being Lorenz Hart. Shortly after Hammerstein's death, Rodgers wrote both words and music to five new songs for the second re-make of the film, *State Fair*, and then, in 1962, he undertook the complete score for *No Strings* which opened at the 54th Street Theatre in New York on 15 March. Rodgers also produced the piece, for which the book was written by the celebrated

playwright, Samuel Taylor, who had impressed the composer with his comedies such as *Sabrina Fair* and *The Pleasure Of His Company*. The black actress, Diahann Carroll, who was spotted by Rodgers on US television on the *Jack Paar Show*, was cast as an American fashion model, Barbara Woodruff, who has moved to Paris. While there, she falls in love with the former Pulitzer Prize-winning novelist, David Jordan (Richard Kiley), whose life has disintegrated to the point that he has given up writing and is just living on hand-outs. She helps in his process of rehabilitation, but they decide to go their separate ways. Rodgers himself hinted later that the reason that the characters split up is because they anticipate racial prejudice on their return to the USA, although the authors were careful not to mention it directly. The director and choreographer, Joe Layton, introduced several innovations such as placing the orchestra onstage instead of in the pit, and having members of the cast move the mobile sets in full view of the audiences. Another neat idea was for Kiley and Carroll to sing the show's lovely hit song, 'The Sweetest Sounds', each accompanied by their own individual instrumental soloist, and this tecnique was also used on some of the other numbers. Carroll excelled throughout on such as 'Loads Of Love', 'You Don't Tell Me', 'An Orthodox Fool', and joined with Kiley for 'Nobody Told Me', 'Maine', 'Look No Further', and the title song. While not in the same money-making class as *The Sound Of Music* and the other Rodgers and Hammerstein blockbusters, *No Strings* had a decent run of 580 performances. Rodgers won the Tony Award for outstanding music - but not, ironically for lyrics - and joint Tonys also went to Diahann Carroll, who shared hers with Anna Marie Alberghetti (*Carnival*); and Joe Layton, whose choreography was adjudged to be equally as excellent as that of Agnes de Mille's for *Kwamina*. In 1963, *No Strings* was presented at Her Majesty's Theatre in London, where it starred Hy Hazell and Art Lund, and ran for 135 performances.

Novello, Ivor

b. David Ivor Davies, 15 January 1893, Cardiff, Wales, d. 6 March 1951, London, England. Born into a highly musical family, Novello was encouraged by his mother, a singing teacher. He took up piano and singing and quickly established a local reputation. That reputation spread throughout the UK when he was only 16, upon the publication of a song which encapsulated the feelings of many families torn apart by World War I. Setting to music a poem by the American Lena Guilbert Ford, Novello's 'Keep The Home Fires Burning' was a huge popular success. He continued to write songs while serving in the military but in 1919 turned mainly to acting, appearing in a number of silent films. His classic profile gained him a

Ivor Novello

huge following amongst the film-going public. Novello's film career continued through into the 30s; however, he kept trying to write for the stage. Not dissuaded by a 1921 flop, *The Golden Moth* written with P.G. Wodehouse, he persevered. Eventually he was rewarded when he suggested to impresario H.M. Tennent that he had the skills needed to counter the transatlantic successes in the West End. Tennant, who was also deeply conscious of the equal success currently being enjoyed by Noël Coward, needed a hit show for his financially beleaguered Drury Lane Theatre. Tennant took a chance and commissioned a show from the playwright, actor and film star who was also a would-be director and manager. Despite the fact that he had not written any music for 10 years, Novello was given *carte blanche*. Novello promptly teamed up with lyricist Christopher Hassall and the result was the hugely popular *Glamorous Night*. Later shows by Novello, who often worked thereafter with Hassall, included *Careless Rapture*, *Crest Of The Wave*, *Perchance To Dream*, *The Dancing Years* and *King's Rhapsody*. With these shows Novello found and profitably mined a market for lushly sentimental music and stories of monumental banality. By customarily taking the non-singing romantic lead in his own shows,he also built a great following with the female audience, despite the fact that in his private life he was homosexual, often flagrantly so. Novello's shows helped fill London's theatres during the darkest days of World War I and he continued to write and produce new ones, amongst them *Arc De Triomphe* and *Gay's The Word*. This last show, which included the song, 'Vitality', sung by Cecily Courtneidge, opened in London in 1951, three weeks before he died during a revival of *King's Rhapsody*. In 1993, the centenary of his birth was celebrated by several special shows around the UK, including one at the Players Theatre in London.
Further reading: *Perchance To Dream: The World Of Ivor Novello*, R. Rose. *Ivor Novello*, S. Wilson. *Ivor Novello: Man Of The Theatre*, Peter Noble.

Nunn, Trevor

b. 14 January 1940, Ipswich, Suffolk, England. Nunn was educated at Downing College, Cambridge, and in 1962 won an ABC Director's Scholarship to the Belgrade Theatre in Coventry where he produced a musical version of *Around The World In 80 Days*. In 1964 he joined the Royal Shakespeare Company, was made an associate director in 1965, and became the company's youngest-ever artistic director in 1968. He was responsible for the running of the RSC until he retired from the post in 1986. As well as his numerous productions for the RSC, he co-directed *Ncholas Nickleby* (winner of five Tony Awards), *Peter Pan*, and *Les Misérables*, which became one of the most-performed musicals in the world. Outside of the RSC

he has directed the Tony Award-winning *Cats*, along with other musicals including *Starlight Express*, *Chess*, *The Baker's Wife*, and *Porgy And Bess*, and operas such as *Cosi Fan Tutte* and *Peter Grimes*. He has also worked in television and directed several films including *Hedda* and *Lady Jane*. Nunn is credited, along with Andrew Lloyd Webber and the late poet T.S. Eliot, with the writing of 'Memory', the hit song from *Cats* which has been recorded in more than 150 versions. In 1992 he directed the RSC's highly acclaimed production of Pam Gems' musical play *The Blue Angel*, and a year later he was back with Lloyd Webber again, staging the London and Los Angeles productions of *Sunset Boulevard*. Also in 1993, he became the ninth recipient of the 'Mr. Abbott Award' given by the US Stage Directors and Choreographers Foundation.

Nunsense

Originally presented at the Duplex nightspot in Greenwich Village in 1984, this spoof on the Catholic sisterhood - 'The Habit Forming Musical Comedy', transferred to the Off Broadway Cherry Lane Theatre on 12 December 1985. It was the brainchild of Dan Goggin, who wrote the book (from an original libretto by Steve Hayes), music, and lyrics, and also staged it. The story concerns the efforts of the convent's five surviving nuns to raise money so that they can bury the last few of their 52 companions who died of botulism after having eaten a meal of vichysoise prepared by the convent chef, Sister Julia. The quintet are still around because they went out to bingo that night. Sister Julia is preparing a cook book containing some of her best recipes, (including barbecued spare-ribs) while the rest of the nuns decide to put on a musical so as to raise enough money to get rid of the bodies, thereby leaving more space in the deep-freeze. The energetic Mother Superior is played by the comedienne, Marilyn Farina, and the rest of a highly talented cast included Suzi Winston, Christine Anderson, Semina De Laurentis, and Vicki Belmonte. The lively and extremely relevant songs included 'Nunsense Is Habit-Forming', 'So You Want To Be A Nun', 'Tackle That Temptation', 'Growing Up A Catholic', 'I Want To Be A Star', 'Just A Coupl'a Sisters', 'I Could've Gone To Nashville', and 'Holier Than Thou'. The show ran and ran, and, in 1992, when it entered its eight 'everlasting' year, was advertising itself as 'The longest-running show in Off-Broadway history'. But what about *The Fantasticks*, which opened in 1960? An explanatory rider was attached which stated: '*The Fantasticks* is more than a show, it is an institution!' In 1993, *Nunsense II: The Second Coming* was on its way to New York with Mother Superior demanding more audience participation on numbers such 'Oh Dear, What Can The Matter Be', in which Franciscan nuns get locked in the lavatory.

Nymph Errant

A vehicle for the delicious Gertrude Lawrence, this show was unusual in that it was written specifically for the London stage by the celebrated American composer Cole Porter. It opened at the Adelphi theatre on 6 October 1933, with book by Romney Brent which was based on James Laver's somewhat risqué novel. The story told of Evangeline Edwards (Gertrude Lawrence), who, after graduating from a Lausanne finishing school, travels around Europe in a fruitless, but amusing search for a man who will love her. Unsuitable candidates included a Russian violinist, a Greek slave trader and a Count of the Holy Roman Empire. The Adelphi's revolving stage was used to excellent effect by costume and set designer Doris Zinkeisen to conjure up stylish locations such as the Carnival at Venice, Athens by moonlight, and the stage of the Folies de Paris. Elisabeth Welch as Haidee Robinson, Austin Trevor as the French impresario André de Croissant, and Morton Selton in the role of a devilish rake, were all outstanding, but the evening belonged to Gertrude Lawrence. As usual, Porter's songs were both tuneful and witty, especially 'The Physician', in which Lawrence complained: 'He said my maxillaries were marvels/And found my sternum stunning to see/He did a double hurdle/When I shook my pelvic girdle/But he never said he loved me'. The rest of the songs, including 'It's Bad For Me', 'How Could We Be Wrong?, 'Nymph Errant', 'Solomon', and 'If You Like Les Belles Poitrines' were all similarly high-class. The show was presented by impresario Charles B. Cochran, so it was inevitable that his 'Young Ladies' should turn up from time to time. Considering the quality of performers and the production he must have been disappointed with a run of only 154 performances.

Of Thee I Sing

After George S. Kaufman's uncompromising book for *Strike Up The Band* had been replaced by a less contentious one by Morrie Ryskind, the two writers collaborated on the libretto for this show which has been called 'the greatest of all American musicals'. It

opened at the Music Box theatre in New York on 26 December 1931, complete with a sharp and witty plot in which most American institutions, especially family life and politics, come in for their fair share of satirical attention. John P. Wintergreen (William Gaxton) and his prospective Vice-President, Alexander Throttlebottom (Victor Moore), have discarded issues such as home and foreign affairs, and are running for office on a ticket of LOVE. In fact, Wintergreen issues a statement that he will propose to his Mary (Lois Moran) in every one of the 48 States. They are elected to the White House with a landslide victory, but, like so many presidents that followed him, Wintergreen's future is threatened by an indiscreet dalliance with the fairer sex - in his case, Diana Devereaux (Grace Brinkley), the current Miss America. Impeachment looms, but Wintergreen keeps his job after Throttlebottom offers to marry the beauty queen because, under the Constitution: 'When the President of the United States is unable to fulfil his duties, his obligations are assumed by the Vice President'. Gaxton and Moore were marvellous, and went on to star in several other musicals together, including *Anything Goes*, *Leave It To Me!*, and *Louisiana Purchase*. Once again, George and Ira Gershwin wrote a score that was both tuneful and entirely complementary to the action. Two of the songs matured into standards, 'Who Cares?' and 'Love Is Sweeping The Country', and the spirited 'Of Thee I Sing (Baby)' was also a hit at the time for Ben Selvin. The remainder of the score consisted of 'Wintergreen For President', 'Hello, Good Morning', 'The Illegitimate Daughter', and 'Because, Because'. As one of the 29 new Broadway musicals that season, *Of Thee I Sing* enjoyed an excellent run of 441 performances, and returned two years later for a brief spell at the Imperial theatre. The show became the first musical to be awarded the prestigious Pulitzer Prize for Drama, although composer George Gershwin's music and name was omitted from the citation. Over the years, *Of Thee I Sing* was a candidate for revival in the US, especially at election time. When the Arena Stage in Washinton D.C. presented the show in November 1992, each patron received a voting slip in their programme. The running total was chalked on the back wall of the auditorium, and, even early on in the campaign, there was a hint of things to come with the Clinton-Gore ticket regularly beating Bush-Quayle by about four to one.

Oh! Calcutta!

A musical revue, devised in 1969 by Kenneth Tynan, the drama critic, and literary manager of Britain's National Theatre for 10 years, *Oh! Calcutta!* is rarely discussed in theatrical reference books. One of the excuses given for its omission is that it was not very good; but the main reason is surely that in most of the sketches the artists appear in the nude, and perform simulated sex acts. Tynan recruited John Lennon, Samuel Beckett, Jules Feiffer, Joe Orton, Sam Shepard, and others, to write material that reflected the sexual revolution that was taking place in the 'swinging sixties'; music and lyrics were credited to Open Window. The show opened in New York in June 1969 at the Off Broadway Eden Theatre, and was such a success that within a few months it was promoted to Broadway, where it stayed for 1,314 performances. The 1970 London production, taking advantage of the abolition of theatre censorship in 1968, ran for 3,918 performances. However, that impressive total paled in the face of the 1976 Broadway revival which notched up an incredible total of 5,852. For some years now the show has been in second place in the Broadway long-running stakes, just behind *A Chorus Line* (6,137), with Andrew Lloyd Webber's *Cats*, coming up fast on the rails. More than 20 years after its inception, *Oh! Calcutta!* continues to be controversial. In 1991, a judge in Chattanooga, Tennessee, overruled local officials and allowed the show to go on in a city-owned theatre. In both London and New York, its prolonged existence was often attributed to the patronage of visiting Japanese businessmen, so it was somewhat ironic that an American production opened in Tokyo in 1993 - albeit with some concessions involving partial body stockings and body paint.

Oh, Boy!

This was the second musical comedy to be written by the young Anglo/American team of Jerome Kern (music), Guy Bolton (book), and P.G. Wodehouse (book and lyrics), and their first to be presented at the the tiny Princess Theatre in New York. When *Oh, Boy!* opened there on 20 February 1917, it blew like a wind of change through the cobwebs of operetta which were hanging around most of the other Broadway shows. It was a jolly, contemporary production, unpretentious and thoroughly entertaining. There were elements of farce, too - people did seem to enter and leave through windows rather a lot - but the story was really about George Budd (Tom Powers). His main problem is to prevent his guardian, Aunt Penelope (Edna May Oliver), from discovering that he has just got married to Lou Ellen (Marie Carroll). If she does - there goes his allowance. When they learn of her imminent arrival, the newly-weds decided to part for a time - Lou Ellen's parents have not been informed of the situation either - and from that moment on, a series of complicted events ensue, during which Tom rescues the lovely actress, Jackie Sampson (Anna Wheaton), from the clutches of an amorous Judge Carter ('Tootles' to her), who eventually turns out to be his (Tom's) father-in-law,

and Aunt Penelope gives the happy couple (George and Lou Ellen) her blessing while under the influence of a glass of spiked lemonade. The cast played it all with a lot of style, aided by a marvellous score which included the romantic couples' naive and wistful 'You Never Knew About Me' ('I'd have let you feed my rabbit/Till the thing became a habit, Dear!/But I never knew about you/Or what might have been/And you never knew about me.'). Jackie and Tom's best chum, Jim (Hal Forde), combined on another of the best numbers, 'Nesting Time In Flatbush', but there was not a dud among the rest of the bunch, which included 'Ain't It A Grand And Glorious Feeling', 'Be A Little Sunbeam', 'Every Day', 'The First Day Of May', 'FlubbyDub, The Cave Man', 'Land Where The Good Songs Go', 'A Pal Like You', 'Words Are Not Needed', 'An Old-Fashioned Wife', and 'A Package Of Seeds.' Another of the songs, 'Till the Clouds Roll By' became popular through recordings by Ann Wheaton with James Harrod, the Prince's Orchestra, and Vernon Dalhart. The tremendous success of *Oh, Boy!*, which ran for 475 performances, meant that the next Kern-Bolton-Wodehouse show, *Leave It To Jane*, which was originally intended for the Princess, had to be diverted to the Longacre Theatre which held more than twice as many people. In 1919, when the show was presented in London, it was retitled *Oh, Joy!*, and starred Beatrice Lillie in her first book musical. The title *Oh, Boy!* did eventually go up in lights in London's West End 60 years later, when a show starring pop stars such as Joe Brown, Shakin' Stevens, and Alvin Stardust, which was based on a the television show, played the Astoria Theatre.

Oh, Joy!
(see **Oh, Boy!**)

Oh, Kay!

This show provides the perfect argument for those who believe that 'they don't write them like that any more'. George and Ira Gershwin introduced four of the their all-time standards in *Oh, Kay!* which opened at the Imperial Theatre in New York on 8 November 1926, and the rest of the score was in the same class. Guy Bolton and P.G Wodehouse, fresh from their successes with Jerome Kern, wrote the book in which the Kay of the title (Gertrude Lawrence in her first Broadway book musical) helps her hard-up ducal brother (Gerald Oliver Smith) - a bootlegger - in the illegal importation of alcoholic beverages into the USA. They stash the booze on the Long Island estate of young and wealthy Jimmy Winter (Oscar Shaw), who is normally away and too busy enjoying himself at various shindigs to notice their comings and goings. However, when he returns, complications ensue, and Kay has to take a job in the houshold for a time, before Jimmy - cold sober - rejects his legion of admirers and decides to marry his 'Dear Little Girl'. That song was not one of the hits from the show, although it was a charming number which Julie Andrews reprised in the Gertrude Lawrence biopic, *Star!* (1968). Kay and Jimmy's romance can only flourish, of course, after the two lovers have duetted on 'Maybe' and 'Do, Do, Do', and danced the night away with 'Clap Yo' Hands'. A more poignant moment occurs when, disguised as a housemaid, Kay 'meditates musically' - as Ira Gershwin put it - with the tender ballad, 'Someone To Watch Over Me'. 'Fidgety Feet' was another lively number by the two Gershwin brothers, but 'Oh, Kay!' and 'Heaven On Earth' both had lyrics by Howard Deitz who helped out when Ira Gershwin was ill for a time. Victor Moore, one of America's favourite funny-men, returned to Broadway for the first time in 15 years in *Oh, Kay!*, and the cast also included Harland Dixon, Marion and Madeleine Fairbanks, Gerald Oliver, and Sascha Beaumont. The show ran for 256 performances, and Gertrude Lawrence recreated her role in the 1927 London production which lasted for six months. *Oh, Kay!* was revived Off Broadway in 1960, and was back in a main house, the Richard Rodgers Theatre, in 1990. The latter production, which started out at the Goodspeed Opera House in 1989, moved the show's location from Long Island to Harlem, and included an all-black cast. It closed after 77 performances, and producer David Merrick's attempt to restage it ended during previews. A reasonably successful West End revival was mounted in 1974, and 10 years later the show was a big hit when it played a season in England at the Chichester Festival Theatre, with the highly acclaimed Michael Siberry as Jimmy.

Oh, Lady! Lady!!

Another of the celebrated Princess Theatre shows with a score by Jerome Kern and P.G. Wodehouse, and a book by Wodehouse and Guy Bolton It opened at the tiny theatre in New York on 1 February 1918, and proved to be the last really successful show that the team wrote together. This time the plot centres on the well-to-do Long Island home belonging to the parents of Mollie Farrington (Vivienne Segal). She is about to marry Willoughby 'Bill' Finch (Carl Randall), that is until May Barber (Carroll McComas) turns up and announces that, in the past, she and Bill have been more than just good friends. Mollie is aghast: could Bill really have a female skeleton in his closet? Actually, it's not Bill that May is after at all, but Mollie's parents' jewels. All ends happily when May is apprehended by Bill's associate (and former crook), Spike Hudgins (Edward Ebeles). A thoroughly entertaining score contained no immediately identifiable hits, although Kern's music

and Wodehouse's lyrics were far superior than those of their contemporaries - always relevant to the libretto - and continually pushing musical comedy forward all the time. The songs included 'Before I Met You', 'Dear Old Prison Days', 'Do Look At Him', 'Do It Now', 'I'm To Be Married Today', 'It's A Hard, Hard World For A Man', 'Little Ships Come Sailing Home', 'Moon Song' 'Not Yet', 'Our Little Nest', 'A Picture I Want To See Of You', 'Some Little Girl', 'Waiting Round The Corner', 'You Found Me And I Found You', and 'Greenwich Village'. The latter number was featured in a spectacular rooftop sequence set in that New York location. One song was discarded during rehearsals because it was not considered suitable for Vivienne Segal's voice. It almost got to Broadway via *Zip Goes A Million* in 1919, but eventually had to wait until 1927, and the film of *Showboat*, before it was introduced to the world by Helen Morgan. The song in question was 'Bill'. Even without it, *Oh, Lady! Lady!!* had an excellent run of 219 performances.

Oh, What A Lovely War!

This 'British musical entertainment' started out at the Theatre Royal, Stratford East in March 1963 before transferring to Wyndham's Theatre on 29 June that year. The cast consisted mainly of members of the Theatre Royal's 'repertory company', such as George Sewell, Avis Bunnage, Brian Murphy, Victor Spinetti, et al. Some of them collaborated with librettist Charles Chilton on the book which purported to reflect the misery and sheer waste of human life during World War I from the coersive recruitment methods ('We Don't Want To Lose You, But We Think You Ought To Go') to the grim reality of the trenches. This was achieved in an intelligent and humorous fashion by the use of more than 20 popular songs of the period, such as 'Your King And Country Need You', 'I'll Make A Man Of You', 'Goodbye ee', 'When This Lousy War Is Over', 'Hush, Here Comes A Whizzbang', 'Belgium Put The Kibosh On the Kaiser', 'Keep The Home Fires Burning', 'I Want To Go Home', and Jerome Kern's lovely ballad 'They Didn't Believe Me'. Although some aspects of what started out at Stratford as a bitter anti-war tract were softened somewhat for West End audiences, the message remained loud and clear, and *Oh, What A Lovely War!* continued to spell it out for more than two years, during which time it won the Evening Standard Award for best musical. The appeal proved not to be so great in America where the show folded after three and a half months. The 1969 film, directed by Richard Attenborough, adopted a different, star-studded approach.

Oklahoma!

If one show can be said to mark the turning-point in

the history of the American musical theatre then it must be *Oklahoma!* Although many of the trend-setting features of the show had been tried before, sometimes successfully so, never before had such things as a ballet sequence and a serious plot been blended so well into a production which had great dramatic merit and was yet filled with many wonderful songs. Set in the early years of the 20th century, as a section of Indian territory was about to become the state of Oklahoma, the story traced the love lives of Curly and Laurey, and of Will Parker and Ado Annie. Conflict between farmers and cowmen, a staple of western films, provided drama as did the personal struggle for Laurey between Curly and Jud Fry, a disreputable farmhand who is finally killed in a knife fight with Curly. An on-stage death in a musical was another 'first' for *Oklahoma!*. Based upon Lynn Riggs's play, *Green Grow The Lilacs*, the book and lyrics for *Oklahoma!* were written by Oscar Hammerstein II with music by Richard Rodgers, the first time the two men had collaborated. Producers and outside commentators were alike in their pre-production reservations about the show. Many felt it was doomed to failure, that the basis of an only moderately successful play, along with a collaboration between Hammerstein, who had been without a hit for some time, and Rodgers, now without his long-time collaborator Lorenz Hart, was a too-shaky foundation. On opening night, the 31 March 1943, despite playing to a less than full house at the St. James Theatre in New York, all doubts vanished. The vivid staging, sparkling choreography by Agnes de Mille, strong central performances, and above all a string of superb songs, made this the most momentous musical event of several decades. The songs included 'Oh, What A Beautiful Mornin'', which opened the show, 'The Surrey With The Fringe On Top', 'Kansas City', 'I Cain't Say No', 'Many A New Day', 'People Will Say We're In Love', 'The Farmer And The Cowman', 'Pore Jud', 'Out Of My Dreams', 'All er Nothin'' and the rousing 'Oklahoma' with which the show ended. The original cast included Alfred Drake as Curly, Joan Roberts as Laurey, Lee Dixon as Will, Celeste Holm as Ado Annie, Howard Da Silva as Jud and Betty Garde as Laurey's Aunt Eller. By the time the show closed, after 2,248 performances, other artists had replaced one or another of the leads, amongst them Howard Keel, Shelley Winters and John Raitt. The 1947 London production starred Keel and Betty Jane Watson and ran for 1,151 performances. London audiences, still war-shocked and starved of spectacle - amongst many other things - were overwhelmed. The show profoundly affected the producers of British shows which were still rooted in the 30s sophistication of Noël Coward and the flimsy Ruritania of Ivor Novello. *Oklahoma!* was the opening wave of a transatlantic musical tide that would take three decades to reverse. The show became a near-permanent feature of the theatrical scenes of both the USA and UK with touring companies seemingly forever on the road. There were major New York revivals in 1951 and 1965. The 1980 London production gave impresario Cameron Mackintosh one of the first of his many West End successes. The 1955 film version, which starred Gordon Macrae and Shirley Jones, had little to offer except the songs and the score, but, not surprisingly, it took the year's Oscar. In 1993, the show's 50th anniversary was marked by a special Tony Award.
Further reading: *OK! The Story Of Oklahoma!*, Max Wilk.

Oliver!

As soon as it opened at the New Theatre in London on 30 June 1960, *Oliver!* was an instant success, winning rave reviews and ecstatic audiences. With book, music and lyrics by Lionel Bart, the show's storyline was reasonably faithful to *Oliver Twist*, the Charles Dickens novel upon which it was based. Filled with memorable songs, from sweet ballads to comic masterpieces, the show had the benefit of a strong cast and one performance that ranks amongst the genre's finest. Ron Moody's Fagin alone was worth the price of admission. Well supported by Georgia Brown, as Nancy, and with a succession of good Olivers and Artful Dodgers, *Oliver!* was excellent entertainment. Bart's songs included 'As Long As He Needs Me', 'Where Is Love?', 'Food, Glorious Food', 'Consider Yourself', 'You've Got To Pick A Pocket Or Two', 'Come Back Soon', 'I Shall Scream', 'Who Will Buy?', 'Oom-Pah-Pah', 'I'd Do Anything' and 'Reviewing The Situation'. The show also had the benefit of extraordinary sets by Sean Kenny, much-admired to the point of outright copying in later years. The show ran for 2,618 performances in London, and Georgia Brown reprised her role for the 1963 New York production which ran for nearly two years. Clive Revill played Fagin, and Lionel Bart won a Tony Award for his outstanding score. The 1968 film version dropped a song or two, inexplicably replaced Brown with Shani Wallis, but fortunately preserved Moody's performance for all time. There were also good child actors in Mark Lester as Oliver and, particularly, Jack Wild as the Artful Dodger. Other young stars in the role included Phil Collins and Steve Marriott.

On A Clear Day You Can See Forever

Alan Jay Lerner's long-time partnership with Frederick Loewe had lapsed by the early 60s partly owing to the composer's ill health, when he decided to write a Broadway show based on his absorbing interest in the subject of extrasensory perception (ESP). Lerner's first choice for a project which was originally entitled *I Picked A Daisy*, was Richard Rodgers, who had been searching for a new partner since the death of Oscar Hammerstein in 1960. According to reports, the collaboration resulted in the irrisistable force meeting the immovable object, so Lerner turned instead to Burton Lane. The new show, now called *On A Clear Day You Can See Forever*, made its debut at the Mark Hellinger theatre on 17 October 1965. In Lerner's book, Dr. Mark Bruckner (John Cullum) discovers that one of his patients, Daisy Gamble (Barbara Harris), can not only foresee the future, and persuade her plants to grow by just talking to them, but is prepared to go into details about her life as Melinda, an early feminist, who lived in 18th century London. They fall in love, but when Daisy begins to believe (mistakenly) that Mark is more interested in Melinda than in her, she walks out. Although miles away, she hears and responds when he gives out with 'Come Back To Me' ('Leave behind all you own/Tell your flowers you'll telephone/Let your dog walk alone/Come back to me!'). McCallum also had two lovely ballads, the title song, 'On A Clear Day (You Can See Forever)', and 'Melinda'. The remainder of a fine score included the delightful 'Hurray! It's Lovely Up Here', 'She Wasn't You', 'Wait Till We're Sixty-Five', 'When I'm Being Born Again', 'What Did I Have That I Don't Have?', 'Don't Tamper With My Sister', and 'Tosy And Cosh'. The show ran for an unsatisfactory 280 performances, and, as usual, while Lerner's lyrics were admired, his book came in for a deal of criticism. Barbara Harris was particularly applauded for her work, but, in the 1970 film, her role was taken by Barbra Streisand, who starred with Yves Montand.

On The Town

Opening on 28 December 1944, *On The Town* was based on the 20-minute ballet, *Fancy Free*, by choreographer Jerome Robbins and composer Leonard Bernstein. Robbins had been on Broadway before, as a dancer, but for Bernstein, and librettists and lyricists Betty Comden and Adolph Green, *On The Town* was their first taste of the glamorous New York musical theatre. The 'almost non-existent book' concerns three sailors, Gaby (John Battles), Ozzie (Adolph Green), and Chip (Cris Alexander) who are on leave in New York for just 24 hours. They meet three girls, Ivy (Sono Osato), Hildy (Nancy Walker), and Claire (Betty Comden), and all enthusiastically take in tourist spots such as Coney Island, The Museum of Natural History, Central Park, Carnegie Hall, Times Square, and a dive called Diamond Eddie's. The score was exhilarating, from the rousing 'New York, New York', through the amusing 'Ya Got Me', 'Come Up To My Place', 'I Can Cook, Too', and 'I Get Carried Way', to the lovely ballads, 'Lonely Town', 'Lucky To Be Me', and 'Some Other Time'. At the end of the boys' day of freedom, the girls see them off at the quay - and another batch of sailors come careering down the gangplank singing 'New York, New York', and the whole process begins all over again. *On The Town* enjoyed a run of 463 performances and was revived twice in New York, Off-Broadway in 1959 (Harold Lang, Wisa D'Orso, and Pat Carroll), and in a main house in 1971, with Ron Husman, Donna McKechnie, Bernadette Peters and Phyllis Newman (Mrs. Adolph Green). A 1963 London production folded after 53 performances. There was renewed interest in the show almost 30 years later, when, in June 1992, a semi-staged version, narrated by Comden and Green, was presented at London's Barbican Hall, and then, in 1993, the Goodspeed Opera House in Connecticut, USA, mounted a well-received production. The 1949 film starred Frank Sinatra, Gene Kelly, Jules Munshin, Vera-Ellen, Ann Miller, and Betty Garrett.

On The Twentieth Century

In the long history of the musical theatre, this was probably not the first occasion on which the critics inferred that 'the audience left the theatre whistling the scenery'. However, that phrase did crop up a lot (along with 'it ran out of steam') in the reviews for this show which opened at the St. James Theatre in New York on 19 February 1978, and was set mostly aboard the fondly remembered train, the Twentieth Century Limited, which used to run from Chicago to New York. The set was certainly spectacular - a splendid art-deco affair - designed by Robin Wagner. The book, by Betty Comden and Adolph Green, which was based on Ben Hecht and Charles MacArthur's farce, *Twentieth Century*, concerns the legendary producer-director, Oscar Jaffee (John Cullum), a Broadway legend - but not recently. He is at the bottom of the barrel, but his former lover and protegée, the temperamental movie star, Lily Garland (Madeline Kahn), is at the top of the tree. His efforts to sign her for a project that will ensure his rehabilitation bring him into contact with the current rivals for her attention, actor Bruce Granit (played by Kevin Kline, himself a film heart-throb of the 80s and 90s), and the film producer, Max Jacobs (George Lee Andrews). The veteran Broadway comedienne, Imogene Coca, making a welcome comeback to the New York musical stage after an absence of over 30 years, played a cooky religious character with a great deal of fervour. The score was written by Comden and Green together with composer Cy Coleman. His music, which is usually jazz-based, like the man himself, was regarded this time as being too flamboyant and out of character, 'alternating much of the time between early nineteenth century comic-opera mannerisms and early twentieth century operetta', in songs such as 'I Rise Again', 'Veronique',

'On The Twentieth Century', 'Our Private World', 'Repent', 'We've Got It', 'She's A Nut', 'Legacy', 'Never', 'Life Is Like A Train', 'Together', 'Stranded Again', and 'Mine'. In spite of the criticism, the show won Tony Awards for score, book, Cullum, and Kline, and stayed on the rails for 449 performances. Cullum is said to have based his portrayal of the mogul on John Barrymore, who appeared with Carol Lombard in the 1934 film *Twentieth Century*. The 1980 West End production of *On The Twentieth Century* starred Julia McKenzie, one of the outstanding leading ladies of the London musical theatre, but it still ground to a halt after only 165 performances.

On With The Dance

Noël Coward's first revue for impresario C.B. Cochran opened at the London Pavilion on 30 April 1925. Coward wrote the book and most of the songs, with Philip Braham providing a few extra numbers. The cast included Hermione Baddeley, Douglas Byng, Ernest Thesiger, Greta Fayne, and Lance Lister. The star was Alice Delysia, who introduced 'Poor Little Rich Girl', a song which Cochran thought 'dreary', although it went on to become one of Coward's most enduring copyrights. The lavish, superbly presented show also contained two ballets created and danced by Leonide Massine, and enjoyed a run of 229 performances.

On Your Toes

Ballet came to Broadway in a big way, courtesy of choreographer George Balanchine, in this show which opened at the Imperial Theatre in New York on 11 April 1936. Richard Rodgers and Lorenz Hart wrote the book, along with George Abbott, and their complex plot involved Junior Dolan (Ray Bolger), who has given up the grind of the vaudeville circuit in favour of teaching music at the Knickerbocker University. When the Russian Ballet just happen to stage a production of a jazzy, insinuating ballet, 'Slaughter On Tenth Avenue', in the locale, Junior becomes involved, both onstage and off, with its prima ballerina, Vera Barnova (Tamara Geva). This Pavlovian *pas de deux* offends both Junior's girlfriend, Frankie Frayne (Doris Carson), and, more importantly, Vera's regular dancing partner, who tries to have Junior bumped off. Bolger, in a part that was originally created for Fed Astaire, was sensational in his first Broadway role, and soon developed into one of America's most cherished clowns. Balanchine's choreography, which included a second ballet, 'Princess Zenobia', was highly praised. The show also marked the acting debut of the former Yale professor, Monty Woolley, as the director of the Russian Ballet company. Rodgers and Hart's lively and tuneful score was right up to their highest standard, and contained

the delightful 'There's A Small Hotel' and It's Got to Be Love', sung by Carson and Bolger, a poignant ballad, 'Glad To Be Unhappy', the amusing 'Too Good For Good For The Average Man', and other equally pleasing numbers such as 'The Heart Is Quicker Than The Eye', 'The Three B's', 'On Your Toes', and 'Quiet Night'. *On Your Toes* danced along for 315 performances, and in 1937 was presented at the Palace Theatre in London with Vera Zorina in the leading role. She also starred in a 1954 Broadway revival with Bobby Van and Elaine Stritch. When *On Your Toes* returned to Broadway again in 1983, the role of Vera was played by the celebrated ballerina, Natalia Makarova, during the early part of a run of 505 performances. Both revivals were staged by George Abbott. Makarova also co-starred with Tim Flavin in a further successful West End presentation in 1984. 'Slaughter On Tenth Avenue' reached a wider audeince when it was danced by Gene Kelly and Vera-Ellen in the Rodgers and Hart biopic, *Words And Music*.

Once Upon A Mattress

This is an expanded musical adaptation of the comical fairy tale, *The Princess And The Pea*, with music by Mary Rodgers, daughter of the famous composer, Richard Rodgers, and lyrics by Marshall Barer. The show opened Off Broadway at the Phoenix Theatre in New York on 11 May 1959, transferring to the Alvin Theatre on Broadway in November. The book, by Jay Thompson, Dean Fuller, and Barer, told of Princess Winnifred (Carol Burnett), who is unable to marry Prince Dauntless the Drab (Joseph Bova), until she can prove to his mother, Queen Agravain (Jane White), that she is a genuine princess of royal blood. She triumphs during a series of tests, the last of which is to get no sleep at all during a night spent on a heap of mattresses with just one pea underneath the bottom one. Comedienne extraordinaire, Carol Burnett, who later went on to star in her own top-rated television series via the the Gary Moore Show, made an auspicious Broadway debut, and the cast also included the ever-reliable funny-man, Jack Gilford. No hits emerged from the score, but there were several pleasant songs, such as 'Shy', 'Sensitivity', 'Normandy', 'Man To Man Talk', 'Many Moons Ago', 'Very Soft Shoes', 'In A Little While', 'Happily Ever After', 'The Swamp Of Home', and 'Yesterday I Loved You'. An encouraging New York run of 460 performances was followed by a brief, one month stay in London.

One Dam Thing After Another

This C.B. Cochran revue, written by Ronald Jeans, opened at the London Pavilion on 20 May 1927. The impressive cast included Sonnie Hale, Leslie 'Hutch' Hutchinson, Melvin Cooper, the accomplished

Kenny Baker and Mary Martin (*One Touch Of Venus*)

American pianist Edythe Baker, and the delightful, vivacious Jessie Matthews in her first leading role. One song, 'The Birth Of The Blues', was written by De Sylva, Brown And Henderson, but the remainder were provided by Richard Rodgers and Lorenz Hart, and included 'My Lucky Star', 'I Need Some Cooling Off', and the enduring standard, 'My Heart Stood Still', which was introduced by Jessie Matthews. The latter number, with Hart's emotional and affecting lyric, played a significant part in the show's success. After the Prince of Wales attended the opening night, he asked for the song to be played at a subsequent function. The orchestra did not know it, so the royal personage hummed it for them. Naturally, the press gave the incident extensive coverage, and also printed the words and music of the song's first 16 bars. The royal seal of approval helped *One Dam Thing After Another* to overcome initial lukewarm reviews, and it became a hit, running for 237 performances.

One Touch Of Venus

After making her initial impact on Broadway in 1938 with Cole Porter's 'My Heart Belongs To Daddy' in *Leave It To Me!*, Mary Martin shot to stardom five years later in this show which opened at the Imperial Theatre in New York on 7 October 1943. The music was written by Kurt Weill, a familiar name in the American musical theatre following his flight from Germany in 1933, but for the two celebrated humorists, poet Ogden Nash (lyrics) and his fellow librettist, S.J. Perelman, *One Touch Of Venus* was their first, and only, book musical. The authors' story, which was based on F. Anstey's *The Tinted Venus*, was a contemporary 'sophisticated and witty variation on the Pygmalion-Galatea myth'. Whitelaw Savory (John Boles) has discovered a 3,000 year-old statue of Venus which he has put on display at his New York museum. While viewing the piece, Rodney Hatch (Kenny Baker), a barber from Ozone Heights, puts his fiancée's ring on Venus's finger, and the statue immediately springs to life in the classic shape of Mary Martin. Complex, and sometimes hilarious situations then develop, during which Whitelaw falls for Venus, but she prefers Rodney - that is until she finds out that he is just a simple barber. Eventually, disillusioned with her animated existence, Venus returns to her marble state, and Rodney falls in love with a girl who looks remarkably like . . . Mary Martin. Weill and Nash's score in which the words and music are always in perfect sympathy, is usually remembered for the haunting torch song, 'Speak Low', but there were several other attractive numbers including 'I'm A Stranger Here Myself', 'How Much I Love You', 'One Touch Of Venus', 'West Wind', 'That's Him', 'Foolish Heart', 'The Trouble With Women', 'Wooden Wedding', 'Very, Very, Very', and two beautiful and highly effective ballets

sequences, 'Forty Minutes For Lunch' and 'Venus In Ozone Heights', both of which were choreographed by Agnes de Mille. Elia Kazan directed a brilliant all-round cast which included Paula Laurence, Teddy Hart, Ruth Bond, Sono Osato, and Harry Clark. The show ran for a respectable 322 performances, and is regarded as one of the classic musical comedies. Surprisingly, revivals have been few and far between, but the Goodspeed Opera House mounted an acclaimed production in 1987 which starred Richard Sabellico, Semina De Laurentis, Michael Piontek, and Lynnette Perry.

Osmond, Donny

b. Donald Clark Osmond, 9 December 1957, Ogden, Utah, USA. The most successful solo artist to emerge from family group, the Osmonds, Donny was particularly successful at covering old hits. His first solo success came in the summer of 1971 with a version of Billy Sherrill's 'Sweet And Innocent', which reached the US Top 10. The follow-up, a revival of Gerry Goffin/Carole King's 'Go Away Little Girl' (previously a hit for both Steve Lawrence and Mark Wynter) took Osmond to the top of the US charts. 'Hey Girl', once a success for Freddie Scott, continued his US chart domination, which was now even more successful than that of the family group. By the summer of 1972, Osmondmania reached Britain, and a revival of Paul Anka's 'Puppy Love' gave Donny his first UK number 1. The singer's clean-cut good looks and perpetual smile brought him massive coverage in the pop press, while a back catalogue of hit songs from previous generations sustained his chart career. 'Too Young' and 'Why' both hit the UK Top 10, while 'The Twelfth Of Never' and 'Young Love' both reached number 1. His material appeared to concentrate on the pangs of adolescent love, which made him the perfect teenage idol for the period. In 1974, Donny began a series of duets with his sister Marie Osmond, which included more UK Top 10 hits with 'I'm Leaving It All Up To You' and 'Morning Side Of The Mountain'. It was clear that Donny's teen appeal was severely circumscribed by his youth and in 1977 he tried unsuccessfully to reach a more mature audience with *Donald Clark Osmond*. Although minor hits followed, the singer's appeal was waning alarmingly by the late 70s. After the break-up of the group in 1980, Donny went on to star in the Broadway musical *Little Johnny Jones* and ceased recording after the mid-70s. A decade later a more rugged Osmond returned with 'I'm In It For Love' and the more successful 'Soldier Of Love', which reached the US Top 30. Most agreed that his attempts at mainstream rock were much more impressive than anyone might have imagined. In the 90s, Osmond proved his versatility once more when he played the lead in Canadian and North American productions of Andrew Lloyd Webber's musical *Joseph And The Amazing Technicolor Dreamcoat*.

Albums: solo *The Donny Osmond Album* (1971), *To You With Love* (1971), *Portrait Of Donny* (1972), *Too Young* (1972), *My Best Of You* (1972), *Alone Together* (1973), *A Time For Us* (1973), *Donny* (1974), *Discotrain* (1976), *Donald Clark Osmond* (1977), *Soldier Of Love* (1988), *Eyes Don't Lie* (1991); with Marie Osmond: *I'm Leaving It All Up To You* (1974), *Make The World Go Away* (1975), *Donny And Marie - Featuring Songs From Their Television Show* (1976), *Deep Purple* (1976), *Donny And Marie - A New Season* (1977), *Winning Combination* (1978), *Goin' Coconuts* (1978).

Our Miss Gibbs

Another vehicle for the vivacious actress and singer, Gertie Miller, with music written for her by her husband, Lionel Monkton in collaboration with Ivan Caryll. *Our Miss Gibbs* opened at the Gaiety Theatre in London on 23 January 1909, and dwelt, like so many similar productions of the time, on the life and loves of the common shop girl. This time the shop is in the county of Yorkshire, England, and sells flowers. Mary Gibbs (Gertie Miller) loves bank clerk Harry Lancaster (J. Edward Fraser), and the romance is going swimmingly until she discovers he is really the well-heeled Lord Eynsford, who has made certain commitments, marriage-wise, to Lady Elizabeth Thanet (Julia James). Wanting to be alone, she dashes off to the 1908 Franco-British Exhibition at London's White City Stadium (capacity 70,000), and emerges to accept the good Lord's apology and nuptial proposal. Most of the songs were written by Monkton or Caryll with lyricists Adrian Ross and Percy Greenbank, but the popular 'Yip-I-Addy-I-Ay', which was sung in the show by George Grossmith Jnr. (as the Hon. Hughie Pierrepoint), was the work of Grossmith Jnr. himself, with Will Cobb and John Flynn. The bulk of the score consisted of 'My Yorkshire Lassie', 'Not That Sort Of Person', 'Yorkshire', 'Mary', 'Hats', 'Country Cousins', 'White City', and 'Our Farm'. The song that created quite a stir, and endured, was the charming 'Moonstruck', which was introduced by Gertie Miller, dressed as a Pierrot, in a party scene. *Our Miss Gibbs* had - for those days - a prodigious run of 636 performances, but, understandably, given its subject matter and setting, flopped in New York, even with Pauline Chase as Mary, and some interpolated songs from Jerome Kern.

Pacific Overtures

Sometimes known as Stephen Sondheim's 'kabuki musical', this ambitious production opened at the Winter Garden, New York, on 11 January 1976. The book was by John Weidman, a student of law at Yale University. It traced the history of Japan from 1852, when naval officer Commander Matthew Perry, and four warships, attempted to establish 'friendly' relations with a 'isolated and peaceful country', through a period of some 120 years of continual change, culminating in the country's emergence as a dominant trading force in the western world. The story was told in an imaginative and original manner, with every aspect of the production heavily influenced by the traditional form of Japanese Kabuki theatre. Most of Sondheim's music was written in the Japanese pentatonic scale, and his lyrics used extremely simple language, with very few rhymes. The songs included 'Pretty Lady', 'Four Black Dragons', "There Is No Other Way", 'Chrysanthemum Tea', 'Please Hello', 'A Bowler Hat', 'Welcome To Kanagawa', 'Someone In A Tree', 'Next'. 'The Advantages Of Floating In The Middle Of The Sea', and 'Poems'. Director Hal Prince received one of the show's several Tony nominations for his staging of a project that was both daring and completely different from anything Broadway had seen in living memory. The actors, who included Mako, Soon-Teck Oh, Yukis Shimoda, and Sab Shimono, were all Asians, even those who played Americans. Prince was among the show's several Tony nominees, but the only winners were Florence Klotz (costumes) and Boris Aronson (scenic design). The show also won the New York Drama Critics' Circle Award for best musical. It ran for 193 performances, and was presented in a revised, small-scale version Off Broadway in 1984.

Paige, Elaine

b. Elaine Bickerstaff, 5 March 1951, Barnet, Hertfordshire, England. An actress, singer, and star of the musical theatre, Elaine Paige was trained at the Aida Foster Stage School. She had already appeared in the musical *Maybe That's Your Problem* (about premature ejaculation!) when she was plucked from near obscurity to appear on stage as Eva Peron in the Tim Rice/Andrew Lloyd Webber musical, *Evita*. Although Julie Covington had sung the part on the original album and had the number 1 hit with 'Don't Cry For Me Argentina', Paige went on to make the

Elaine Paige

role her own. Despite the twin disappointments of being unable to play the role on Broadway (because of American union rules), and missing out on the film, *Evita* turned Paige into a star almost overnight. In 1978 she recorded an album with Peter Oliver but her first solo album came in 1981. Featuring a variety of songs – mostly with lyrics by Tim Rice – the album was recorded with the assistance of Stuart Elliot (ex-Cockney Rebel), Ian Bairnson and David Paton from Pilot, and Mike Moran. As well as a version of Paul Simon's 'How The Heart Approaches What It Yearns', there was a rare Paul McCartney instrumental ('Hot As Sun') with words by Rice. Subsequent releases were show and film themes and she gained a number 1 single duetting with Barbara Dickson on the striking 'I Know Him So Well' from *Chess*, in which she also starred. Her most unusual album came out in 1988 and was full of cover versions of Queen songs. In 1989 she turned her attention to acting and made two films for the BBC including the acclaimed *Unexplained Laughter*, with Diana Rigg. She had previously worked in the television soap-opera *Crossroads*. In 1990 her long-term relationship with Tim Rice dissolved and she threw herself into her work. During the early 90s she toured the UK, acompanied in concert by a 26-piece symphony orchestra, and in 1993 was highly acclaimed for her powerful and dramatic performance in Pam Gems' play with music *Piaf*, at the Piccadilly Theatre in London.

Albums: with Peter Oliver *Barrier* (1978), *Elaine Paige* (1982), *Stages* (1983), *Cinema* (1984), *Sitting Pretty* (1985), *Love Hurts* (1985), *Christmas* (1986), *The Queen Album* (1988), *Love Can Do That* (1991), with Barbara Dickson *Together* (1992), *Romance And The Stage* (1993), and Original Cast recordings. Compilation: *Memories - The Best Of Elaine Paige* (1987).

Paint Your Wagon

Despite the qualities of its writers, the stage musical *Paint Your Wagon* had only modest success. It opened at the Shubert Theatre in New York on 12 November 1951, and ran for only 295 performances. Well-staged and with excellent choreography by Agnes de Mille, *Paint Your Wagon* was set in California during the 1850s gold rush. With music by Frederick Loewe and book and lyrics by Alan Jay Lerner, the cast, which included James Barton, Tony Bavaar, Olga San Juan, Rufus Smith and James Mitchell, portrayed hard-bitten prospectors and their equally tough girlfriends. There were several appealing songs in the score, such as 'They Call The Wind Maria', 'I Still See Elisa', 'There's A Coach Comin' In', 'I Talk To The Trees', and 'Wand'rin' Star', which became a UK number 1 hit for the actor Lee Marvin after he had performed it in a gruff whisper in the 1969 film version. In 1953, London audiences were delighted with the show and it ran at Her Majesty's Theatre for over a year with Bobby Howes and his real-life daughter Sally Ann Howes. In 1992, the Goodspeed Opera House in Connecticut gave theatregoers another chance to hear what is now – over 40 years on – regarded as an outstanding score.

Pajama Game, The

With a book by Richard Bissell and George Abbott from Bissell's novel 7 1/2 Cents, The Pajama Game opened at the St. James Theatre in New York on 13 May 1954 with only limited expectations. For one thing, the show's writers, Richard Adler and Jerry Ross, were relatively unknown to Broadway audiences, as was choreographer Bob Fosse; and for another, mid-May is late in the season for a show to have a chance to take off. However, take off it did, eventually running for 1,063 performances. The score was full of amusing and romantic numbers, such as 'I'll Never Be Jealous Again', 'There Once Was Man', 'Once A Year Day', 'Small Talk', 'I'm Not At All In Love' 'Hernando's Hideaway', 'Steam Heat', and 'Hey, There'. Set against the unlikely backdrop of a factory manufacturing pajamas and with an industrial dispute as its central dramatic device, the show had strong central performances from Janis Paige, John Raitt and Carol Haney. It won Tony Awards for best musical, featured actress (Haney), and Bob Fosse's choreography which was an outstanding feature of the show. The 1955 London production, which ran for 501 performances and is remembered with great affection, starred Max Wall, Joy Nichols, Edmund Hockridge, and Elizabeth Seal. Hockridge was subsequently always associated with 'Hey, There', although in fact the song was a UK hit for Rosemary Clooney, Johnnie Ray, Lita Roza, and Sammy Davis Jnr. The Pajama Game was revived briefly on Broadway in 1973 with Barbara McNair, Hal Linden, and Cab Calloway. The 1957 film version achieved the impossible and actually improved upon the original with dazzling performances from Doris Day, Raitt, Haney, and Eddie Foy Jnr. In 1958, the musical Say Darling, which was based on Richard Bissell's experiences with The Pajama Game, opened on Broadway and ran for 332 performances. The cast was headed by Vivian Blaine, David Wayne, and Johnny Desmond, and the score was by Betty Comden and Adolph Green.

Pal Joey

One of the first musical comedies to break with tradition, Pal Joey opened at the Ethel Barrymore Theatre in New York on Christmas Day 1940. With a libretto by John O'Hara, based on his own short stories, the plot had tough, realistic characters whose lives were a mess of sex and blackmail, and was far from the usual escapism. Also breaking new ground were the songs, which had music by Richard Rodgers and lyrics by Lorenz Hart. They were cleverly integrated into the plot, advancing both it and the development of characters. Joey was played by Gene

Kelly and other cast members included Leila Ernst and Vivienne Segal (as just two of the women in his life), June Havoc and Van Johnson. The rich and amusing score included 'I Could Write A Book', 'Bewitched, Bothered, And Bewildered', 'That Terrific Rainbow', 'You Musn't Kick It Around', 'Do It The Hard Way', 'Take Him', 'The Flower Garden Of My Heart', 'What Is A Man?', 'Our Little Den Of Iniquity', and the intellectual striptease 'Zip'. Pal Joey ran for 374 performances but its 1952 revival did better, lasting for 542 performances, and winning Tony Awards for best featured actress (Helen Gallagher), choreographer (Robert Alton), and musical director (Max Meth). The remainder of the cast included Harold Lang, Vivienne Segal, and Elaine Stritch. The new production was widely applauded by critics and audiences who were by this time familiar with at least some of the shows songs and themes. The 1954 London production also starred Harold Lang with Carol Bruce. Over the years, revivals continued to be mounted, and in the early 90s the show was presented by the Goodspeed Opera House, Connecticut, the Long Beach Civic Light Opera, California, the Huntington Theatre Company in Boston, and the Old Vic in Bristol, UK. A film version was released in 1957 with Frank Sinatra, Rita Hayworth, and Kim Novak.

Panama Hattie

Considered to be similar in some ways to Dubarry Was A Lady (1939), this show was nevertheless felt to be inferior to that one, although it employed the same creative team, and ran for some four months longer. Panama Hattie opened at the 46th Street Theatre on 30 October 1940, with a Cole Porter score, a book by Herbert Fields and B.G. 'Buddy' DeSylva, and with the dynamic Ethel Merman on hand to belt out the songs. She plays Hattie Maloney, the owner of a nightclub in Panama City. Outwardly cynical, but a real pussy-cat deep down inside (a perfect Merman character) her prospective marriage to well-heeled divorcé, Nick Bullitt (James Dunn), hangs on the approval of Geraldine – sometimes known as Jerry – (Joan Carroll), the precocious eight-year-old daughter from his first marriage. Hattie wins her over during the conciliatory 'Let's Be Buddies' (Hattie: 'Would you like a big box of chocolate creams?'/Jerry: 'No, for candy I never did care'/Hattie: 'Then will you let me get you a cute little dog?'/Jerry: 'Do you think you could make it a bear?'). Merman had several other clever Porter numbers, including 'Make It Another Old Fashioned, Please', 'I'm Throwing A Ball Tonight', and 'I've Still Got My Health' ('I can't count my ribs, like His Nibs, Fred Astaire/But I've still got my health, so what do I care!'). The rest of the songs included 'All I've Got To Get Now Is My Man', 'Fresh As A Daisy', 'My Mother Would Love

You', 'Who Would Have Dreamed?', and 'Visit Panama'. The cast included some familiar names of the future such as Betty Hutton, along with June Allyson and Vera-Ellen who were both in the chorus. *Panama Hattie*, which was the fourth in a series of five musicals that Porter and Merman did together, enjoyed a run of 501 performances. It marked the beginning of a decade during which they both produced some of their finest work: Porter with *Kiss Me, Kate* (1948), and Merman with *Annie Get Your Gun* (1946). *Panama Hattie* also had a decent run of 308 performances in London's West End, where it starred Bebe Daniels, Max Wall, Ivan Brandt, Claude Hulbert, and Richard Hearne.

Peggy-Ann

With a score by Richard Rodgers and Lorenz Hart, and a book by Herbert Fields, this show opened at the Vanderbilt Theatre in New York on 27 December 1926. It was sandwiched between *Lido Lady* and *Betsy*, two fairly unsatisfactory Rodgers and Hart shows that were produced in the same year. *Peggy-Ann* was sub-titled 'The Utterly Different Musical Comedy', and, in some respects, that proved to be true - for a start, it was a hit. Although Fields's book was based on the Edgar Smith and A. Baldwin Sloane's 1910 musical, *Tillie's Nightmare*, in which Marie Dressler had enjoyed great success, it had highly topical overtones. 1926 was the year of the Surrealists, a new movement in poetry and painting whose members believed in the 'omnipotence of the dream', and were heavily influenced by Sigmund Freud. The libretto for *Peggy-Ann* was liberally sprinkled with Freudian references, and follows Peggy-Ann Barnes (Helen Ford), a domestic servant in a boarding house in Glen Falls, New York, into her own private fantasy world. In a trice, she is travelling the globe, tasting the high-life at the race track, aboard a yacht, shopping on New York's Fifth Avenue - and getting married in her underwear. There were some other unusual touches, too: no songs were sung in the opening 15 minutes of the show, and there was no rousing finale. Also, the sets and props were moved around in full view of the audience, a device used by Rodgers again, 36 years later, in *No Strings*. The songs, when they eventually came, were a pleasing bunch, and one of them, 'A Tree In The Park', achieved some popularity through recordings by Helen Morgan and Frank Black. 'Where's That Rainbow?' also endured, and is often performed by supper-club singers such as Bobby Short. The rest of the score included 'A Little Bird Told Me So' 'and 'Maybe It's Me'. A New York run of 333 performances was followed by a further 130 in London, where the role of Peggy-Ann was played by Dorothy Dickson.

Perchance To Dream

When this show opened at the London Hippodrome on 21 April 1945, it was conceived as Ivor Novello's 'victory presentation'. With blithe disregard for the grimness of post-war Britain in the streets outside, Novello set out to recreate the kind of musical nostalgia with which he had been linked so successfully in the 30s. His story, which traced the lives of members of a family over several generations from Regency times to the present, was unashamedly romantic. In much the same manner as before the war, Novello unerringly found a buried desire in the hearts of London's theatre-goers for the kind of musical that had never really been truly British. Owing more to Viennese operetta of an earlier century than it did to the harsh reality of still war-shocked Britain, *Perchance To Dream* proved to be one of the composer's greatest successes. With several of his regular favourites in the cast, amongst them Olive Gilbert, Roma Beaumont and Muriel Barron, and songs like 'A Woman's Heart', 'This Is My Wedding Day', and especially 'Love Is My Reason' and 'We'll Gather Lilacs', Novello had yet another major success on his hands. The show ran for 1,022 performances.

Peter Pan

A musical adaptation of J.M. Barrie's classic story were presented in New York as early as 1905 when Maude Adams and Ernest Lawford starred in a Charles Frohman production. It was revived in 1924, with Marilyn Miller in the leading role, and included two Jerome Kern songs, 'The Sweetest Thing In Life' and 'Just Because You're You'. The 1950 version, which ran for 321 performances, starred Jean Arthur and Boris Karloff. Leonard Bernstein wrote the music and lyrics for several songs, such 'Who Am I?', 'Never-Land', 'Peter, Peter', and 'My House', and Alec Wilder also provided some incidental music. In the fourth interpretation, which opened at the Winter Garden in New York on 20 October 1954, Mary Martin, returning to Broadway for the first time since her triumph in *South Pacific*, made a spirited, high-flying Peter, to Cyril Ritchard's amusingly degenerate Captain Hook. The initial score, which was written by Moose Charlap and Carolyn Leigh, contained songs such as 'Tender Shepherd', 'I've Got To Crow', 'I'm Flying', and 'I Won't Grow Up'. Before the show reached Broadway, director and choreographer, Jerome Robbins, enlisted the help of Jule Styne, along with Betty Comden and Adolph Green. They provided the music and lyrics for several additional numbers, including 'Captain Hook's Waltz', 'Wendy', 'Mysterious Lady', and the lovely 'Never Never Land', which is still sung occasionally, and received a sensitive reading from Lena Horne on her *Lena At The Sands*. Mary Martin received the Tony Award for best actress, and this version ran for

152 performances before it was taped, and shown on US television, giving non theatre-going audiences a rare opportunity to see a Broadway show. A 1979 New York revival, starring Sandy Duncan and George Rose, beat all the previous versions and lasted for 551 performances. Six years later the same basic production played the West End, with Joss Ackland, Judith Bruce, and Bonnie Langford. In 1990, Cathy Rigby and Stephan Hanon played Peter and Hook when *Peter Pan* looked in on Broadway again for a limited six-week engagement as part of its nation-wide tour. Another, quite different adaptation of J.M. Barrie's *Peter Pan*, with music and lyrics by Stephen Oliver, was presented at the Barbican Theatre in London in December 1982.

Further reading: *The Peter Pan Chronicles*, Bruce K. Hanson.

Peters, Bernadette

b. Bernadette Lazzara, 28 February 1948, Ozone Park, Queens, New York City, New York, USA. She has been called 'the finest singing actress since Streisand', and is certainly one of the few leading ladies of the last decade whose name on a Broadway marquee can cause box-office queues to form before the show has gone into previews. Peters was tap-dancing and acting at an early age, and joined Actors' Equity when she was nine. Soon afterwards she changed her name to Peters, and played Tessie in the 1959 revival of *The Most Happy Fella* at the New York City Centre. After appearing in the role of Baby June in a road tour of *Gypsy*, she gave up performing for a time, and studied acting and singing in her teens, before returning to the stage in a number of fairly mediocre productions. In 1968 she received favourable notices, and a Theatre World citation, for her portrayal of George M. Cohan's sister in *George M!*, and, in the same year, won a Drama Desk Award for her 'hilarious performance' as the zany Ruby in *Dames At Sea*, a 30s movie-spoof which enjoyed a good run Off Broadway. In between several theatrical disappointments in the late 60s and early 70s with *La Strada* (one performance), a New York revival of *On The Town*, *W.C.* (a musical about W.C. Fields), and *Mack And Mabel* (1974), she turned to films and television, often playing straight roles, but without any notable success. In 1977 Peters formed a private and professional partnership with the comedian Steve Martin, and they appeared together in two movies, *The Jerk* (1979), and the highly expensive box-office disaster *Pennies From Heaven* (1981), for which Peters won a Golden Globe Award. Her other films around this time included the musical, *Annie*, in which she played Lily, the fiendish social worker. In the 80s she starred in three Broadway musicals, two of which had scores by Stephen Sondheim, *Sunday In The Park With George* (1984) and *Into The Woods* (1987). She also won a Tony Award for her brilliant solo

Bernadette Peters

performance in Andrew Lloyd Webber and Don Black's *Song And Dance*. During the latter part of the decade, Peters developed her cabaret act which revolved around Broadway show tunes but also contained a lovely version of Hank Williams' 'I'm So Lonesome I Could Cry', and a highly effective Harold Arlen medley. In 1993 she was back on Broadway with Martin Short and Carol Woods in the eagerly awaited musical, *The Goodbye Girl*. In spite of Neil Simon's witty book, and a score by Marvin Hamlisch and David Zippel, the show folded after only 188 performances.

Selected albums: *Bernadette Peters* (1980), *Now Playing* (1981), and Original Cast and film soundtrack recordings.

Phantom Of The Opera, The

This is probably Andrew Lloyd Webber's most highly regarded and critically acclaimed work to date. Of course, the vast majority of his other productions, including those he wrote with Tim Rice and the later ones where people pretend to be cats and trains, have been enormously successful all over the world for many years now, but *The Phantom Of The Opera* seems to be the show that gives audiences the deepest and most enduring satisfaction. It opened at Her Majesty's Theatre in London on 9 October 1986. The score was by Lloyd Webber (music) and Charles Hart (lyrics), with additional lyrics by Richard Stilgoe. The book, which was based on Gaston Leroux's classic 1911 novel, was written by Lloyd Webber and Stilgoe. The familiar story is set in the Paris Opera House during the 19th century, where the facially disfigured masked Phantom (Michael Crawford) haunts and terrorizes the occupants. He is obsessed with the young and beautiful soprano, Christine (Sarah Brightman or Claire Moore), and whisks her away below the theatre, steering her through the candlelit sewers to his richly furnished rooms deep under the streets of the city. He teaches her to sing 'like an angel' and she initially becomes entranced by him, but she loves another. In his rage, the Phantom threatens to blow up the opera house if she refuses to stay with him. She agrees to his blackmail, but when she kisses him without any apparent sign of revulsion at his deformity, he is so moved that he releases her into the arms of Raoul (Steve Barton), her leading man. Lloyd Webber's 'ravishing' music was his most romantic and overtly operatic so far - and arguably his best. The outstanding numbers were the major love ballads, 'All I Ask Of You', sung by Brightman and Barton, and 'The Music Of The Night', impressively rendered by Crawford, but there were others equally attractive, including 'Masquerade', 'Wandering Child', 'The Phantom Of The Opera', 'Angel Of Music', 'Think Of Me', 'Wishing You Were Somehow Here Again', and 'The Point Of No Return'. Hal Prince's highly impressive staging featured the by-now famous scene in which the great chandelier crashes down from the ceiling on to the stage - one of the Phantom's pranks in reprisal for his protegée not being given the lead. Crawford, who maintains that he only got the job because Lloyd Webber heard him singing while waiting to collect his wife, Sarah Brightman from her lesson, dominated in the leading role. After appearing on the London stage in the musicals *Billy* and *Barnum*, and on film in *Hello, Dolly!*, this show marked a new beginning in his career. He had a UK Top 10 hit with 'The Music Of The Night', and won the Olivier Award for best actor; the show itself won for best musical. Sarah Brightman and Cliff Richard almost made the top of the UK chart (number 3) with their duet of 'All I Ask Of You'. While *The Phantom Of The Opera* settled in for a long London run, Crawford, Brightman, and Barton recreated their roles for the Broadway production which opened at the Majestic Theatre on 26 January 1988. 'A muted triumph' was the consensus of opinion, but there was nothing muted about the show's appeal when Tony Awards time came round, and it won for best musical, actor (Crawford), featured actress (Judy Kaye), sets, costumes, lighting, and director (Prince). Since that time, both the UK and US production have continued to be the hottest tickets in town, and touring versions have proliferated in many countries. In 1993, as the London production celebrated its seventh anniversary, a second company was dispatched to the provinces, and, in the same year, it was estimated that the show had grossed over $1 billion worldwide.

There have been several other musical adaptations of Gaston Leroux's famous story. The two best-known versions are *Phantom Of The Opera* by Ken Hill, and *Phantom* with a book by Arthur Kopit and music and lyrics by Maury Yeston. Ken Hill's show, which is billed as 'The Original Stage Musical', was first seen in 1984 at the Theatre Royal, Stratford East in London. After revisions, and the negative impact of the Lloyd Webber version, it ran for six months at the Shaftesbury Theatre in the West End from 1991-92, with Peter Straker as the Phantom, music by composers such as Offenbach, Gounod, Verdi, Weber, Bizet, and Mozart, and witty and original lyrics by Hill. The Yeston-Kopit version ('A New Musical Thriller') first emerged in 1990 as a four-hour mini-series on US television with Burt Lancaster and Charles Dance, and was later presented on stage at such venues as the Music Hall, Texas, and the Paper Mill Playhouse, New Jersey. The *Phantom* phenomenon continues in many forms, but as far as the public at large are concerned it probably all started with the 1925 film which starred Lon Chaney. Subsequent screen versions were released in 1943

Michael Crawford (*The Phantom Of The Opera*)

(with Claude Rains, Susanna Foster and Nelson Eddy), 1962 (Herbert Lom, Heather Sears, and Thorley Walters), 1983 (Maxamilian Schell, Jane Seymour and Michael York), and 1989 (Robert Englund, Jill Schoelen and Alex Hyde-Whyte).
Further reading: *The Complete Phantom Of The Opera*, George Perry.

Phil The Fluter

This show began its life in Dublin as a radio play by Donal Giltinan, based on the life of the celebrated Irish entertainer Percy French, who composed such memorable songs as 'The Mountains Of Mourne' and 'Phil The Fluter's Ball'. The radio show evolved into the stage musical *The Golden Years* which was presented successfully at the Gaiety Theatre in Dublin where it caught the eye of one of London's leading theatrical producers, Harold Fielding. He determined to produce the show in London, and engaged Beverly Cross to collaborate with Giltinan on the book, and composer David Heneker, of *Half A Sixpence* fame, to supplement Percy French's original score. The result, *Phil The Fluter*, opened in the West End at the Palace Theatre on 13 November 1969. The popular singer Mark Wynter, in the role of Percy French, was retained from the cast of *The Golden Years*, and he was joined by comedian and impressionist Stanley Baxter and one of the most celebrated leading ladies of the London musical stage, Evelyn Laye. Her rendition of Heneker's poignant 'They Don't Make Them Like That Any More' ('In those days men gave orchids by the dozen/Today they think forget-me-nots will do') still burns brightly in the memory more than 20 years later. She also had a charming duet with Wynter, 'You Like It'. The remainder of the score, a mixture of French and Heneker, included 'If I Had A Chance', 'Mama', 'A Favour For A Friend', 'Good Money', 'How Would You Like Me?', 'Abdoul Abulbul Ameer', 'I Shouldn't Have To Be The One To Tell You', 'Follow Me', 'Are You Right There, Michael?', 'That's Why The Poor Man's Dead', and 'Wonderful Woman'. Following a set of mixed reviews, the show never really caught on with the public, and closed after 125 performances.

Piaf

Legend has it that when Pam Gems was writing this musical play about Edith Piaf, 'the mid-20th century chanteuse who took to young men, drugs and fame, and regretted nothing', she saw Elaine Paige in a West End show and decided that she would be the ideal choice for the lead. But in the early 70s Paige was too young, and had yet to make a name for herself, so the role went to Jane Lapotaire, whose nerve-shattering performance earned her a Tony award when the show transferred to Broadway. Since then, Elaine Paige has established herself as one of the outstanding leading ladies on the London musical stage, and was therefore first in line to star in Peter Hall's revival which began its limited run on 13 December 1993. However, Miss Paige was not too happy with Hall's choice of theatre - the Piccadilly - because of its recent association with a series of flop musicals which included *Mutiny!*, *Metropolis*, *King*, *Moby Dick*, and *Which Witch*. She need not have worried: the critics were unanimous in their praise for her 'astonishingly poignant performance as the tiny, black-garbed creature - a powerhouse of emotion'. She matched Piaf vulgarity for vulgarity, but her finest moments came when she sang those resounding anthems, 'Mon Dieu', 'Je Ne Regrette Rein', and the impassioned aria of loss, 'Hymne A L'Amour'. Lapotaire still lingers in the memory, but, with her powerful vocal range and heart-rending, emotional vibrato, Elaine Paige was Edith Piaf to the life.

Pickwick

Devised as a vehicle for the popular British comedian and singer Harry Secombe, *Pickwick* had a book by Wolf Mankowitz which was based on Charles Dickens' novel, *The Pickwick Papers*. Leslie Bricusse, fresh from his triumph with *Stop The World - I Want To Get Off*, wrote the lyrics, and the music was composed by Cyril Ornadel. The show opened at the Saville Theatre in London on 4 July 1963, and was what one critic described as 'comic-strip Dickens'. Secombe made a jovial, likeable Pickwick, and his adventures with familiar characters such as Sam Weller (Teddy Green), Tony Weller (Robin Wentworth), Mrs. Bardell (Jessie Evans), Augustus Snodgrass (Julian Orchard), and Mr. Jingle (Anton Rodgers), made for an extremely enjoyable evening. The score, a mixture of lively and amusing numbers and one or two spirited ballads, included 'There's Something About You', 'That's What I Want For Christmas', 'The Trouble With Women', 'You Never Met A Feller Like Me', 'A Bit Of Character', 'Look Into Your Heart', 'Talk', 'Learn A Little Something', and 'Do As You Would Be Done By'. The show's big hit, 'If I Ruled The World', is sung by Mr. Pickwick when he is mistaken for a parliamentary candidate. It gave Secombe a UK Top 20 hit, and is probably the song most associated with him. After a satisfying London run of some 20 months, *Pickwick* travelled to New York, via a successful stop-over in San Francisco, but Broadway audiences were unimpressed, and the show folded after only 56 performances. Roy Castle, the UK all-round entertainer and a good friend of Secombe's, played the role of Sam Weller in the American production. Thirty years later, when *Pickwick*, was revived at the Chichester Festival Theatre, prior to a season at London's Sadler's Wells, Castle joined Secombe again - this time as Sam's father, Tony.

Pink Lady, The

After writing the music for several successful shows on the London stage between 1894 and 1909, Ivan Caryll moved to America and collaborated with C.M.S. McLellan on the celebrated operetta, The Pink Lady, which opened at the New Amsterdam theatre in New York on 13 March 1911. McLellan's book was based on a French play, Le Satyre, by Georges Berr and Marcel Guillemand, and concerns Lucien Garidel (William Elliot), who is soon to marry Angele (Alice Dovey). Before he 'puts the ball and chain on', he decides that he would like to 'bring champagne on', and invites an old flame, Claudine (Hazel Dawn), for one last farewell dinner. Unluckily for him, his future wife is dining at the same restaurant, and cannot help noticing Lucien's companion, who is known as 'The Pink Lady' because of her blushing wardrobe. The embarrassing situation leads to some bewildering twists and turns in the plot, culminating in the reunion of the happy couple as Lucien sings 'My Beautiful Lady' to his Angele. The lovely waltz became widely successful through versions by Lucy Isabelle Marsh, Grace Kerns, and Elizabeth Spencer, and another song from the show, 'By The Saskatchewan' ('Flow river, flow, down to the sea'), was made popular by Reinald Werrenrath and the Hayden Quartet, amongst others. The rest of a romantic and tuneful score included 'The Kiss Waltz', 'The Right To Love', 'Parisian Two-Step', 'Bring Along The Camera', 'The Hudson Belle', 'I Like It', and 'Donny Didn't, Donny Did'. Critics agreed that, unlike most operettas, the songs emerged quite naturally from the plot. It all added up to a tremendous success, and a run of 312 performances. Hazel North, who not only sang and danced in a charming manner, but also played the violin, delighted London audiences when The Pink Lady opened at the Globe theatre in 1912. Since those days it has been revived on many occasions.

Pins And Needles

Originally presented by members of the International Ladies Garment Workers Union at the tiny Labor Stage (formerly the Princess Theatre) for the enjoyment of their fellow workers, this revue subsequently transferred to the Windsor Theatre (which had nearly three times as many seats), and ran for a (then) record 1,108 performances. Armed with a liberal, pro-union point of view, it opened on 27 November 1937, and proceeded to take a satirical swipe at the usual targets, Fascists, Nazis, and Britain's injustice to its long-established Empire. Anyone who could 'Sing Me A Song Of Social Significance', as its most popular number demanded, was OK, of course, and if you could take your partner for 'Doin' The Reactionary', well, that was even better. The sketches were by the show's director, Charles Freidman,

amongst several others, and the music and lyrics wre provided by a newcomer to Broadway, Harold Rome. His other songs included 'Sunday In The Park', 'Nobody Makes A Pass At Me', 'One Big Union For Two', 'I've Got The Nerve To Be In Love', 'Chain Store Daisy (Vassar Girl Finds A Job)', 'It's Better With A Union Man', 'Not Cricket To Picket', and 'Four Little Angels Of Peace'. When it moved to the Windsor Theatre in 1939, the show was retitled New Pins And Needles, and continued on its honest, angry, but good-humoured way, constantly up-dating the material as it went.

Pippin

Although the book was written by Roger O. Hirson, much of the credit for the success of the stage musical Pippin is owed to Bob Fosse. As director and choreographer, and through his collaboration with Hirson in the writing of the show, Fosse gave Pippin the sparkle needed to attract critical plaudits. The show opened at the Imperial Theatre in New York on 23 October 1972 and starred Ben Vereen in the lead role. The revue format, with its fast paced great dancing, and the remarkable sets helped overcome any audience resistance to a story set in the Middle Ages. John Rubinstein played the title role, a character based upon Pepin, the son of Emperor Charlemagne. Eric Berry, Jill Clayburgh, Leland Palmer, and Irene Ryan (Grandma in television's The Beverly Hillbillies) were also in the original cast but Irene Ryan died during the show's run and was replaced by Dorothy Stickney. The score was by Stephen Schwartz, whose songs included 'Magic To Do', Morning Glow', 'On The Right Track', 'Corner Of The Sky', 'No Time At All', 'Simple Joy', and 'Extraordinary'. That last song title describes perfectly this show's success and its run of 1,944 performances. Pippin won Tony awards for best actor (Vereen), director and choreographer (Fosse), scenic design (Tony Walton), and lighting design (Jules Fisher). The 1973 London production didn't appeal, in spite of the inclusion in the cast of John Turner, Patricia Hodge, Diane Langton, Paul Jones, and Elisabeth Welch, and folded after 85 performances.

Plain And Fancy

Rock 'n' roll music had begun to take a hold in America by the mid-50s, but the 1954/5 Broadway season was full of more traditional fare, such as The Boy Friend, Peter Pan, Silk Stockings, and Damn Yankees, amongst others. One of the others was Plain And Fancy, which opened at the Mark Hellinger Theatre on 27 January 1955. Joseph Stein and Will Glickman's book was set in Bird-in-Hand, Pennsylvania, the home territory of the Amish people, members of a fundamentalist religious sect who have no time or use for even the most basic modern aids. Don King (Richard Derr) has inherited a farm in the area, and he travels there from New York with Ruth Winters (Shirl Conway) to try to sell it to an Amish farmer, Papa Yoder (Stefan Schnabel). Yoder's daughter, Katie (Gloria Marlowe), is about to go through with an arranged marriage to Ezra Reber (Douglas Fletcher Rodgers), but she is still in love with an old flame, Ezra's brother, Peter, (David Daniels). Peter has left the Amish community, and, when he returns just before the wedding, he is shunned by the traditionalists. Matters resolve themselves when Peter's bravery in a crisis gains him the respect of Katie's father, and the young people are allowed to marry. Don and Ruth make it a double wedding. The score, by composer Albert Hague - who was making his Broadway debut - and lyricist Arnold Horwitt, contained a ballad that many feel to be one of the loveliest of all popular songs, 'Young And Foolish'. It was introduced by Daniels and Marlowe, and they also had 'Follow Your Heart' with Barbara Cook, who made a favourable impression in the role of Hilda Miller. Cook sang 'This Is All Very New To Me', 'I'll Show Him', and 'Take Your Time And Take Your Pick' (with Richard Kerr and Shirl Conway). The remainder of the delightful and romantic score included 'You Can't Miss It', 'It Wonders Me', 'Plenty Of Pennsylvania', 'Why Not Katie?', 'It's A Helluva Way To Run A Love Affair', 'Plain We Live', 'How Do You Raise A Barn?' (a spectacular scene to open Act II), 'Follow Your Heart', and 'City Mouse, Country Mouse'. Sophisticated New York audiences obviously loved this folksy view of their country cousins, and *Plain And Fancy* had a decent run of 461 performances. Barbara Cook went on to become Broadway's favourite ingénue during the 50s in shows such as *Candide*, *The Music Man*, and *The Gay Life*.

Poppy

After a brief career in vaudeville, and appearances in several editions of the the Ziegfeld Follies, W.C. Fields, the bulbous-nosed comic with the 'never-give-a-sucker-an-even-break' attitude, came to Broadway in this production which opened at the Apollo Theatre in New York on 3 September 1923. The star was supposed to be Madge Kennedy who plays Fields's foster child, Poppy, but, during the New York run and the subsequent tour, the comedian gradually emerged as the principal attraction. In Dorothy Donnelly's book, Professor Eustace McGargle (Fields) is a card-sharp, a juggler (Fields used to juggle in vaudeville), and an all-round trickster and con-man around the carnivals. Poppy is an orphan girl from the same background, who eventually discovers that she is an heiress. Donnelly also wrote the lyrics for several of the songs, with music by Stephen Jones and Arthur Samuels. These

included 'Two Make A Home', 'Steppin' Around', 'Hang Your Sorrows In The Sun', 'When You Are In My Arms', and 'A Picnic Party With You'. However the most popular numbers were the interpolated 'What Do You Do Sunday, Mary?' (music: Jones, lyric: Irving Caesar), which was introduced by Luella Gear and Robert Woolsey, and became a hit for the American Quartet; and 'Alibi Baby' (music: Samuels, lyric: Howard Dietz). 'Alibi Baby' was Howard Dietz's first successful song. Years later, when he was doing some of his best work with Arthur Schwartz, it turned up in the US Hit Parade in a version by Tommy Dorsey. Fans of W.C. Fields continued to flock to see *Poppy* for 346 performances, and the London production, which starred W.H. Berry and Annie Croft, stayed at the Gaiety Theatre for five months. Fields dominated the two films that were based on the show: a 1925 silent, renamed *Sally Of The Sawdust*, and the 1936 *Poppy*, with Rochelle Hudson. Another, quite different show named *Poppy*, with music by Monty Norman and a book and lyrics by Peter Nichols, played in London's West End in 1982.

Porgy And Bess

The most acclaimed and performed American opera, *Porgy And Bess* was premiered in Boston, Massachusetts, on 30 September 1935. Composed by George Gershwin, the opera was based upon the play *Porgy* by DuBose and Dorothy K. Heyward. DuBose Heyward was also librettist and co-author with Ira Gershwin of the lyrics. The cast included Todd Duncan as Porgy, Anne Brown as Bess, and John Bubbles as Sportin' Life. Among the songs were 'Summertime', 'Bess, You Is My Woman Now', 'Oh, I Got Plenty O' Nuttin''. 'It Ain't Necessarily So', 'A Woman Is A Sometime Thing' and 'There's A Boat Dat's Leavin' Soon For New York'. The story told of events in the lives of urban blacks, enduring conditions of acute deprivation and attempting to survive in the face of indifference and the temptation of drink and drugs. In choosing to set his major work in a context and with characters so far removed from anything to which white middle-class Americans were accustomed, Gershwin took a great risk. Despite a poor reception in New York where *Porgy And Bess* ran for just 24 performances, in the long term the composer's gamble paid off. Despite the lyricists' debasing of language in an attempt to recreate the speech patterns of black Americans, which today appears patronising but was commonplace for its time, *Porgy And Bess* must be regarded as a major accomplishment. Not only does it have merit as musical theatre but much of the music stands up out of context. 'Summertime' in particular has been recorded many times by a wide range of artists. Additionally, concert suites have been performed by symphony orchestras around the world. *Porgy And Bess* was produced in London in 1952 and was brought to the screen in 1959, heavily directed by Otto Preminger, and starring Sidney Poitier, Dorothy Dandridge, Sammy Davis Jnr., Brock Peters and Pearl Bailey. In 1986 the opera was given a sumptuous production by Trevor Nunn at Glyndebourne with a cast including Willard White, Cynthia Haymon, Damon Evans and Harolyn Blackwell. The highly acclaimed production repeated its triumph at the Royal Opera House, Covent Garden in 1992, and was televised two years later.

Porter, Cole

b. 9 June 1891, Peru, Indiana, USA, d. 15 October 1964, Santa Monica, California, USA. Born into a rich family, Porter was taught privately, with music prominent amongst his studies. He composed his first songs before reaching his teens. At the age of 15 he attended school, where he excelled in many academic subjects and continued to write songs and play piano for his own amusement - activities he later pursued at Yale University. Later he attended Harvard where he reluctantly studied law. Fortunately, his other talents had been noted and on faculty advice he switched to the study of music. While still at college some of his songs were used in Broadway productions and in 1916 his first full score, for *See America First*, opened and closed almost at once. The Porter family's wealth allowed him to travel extensively and he visited Europe both before and after World War I. In 1920 another Broadway show, the revue *Hitchy-Koo*, opened and was almost as disastrously received as his first effort. He persevered, however, and some of the songs from these earlier shows survived in their own right. It was a song written for the 1928 show, *Paris*, that gave him his first major song success with 'Let's Do It' and the following year his persistence paid off with two moderately successful Broadway shows, *Fifty Million Frenchmen* and *Wake Up And Dream*, which included, respectively, 'You Do Something To Me' and 'What Is This Thing Called Love?'. During the early 30s Porter wrote for several shows and among the songs which became standards were 'Love For Sale' and 'Night And Day'. In 1932 he had his first major Broadway hit with *Anything Goes*, which included 'Blow, Gabriel, Blow', 'I Get A Kick Out Of You', 'You're The Top' and the title song. Other 30s shows, while less popular than *Anything Goes*, had their own hit songs: 'My Heart Belongs To Daddy', 'Get Out Of Town', 'Friendship', 'Do I Love You?', 'Begin The Beguine', 'Just One Of Those Things' (these last two from the unsuccessful *Jubilee*), 'It's De-Lovely' and 'At Long Last Love'.
Not surprisingly, Porter was lured to Hollywood, where he began his screen musical career with 'I've Got You Under My Skin' and 'Easy To Love',

written for the 1936 film *Born To Dance*. His second film, *Rosalie* (1937), had hits with 'Rosalie' and 'In The Still Of The Night'. In 1937 Porter was seriously injured in a riding accident. Astonishingly, a series of more than two dozen operations, several years in a wheelchair and almost constant pain (his right leg would be amputated in 1958), seemed to have little effect on his creative ability. Among his songs of the early 40s were 'I Concentrate On You', 'I've Got My Eyes On You', 'Let's Be Buddies', 'Ace In The Hole', 'Everything I Love' and 'I Love You'. During this time Porter was dividing his time and talent between stage and films and his song successes came in both mediums: 'You'd Be So Nice To Come Home To' from the film *You'll Never Get Rich* (1941) and 'Ev'ry Time We Say Goodbye', from the 1944 show *Seven Lively Arts*. Although written some years before for an aborted film project, another song, 'Don't Fence Me In', was used in *Hollywood Canteen* (1944). Two unsuccessful Porter scores followed in the late 40s, one a show, the other a film, but in 1948 he had his biggest Broadway hit with *Kiss Me, Kate*, for which he wrote 'So In Love', 'Always True To You In My Fashion', 'Wunderbar', 'I Hate Men', 'Too Darn Hot' and 'Brush Up Your Shakespeare'. In 1950, Porter followed *Kiss Me, Kate* with another unsuccessful show, *Out Of This World*, but even this had its hit song, 'From This Moment On'.
The mid-50s found Porter still capable of bringing Broadway to its feet with two more smash hits: *Can-Can* (1953) from which came 'I Love Paris', 'C'est Magnifique' and 'It's All Right With Me'; and *Silk Stockings* (1955) with 'Paris Loves Lovers' and 'Without Love'. Porter then returned to Hollywood with two film scores: *High Society* (1956) and *Les Girls* (1957). From the former came 'True Love', 'Samantha' and 'Did You Ever', while the latter included 'Ça C'est Amour'. Marked by wit and sophistication often far ahead of the times in which he lived, Porter's music and lyrics set standards which were the envy of most of his contemporaries and even so distinguished a composer as Irving Berlin was fulsome in his praise. Although Porter stopped writing in the late 50s, his music continued to be used in films and on television and he was the subject of television specials and numerous honours and awards. In 1991, the centenary of his birth, there were tributes galore. In a gala concert at Carnegie Hall, artists such as Julie Wilson, Kathryn Grayson, and Patricia Morison paid tribute to him, as did songwriters Jule Styne, Sammy Cahn, and Burton Lane. Among the other special events were an Off Broadway revue *Anything Cole*, the West End production *A Swell Party*, and a London concert entitled *Let's Do It*, starring Elaine Delmar and Paul Jones. The special occasion was also marked by the release of complete recordings of his scores for *Nymph Errant* and *Kiss Me, Kate*.

Cole Porter

Further reading: *The Cole Porter Story*, David Ewen. *Cole: A Biographical Essay*, Brendan Gill and Richard Kimball. *The Cole Porter Story*, Cole Porter and Richard Hubler. *Cole Porter: The Life That Late He Led*, George Eells. *Travels With Cole Porter*, Jean Howard.

Preston, Robert

b. Robert Preston Meservey, 8 June 1918, Newton Highlands, Massachussetts, USA, d. 21 March 1987, Santa Barbara, California, USA. An actor and singer, Preston had already had a busy, but undistinguished career in Hollywood for nearly 20 years when he landed the role of a lifetime on Broadway in *The Music Man* (1957). He grew up in Hollywood, and spent several of his teenage years in the theatre before signing for Paramount and making his first movie, *King Of Alcatraz*, in 1938. From then, until 1942, he made some 15 films, including *Union Pacific, Beau Geste, Typhoon, Moon Over Burma, Northwest Mounted Police*, and *This Gun For Hire* (1942). After serving in the US Army Air Force during World War II, Preston resumed his film career in features such as *The Macomber Affair, Tulsa*, and *When I Grow Up*, until 1951 when he moved to New York. He appeared on Broadway in number of straight plays including *Twentieth Century, The Tender Trap*, and *Janus*, and was out of town in Philadelphia with *Boy Meets Girl* when he was asked to audition for *The Music Man*. His portrayal of the likeable con-man, Harold Hill, who travels to small US towns such as Iowa, selling band instruments (which never materialise) to parents for their children to play, made Preston a gilt-edged Broadway star. Meredith Willson's fine score contained numbers such as 'Seventy-Six Trombones', ''Til There Was You', and Preston's *tour de force* 'Ya Got Trouble'. He won the Tony Award for best actor in a musical, and stayed with the show for over two years. After being virtually ignored during initial casting, he recreated the part in the 1962 film version. Cary Grant, who was one of the actors to whom the role was offered, reportedly said: 'Not only won't I play it, but unless Robert Preston plays it, I won't even go see it.' After appearing in several more straight parts, Preston returned to the musical stage in 1964 with *Ben Franklin In Paris*, but, unlike the large on-stage floating balloon in which Preston rode, the show did not really take off. Much more satisfying was *I Do! I Do!*, a two-hander with Mary Martin for which Preston won another Tony Award. His final Broadway musical appearance came in 1974 with *Mack And Mabel*, which, despite a splendid Jerry Herman score, only lasted for six weeks. During the 50s and 60s he had continued to make films, and in the 70s and early 80s he appeared in several more, including the musical *Mame* (1973), with Lucille Ball, and *S.O.B.* and *Victor/Victoria* (1982), both with Julie

Andrews. He also starred in several television movies, including the highly regarded *Finnegan Begin Again*, a poignant story of the love of an older man for a young woman played by Mary Tyler Moore. Preston died of lung cancer in 1987, and in the same year was awarded a special posthumous Tony, the Lawrence Langner Memorial Award for Distinguished Lifetime Achievement in the American Theatre.

Prince, Harold (Hal)

b. 30 January 1928, New York, USA. A distinguished director and producer - the supreme Broadway showman - whose career has lasted for nearly 40 years, and is still going strong. Prince served his theatrical apprenticeship in the late 40s and early 50s with the esteemed author, director, and producer George Abbott. He presented his first musical, *The Pajama Game*, in 1954, in collaboration with Robert Griffith and Frederick Brisson. His association with Griffith continued until Griffith's death in 1961, mostly with hits such as *Damn Yankees, New Girl In Town, West Side Story*, and *Fiorello!* (1959). *Tenderloin* (1960) was a disappointment, as was Prince's first assignment as a director, *A Family Affair* (1962). From then on, he has been the producer or co-producer and/or director for a whole range of musicals such as *A Funny Thing Happened On The Way To The Forum* (1962), *She Loves Me* 1963), *Fiddler On The Roof* (1964), *Baker Street* (1965), *Flora, The Red Menace* (1965), *It's A Bird, It's A Plane, It's Superman* (1966), *Cabaret* (1966), *Zorba* (1968), *Company* (1970), *Follies* (1971), *A Little Night Music* (1973), *Candide* (1974), *Pacific Overtures* (1976), *On The Twentieth Century* (1978), *Evita* (1978), *Sweeney Todd* (1979), *Merrily We Roll Along* (1981), *A Doll's Life* (1982), *Grind* (1985), *The Phantom Of The Opera* (1986), *Roza* (1987), and *Kiss Of The Spider Woman* (1992). The list does not include re-staging and directing the original productions in several different countries, nor his work with American opera companies such as the New York Opera, the Houston Opera, and the Chicago Lyric Opera. For his innovative concepts, the ability to find the exact visual framework for the musical-narrative content, and his role, notably with Stephen Sondheim, in the drastic reshaping of the modern theatre musical, Prince has received 16 Tony Awards - more than anyone else - and he is not finished yet.

Further reading: *Contradictions*, Harold Prince. *Harold Prince And The American Musical Theatre*, Foster Hirsch. *From Pajama Game To The Phantom Of The Opera And Beyond*, Carol Ilson.

Princess Theatre Musicals

A short but legendary series of significant musical productions presented at the tiny 299-seater house in New York in the period leading up to the Roaring

Harold (Hal) Prince with Helen Gurley Brown

Twenties. The Princess Theatre was built in 1913 at the corner of 39th Street and Sixth Avenue as a home for intimate one-act plays. However, in 1915 the theatre's owner, F. Ray Comstock, decreed that there should be musicals, so Jerome Kern, Guy Bolton and lyricist Schuyler Greene created *Nobody Home*, which, although it contained several interpolated numbers, was the first of what were subsequently regarded as landmarks in the history of American musical comedy. Instead of the usual old-fashioned, scarcely credible operettas, the new shows were funny and fast-moving, with the stylish, contemporary songs and situations integrated to an extent never attempted before. Kern, Bolton and Greene came together later that year for *Very Good Eddie*, before Schuyler was replaced by P.G. Wodehouse and the magic really began. Not straight away though, because the new team considered that it would be inappropriate to add music and lyrics to Charles Hoyt's play, *A Milk White Flag*, and so the third Princess Theatre musical, *Go To It* (1916), had a score by John Golden and Anne Caldwell. However, Kern, Bolton and Wodehouse came into their own with *Oh, Boy!* (1917) and *Oh, Lady! Lady!!* (1918). Another of their shows, *Leave It To Jane* (1917), was also a contender for the Princess Theatre but was unable to play there because *Oh, Boy!* was in residence for over a year. When it was finally withdrawn, Bolton and Wodehouse collaborated with composer Louis Hirsch for *Oh, My*

Dear! (1918), and the final show in the Princess series was *Toot Sweet*, a revue with a score by Richard Whiting and Raymond B. Egan. Some 75 years later it is hardly credible that just a few small productions had such an influence on the future course of Broadway, and by definition, world musical theatre, but it is said to be so. In later years the Princess Theatre presented straight plays and was also used for extended periods as a cinema. In 1936 the theatre was re-named the Labor Stage when it was taken over by the International Ladies Garment Workers Union who produced the popular revue *Pins And Needles* there, and was finally demolished in the 50s.

Promises, Promises

Although they had previously enjoyed enormous success writing popular songs, television shows and films, *Promises, Promises* was the first Broadway musical with a score by Burt Bacharach and Hal David. The show, which opened at the Shubert Theatre in New York on 1 December 1968, was adapted by Neil Simon from the successful Billy Wilder film *The Apartment* (1960). The story follows the tormented love affair of Chuck, a clerk who achieves promotion by renting his room to his bosses for their extra-marital affairs. In the course of his career rise, Chuck learns that one of these 'temporary tenants' is having an affair with Fran, the girl he loves. Jerry Orbach headed a cast which also included Jill

Burt Bacharach (*Promises, Promises*) with Carole Bayer Sager

O'Hara, Marian Mercer, A. Larry Haines and Edward Winter. Amongst the score's many delightful songs were 'Whoever You Are', 'Knowing When To Leave', 'You'll Think Of Something', 'Wanting Things', 'Upstairs', 'She Likes Basketball', 'Our Little Secret', and 'I'll Never Fall in Love Again', which became a hit for Dionne Warwick in the US, and was a UK number 1 for Bobby Gentry. *Promises, Promises* won Tony Awards for best actor (Orbach) and supporting actress (Mercer), and ran for a remarkable 1,281 performances. Betty Buckley and Anthony Roberts starred in the 1969 London production which was in residence at the Prince of Wales Theatre for well over a year, a total of 560 performances.

Purlie

With a score by two newcomers to the New York musical theatre, Gary Geld (music) and Peter Udell (lyrics), this amusing satire on the serious subject of racial bigotry opened at the Broadway Theatre on 15 March 1970. The book, by Ossie Davis, Philip Rose, and Peter Udell, was based on Davis's 1961 play, *Purlie Victorious*, and set in southern Georgia. It deals mainly with the struggle between the young evangelist, Purlie (Cleavon Little), who wants to take over the Big Bethel Church, and the intolerant plantation owner, Cap'n Cotchipee (John Heffernan). Fortunately, the Cap'n's son, Charlie (C. David Colson), has not inherited his father's twisted views, and he defects to Purlie's cause. In the end, the new preacher man gets the church - and the girl, Lutiebelle. She was played by Melba Moore, an actress who made a big impression in *Hair* (1968), and has since had several hits in the wider world of pop music, including a UK Top 10 entry with 'This Is It' (1976). In Purlie, Moore gave a beautiful, understated performance, and introduced the tender 'I Got Love'. There was also the spirited 'New Fangled Preacher Man', which celebrates the Cap'n's death early on (the story is told in flashback), and sets the scene for one of those feel-good, 'hallelujah'-style evenings complete with songs such as 'Walk Him Up The Stairs', 'Purlie', 'Skinnin' A Cat', 'First Thing Monday Mornin', 'He Can Do It', 'Big Fish, Little Fish', 'The Harder They Fall', and 'God's Alive'. Cleavon Little and Melba Moore won Tony Awards for their work in a show that attracted more black audiences than usual to Broadway, and ran for 688 performances. Gary Geld and Peter Udell went on to further success with *Shenandoah* (1975), another show with a relevant, contemporary theme.

Quaker Girl, The

Lionel Monkton was one of the most successful composers for the London musical stage at the turn of the century and for several years afterwards. He wrote the score for this show with lyricists Adrian Ross and Percy Greenbank just 18 months after one of his biggest hits, *The Arcadians*, began its West End run. Presented by George Edwardes, *The Quaker Girl* opened at London's Adelphi Theatre on 5 November 1910. The book was by James T. Tanner, and Gertie Miller starred as Prudence Pym, an English girl who has been brought up in the Quaker faith by her strict aunt and uncle. She is entranced by a visiting American, Tony Chute (Joseph Coyne), and he tempts her to taste some of the 'forbidden' champagne at a wedding reception. Disowned by her family for the dreadful act, she travels to Paris where Tony is a naval attaché at the American Embassy, and works for a time as a mannequin at a fashion house. She attracts the attention of a well-known roué, Prince Carlo (George Carvey), who tries to seduce her, and she and Tony part for a time, before meeting up again at a masked ball when all their misunderstandings are forgotten as they go into 'The First Dance'. The happy and melodious score was full of delightful numbers such as 'Take A Step', 'Tony From America', 'The Quaker Girl', 'A Bad Boy And A Good Girl', 'I Wore A Little Grey Bonnet', 'Tip Toe', and the ravishing 'Come Come The Ball', which was introduced by George Carvey. *The Quaker Girl* played for a remarkable 536 performances in London, and added another 240 to that total in New York, when Ina Claire took the role of Prudence. One London revival was presented in 1938, and two more in the 40s. Since then, *The Quaker Girl* has been kept alive through many amateur productions.

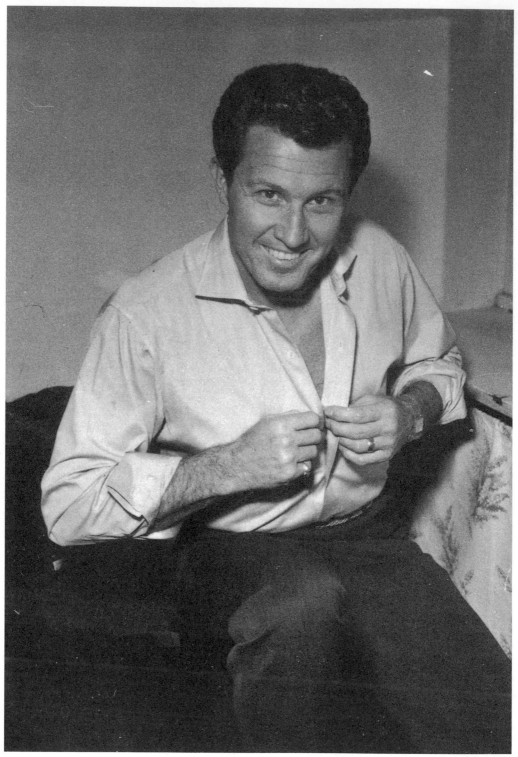

John Raitt

R

Raisin

During a Broadway season in which good original musicals were scarce, and one-person shows by such as Sammy Davis Jnr., Liza Minnelli, and Sammy Cahn proliferated, *Raisin* came as a welcome relief. It opened at the 46th Street Theatre on 18 October 1973, with a book by Robert Nemiroff and Charlotte Zaltzburg which was based on Lorraine Hansbury's 1959 play *A Raisin In The Sun*. Set in a Chicago ghetto during the 50s, the story told of the efforts of a black family to change their lives once and for all. Newly widowed Lena Younger (Virginia Capers), decides to use her late husband's inheritance to buy a liquor store for her son, Walter (Joe Morton), put her daughter, Beneatha (Deborah Allen), through medical school, and buy a house somewhere away from the ghetto. Lena's plans are in jeopardy for a time when Walter's sometime business partner flees with part of the money, but her ambitious plans eventually come to fruition, and the family moves into the house of their dreams. It was a moving, heart-warming story, complemented perfectly by a score from Broadway newcomers, Judd Woldin (music) and Robert Brittan (lyrics). Songs such as 'Sweet Time', 'He Come Down This Morning', 'Whose Little Angry Man', 'Not Anymore', 'Measure The Morning', and 'A Whole Lotta Sunlight', were put over with a great deal of verve and zeal by a high-quality cast, which also included Ernestine Jackson, Ralph Carter, Ted Ross, and Robert Jackson. Virginia Capers won a Tony Award for her outstanding performance, and the show itself won one for best musical. No doubt the kudos helped *Raisin* to surprise a lot of people, and stay in New York for two years.

Raitt, John

b. John Emmett Raitt, 19 January 1917, Santa Ana, California, USA. An actor and singer with a fine voice, Raitt sang in light opera and concerts before playing the lead in a Chicago production of *Oklahoma!* (1944). In the following year he was on Broadway in 'the season's triumph', Richard Rodgers/Oscar Hammerstein II's *Carousel*, playing the lead role of Billy Bigelow, and introducing 'immortal' numbers such as 'If I Loved You' and 'Soliloquy'. Three years later, he appeared on Broadway again, in the short-lived and 'unconventional' *Magdalena*. This was followed, in 1952, by the 'whimsical' *Three Wishes For Jamie*, which was 'too treacly' to run for long. *Carnival In Flanders* (1953), despite a score by Johnny Burke and Jimmy Van Heusen which contained 'Here's That Rainy Day', provided less than a week's employment, but help was at hand in the shape of a job which lasted nearly two-and-a-half years, as the factory superintendent in *The Pajama Game* (1954). With songs from the Richard Adler and Jerry Ross score such as 'There Once Was A Man' and 'Small Talk' (both with Janis Paige), plus 'Hey There', a duet with a dictaphone machine, Raitt made sufficient impact to be cast opposite Doris Day in the 1957 film version, despite being a complete newcomer to that medium. In the 50s and 60s he appeared frequently on US television and, in 1960, toured with *Destry Rides Again*. In the spring of 1966, he re-created his original role in a music theatre revival of *Carousel* and, later in the year, spent a brief tenure amid the 'newly created folk songs' of *A Joyful Noise*. Raitt continued to tour, and in 1975 was back on Broadway, along with Patricia Munsell, Tammy Grimes, Larry Kert, Lillian Gish and Cyril Ritchard in *A Musical Jubilee*, a 'potpourri' claiming to demonstrate the development of the American musical. By then, his daughter, Bonnie Raitt, was well into her stride as one of the best female singer/guitarists of the 70s and 80s. John Raitt himself continued to be active, and in 1992 he received a Ovation Award in Hollywood for services to the Los Angeles theatre scene.
Selected albums: *Mediterranean Magic* (c.50s), *Songs The Kids Brought Home* (c.50s), and Original Cast recordings.

Red Mill, The

As an operetta with a sense of humour, this has to be one of the most cherished productions of its time. The Red Mill opened at the Knickerbocker Theatre in New York on 24 September 1906, and was a vehicle for the ex-vaudeville comedy duo of David Montgomery and Fred Stone who had made their first impact on Broadway in The Wizard Of Oz (1903). Their adventures as a couple of naïve American tourists, Kid Connor and Con Kidder, stranded without money in Katwyk-aan-Zee, Holland, involve them in some hair-raising situations, and force them to adopt a number of disguises, one of which finds them masquerading as Sherlock Holmes and Doctor Watson. Henry Blossom's book and lyrics, and Victor Herbert's fine music combined in a score that is generally considered to have crossed the divide from operetta into musical comedy. Romantic and engaging songs such as 'Every Day Is Ladies Day With Me', 'Because You're You', 'When You're Pretty And The World Is Fair', 'The Isle Of Our Dreams', 'Moonbeams', and 'The Streets Of New York' (which became a hit for Billy Murray), ensured a run of 274 performances, the longest for any of Victor Herbert's book musicals. The 1945 revival,

Bob Hope (*Red, Hot And Blue*)

which starred Eddie Foy Jnr. and Michael O'Shea, and had additional lyrics by Forman Brown, did even better and stayed at the Ziegfeld Theatre for well over a year. A 1919 London production, with Little Tich as Kid Connor, folded after only 64 performances. A 1947 radically revised revival with 'a tedious new libretto', and starring on of Britain's top comedy double acts, Jewel And Warriss, lost a lot of money in a very short time.

Red Shoes, The

'Cobbling' and 'cobbled', two words that are dangerously close to 'cobblers' - which does not perhaps have the same connotations in America as is it does in Britain - were prominent in several US critics' reviews of this 'mishmash musical version of the beloved 1948 ballet film *The Red Shoes*' which opened at the Gershwin Theatre in New York on 16 December 1993. The score was mostly the work of veteran composer Jule Styne and his lyricist and librettist Marsha Norman, but Styne brought in Paul Stryker (a *nom de guerre* for his *Funny Girl* collaborator Bob Merrill) at a late hour to help out with the lyrics. Other pre-Broadway changes resulted in director Susan Schulman being replaced by Hollywood legend Stanley Donen, and the departure of Roger Rees, one of the principals. The well-known story tells of a young dancer, Victoria Page (Margaret Illman), who is torn between the impresario who has made her a star, Boris Lermontov (Steve Barton), and the young and dashing composer, Julian Craster (Hugh Panaro), who creates her 'role of a lifetime' and falls in love with her. The 'banal and melodramatic' score included 'Swan Lake', 'Corps de Ballet', 'When It Happens To You', 'It's A Fairy Tale', 'Be Somewhere', 'The Rag', 'Come Home', and 'When You Dance For A King'. Lyric lines such as 'Now we learn what no one's known/The shoes have passions of their own' and 'Most of us are bound to a lifetime on the ground/You won't stop 'til you reach the top of the sky', were siezed on with derisory glee by the critical fraternity. The meeting of classical dance and musical comedy just did not work, although Margaret Illman was applauded for her performance overall (in a role that was immortalised in the film by Moira Shearer), and in particular for her elegance and style in the second-act showpiece, 'The Red Shoes Ballet' - the longest dance sequence of its type since Richard Rodgers' 'Slaughter On Tenth Avenue' for *On Your Toes* (1936). Heidi Landesman's sets, which included a baroque false proscenium, were applauded too, but the knives were out, and *The Red Shoes* was withdrawn after only three days. The reported loss of $8 million could be a Broadway record.

Red, Hot And Blue!

This attempt to repeat the success of *Anything Goes*

(1934), went wrong somewhere on the road to the Alvin Theatre in New York, where it opened on 20 October 1936. Victor Moore and William Gaxton, two of the reasons for the earlier show's appeal, were absent this time, but librettists Howard Lindsay and Russel Crouse and songwriter Cole Porter were on hand, and Ethel Merman's presence ensured that the audience heard every word and note. Her co-star was comedian Jimmy Durante, and disagreement over top billing resulted in a design in which their names formed a cross, with 'Jimmy' appearing on the upper left-hand diagonal arm, and 'Merman' on the right. Bob Hope's name was below and in the middle, and a good deal easier to read. Together with Merman, he introduced 'You've Got Something', as well as one of Porter's most durable standards, 'It's De-Lovely'. Merman had the first stab at two more of the composer's most memorable songs, the exuberant 'Ridin' High', and 'Down In The Depths (On the Ninetieth Floor)' ('When the only one you wanted wants another/What's the use of swank and cash in the bank galore?/Why, even the janitor's wife/Has a perfectly good love life/And here am I/Facing tomorrow/Down in the depths on the ninetieth floor'). Durante had 'A Little Skipper From Heaven Above', as part of his role as 'Policy' Pinkle, the captain of the polo team at Lark's Nest Prison. 'Policy' is one of several inmates who are released in an effort to assist with a national lottery organized by 'Nails' O'Reilly Duquesne (Ethel Merman) and her lawyer, Bob Hale (Bob Hope). The winner of the lottery has to find the whereabouts of Hale's childhood sweetheart. The search is made easier by the knowledge that the girl sat on a waffle iron when she was four, so identification should prove to be a fairly simple matter. The whole thing becomes academic anyway when the Supreme Court rules that any such contest which benefits the American people is unconstitutional. The show's political overtones and other aspects of the production, meant that *Red, Hot And Blue!* was often compared to the 1931 political musical satire *Of Thee I Sing*. It was not nearly as successful though, and closed after only 183 performances.

Redhead

Composer Albert Hague, and the veteran lyricist and librettist Dorothy Fields, came together for the first time to write the score for this musical which opened at the 46th Street Theatre in New York on 5 February 1959. Fields, together with her brother, Herbert, and their fellow authors, Sydney Sheldon and David Shaw, came up with what was an unusual subject for a Broadway musical - a murder mystery. Set in Victorian London at around the time of the Jack the Ripper killings, the story has Essie Whimple (Gwen Verdon) and Tom Baxter (Richard Kiley) chasing suspects around various parts of the metropolis, including a waxworks museum bearing a remarkable resemblance to Madame Tussaud's emporium. Hague and Fields's score is not considered to be remarkable, but any show that contains such engaging songs as 'I Feel Merely Marvellous', 'The Right Finger Of My Right Hand', and 'Look Who's In Love', merits serious consideration. Add to those, Gwen Verdon's music hall version of 'Erbie Fitch's Twitch', and several other bright numbers, including 'I'm Back In Circulation', The Uncle Sam Rag', 'My Girl Is Just Enough Woman For Me', and 'We Loves Ya, Jimmy', and it certainly was not all bad news. The Tony Awards committee certainly did not think so, and their kudos went to Verdon, Kiley, and Hague, along with others for best musical, libretto, and Bob Fosse's brilliant choreography. The public gave the show their vote, too, and it ran for well over a year, a total of 452 performances.

Return To The Forbidden Planet

Based very loosely on the 1956 film *Forbidden Planet* which was a sci-fi version of William Shakespeare's play, *The Tempest*, this show - 'it's all a-Bard for an intergalactic rock extravaganza' - opened at the Cambridge Theatre in London on 18 September 1989. It was written and directed by Bob Carlton, who had mounted a miniature production for the Bubble Theatre Company in the mid-80s. The story, which retains only three names from the original source, Prospero, Miranda, and Ariel, is set on a spaceship that lands on the uncharted planet D'Illyria, the very place that the mad scientist Doctor Prospero (Christian Roberts) and his daughter Miranda (Allison Harding) had ended up several years previously, after the Doctor's wife had rather carelessly tinkered with his formula which was about to change the world. The spaceship's commander is Captain Tempest (John Ashby), 'a square-jawed, *Boys Own*-paper-hero and pipe-smoker', and the antithesis of the devilishly devious Prospero. Examples of the fractured Shakespearean dialogue include 'Two bleeps, or not two bleeps?' 'That is the question', and 'Shall I compare thee to a chemist's shop?', but it was the music and the high-tech effects (credited to *Thunderbirds* creator Gerry Anderson) that gave the show its wide appeal. Rock classics such as 'Wipeout', 'Telstar', 'Great Balls Of Fire', 'Don't Let Me Be Misunderstood', 'Good Vibrations', 'A Teenager In Love', 'Go Now', 'We've Gotta Get Out Of This Place', and many more, accompany the crazy antics aboard the space vehicle. Patrick Moore, the doyen of the high-powered telescope and star of UK television's long-running *The Sky At Night*, materialises in video form as a galactic guide, and, of all the comic-book characters, Kraig Thornbar excelled as Ariel, the roller-skating robot. The show

won the 1990 Olivier Award for best musical and became a tremendous success, running for 1,516 performances before its closure in January 1993. A 1991 Off Broadway production stayed at the Variety Arts Theatre for six months.

Rice, Tim

b. Timothy Miles Bindon Rice, 10 November 1944, Amersham, Buckinghamshire, England. A librettist, journalist, broadcaster and cricket captain. Around the time he was briefly studying law, Rice met the 17-year-old Andrew Lloyd Webber, and in 1965, they collaborated on *The Likes Of Us*, a musical version of the Dr. Barnardo story. Lloyd Webber then went off to concentrate on serious music, and Rice worked for EMI Records, progressing later to the Norrie Paramor Organization. In 1968 they resumed their partnership with *Joseph And The Amazing Technicolor Dreamcoat*, a 20-minute 'pop cantata' based on the biblical character of Joseph, for an end-of-term concert at Colet Court boys' school in the City of London. Subsequently, the piece reached a wider audience with performances at the Edinburgh Festival, and venues such as the Old Vic, St. Paul's Cathedral, and the Central Hall, Westminster, where Rice played the part of Pharaoh. In 1970, Rice and Lloyd Webber raided the 'good book' again for the score of *Jesus Christ Superstar*, a 'rock opera', presented on a double album, which, when exploited by producer Robert Stigwood, topped the US chart, and spawned successful singles by Murray Head ('Superstar'), and Yvonne Elliman ('I Don't Know How To Love Him'). After several concert performances of the piece in the USA, some of them unauthorized and unlicensed the show was 'extravagantly' staged on Broadway in 1972, and ran for over 700 performances despite some reviews such as 'nearer to the rock bottom than rock opera', and a good deal of flak from the religious lobby. It did even better in London, running for a total of 3,358 performances over a period of eight years. In 1992 a concert version, celebrating the show's 20th anniversary, toured the UK, starring Paul Nicholas and Claire Moore. The 1973 film version, in one critic's opinion, was 'one of the true fiascos of modern cinema'.

Meanwhile, *Joseph And The Amazing Technicolor Dreamcoat* had risen again, and when extended, and paired with a new one-act piece, *Jacob's Journey*, played in the West End for nearly 250 performances during 1973. Lengthened even further, it became extremely popular throughout the world, and stayed on Broadway for 20 months in 1981, during which time Joseph was personified by pop stars such as Andy Gibb and David Cassidy. Hardly any subject could have been further from Joseph, Jesus and Jacob, than Rice and Lloyd Webber's next collaboration, *Evita*

Tim Rice with Elaine Paige

'an opera based on the life of Eva Peron'. Conceived as an album in 1976, Julie Covington, who sang the part of Eva, went to number 1 in the UK with 'Don't Cry For Me Argentina', and 'Another Suitcase, Another Hall' was successful for Barbara Dickson. When the project reached the West End in 1978, Elaine Paige became a star overnight as Eva, and David Essex, in the role of Che, made the Top 10 with 'Oh What a Circus'. Four years later, Essex climbed to the UK number 2 spot with Rice's 'A Winter's Tale', written in collaboration with Mike Batt. The original production of *Evita* was 'a technical knockout, a magnificent earful, a visual triumph', which stayed at the Prince Edward Theatre for nearly eight years, and spent almost half that time on Broadway. Rice's next musical, with composer Stephen Oliver, was *Blondel* (1983), 'a medieval romp' which ran for eight months. Three years later Rice was back in the West End with *Chess* (1986), which replaced *Evita* at the Prince Edward Theatre. Written with Benny Andersson and Bjorn Ulvaeus, both ex-members of Abba, the score was released two years earlier on an album which produced 'You Know Him So Well', a UK number 1 for Elaine Paige And Barbara Dickson, and 'One Night In Bangkok', a Top 20 entry for Murray Head. *Chess* ran for three years in London, but was 'a £5 million flop' in New York. Over the years, Rice tinkered with various aspects of the show, and the 1992 off-Broadway version had a drastically revised book. At that stage of his career, *Chess* remained his last major production. In the same year, his first, albeit small theatrical effort, *Joseph And The Amazing Technicolor Dreamcoat* was re-staged at the London Palladium, starring, at various times, the children's television entertainer Phillip Schofield, and actor/pop star Jason Donovan, who topped the UK chart with the show's big number, 'Any Dream Will Do'. Schofield also had a UK chart hit with another song from the show, 'Close Every Door'. It was estimated that Rice and Lloyd Webber were each receiving £16,000 each week from the box office, besides the peripherals.

Rice's smaller-scale projects include *Cricket* (1986) (with Andrew Lloyd Webber) and *Tycoon*, an English-language version Michel Berger's hit French musical *Starmania* (1991). He has also contributed songs to several films, including *The Fan*, *The Odessa File*, *Gumshoe* and *The Entertainer*, and worked with Elton John, Francis Lai, Vangelis, Rick Wakeman and Marvin Hamlisch. In 1993, Rice, taking over from the late Howard Ashman, as Alan Menken's lyricist, won a Golden Globe Award and an Academy Award, for the song, 'Whole New World', from the Walt Disney movie, *Aladdin*. The number went to the top of the US charts in a version by Peabo Bryson and Regina Belle. In 1993/4, Rice was working with Elton John on the score for a forthcoming Disney film *The Lion And King*, and collaborating with Alan Menken on the stage version of *Beauty And The Beast*. As a journalist, Rice has written regular columns for UK national newspapers and for cricket magazines, reflecting his abiding interest in the game which manifested itself in him forming and leading his own regular side, the Heartaches, complete with team colours and year-book. His other more lucrative publications include co-authorship, with his brother Jonathan, and Paul Gambaccini, of the *Guinness Book Of British Hit Singles* and over 20 associated books. His interest in, and knowledge of, popular music was rewarded with the title of 'Rock Brain Of The Year' on BBC Radio in 1986. He also wrote the script for a 15-part series on the history of Western popular music. His other radio and television work includes *The Musical Triangle*, *Many A Slip*, *American Pie*, *Lyrics By Tim Rice*, *Just A Minute* and *Three More Men In A Boat*. As well as his Golden Globe and Oscar, he has gained two Tony Awards, two Grammy Awards, and several Ivor Novello Awards (including five for 'Don't Cry For Me Argentina'), but would probably swap them all for the chance to open the batting for England at Lord's cricket ground.

Richman, Harry

b. Harry Reichman, 10 August 1895, Cincinnati, Ohio, USA. Basically a nightclub entertainer, Richman was very popular during the 20s and 30s. A flamboyant character, with a debonair 'man-about-town' image, complete with top hat, or straw boater and cane, he had an uninhibited vocal style, often compared to Al Jolson. At the age of 12, together with a friend, he formed a musical act, Remington and Reichman, and appeared at the Casino Theatre, Chicago. When he was 18 he changed his name to Richman and played regular cafe engagements in San Francisco as a comedian, then appeared in vaudeville as a song and dance man, and as a pianist for headliners, the Dolly Sisters, Mae West and Nora Bayes. In 1922 he made his Broadway debut, with Bayes, in *Queen O' Hearts*, which ran for only 39 performances. Much more successful was *George White's Scandals* of 1926, in which Richman introduced the songs 'Lucky Day' and 'The Birth Of the Blues', the latter being one of his biggest hits. Richman also starred in the 1928 edition of the *Scandals*, in which he sang 'I'm On the Crest Of A Wave'. His next Broadway show was in 1930 Lew Leslie's lavish *International Revue*, was another comparative flop, despite the presence of England's Gertrude Lawrence, dance direction by Busby Berkely, and Richman's renditions of two of Dorothy Fields and Jimmy McHugh's best songs, 'Exactly Like You' and 'On The Sunny Side Of The Street'. He introduced another all-time standard, Joseph McCarthy and Jimmy Monaco's 'You Made Me Love

You', in the *Ziegfeld Follies* in 1931, which also co-starred Helen Morgan and Ruth Etting, and a year later, in *George White's Musical Hall Varieties*, his big numbers were 'I Love A Parade', and one of Herman Hupfield's select songs, 'Let's Put Out The Lights And Go To Sleep'. Richman's last 30s Broadway musical was *Say When*, in 1934.

From early in his career he had co-written songs and made hit recordings of some of them, including 'Walking My Baby Back Home', 'There's Danger In Your Eyes, Cherie', 'Singing A Vagabond Song', 'Miss Annabelle Lee', 'C'est Vous (It's You)' and 'Muddy Water'. As well as records and stage appearances, he was enormously popular during the 30s in cabaret and on radio. He also made a few films, including *Putting On The Ritz* (1930), *The Music Goes Round* (1936) and *Kicking The Moon Around* (1938), which was made in England, and co-starred top bandleader, Ambrose And His Orchestra. Richman was very popular in the UK, playing the London Palladium, and other theatres, several times. During the 40s, he appeared in the revue, *New Priorities Of 1943*, and continued to play clubs and theatres. By the late 40s he had become semi-retired, but emerged to give the occasional performance until the early 60s. He died on 3 November 1972 in Hollywood, California, USA. Always a high-living individual, it is said that, at the peak of his career, he drove along Broadway in his Rolls Royce, dispensing 10 dollar gold pieces to his admirers. He also owned a speakeasy establishment, Club Richman, in New York. In his leisure time he was an accomplished pilot. In 1935 he set the world altitude record for a single-engine amphibious plane, and a year later, with his partner Dick Merrill, created another record by flying from New York to the UK, and back again, in a single-engine plane. They reputedly packed the aircraft with 50,000 ping-pong balls as an aid to buoyancy in case they ditched in the sea. After all that, the title of Richman's autobiography, *A Hell Of A Life*, would seem to be a reasonable one.

Album: *Harry Richman And Sophie Tucker* (1979).
Further reading: *A Hell Of A Life*, Harry Richman.

Rio Rita

An historic show, in that it was the first to be presented at New York's brand new Ziegfeld Theatre, on 2 February 1927. Florenz Ziegfeld himself produced this hybrid of musical comedy and operetta, so it goes without saying that it was a colourful and spectacular affair, populated by lots of beautiful girls. Guy Bolton and Fred Thomson's story is firmly in the operetta tradition, and concerns the hunt for a desperado known as the Kinkajou. The search across the Rio Grande is led by Capt. James Stewart (J. Harold Murray), with his Texas Rangers. Captain Stewart is in love with the wild and passionate Rita Ferguson (Ethelind Terry), but has to wait for her hand until her other suitor, General Esteban (Vincent Serrano), has been revealed as the Kinkajou. Composer Harry Tierney and lyricist Joseph McCarthy were collaborating on their third, and last, successful Broadway musical, following *Irene* and *Kid Boots*. Their score was notable for the rousing 'Rangers' Song' and the delightful 'If You're In Love, You'll Waltz'. Terry and Murray combined on another lovely ballad, 'Rio Rita', and the rest of the songs included the lively 'The Kinkajou', 'Following The Sun Around', and 'You're Always In My Arms'. *Rio Rita* was an enormous hit, and ran for 494 performances - even longer than *The Desert Song* which had opened earlier in that same season. Coincidentally, when the show reached London, where it starred Edith Day, it inaugurated yet another theatre, the Prince Edward, but only stayed there for 59 performances. Many more people had the opportunity to enjoy the early-talkie film version, with Bebe Daniels and John Boles, which was released in 1929.

Rivera, Chita

b. Dolores Conchita Figueroa del Rivero, 23 January 1933, Washington, DC, USA. A vivacious, sometime fiery, singer, dancer and actress, Rivera was born to Puerto Rican parents and grew up in the Bronx. She started dancing when she was seven, and from the age of 11, trained for a career in classical ballet. After studying at the New York City Ballet via a scholarship from choreographer George Balanchine, in 1952 she turned from classical dance and joined the chorus of *Call Me Madam* on Broadway. Further chorus work in *Guys And Dolls* and *Can-Can*, was followed by appearances in *Shoestring Revue*, *Seventh Heaven*, and *Mr. Wonderful* (1956). She rocketed to stardom in 1957 as Anita in *West Side Story*, and stopped the show nightly by singing and dancing herself in a frenzy to the whooping tempi of 'America'. She caused even more of a sensation when *West Side Story* opened in London on 12 December 1958; it is still regarded by many as the most exciting first night of the post-year years. Two years later she was back on Broadway as Dick Van Dyke's secretary Rose in the first hit rock 'n' roll musical, *Bye Bye Birdie*; she went to London with that production, too. A musical adaptation of the *The Prisoner Of Zenda* (1963) in which she starred with Alfred Drake folded before it reached New York, but a year later, Rivera was acclaimed for her role as a gypsy princess in *Bajour* on Broadway. In the late 60s she toured in various productions including *Sweet Charity*, and also appeared in the 1969 film version with Shirley MacLaine. After more national tours in the early 70s in musicals such as *Jacques Brel Is Alive And Well And Living In Paris* and *Kiss, Me Kate*, in addition to several straight roles, she co-starred with Gwen Verdon in *Chicago* (1975). John Kander and Fred Ebb wrote the score, and they also devised and developed Chita Rivera's cabaret act which included a number called 'Losing', a reference to the number of Tony nominations she had received. She gained one more nomination for her performance in *Bring Back Birdie* (1981) which closed after only four nights, and *Merlin* (1983) was unsuccessful too. Rivera was finally awarded the coveted Tony - and a Drama Desk Award - when she co-starred with Liza Minnelli in *The Rink* (1984), another of Kander and Ebb's projects. Shortly afterwards, she was was involved in a serious car accident which: 'mangled my leg from the knee down'. After having 12 bolts inserted in the bones, she was back on Broadway, along with Leslie Uggams, Dorothy Loudon, and others, in *Jerry's Girls*, a tribute to the composer Jerry Herman. During the rest of the 80s, she performed in cabaret and continued to tour in America and other countries including the UK. In 1988/9, she joined the Radio City Music Hall Rockettes in a national tour of *Can-Can* which lasted for over a year. In 1991, she was inducted into New York's Theatre Hall Of Fame, along with - nice touch - Kander and Ebb. A year later she was widely applauded, and won a London *Evening Standard* Award for her outstanding performance in the musical *Kiss Of the Spider Woman*. When she reprised her dual role as the movie star Aurora and the Spider Woman, in New York, she won her second Tony and can now definitely not include the song 'Losing' in her cabaret act any more.

Roar Of The Greasepaint-The Smell Of The Crowd, The

Leslie Bricusse and Anthony Newley's follow-up to their smash-hit *Stop The World - I Want To Get Off* floundered in the UK provinces with the popular knockabout comedian, Norman Wisdom, in the leading role. Adjudged unfit to face the rigours of the West End in its present condition, producer David Merrick persuaded Newley to take over from Wisdom, and sent the show on a successful three month tryout tour of the USA and Canada before the Broadway opening at the Shubert Theatre on 16 May 1965. It proved to be very similar in style to its predecessor - an allegorical piece in which the irrepressible Cocky (Newley) and the imperious Sir (Cyril Ritchard) play the 'game' (of life) in a small arena-like area. Cocky, the litle man, alway plays by the rules, while the conniving Sir simply ignores them and goes his own way. Towards the end, Cocky, with the help of the Negro (Gilbert Price), begins to assert himself, and eventually he and Sir agree that the 'game' should be a tie. The British actress, Sally Smith, made her Broadway debut as The Kid, and Murray Tannenbaum was pretty scarey as The Bully.

Bricusse and Newley's score was full of good things, not all of them immediately appreciated. 'Who Can I Turn To? (When Nobody Needs Me)', which was introduced by Newley, emerged as the biggest hit, particularly in a version by Tony Bennett. Price created quite an impact with 'Feeling Good', and Ritchard, with a group of 'urchins', sang 'A Wonderful Day Like Today'. The remainder of the fine score consisted of 'The Beautiful Land', 'It Isn't Enough', 'Things To Remember', 'Put It In The Book', 'This Dream', 'Where Would You Be Without Me', 'Look At That Face', 'My First Love Song', 'The Joker', 'A Funny Funeral', 'That's What It's Like To Be Young', 'What A Man', 'Nothing Can Stop Me Now', and 'Sweet Beginning'. Several them were recorded by Sammy Davis Jnr., an enthusiastic promoter of the composers' work. Newley directed the show himself, and the musical staging was by Gillian Lynne, a highly regarded choreographer and director, whose subsequent credits included Andrew Lloyd Webber's mega-hits, *Cats* and *The Phantom Of The Opera*. *The Roar Of The Greaspaint* could only manage a disppointing run of 232 performances, but, fortunately for David Merrick, most of the show's original costs had been recouped during the pre-Broadway tour. To date, a West End production would seem unlikely.

Robbins, Jerome

b. Jerome Rabinowitz, 11 October 1918, New York, USA. A director, choreographer, and dancer, Robbins began his career with the celebrated Ballet Theatre in New York, and subsequently appeared as a dancer on Broadway in shows such as *Great Lady*, *The Straw Hat Revue*, and *Stars In Your Eyes*. In 1944, he and composer Leonard Bernstein conceived a short ballet, *Fancy Free*, which, with the participation of Betty Comden and Adolph Green, evolved into the musical *On The Town* - and Robbins was off and running (or rather, dancing). During the 40s and early 50s he was constantly acclaimed for his stylish and original choreography for shows such as *Billion Dollar Baby* (1945), *High Button Shoes* (Tony Award), *Look Ma, I'm Dancing*, *Miss Liberty*, *Call Me Madam*, *The King And I*, and *Two's Company* (1952). From then on, he also served as the director on series of notable productions: *The Pajama Game*, *Peter Pan*, *Bells Are Ringing*, *West Side Story* (Tony Award), *Gypsy*, *A Funny Thing Happened On The Way To The Forum*, *Funny Girl*, and *Fiddler On The Roof*. For the last-named show, one of his greatest achievements, he won Tony Awards for choreographer and director. He and Robert Wise were also awarded Oscars when they co-directed the film version of *West Side Story* in 1961. After working on the London productions of *Funny Girl* and *Fiddler On The Roof* in 1966 and 1967, Robbins turned away from the Broadway musical

June Bronhill (*Robert And Elizabeth*)

theatre and devoted his life to ballet. He came back in February 1989 to direct a celebratory revue of his work entitled *Jerome Robbins' Broadway*. In a season which was so bereft of original musicals that *Kenny Loggins On Broadway* and *Barry Manilow At The Gershwin* were catagorized as such, this reminder of Broadway's glory days was greeted with relief and rejoicing (and six Tony Awards). With its extended sequences from *West Side Story* and *Fiddler On The Roof*, along with other delights such as the gloriously incongruous 'You Gotta Have A Gimmick' from *Gypsy*, and the famous Keystone Cops chase from *High Button Shoes*, all sandwiched between excerpts from Robbins' first hit, *On The Town*, which opened and closed the show, it was enormously expensive at $8 million, and reportedly lost around half of that even though it ran for 538 performances.

Robert And Elizabeth

A musical adaptation of the 1930 play, *The Barretts Of Wimpole Street* by Rudolph Besier, with music by Ron Grainer and a book and lyrics by Ronald Millar. The source of this piece was an unproduced musical, *The Third Kiss*, by the American composer and lyricist Fred G. Moritt. *Robert And Elizabeth*, which opened at the Lyric theatre in London on 20 October 1964, was set in 1845-46 and based on the true story of two poets, the bed-ridden Elizabeth Moulton-Barrett (June Bronhill) and Robert Browning (Keith Michell). After corresponding with each other for some time, they fall in love and eventually marry in spite of stern opposition from Elizabeth's tyrannical father, Edward Moulton-Barrett (John Clements). The production, directed and choreographed by Wendy Toye, captured the period perfectly, with Bronhill and Michell leading an outstanding cast. They made the most of Grainer and Millar's highly romantic score which included 'The Girls That Boys Dream About', 'I Know Now', 'The World Outside', 'Escape Me Never', 'In A Simple Way', and 'I Said Love'. *Robert And Elizabeth* ran for well over two years, a total of 948 performances. The show never played Broadway, but has been presented in Chicago (1974), Maine (1978), and at the Paper Mill Playhouse (1982). An acclaimed production was mounted in England at the Chichester Festival Theatre in 1987, starring Mark Wynter and Gaynor Miles.

Roberta

Opening at the New Amsterdam Theatre in New York on 18 November 1933, this show was based on Alice Duer Miller's novel, *Gowns By Roberta*, and set, appropriately enough, in the high fashion capital of the world - Paris. Otto Harbach's book concerned John Kent (Ray Middleton), who used to be an All-American full-back before he inherited an interest in a dress shop named Roberta, which is operated by his Aunt Minnie (Fay Templeton). He takes on a partner, Stephanie (Tamara), who leaves it until they are almost married before revealing that she is a Russian Princess. This was a visually stunning production, the highlight of which was an elegant, lavishly mounted fashion show. Jerome Kern and Otto Harbach's score was pretty spectacular, too. It contained the ravishing trio, 'Smoke Gets In Your Eyes', 'The Touch Of Your Hand', and 'Yesterdays', which was introduced by Fay Templeton who was making her final Broadway appearance in a career that had lasted for 50 years. Most of the laughs were provided by Bob Hope and George Murphy, prior to them both going off to Hollywood. They were involved in 'Let's Begin' (with Tamara), and Hope also had the amusing 'You're Devastating', and 'Something Had To Happen', with Ray Middleton and Lyda Roberti. The latter, who was described as 'a supple, Polish-accented blond', also registered strongly with 'I'll Be Hard To Handle' (lyric by Bernard Dougal). This was Jerome Kern's last Broadway hit, and although 295 performances was alright, it could have been better The composer who had been the catalyst for what became accepted as America's own popular music, as opposed to the European imported variety, was to spend most of the rest of his life writing music for films, including the lovely Academy Award-winning song, 'The Way You Look Tonight'. Hollywood had two attempts at filming *Roberta*. The first, in 1935, starred Irene Dunn, Fred Astaire and Ginger Rogers, and the second, retitled *Lovely To Look At*, had Howard Keel, Kathryn Grayson and Ann Miller.

Robeson, Paul

b. 9 April 1898, Princeton, New Jersey, USA, d. 23 January 1976. Robeson's father was born into slavery, but he escaped at the age of 15 and eventually studied theology and became a preacher. His mother was a teacher, but she died in 1904. Education was of paramount importance to the Robeson family, one son became a physician, and the daughter was a teacher. Of all the family, Paul Robeson was by far the most gifted. In 1911 he was one of only two black students at Somerville High School in New Jersey, yet maintained a potentially dangerous high profile. He played the title role in *Othello*, sang in the glee club and also played football. He graduated with honours and won a scholarship to Rutgers University. A formidable athlete, he played football at All-American level and achieved scholastic success. In the early 20s, while studying law at Columbia University, he took part in theatrical productions and sang. In 1922 he visited England where he toured in the play *Taboo* with the noted actress Mrs Patrick Campbell. During this visit he also met pianist Lawrence Brown, with whom he was to have a close professional

Paul Robeson

relationship for the rest of Brown's life. In 1923 Robeson was in the chorus of Lew Leslie's *Plantation Revue*, which starred Florence Mills, and the following year made his first film, *Body And Soul*, for Oscar Micheaux, one of the earliest black film-makers. He appeared in prestigious stage productions, including *All God's Chillun Got Wings* (1924) and *The Emperor Jones* (1925).

In 1924 he had his first brush with the Ku Klux Klan over a scene in *All God's Chillun* in which he was required to kiss the hand of a white woman. In 1925 he made his first concert appearance as a singer. The impact of this concert, which awakened Americans to the beauty of his rich bass-baritone voice, was such that he was invited to tour Europe, appearing in London in 1928 in *Show Boat* with Alberta Hunter. Also in 1928 he played the title role of Porgy in the play by DuBose and Dorothy Heyward which formed the basis of George Gershwin's *Porgy And Bess*. In 1930 he was again in London, where he took the leading role in *Othello*, playing opposite Peggy Ashcroft and Sybil Thorndike. During the 30s he made a number of films including, *The Emperor Jones* (1933) and several in the UK, among them *Sanders Of The River* (1935) and *The Proud Valley* (1939) and in 1936 he made the screen version of *Show Boat*. As in the stage production, his part was small but his rendition of 'Ol' Man River' was one of the outstanding features. The 30s also saw his first visit to Russia and he travelled to Spain to sing for the loyalist troops. He also developed an amazing facility with languages, eventually becoming fluent in 25, including Chinese and Arabic. He incorporated folk songs of many nations in his repertoire, singing them in the appropriate language. This same period saw Robeson's political awareness develop and he extended his studies into political philosophy and wrote on many topics. In 1939 he again played Othello in England, this time at Stratford-upon-Avon, and also played the role in Boston, Massachusetts, in 1942 and on Broadway in 1943. In the 40s Robeson's politicization developed, during another visit to Russia he embraced communism, although he was not blind to the regime's imperfections and spoke out against the anti-Semitism he found there. Reaction in his home country to his espousal of communism was hostile and a speech he delivered in Paris in 1949, in which he stated that although he loved America he loved Russia more than he loved those elements of America which discriminated against him because of his colour, was predictably misunderstood and widely misquoted. Also in 1949, Robeson led protests in London against the racist policies of the government of South Africa. The FBI began to take an interest in Robeson's activities and conflict with right-wing elements and racists, especially during a rally at Peekskill in upstate

New York, which drew the attention of the media away from his artistic work. An appearance before the Un-American Activities Committee drew even more attention to his already high political profile. In 1950 his passport was withdrawn because the State Department considered that his 'travel abroad at this time would be contrary to the best interests of the United States'. Ill health in the mid-50s allied to the withdrawal of his passport, severely damaged his career when he was in his vocal prime. He continued to address rallies, write extensively on political matters and make occasional concert performances by singing over telephone links to gatherings overseas. Repeated high-level efforts by other governments eventually caused the US State Department to reconsider and during his first New York concert in a decade, to a sell-out audience at Carnegie Hall, he was able to announce that his passport had been returned. This was in May 1958 and later that year he appeared on stage and television in the UK and in Russia. His comeback was triumphant and he made several successful tours of Europe and beyond. He was away for five years, returning to the USA in 1963 for more concerts and political rallies. However, pressures continued to build up and he suffered nervous exhaustion and depression. His wife of 44 years died in 1965.

Another comeback, in the late 60s, was greeted with considerable enthusiasm, but the power and quality of his voice had begun to fade. During the final years of his life Robeson toured, wrote and spoke, but his health was deteriorating rapidly and he died on 23 January 1976. Although Robeson possessed only a limited vocal range, the rich coloration of his tone and the unusual flexibility of his voice made his work especially moving. He brought to the 'Negro spiritual' an understanding and a tenderness that overcame their sometimes mawkish sentimentality, and the strength and integrity of his delivery gave them a quality no other male singer has equalled. His extensive repertoire of folk songs from many lands was remarkable and brought to his concert performances a much wider scope than that of almost any regular folk singer. Although beyond the scope of this work, Robeson's career as actor, writer and political activist cannot be ignored. His independence and outspokenness against discrimination and political injustice resulted in him suffering severely at the hands of his own government. Indeed, those close to him have intimated a belief that his final illness was brought about by the deliberate covert action of government agents. Perhaps as a side-effect of this, he is frequently omitted from reference works originating in his own country, even those which purport to be black histories. For all the dismissiveness of his own government, Robeson was highly regarded by his own people and by audiences in many

To Wells with best wishes always Bill Robinson '36

Bill 'Bojangles' Robinson

lands. His massive intellect, his powerful personality and astonishing charisma, when added to his abilities as a singer and actor, helped to make him one of the outstanding Americans of the 20th century.

Selected albums: all various dates *Green Pastures, A Lonesome Road, Songs Of Free Men, Songs Of The Mississippi, The Essential Paul Robeson.*

Further reading: *Here I Stand*, Paul Robeson. *Paul Robeson Speaks: Writings Speeches Interviews 1918-1974*, Paul Robeson. *Paul Robeson*, Martin Bauml Duberman.

Robinson, Bill 'Bojangles'

b. 25 May 1878, Richmond, Virginia, USA, d. 25 November 1949. As a child Robinson worked in racing stables, nursing a desire to become a jockey. He danced for fun and for the entertainment of others, first appearing on stage at the age of eight. Three years later he decided that dancing was likely to prove a more lucrative career than horseback riding. He became popular on the black vaudeville circuit and also appeared in white vaudeville as a 'pick', from pickaninny, where his dancing skills gave a patina of quality to sometimes second-rate white acts. As his reputation grew so did his prominence in showbusiness. In 1921 while working at the Palace in New York, he danced up and down the stairs leading from the stage to the orchestra pit and out of this developed his famous 'stair dance'. Although Robinson was not the first to dance on stairs, he refined the routine until it was one of the most spectacular events in the world of vernacular dance. Towards the end of the decade, though he was now 60-years-old, he was a huge success in the smash-hit production of Lew Leslie's *Blackbirds Of 1928*. In the mid-30s he appeared at nightclubs in revues, musical comedies and other stage shows, amongst which was *The Hot Mikado*. He was so active in these years that he sometimes played different shows in different theatres on the same night. Robinson had no doubts that he was the best at what he did, a self-confidence that some took to be arrogance and which was mixed with a sometimes brooding depression at the fact that, because he was black, he had to wait until he was in his 60s before he could enjoy the fame and fortune given to less talented white dancers. In fact, he appears to have been a remarkably generous man and in addition to his massive work-load, he never refused to appear at a benefit for those artists who were less successful or ailing. It has been estimated that in one year he appeared in a staggering 400 benefits. In 1930 Robinson had made a film, *Dixiana*, but it was not until he went to Hollywood in the middle of the decade that he made a breakthrough in this medium. He danced in a string of popular films, including some with Shirley Temple. By 1937 Robinson was earning $6,600 a week for his films, a strikingly high sum for a black entertainer in Hollywood at the time. In 1943 he played his first leading role in *Stormy Weather*, an all-black musical in which he starred opposite Lena Horne. Despite being in his early 70s when he made the film he performed his stair dance and even if he was outglossed by the Nicholas Brothers, his was a remarkable performance. In addition to dancing, Robinson also sang in a light, ingratiating manner, memorably recording 'Doing The New Low Down' in 1932 with Don Redman and his orchestra. Although his high salary meant that he was estimated to have earned more than $2 million during his career, Robinson's generosity was such that when he died in November 1949 he was broke. Half a million people lined the funeral route of the man who was known with some justification as the Mayor of Harlem. In 1993, a potential Broadway show entitled *Bojangles*, with a book by Douglas Jones and a score by Charles Strouse and the late Sammy Cahn, was being workshopped in various provincial theatres.

Rocky Horror Show, The

One of the phenomenons of the UK musical theatre in the 70s and 80s, this rock musical opened at the Royal Court Theatre Upstairs on 19 June 1973. The book, music and lyrics were by Richard O'Brien who had been played a minor role in the London production of *Jesus Christ Superstar*. Nearly five years on from the abolition of theatrical censorship in Britain, provided the opportunity for what turned out to be a jumble of 50s and 60s sexual deviation, drug abuse, horror and science fiction movies, rock 'n' roll music, and much else besides. The story followed a young all-American couple, Brad (Christopher Malcolm) and Janet (Julie Covington) who take refuge in a remote castle. It is the home of several weird characters, including Frank 'n' Furter (Tim Curry), a 'sweet transvestite from Transexual, Transylvania', Magenta (Patricia Quinn), an usherette, Columbia (Little Nell), who tap-danced a lot, and the satanic Riff Raff (Richard O'Brien). The outrageously charismatic Frank 'n' Furter, dressed in the obligatory black stockings and suspenders, creates his perfect man, Rocky Horror, when he is not ravishing both Brad and Janet, and the remainder of the plot has to be experienced to be believed. The mostly 50s-style songs included 'Science Fiction, Double Feature', 'Dammit, Janet', 'Over At The Frankenstein Place', 'Sweet Transvestite', 'Time Warp', 'Sword Of Damocles', 'Hot Patootie (Bless My Soul)', 'Touch-A-Touch-A-Touch-A-Touch Me', 'Once In A While', 'Rose Tint My World', 'I'm Going Home', and 'Superheroes'. This 'harmless indulgence of the most monstrous fantasies' caught on in a big way, especially when it moved in August 1973 to the ideal enviroment of a seedy cinema in the trendy King's Road, Chelsea. After an incredible

Tim Curry (*The Rocky Horror Show*)

period of five and a half years, Frank 'n' Furter and his pals finally made it to the West End's Comedy Theatre in April 1969, where they stayed until September of the following year. The total London run amounted to 2,960 performances, but New York audiences demurred, and that production closed after only 45 performances at the Belasco theatre in 1975. In the following year, several of the original cast reassembled to film the *The Rocky Horror Picture Show* which proved to be a critical and financial disaster in the UK, but, ironically, in the USA where the original show had flopped, the movie became a hot cult item on university campuses. However, legend has it that the Waverly Theatre in New York was the scene of the first example of the audience participation craze which has since become the norm. Fanatical fans in America and many other countries in the world, including Britain, who return again and again to see the movie, now dress up in clothes similar to those worn on the screen, and join in with the dialogue and lyrics on the screen and constantly heckle, and introduce their own ad-lib material. The movie's success helped the stage show's survival in the UK, where, on various provincial tours, the audiences repeated the excesses of the cinema. One of the 'highspots' comes when Brad and Jane are married, and a barrage of rice and various other celebratory souvenirs are despatched from the auditorium, threatening the life and limbs of the participating thespians. It even happened when the show was revived briefly at the Piccadilly Theatre in London in 1990. Two years later, in addition to *The Rocky Horror* fan clubs that have sprung up around the world, the first convention of a British version, snappily called Timewarp, was held in London.

Rodgers, Richard

b. 28 June 1902, Hammells Station, Arverne, Long Island, USA, d. 30 December 1979. Raised in a comfortable middle-class family, Rodgers developed an early love for the musical theatre. He first attempted songwriting at the age of 14 and within two years he had composed several dozen songs. In 1918, a family friend, aware of Rodgers's potential but realizing that he needed a collaborator, introduced him to Lorenz Hart. Together, Rodgers and Hart wrote many songs in their first year as partners, some of which were taken up for current Broadway shows. However, it was not until 1925 and the appearance of 'Manhattan' and 'Sentimental Me', both written for *The Garrick Gaieties*, that the public became aware of this new songwriting team. That same year their first complete Broadway show, *Dearest Enemy*, was staged. Included in this show was 'Here In My Arms'. The following year they brought *The Girl Friend* to Broadway, with hits in the title song and 'Blue Room' and wrote 'Mountain Greenery' and for

Peggy-Ann, 'A Tree In The Park'. In 1927 came 'Thou Swell' for *A Connecticut Yankee*, a show which also featured 'My Heart Stood Still', a song written originally for an earlier show. In the late 20s and early 30s, although their shows met with only moderate success, the songs from them were exceptional and became independently successful. Among these hit songs were 'You Took Advantage Of Me', 'With A Song In My Heart', 'A Ship Without A Sail', 'Ten Cents A Dance' and 'Dancing On The Ceiling'.

In the early 30s Rodgers and Hart worked together in Hollywood, their songs including 'Isn't It Romantic', 'Love Me Tonight', 'Lover' and 'It's Easy To Remember'. Back on Broadway, in 1935 they wrote *Jumbo*, which included 'My Romance', 'Little Girl Blue' and 'The Most Beautiful Girl In The World'. *On Your Toes* (1936) followed, which included 'There's A Small Hotel', then *Babes In Arms* (1937) with 'Where Or When', 'My Funny Valentine' and 'The Lady Is A Tramp' and *I'd Rather Be Right* (1937), which had 'Have You Met Miss Jones?'. Their two shows of 1938 were *I Married An Angel*, with hits in the title song and 'Spring Is Here', and *The Boys From Syracuse*, which featured 'Falling In Love With Love' and 'This Can't Be Love'. The partnership's song successes continued with 'I Didn't Know What Time It Was', from *Too Many Girls* (1939), 'It Never Entered My Mind' from *Higher And Higher* (1940) and 'Bewitched, Bothered And Bewildered' and 'I Could Write A Book' from *Pal Joey* (1940). Their last show together was *By Jupiter* (1942), from which came 'Careless Rhapsody'. The seamless nature of their work together belied the fact that Rodgers and Hart were very different characters. Unlike Hart, who was undisciplined, casual, unpunctual, unreliable and irresponsible, Rodgers was a dedicated individual who set for himself and maintained strict working habits. Despite the problems he experienced in working with the mercurial Hart, Rodgers was fully aware how much they needed one another and was distressed when, in 1942, Hart indicated that he no longer wished to continue writing.

Fortunately, Rodgers's practical nature took over and he set about finding a new collaborator. He found a kindred spirit in Oscar Hammerstein II. Utterly different, both musically and in his personal characteristics, from Hart, Hammerstein brought to the new partnership an appreciation of an earlier kind of musical show (he was seven years older than Rodgers). Structurally, the shows Rodgers and Hammerstein created owed much to the formalities of operetta, while maintaining a sprightly contemporary approach to music and lyrics. Significantly for the development of the American musical, the songs were integral to the libretto, furthering plot and character development. Their first show together was

Richard Rodgers

Oklahoma!, which opened on Broadway on 31 March 1943 and ran for 2,248 performances. The songs from the show included 'Oh, What A Beautiful Mornin'', 'The Surrey With A Fringe On Top' and 'People Will Say We're In Love'. Rodgers and Hammerstein followed the success of *Oklahoma!* by collaborating on a musical film. This was *State Fair* (1945), which featured 'It Might As Well Be Spring', 'That's For Me' and 'It's A Grand Night For Singing'. Before the film was released the pair were already working on a new Broadway show, *Carousel*, which opened in April 1945. The show's 890 performances made it a huge hit helped by such songs as 'If I Loved You', 'June Is Bustin' Out All Over' and 'You'll Never Walk Alone'. The partnership's next Broadway show was strikingly less successful but *Allegro* included some fine songs, among them 'A Fellow Needs A Girl' and 'The Gentleman Is A Dope'. The comparative failure of *Allegro* was probably due to the abstract sets and the unusual staging. If that was the case, then Rodgers and Hammerstein clearly learned from their mistakes, returning to more orthodox ways with their next production. This was *South Pacific* (1949), which ran for almost 2,000 performances and followed the example of *Oklahoma!* by becoming a hugely successful film. The songs from the show included several hits: 'Some Enchanted Evening', 'Younger Than Springtime', 'A Wonderful Guy', 'Bali Ha'i', 'I'm Gonna Wash That Man Right Out Of My Hair' and 'There Is Nothing Like A Dame'. Rodgers and Hammerstein began the 50s with *The King And I*, another major success both on stage and as a film and, like its predecessors, the subject of numerous revivals. Songs included 'Shall We Dance', 'Hello, Young Lovers' and 'We Kiss In The Shadow'.

Other 50s' shows were less successful but there were still good songs to be heard, among them 'No Other Love', from *Me And Juliet*. During this same period Rodgers developed a long-suppressed interest in writing music of a quasi-symphonic kind. Most successful of these ventures were his scores for the television series *Victory At Sea* (1952) and *The Valiant Years* (1960). Another collaboration of Rodgers and Hammerstein, the musical, *Cinderella* (1957), was also for television. In 1958 the pair returned to Broadway with *The Flower Drum Song*, from which came the hit 'I Enjoy Being A Girl'. The following year the partners ended their Broadway career with the opening of one of their greatest successes, *The Sound Of Music*. In addition to the title song the score included 'Do Re Mi', 'Edelweiss', 'My Favourite Things' and 'Climb Ev'ry Mountain'. Hammerstein's death in 1960 was a serious blow to Rodgers and thereafter his work lost some of its sparkle. Nevertheless, he continued to write, creating the score and writing the lyrics for *No Strings* (1962), from which came 'The Sweetest Sounds'. He

followed this with collaborations with Stephen Sondheim on *Do I Hear A Waltz ?* (1965) and Martin Charnin on *Two By Two* (1970). Although he continued working into the 70s, Rodgers was by now a sick man. His last shows, *Rex* (1976) and *I Remember Mama* (1979), were box office failures. Rodgers was a marvellously adaptable composer. In his collaboration with Hart, he wrote the music first, to which his partner fitted his sophisticated and witty lyrics. Contrastingly, with Hammerstein, Rodgers wrote the music to suit the completed lyrics, which were necessarily structured to forward the tale being unfolded on stage. Much honoured during the closing years of his life, including a special Tony Award, Rodgers died in December 1979. In 1993, on the 50th anniversary of the birth of his second momentous partnership, a celebratory revue, *A Grand Night For Singing*, which was crammed with Rodgers and Hammerstein's songs, played on Broadway.

Selected album: *Mary Martin Sings Richard Rodgers Plays* (1958).

Further reading: *Musical Stages: His Autobiography*, Richard Rodgers. *Some Enchanted Evening: The Story Of Rodgers And Hammerstein*, J.D. Taylor. *With A Song In His Heart*, David Ewen. *The Rodgers And Hammerstein Story*, Stanley Green. *Rodgers And Hart: Bewitched, Bothered And Bedevilled*, S. Marx and J. Clayton. *The Sound Of Their Music: The Story Of Rodgers And Hammerstein*, Frederick Nolan.

Rogers, Will
(see **Will Rogers Follies, The**)

Romberg, Sigmund
b. 29 July 1887, Nagykanizsa, Hungary, d. 9 November 1951. After formal training as a violinist, Romberg began writing music while in his late teens. Despite these early interests, Romberg's main studies were in engineering and it was not until 1909, after completing a period of service in the Hungarian army, most of which was spent in Vienna, that he decided to make his career in music. Romberg showed a practical streak by recognizing that he would do better away from the Viennese 'hot house', which already contained numerous important composers. He emigrated to the USA, taking up residence in New York City where he found work in a factory, supplementing his income playing piano in restaurants and bars. He graduated to leading an orchestra, which proved very popular but his heart was set on composing for the musical stage. His first show, written in collaboration with lyricist Harold Atteridge, was *The Whirl Of The World*, which opened in 1914, the year in which Romberg became an American citizen. Romberg and Atteridge continued their partnership for several years, creating numerous shows, few of which were especially

successful despite starring such leading theatrical personalities as Marilyn Miller, Nora Bayes and Al Jolson. The shows that fared best were *The Blue Paradise* (1915) and *Maytime* (1917); in both Romberg drew upon his musical heritage, writing waltzes in the Viennese manner. This was a practice he revived in 1921 with *Blossom Time*, which told a fanciful version of the life of classical composer Franz Schubert. The score included 'Song Of Love', by far Romberg's most popular song up to this time. Convinced that the operetta was where he was most at ease, Romberg turned increasingly to this form even though he was obliged to write in other contexts to make a living. It was not until 1924 and the opening of *The Student Prince*, that he was able to prove conclusively that he was right in his belief. *The Student Prince*, in which Romberg was joined by lyricist Dorothy Donnelly, included such major song successes as 'Deep In My Heart', 'Serenade', 'Golden Days' and the 'Drinking Song'. With the evidence of this show as his guide, he concentrated on operettas and, despite some failures, soon became America's leading exponent of this type of musical theatre. In 1926 he wrote *The Desert Song* (lyrics by Otto Harbach and Oscar Hammerstein II), from which came 'Blue Heaven', 'One Alone' and the rousing 'Riff Song'. Romberg followed this with *The New Moon* (1928), for which his collaborator was Hammerstein. Both on stage and as a film, in 1930, *The New Moon* was hugely popular, with hit songs in 'Lover, Come Back To Me', 'One Kiss', 'Stouthearted Men' and 'Softly, As In A Morning Sunrise'. Inevitably, Romberg's inclination towards operetta endangered his continuing popularity through the 30s. Changing musical tastes conspired against him, although he still wrote many engaging songs, among them 'When I Grow Too Old To Dream', written with Hammerstein for the 1934 film *The Night Is Young*. In 1935 he adapted to the vogue for musical comedy with *May Wine*, before settling in California to write for films. In the early 40s he was relatively inactive but he made a comeback on Broadway in 1945 with *Up In Central Park*. With lyrics by Dorothy Fields, the show included such songs as 'Close As Pages In A Book' and 'Carousel In The Park'. Despite this show's success, Romberg's subsequent work drifted between operetta and musical comedy and met with little interest from audiences. He died in 1951.

Rome, Harold

b. 27 May 1908, Hartford, Connecticut, USA, d. 26 October 1993. While still attending school Rome played piano in local dance bands and was already writing music. Despite this early interest in music, he went on to study architecture and law at Yale. In 1934 he practised as an architect in New York City, but studied piano and composition in his spare time. This was a fortunate decision because by the following year, with work opportunities diminishing with the Depression, he was obliged to turn more and more to his second string activity for support. Much of the music Rome was writing at this time was socially-conscious and was thus of little interest to Tin Pan Alley. Nevertheless, he was engaged to write a revue for the International Garment Workers' Union. To everyone's surprise, the revue, *Pins And Needles* (1937), put on for members of the union, became a popular success and one song, 'Sunday In The Park', established a life outside the show. Rome was now sought-after, although his next show displayed similarly political concerns. This was *Sing Out The News* (1939) and, once again, there was a universally-accepted hit song, 'F.D.R. Jones'. In the early 40s Rome wrote songs for several revues and shows, but it was not until after the end of World War II that he had his first major success. This was *Call Me Mister* (1946), from which came 'South America, Take It Away'. More revues followed until his first full-fledged musical show, *Wish You Were Here*, in 1952. Two years later he wrote *Fanny*, his most popular Broadway show, which included 'Love Is A Very Light Thing'. This was followed by *Destry Rides Again* (1959) and *I Can Get It For You Wholesale* (1962), in which Barbra Streisand made her Broadway debut. In the mid-60s Rome showed that the social conscience which had marked his early work was still intact when he wrote *The Zulu And The Zayda* (1965), which dealt with racial and religious intolerance. In 1970 he wrote *Scarlett*, based upon the novel *Gone With The Wind*, for a Japanese production in Tokyo. More than with any other American composer in the field of mainstream popular music, Rome's work consistently showed an awareness of social issues, often to the extent that it kept him from the massive successes enjoyed by many of his contemporaries. He was also a gifted painter and a dedicated art collector.

Rosalie

Two composers representing entirely different worlds of popular music contributed to this lavish Florenz Ziegfeld production which opened at the New Amsterdam Theatre in New York on 10 January 1928. Composers George Gershwin and Sigmund Romberg squeezed this show into their busy schedules, and were rewarded with an excellent run of 335 performances. The book, by William Anthony McGuire and Guy Bolton, capitalised on the American public's fascination with early aviators in general, and Captain Charles Lindbergh's record-breaking solo flight to Paris in particular. No doubt the latter's achievement pales in comparison with the exploits of West Point high flyer, Lieutenant Richard Fay (Oliver McLennan), who loves Princess Rosalie of Romanza (Marilyn Miller), and risks life and limb to make a trans-Atlantic flight to be near her. However, she is unable to marry a commoner unless her father, King Cyril (Frank Morgan), abdicates. As this appears to be the European thing to do, the King is pleased to oblige. One of the George Gershwin songs, a future standard, 'How Long Has This Been Going On?' (lyric: Ira Gershwin), which had been cut from Funny Face, resurfaced here, but did not catch on, and another other of the brothers' numbers, 'Ev'rybody Knows I Love Somebody', was also in the score. The rest of the songs included 'Say So!' and 'Oh Gee! Oh Joy!' (music: George Gershwin, lyrics: Ira Gershwin and P.G. Wodehouse), and 'West Point Song' (music: Sigmund Romberg, lyric: Wodehouse). The highly commercial combination Ziegfeld's elegant production, a singable, danceable score, and the enormous box-office appeal of the petite and lovely Marilyn Miller, ensured that Rosalie stayed on Broadway for over 10 months. An attempt by Hollywood to make a film version with Marion Davies was never released, but some of the footage was used in the 1937 movie, which starred Nelson Eddy and Eleanor Powell. Several pieces of classical music were incorporated, and the orginal stage score was neatly removed in favour of one by Cole Porter - and Rosalie got a title song at last.

Rose, Billy

b. William Samuel Rosenberg, 6 September 1899, New York, USA. d. 10 February 1966. An important lyricist and impresario, Rose was a small, dynamic man, once called 'the little Napoleon of showmanship'. He was married twice, firstly to star comedienne Fanny Brice, and then to champion swimmer Eleanor Holm. As a lyric writer, it is sometimes said that he often insisted on collaborating with songwriters who were contributing to shows that he was producing. His first successful songs came in the early 20s. 'Barney Google', based on the popular cartoon strip, and 'You've Got To See Mama Every Night', were both written with Con Conrad in 1923. 'Does The Spearmint Lose Its Flavor On The Bedpost Overnight?' in 1924, on which Rose collaborated with Marty Bloom and Ernest Brever, was a hit, along with the previous titles, for US radio's popular tenor-baritone team of Ernest Hare and Billy Jones. With a slightly modified title, the latter song resurfaced in the US charts in 1961, sung by UK artist, Lonnie Donegan. Hare and Jones again, and Billy Murray (the 'Denver Nightingale'), also had success with 'Don't Bring Lulu', which Rose wrote with Lew Brown and Ray Henderson. Some of the other well-known Rose songs, with his collaborators, included 'The Night Is Young And You're So Beautiful' (Irving Kahal and Dana Suesse), 'I've Got A Feeling I'm Falling' (Fats Waller and Harry Link), 'That Old Gang Of Mine' (Mort Dixon and Ray

Henderson), 'Clap Hands! Here Comes Charley' (Ballard MacDonald and Joseph Meyer), 'Tonight You Belong To Me' (Lee David), 'It Happened In Monterey' (Mabel Wayne), 'Back In Your Own Backyard', 'There's A Rainbow 'Round My Shoulder' and 'Me And My Shadow' (written with Al Jolson and Dave Dreyer).

In 1926 he started to contribute songs to Broadway shows and revues, including 'A Cup Of Coffee, A Sandwich And You', for Gertrude Lawrence to sing in the Charlot Revue of that year. Three years later he wrote his first Broadway score for Great Day!, with Edward Eliscu and Vincent Youmans. This included the songs 'More Than You Know', 'Happy Because I'm In Love', 'Without A Song' and 'Great Day'. Rose's first Broadway production, in 1930, was the revue Sweet And Low, which also contained two of his songs, 'Cheerful Little Earful' (with Ira Gershwin and Harry Warren) and 'Would You Like To Take A Walk?' (with Mort Dixon and Warren). When the show was revised in 1931 as Crazy Quilt, Rose, Warren and Dixon had added another song, 'I Found A Million Dollar Baby (In A Five And Ten Cent Store)', which was sung by Rose's wife, Fanny. Rose's 1935 Broadway project, Jumbo, was not quite a 'million-dollar-baby', but it apparently did cost somewhere in the region of $350,000 to produce - a lot of money for a show in those days. For this musical comedy-vaudeville-circus extravaganza, much of the cash was spent in gutting Broadway's Hippodrome Theatre and refitting it to resemble a circus arena, with a circular revolving stage, and the audience seating sloping in grandstand fashion. Jumbo was spectacular in every way. The extravaganza featured Jimmy Durante, bandleader Paul Whiteman seated on a white horse, an elephant named Big Rosie, a human cast of around 90, and almost as many animals. Despite a book by Ben Hecht and Charles MacArthur, and a Richard Rodgers/Lorenz Hart score (no Rose lyrics in this one), which featured songs such as 'The Most Beautiful Girl In The World', 'My Romance', and 'Little Girl Blue', and a healthy New York run of five months, Jumbo closed without getting near to recovering its costs. In complete contrast was Rose's production of Hecht and MacArthur's play, The Great Magoo, the story of a Coney Island barker, which contained only one song, 'It's Only A Paper Moon', written by Rose, Yip Harburg, and Harold Arlen. Rose, in collaboration with Maceo Pinkard, also contributed one additional song, 'Here Comes The Showboat' to the original Jerome Kern/Oscar Hammerstein II/P.G. Wodehouse score for the 1936 film version of the musical, Show Boat.

During the 40s, Rose's two main Broadway productions were Carmen Jones in 1943, and Seven Lively Arts in 1944. Despite Rose's failure to get Sir

Thomas Beecham, his first choice conductor for the show, Oscar Hammerstein II's re-setting of Georges Bizet's opera *Carmen* was extremely well received by critics and public alike. By contrast, *Seven Lively Arts*, with a concept embracing opera, ballet, Broadway, vaudeville, jazz, concert music, and modern painting, and a Cole Porter score which included 'Ev'ry Time We Say Goodbye', was thought to be somewhere between a 'disappointment' and a 'disaster'. As well as his Broadway projects, Rose produced aquacades at many locations including the *New York World's Fair* in 1937, and the *San Francisco World's Fair* in 1940. He also owned two top New York nightspots, (the New York Supper Club and the Diamond Horseshoe) and two Broadway theatres, the Ziegfeld and the Billy Rose Theatre. One of the most colourful show business characters of his time, Rose retired in the 50s, and repeated his previous success, this time as a stock market speculator. He died in 1966 in Jamaica.
Further reading: *Billy Rose: Manhattan Primitive*, Earl Conrad. *The Nine Lives Of Billy Rose*, Pearl Rose Gottlieb (Billy Rose's sister). *Wine, Women And Words*, Billy Rose.

Rose-Marie

First staged on Broadway at the Imperial Theatre on 2 September 1924, *Rose-Marie* had music by Rudolf Friml and Herbert Stothart, and a libretto and lyrics by Otto Harbach and Oscar Hammerstein II. Set in Canada and telling the love story of Jim Kenyon (Dennis King) and Rose-Marie La Flamme (Mary Ellis), the rich and romantic score included several memorable numbers including 'Indian Love Call', 'The Door Of My Dreams', 'The Mounties', 'Why Shouldn't We?', and 'Rose-Marie'. This kind of show still had enormous appeal in the 20s - and for some time afterwards - and *Rose-Marie* enjoyed a good run of 557 performances. The London production, with Edith Day and Derek Oldham, was even more successful and stayed at the Drury Lane Theatre for over two years. The show also proved to be popular in Europe, particularly in France, and it was presented there on several occasions through until 1981. *Rose-Marie* was revived in London in 1925, 1929, 1942, and 1960. The latter production included the popular singer David Whitfield. Film versions were released in 1928 (silent) with Joan Crawford; in 1936, with Jeanette MacDonald and Nelson Eddy; and in 1954, with Ann Blyth, Fernando Lamas and Howard Keel. In 1955, Slim Whitman took 'Rose Marie' to the top of the UK charts for an incredible 11 weeks and enjoyed a successful follow-up from the show with 'Indian Love Call'.

Ross, Jerry
(see **Adler, Richard**)

Rothschilds, The

Six years after their smash-hit *Fiddler On The Roof*, Jerry Bock (music) and Sheldon Harnick (lyrics) collaborated with librettist Sherman Yellen on another tale which centred on the plight of oppressed Jews in Europe. *The Rothschilds* opened at the Lunt-Fontanne Theatre in New York on 19 October 1970. Yellen's book was based on a best-selling biography by Frederic Morton, which detailed the rise of the Rothschilds, the fabulously wealthy banking family, and, in particular, one of its driving influences, Mayer Rothschild (Hal Linden). Paul Hecht, as the son, Nathan, and Keene Curtis, who took on several roles throughout the piece, both gained favourable notices. Unlike *Fiddler On The Roof*, *The Rothschilds'* score contained no durable hits, but apposite and engaging songs such as 'He Tossed A Coin', 'Rothschild And Sons', 'One Room', 'Sons', 'I'm In Love! I'm In Love!', 'In My Own Lifetime', 'Everything', and 'Pleasure And Privilege', ensured a run of 507 performances. Linden won a Tony Award for his vigorous performance, and Bock and Harnick split up after writing seven scores together.

Ruby, Harry

b. Harry Rubinstein, 27 January 1895, New York, USA, d. 23 February 1974, Woodland Hills, California, USA. Ruby was a successful composer for stage and film over a long career, mostly in collaboration with lyricist Bert Kalmar (b. 16 February 1884, New York, USA, d. 18 September 1947, Los Angeles, California, USA). Ruby played piano in music publishing houses, and accompanied vaudeville acts such as the Messenger Boys, before starting to write songs. He had an early hit in 1919 with 'And He'd Say Oo-La-La, Wee-Wee', written with comedian George Jessel, and a hit for the specialist novelty singer Billy Murray. From 1918-28 Kalmar and Ruby wrote songs for Broadway shows, with Ruby sometimes contributing to the libretto. These included *Helen Of Troy, New York* ('I Like A Big Town', 'Happy Ending'); *The Ramblers* ('All Alone Monday', 'Just One Kiss', 'Any Little Tune'); *Five O'Clock Girl* ('Thinking Of You', 'Up In The Clouds'); *Good Boy* ('Some Sweet Someone', 'I Wanna Be Loved By You', the latter memorably revived by Marilyn Monroe in the 1959 Billy Wilder movie, *Some Like It Hot*); and *Animal Crackers* ('Watching The Clouds Roll By, 'Who's Been Listening To My Heart?', 'Hooray For Captain Spaulding'). While working on *Animal Crackers*, Kalmar and Ruby formed a friendship with the Marx Brothers, and, after moving to Hollywood in 1928, supplied songs for some of the Marx Brothers' early movies, including *Horse Feathers* (1932) and *Duck Soup* (1933), and the film version of *Animal Crackers*. Groucho Marx later used their 'Hooray For Captain

Spaulding' as a theme for his radio and television shows. While in Hollywood, Kalmar and Ruby wrote what was probably their most popular song, 'Three Little Words', for the comedy film *Check And Double Check* (1930), featuring radio's famous double-act, Amos 'N Andy. The songwriting team continued to write consistently for films through the 30s, including: *The Cuckoos* (1931) ('I Love You So Much', 'Dancing The Devil Away'); *The Kid From Spain* (1932) ('Look What You've Done', 'What A Perfect Combination'); *Hips, Hips, Hooray* (1934) ('Keep On Doin' What You're Doin''); and *Kentucky Kernels* (1934) ('One Little Kiss'). Their last film together, in 1939, was *The Story Of Vernon And Irene Castle* ('Only When You're In My Arms', 'Ain'tcha Comin' Out?'), starring Fred Astaire and Ginger Rogers, although their 1947 song, 'A Kiss To Build A Dream On', written with Oscar Hammerstein II, featured in the 1951 movie, *The Strip*, and was nominated for an Academy Award. In 1941, they also contributed to another Broadway show, *The High Kickers* ('You're On My Mind', 'A Panic In Panama', 'Time To Sing'). In the 1950 bio-pic, *Three Little Words*, Red Skelton played Ruby, and Fred Astaire was cast as Kalmar. The film featured most of their big hits including 'Who's Sorry Now', 'Nevertheless', and the novelty, 'So Long, Oo-Long (How Long You Gonna Be Gone?)'. During the 40s, Ruby also wrote songs with other lyricists, including Rube Bloom, ('Give Me The Simple Life'), and provided both music and lyrics for the title song to the Dick Haymes-Maureen O'Hara film, *Do You Love Me?* (1946). After the early 50s Ruby was semi-retired, emerging occasionally to appear on television programmes to celebrate songwriters and associated artists.

S

Salad Days

Hastily assembled to fill a three-week gap in the schedule of the Bristol Old Vic in 1954, *Salad Days* was swiftly transferred to London where it opened at the Vaudeville Theatre on 5 August that same year. With music by Julian Slade who also wrote the book and lyrics with Dorothy Reynolds, the show told a slight story of two graduating students, Jane (Eleanor Drew) and Timothy (John Warner), who meet the Tramp (Newton Blick) in the park, and agree to take

care of his mobile piano for a month in return for a payment of £7 per week. The instrument is a magic one, and makes everybody dance. So did the delightful and jolly score, which included 'The Things That Are Done By A Don', 'It's Easy To Sing', 'We're Looking For A Piano', 'We Said We'd Never Look Back', 'I Sit In The Sun', 'Oh, Look At Me, I'm Dancing!' 'Find Yourself Something To Do', Hush-Hush', 'The Saucer Song', 'Cleopatra', and 'The Time Of My Life'. Julian Slade himself played one of the two accompanying pianos, and *Salad Days* ran on and on for 2,283 performances - a remarkable achievement in the days long before the Andrew Lloyd Webber blockbusters. Sophisticated New Yorkers were not impressed, and the 1958 US production folded after only 10 weeks. Londoners retained their enormous affection for this curiously British phenomenon, and there were West End revivals in 1961, 1964 and again in 1976. In 1983 a television version was screened in the UK.

Sally

One of the most popular musicals of the 20s, this was really another version of the Cinderella rags-to-riches story which has been used in shows such as *Irene*, *Mlle. Modiste*, *My Fair Lady*, and *42nd Street*, amongst others. *Sally* opened at the New Amsterdam Theatre in New York on 21 December 1921, and was intended as a showcase for producer Florenz Ziegfeld's current protegée, Marilynn (later Marilyn) Miller. Guy Bolton's book portrayed Miss Miller as poor Sally Green, who dreams of becoming a famous dancer while washing dishes at a Greenwich Village cafe. One of the waiters (who, not surprisingly, is the exiled Duke of Czechogovinia in disguise) encourages her when a theatrical agent, Otis Hopper (Walter Catlett), suggests that she masquerades as prima ballerina Mme. Nookarova at an elegant party. Of course, it is her big chance, and leads to a starring role in the *Ziegfeld Follies*, where she dances the 'Butterfly Ballet' with music by Victor Herbert. Leon Errol, as the disguised Duke, provided most of the comedy, along with Walter Catlett. The score was rather a mixed-up affair. All the music was written by Jerome Kern, but several lyricists were involved. P.G. Wodehouse, who, at one stage, was to have written all the song lyrics, ended up by collaborating with Clifford Grey on just two: 'The Church 'Round The Corner' and 'You Can't Keep A Good Girl Down' (Joan Of Arc). Grey also wrote the words for 'Wild Rose', 'Sally', 'On With The Dance', and 'The Schnitza Komisski'. Two of the numbers, with lyrics by Buddy De Sylva, came from *Zip Goes A Million* which folded before it reached Broadway. One of them, 'Whip-Poor-Will', did not cause much of a stir, but the other, 'Look For The Silver Lining', eventually became a sentimental standard. One more song, 'The Lorelei' (lyric: Anne Caldwell), was also 'borrowed' from an earlier Kern score for *The Night Boat*. It all added up to a tremendous hit. 570 performances in a season when 42 other musicals made their Broadway debut, was quite phenomenal. When *Sally* returned to New York in 1948 with Bambi Linn in the leading role, it was only for a brief run. London audiences took to the show in 1921 when it starred Dorothy Dickson and Leslie Henson, and stayed at the Winter Garden for nearly a year. They also enjoyed a revised version, entitled *Wild Rose*, which spent six months at the Prince's Theatre in 1942 with Jessie Matthews as Sally. There have been two films of the story: a silent version in 1925, and the 1929 early talkie, with Marilyn Miller.

Schofield, Phillip

b. 1962, Oldham, Lancashire, England. When Schofield took over the leading role of *Joseph And The Amazing Technicolor Dreamcoat* at the London Palladium while Jason Donovan went on holiday early in 1992, it proved to be one of Andrew Lloyd Webber's most (commercially) inspired decisions. Having been obsessed with broadcasting from an early age, Schofield eventually got a job as a bookings clerk with the BBC in 1979. Later that year he emigrated to New Zealand with his family, and began his television career there on a pop show called *Shazam!*. He stayed in New Zealand for three and a half years, and, on his return, landed a late-night spot on Capital Radio in London. During the 80s he became one of the most popular presenters on children's television, especially on the Saturday morning programme *Going Live!*, and other shows such as the travelogue, *Schofield's Europe*, and *Television's Greatest Hits*. He also had his own record programmes on BBC Radio One. In October 1991, while hosting the *Smash Hits Pollwinners Party* on live television, he was 'assaulted' by the guitarist Fruitbat, a member of the eccentric pop group Carter USM. When he recovered, he named Jason Donovan as best male singer – and, just under three months later, took over from Donovan at the Palladium on 13 January 1992. After receiving a five-minute standing ovation on the first night, he was offered the part full-time from May when Donovan's contract ended. The theatre's box-office was besieged, and, from then on, until Donovan took over for the last few weeks before the show closed in January 1994, Scofield played the role for extended periods and was widely acclaimed – particularly by the young girls who arrived by the coachload. Many of them must also have bought his record of 'Close Every Door', one of the songs from the show, enabling it reach the UK Top 30.

Schönberg, Claude-Michel

b. 1944, France. A composer, author, and record producer, Schönberg began his collaboration with Alain Boublil in 1973 with the first-ever staged French rock opera *La Revolution Francaise*, which played to capacity audiences and sold over 350,000 double-albums. A year later he sang his own music and lyrics on an album which spawned the hit single 'Le Premier Pas'. In 1978, he and Boublil started work on the musical *Les Misérables* which was presented at the Palais des Sports in Paris in September 1980. The concept album won two gold discs in 1981. *Les Misérables* (with English lyrics by Herbert Kretzmer) opened at the Barbican Theatre in London on 30 September 1985, and transferred to the Palace Theatre in December of that year before settling in for a long run. When the show was produced on Broadway in 1987, Schönberg won Tony Awards for best score and book, and a Grammy for Best Original Cast recording. In January 1994, *Les Misérables* became the third longest-running musical in London theatre history. Schonberg and Boublil's next project, *Miss Saigon*, was acclaimed both in London (1989) and New York (1991). Two more of the partners' compositions, 'Rhapsody For Piano And Orchestra' and 'Symphonic Suite', were premiered at London's Royal Albert Hall in 1992.

Schwartz, Arthur

b. 25 November 1900, New York City, New York, USA, d. 3 September 1984. Prohibited by his family from learning music, Schwartz began composing while still a teenager at high school. He studied law and continued to write as a hobby but in 1924 he met Lorenz Hart, with whom he immediately began to collaborate on songs. They enjoyed some modest success but not enough to turn Schwartz from his path as a lawyer. In the late 20s he practised law in New York City, continuing to write songs in his spare time with a string of lyricists as collaborators until Hart convinced him that he could make a career in music. He took time off from his practice and was advised to seek a permanent collaborator. He was introduced to Howard Dietz, with whom he established immediate rapport. Among their first joint efforts were some contributions to the music for *The Little Show* (1929). For this revue, one of the songs Schwartz had written with Hart, 'I Love To Lie Awake In Bed', was given a new lyric by Dietz. This now became 'I Guess I'll Have To Change My Plan'. Later songs for revues included 'Something To Remember You By' and 'The Moment I Saw You'. In 1931, Schwartz and Dietz had a major success with *The Band Wagon*, which starred Fred Astaire and his sister Adele. The partners' score included their most important song success, 'Dancing In The Dark'. Other shows of the 30s were less successful but there were always excellent songs: 'Louisiana Hayride', 'Alone Together', 'A Shine On Your Shoes', 'What

Harry Secombe

A Wonderful World', 'Love Is A Dancing Thing' and 'You And The Night And The Music'. The pair also wrote for radio and interspersed their collaborations with songs written with other partners. Schwartz wrote songs for shows such as *Virginia* (1937) and *Stars In Your Eyes* (1939) and during the late 30s and early 40s he was heavily involved in writing for films with such successes as 'They're Either Too Young Or Too Old' (with Frank Loesser) and 'A Gal In Calico' (Leo Robin). Schwartz was reunited with Dietz in 1948 on a revue, *Inside USA*, and in 1953 they wrote a new song, 'That's Entertainment', for the screen version of *The Band Wagon*. In 1951, Schwartz collaborated with Dorothy Fields on *A Tree Grows In Brooklyn*, from which came 'Love Is The Reason' and 'I'll Buy You A Star'. Schwartz and Fields also wrote *By The Beautiful Sea* (1954), which included 'Alone Too Long'. Later Broadway shows by Schwartz and Dietz proved unsuccessful and although their songs, such as 'Something You Never Had Before' and 'Before I Kiss The World Goodbye', were pleasant and lyrically deft, they were not of the high standard they had previously set themselves. In the late 60s Schwartz settled in London, England, for a while where he wrote *Nicholas Nickleby* and *Look Who's Dancing* (a revised version of *A Tree Grows In Brooklyn* with several new songs). In the 70s he returned to the USA, where he released an album of his own songs, *From The Pen Of Arthur Schwartz*. He died in September 1984.
Album: *From The Pen Of Arthur Schwartz* (1976).

Secombe, Harry

b. Harold Donald Secombe, 8 September 1921, Swansea, West Glamorgan, Wales. Harry Secombe's development as an all-round entertainer began as a product of the post-war 'fair play' policy of London's West End Windmill Theatre. This ensured that men recently, or soon-to-be demobbed from the armed forces, were given the chance to prove themselves to an audience and get noticed by agents. Secombe worked at the theatre before becoming a regular on the variety circuit in the late 40s. In 1949 he teamed up with Peter Sellers, Spike Milligan and Michael Bentine to form the highly-influential British radio comedy team, the Goons, taking on characters, created by Spike Milligan, such as the popular Neddy Seagoon. With his large build, gentle humour and resonant Welsh baritone, which he put to good effect on light operatic arias as well as popular tunes, Secombe became a regular fixture at the London Palladium, including Royal Command performances from the 50s through to the 80s. His screen appearances included both comedy and 'straight' roles including *Helter Skelter* (1949, his debut), *Fake's Progress* (1950), *Down Among The Z Men* (1952), *Davy* (1957), *Oliver!* (1968), *The Bedsitting Room* (1968),

Song Of Norway (1969), *Rhubarb* (1969) and *The Magnificent Seven Deadly Sins* (1971). He appeared regularly on UK television screens, in variety shows and his own series in the 60s and 70s. He scored his first solo UK chart hit with 'On With The Motley' in 1955, which reached number 16. It was not until 1963 that Secombe recorded the song that was to become one of the singer's theme tunes, the Leslie Bricusse and Cyril Ornadel- penned 'If I Ruled The World', reaching the UK Top 20. After another hiatus, he achieved his biggest hit to date in 1967 with Charlie Chaplin's 'This Is My Song', reaching number 2 and prevented from reaching the number 1 slot by Petula Clark's version of the very same song. During his career this multi-faceted performer has also managed to appear in the London stage musicals *Pickwick* (1963), *The Four Musketeers* (1967) and *The Plumber's Progress* (1975). Following a massive reduction in his weight (for medical reasons) a trimmed-down Secombe has in recent years carved out a career since 1983 as the presenter of Independent Television's religious programme, *Highway* which required Secombe to master another skill, that of the interview technique. He has over the years been actively involved in charity organizations and fund-raising and after being awarded the CBE in 1963, Harry Secombe was knighted in 1981. In 1993, 30 years after creating the leading role in *Pickwick*, he appeared in a UK revival of the show with his old friend Roy Castle.
Albums (excluding Goons and other comedy albums): *At Your Request* (late 50s), *Operatic Arias* (late 50s), *Richard Tauber Favourites* (late 50s), *Secombe Sings* (1959), *Harry Secombe Showcase* (1960), *Sacred Songs* (1961), *Vienna, City Of My Dreams* (early 60s), *Show Souvenirs* (early 60s), *Sacred Songs* (early 60s), *Immortal Hymns* (early 60s), *Secombe's Personal Choice* (1967), *If I Ruled The World* (1971), *Songs For Sunday* (1972), *This Is Harry Secombe, Volume Four* (1974), *A Man And His Dreams* (1976), *Far Away Places* (1977), *Twenty Songs Of Joy* (1978), *Bless This House* (1979), *Songs Of My Homeland* (1979), *These Are My Songs* (1980), with Moira Anderson *Golden Memories* (1981, reissued as *This Is My Lovely Day* on CD), *A Song And A Prayer* aka *How Great Thou Art* (1981), *The Musical World Of Harry Secombe* (1983), *Highway Of Life* (1986), *The Highway Companion* (1987), *Onward Christian Soldiers* (1987), *Yours Sincerely* (1991), *Sir Harry* (1993). Compilations: *Spotlight On Harry Secombe* (1975), *The Harry Secombe Collection* (1976), *Portrait* (1978).
Further reading: *Arias And Raspberries*, Sir Harry Secombe.

Secret Garden, The

This charming and stylish musical was welcomed by one critic as 'one of the most aggressively pretty shows ever to grace a Broadway stage' when it opened at the St. James Theatre in New York on 25 April 1991. Marsha Norman's book was based on the much-loved Edwardian children's novel by Frances Hodgson Burnett, and tells of Mary Lennox (Daisy Eagan), who returns to England and the custody of her hunchbacked uncle, Archibald Craven (Mandy Patinkin), after her family, who were in the Colonial Service in India, are wiped out by an outbreak of cholera. Mary discovers Craven's sickly young son, Colin (John Babcock), who is being left to wither and die in a secluded room in the large, dreary mansion on the Yorkshire moors. She also finds the key to the secret walled garden which has been locked up since Craven's wife, Lily (Rebecca Luker), died in childbirth some 10 years earlier. Lily returns to the scene in saintly form, and has one of the show's most effective numbers, 'Come To My Garden'. Several other departed souls also materialise, including Mary's parents and several of the young victims of the cholera outbreak who form the chorus. The spirits lead Mary, Colin, and Craven 'towards vitality and joy in such captivating numbers as 'I Hear Someone Crying' and 'Come Spirit, Come Charm'. The remainder of composer Lucy Simon and lyricist Marsha Norman's 'sentimental and old-fashioned' score included 'Opening Dream', 'There's A Girl', 'The House Upon A Hill', 'A Girl In the Valley', 'Lily's Eyes', 'The Girl I Mean To Be', 'A Bit Of Earth', 'Letter Song', 'Where In The World', and 'How Could I Ever Know?'. General opinion was that the whole show was 'warm and wonderful', especially the gorgeous costumes, and designer-producer Heidi Landesman's ingenious placing of the action inside a toy theatre complete with drops and wings. She won a Tony Award for her dazzling effects, as did 11-year old Daisy Eagan for her fine performance. For a children's story The Secret Garden did pretty well - even with a $60 top price - and ran until January 1993, a total of 706 performances, before embarking on a successful US tour. Another, much smaller adaptation of Frances Hodgson Burnett's story, with a book and lyrics by Diana Morgan and music by Steven Markwick, was presented in 1993 at the King's Head Islington, on the London Fringe. The novel has been filmed at least three times: as a feature film with Margaret O'Brien in 1949; a television movie with Gennie James and Derek Jacobi in 1987; and another feature film in 1993 with Maggie Smith, Kate Maberly, John Lynch, and Haydon Prowse.

1776

America's obsession with its history had already resulted in two musicals based on momentous national events before this show opened at the 46th Street Theatre on 16 March 1969. Exactly 20 years before that, Miss Liberty, with a score by Irving Berlin,

concerned itself with the period leading up to the dedication ceremony for the lady with the torch, and, in 1925, songwriters Richard Rodgers and Lorenz Hart, together with librettist Herbert Fields, offered Dearest Enemy, which was 'inspired' by the American Revolution. Naturally, with a title like 1776, Peter Stone's book and Sherman Edwards's score relates to the culmination of that Revolution - the signing of the Declaration of Independence. Edwards, a newcomer to Broadway, had worked on the project for several years before collaborating with the more experienced Stone on the final draft. It stayed closely to historical fact, both in regard to the dramatic circumstances, and the personalities involved in them. The performances of Howard Da Silva (Benjamin Franklin), William Daniels (John Adams), and Ken Howard (Thomas Jefferson) were particularly applauded. In many ways, the show was more like a straight play - a powerful and emotional piece of theatre. Edwards's sympathetic, and sometimes poignant score included songs such as 'Momma Look Sharp', 'Cool, Cool Considerate Man', 'Sit Down, John', 'But Mr. Adams', 'The Lees Of Old Virginia', 'He Plays The Violin', 'Is Anybody There?', 'Yours, Yours, Yours!', 'Molasses To Rum', and 'Till Then'. The show was acclaimed from the start, and became a tremendous success, running for 1,217 performances. It won three Tony Awards: for best musical, supporting actor (Ronald Holgate in the role of Richard Henry Lee) and director (Peter Hunt). There was a short-lived London production in 1970. The 1972 film version retained several of the Broadway cast.

70, Girls, 70

Another celebrated flop, this show closed some five weeks after it emerged into the lights of the Broadhurst Theatre on 15 April 1971. Some critics attributed its failure to Stephen Sondheim's Follies, which had arrived on Broadway just 11 days earlier, and also concerned itself with the celebration of old troupers from the past. However, the glamorous settings of the 'Wiesmann Follies' could hardly be compared to the more down-to-earth situation in 70, Girls, 70, where the action switches between a group of veteran vaudevillians returning to Broadway, and 'some equally venerable ladies and a few gentlemen living at The Sussex Arms, a senior Citizens' run-down hotel in New York City'. One of the establishment's favourite residents, Ida Dodd (Mildred Natwick), forms a shop-lifting gang to get her own back on rude traders. After one job the aged criminals just make their getaway, but Ida gets caught. Before they can put her away, she escapes - by dying. The book, by Fred Ebb and Norman L. Martin, was based on the English comedy, Breath Of Spring, which was filmed as One Touch Of Mink. The show opened with a rousing, defiant anthem: 'Old Folks' . . . 'don't go out, strangers make them ill at ease/Old folks stay at home, nursing their infirmities' . . . 'So take a look at the old folks, they're quite an interesting sight/But if you want to see old folks/You're in the wrong hall tonight!'). From then on, Fred Ebb and composer John Kander cleverly interpolated numbers such as 'Broadway, My Street', 'Go Visit' and 'Coffee In A Cardboard Cup' by the old vaudeville performers, Melba (Lillian Hayman) and Fritzi (Goldye Shaw), among the 'plot' songs which included 'Home', 'The Caper', 'You And I, Love', 'Do We?', 'Hit It, Lorraine', 'See The Light', 'Boom Ditty Boom', 'Believe', 'The Elephant Song', and 'Yes'. Whatever the reason for the shows miserable run of 35 performances (*Follies* scooped the Tony Awards), it certainly was not the fault of the score, which was witty and entertaining throughout. Twenty years later, *70, Girls, 70* finally reached the West End, where Dora Bryan was 'irresistible' in the leading role.

She Loves Me

This chamber musical ostensibly set in Budapest in the mid-30s, was the first to be both produced and directed by Harold Prince. It was based on the play, *Parfumerie* by Miklos Laszlo, which had been filmed twice, as *The Shop Around The Corner* and *The Good Old Summertime*. *She Loves Me* opened at the Eugene O'Neill Theatre in New York on 23 April 1963, with music and lyrics by Jerry Bock and Sheldon Harnick. Jose Masteroff's book concerns certain members of the sales staff at Maraczek's Parfumerie, particularly the shop's manager, Georg Nowack (Daniel Massey), and the new salesgirl, Amalia Balash (Barbara Cook). They bicker with each other all day long, little knowing that each is the other's penfriend. Georg is the first to realize that they have been pouring their hearts out to each other via the US Mail, but he keeps it to himself. He finally reveals the true situation - and his feelings for her - by presenting her with some 'Ice Cream' (vanilla), and then reading aloud one of the letters she has written to her 'correspondent', whom she always refers to as 'Dear Friend'. The charming and tender story was perfectly complemented by the score, which has become one of the most cherished of all Broadway musicals. The songs included 'Days Gone By', 'No More Candy', 'Tonight At Eight', 'I Don't Know His Name', 'Will He Like Me?', 'Dear Friend', 'Try Me', 'Ice Cream', 'She Loves Me', 'A Trip To The Library', 'Grand Knowing You', 'Twelve Days To Christmas'. *She Loves Me* ran for 301 performances, and gained one Tony Award for featured actor (Jack Cassidy), but lost out in the rest of the categories to the brash and brassy *Hello, Dolly!*. The 1964 London production, with Anne Rogers, Gary Raymond, and the popular singer Gary Miller,

lasted for nearly six months. In 1993, a 30th anniversary revival starring Judy Kuhn and Boyd Gaines, was welcomed with open arms by Broadway audiences starved of good, original American musicals. In the same year, Barbara Cook was still closing her classy cabaret act with an exhilarating version of 'Ice Cream'.

Shenandoah

This musical was based on the critically acclaimed movie of the same name which starred James Stewart and was released in 1965. James Lee Barrett, the author of the screenplay, collaborated with Philip Rose and Peter Udell on the libretto for the stage adaptation which opened at the Alvin Theatre in New York on 7 January 1975. Set in the Shenandoah Valley at the time of the American Civil War, the strongly anti-war story concerns a widowed Virginian farmer, Charlie Anderson (John Cullum), who refuses to allow the North versus South conflict to intrude upon his life until some Yankee troops abduct his youngest son (Joseph Shapiro) because he is wearing a Rebel cap. Several members of Anderson's family are killed in tragic circumstances in the days that follow. The score, by Peter Udell (lyrics) and Gary Geld (music), had a rousing 'wide open spaces' feel about it, with numbers such as 'Raise The Flag Of Dixie', 'I've Heard It All Before', 'Why Am I Me', 'Next To Lovin' (I Like Fightin')', 'Over The Hill', 'The Pickers Are Comin'', 'Meditation', 'We Make A Beautiful Pair', 'Freedom', 'Violets And Silverbells', 'Papa's Gonna Make It Alright', and 'Meditation'. It is sometimes said that *Shenandoah*'s remarkably long run of 1,050 performances owed something to the feelings of revulsion towards war in general - and Vietnam in particular - that were prevalent in America around that time. At any rate, the show won Tony Awards for its book, and for John Cullum's fine performance. He recreated his original role when *Shenandoah* was revived for a limited period on Broadway in 1989.

Show Boat

A major theatrical triumph of the 20s which has never completely lost its original magic, *Show Boat* opened at the Ziegfeld Theatre in New York on 27 December 1927. For the basis of his show, Jerome Kern took the Edna Ferber novel of the life and loves of the travelling entertainers on a Mississippi riverboat. With book and lyrics by Oscar Hammerstein II, the magnificent score included many songs which have become an integral part of American popular music. Perhaps the best known is 'Ol' Man River', sung in the original staging by Jules Bledsoe as Joe but made internationally famous by Paul Robeson who also played the role. Other fine songs included 'Make Believe', 'You Are Love', 'Can't Help Lovin' Dat Man', sung by Helen Morgan

as Julie, and 'Why Do I Love You?'. Another song, 'Bill', written by Kern for an earlier show, with a lyric by P.G. Wodehouse, had remained unused and was revived for Morgan. It became one of the hits of the show and was ever afterwards associated with the singer. The show ran on Broadway for 572 performances. When it was staged in London in the 1928/9 season, the cast included Alberta Hunter as Queenie and Robeson. A new song had been added for Robeson, 'I Still Suits Me'. The show was revived briefly in London in 1942. Broadway had not seen the last of *Show Boat*, however, and it was revived in 1946, running for 418 performances. For this version Kern and Hammerstein added a new song, 'Nobody Else But Me', which was Kern's last composition. The show was revived again in 1948, 1954, 1966, the latter with an excellent production and cast, which included William Warfield, Barbara Cook, Stephen Douglas and Constance Towers, and yet again in 1982. In 1990, Opera North and the Royal Shakespeare Company presented the show at the London Palladium for a limited season, and, three years later, yet another revival, staged by Harold Prince, was out of town in the US, heading for New York. Several film versions have appeared, first in 1929 as a silent with sound added. The 1936 version starred Morgan, Robeson, Allan Jones and Hattie McDaniel, and in the 1951 remake the leads were sung by Howard Keel and Kathryn Grayson. In 1988, EMI released what they claimed was 'the first ever complete recording of Jerome Kern and Oscar Hammerstein II's great musical'. It featured Frederick von Stade, Jerry Hadley, Teresa Stratas, Bruce Hubbard, Karia Burns, Lillian Gish, and the London Sinfonietta conducted by John McGlinn.
Further reading: *Show Boat: The Story Of A Classic American Musical*, M. Kreuger.

Show Is On, The

One of the last of the smart and sophisticated Broadway revues that were so popular in the late 20s and early 30s. This one, which was a vehicle for the extravagant comedic talents of Beatrice Lillie and Bert Lahr, opened at the Winter Garden in New York on 25 December 1936. David Freedman and Moss Hart wrote the sketches which emphasised the production's celebration of 'show business', and lampooned contemporary figures such as John Gielgud and Leslie Howard, who were both offering their 'Hamlets' in New York. The songs came from a variety of composers and lyricists, but 'Little Old Lady' (Hoagy Carmichael and Stanley Adams) and 'By Strauss' (George Gershwin-Ira Gershwin) are probably the best-remembered items from the score. There were several other appealing numbers, including 'Long As You've Got Your Health' (Will Irwin-E.Y. 'Yip Harburg-Norman Zeno), 'Song Of

The Woodman' (Harold Arlen-Harburg), 'Now' (Vernon Duke-Ted Fetter), 'Rhythm' (Richard Rodgers-Lorenz Hart), and 'Buy Yourself A Balloon' (Herman Hupfield), during which Beatrice Lillie distributed garters to gentlemen members of the audience while perched on a 'moon seat', which was swung out into the auditorium. The show was stylishly directed by Edward Clark Lilley and Vincente Minnelli several years before the start of the latter's distinguished Hollywood career. It ran for 237 performances, and, in some ways, marked the end of an elegant and rather special era.

Shuffle Along

This show started its life in America as a vaudeville sketch, and was then adapted into the 'longest-running musical to be produced, directed, written, and acted by Negroes'. Naturally, given the era in which it was created and the kind of people who were concerned with it, *Shuffle Along* was not invited to occupy a prime site. Rather it was shuffled off to the 63rd St. Music Hall at the northern end of Broadway, where it opened on 23 May 1921. Much to everyone's surprise, the show was a big hit, and ran for 504 performances. This was not neccessarily due to the book, which was written by Flournoy Miller and Aubrey Lyles, and provided the authors with two of the leading roles. Their story of political corruption in Jimtown, Dixieland, tells of how the leading candidates for the office of mayor, Steve Jenkins (Miller) and Sam Peck (Lyles), fix it so that whichever one of them wins - the other cannot lose. Eventually they are both kicked out of office by a knight in shining armour, the high-principled Harry Walton (Roger Matthews). Noble Sissle and Eubie Blake also took part in the show, but their main role was to write the score which contained one enormous hit, 'I'm Just Wild About Harry', as well as a varied selection of songs including the charming 'Love Will Find A Way', 'Bandana Days', 'If You've Never Been Vamped By a Brownskin (You've Never Been Vamped At All)', 'Everything Reminds Me Of You', 'Low Down Blues', 'Shuffle Along', and several more. Paul Robeson joined the Broadway cast for a time in as member of a vocal group, and, when the show eventually went on the road, Joséphine Baker was a member of the chorus. This was a tremendous, fast moving production, with a lot of style, humour, and pulsating music. Subsequent attempts to recreate the formula in 1928, 1932, and 1952, were all unsuccessful. Eubie Blake lived to be over 100, and a musical anthology of some of his work, entitled *Eubie!*, played on Broadway in 1978.

Shuman, Mort

b. 12 November 1936, Brooklyn, New York, USA, d. 2 November 1991, London, England. After studying music, Shuman began writing songs with blues singer, Doc Pomus, in 1958. Early in 1959 two of their songs were Top 40 hits: 'Plain Jane' for Bobby Darin, and Fabian's 'I'm A Man'. During the next six years, their catalogue was estimated at over 500 songs, in a mixture of styles for a variety of artists. They included 'Surrender', 'Viva Las Vegas', 'Little Sister' and 'Kiss Me Quick' (Elvis Presley), 'Save The Last Dance For Me', 'Sweets For My Sweet' and 'This Magic Moment' (the Drifters), 'Teenager In Love' (Dion And The Belmonts), 'Can't Get Used To Losing You' (Andy Williams), 'Suspicion' (Terry Stafford); 'Seven Day Weekend' (Gary 'U.S.' Bonds) and 'Spanish Lace' (Gene McDaniels). Around the time of the team's break-up in 1965, Shuman collaborated with several other writers. These included John McFarland for Billy J. Kramer's UK number 1, 'Little Children', Clive Westlake for 'Here I Go Again' (the Hollies), ex-pop star, Kenny Lynch, for 'Sha-La-La-La-Lee' (Small Faces), 'Loves Just A Broken Heart' (Cilla Black), producer Jerry Ragavoy for 'Get It While You Can' and 'Look At Granny Run, Run' (Howard Tate). Subsequently, Shuman moved to Paris, where he occasionally performed his own one-man show, and issued solo albums such as *Amerika* and *Imagine...*, as well as writing several songs for one of France's few rock 'n' roll stars, Johnny Halliday. In 1968 Shuman translated the lyrics of French composer Jacques Brel ; these were recorded by many artists including Dusty Springfield, Scott Walker and Rod McKuen. Together with Eric Blau, he devised, adapted and wrote lyrics for the revue, *Jacques Brel Is Alive And Well And Living In Paris*. Shuman also starred in the piece, which became a world-wide success. In October 1989, *Budgie*, a musical set in London's Soho district, with Schuman's music and Don Black's lyrics, opened in the West End. It starred former pop star, turned actor and entrepreneur, Adam Faith, and UK soap opera actress, Anita Dobson. The show closed after only three months, losing more than £1,000,000. Shuman wrote several other shows, including *Amadeo, Or How To Get Rid Of It*, based on an Ionesco play, a Hong Kong portrayal of *Madame Butterfly* and a re-working of Bertolt Brecht and Kurt Weill's opera, *Aufstieg Und Fall Der Stadt Mahogonny*. None has yet reached the commercial theatre. After undergoing a liver operation in the spring of 1991, he died in London.

Silk Stockings

Cole Porter's final Broadway show was based on the 1939 film *Ninotchka*, which starred Greta Garbo. During the out-of-town try-outs, Abe Burrows' name was added to those of librettists George S. Kaufman and Leueen McGrath, and Kaufman was replaced as director by Cy Feur. *Silk Stockings* opened at the Imperial Theatre in New York on 24 February 1955.

In this musical version of the by now familiar story, Ninotchka (Hildegarde Neff) is seduced by a glib Hollywood talent agent, Steve Canfield (Don Ameche), who is trying to persuade a famous Russian composer, Peter Ilyich Boroff (Philip Sterling), to expand his 'Ode To A Tractor' into the score for a ritzy movie version of *War And Peace*. The score was not top-drawer Porter by any means, but there were some worthwhile numbers especially the gorgeous ballad, 'All Of You', the amusing and contemporary 'Stereophonic Sound', and several more varied and entertaining items including 'Paris Loves Lovers', 'Without Love', 'It's A Chemical Reaction, That's All', 'Too Bad', 'Silk Stockings', 'The Red Blues', 'As On The Seasons We Sail', 'Satin And Silk', 'Josephine', and 'Siberia'. The show enjoyed a run of 478 performances and was filmed in 1957 with Fred Astaire and Cyd Charisse.

Simple Simon

One of America's most cherished clowns, Ed Wynn, brought his fumbling style, nervous laugh, and excruciating puns to this Florenz Ziegfeld production which opened at the impresario's own Broadway theatre on 18 February 1930. Wynn also collaborated with Guy Bolton on the book in which he was cast a a newspaper vendor who, rather than accept that bad news exists, spends his time in a kind of fairy-tale land. This gave Ziegfeld and his designer Joseph Urban the opportunity to display the lavish sets and costumes for which he was justifiably famous. Richard Rodgers and Lorenz Hart wrote the score, and it contained one of their most enduring numbers, 'Ten Cents A Dance', which was emphatically introduced by Ruth Etting. She had a big record hit with the song, and it figured prominently in her film biography, *Love Me Or Leave Me*, in which she was played by Doris Day. Ironically, the song 'Love Me Or Leave Me' (Gus Kahn-Walter Donaldson) was added to the score of *Simple Simon* a couple of months after the show opened. One of the numbers that was cut during the Broadway try-out, 'Dancing On The Ceiling', was later sung by Jessie Matthews in the London production of *Ever Green*, and became forever associated with her. The remainder of the score for *Simple Simon* included 'I Can Do Wonders With You', 'Don't Tell Your Folks', 'Send For Me', and 'I Still Believe In You'. The show ran for 135 performances, and returned early in 1931 for a further brief engagement.

Sinbad

This vehicle for the ebullient entertainer Al Jolson, opened at the Winter Garden in New York on 14 February 1918. His regulation blackface came in handy as he travelled to the exotic locations demanded by Harold Atteridge's book which was apparently something to do with the Arabian Nights. In Jolson's shows a simple plot was essential anyway because he continually stopped the action to sell the songs, and the evening always threatened to become a one-man concert. The basic score was credited to Sigmund Romberg and Harold Atteridge, but the interpolated numbers were far more popular, and several of them became Jolson specialities. They included 'Rock-A-Bye Your Baby With A Dixie Melody' and 'Why Do they All Take The Night Boat To Albany?', both written by Jean Schwartz, Sam M. Lewis, and Joe Young; and ''N Everything' by Buddy De Sylva and Gus Kahn. During the show's run of 388 performances, two more songs were added, 'Avalon' (Jolson-Vincent Rose) and 'My Mammy' (Lewis-Joe Young-Walter Donaldson). On the subsequent road tour of *Sinbad*, Jolson introduced yet another one of his enormous crowd-pleasers, 'Swanee', which had a lyric by Irving Caesar, and gave composer George Gershwin his first big hit. Many years later the song became identified with Judy Garland after she performed it so memorably in the film *A Star Is Born*.

Sissle, Noble

b. 10 July 1889, Indianapolis, Indiana, USA, d. 17 December 1975. Sissle's early career was spent largely in vaudeville as a singer and he also sang with the orchestra of James Reese Europe. However, his talents as a songwriter gradually drew him to Broadway where, in collaboration with Eubie Blake, he achieved a major breakthrough. Before Sissle and Blake it was rare for a black entertainer to gain acceptance along the 'Great White Way', but the success of their 1921 show, *Shuffle Along*, changed all that. *Shuffle Along* starred Florence Mills and among its memorable tunes were 'In Honeysuckle Time', 'Love Will Find A Way' and the hit of the show, 'I'm Just Wild About Harry'. In this and succeeding shows, such as *Chocolate Dandies*, the collaborators presented a succession of songs, dances and sketches that were attuned to the new musical sounds of the day - unlike most other Broadway shows which also performed by all-black casts, had ignored ragtime and the emergence of jazz. In these and later years Sissle led a number of fine orchestras that featured some of the best musicians available, among them Sidney Bechet, Otto 'Toby' Hardwicke, Tommy Ladnier and Buster Bailey. In the late 20s Sissle led a band in Paris and London and during the 30s led successful bands in New York and elsewhere in the USA. He continued touring during the 40s and 50s but gradually directed his attention to music publishing. Albums: *Sissle And Blake's 'Shuffle Along' (1921)* (80s), *Sissle And His Sizzling Syncopators (1930-31)* (80s).

1600 Pennsylvania Avenue

The title is the location of the White House in Washington, where, in 1974, the current resident, Richard Nixon, reluctantly vacated the premises. Two years later, on 4 May 1976, the show bearing that fancy address took up residence at the Mark Hellinger Theatre in New York - and was evicted after only seven performances. The early departure was all the more suprising since the men concerned were two of the American musical theatre's most illustrious names: Leonard Bernstein and Alan Jay Lerner. As usual in this kind of debacle, the book got most of the blame. It was a fascinating idea to tell the White House story - the first 100 years of its history from George Washington to Theodore Roosevelt - through the eyes of three generations of Lud Simmons, a family dynasty of black servants who worked at the White House. They oversee the action and represent the American people. Gilbert Price stood in for all the servants, and the presidents were played by one actor, Ken Howard, and the First Ladies by the British actress, Patricia Routledge. It is impossible to say where it all went wrong - after all, not many people saw it - but at least the score contained several engaging pieces such as 'Duet For One', 'Take Care Of This House', and 'We Must Have A Ball'. Sixteen years later, on 11 August 1992, a major revival opened - appropriately enough at the John F. Kennedy Centre for the Performing Arts in Washington.

Slade, Julian

b. 28 May 1930, London, England. Slade was a composer, lyricist, librettist and pianist. He started to write when he was at Cambridge University, and his first two musicals, The *Meringue* and *Lady May* were presented by the Cambridge Amateur Dramatic Club. He then went to the Bristol Old Vic Theatre School, and in 1952 was invited by Denis Carey to join the company as a small part actor and musical director. In the same year he provided the music for a highly successful version of Sheridan's *The Duenna*, and it was at Bristol that he met Dorothy Reynolds, a leading actress, who collaborated with him on libretto and lyrics. Their long association began with *Christmas In King Street* and *The Merry Gentlemen*, written for the Theatre Royal, Bristol, and then, in 1954, *Salad Days*, which transferred to the Vaudeville Theatre in London. It ran until 1960, the longest running British musical of its era. Slade played the piano in the pit for the first 18 months, while onstage, a magic piano in a London park caused passers-by to dance uncontrollably. The piece was typical Slade - a simple plot and inconsequential humour, accompanied by charming, hummable songs, such as 'We Said We Wouldn't Look Back', 'I Sit In The Sun', 'It's Easy To Sing', 'The Time Of My Life' and

'Cleopatra'. In 1956, *The Comedy Of Errors*, a comic operetta adapted from Shakespeare's play, for which Slade wrote the music, played a season at the Arts Theatre. It had originally been performed on BBC Television two years earlier. In 1957, Slade and Reynolds wrote *Free As Air*, which lasted for a over a year. This was succeeded by *Follow That Girl*, *Hooray For Daisy* and *Wildest Dreams*, which even contained a 'rock' number. However, these shows seemed out of place in the theatre of the 'angry young men'. 'Our shows went well out of town, but London didn't seem to want them' Slade recalled. *Vanity Fair*, with lyrics by Roger Miller, faded after 70 performances at the Queen's Theatre, and Slade's first solo effort, *Nutmeg And Ginger* (1963), based on Francis Beaumont's 1609 comedy, *The Knight Of The Burning Pestle*, did not play the West End. Neither did some of the others, such as *The Pursuit Of Love* and *Out Of Bounds* (1973), although *Trelawney* (1972) stayed at the Prince of Wales Theatre for over six months. Slade received his warmest reviews for that show, the last time London saw his work until 1991, when a revival of his *Nutmeg And Ginger* opened to enthusiastic reviews at the Orange Tree Theatre in Richmond, Surrey.

Slice Of Saturday Night, A
After a stay of nearly two years at London's tiny Arts Theatre, and many other productions worldwide, the Heather Brothers' most successful musical finally opened in the West End at the Strand theatre on 6 September 1993 for a limited run of 12 weeks. Set in the Club A Go-Go on a typical Saturday night, the story concerns itself with the teenage mating habits that were currently in vogue around 1964. The message is spread via some 30 songs which sound as though they might have been written in the 60s, and hardly any dialogue. There are several amusing and engaging numbers, including 'Love On Our Side', 'The Boy Of My Dreams', 'Oh, So Bad', 'Baby I Love You', 'Please Don't Tell Me', and 'Twiggy'. The 70s UK pop star, Alvin Stardust, played the club's manager, Eric 'Rubber Legs' Devine, in the provinces, but Dennis Waterman, renowned for his work in top-rated television programmes such as *Minder* and *The Sweeney*, took over for the West End run. Also added for the London production were Danny McCall (from the television soap *Brookside*), and Sonia, the UK entrant in the 1993 Eurovision Song Contest. The remainder of the energetic young cast, who had been with the show for some time, consisted of Nikki Brooks, Judith Ellis, Joanne Engelsman, Peter Heppelthwaite, and Sean Oliver.

Some Like It Hot
(see *Sugar*)

Sondheim, Stephen
b. Stephen Joshua Sondheim, 22 March 1930, New York, USA. Sondheim is generally regarded as the most important theatrical composer of the 70s and 80s due to his introduction of the concept musical (some say, anti-musical) or 'unified show', which has made him a cult figure. Born into an affluent family, his father was a prominent New York dress manufacturer, Sondheim studied piano and organ sporadically from the age of seven. When he was 10, his parents divorced, and he spent some time at military school. His mother's friendship with the Oscar Hammerstein family in Philadelphia enabled Sondheim to meet the lyricist, who took him under his wing and educated him in the art of writing for the musical theatre. After majoring in music at Williams College, Sondheim graduated in 1950 with the Hutchinson Prize For Musical Composition, a two-year fellowship, which enabled him to study with the innovative composer Milton Babbitt. During the early 50s, he contributed material to television shows such as *Topper*, and wrote the songs for a proposed Broadway musical, *Saturday Night* (1955), which was never staged due to the death of producer Lemuel Ayres. Sondheim also wrote the incidental music for the play, *Girls Of Summer* (1956). His first major success was as a lyric writer, with Leonard Bernstein's music, for the 1957 Broadway hit musical *West Side Story*. Initially, Bernstein was billed as co-lyricist, but had his name removed before the New York opening, giving Sondheim full credit. The show ran for 734 performances on Broadway, and 1,039 in London. The songs included 'Jet Song', 'Maria', 'Something's Coming', 'Tonight', 'America', 'One Hand, One Heart', 'I Feel Pretty', 'Somewhere' and 'A Boy Like That'. A film version was released in 1961 and there were New York revivals in 1968 and 1980. Productions in London during in 1974 and 1984 were also significant in that it marked the first of many collaborations between Sondheim and producer Harold Prince.

It was another powerful theatrical figure, David Merrick, who mounted *Gypsy* (1959), once again a Laurents-Robbins project, based on stripper Gypsy Rose Lee's book, *Gypsy: A Memoir*, and considered by some to be the pinnacle achievement of the Broadway musical stage. Sondheim was set to write both music and lyrics before the show's star Ethel Merman demanded a more experienced composer. Jule Styne proved to be acceptable, and Sondheim concentrated on the lyrics, which have been called his best work in the musical theatre, despite the critical acclaim accorded his later shows. *Gypsy's* memorable score included 'Let Me Entertain You', 'Some People', 'Small World', 'You'll Never Get Away From Me', 'If Momma Was Married', 'All I Need Is The Girl', 'Everything's Coming Up Roses',

Stephen Sondheim

'Together, Wherever We Go', 'You Gotta Have A Gimmick' and 'Rose's Turn'. Merman apparently refused to embark on a long London run, so the show was not mounted there until 1973. Angela Lansbury scored a personal triumph then as the domineering mother, Rose, and repeated her success in the Broadway revival in 1974. In 1989, both the show and its star, Tyne Daly (well known for television's *Cagney and Lacey*), won Tony Awards in the 30th anniversary revival,which ran through until 1991. Rosalind Russell played Rose in the 1962 movie version, which received lukewarm reviews. For *Gypsy*, Sondheim had interrupted work on *A Funny Thing Happened On The Way To The Forum* (1962), to which he contributed both music and lyrics. Based on the plays of Plautus, it has been variously called, 'a fast moving farce', 'a vaudeville-based Roman spoof' and 'a musical madhouse'. Sondheim's songs, which included the prologue, 'Comedy Tonight' ('Something appealing, something appalling/Something for everyone, a comedy tonight!') and 'Everybody Ought To Have A Maid', celebrated moments of joy or desire and punctuated the thematic action. The show won several Tony awards, including 'Best Musical' and 'Best Producer' but nothing for Sondheim's score. The show was revived on Broadway in 1972 with Phil Silvers in the leading role, and had two London productions (1963 and 1986), both starring British comedian Frankie Howerd. A film version, starring Zero Mostel and Silvers, dropped several of the original songs. *Anyone Can Whistle* (1964), 'a daft moral fable about corrupt city officials', with an original book by Laurents, and songs by Sondheim, lasted just a week. The critics were unanimous in their condemnation of the musical with a theme that 'madness is the only hope for world sanity'. The original cast recording, which included 'Simple', 'I've Got You To Lean On', 'A Parade In Town', 'Me And My Town' and the appealing title song, was made after the show closed, and became a cult item.

Sondheim was back to 'lyrics only' for *Do I Hear A Waltz?* (1965). The durable Broadway composer, Richard Rodgers, supplied the music for the show that he described as 'not a satisfying experience'. In retrospect, it was perhaps underrated. Adapted by Arthur Laurents from his play, *The Time Of The Cuckoo*, the show revolved around an American tourist in Venice, and included 'Moon In My Window', 'This Week's Americans', 'Perfectly Lovely Couple' and 'Here We Are Again'. Broadway had to wait until 1970 for the next Sondheim musical, the first to be directed by Harold Prince. *Company* had no plot, but concerned 'the lives of five Manhattan couples held together by their rather excessively protective feelings about a 'bachelor friend'. Its ironic, acerbic score included 'The Little Things You Do Together' ('The concerts you enjoy together/Neighbours you annoy together/Children you destroy together...'), 'Sorry-Grateful', 'You Could Drive A Person Crazy', 'Have I Got A Girl For You?', 'Someone Is Waiting', 'Another Hundred People', 'Getting Married Today', 'Side By Side By Side', 'What Would We Do Without You?', 'Poor Baby', 'Tick Tock', 'Barcelona', 'The Ladies Who Lunch' ('Another chance to disapprove, another brilliant singer/Another reason not to move, another vodka stinger/I'll drink to that!') and 'Being Alive'. With a book by George Furth, produced and directed by Prince, the musical numbers staged by Michael Bennett, and starring Elaine Stritch and Larry Kert (for most of the run), *Company* ran for 690 performances. It gained the New York Drama Critics' Circle Award for Best Musical, and six Tony Awards, including Best Musical, and Best Music and Lyrics for Sondheim, the first awards of his Broadway career. The marathon recording session for the original cast album, produced by Thomas Z. Shepard, was the subject of a highly-acclaimed television documentary. The next Prince-Bennett-Sondheim project, with a book by James Goldman, was the mammoth *Follies* (1971), 'the story of four people in their early 50s: two ex-show girls from the *Weismann Follies*, and two stage-door-Johnnies whom they married 30 years ago, who attend a reunion, and start looking backwards...'. It was a lavish, spectacular production, with a cast of 50, and a Sondheim score which contained 22 'book' songs, including 'Who's That Woman?' (sometimes referred to as the 'the mirror number'), 'Ah Paris!', 'Could I Leave You?', 'I'm Still Here' ('Then you career from career, to career/I'm almost through my memoirs/And I'm here!'); and several 'pastiche' numbers in the style of the 'great' songwriters such as George Gershwin and Dorothy Fields ('Losing My Mind'); Cole Porter ('The Story Of Lucy and Jessie'); Sigmund Romberg and Rudolf Friml ('One More Kiss'); Jerome Kern ('Loveland'); Irving Berlin (the prologue, 'Beautiful Girls') and De Sylva, Brown, And Henderson ('Broadway Baby'). Although the show received a great deal of publicity and gained the Drama Critics Circle Award for Best Musical, plus seven Tony awards, it closed after 522 performances with the loss of its entire $800,000 investment. A spokesperson commented: 'We sold more posters than tickets'. *Follies In Concert*, with the New York Philharmonic, played two performances in September 1985 at the Lincoln Center, and featured several legendary Broadway names such as Carol Burnett, Betty Comden, Adolph Green, Lee Remick, and Barbara Cook. The show was taped for television, and generated a much-acclaimed RCA album, which compensated for the disappointingly truncated recording of the original show. The show did not reach London until 1987, when the young Cameron

Mackintosh produced a 'new conception' with Goldman's revised book, and several new songs replacing some of the originals. It closed after 600 performances, because of high running costs. *A Little Night Music* (1973), was the first Sondheim-Prince project to be based on an earlier source; in this instance, Ingmar Bergman's film, *Smiles Of A Summer Night*. Set at the turn of the century, in Sweden it was an operetta, with all the music in three quarter time, or multiples thereof. The critics saw in it echoes of Mahler, Ravel, Rachmaninoff, Brahms, and even Johann Strauss. The score contained Sondheims's first song hit for which he wrote both words and music, 'Send In The Clowns'. Other songs included 'Liaisons', 'A Weekend In The Country', 'The Glamorous Life', 'In Praise Of Women', 'Remember' and 'Night Waltz'. The show ran for 601 performances, and was a healthy financial success. It gained the New York Drama Critics Award for Best Musical, and five Tony awards, including Sondheim's music and lyrics for a record third time in a row. The London run starred Jean Simmons, while Elizabeth Taylor played Desiree in the 1978 movie version.

On the back of the show's 1973 Broadway success, and the composer's increasing popularity, a benefit concert, *Sondheim: A Musical Tribute*, was mounted at the Shubert Theatre, featuring every available performer who had been associated with his shows, singing familiar, and not so familiar, material. *Pacific Overtures* (1976), was, perhaps, Sondheim's most daring and ambitious musical to date. John Weidman's book purported to relate the entire 120 years history of Japan, from Commodore Perry's arrival in 1856, to its emergence as the powerful, industrial force of the 20th century. The production was heavily influenced by the Japanese Kabuki Theatre. The entire cast were Asian, and Sondheim used many Oriental instruments to obtain his effects. Musical numbers included 'Chrysanthemum Tea', 'Please Hello', 'Welcome To Kanagawa', 'Next', 'Someone In A Tree' and 'The Advantages Of Floating In The Middle Of The Sea'. The show closed after 193 performances, losing its entire budget of over half-a-million dollars, but it still won the Drama Critics Circle Award for Best Musical. It was revived Off-Broadway in 1984.

The next Broadway project bearing Sondheim's name was much more successful, and far more conventional. *Side By Side By Sondheim* (1977), an anthology of some of his songs, started out at London's Mermaid Theatre the year before. Starring the original London cast of Millicent Martin, Julia McKenzie, David Kernan and Ned Sherrin, the New York production received almost unanimously favourable notices, and proved that many of Sondheim's songs, when presented in this revue form and removed from the sometimes bewildering librettos, could be popular items in their own right. In complete contrast, was *Sweeney Todd, The Demon Barber Of Fleet Street* (1979), Hugh Wheeler's version of the grisly tale of a 19th century barber who slits the throats of his clients, and turns the bodies over to Mrs Lovett (Angela Lansbury), who bakes them into pies. Sondheim's 'endlessly inventive, highly expressive score', considered to be near-opera, included the gruesome, 'Not While I'm Around', 'Epiphany', 'A Little Priest', the more gentle 'Pretty Women' and 'My Friends'. Generally accepted as one of the most ambitious Broadway musicals ever staged ('a staggering theatrical spectacle'; 'one giant step forward for vegetarianism'), *Sweeney Todd* ran for over 500 performances, and gained eight Tony Awards, including Best Musical, Score and Book.

In 1980, it played in London for four months, and starred Denis Quilley and Sheila Hancock. *Merrily We Roll Along* (1981), with a book by George Furth, based on the 1934 play by George S. Kaufman and Moss Hart, was probably the nearest that Sondheim reached to writing a 'good, old fashioned musical comedy'. Despite a run of only 16 performances, the pastiche score contained some 'insinuatingly catchy numbers'. It also marked the end, for the time being, of Sondheim's association with Harold Prince, who had produced and directed nearly all of his shows. Depressed and dejected, Sondheim threatened to give up writing for the theatre. However, in 1982, he began working with James Lapine, who had attracted some attention for his direction of the off-Broadway musical, *March Of The Falsettos* (1981).

The first fruits of the Sondheim-Lapine association, *Sunday In The Park With George* also started off-Broadway, as a Playwrights Horizon workshop production, before opening on Broadway in 1984. Inspired by George Seurat's 19th century painting, *Sunday Afternoon On The Island Of La Grande Jatte*, with book and direction by Lapine, the two-act show starred Mandy Patinkin and Bernadette Peters, and an 'intriguingly intricate' Sondheim score that included 'Finishing The Hat', 'Lesson No.8', and 'Move On'. The run of a year-and-a-half was due in no small part to energetic promotion by the *New York Times*, which caused the theatrical competition to dub the show, *Sunday In The Times With George*. In 1985, it was awarded the coveted Pulitzer Prize for Drama, and in 1990 became one of the rare musicals to be staged at London's Royal National Theatre. In 1987, Sondheim again received a Tony award for *Into the Woods*, a musical fairy tale of a baker and his wife, who live under the curse of a wicked witch, played by Bernadette Peters. The critics called it Sondheim's most accessible show for many years, with a score that included 'Cinderella At The Grave', 'Hello, Little Girl' and 'Children Will Listen'. It won the New York Drama Critics Circle, and Drama Desk Awards, for Best Musical, and a Grammy for Best Original Cast album. 'Angry', rather than accessible, was the critics' verdict of *Assassins*, with a book by John Weidman, which opened for a limited run Off Broadway early in 1991, and played the Donmar Warehouse in London a year later. Dubbed by *Newsweek*: 'Sondheim's most audacious, far out and grotesque work of his career', it 'attempted to examine the common thread of killers and would-be killers from John Wilkes Booth, the murderer of Lincoln, through Lee Harvey Oswald to John Hinckley Jnr, who shot Ronald Reagan'. The pastiche score included 'Everybody's Got The Right', 'The Ballad Of Booth' and 'The Ballad Of Czolgosz'. In 1993, a one-night tribute *Sondheim: A Celebration At Carnegie Hall*, was transmitted on US network television in the 'Great Performers' series, and, on a rather smaller scale, the Off Broadway revue *Putting It Together*, which was packed with Sondheim songs, brought Julie Andrews back to the New York musical stage for the first time since *Camelot*.

Besides his main Broadway works over the years, Sondheim provided material for many other stage projects, such as the music and lyrics for *The Frogs* (1974), songs for the revue *Marry Me A Little* and a song for the play *A Mighty Man Is He*. He also contributed the incidental music to *The Girls Of Summer*, 'Come Over Here' and 'Home Is the Place' for Tony Bennett. In addition, Sondheim wrote the incidental music for the play *Invitation To A March*, the score for the mini-musical *Passionella*, the lyrics (with Mary Rodgers' music) for *The Mad Show* and new lyrics for composer Leonard Bernstein's 1974 revival of *Candide*. Sondheim's film work included the music for *Stravinsky*, *Reds* and *Dick Tracy*. Sondheim also wrote the screenplay, with Anthony Perkins, for *The Last Of Sheila*, a film 'full of impossible situations, demented logic and indecipherable clues', inspired by his penchant for board games and puzzles of every description. For television, Sondheim wrote the music and lyrics for *Evening Primrose*, which starred Perkins, and made his own acting debut in 1974, with Jack Cassidy, in a revival of the George S. Kaufman-Ring Lardner play, *June Moon*. While never pretending to write 'hit songs' (apparently the term 'hummable' makes him bristle), Sondheim has nevertheless had his moments in the charts with songs such as 'Small World' (Johnny Mathis); 'Tonight' (Ferrante And Teicher); 'Maria' and 'Somewhere' (P.J. Proby); 'Send In The Clowns' (Judy Collins), and 'Losing My Mind' (Liza Minnelli). Probably Sondheim's greatest impact on records, apart from the Original Cast albums which won seven Grammys, was Barbra Streisand's, *The Broadway Album*, in 1985. Seven tracks, involving eight songs, were Sondheim's (two in collaboration with Bernstein), and he re-wrote three of them for

Streisand, including 'Send In The Clowns'. *The Broadway Album* stayed at number 1 in the US charts for three weeks, and sold over three million copies. Other gratifying moments for Sondheim occurred in 1983 when he was voted a member of the American Academy and the Institute of Arts and Letters, and again in 1990, when he became Oxford University's first Professor of Drama. As for his contribution to the musical theatre, opinions were sharply divided. John Podhoretz in the *Washington Times* said that 'with *West Side Story*, the musical took a crucial, and in retrospect, suicidal step into the realm of social commentary, and created a self-destructive form in which characters were taken to task and made fun of, for doing things like bursting into song'. Others, like Harold Prince, have said that Stephen Sondheim is simply the best in the world.

Further reading: *Sondheim & Co.*, Craig Zadan. *Sondheim And The American Musical*, Paul Sheran and Tom Sutcliffe. *Song By Song By Sondheim (The Stephen Sondheim Songbook)*, edited by Sheridan Morley. *Sunday In the Park With George*, Stephen Sondheim and James Lapine. *Sondheim*, Martin Gottfried.

Song And Dance

A 'concert for the theatre' consisting of the 'song cycle', *Tell Me On Sunday*, with music by Andrew Lloyd Webber and lyrics by Don Black, and *Variations* composed by Lloyd Webber on a theme of Paganini for his 'cellist brother, Julian. *Tell Me On Sunday* was first performed at Lloyd Webber's Sydmonton Festival in 1979. When it subsequently played to an invited audience at London's Royalty Theatre in January 1980, and was transmitted by BBC Television during the following month, the piece was sung by Marti Webb. In the same year, she had UK chart hits with two of of the songs, 'Tell Me On Sunday' and 'Take That Look Off Your Face'. The latter number also won an Ivor Novello Award. She was present again when *Tell Me On Sunday* was expanded to 50 minutes and became the first part of *Song And Dance*, while Wayne Sleep, with his team of eight dancers, performed *Variations* in the second half. The complete work opened at the Royalty theatre in London on 7 April 1982. *Tell Me On Sunday* is a simple tale of a young English woman in New York, and the trials and tribulations she experiences during a series of unhappy love affairs. The songs are considered to be among the composer's - and Don Black's - very best work, and included 'You Made Me Think You Were In Love', 'I Love New York', 'Come Back With The Same Look In Your Eyes', 'I'm Very You, You're Very Me', 'Let's Talk About Me', and 'When You Want To Fall In Love'. Black, who had spent some time in America, came up with what he thought was an apposite song title that pleased him considerably, 'Capped Teeth And Caesar Salad'. *Song And Dance* enjoyed a run of 781 performances, closing in March 1984. During the run, Marti Webb was replaced by several actresses including Sarah Brightman, and in August 1984, she played the lead when the show was shown on UK television. In 1985, much to the reported chagrin of Don Black, *Song And Dance* was expanded even further, and presented at the Royale Theatre in New York, where it stayed for 474 performances. Bernadette Peters won a Tony Award for her performance in the leading role.

Song Of Norway

The first of several shows in which Robert Wright and George Forrest adapted works by the classical composers for the Broadway stage. In this case, they turned for their inspiration to the life and music of Edvard Grieg. *Song Of Norway* began its life on the west coast with the San Francisco and the Los Angeles Opera companies, before opening at the Imperial Theatre in New York on 21 August 1944. The book by Milton Lazarus, based on a play by Homer Curran, tells a fanciful story in which Grieg (Lawrence Brooks) and his poet friend, Rikard Nordraak (Robert Shafer), are diverted from their work by the tempestuous Italian prima donna Louisa Giovanni (Irra Petina). After the poet's death, Grieg is supposedly inspired to write the A-Minor Piano Concerto. Wright and Forrest's music and lyrics combined with Grieg's music in a score which included 'Freddy And The Fiddle', 'Midsummer's Eve', 'Three Loves', 'Hill Of Dreams', 'The Legend', 'Strange Music', 'Now!', 'Hymn Of Betrothal', and 'I Love Thee'. *Song Of Norway* was one of Broadway's biggest wartime hits, running for 860 performances. The 1946 London production, with John Hargreaves, ran for over a year. A film version, starring Florence Henderson and Toralv Maurstad was released in 1970. In 1981, the show was revived on Broadway by the New York City Opera. Many recordings have been issued over the years, but the complete score was not available until 1992,when a version with Valerie Masterson, Diana Montague, David Rendall, and Donald Maxwell, was released on two CDs.

Sony Broadway

The Masterworks division of Columbia Records under the leadership of Goddard Lieberson, dominated the recording of Original Broadway Cast albums from the early 50s onwards. By that time, Columbia Records had become part of the Columbia Broadcasting System (CBS), having been bought out in 1938 for the sum of $700,000. Exactly 50 years later, the Japanese conglomerate, Sony Music, reportedly paid $2 billion for CBS. That is how, in the early 90s, the Sony Broadway label was in a position to begin to re-release all those (mostly) marvellous musicals from the genre's vintage years on mid-price CDs. Early in 1994 the list was substantial, and included *Goldilocks, Miss Liberty, Mr. President, Candide, West Side Story, Wonderful Town, The Apple Tree, The Rothschilds, On The Twentieth Century, The Girl Who Came To Supper, 1776, Ballroom, Dear World, 70, Girls, 70, The Most Happy Fella, Bajour, Irma La Douce, Out Of This World, Do I Hear A Waltz?, Flower Drum Song, The Sound Of Music, South Pacific, Two By Two, A Tree Grows In Brooklyn, Over Here, All American, It's a Bird, It's a Plane, It's Superman, Gentlemen Prefer Blondes, Hallelujah, Baby!, Irene, Here's Love, Dames At Sea*, and *Raisin*. The CD booklet covers are reconstructions of the original album sleeve graphics, but the liner notes are all newly written by contemporary experts such as Ken Mandelbaum. As well as those recording of the originals casts, the label has also released several studio recordings of Broadway shows, and various compilations such as *There's No Business Like Show Business - Broadway Showstoppers, There's Nothing Like A Dame - Broadway's Broads, Embraceable You - Broadway In Love, The Party's Over - Broadway Sings The Blues*, and tributes to leading songwriters, including Stephen Sondheim, Richard Rodgers and Oscar Hammerstein II, and Betty Comden and Adolph Green. Another label devoted to re-issuing Broadway musicals, most of which have only been available for many years, second-hand, at inflated collectors' prices, is Broadway Angel.

Sophisticated Ladies

This revue which celebrated the music of the great American composer Duke Ellington, was conceived by Donald McKayle and opened at the Lunt-Fontanne Theatre in New York on 1 March 1981. McKayle was also one of the choreographers, along with director Michael Smuin and Henry LeTang, for what was essentially a dynamic song and dance show with an awful lot of class. From a large on-stage orchestra led by Mercer Ellington, Duke's son, there flowed a constant stream of classics from the world of popular music and jazz, such as 'I'm Beginning To See The Light', 'Satin Doll', 'Mood Indigo', 'Take the 'A' Train', 'I Got It Bad (And That Ain't Good)', 'It Don't Mean A Thing (If It Ain't Got That Swing)', and some 30 more. Tap dancer extraordinaire, Gregory Hines, headed a cast of dedicated singers and dancers including Gregg Burge, Judith Jamison, Hinton Battle, P.J. Benjamin, Phyllis Hyman, and Terri Klausner. The original book was dispensed with, and it was left to the superb music to carry the evening. This it did - and for a remarkable 767 performances. For some reason, it was 1992 before the show reached London, and by that time the West End was full of tributes to icons such as Buddy Holly, Louis Jordan, and Cole Porter. *Sophisticated Ladies* joined them for just three months.

Sound Of Music, The

Even before its Broadway opening at the Lunt-Fontanne Theatre on 16 November 1959, *The Sound Of Music* was set to become a financial success. Advance sales exceeded three million dollars and with numerous touring versions, best-selling albums and a blockbuster film, it made a fortune for its composers, Richard Rodgers and Oscar Hammerstein II. The show had a strong narrative book, by Howard Lindsey and Russel Crouse, which was based upon the real-life story of Maria Rainer, her marriage to George von Trapp and her relationship with his family of singing youngsters. The family's evasion of capture by the Nazis during World War II gave the story a tense dramatic core and the fact that the family became professional singers meant that music and song blended well into the narrative, even if, at times, there seemed to be rather more sentiment than reality would have allowed. Starring Mary Martin as Maria, Theodore Bikel and Patricia Neway, the show was filled with songs which became very popular, including the title song, 'Do-Re-Mi', 'My Favorite Things', 'Edelweiss', 'So Long, Farewell', 'Sixteen Going On Seventeen', 'How Can Love Survive?', 'Maria', 'The Lonely Goatherd', and 'Climb Ev'ry Mountain'. Sentimental or not, it is hard to imagine that at the time he was working on this show, Hammerstein was a sick man; less than a year after the Broadway opening he was dead. *The Sound Of Music* played for 1,443 performances, and won Tony Awards for best musical (tied with *Fiorello!*), actress (Martin), featured actress (Neway), musical director (Frederick Dvonch), and scenic design (Oliver Smith). Jean Bayliss and Roger Dann headed the cast of the 1961 London production which surpassed the original and ran for 2,385 performances. New York revivals included one in 1967 at the City Centre, and another in 1990, presented by the New York City Opera, in which the ex-chart-topper Debby Boone played Maria. London audiences saw the show again in 1992 when it was presented at Sadlers Wells, with Liz Robertson and Christopher Cazenove. The 1965 film version, which starred Julie Andrews, won three Oscars and spawned one of the best-selling soundtrack albums of all-time.

South Pacific

Opening on Broadway at the Majestic Theatre on 7 April 1949, *South Pacific* became one of the best-loved and most successful of the fruitful collaborations between Richard Rodgers and Oscar Hammerstein II. The libretto, by Hammerstein and Joshua Logan, was based on stories in James Michener's book *Tales Of The South Pacific*. Its story was set during World War II and dealt in part with racism, a subject not exactly commonplace in American musical comedies. Mary Martin starred as Nellie Forbush, an American nurse who falls in love with a middle-aged French planter, Emil de Becque (Ezio Pinza), but is disturbed by the fact that he has two children by a Polynesian woman who is now dead. Meanwhile, a US Navy lieutenant, Joe Cable (William Tabbert), is attracted to an island girl, Liat (Betta St. John), but, like Nellie, his underlying racial fears cause him to reject her (or it could just be that is is scared stiff of her mother, Bloody Mary [Juanita Hall]). In any event, Joe dies in action and Nellie comes to terms with the colour issue and is reunited with Emile. The marvellous score, which contained several big hits, included 'Some Enchanted Evening', 'Younger Than Springtime', 'Wonderful Guy', 'I'm Gonna Wash That Man Right Outa My Hair', 'Honey Bun', 'There Is Nothin' Like A Dame', 'A Cockeyed Optimist', 'You've Got To Be Carefully Taught', 'This Nearly Was Mine', and two songs which were sung by Juanita Hall, 'Bali Ha'i' 'Dites-moi', and 'Happy Talk'. Myron McCormick played the endearing character of US marine Luther Billis, and he was the only member of the cast to appear in every one of *South Pacific*'s 1,925 performances. The show scooped the Tony Awards, winning for best musical, score, libretto, actress (Martin), actor (Pinza), supporting actress (Hall), supporting actor (McCormick), and director (Joshua Logan). It also became only the second musical (not counting *Oklahoma!*'s special award) to win the prestigious Pulitzer Prize for Drama. Mary Martin reprised her role in 1951 at the Drury Lane Theatre, with Wilbur Evans as de Becque. London audiences were delighted with her performance, and were particularly intrigued by her nightly ritual of washing her hair on-stage. Over the years American revivals have proliferated, but the 1988 London production, with a cast headed by Gemma Craven, which ran for over 400 performances, was said to be the first since 1951. The enormously popular 1958 screen version starred Mitzi Gaynor and Rossano Brazzi, and its soundtrack album spent over five years in the UK chart.

St. Louis Woman

After collaborating with Hoagy Carmichael on the flop show, *Walk With Music* (1940), Johnny Mercer turned to Harold Arlen, the perfect theatrical composer, for this show which opened at the Martin Beck Theatre in New York on 30 March 1946. It did not run for much longer than his previous effort, but it did contain at least one song that is still remembered nearly 50 years later. Arna Bontemps and Countee Cullen wrote the book which was based on Bontemps novel, *God Sends Sunday*. The setting is St. Louis in 1898, where Della Green (Ruby Hill), is happily in harness with saloon owner Biglow Brown (Rex Ingram) before jockey Little Augie (Harold Nicholas) experiences a phenomenal winning streak.

Della is impressed, and switches her affections to the jockey. However, Biglow puts a curse on them both just before he dies, which ruins both the racing and their relationship for a time. 'Come Rain Or Come Shine' is the song from the show that has endured more than any other, but Pearl Bailey, who played the comical character, Butterfly, also delighted audiences with the witty 'Legalize My Name' and 'A Woman's Prerogative'. The remainder of a fine score included 'Any Place I Hang My Hat Is Home', 'I Had Myself A True Love', 'Ridin' On the Moon', 'Sleep Peaceful, Mr. Used-To-Be', 'Lullabye', 'Leavin' Time', and 'Cakewalk My Lady'. The Nicholas Brothers, Harold and Fayard, the acrobatic dancers who featured in several Hollywood musicals during the 40s, performed some extraordinary feats, but, for some reason - certainly not because of the score - the public just would not attend, and St. Louis Woman closed after only 113 peformances. Arlen and Mercer persevered, and adapted some of the material into a 'blues opera', Free And Easy, which spent a brief time in Europe in 1959. The original score - totalling only 29 minutes - was released on CD in 1993.

Stand Up And Sing

After their tremendous successs together in That's A Good Girl (1928), Jack Buchanan and Elsie Randolph teamed up again for this delightful musical comedy which was presented at the London Hippodrome on 5 March 1931. The score was by Phil Charig and Vivian Ellis (music) and Douglas Furber (lyrics). Furber also collaborated with Buchanan on a book which turned out to be a mini-world tour. Much of the action takes place on the cruise ship S.S. Ambrosia and in Egypt where Buchanan, who is pretending to be a valet but is really a toff, goes to retrieve some important papers for his girl's father. The ingénue was played by Anna Neagle in her first important stage role before launching into a long and distinguished film career. She sang 'There's Always Tomorrow', the show's big ballad, with Buchanan, but he and Elsie Randolph (who rather conveniently was a maid to his valet) handled most of the other songs which included 'Take It Or Leave It', 'Mercantile Marine', 'I Would If I Could', 'It's Not You', 'Nobody To Take Care Of Me', 'Keep Smiling', 'Night Time', and Buchanan's speciality 'inebriated dance' routine, 'Hiccup Time In Burgundy'. Also in the cast were familar names such as Sylvia Leslie, Richard Dolman, Richard Murdoch, Vera Pearce, Morris Harvey, and Anton Dolin who occasionally brought his brilliant brand of dancing from the ballet theatre to revue and musical comedy. Stand Up And Sing was an instant hit - West End audiences rejoiced in having Buchanan back on stage after a break of three years. The show ran for 325 performances at the Hippodrome and then toured successfully. During the run the entire second act was broadcast by the BBC, and several years later, in 1945, the complete show, still with Jack Buchanan and Elsie Randolph, was adapted for radio.

Starlight Express

Andrew Lloyd Webber is quoted as saying that this show, which was nick-named 'Squeals On Wheels' by one unkind critic, started out in 1975 as an entertainment intended for children. In 1983 he rewrote it for the benefit of his own children, Imogen and Nicholas, and then, with the help of lyricist Richard Stilgoe, it became the full-blown musical which opened at the Apollo Victoria in London on 27 March 1984. As for so many of Lloyd Webber's shows, the theatre's interior had to be completely re-designed - in this case to accommodate a series of racetracks, gantrys, ramps, and bridges which encircled and dominated the auditorium. More than 20 rollerskaters, pretending to be trains, zoom along the tracks enacting a story in which, after a number of races, Rusty (Ray Shell), a shy little steam engine, triumphs over Greaseball (Jeff Shankley) the flashy diesel locomotive, and gets hitched up to his favourite carriage, Pearl (Stephanie Lawrence). The high-tech effects plus Arlene Phillips' imaginative choreography and Trevor Nunn's direction created what seemed almost like a giant computer game. The loudly amplified score contained elements of rock, blues, country, and many other influences in songs such as 'Call Me Rusty', 'Only He (Has The Power To Move Me)', 'Pumping Iron', 'U.N.C.O.U.P.L.E.D', 'AC-DC', 'Right Place, Right Time', 'One Rock 'N' Roll Too Many', and 'Light At The End Of The Tunnel'. The show proved to be a consistently popular attraction, and in April 1992 became the second longest-running British musical after Cats. Later in the year the production was revised and re-choreographed, and five new songs added before it resumed its record-breaking journey. One member of the new cast, Lon Satton, had played Poppa the old steam locomotive since the first night in 1984. Starlight Express was also reworked for its Broadway run which began in March 1987 and lasted for 761 performances. In September 1993, a 90 minute edition of the show opened at the Las Vegas Hilton in the USA, the first major legitimate production ever to play the gambling capital.

Steele, Tommy

b. Thomas Hicks, 17 December 1936, Bermondsey, London, England. After serving as a merchant seaman Hicks formed the skiffle trio, the Cavemen with Lionel Bart and Mike Pratt, before being discovered by entrepreneur John Kennedy in the 2 I's coffee bar in Soho, London. A name change to Tommy Steele followed and after an appearance at London's Condor Club the boy was introduced to manager Larry

Tommy Steele

Parnes. From thereon, his rise to stardom was meteoric. Using the old 'working-class boy makes good' angle, Kennedy launched the chirpy cockney in the unlikely setting of a debutante's ball. Class conscious Fleet Street lapped up the idea of Tommy as the 'Deb's delight' and took him to their hearts. His debut single, 'Rock With The Caveman' was an immediate Top 20 hit and although the follow-up 'Doomsday Rock'/'Elevator Rock' failed to chart, the management was unfazed. Their confidence was rewarded when Steele hit number 1 in the UK charts with a cover of Guy Mitchell's 'Singing The Blues' in January 1957. By this point, he was Britain's first and premier rock 'n' roll singer and, without resorting to sexual suggestiveness, provoked mass teenage hysteria unseen since the days of Johnnie Ray. At one stage, he had four songs in the Top 30, although he never restricted himself to pure rock 'n' roll. A bit part in the film Kill Me Tomorrow led to an autobiographical musical The Tommy Steele Story, which also spawned a book of the same title. For a time Steele performed the twin role of rock 'n' roller and family entertainer but his original persona faded towards the end of the 50s. Further movie success in The Duke Wore Jeans (1958) and Tommy The Toreador (1959) effectively redefined his image. His rocking days closed with covers of Ritchie Valens' 'Come On Let's Go' and Freddy Cannon's 'Tallahassee Lassie'. The decade ended with the novelty 'Little White Bull', after which it was goodbye to rock 'n' roll.

After appearing on several variety bills during the late 50s, Steele sampled the 'legit' side of show business in 1960 when he played Tony Lumpkin in She Stoops To Conquer at the Old Vic, and he was back in the straight theatre again in 1969, in the role of Truffaldino in The Servant Of Two Masters at the Queen's Theatre. In years between those two plays, he experienced some of the highlights of his career. In 1963, he starred as Arthur Kipps in the stage musical, Half A Sixpence, which ran for 18 months in the West End before transferring to Broadway in 1965; Steele re-created the role in the film version in 1967. A year later, he appeared in another major musical movie, Finan's Rainbow, with Fred Astaire and Petula Clark. His other films included Touch It Light, It's All Happening, The Happiest Millionaire and Where's Jack? In 1974, Steele made one of his rare television appearances, in the autobiographical, My Life, My Song, and, in the same year, appeared at the London Palladium in Hans Anderson, the first of three stage adaptations of famous Hollywood films. He also starred in the revival three years later. In 1979-80 his one-man musical show was resident at London's Prince of Wales Theatre for a record 60 weeks - the Variety Club Of Great Britain made him their Entertainer Of The Year. He was also awarded the OBE. Steele was back at the Palladium again in 1983

and 1989, in the highly popular Singin' In The Rain, which he also directed. In the latter capacity he tried, too late as it transpired, to save impresario Harold Fielding's Ziegfeld (1988) from becoming a spectacular flop. Fielding had originally cast Steele in Half A Sixpence some 25 years earlier. Off-stage in the 80s, Steele published his first novel, a thriller, The Final Run; had one of his paintings exhibited at the Royal Academy; was commisioned by Liverpool City Council to fashion a bronze statue of 'Eleanor Rigby' as a tribute to the Beatles; and composed 'A Portrait Of Pablo' and 'Rock Suite - An Elderly Person's Guide To Rock'. The third, and least successful of Steele's movie-to-stage transfers was Some Like It Hot (1992). A hybrid of Billy Wilder's classic film, and the Broadway stage musical Sugar (1972), it received derisory reviews ('The show's hero is Mr Steele's dentist'), and staggered along for three months in the West End on the strength of its star's previous box-office appeal. In 1993 Steele was presented with the Hans Andersen Award at the Danish Embassy in London. A year later he was back on the road again with 'A Dazzling New Song & Dance Spectacular' entitled What A Show!.

Albums: The Tommy Steele Stage Show (1957), The Tommy Steele Story (1957), Stars Of 6.05 (late 50s), The Duke Wore Jeans (1958, film soundtrack), Tommy The Toreador (1959, film soundtrack), So This Is Broadway (1964), Light Up The Sky (1959), Cinderella (1959, stage cast), Get Happy With Tommy (1960), It's All Happening (1962), Half A Sixpence (1963, stage recording), Everything's Coming Up Broadway (1967), The Happiest Millionire (1967), My Life My Song (1974), Hans Andersen (1978, London stage cast), with Sally Ann Howes Henry Fielding's Hans Anderson (1985). Compilations: The Happy World Of Tommy Steele (1969), The World Of Tommy Steele, Volume 2 (1971), Focus On Tommy Steele (1977), The Family Album (1979), 20 Greatest Hits (1983), Tommy Steele And The Steelmen - The Rock 'N' Roll Years (1988), Handful Of Songs (1993).

Further reading: Quincy's Quest, Tommy Steele, based on the children's television programme he scripted. Tommy Steele, John Kennedy.

Stilgoe, Richard

b. 28 March 1943, Camberley, Surrey, England. Now known as a television presenter and entertainer, Richard Stilgoe came into showbusiness via the Cambridge Footlights. He also played piano in a 60s beat group called Tony Snow And The Blizzards. Arriving at the BBC in the 70s he appeared regularly on shows such as A Class By Himself, Nationwide, That's Life, and Stilgoe's Around, often performing a self-written, highly topical little ditty. Undoubtedly talented - he plays 14 instruments and sings in opera - Stilgoe broke new ground in the 80s when he teamed up with composer Andrew Lloyd Webber to write the lyrics for the hit shows *Starlight Express* and *Phantom Of The Opera*. In 1985, he performed in a show with Peter Skellern for the charity organization, the Lords Taverners, called 'Stilgoe And Skellern Stompin' At The Savoy'. This led to a number of successful tours as a partnership. In 1991, Stilgoe was writing children's musicals while also devoting time to a small forest which he is growing for the sole purpose of making musical instruments.

Albums: *Live Performance* (1977), *Bodywork* (1988).

Stop The World - I Want To Get Off

This fresh, novel - some say unique - entertainment with book music and lyrics by the new team of Anthony Newley and Leslie Bricusse, opened at the Queen's Theatre in London on 20 July 1961. Newley also directed, and played the leading role of Littlechap whose travels through the Seven Ages of Man - from factory teaboy to an Earldom - inevitably end in disillusionment. After taking the first step by marrying his boss's daughter, Evie (Anna Quayle), Littlechap's rise to fame and power is swift. His new life-style brings him into contact with other women (all played by Quayle), including an athletic Russian, Anya ('I will come to your room at two o'clock. Please be ready - I'm playing football at half past'), the American nightclub singer Ginnie, and Ilse, an au pair from Germany. Throughout it all, he is unable to find true happiness for himself and his family, or father the son he constantly yearns for. All the action takes place on a set designed by Sean Kenny, which resembles a section of a circus tent with bare planks representing the seating. Newley, dressed like a clown with white face, and wearing baggy pants held up by big braces, sang the show's three big numbers, 'Gonna Build A Mountain', 'Once In A Lifetime', and 'What Kind Of Fool Am I?', and he also had the amusing 'Lumbered', and a lovely ballad, 'Someone Nice Like You'. The score also included 'I Wanna Be Rich', 'Glorious Russia', 'Meilinki Meilchick', 'Typische Deutsche', 'Nag Nag Nag', 'All-American', and 'Mumbo Jumbo'. The London run of 556 performances was followed by an almost identical stay in New York, where Anna Quayle won a Tony Award, but Newley was beaten by Zero Mostel's bravura performance in *A Funny Thing Happened On The Way To The Forum*. Sammy Davis Jnr., who had a hit with 'What Kind Of Fool Am I?' in the US and UK, starred in a revised revival of the show on Broadway in 1978, and Newley recreated his original role in a 1989 West End production which lasted for five weeks and reportedly lost £600,000. There have been two unsuccessful film versions: in 1966 with Tony Tanner and Millicent Martin; and a 1979 'disaster', *Sammy Stops The World*, with Sammy Davis Jnr. and Marian Mercer.

Streisand, Barbra

b. 24 April 1942, New York City, New York, USA. From childhood Streisand was eager to make a career in show business, happily singing and 'playacting' for neighbours in Brooklyn, where she was born and raised. At the age of 15, she had a trial run with a theatrical company in upstate New York and by 1959, the year she graduated, was convinced that she could make a success of her chosen career. She still sang for fun, but was set on being a stage actress. The lack of opportunites in straight plays drove her to try singing instead and she entered and won a talent contest at The Lion, a gay bar in Greenwich Village. The prize was a booking at the club and this was followed by more club work, including an engagement at the Bon Soir which was later extended and established her as a fast-rising new singer. Appearances in off-Broadway revues followed, in which she acted and sang. Towards the end of 1961 she was cast in *I Can Get It For You Wholesale*, a musical play with songs by Harold Rome. The show was only moderately successful but Streisand's notices were excellent (as were those of another newcomer, Elliott Gould). She was invited to appear on an 'original cast' recording of the show, which was followed by another record date, to make an album of Rome's *Pins And Needles*, a show he had written 25 years earlier. The records and her Bon Soir appearances brought a television date and in 1962, on the strength of these, Columbia Records offered her a recording date of her own. With arrangements by Peter Matz, who was also responsible for the charts used by Noël Coward at his 1955 Las Vegas appearance, Streisand made her first album, which included such songs as 'Cry Me A River', 'Happy Days Are Here Again' and 'Who's Afraid Of The Big, Bad Wolf?'. Within two weeks of the album's release, in February 1963, Streisand was the top-selling female vocalist in the USA. Two Grammy Awards followed, for Best Album and for Streisand as Best Female Vocalist (for 'Happy Days Are Here Again'). Streisand's career was now unstoppable.

She had more successful club appearances in 1963 and released another strong album, which she followed by opening for Liberace at Las Vegas and appearing at Los Angeles's Coconut Grove and the Hollywood Bowl. That same remarkable year she married Elliott Gould and she was engaged to appear in a forthcoming Broadway show, *Funny Girl*. Based upon the life of Fanny Brice, *Funny Girl* had a troubled pre-production history, but once it opened it proved to have all the qualities its principal producer, Ray Stark, (who had nurtured the show for 10 years), believed it to have. With songs by Jule Styne and Ray Merrill, amongst which were 'People' and 'Don't Rain On My Parade', the show was a massive success, running for 1,348 performances and giving Streisand

Barbra Streisand

cover stories in *Time* and *Life* magazines. Early in 1966 Streisand opened *Funny Girl* in London but the show's run was curtailed when she became pregnant. During the mid-60s she starred in a succession of popular and award-winning television spectaculars. Albums of the music from these shows were big-sellers and one included her first composition, 'Ma Premiere Chanson'. In 1967, she went to Hollywood to make the film version of *Funny Girl*, the original Styne-Merrill score being extended by the addition of some of the songs Fanny Brice had performed during her own Broadway career. These included 'Second-Hand Rose' and 'My Man'. In addition to *Funny Girl*, Streisand's film career included roles in *Hello, Dolly!* and *On A Clear Day You Can See Forever*. The film of *Funny Girl* (1968) was a hit, with Streisand winning one of two Oscars awarded that year for Best Actress (the other winner was Katharine Hepburn).

By the time she came to the set to make her second Hollywood film, *Hello, Dolly!* (1969), Streisand had developed an unenviable reputation as a meddlesome perfectionist who wanted, and usually succeeded in obtaining, control over every aspect of the films in which she appeared. Although in her later films, especially those which she produced, her demands seemed increasingly like self-indulgence, her perfectionism worked for her on the many albums and stage appearances which followed throughout the 70s. This next decade saw changes in Streisand's public persona and also in the films she worked on. Developing her childhood ambitions to act, she turned more and more to straight acting roles, leaving the songs for her record albums and television shows. Among her films of the 70s were *The Owl And The Pussycat* (1970), *What's Up, Doc?* (1972), *The Way We Were* (1973), *Funny Lady* (1975), a sequel to *Funny Girl*, and *A Star Is Born* (1976). For the latter she co-wrote (with Paul Williams) a song, 'Evergreen', which won an Oscar as Best Song. Streisand continued to make well-conceived and perfectly executed albums, most of which sold in large numbers. She even recorded a set of the more popular songs written by classical composers such as Debussy and Schumann.

Although her albums continued to attract favourable reviews and sell well, her films became open season for critics and were markedly less popular with fans. The shift became most noticeable after *A Star Is Born* was released and its damaging self-indulgence was apparent to all. Nevertheless, the film won admirers and several Golden Globe Awards. She had an unexpected number 1 hit in 1978 with 'You Don't Bring Me Flowers', a duet with Neil Diamond, and she also shared the microphone with Donna Summer on 'Enough Is Enough', a disco number which reached Platinum, and with Barry Gibb on the album, *Guilty*. Her film career continued into the early 80s

with *All Night Long* (1981) and *Yentl*, (1983) which she co-produced and directed. By the mid-80s Streisand's career appeared to be on cruise. However, she starred in and wrote the music for *Nuts* (1987), a film which received mixed reviews. Growing concern for ecological matters revealed themselves in public statements and on such occasions as the recording of her 1986 video/album, *One Voice*. In 1991 she was criticized for another directorial assignment on *Prince Of Tides*. As a performer, Streisand was one of the greatest showbiz phenomenons of the 60s. Her wide vocal range and a voice which unusually blends sweetness with strength, helps make Streisand one of the outstanding dramatic singers in popular music. Her insistence upon perfection has meant that her many records are exemplars for other singers. Her 1991 movie, *Prince Of Tides*, which she also directed, was nominated for seven Oscars. Two years later, she was being talked of as a close confidante and advisor to the newly elected US President Clinton, although she still found the time to return - on record at least - to where it all started, when she released *Back To Broadway*. In November 1993 it was reported that the singer had given away her £10 million Californian estate 'in an attempt to save the earth'. The 26 acres of landscaped gardens with six houses and three swimming pools would become the Barbra Streisand Centre For Conservancy Studies. She recouped the money early in January 1994, by giving two 90-minute concerts at MGM's new Grand Hotel and theme park in Las Vegas for a reported fee of £13 million.

Selected albums: *The Barbra Streisand Album* (1962), *The Second Barbra Streisand Album* (1963), *Barbra Streisand: The Third Album* (1964), *Funny Girl* (1964), *People* (1964), *My Name Is Barbra* (1965), *Color Me Barbra* (1966), *Je M'Appelle Barbra* (1967), *What About Today?* (1969), *Stoney End* (1970), *Greatest Hits* (1970), *Barbra Joan Streisand* (1971), *Classical Barbra* (1974), *Butterfly* (1975), *Lazy Afternoon* (1975), *Streisand Superman* (1977), *Songbird* (1978), *Wet* (1979), *Guilty* (1980), *Memories* (1981), *Yentl* (1983, soundtrack), *Emotion* (1984), *The Broadway Album* (1985), *One Voice* (1986), *Nuts: Original Motion Picture Soundtrack* (1987), *Til I Loved You* (1988), *A Collection: Greatest Hits...And More* (1989), *Just For The Record...* (1991), *The Prince Of Tides* (1991, soundtrack), *Butterfly* (1992), *Back To Broadway* (1993).

Further reading: *Streisand: The Woman and the Legend*, James Spada. *Barbra Streisand, The Woman, The Myth, The Music*, Shawn Considine.

Strike Up the Band

Regarded by some as having been ahead of its time, this somewhat bitter satirical spoof on war, big business, and politics in America at the time of the Depression, proved too much for the public to take first time round. In 1927, it closed during out-of-town tryouts, and only made Broadway in a revised and toned-down version some three years later. By the time the show opened at the Times Square Theatre on 14 January 1930, George S. Kaufman and his acerbic book about a 'cheese tariff' war between the US and the Swiss, had been replaced by Morrie Ryskind and a sweeter plot about chocolate. Nevertheless, it was still a radical departure from the usual 'moon and June' style of musical comedy, and paved the way for other more socially relevant shows such as *Of Thee I Sing*, *I'd Rather Be Right*, and *Let 'Em Eat Cake*. The comedy team of Bobby Clark and Paul McCullough led the cast, along with Blanche Ring, Jerry Goff, Dudley Clements, and Doris Carson. George and Ira Gershwin wrote the score which contained at least three enduring items, including the rousing title song. 'Soon' which has received many memorable readings over the years, including one by Ella Fitzgerald on her tribute album to the composers, and 'I've Got A Crush On You', and in 1993 by Frank Sinatra and Barbra Streisand on his album *Duets*. The rest of the numbers, which included 'Madamoiselle In New Rochelle', 'Hanging Around With You', 'If I Became President', 'I Mean To Say', and the highly amusing 'A Typical Self-Made American', were played in fine style by Red Nichols Orchestra, whose personnel included Glenn Miller, Gene Krupa, Jimmy Dorsey, Jack Teagarden and Benny Goodman. Given the show's innovative and original approach, a run of 191 performances was probably as much as the producers could have expected.

Strouse, Charles

b. 7 June 1928, New York City, New York, USA. A composer who has experienced the sweet taste of Broadway success - but not for some considerable time. When Strouse graduated from the Eastman School of Music he intended to make a career in the classical field, and studied for a time with Aaron Copland. After meeting lyricist Lee Adams in 1949, he changed course, and during the early 50s they contributed songs to revues at the popular Green Mansions summer resort, and in 1956 they had some numbers interpolated into the Off Broadway shows *The Littlest Revue* and *Shoestring '57*. Their big break came four years later with *Bye Bye Birdie*, which starred Dick Van Dyke and Chita Rivera and ran for 607 performances. The witty and tuneful score included 'Kids!', 'A Lot Of Livin' To Do', and 'Put On A Happy Face'. *All American* (1962), a musical about college football, failed to score heavily, but *Golden Boy* (1964) lasted for 569 performances. on the sheer strength of Sammy Davis Jnr.'s appeal. *It's A Bird, It's A Plane, It's Superman* (1966), which was based on the syndicated comic-strip, came down to

earth with a bump after only 129 performances. It was four years before Strouse and Adams took off again with *Applause*, their second big hit which ran for over two years, and, like *Golden Boy*, had a gilt-edged box office star in Lauren Bacall. In 1971 Strouse wrote his own lyrics for *Six* - which ran for eight - performances, that is, Off Broadway. The composer collaborated once again with Adams for *I And Albert* in 1972 - presented in London only - but audiences there were definitely not amused. Strouse's hit-of-a-lifetime came five years later - but not in collaboration with Lee Adams. Martin Charnin provided the lyrics for another Strouse show that was based on a comic-strip - in this case Little Orphan Annie. Together with librettist Thomas Meehan they turned it into *Annie*, the hottest Broadway ticket of the 70s which ran for 2,377 performances. From then, until 1990, Strouse had nothing but flops - and some real beauties at that: *A Broadway Musical* (one performance), *Flowers For Algernon* (London 28 performances) - retitled for New York as *Charley And Algernon* (17), *Bring Back Birdie* (four), *Dance A Little Closer* (one), *Mayor* (268, but still a failure), *Rags* (four), and the follow-up to his mega-hit, *Annie 2* (closed in Washington). In August 1993, the latter show, scaled-down and retitled *Annie Warbucks*, opened Off Broadway. Experienced Broadway watchers say that, in spite of all the setbacks, the musical theatre has not seen the last of Charles Strouse.

Student Prince In Heidelberg, The

The geographical qualification 'In Heidelberg' was dropped from the title after the original production which opened at the Jolson's Theatre in New York on 2 December 1924, and went on to become the longest-running Broadway musical of the 20s. With music by Sigmund Romberg and book and lyrics by Dorothy Donnelly, this operetta was based on the play, *Old Heidelberg*, by Rudolf Bleichman, which was adapted from Wilhelm Meyer-Forster's *Alt Heidelberg*. Set in 1860, the story concerns Prince Karl-Franz of Karlsberg (Howard Marsh), who takes lodgings at the Inn of the Three Golden Apples while he is studying at Heidelberg University. He falls in love with a waitress there, Kathie (Ilse Marvenga), and is about to elope with her when he hears that his father, the king, is dying. Karl-Franz must leave to assume his regal responsibilites. When they are re-united two years later, they realise that, although they still love each other, their lives will be better spent apart. Romberg and Donnelly's score was in the grand operetta style, and contained several memorable numbers, including 'The Drinking Song', 'Serenade', 'Deep In My Heart, Dear', 'Just We Two', and 'Golden Days'. After an impressive run of 608 performances, Ilse Marvenga recreated her role in the 1926 London production which folded after less than three months. Rather more successful revivals were presented in 1929, 1944, and particularly in 1968 when a revised version, with extra songs, and starring the highly popular actor-manager John Hanson, played at the Cambridge Theatre. Broadway audiences saw the show again in 1931 and 1943, and there was a production by the New York City Opera in 1980. Film versions were released in 1927, with Ramon Navarro and Norma Shearer, and in 1954, with Edmund Purdom (sung by Mario Lanza) and Ann Blyth.

Styne, Jule

b. Julius K. Stein, 31 December 1905, London, England. Even before his family emigrated to the USA when he was aged seven, Styne had become an accomplished pianist. His studies continued in his new homeland and he was soon appearing as piano soloist with symphony orchestras. Deflected from a career as a concert pianist because his hands were thought to be too small, Styne tried composing popular songs. His first attempts included 'The Guy With The Polka-Dot Tie' and 'The Moth And The Flame'. After leaving school in 1922 he formed a band, which at one time included Benny Goodman in its ranks, but continued writing music. He had his first big success in 1926 with 'Sunday' (lyrics by Ned Miller) and continued working with Chicago-based jazz-orientated dance groups including the band led by Ben Pollack. In 1932 he adopted the spelling of his name by which he was thereafter known to avoid confusion with another musician named Jules Stein. Styne spent the mid-30s working in New York as a vocal coach and it was in this capacity that in 1937 he was hired to work in Hollywood. He continued to write songs and background music for films. Amongst his song successes from the 40s are 'Who Am I?' (lyrics by Walter Bulock), 'I've Heard That Song Before' (Sammy Cahn) and 'I Don't Want To Walk Without You' (Frank Loesser). Soon, Styne and Cahn formalized their partnership and theirs proved to be one of the most fruitful of such collaborations. Amongst their songs were 'I'll Walk Alone', 'There Goes That Song Again', 'And Then You Kissed Me', 'Five Minutes More', 'Time After Time', 'It's Magic', 'Three Coins In The Fountain', 'It's Been A Long, Long Time', 'Saturday Night (Is The Loneliest Night Of The Week)', 'Let It Snow! Let It Snow! Let It Snow!', 'The Things We Did Last Summer', 'I Fall In Love Too Easily', 'I Believe' and 'Give Me A Song With A Beautiful Melody'. In 1947, Styne and Cahn collaborated on a stage musical, High Button Shoes, which ran for 727 performances. The following year Styne formed a new partnership, this time with Leo Robin as his lyricist. This team wrote Gentlemen Prefer Blondes which ran for 740 performances thanks partly to the dynamism of Carol Channing in the lead and

songs like 'Diamonds Are A Girl's Best Friend' and 'Bye Bye, Baby'. Styne's next few Broadway shows were undistinguished but he continued to write good songs for them, including 'Hold Me-Hold Me-Hold Me' (lyrics by Betty Comden and Adolph Green), 'How Do You Speak To An Angel?', 'Ev'ry Street's A Boulevard In Old New York' (both with Bob Hilliard) and 'Distant Melody' (Comden and Green). Styne hit again with Bells Are Ringing from which came 'Just In Time', 'Long Before I Knew You' and 'The Party's Over', all with lyrics by Comden and Green. In 1959 Styne had another Broadway success with Gypsy, from which came 'Everything's Coming Up Roses', 'Let Me Entertain You', and 'Together Wherever We Go', all with lyrics by Stephen Sondheim.

Although his next Broadway shows were less popular Styne still wrote some good songs, including 'Make Someone Happy' (Comden and Green) from Do Re Mi and 'Come Once In A Lifetime' (Comden and Green) from Subways Are For Sleeping. Next in Styne's musicals was Funny Girl, his greatest success, which made a star of Barbra Streisand. Styne's collaborator on this show was Bob Merrill and their songs included 'People' and 'Don't Rain On My Parade'. Later musicals for which Styne wrote suffered in comparison with Funny Girl's huge success although Sugar, based upon Billy Wilder's 1959 film, Some Like It Hot, was better than several. He has continued to be active into the 90s, although his 1993 Broadway musical Red Shoes closed after only three days. Apart from writing for Broadway, Styne has also produced shows including the successful 1952 revival of Pal Joey. One of the most respected American songwriters, Styne has been the recipient of numerous awards and honours and even found time during the 80s to teach at New York University.

Sugar

Based on the enormously popular 1959 film Some Like It Hot, this musical, which had a score by the Funny Girl team of Jule Styne and Bob Merrill, opened at the Majestic Theatre in New York on 9 April 1972. Peter Stone's book stayed closely to the original story of two musicians who, having accidentally witnessed the notorious St. Valentine's Day Massacre in Chicago, flee to Miami disguised as members of an all-female orchestra. Robert Morse and Tony Roberts played the roles that were taken in the film by Jack Lemmon and Tony Curtis, Cyril Ritchard was the eccentric millionaire who found himself completely beguiled by Morse in drag, and Elaine Joyce did her best to make people forget the unforgettable Marilyn Monroe. The score was suitably 20s in style and included numbers such as 'When You Meet A Man In Chicago', '(Doing It For) Sugar', 'Sun On My Face', 'What Do You Give To A Man Who's Had

Mickey Rooney (*Sugar Babies*)

Everything?', 'Beautiful Through And Through', 'We Could Be Close', 'It's Always Love', 'Hey, Why Not!', and 'Penniless Bums'. Gower Champion contributed some slick choreography, and *Sugar* stayed around for 505 performances. Twenty years later a revised edition with the orginal film title, *Some Like It Hot*, reached London's West End. The emphasis was switched from the character of Sugar to the show's star, Tommy Steele, and when he had to leave the cast for a time following an on-stage accident, the production went rapidly downhill and closed after a run of three months with losses estimated at around £2 million.

Sugar Babies

This celebration of the golden age of American burlesque entertainment between 1905 and 1930, opened at the Mark Hellinger Theatre in New York on 8 October 1979. It was conceived by Ralph G. Allen and Harry Rigby, two students of the burlesque form, who based several of the numbers directly on famous historic routines. Most of the music came from the catalogue of the distinguished American composer Jimmy McHugh, with lyrics by Dorothy Fields, Harold Adamson, and Al Dubin. Additional music and lyrics were by Arthur Malvin. The obvious choice for the comedian and song and dance man to follow in the oversized footsteps of legendary burlesque comics such as Bert Lahr, Bobby Clark, and W.C. Fields, was one of America's most cherished clowns, Mickey Rooney. His co-star was Ann Miller, whose long legs and precision dancing style showed no noticeable signs of deterioration since she appeared in movies such as *Kiss Me, Kate* and *On The Town* more than 25 years previously. The sketch material was strictly 'adults only', but the songs, which included classics such as 'Exactly Like You', 'I Feel A Song Comin' On', 'I'm In The Mood For Love', and 'On Sunny Side Of The Street', appealed to young and old alike. The show ran for a remarkable 1,208 performances and then undertook succcessful US road tours. The 1988 London production, with Rooney and Miller, appealed at first, but then went under after a run of just over three months.

Sunday In The Park With George

Stephen Sondheim and his librettist and director James Lapine used a painting by the 19th century impressionist painter Georges Seurat as the basis for this innovative musical which opened at the Booth Theatre in New York on 2 May 1984. 'A Sunday Afternoon On The Island Of La Grande Jatte' has been described as 'a multi-layered panorama of Parisian life and a masterpiece of pointillism - the method of building a painting from minute dots of blending colours'. In the show's first act the painting gradually comes to life as George (Mandy Patinkin) obsessively creates the characters and places them on the canvas, eventually progressing to the complete tableau. Meanwhile, the relationship with Dot (Bernadette Peters), his mistress–model, falls apart, and although they are expecting a child, she leaves him to marry someone else. The second act advances the plot by 100 years. The setting is now present-day New York, and Seurat and Dot's great-grandson, also named George, is 'an American mulitmedia sculptor likewise bedevilled by a philistine society'. Sondheim and Lapine's point of view about 'the angst of artistic creation' comes over loud and clear throughout the piece. Sondheim's score was complex and intricate, and included 'Sunday In The Park With George', 'No Life', 'Colour And Light', 'Gossip', 'The Day Off', 'Everybody Loves Louis', 'Finishing The Hat', 'We Do Not Belong Together', 'Beautiful', 'Sunday', 'It's Hot Up Here', 'Chromolume No. 7', 'Putting It Together', 'Children And Art', 'Lesson No. 8', and 'Move On'. Considering the quality of the piece, a run of 604 performances was somewhat disappointing. There were Tony Awards for the brilliant scenic design (Tony Straiges) and lighting (Richard Nelson), and the show was voted best musical by the New York Drama Critics Circle. It also won the 1985 Pulitzer Prize for Drama. Five years later, *Sunday In The Park With George* was presented in London by the Royal National Theatre. That production gained Olivier Awards for best musical and actor (Philip Quast).

Sunny

After Marilyn Miller's great success in Florenz Ziegfeld's *Sally* (1920), another distinguished American producer, Charles Dillingham, arranged for her to board this vehicle for her singing and dancing talents which arrived at the New Amsterdam Theatre in New York on 22 September 1925, and stayed for 517 performances. Otto Harbach and Oscar Hammerstein II wrote the more than fanciful book in which Sunny Peters (Miller), a star equestrian performer in an English circus, stows away on an ocean liner to be near her beloved, Tom Warren (Paul Frawley). Almost 70 years later, it is difficult to understand why Sunny has to marry - not Tom - but his best friend, Jim Deming (Jack Donahue), in order to disembark in the USA. Also in the cast were Clifton Webb, Mary Hay, Joseph Cawthorn, Cliff Edwards, and George Olsen And His Orchestra. The score, with music by Jerome Kern and lyrics by Harbach and Hammerstein, included 'Let's Not Say Goodnight Till It's Morning', 'Sunny', 'D'Ye Love Me?', 'Two Little Bluebirds', 'I Might Grow Fond Of You', and 'Who'. Jack Buchanan made the latter number his own when *Sunny* opened in London at the Hippodrome in 1926. Joining him in the West End production which ran for 363 performances, were Elsie Randolph, Binnie Hale, Maidie Hope, and Claude Hulbert. An early 'talkie' version of *Sunny* released in 1930 starred Marilyn Miller, Lawrence Grey, and Jack Donahue, and there was a remake in 1941 with Anna Neagle and Ray Bolger.

Sunset Boulevard

Composer Andrew Lloyd Webber's long awaited musical adaptation of Billy Wilder's classic black and white movie which starred Gloria Swanson and William Holden, finally surmounted a host of technical problems and opened at the refurbished Adelphi Theatre in London on 12 July 1993. The book and lyrics were by Don Black, who had previously collaborated with Lloyd Webber, and the author Christopher Hampton who was making his debut in the musical theatre. Their libretto, which stayed closely to the original screenplay, told the familiar story of Norma Desmond (Patti LuPone), the ageing silent movie queen, who enlists the help of the failed and penniless scriptwriter Joe Gillis (Kevin Anderson) in her efforts to make a comeback. Too late he finds that he is hopelessly trapped. The score contained several powerful ballads, particularly 'With One Look' and 'As If We Never Said Goodbye', and there were others which could prove just as durable such as 'Surrender', 'New Ways To Dream', 'The Perfect Year', and 'Too Much In Love To Care'. There were also a couple of amusing comedy numbers, 'The Lady's Paying' and 'Let's Have Lunch'. The £3 million production received generally good, if not enthusiastic reviews. Most critics thought that Patti LuPone looked too young for the role, but there were no reservations about her voice. There was also praise for John Napier's 'wonderfully elaborate rococo set'. Going against convention, *Sunset Boulevard* had its US premiere, not on Broadway, but in Los Angeles. By the time the show opened there in December 1993, it had been drastically reworked and a new song, 'Every Movie's A Circus', added. There was a first night standing ovation for film actress Glenn Close who played Norma, and the lavish post-premiere party was held at Paramount Studios where the original 1950 film was made.
Further reading: *Sunset Boulevard - From Movie To Musical*, George Perry.

Sweeney Todd

A 'Musical Thriller' which is often regarded as Stephen Sondheim's best work to date - certainly his most grisly - *Sweeney Todd* opened at the Uris Theatre in New York on 1 March 1979. Sondheim and librettist Hugh Wheeler based their musical adaptation of the legendary 'demon barber of Fleet Street' on Christopher Bond's play, *Sweeney Todd*, which played at the Theatre Royal, Stratford East in

1973. As Wheeler's story begins, the barber Sweeney Todd (Len Cariou) is just returning to London after 15 years in enforced exile. He discovers that his wife has been driven to her death (or so he thinks) and his daughter made a ward of court by the man who sentenced him - the evil Judge Turpin (Edmund Lyndeck). Intent on revenge, he rents a room above a shop run by Mrs. Lovett (Angela Lansbury), who sells 'The Worst Pies In London'. While waiting for his chance to dispose of Judge Turpin, Todd lures other unsuspecting victims to his barbers' chair. He slits their throats before passing them over to Mrs. Lovett, who uses her meat grinder and oven to turn them into pies. Although he gets the Judge in the end, justice is seen to be done when Sweeney Todd is slain with one of his own razors, and lies beside the body of his wife who he has inadvertently murdered. Sondheim's superb 'near-operatic' score, which has been called 'Grand Guignol' and 'quasi-Brechtian' in style, ranged from the witty list song 'A Little Priest' to tender ballads such as 'Not While I'm Around' and 'Johanna', along with other numbers such as 'Pretty Women', 'By The Sea', 'Epiphany', 'Poor Thing', 'God, That's Good', and 'The Ballad Of Sweeney Todd'. The show ran for 558 performances and won eight Tony Awards, including best musical, book, score, actor (Cariou), actress (Lansbury) and director (Harold Prince). A New York revival was presented at the Circle In the Square in 1989, with Bob Gunton and Beth Fowler, and the Paper Mill Playhouse offered a version with George Hearn and Judy Kaye in 1992. The 1980 London production at Drury Lane, with Denis Quilley and Sheila Hancock, was generally held to be unsatisfactory, but the 1993 'chamber version', presented by the Royal National Theatre and starring Julia McKenzie and Alun Armstrong, was widely acclaimed.

Sweet Adeline

Following her tremendous success in *Showboat* (1927), Jerome Kern and Oscar Hammerstein II wrote this 'Musical Romance Of the Gay Nineties' for Helen Morgan, the bluesy torch singer who could wring a tear from even the most innocuous ballad. Not that there are any of those in this score which included 'Why Was I Born?', one of the composers' most heart-felt and enduring numbers, along with several other bitter-sweet items which were introduced by Morgan, including 'Here Am I', 'Don't Ever Leave Me', and ''Twas Not so Long Ago'. *Sweet Adeline* opened at Hammerstein's Theatre in New York on 3 September 1929, with a book by Hammerstein which was set in 1898 and concerns Addie Schmidt who leaves her father's beer garden in Hoboken, New Jersey, for singing stardom amid the bright lights of Broadway. There were several more appealing numbers in what is accepted as one of the loveliest of

Kern's early scores, including a bluesy piece, 'Some Girl Is On Your Mind' which was sung by a group of Addie's boyfriends, the waltz ballad 'The Sun Is About To Rise', 'Spring Is Here', 'Out Of The Blue', and the lively 'Play Us A Polka Dot'. *Sweet Adeline* was an immediate success and looked set for a long run. Then came the Wall Street Crash, and although the show rode out the storm for a while, it was forced to close in April 1930 after a total of 234 performances. The 1935 film version had a revised book, and Irene Dunne.

Sweet Charity

Veteran lyricist Dorothy Fields teamed with the much younger composer Cy Coleman on the score for this warm-hearted musical which opened at the Palace Theatre in New York on 29 January 1966. Neil Simon's book, which was based on the Federico Fellini film *Nights Of Cabiria*, changed the movie's main character from a prostitute to a dance hall hostess named Charity (Gwen Verdon) who is desperately seeking love, marriage, and respectability. She becomes romantically involved with an Italian film star, Vittorio Vidal (James Luisi), and a neurotic accountant, Oscar Lindquist (John McMartin) who she is set to marry until her job comes between them. Bob Fosse won a Tony Award for his innovative and exciting choreography, and there was not a dull moment in a score that contained a whole range of marvellous songs, including 'Big Spender', 'Rich Man's Frug', 'If My Friends Could See Me Now', 'Too Many Tomorrows', 'There's Gotta Be Something Better Than This', 'Rhythm Of Life', 'Baby, Dream Your Dream', 'Where Am I Going?', 'I'm A Brass Band', and 'I Love to Cry At Weddings'. Gwen Verdon's portrayal of the loveable Charity was funny and tender, but she was edged out of the Tonys by Angela Lansbury who triumphed for her performance in *Mame*. *Sweet Charity* ran for 608 performances and was revived in 1986 with Debbie Allen in the lead. The 1967 London production starred the South African actress Juliet Prowse, and two years later a film version was released with Shirley MacLaine, John McMartin, Chita Rivera, and Sammy Davis Jnr..

Sweethearts

Most operettas are cherished for their sometimes glorious music, and gently mocked for their 'you cannot be serious' librettos. *Sweethearts*, which opened at the New Amsterdam Theatre in New York on 8 September 1913, was typical of the genré. Even so, Harry B. Smith and Fred De Gresac's book for this show stretched credibilty to breaking point and beyond. The romantic story begins when the infant Sylvia (Christie MacDonald) is found in a tulip garden by Dame Paula (also known as Mother Goose) who is

in charge of the Laundry of the White Geese. Sylvia is raised as her daughter until one day, purely by chance, she meets Prince Franz (Thomas Conkey) and they fall in love. Everything works out well because Sylvia is really the Crown Princess of the Kingdom of Zilania, so there is a big royal wedding and the couple ascend the vacant throne together. In contrast to that somewhat bizarre tale, the score, by Victor Herbert (music) and Robert B. Smith (lyrics), was rich and grand. Christie Macdonald introduced the gorgeous waltz, 'Sweethearts', and there were other numbers almost as fine, including 'The Angelus', 'Every Lover Must Meet His Fate', 'Pretty As A Picture', 'The Cricket On the Hearth', and 'Jeannette And Her Little Wooden Shoes'. The show ran for 136 performances and returned to New York briefly in 1929. A far more successful Broadway revival was mounted in 1947, when, following the successful resuscitation of Herbert's *The Red Mill* two years before, *Sweethearts* enjoyed a run of 288 performances at the Shubert Theatre. With a revised book by John Cecil Holm, the show was now a vehicle for comedian Bobby Clark, whose own particular brand of mayhem gave the piece a lighter and funnier touch. The 1938 film version starred Jeanette MacDonald and Nelson Eddy.

T

Take A Chance

The stories of the changes that are made to shows on the road during their pre-Broadway or West End try-outs are legendary, but not many can have undergone such radical reforms as this one. In September 1932 it was a revue entitled *Humpty Dumpty* with sketches and songs that dealt in an amusing way with certain aspects of American history. The material was linked by two members of the company seated in one of the theatre boxes, but the remainder of the audience in Pittsburg, Pennsylvania did not see the joke, and *Humpty Dumpty* had a great fall after just five days up there on the wall. However, when the show - re-titled *Take A Chance* - opened at the Apollo Theatre on Broadway on 26 November, it had been turned into a conventional book musical, in which the stars, Jack Whiting and June Knight, are appearing together in a revue called *Humpty Dumpty* with songs and sketches, that naturally enough, deal in an amusing way with certain aspects of American history. The original score by Richard Whiting and Nacio Herb Brown (music) and Buddy De Sylva (lyrics) had been strengthened by several numbers by the composer Vincent Youmans. There were also some important changes in the cast, but fortunately Ethel Merman survived to sing (clearly and fairly loudly) the pick of the output from this impressive array of songwriters. She introduced the show's three big hits, 'Eadie Was A Lady' (De Sylva-Whiting-Roger Edens), 'Rise 'n' Shine' (De Sylva-Youmans), and 'You're An Old Smoothie' (De Sylva-Whiting-Brown) on which she duetted with 'innocent-abroad' comedian Jack Haley. The love-interest, Jack Whiting and June Knight, shared most of the other numbers which included 'Should I Be Sweet?', 'Oh, How I Long to Belong To You' and 'So Do I' (all three by De Sylva and Youmans), along with 'Turn Out The Lights' (De Sylva-Whiting-Brown), for which Whiting and Knight were joined by Haley and the show's other funny man, Sid Silvers. He also collaborated on the book with De Sylva and Laurence Schwab. With America emerging slowly from the Depression, *Take A Chance* was just the tonic that Broadway audiences needed, and they kept on coming for 243 performances. Towards the end of the run, Haley and Silvers were replaced by Olsen and Johnson, the vaudeville comedy team who were making their debut in a legitimate Broadway musical. June Knight appeared in the 1933 film version, which came up with yet another variation on the original theme, along with Lillian Roth, James Dunn, and Cliff Edwards ('Ukelele Ike').

Take Me Along

Bob Merrill, the composer and lyricist for a host of pop hits during the 50s, wrote his first Broadway score in 1957 for a musical adaptation of Eugene O'Neill's classic drama *Anna Christie*. Two years later, for *Take Me Along*, he tackled another of the playwright's works, but one with a much lighter theme - *Ah, Wilderness!* It opened at the Shubert Theatre in New York on 22 October 1959 with a strong cast which was headed by a legendary Hollywood leading man of the 30s and 40s, Walter Pidgeon, and Jackie Gleason, whose main claim to fame at that time was as a comedian on US television. Joseph Stein and Robert Russell wrote the book which was set in the homely town of Centerville, Connecticut in 1910. Pidgeon plays Ned Miller, the publisher of the local newspaper, and the father of Richard, whose adolescent problems with his girlfriend, Muriel Macomber (Susan Luckey), and the devil drink, are resolved when he enters the hallowed halls of Yale University. The sub-plot concerns Sid Davis (Jackie Gleason), a far more serious drinker, who would like to settle down with Ned's sister, Lily

(Eileen Herlie), but he will have to sober up before she will have him. Pidgeon and Gleason duetted on the the lively 'Take Me Along', and the rest of Merrill's score, which has been called 'wistful and enchanting', included 'I Would Die', 'Staying Young', 'I Get Embarrassed', 'Sid Ol' Kid', 'We're Home', 'Promise Me A Rose', 'Nine O'Clock', and 'But Yours'. Walter Pidgeon and Jackie Gleason were both nominated for the Tony for best actor, and Gleason won for the most satisfying stage role of his career. He was succeeded during the show's run of 448 performances by William Bendix, the movie tough-guy with a heart of gold; it sounds like perfect casting. *Take Me Along* returned to Broadway during the 1984/5 season, which, according to experienced Broadway watchers, was one of the worst in living memory. The climate was not right for the show's warm and charming approach, and it closed after only one performance.

That's A Good Girl

The first of several highly popular and successful musical comedies in which Jack Buchanan and Elsie Randolph starred together and delighted London theatre audiences with their elegant and graceful blend of song and dance - and the usual frothy plot. *That's A Good Girl* opened at the London Hippodrome on 5 June 1928 with a book by Douglas Furber in which Buchanan was pursued throughout England and the South of France by Randolph in the role of a detective who adopted so many disguises that she probably did not know who she was herself. There were plenty of smart and witty lines, but the audiences really came to see the 'dynamic duo', Britain's answer to Fred Astaire and his sister Adele. The music for *That's A Good Girl* was composed by the Americans Phil Charig and Joseph Meyer, and another distinguished American, Ira Gershwin, provided some of the lyrics, along with Douglas Furber and Desmond Carter. The big hit song, introduced by the two stars, was 'Fancy Our Meeting', and this remained forever associated with Jack Buchanan. The rest of the numbers included another duet, 'The One I'm Looking For', along with 'Sweet So-And-So', 'Tell Me Why', 'Chirp, Chirp', 'Marching Song', 'Let Yourself Go', and 'Parting Time'. This show found Buchanan at the peak of his powers. It's sometimes difficult to realise how enormously popular and versatile he was. As well as performing in *That's A Good Girl*, he also presented the show, and choreographed and directed it as well. It ran for nearly a year, a total of 363 performances, and Jack Buchanan and Elsie Randolph recreated their roles for the film version which was released in 1933.

They're Playing Our Song

After composer Marvin Hamlisch's tremendous success with the long-running *A Chorus Line* (1975), he turned to his real-life partner, Carole Bayer Sager, for the lyrics to this miniscule musical which opened at the Imperial Theatre in New York on 11 February 1979. Miniscule that is, as regards the cast, for there were only two principal players, Lucie Arnaz and Robert Klein, although they each had three singing alter egos. Neil Simon's book, which is said to have been based on Hamlisch and Sager's own stormy relationship, concerns Vernon Gersch (Klein) and Sonia Walsk (Arnaz), two hip young songwriters whose developing romantic entanglement is hampered by Sonia's ex-boyfriend's telephone calls at any time of the day or night, and the feeling that they should keep things on a professional level anyway. The pleasing, melodic score included 'Fallin'', 'Workin' It Out', 'If He Really Knew Me', 'They're Playing My Song', 'Just For Tonight', 'When You're In My Arms', 'Right', and 'I Still Believe In Love'. No doubt the absence of a large chorus and similar overheads contributed to the show's abililty to last out for 1,082 performances. Subsequent road shows were equally successful, and the West End production with Tom Conti and Gemma Craven was the highlight of the 1980 London theatre season.

This Is The Army

Apart from George M. Cohan, no personality in American show business could wave the stars and stripes like Irving Berlin. He did it to great effect during World War I with the stage show *Yip Yip Yaphank*, and he rekindled the patriotic flames again in 1942 with *This Is The Army*. This all-soldier revue, which opened at the Broadway Theatre in New York on July 4 (naturally), was a mixture of songs and sketches designed to spread the belief that it was just a matter of time before the boys would all be home – and for good. Most of the songs were new, but Berlin himself sang one of fondly rememberd oldies, 'Oh, How I Hate To Get Up In the Morning', surrounded by his buddies dressed in 1917 soldiers' uniforms just as he had in *Yip Yip Yaphank* all those years ago. The rest of the fine score included 'This Is The Army, Mr. Jones' ('You've had your breakfast in bed before/But you won't get it there anymore'), 'The Army's Made A Man Of Me', 'I'm Getting Tired So I Can Sleep', 'This Time', and 'American Eagles'. For the 'I Left My Heart At The Stage Door Canteen' number, male cast members impersonated female celebrities such as Gypsy Rose Lee and Lynn Fontanne representing the stars who really did wait on members of the US Armed Services at the real-life Stage Door Canteen in New York. Those taking part in the show at various times included Ezra Stone, Burl Ives, Robert Sidney, Earl Oxford, Gary Merrill, and Alan Manson. The rousing finale, with everyone dressed in full uniform, brought a tear to the eye every night. *This Is the Army* ran for 113 performances in New York, and then toured in the US and overseas until the end of the war. The 1943 film version starred George Murphy and Joan Leslie (and Irving Berlin).

This Year Of Grace!

One of the most popular Noël Coward – C.B. Cochran revues, *This Year Of Grace!* opened at the London Pavilion on 22 March 1928. The book, music and lyrics were by Coward, and the all-star cast included Sonnie Hale, Douglas Byng, Maisie Gay, Tilly Losch, Jessie Matthews, Lance Lister, and Moya Nugent. The score contained several memorable numbers, such as 'Dance, Little Lady', 'A Room With A View', 'Teach Me To Dance Like Grandma', 'Lorelei', 'Mary Make-Believe', 'I'm Mad About You', and 'Try To Learn To Love'. The show ran for 316 performances in London, and Coward himself starred in the American edition which began its run of 158 performances in November 1928. With him in the New York cast were Florence Desmond, and Beatrice Lillie who introduced an extra Coward composition, 'World Weary'.

Three's A Crowd

Just a year after they appeared together in the legendary revue *The Little Show*, the main participants in that show were reunited for this similar kind of song and sketch entertainment which opened at the Selwyn Theatre in New York on 15 October 1930. Most of the songs were by Arthur Schwartz and Howard Dietz, who combined with the suave and sophisticated song-and-dance man Clifton Webb, deadpan comedian Fred Allen, and torch singer *extraordinaire* Libby Holman, to make this an amusing and innovative show. The sketches came from a variety of writers such as Dietz himself, Laurence Schwab, William Miles, Donald Blackman, Groucho Marx, and Arthur Sheekman. Schwartz and Dietz's musical numbers included 'The Moment I Saw You', 'Right At The Start Of It', and the gentle and wistful 'Something To Remember You By', which was introduced by Holman and became popular via her recording and another, several years later, by Dinah Shore. Holman also sang the most enduring song in the piece, the lovely ballad 'Body And Soul', by Johnny Green, Edward Heyman, Frank Eyton and Robert Sour. After early recordings by Paul Whiteman, Leo Reisman with Eddy Duchin at the piano, and Ruth Etting, it went on to become an all-time standard in the popular field, and was a particular favourite of jazz artists such as the pioneering tenor saxophonist Coleman Hawkins. The rest of the score for *Three's A Crowd* included 'Talkative Toes' (Dietz-Vernon Duke), 'Out In The Open Air' (Dietz-

Burton Lane), 'All The King's Horses' (Dietz-Edward Brandt-Alec Wilder), amd 'Yaller' (Richard Myers-Charles Schwab). The show ran for 272 performances, and set the mood and style for many other musicals of the 30s.

Threepenny Opera, The

A dramatic play with music by Kurt Weill and a book and lyrics by Bertolt Brecht, this three-act production was first presented at the Theatre am Schiffbauerdam in Berlin on 31 August 1928 under the title of *Die Dreigroschenoper*. That was 200 years after the show on which it was based, *The Beggar's Opera* by John Gay, was first seen in London. *The Threepenny Opera* had its first English language production on Broadway in 1933, and then returned to New York in 1954. This revised version, with an English book and lyrics by Marc Blitzstein, opened Off Broadway at the Theatre de Lys on 10 March and ran for just three months. Public demand caused it to return in September 1955, and this time it stayed for an incredible 2,706 performances. The cynical and satirical tale of morality which had seemed so appropriate, yet futile, in the Germany of the 20s, remained the same, with its familiar characters which included: the outlaw Macheath, otherwise known as Mack the Knife (Scott Merrill), his wife Polly Peachum (Jo Sullivan), the police chief's daughter Lucy Brown (Beatrice Arthur), and Jenny Diver, the whore, played by Lotte Lenya (Weill's widow), the actress who had created the role in Germany. The score included 'The Ballad Of Mack The Knife', 'Love Song', 'Army Song', 'Pirate Jenny', 'Tango-Ballad', 'Useless Song', 'Ballad Of The Easy Life', 'Barbara Song', 'Solomon Song', and 'Instead-Of-Song'. During the show's extremely long run many well-known actors and actresses took part, including Charlotte Rae, James Mitchell, Jerry Orbach, Carole Cook, Nancy Andrews, and Edward Asner. The English actress Georgia Brown played Lucy for a time, and she recreated her role, along with Bill Owen, Daphne Anderson, Lisa Lee, Eric Pohlmann, and Warren Mitchell for the 1956 London production which ran for 140 performances. Thirty years later in March 1986, a UK National Theatre production starred Tim Curry. A new adaptation of the piece, by Ralph Manheim and John Willett, spent 10 months on Broadway in 1976, and yet another version, billed as *3 Penny Opera* and translated by Michael Feingold, gave 65 performances at the Lunt-Fontanne Theatre in November 1989. Perhaps in an attempt to attract a different kind of audience, the cast for that production included rock star Sting as Macheath, along with popular singers Maureen McGovern and Kim Criswell. Several film version have been released, notably in 1931 with Lotte Lenya, and in 1964 with Hildegarde Neff and Curt Jurgens. The show is best-remembered by many people for one song - 'Mack the Knife' (originally entitled 'Moriat'). It was introduced by Lotte Lenya in the tinkly Victorian-style of most of the show's music, and became successful in 1956 in the USA for several artists including the Dick Hyman Trio, Richard Hayman with Jan August, Lawrence Welk, Louis Armstrong, and Billy Vaughn. Three years later the song became a massive number 1 hit on both sides of the Atlantic in a superb swinging version by Bobby Darin. Shortly afterwards, Ella Fitzgerald made a popular recording, and in 1984, yet another version, by the vocal-instrumental group King Kurt, entered the UK chart.

Tierney, Harry

b. Harry Austin Tierney, 21 May 1890, Perth Amboy, New Jersey, USA, d. 22 March 1965, New York, USA. A popular composer for the Broadway musical stage during the 20s, Tierney intended to study classical music, and attended the Virgil School of Music in New York. After touring the USA and other countries as a concert pianist, he worked for some time at the famous Remick's publishing house in New York, and started to write popular songs. From 1916-18, he had several songs interpolated into Broadway shows, including *The Passing Show Of 1916* ('So This Is Paris'); *Hitchy-Koo* ('M-I-S-S-I-S-S-I-P-P-I', a hit for Ann Wheaton and Ada Jones); *Everything* ('On Atlantic Beach' and 'Honky Tonk Town'); *The Canary* ('Jazz Marimba' and 'Oh, Doctor'); *So Long Letty* and *Follow Me*. With Joseph McCarthy, who was to be his chief collaborator, Tierney contributed 'My Baby's Arms' to *The Ziegfeld Follies Of 1919*, generally held to be the best of the series. In the same year, Tierney and McCarthy wrote the songs for *Irene*, the season's biggest hit. The show starred Edith Day, and featured musical numbers such as 'Alice Blue Gown', 'Talk Of The Town' and 'Castle Of Dreams'. The show became one of America's most treasured musicals. It was filmed in 1940, starring Anna Neagle and Ray Milland, and was successfully revived at the Minskoff Theatre in 1973 with Debbie Reynolds as Irene.

In 1920, Tierney and McCarthy added several songs to the European score of Charles Cuvillier's *Afagar* when it was staged on Broadway starring the toast of London and Paris, Alice Delysia. After contributing to the revue, *The Broadway Whirl* ('All Girls Are Like A Rainbow' and 'Oh, Dearie'); *Up She Goes* ('Let's Kiss And Make Up', 'Journey's End' and 'Lady Luck, Smile On Me') and the disappointing *Glory*, the team wrote the score for Ziegfeld's 1923 hit, *Kid Boots* with songs such as 'Someone Loves You', 'After All' and 'If Your Heart's In The Game'. In 1924, Tierney teamed with Sigmund Romberg to 'doctor' Clare Kummer's score to another Ziegfeld show, *Annie Dear*, and he also wrote 'Adoring You' for the impresario's *Follies* of that year. Three years later he was back with McCarthy for the double event of the theatrical year. The show was the operetta, *Rio Rita*, the season's biggest musical hit, and it was the first show to be staged at 'the finest musical playhouse ever constructed in America', the Ziegfeld. Tierney's robust and romantic score included 'The Rangers' Song', 'If You're In Love, You'll Waltz', 'You're Always In My Arms', 'Following The Sun Around', 'The Kinkajou' and the main duet, 'Rio Rita', sung by the show's stars, Ethelind Terry and J. Harold Murray. It ran for nearly 500 performances and was filmed in 1929, starring Bebe Daniels, John Boles and Wheeler and Wolsey, and again in 1942, with Abbott and Costello, Kathryn Grayson and John Carroll. Tierney and McCarthy's last Broadway show was *Cross My Heart*, in 1928, which ran for only eight weeks. After that, Tierney went to work in Hollywood during the 30s. His few movie scores included *Dixiana* ('Here's To The Good Old Days'), *Half Shot At Sunrise* (the Bert Wheeler/Robert Woolsey comedy) and *Juliana*. His attempts to write again for Broadway were unsuccessful, and his career declined in what ironically was a golden era of popular song. He died in March 1965.

Time

Cliff Richard, the UK 'Peter Pan of Pop', finally realised a long-cherished ambition to star in a lavish stage musical when this production opened at the Dominion Theatre in London on 9 April 1986. It was devised and produced by Dave Clark, leader of the popular 60s group the Dave Clark Five who had major chart hits with 'Glad All Over' and 'Bits And Pieces'. Clark also wrote the book and lyrics with David Soames, and composed the music with Jeff Daniels. The show's theme is one of human survival. Earth itself is on trial before the High Court of the Universe, and Cliff Richard, in the role of a spiritual rock star, is beamed out to the Andromeda galaxy to face the music on Earth's behalf. The planet is saved from extinction by the intervention of a galactic sage, known as the universe's Ultimate Word of Truth, in the shape of a huge holographic speaking image of the distinguished British actor Laurence Olivier. All this was enhanced by the use of spectacular sets and sensational special effects, the like of which London had never seen before. Arlene Phillips, formerly of the pop dance group Hot Gossip, engineered some appropriately high-tech choreography, and the score included several cosmic musical numbers such as 'Time Talkin'', 'The Music Of The Spheres', 'Law Of The Universe', 'What On Earth', and 'We're The UFO'. Despite a luke-warm reception from the critics, *Time* became a popular tourist attraction, particularly for its imaginative use of the space-age technology, and stayed at the Dominion for two years, a total of 777 performances. During the run Cliff Richard was succeeded by David Cassidy.

Tip-Toes

Although this show, which opened at the Liberty Theatre in New York, on 28 December 1925, had more or less the same creative team as the 1924 hit, *Lady, Be Good!*, one of the reasons why it was not nearly so successful may well have been that the brilliant dance team, Fred Astaire and his sister Adele, were not present this time. Guy Bolton and Fred Thompson's book was not considered to be up to much either - another rags-to-riches story, this time about a hard-up family vaudeville trio, consisting of Tip-Toes Kaye (Queenie Smith) and her two uncles, who are stranded in Palm Beach. One route to financial security would be for Tip-Toes to marry someone rich, but she loves Steve Burton (Allen Kearns) and he maintains that he is penniless - or is he? Surely he's that guy who made fortune out of glue? Andrew Tombes and Harry Watson Jnr. played Tip-Toes' vaudevillian uncles, and also in the cast was the young singer Jeanette MacDonald, just four years before she burst onto the Hollywood scene in the *The Love Parade*. George and Ira Gershwin's score was delightful in every way - a perfect blend of melody and witty and sentimental lyrics. Queenie Smith introduced the lovely 'That Certain Feeling' and 'Looking For A Boy', and joined in with 'These Charming People' and the gentle 'Nightie Night'. The rest of the score included the rousing 'Sweet And Low-Down', which was 'sung, kazooed, tromboned, and danced by the entire ensemble at a Palm Beach party'; 'Harlem River Shanty', 'When Do We Dance?', and 'Nice Baby'. *Tip-Toes* was yet another of those 'feel-good' musicals that proliferated during the 20s, and it attracted appreciative audiences for 194 performances. Allen Kearns briefly recreated his role for the London production which also starred Dorothy Dickson and ran for 194 performances. The 1927 film version was made in England with Dorothy Gish and Will Rogers.

Tobias Brothers

This family group of songwriters comprised Charles Tobias (b. 15 August 1898, New York, USA, d. 7 July 1970), Harry Tobias (b. 11 September 1895, New York, USA) and Henry Tobias (b. 23 April 1905, Worcester, Massachusetts, USA). Charles Tobias was the most prolific of the trio, writing mainly lyrics, and occasionally music. After singing for publishing houses, on radio, and in Vaudeville, he formed his own New York publishing company in 1923, and started writing songs soon afterwards. In the late 20s these included 'On A Dew-Dew-Dewy Day' and 'Miss You' (with brothers Henry and Harry), which became hits for Dinah Shore, Bing

Crosby and Eddie Howard. From 1928 through to the early 40s, Charles wrote sundry songs for Broadway shows, such as *Good Boy*, *Earl Carroll's Sketch Book* (1929 and 1935), *Earl Carroll's Vanities Of 1932*, *Hellzapoppin'*, *Yokel Boy* and *Banjo Eyes*. His contributions to films continued for another 10 years, until the early 50s. These included: *Life Begins In College* (1937), *Private Buckaroo* (1942), *Shine On, Harvest Moon* (1944), *Saratoga Trunk* (1945), *Tomorrow Is Forever* (1946), *Love And Learn* (1947), *The Daughter Of Rosie O'Grady* (1950), *On Moonlight Bay* (1951) and *About Face* (1952). From the shows, films and Tin Pan Alley, came popular songs such as 'When Your Hair Has Turned To Silver', 'Throw Another Log On The Fire', 'Don't Sweetheart Me', 'No Can Do', 'A Million Miles Away', 'Coax Me A Little Bit' and 'The Old Lamplighter'. His collaborators included Joe Burke, Murray Mencher, Sam Stept, Peter DeRose, Cliff Friend, Sammy Fain, Nat Simon, Jack Scholl, Lew Brown, Roy Turk and Charles Newman. In 1962, after a period of relative inactivity, Tobias wrote 'All Over The World' (with Al Frisch) and 'Those Lazy, Hazy, Crazy Days Of Summer' (with Hans Carste), both of which were successful for Nat 'King' Cole.

Charles' older brother Harry wrote lyrics for some songs in 1916, including 'That Girl Of Mine' and 'Take Me To Alabam' (both with Will Dillon). After military service in World War I, he spent several years in the real estate business before returning to songwriting in the late 20s. In 1931, with bandleader Gus Arnheim and Jules Lemare, he wrote 'Sweet And Lovely', which became Arnheim's theme song, and a big hit in the UK for Al Bowlly; and 'Goodnight My Love', which was featured in the film *Blondie Of The Follies* (1932). During the next 20 years, many of Tobias's lyrics were heard in films such as *Gift Of The Gab*, *Dizzy Dames*, *The Old Homestead*, *With Love And Kisses*, *Swing While You're Able*, *It's A Date*, *Stormy Weather*, *You're A Lucky Fellow, Mr. Smith*, *Sensations Of 1945*, *Brazil*, and *Night Club Girl*. His best-known songs included 'It's A Lonesome Old Town', 'Sail Along Sil'vry Moon', 'Wait for Me', 'No Regrets', 'Fascinating You', 'Go To Sleep, Little Baby', 'Oh Bella Maria' and 'Take Me Back To Those Wide Open Spaces'. His collaborators included Al Sherman, Roy Ingraham, Pinky Tomlin, Harry Barris, Neil Moret and Percy Wenrich. In the 50s he concentrated more on his music publishing interests.

The youngest of the three brothers, Henry Tobias, had a varied career. He wrote special material for artists such Sophie Tucker, Eddie Cantor and Jimmy Durante, was a producer and director for summer stock shows, and also worked for CBS Television as a producer and musical director. With his brother Charles he contributed to the Earl Carroll revues in the 30s, and also wrote many other popular numbers

with Will Dillon, David Ormont, David Oppenheim, Don Reid, Milton Berle and Little Jack Little. These included 'Katinka', 'Cooking Breakfast For The One I Love', 'We Did It Before And We Can Do It Again', 'The Bowling Song, 'You Walked Out Of The Picture', 'Easter Sunday With You' and 'I've Written A Letter To Daddy' (with Larry Vincent and Mo Jaffe), which was featured in the 1979 Janis Joplin bio-pic, *The Rose*, starring Bette Midler.

Tobias, Charles
(see **Tobias Brothers**)

Tommy
(see **Who's Tommy, The**)

Tonight At 8.30
A series of nine one-act plays written by Noël Coward, and presented in two groups at London's Phoenix Theatre in successive weeks in January 1936, starring Coward and Gertrude Lawrence. After the curtain-raiser, *We Were Dancing*, with its title song, three of the other pieces were significant because of their musical content: *Shadow Play*, a romantic musical fantasy, which contained 'Then', 'Play Orchestra, Play', and 'You Were There'; *Red Peppers*, the most popular item in the set which dealt with a sleazy, quarrelsome music-hall duo in terminal decline, and included 'Has Anybody Seen Our Ship?' and 'Men About Town'; and *Family Album*, a 'mock-Victorian comedy about a missing will' with two songs, 'Here's A Toast' and 'Hearts And Flowers'. This was Coward at his versatile best, both in writing and performing. After a run of 157 performances he and Gertrude Lawrence enjoyed similar success later in the year in New York. Lawrence also starred with one of Coward's protégés, Graham Payn in a brief 1948 Broadway revival. Four years later, three of the plays, including *Red Peppers*, were filmed under the collective title of *Meet Me Tonight*, with Ted Ray and Kay Walsh. In 1991, the actress Joan Collins and her ex-husband Anthony Newley, appeared in the complete series of nine plays on UK television.

Tonight's The Night
World War I was just a few months old when this British musical opened - not in London - but at the Shubert Theatre in New York on 24 December 1914. Fred Thompson's book, which was based on the popular 19th century farce *The Pink Dominoes* by James Albery, was typical of the genre and involved a 'did-they-know-or-not' story about two society chaps, Dudley Mitten (George Grossmith) and his pal, Albert (Dave Burnaby), who are cajoled into romancing a certain two young ladies at a masked ball. When it is revealed that the female duo are the men-about-towns' current girlfriends, June (Emmy

Wehlen) and Beatrice (Iris Hoey), they staunchly insist that they were aware of the joke all the time - and went along with it. *Tonight's The Night* had a reasonably successful New York run of 108 performances, but found its true audience when it returned to London and the Gaiety Theatre on 28 April 1915. Paul Rubens and Percy Greenbank' score, which included 'Murders', 'The Only Way', 'Boots And Shoes', 'I'm A Millionaire', 'Dancing Mad', 'Please Don't Flirt With Me', 'When the Boys Come Home To Tea', 'Too Particular', and 'Round The Corner', was strengthened by the scatty 'I'd Like To Bring My Mother', and two interpolated songs, 'Any Old Night (Is A Wonderful Night)' (music by Otto Motzan and Jerome Kern, lyric by Schuyler Greene and Harry B. Smith), and 'They Didn't Believe Me' (music by Jerome Kern, lyric by Herbert Reynolds). Comedian Leslie Henson who had originally had a minor part in the Broadway production, was elevated to the role of Henry, 'a naughty schoolboy out for a spree and a flirt with a pretty maid', and was oustanding in the first of his many West End successes. *Tonight's The Night* ran on and on for 460 performances, and was revived at the Winter Garden in 1924 with several of the original cast, including Leslie Henson.

Tony Awards

The Antoinette Perry Awards, America's most prestigious theatrical awards - the equivalent to the Hollywood Oscars - were inaugurated in 1947. Their fascinating history begins during World War I when an obsure playwright, Rachel Crothers, and a few other women, organized theatre people to sell Liberty Bonds and run a canteen for servicemen in Times Square. In 1939 Crothers and her voluntary workers, including an actress–director named Antoinette Perry, surfaced again and formed the American Theatre Wing War Service. The Wing founded two famous institutions: the Stage Door Canteen, where stars of stage, screen and radio served coffee and doughnuts and entertained visiting service personnel, and which was immortalized in the 1943 film of the same name; and the annual award given in the memory of Antoinette Perry's pioneering work for women and young people in the theatre and for the American Theatre Wing itself, which still organizes the Awards. In 1993 the nominations for the 19 categories were selected by an independent committee of 12 theatre professionals, and they in turn were voted on by 670 theatre professionals and journalists. In that year the specific musical sections consisted of best musical, book, original score, performance by a leading actor, leading actress, featured actor, and featured actress; and best direction and choreography. Musical productions could also win in the best scenic, costume, and lighting design categories, and the best

revival of a play or musical. In most years one or more special Tonys are awarded for outstanding service to the theatre, and in 1993 one of these celebrated the 50th anniversary of Richard Rodgers and Oscar Hammerstein II's *Oklahoma!*. Over the years the Award itself has taken many forms. The current honour is in the shape of a Tony Medallion, the product of a Stage Designer's Union competition won by Herman Rose in 1950. An annual live television audience of some 10 million watch the ceremony, the outcome of which often means the difference between success and failure on Broadway. Further reading: *The Tony Award Book*, Lee Alan Morrow. *The Tony Award*, Crown Publishers USA.

Too Many Girls

Another musical set at an American college where football consistently scores over schoolbooks, the lively and entertaining *Too Many Girls* opened at the Imperial Theatre in New York on 19 October 1939. George Marion Jnr.'s book concerns Consuelo (Marcy Westcott), whose wealthy father, Harvey Casey (Clyde Fillmore), sends her to Pottawatomie College in New Mexico in search of a little discipline. Just to be on the safe side he hires four All-American footballers, Manuelito (Desi Arnaz), Jojo Jordan (Eddie Bracken) Al Terwilliger (Hal LeRoy), and Clint Kelley (Richard Kollmar), to serve as her bodyguards. Complications ensue when Consuelo falls for Clint, but everything is sorted out by the day of the BIG GAME!!. Richard Rodgers and Lorenz Hart's score was full of good things although there was only one enduring number, 'I Didn't Know What Time It Was', which was introduced by Westcott and Kollmar. It became popular for Benny Goodman and Jimmy Dorsey, and Frank Sinatra gave the song a pleasant reading when it was interpolated into the film score of *Pal Joey* (1957). Westcott and Kalmar also duetted on 'Love Never Went To College', and the rest of the score consisted of lively and amusing numbers such as the Latin-styled 'All Dressed Up (Spic And Spanish)', 'She Could Shake The Maracas', in which Arnaz, quite naturally, was involved; 'Give It Back To The Indians', and the songwriters' witty plea - in the face of the blare of the Big-Band Era - for a return to musical sanity in 'I Like To Recognize The Tune' ('A guy Krupa plays the drums like thunder/But the melody is six feet under/There isn't anyone immune - they kill the Billy Roses and Puccinis/Don't be meanies/Must you bury the tune?'). Mel Tormé made an excellent recording of that one. Rumour has it that Lorenz Hart was frequently absent during preparations for this show and Rodgers had to write some of his own lyrics. The future movie heartthrob Van Johnson was in the chorus, and he succeeded Richar Kollmar when the show toured directly after its New York run of 249 performances. Several of the original cast were in the 1940 film version including Desi Arnaz, whose meeting on the set with Lucille Ball led to their stormy marriage and the long-running television series *I Love Lucy*.

Tree Grows In Brooklyn

With a book by George Abbott and Betty Smith which was adapted from Smith's best-selling novel of the same name, this sentimental story of an ordinary, working-class Brooklyn family opened at the Alvin Theatre in New York on 19 April 1951. Set in the early 1900s, the story follows the fortunes of the hard-drinking Johnny Nolan (Johnny Johnston), a singing waiter who meets and marries Katie (Marcia Van Dyke). She has a sister named Cissy who 'collects' husbands and calls them all Harry. Eventually, her current spouse becomes so used to the name that he objects to being called by his real name of Oscar. Meanwhile, Johnny and Katie have a daughter, Francie (Nomi Mitty), but Johnny's drinking is getting worse. He loses his job, and leaves home to find other work, only to get killed in the process. However, he has left sufficient money to enable Francie to finish her education, and the curtain falls on the celebrations following her graduation. In Smith's original book, and in the 1945 film, the story focussed on the daughter Francie, but for this musical treatment the authors shifted the emphasis onto the older players, particularly Shirley Booth who gave a wonderfully humorous performance, particularly when reflecting on her 'late' Harry in 'He Had Refinement' ('One time he said: "May I suggest/You call a ladies' chest, a chest/Instead of her points of interest?'/Dainty, ain't he?'). The remainder of Dorothy Fields and Arthur Schwartz's warmly romantic and sometimes lively score included the lovely 'Make The Man Love Me', 'Look Who's Dancing', 'Love Is The Reason', 'I'm Like A New Broom', 'Growing Pains', 'Mine 'Til Monday', 'Don't Be Afraid', and 'If You Haven't Got A Sweetheart'. One of the other numbers, 'I'll Buy You A Star', was sung by Johnny Mathis on his 1961 album with the same title. *A Tree Grows In Brooklyn* had a decent run of 270 performances, but is rarely revived.

Tribute To The Blues Brothers, A

Inspired by the American television satire-comedy institution *Saturday Night Live*, which spawned the cult 1980 film *The Blues Brothers*, this 'couple of hours of high-octane serious partying' began as a pub (or bar) entertainment in the English seaside town of Brighton before moving to the up-market London suburb of Hampstead. From there it was just a short distance to the West End and the Whitehall Theatre, where this 'good-time' entertainment opened on 12 August 1991. Jake and Elwood Blues, two Chicago petty crooks-turned R&B singers, complete with the dark blue suits, narrow-brim hats, and Ray Ban shades, were the creations of film actors John Belushi and Dan Aykroyd. Their on-stage counterparts, played by Con O'Neill and Warwick Evans, retain the uniform, but claim to come from Halifax in Yorkshire, and have hobbies which include train-spotting and collecting cardigans ('a couple of nerds'). The story remains nominal, but the music more than makes up for it. A dazzling array of mostly great old songs include 'Hey Bartender', 'I Need You, Flip Flop Fly', 'I Can Dance', 'Gimme Some Lovin'', 'Minnie The Moocher', 'Soul Man', 'Cell Block No.9', 'Jailhouse Rock', 'Who's Making Love To Your Old Lady While You're Out Making Love?', and somewhat surprisingly, the 'Theme From Rawhide'; and a rap version of the Rolf Harris hit 'Two Little Boys'. The 'brothers' are supported by singers Greg Brown, who gives an immaculate reading of 'In The Midnight Hour', Ian Roberts, whose outstanding solo is 'On The Boardwalk', Liza Spenz, and a hot six-piece band. The 'initial onslaught' was greeted enthusiastically by the critics, and the singing and dancing on the stage (and in the aisles) continued for 10 months at the Whitehall, prior to UK and European tours.

Tucker, Sophie

b. Sophie (or Sonia) Kalish-Abuza, 13 January 1884, in transit between Russia and Poland, d. 9 February 1966. She was a singer of generous proportions, brassy and dynamic, who claimed to be 'The Last Of The Red-Hot Mamas'. The daughter of Russian parents, Tucker was taken to the USA when she was three years old. Sophie's father took the man's name and papers in an attempt to evade the Russian authorities. By the time she was 10-years-old Tucker was a singing waitress in her father's cafe in Hartford, Connecticut, and in 1906 she moved to New York to work at the Café Monopole, the German Village Cafe and then in burlesque, vaudeville and cabaret. Sometimes, because of her plain appearance she was persuaded to work in blackface, and made a reputation as a 'Coon-Shouter' in the ragtime era. After a teenage marriage failed (as did two later attempts), she added 'er' to her ex-husband's name of 'Tuck' to create her new stage name. In 1909 she played a small, but telling part in the Ziegfeld Follies. By 1911 she was a headliner, and was able to drop the dreaded blackface for good. In the same year she made her first recording of the song which was to become her life-long theme, forever associated with her. 'Some Of These Days' was written by composer-pianist Shelton Brooks (b. 4 May 1886, Amesburg, Ontario, Canada), who also wrote 'The Darktown Strutters Ball', and special material for Nora Bayes and

Sophie Tucker

Al Jolson. Other hits around this time were 'That Lovin' Rag', 'That Lovin' Two-Step Man', 'That Loving Soul Kiss' and 'Knock Wood'. When jazz music became the new craze during World War I, Tucker became known as 'The Queen Of Jazz', and toured with the band 'Sophie Tucker And Her Five Kings Of Syncopation'.

In 1919 she replaced 'shimmy dance' specialist, Gilda Gray in the Broadway show, *Schubert Gaieties*, and in 1921 hired pianist Ted Shapiro, who as well as writing some of her risque material, became her accompanist and musical director for the rest of her career. In the following year she made the first of many performances in London in the revue, *Round In 50*, based on the novel *Around The World In 80 Days*, by Jules Verne. She was back on Broadway in 1924 for the *Earl Carroll Vanities*, and was by now a major star. Her hits during the 20s included 'High Brown Blues', 'You've Gotta See Mama Ev'ry Night (Or You Won't See Mama At All)', 'Aggravatin' Papa', 'The One I Love Belongs To Somebody Else', 'Red-Hot Mama', 'Bugle Call Rag' (with Ted Lewis and his band), 'Fifty Million Frenchmen Can't Be Wrong', 'After You've Gone', 'I Ain't Got Nobody', 'Blue River', 'There'll Be Some Changes Made', 'The Man I Love', 'I'm The Last Of The Red-Hot Mamas', and two reputed million-sellers, a re-recording of her trademark song, 'Some Of These Days', and 'My Yiddishe Momme', written for her by Jack Yellen and Lew Pollack. She recorded the song in English on one side of the record, and in Yiddish on the other.

In 1929 Tucker made her movie debut in an early talkie, *Honky Tonk*, with songs by Yellen. She made several more films until 1944, including *Gay Love*, *Follow The Boys* and *Sensations Of 1945* - usually as a guest artist playing her larger-than-life self - although she gave critically acclaimed performances in *Thoroughbreds Don't Cry* and *Broadway Melody Of 1938*, co-starring with Judy Garland. In 1930 she returned to London's West End to star with Jack Hulbert in the musical comedy, *Follow A Star*. The London *Observer's* theatre critic wrote: 'She hurls her songs like projectiles, in a very explosive manner'. Four years later she was back in London for the first of several Royal Command Performances, besides regular appearances at London's Kit Kat Club, music hall tours and cabaret. She made her final Broadway appearances in Cole Porter's *Leave It To Me* (1938), in which she sang 'Most Gentlemen Don't Like Love (They Just Like To Kick It Around)' and *High Kickers* (1941). Her fame faded somewhat in the 50s and 60s, although she still worked in clubs and occasionally on television, including several appearances on the *Ed Sullivan Show*. She also played an effective cameo role in the biopic of comedian Joe E. Lewis, *The Joker Is Wild* (1957). In her later years, when her voice declined, she specialized in half-sung, half-spoken, philosophical songs and monologues, many written by Jack Yellen, sometimes in partnership with Ted Shapiro or Milton Ager. Her specialities included 'Life Begins At 40', 'I'm Having More Fun Now I'm 50', 'I'm Having More Fun Since I'm 60', 'I'm Starting All Over Again', 'The Older They Get', 'You've Got To Be Loved To Be Healthy', 'No One Man Is Ever Going To Worry Me' and 'He Hadn't Till Yesterday'. Her last appearances included New York's Latin Quarter, and The Talk Of The Town in London. She died in February 1966 in New York, USA. The 1963 Broadway musical *Sophie*, was based on her life.

Compilations: *Miff Mole's Molers 1927* (1971), *The Great Sophie Tucker* (1974), *Some Of These Days* (1976), *Harry Richman And Sophie Tucker* (1979), *Last Of The Red-Hot Mamas* (1983), *The Golden Age Of Sophie Tucker* (1985), *Follow A Star* (1987), *The Sophie Tucker Collection* (1987).

Further reading: *Some Of These Days*, Sophie Tucker.

Tune, Tommy

b. Thomas James Tune, 28 February 1939, Wichita Falls, Texas, USA. An actor, dancer, choreographer, and director. His father worked in the oil industry, and Tune grew up in Houston, Texas. He took dancing lessons from the age of five, directed and choreographed musicals at high school, and majored in performing arts at the University of Texas. Soon after he moved to New York, he moved right out again with a touring version of *Irma La Douce*. Ironically, his height of six feet nine inches, which he thought might be a hindrance, helped him to gain his first part on Broadway - as one of three tall men in the chorus of the musical, *Baker Street* (1965). After further modest roles in *The Joyful Noise* and *How Now Dow Jones*, he choreographed the 1969 touring version of *Canterbury Tales*, and appeared in two films, *Hello, Dolly!* (1969) and *The Boyfriend* (1971). His big break came firstly as a performer in *Seesaw* (1973), in which he stopped the show almost every night with 'It's Not Where You Start (It's Where You Finish)', a number that he choreographed himself. He won a Tony Award for best featured actor, and then did not work on a Broadway musical for five barren years ('I couldn't even get arrested'). His role as choreographer-director on *The Best Little Whorehouse In Texas* (1978) changed all that, and, during the next decade, Tune became the natural successer to past masters such as Bob Fosse, Jerome Robbins, Gower Champion, and Michael Bennett. He brought his own brand of 'infectious, eye-popping pizzazz' to a string of hit shows: *A Day In Hollywood, A Night In The Ukraine* (1980), *Nine* (1982), *My One And Only* (1983, in which he also co-starred with Twiggy), *Grand Hotel* (1989), and *The Will Rogers Follies* (1991).

They gained him a total of nine Tony Awards, and induction into New York's Theatre Hall of Fame in 1991. In the following year, Tune took time out from appearing in a lucrative US tour of *Bye, Bye Birdie* to stage the London production of *Grand Hotel* which was greeted with apathy by the critics and public alike. In December 1992 he presented his own *Tommy Tune Tonight!* on Broadway for a limited period, prior to a 20-week 1993 national tour. Also in 1993, he directed the Takarazuka Theatre Company in Japan, and prepared a new production of *Grease* for Broadway.

Twang!!

The Robin Hood legend has been the subject of many a musical production since it was presented, usually as a comic operetta, in both the USA and England in the late 19th, and early 20th century. The 'burlesque' version which opened at London's Shaftesbury Theatre on the 20 December 1965, had music and lyrics by Lionel Bart, who also wrote the book in collaboration with an American talent agent and television personality, Harvey Orkin. Several members of Bart's successful 1960 production, *Fings Ain't Wot They Used T'Be*, were involved in his new venture, including Joan Littlewood (director), Anthony Booth (Robin Hood, a con-man), and Barbara Windsor (Delphina, a nymphomaniac). In addition, the diminutive Ronnie Corbett played Will Scarlett, and Long John Baldry, who was to have a UK number 1 hit with 'Let The Heartaches Begin' two years later, was billed as 'Mystery Voice'. Bart said it was all supposed be a 'giggle'. From an early stage, *Twang!!* was perceived to be in trouble, and the persistent rumours were confirmed when, after being set for a provincial tryout in October in Birmingham, the show was reluctantly presented to the public for the first time on the 3 November - in Manchester. On the following day, Littlewood departed, Booth was said to be suffering from nervous exhaustion, and soon afterwards Bernard Delfont Ltd withdrew its financial backing. Bart was determined to open in London, and, disregarding his friend Noël Coward's advice, invested his own money in the show. It was the beginning of his slide into bankruptcy which led to many years in the wilderness. Naturally, the script changed daily, as did the score. At various stages in the production the songs included 'Make An Honest Woman Out Of Me', 'Roger The Ugly', 'Whose Little Girl Are You?', 'Follow Your Leader', 'With Bells On', and a delicate piece called 'Sighs'. The critics had a field day: 'The worst musical for years', 'a dank, bedraggled, feeble thing', were two of the more favourable reviews. The word 'shambles' was used a lot, as *Twang!!* staggered on for 43 performances. Perhaps there's a jinx on the whole Robin Hood musical concept: in 1993, *Robin, Prince Of Sherwood*

('a doomed farrago'), with music and lyrics by Rick Fenn and Peter Howarth, and directed by Bill Kenwright - an impresario with the 'magic touch' - closed in London after a run of eight weeks, losing £500,000.

Two Gentlemen Of Verona

Galt MacDermot, who burst on the Broadway scene in 1967 with his music for *Hair*, collaborated with lyricist John Guare on the score for this rock musical version of William Shakespeare's play which concerns, according to one critic, 'two sets of lovers, who are by turns, skittish, treacherous, endearing and eccentric'. This modern conception of the *Two Gentlemen Of Verona* was first presented as part of a series of open-air productions in New York's Central Park in the summer of 1971, and proved to be so successful that it transferred to Broadway at the St. James Theatre on December 1 that year. Librettists John Guare and the show's director Mel Shapiro, skilfully interpolated contemporary language and references into the original and well-worn story of odious Proteus (Raul Julia) who not only plays fast and loose with his lady friend Julia (Diana Davila), but also tries to muscle in on Silvia (Jonelle Allen), the mistress of his best friend Valentine (Clifton Davis). The cast also included Stockard Channing who was to blossom into a fine stage actress, and made such an impact as the cynical Rizzo in the film of *Grease*. The score was not considered by the critics to be in the same class as *Hair*, but numbers such as 'Bring All The Boys Back Home', 'Follow The Rainbow', 'Night Letter', 'Who Is Silvia?' (lyric: Shakespeare), and 'Calla Lily Lady', when reproduced at extremely high levels of sound, appealed sufficiently to sustain a run of 627 performances. To the surprise of many the show won Tony Awards for best musical and book, but *Follies* took most of the rest of the prizes that season. More than 20 years later, in October 1993, the Royal Shakespeare Company in Britain approached *Two Gentlemen Of Verona* in quite a different way. Their much-praised production at the Barbican in London was conceived by David Thacker, and gave the piece an elegant and stylish 30s setting in which singer Hilary Cromie accompanied by a seven-piece band, drifted in and out of the action with bitter-sweet songs of the era such as 'Love Is The Sweetest Thing', 'More Than You Know', 'What'll I Do?', 'Heartaches', and 'In The Still Of The Night'. As with the Broadway production, the song 'Who Is Silvia?' was present, although this time the melody was by Guy Woolfenden who composed the original music for the entire production.

U

Under Your Hat

This musical comedy reunited the husband and wife team of Cicely Courtneidge and Jack Hulbert on the West End stage for the first time since they appeared together in the revue *The House Jack Built* (1929). It opened on 24 November 1938 at the Palace Theatre, and, after being withdrawn for two months at the beginning of World War II, ran until April 1940, a total of 512 performances. The book was the result of a collaboration between Archie Menzies, Arthur Macrae, and Jack Hulbert, and the music and lyrics were by Vivian Ellis, with additional numbers by the Rhythm Brothers and Claude Hulbert. Almost inevitably, Courtneidge and Hulbert were once again cast as husband and wife, this time as the smart filmstar twosome Kay Porter and Jack Millet. The plot has them travelling to various home and foreign locations on behalf of the British Government in an effort to retrieve a valuable carburettor which has been stolen by the glamorous spy, Carol Markoff (Leonora Corbett), who has given it to the the Russians' representative, Boris Vladimir (Frank Cellier). It was an ideal excuse for everyone to dress up in a variety of disguises, especially Courtneidge, who provided one of the show's many highlights when her impersonation of a waitress in a red wig develops into an hilarious burlesque of a French cabaret performer in the number, 'Dance, C'est Moi'. Vivian Ellis's consistently tuneful and witty score also included 'Together Again', 'If You Want To Dance', 'Keep It Under Your Hat', 'Swingin'', and 'The Hat Ballet'. As usual there was one particularly outstanding song for Cicely Courtneidge. This time it was 'The Empire Depends On You', in which she lectured them, not necessarily, severely, thus: 'Now I'm a soldier's daughter, our family thrive on war/Why, all my folk were Army, they fought at Agincourt/My dear old Dad, the Major, he served at Crecy too/A touch of gout just put him out/He was late for Waterloo'. This 'lavish, witty, fool-proof entertainment . . . the funniest musical comedy for years' lightened the early, uneasy years of the war, and was filmed under the title of *Grand National* in 1940, when Courtneidge and Hulbert recreated their roles.

Unsinkable Molly Brown, The

Not as successful or as satisfying as Meredith Willson's earlier smash-hit, *The Music Man*, but then that show was all his own work and is considered to be a masterpiece of the American musical theatre. Willson only provided the music and lyrics for this one, and left the book to Richard Morris who also collaborated with him on *1491*, Willson's final musical which did not reach Broadway. *The Unsinkable Molly Brown* opened at the Winter Garden in New York on 3 November 1960. The story was set in the early part of the 20th century and cncerned the indefatigable Molly Brown, a legendary figure in US history, who was born on the wrong side of the tracks in Hannibal, Missouri, but is determined to progress swiftly from that unfortunate condition. She moves to the mining town of Colorado, and and marries Johnny 'Leadville' Brown (Harve Presnell), a prospector with the 'golden touch'. Their initial attempts to break into Denver high society fail dismally, but after conquering Europe - especially Monte Carlo - with her personality and Johnny's money, and becoming something of a hero (and a survivor) during the *Titanic* disaster, she returns to find that Denver and its high-falutin citizens are at her feet. Willson's score had the same kind of folksy, all-American down-home charm, that worked so well in *The Music Man*. The highlight was Molly's spirited anthem to survival, 'I Ain't Down Yet', and there were several other rousing numbers among the rest of the songs which included 'My Own Brass Bed', 'Belly Up To The Bar, Boys', 'I'll Never Say No', 'Colorado, My Home', 'Are You Sure?', 'Bea-u-ti-ful People Of Denver', 'Chick-A-Pen', and 'Dolce Far Niente'. Tammy Grimes won a Tony Award for her lively and gutsy performance, and New York theatregoers liked this glimpse of their pioneering past sufficiently for the show to run for 15 months. Harve Presnell reprised his role for the 1960 film in which he co-starred with Debbie Reynolds.

Up In Central Park

More than 15 years had passed since composer Sigmund Romberg's last big hit, *New Moon*, when he teamed with lyricist Dorothy Fields to write the score for this show which opened at the New Century Theatre in New York on 27 January 1945. Fields also collaborated with her brother Herbert on the book, a tale of intrigue and corruption set in the late 19th century in which newspaper reporter John Matthews (Wilbur Evans) is intent on exposing an infamous Tammany Hall political group, led by William Macey Tweed (Noah Beery), who are siphoning off monies that have been allotted for the creation of Central Park. Complications ensue when Matthews falls for Rosie Moore (Maureen Cannon), the daughter of one of the fraudsters. The lovers have the show's outstanding ballad, the lovely 'Close As Pages In A Book', which became a bestseller for Benny Goodman at the time, and was later given memorable readings by Margaret Whiting and Maxine Sullivan, amongst others. It also titled Barbara Cook's 1993 tribute album to Dorothy Fields. Evans and Cannon introduced yet another superior song, 'April Snow', and the remainder of Romberg's typically 'operetta-tinged' score included 'Carousel In The Park', 'When You Walk In The Room', and 'The Big Back Yard'. The outstanding moment came with the celebrated 'Currier And Ives Ballet', a stunning sequence set in the Park, and choreographed by Helen Tamaris. The show, which is said to have some basis in fact, ran for 504 performances, and was filmed in 1948 with Dick Haymes and Deanna Durbin.

Up On The Roof

Following a brief run at the Theatre Royal, Plymouth, this show spent a few weeks at London's Donmar Warehouse before transferring to the Apollo theatre in the West End on June 8 1987. The play, which was written by Simon Moore and Jane Prowse (who also directed) was originally developed from improvisation with Beverley Hills, Mark McGann, Felicity Montagu, Michael Mueller, and Gary Olsen. Olsen has gone on to various UK television successes, including 2point4 Children, and Mark McGann, one of the four theatrical brothers from Liverpool, is renowned for his portrayal of John Lennon in several productions. McGann was also present in 1991 when The Hunting Of The Snark proved to be a fruitless expedition. As Up On The Roof opens, the time is the summer of 1975. Five university students have had their examination results, and are spending their last night on the roof of their student house discussing life and what the future holds for them. They decide to meet up for a reunion in 10 years time at a villa in the south of France, and the story follows them through those years, reflecting in a dramatic and often amusing way, the gradual changes in their attitudes and ideals. The 70s songs which accompany this journey are performed appealingly by the cast, a cappella, and include 'Never Can Say Goodbye', 'When Will I See You Again', 'Sad Sweet Dreamer', 'Band Of Gold', 'What Becomes Of The Broken Hearted?', 'My Eyes Adored You', and, of course, 'Up On The Roof'. The production gained three Laurence Olivier Award nominations, including best musical, and, in the subsequent touring version, Steve McGann replaced his brother Mark, and also served as the musical director.

V

Vagabond King, The

With music by Rudolph Friml and lyrics by Brian Hooker, this operetta was presented at the Casino Theatre in New York on 21 September 1925. The book, by Hooker, Russey Janney, and W.H. Post was based on the play and novel If I Were A King, and was a highly imaginative piece - even for this era. It was set in 15th century Paris and concerned the outlaw Francois Villon (Dennis King) who escapes the guillotine by becoming the King of France for a day and defeating the Duke of Burgundy. His reward is the the the hand in marriage of the lovely Katherine de Vaucelles (Carolyn Thompson). The score was a mixture of rousing songs and ballads, and included such enduring favourites as 'Song Of the Vagabonds', 'Only A Rose', 'Some Day', 'Hugette Waltz', 'Love Me Tonight', and 'Love For Sale'. The New York run of 511 performances was followed by a further 480 in London in 1927, and the show has remained a staple item in the repertoires of amateur and professional operatic societies ever since. Two film versions have been released: in 1930 with Dennis King and Jeanette MacDonald, and 1956 with Oreste and Kathryn Grayson.

Vallee, Rudy

b. Hubert Prior Vallee, 28 July 1901, Island Pond, Vermont, USA, d. 3 July 1986, North Hollywood, California, USA. Vallee was an immensely popular singer during the 20s and 30s and generally accepted as the first pop idol. He sang through a megaphone, and is usually regarded as the first 'crooner'; a precursor of Russ Columbo and Bing Crosby. Vallee was also one of the first entertainers to generate mass hysteria among his audiences. Vallee was brought up in Westbrook, Maine. learning to play the saxophone in his teens, and took the name 'Rudy', because of his admiration for saxophonist, Rudy Weidoft. During 1924-25 he took a year off from university to play the saxophone in London with the Savoy Havana Band led by Reginald Batten. At this time his singing voice, which was somewhat slight and nasal, was not taken seriously.In 1928 he led his first band, at the exclusive Heigh-Ho Club on New York's 53rd Street. Billed as Rudy and his Connecticut Yankees, Vallee made a good front man, with his famous greeting: 'heigh-ho, everybody', and his smooth vocal delivery of his theme song at that time, Walter Donaldson's 'Heigh-Ho Everybody, Heigh-Ho'. When radio stations started to carry his shows in the club, he became an instant success, and admitted that he was 'a product of radio'. His next venue was the Versaille Club on 50th Street. After a few weeks, business was so good they renamed it the Villa Vallee. His success continued when he transferred his show to vaudeville. In 1929 he starred in his first feature film, the poorly- received *I'm A Vagabond Lover*, and in the same year began a weekly NBC network radio variety show sponsored by the Fleischmann's Yeast company (*The Fleischmann Hour*), which became a top show and ran for 10 years. His theme song for this show was 'My Time Is Your Time'. Artists he promoted on the show included radio ventriloquist Edgar Bergen, Frances Langford and Alice Faye. In 1931 and 1936, Vallée appeared on Broadway in *George White's Scandals*, and in 1933 starred in a film version of the show. From early in his career he had co-written several popular songs including 'I'm Still Caring', 'If You Haven't Got A Girl', 'Don't Play With Fire', 'Two Little Blue Little Eyes' and 'Oh, Ma-Ma'. He had big hits with some of his own numbers including 'I'm Just A Vagabond Lover', 'Deep Night', 'Vieni Vieni' and 'Betty Co-ed' (a song mentioning most of the US colleges).

Other record successes included 'Marie', 'Honey' (a number 1 hit), 'Weary River', 'Lonely Troubadour', 'A Little Kiss Each Morning (A Little Kiss Each Night)', 'Stein Song (University Of Maine)', 'If I Had A Girl Like You', 'You're Driving Me Crazy', 'Would You Like To Take A Walk?', 'When Yuba Plays The Rhumba On The Tuba', ' Let's Put Out The Lights', 'Brother Can You Spare A Dime?', 'Just An Echo In The Valley', 'Everything I Have Is Yours', 'Orchids In The Moonlight', 'You Oughta Be In Pictures', 'Nasty Man', 'As Time Goes By' and 'The Whiffenpoof Song'. In the late 30s and early 40s, he started new movie career as a comedy actor. Discarding his romantic image, he began portraying a series of eccentric, strait-laced, pompous characters in films such as *The Palm Beach Story* (1942). During World War II, Vallée led the California Coastguard orchestra, which he augmented to 45 musicians. After the war he was back on the radio, in nightclubs, and making more movies including, *The Bachelor And The Bobbysoxer* (1947), *I Remember Mama* (1948), *So This Is New York* (1948) and *Unfaithfully Yours* (1948). During the 50s he appeared regularly on television, especially in talk shows and he appeared in the film *Gentlemen Marry Brunettes* (1955). In 1961 he was a tremendous success as J.B. Biggley, a caricature of a collegiate executive figure, in Frank Loesser's smash hit musical, *How To Succeed In Business Without Really Trying*. Vallee re-created the role in the 1967 movie, and in a San Francisco show revival in 1975. In 1968 Vallee contributed the narration to the William Friedkin film *The Night They Raided Minsky's*. He continued to make movies into the 70s (his last feature was the 1976 film *Won Ton Ton, The Dog Who Saved Hollywood*), and continued to perform his one-man show up until his death from a heart attack in Hollywood.

Album: *How To Succeed In Business Without Really Trying* (1961, US Broadway soundtrack). Compilations: *Rudy Vallee And His Connecticut Yankees* (1986), *'Heigh-Ho Everybody, This Is...'* (1981), *Sing For Your Supper* (1989). Further reading: *Vagabond Dreams Come True*, Rudy Vallee. *My Time Is Your Time*, Rudy Vallee. *I Digress*, Rudy Vallée.

Valmouth

A British cult musical which shocked some, is fondly remembered by many, and, so the story goes, understood by relatively few. *Valmouth* opened at the Lyric, Hammersmith, which is located a few miles away from the glamorous West End, on 2 October 1958. It was adapted from the 'scandalous' works of Ronald Firbank by Sandy Wilson, whose smash-hit *The Boy Friend*, was coming to the end of its five-year run at Wyndhams Theatre. Many wise and learned beings have attempted unsuccessfully to fathom the mysteries of this show, but what seems to be clear is that Valmouth is one of those essentially English spa towns where life-enhancing benefits of a somewhat bizarre kind can be had by visitors and residents alike. In the case of Valmouth, the residents are mostly centenarians, and the main benefits include an abnormally long and active sex life. The inhabitants include Mrs. Yajnavalka (Bertice Reading), the black masseuse with the 'magic fingers' who provides a variety of advice and services to Grannie Took (Doris Hare) and her grand-daughter Thetis (Patsy Rowlands). Thetis imagines she is to be the bride of Captain Dick Thoroughfare (Alan Edwards), heir to Mrs Hurstpierpoint (Barbara Couper) the Catholic châtelaine of Hare Hatch House ('the former favourite of a King, but for just a few minutes'). In actual fact, Captain Dick has already married Mrs. Yajnavalk's niece, Niri-Esther (Maxine Daniels) - it's that complicated. Another familiar figure in the area is Lady Parvula de Panzoust (Fenella Fielding), an ageing nymphomaniac - but she is just visiting.

The song mostly associated with the show is 'My Big Best Shoes' joyously performed by Bertice Reading, but there were other memorable moments too in Wilson's wonderfully witty score which included Fenella Fielding's 'Just Once More' and 'Only A Passing Phase', along with 'Magic Fingers', 'Mustapha', 'The Cry Of The Peacock', 'Little Girl Baby' (all Reading), 'I Will Miss You' (Hare and Reading), and 'I Loved A Man', 'What Then Can Make Him Come So Slow', 'All The Girls Were Pretty', 'Lady Of The Manor', What Do I Want With Love', 'Where The Trees Are Green With Parrots', and 'My Talking Day'. *Valmouth* ran for 84 performances at the Lyric, but by the time the show transferred to Saville Theatre in the West End on 27 January 1959, Bertice Reading had returned to America and was replaced by the young up-and-coming jazz singer Cleo Laine. A further run of 102 performances to frequently puzzled and offended audiences was followed by complete rejection in New York where the show was withdrawn after less than two weeks. Over 20 years later, in May 1982, *Valmouth* was revived at the Chichester Festival Theatre with several of the original cast including Bertice Reading and Fenella Fielding, and with pop-star-turned-actor Mark Wynter as Captain Dick. The production was highly acclaimed, and although it is inconceivable that 80s audiences would be even slightly outraged, no impresario would take a chance on London.

Verdon, Gwen

b. Gwyneth Evelyn Verdon, 13 January 1926, Culver City, California, USA. A vivacious, red-headed dancer, actress and singer, Verdon can be funny or tender, sassy or seductive, depending on the music and the mood. She studied dancing from an early age, and, after assisting the noted choreographer Jack Cole on *Magdalena* (1948), made her first appearance on Broadway two years later in *Alive And Kicking*. However, it was Cole Porter's *Can-Can* that made her a star in 1953. She played the (very) high-kicking Claudine, and won her first Tony Award. She won another for her portrayal of the bewitching Lola in *Damn Yankees* (1955), which was brilliantly choreographed by her future husband, Bob Fosse. He re-staged his innovative dance sequences for the 1958 film version, for which, instead of casting an already established film star, Verdon was invited to reprise her Broadway role. From then on, Fosse choreographed and/or directed all Verdon's shows. In 1957 she played Anna Christie in *New Girl In Town*, a musical adaptation of Eugene O'Neill's 1921 play, and on this occasion she shared the Tony with a fellow cast member, Thelma Ritter - the first time there had been a Tony-tie. In 1959, Verdon won outright - and for the last time - when she starred with Richard Kiley in *Redhead*. After that, Broadway audiences had to wait another seven years before they saw Verdon on the musical stage, but the wait was more than worthwhile. In *Sweet Charity* (1966) she played a dancehall hostess with a heart of gold who yearns for marriage and roses round the door. Cy Coleman and Dorothy Fields provided her with some lovely songs, including 'If My Friends Could See Me Now' and 'There's Gotta Be Something Better Than This'. Gwen Verdon's final Broadway musical (to date) was *Chicago* (1975), a razzle-dazzle affair set in the roaring 20s, full of hoods and Chita Rivera. In more recent times she has turned once more to films. She had

appeared in several during the 50s, including *On The Riviera*, *Meet Me After The Show*, *David And Bathsheba*, *The Merry Widow*, *The I Don't Care Girl*, *The Farmer Takes A Wife*, as well as *Damn Yankees*. In 1983 she played a choreographer in the television movie *Legs*, and had several other good roles in big-screen features such as *The Cotton Club*, *Cocoon*, *Nadine*, *Cocoon-The Return*, and *Alice* (1990). In 1992 she donated a substantial amount of material documenting her own career and that of her late husband, Bob Fosse (he died in 1987), to the Library of Congress.

Very Good Eddie

The second of the renowned Princess Theatre shows written by Jerome Kern and Guy Bolton immediately before they began their fruitful partnership with P.G. Wodehouse. It was an early attempt to write jolly, tuneful musical comedies on a small, inexpensive scale, which would be quite different from the prevailing imported operettas. Bolton's book, written with Philip Bartholomae, and adapted from the latter's play, *Over Night*, told of two honeymoon couples on a Hudson River cruise boat, who become embarrassingly separated when the husband from one couple and the wife from the other pair are accidentally left on shore. Explanations are offered and accepted when the quartet are subsequently reunited at the Rip Van Winkle Inn. The young and talented cast included Ernest Truex, Oscar Shaw, Alice Dovey, Helen Raymond, and John E. Hazzard. Kern's light-hearted and appealing score, with lyrics mostly by Schuyler Greene and Herbert Reynolds, contained two of his early hits, 'Some Sort Of Somebody' and 'Babes In The Wood', along with others such as 'I'd Like To Have A Million In The Bank', 'Nodding Roses', 'On The Shore At Le Lei Wi', 'Isn't It Great To Be Married?', 'Thirteen Collar', 'Old Boy Neutral', and 'If I Find The Girl'. The plausible book and the skilfully integrated songs attracted a great deal of approval for a show which is now considered to be a landmark in the history of the American musical. *Very Good Eddie* ran for 341 performances in New York, but the 1918 London production could only add another 46 to that total. The show was successfully revived on Broadway in 1975.

Von Tilzer, Albert

b. Albert Gumm, 29 March 1878, Indianapolis, Indiana, USA, d. 1 October 1956, Los Angeles, California, USA. Albert changed his name from Gumm following his elder brother, Harry Von Tilzer's success as a composer and song publisher, and worked for him for a while as a song-plugger. In 1903 he started his own publishing company with another brother, Jack, and, in the following year wrote his first song hit, 'Teasing', with lyricist Cecil

Mack. He contributed songs to several Broadway shows, including *About Town* ('I'm Sorry'), *The Yankee Girl* ('Nora Malone') and *Madame Sherry* ('Put Your Arms Around Me Honey' (with Junie McCree). The last was a big hit in 1911 for several artists, including Arthur Collins, Byron Harlan and Ada Jones, and was revived in 1943 after it was featured in the Betty Grable movie, *Coney Island*. The composer also contributed to the 1917 revue, *Hitchy-Koo* in which Albert's war song, 'I May Be Gone For A Long, Long Time', written with Lew Brown, was the main hit, and *Linger Longer Letty* which included another collaboration with Brown, 'Oh, By Jingo'. Von Tilzer's complete Broadway scores included *The Happiest Night Of His Life* (lyrics by Junie McCree), *Honey Girl*, (with an impressive score, written with Neville Fleeson), *The Gingham Girl*, *Adrienne* and *Bye Bye Bonnie*.

His many other successful compositions included 'Honey Boy' (with Jack Norworth), a hit in 1907 for the Peerless Quartet and Billy Murray, 'Smarty' (Ada Jones and Billy Murray), 'Take Me Out To The Ball Game' (with Norworth), sung at the time by Billy Murray And The Haydn Quartet and revived by Frank Sinatra and Gene Kelly in the 1949 film of the same name, 'I'll Be With You In Apple Blossom Time' (with Fleeson), recorded by Charles Harrison, Henry Burr and Albert Campbell in 1920. Other hits included a big war-time speciality for the Andrews Sisters (1941), 'My Cutey's Due At Two-To-Two Today', a 'tale of amatory fidelity', amusingly performed by Bobby Darin and Johnny Mercer on their 1961 album, *Two Of A Kind*, and several songs with lyrics by Lew Brown, such as 'Give Me The Moonlight, Give Me The Girl' (the theme song of UK entertainer, Frankie Vaughan), 'I Used To Love You (But It's All Over Now)' and 'Dapper Dan', a hit in 1921 for the singer of comic novelties, Frank Crumit.

Von Tilzer's other collaborators included Arthur J. Lamb and Edward Madden. In the late 20s, after the *Bye Bye Bonnie* show, Von Tilzer's songwriting output declined, although he did write a few minor film scores in the 30s, including *Here Comes The Band* (1935), which included 'Roll Along Prairie Moon'. The latter boasted a lyric by Ted Fio Rito and Cecil Mack, and became successful for the singing bandleader, Smith Ballew. In the early 50s, he wrote 'I'm Praying To St. Christopher' with Larry McPherson, which was recorded in the UK by Anne Shelton, Joyce Frazer and Toni Arden.

Von Tilzer, Harry

b. Harold Gumm, 8 July 1872, Detroit, Michigan, USA, d. 10 January 1946. Von Tilzer was a prolific composer, publisher and producer. He grew up in Indianapolis, where he learned to play the piano. As a teenager he worked in a circus, touring in shows, singing and playing the piano, performing his own material. In 1892 he moved to New York, and started writing special material for vaudeville performers, and in 1898 had his first song hit, 'My Old Hampshire Home' (lyric by Andrew B. Sterling, his chief collaborator). This was followed soon after by 'I'd Leave My Happy Home For You' (with Will A. Heelan). For a time Von Tilzer worked for music publishers Shapiro & Bernstein and while there, wrote 'A Bird In A Gilded Cage' (with Arthur Lamb), which sold over two million copies as sheet music. With his share of the royalties, Harry set up his own music publishing company on West 28th Street, New York in 1902, becoming one of the first residents in what became known as 'Tin Pan Alley', a term that, it is claimed, was coined in his office. In the same year he wrote 'Down Where The Wurzburger Flows' (with Vincent Bryan), which was a hit for the flamboyant entertainer Nora Bayes, who became known as the 'Wurzburger Girl'. A year later Harry wrote his first and only complete Broadway score, for the comic opera, *The Fisher Maiden*; it closed after only a month.

Later, he contributed the occasional number to several other musicals, including *The Liberty Belles*, *The Girls Of Gottenburg*, *The Kissing Girl*, *The Dairy Maids*, *Lifting The Lid* and *The Honeymoon Express* (1913), but it was the individual songs with which he had his biggest hits. These included the extremely successful 'The Mansion Of Aching Hearts' 'On A Sunday Afternoon', 'Please Go 'Way And Let Me Sleep', 'Wait Till The Sun Shines, Nellie', 'Cubanola Glide', 'I Want A Girl (Just Like The Girl That Married Dear Old Dad)' with Willian Dillon, as well as 'In The Evening By The Moonlight' and 'They Always Pick On Me'. He also wrote 'Under The Anheuser Tree' with Sterling, Percy Krone and Russell Hunting, better known in its rearranged version as 'Down At The Old Bull And Bush', a perennial singalong favourite in the UK. Also popular was the anti-Prohibition number, 'If I Meet The Guy Who Made This Country Dry' (1920). Harry Von Tilzer's last big song was 'Just Around The Corner' (1925). When it was followed a year later by 'Under The Wurzburger Tree', a throwback to one of his biggest early hits, the end of his songwriting career was in sight, and he retired to supervize his publishing interests. He died in 1946 in New York. Some of his songs were used in the 1975 Broadway musical, *Doctor Jazz*, starring Bobby Van. His other collaborators included William Jerome, Bert Hanlon and Arthur J. Lamb.

W

Waller, Fats

b. Thomas Wright Waller, 21 May 1904, Waverley, New York, USA, d. 15 December 1943, Kansas City, Missouri, USA. Influenced by his grandfather, a violinist, and his mother Waller was playing piano at students' concerts, and organ in his father's church by the time he was 10 years old. In 1918, while still in high school, he was asked to fill in for the regular organist at the Lincoln Theatre, and subsequently gained a permanent seat at the Wurlitzer Grand. A year later, he won a talent contest, playing ragtime pianist James P. Johnson's, 'Carolina Shout'. While a protege of Johnson's, Waller adopted the Harlem stride style of piano playing, 'the swinging left hand', emphasizing tenths on the bass, to which Waller added his own distinctive touch. In 1919, while on tour as a vaudeville pianist, he composed 'Boston Blues' which, when the title was later changed to 'Squeeze Me', with a lyric by Clarence Williams, became one his best known songs. In the early 20s, with the USA on the brink of the 'jazz age', and Prohibition in force, Waller's piano playing was in demand at rent-parties, bootleg joints, in cabaret and vaudeville. Inevitably, he mixed with gangsters, and it is said that his first $100 bill was given to him by Al Capone, who fortunately enjoyed his piano playing. Around this time Waller made his first records as accompanist to one of the leading blues singers, Sara Martin. He also recorded with the legendary Bessie Smith, and toured with her in 1926. His first solo piano recording was reputedly 'Muscle Shoal Blues'. From 1926-29 he made a series of pipe organ recordings, in a disused church in Camden, New Jersey. Having studied composition from an early age with various teachers including Leopold Godowski and Carl Bohm, Waller collaborated with James P. Johnson and Clarence Todd on the music for the Broadway revue, Keep Shufflin' (1928). This was a follow-up to Noble Sissle and Eubie Blakes' smash hit, Shuffle Along (1921), which starred Joséphine Baker, and was the show which is credited with making black music acceptable to Broadway audiences. Although not on stage in Keep Shufflin', Waller made a considerable impression with his exuberant piano playing from the show's orchestra pit at Daly's Theatre. Andy Razaf, who wrote most of the show's lyrics, including the outstanding number, 'Willow Tree', would become Waller's most regular collaborator, and his closest friend. Just over a year later, in June 1929, Waller again combined with

Razaf for Hot Chocolates, another Negro revue, revised for Broadway. In the orchestra pit this time, was trumpeter, Louis Armstrong, whose role was expanded during the show's run. The score for Hot Chocolates also contained the plaintive ('What Did I Do To Be So) Black, And Blue?'; and one of the team's most enduring standards, 'Ain't Misbehavin'', an instrumental version of which became Waller's first hit and years later, was selected for inclusion in the NARAS Hall of Fame. Both Keep Shufflin' and Hot Chocolates were first staged at Connie's Inn, in Harlem, one of the biggest black communities in the world. Waller lived in the middle of Harlem, until he hit the really big time and moved to St. Albans, Long Island, where he installed a built-in Hammond organ. In the late 20s and early 30s, he was still on the brink of that success. Although he endured some bleak times during the Depression he was writing some of his most effective songs, such as 'Honeysuckle Rose', 'Blue, Turning Grey Over You', and 'Keepin' Out Of Mischief Now' (all with Razaf); 'I've Got A Feeling I'm Falling' (with Billy Rose and Harry Link); and 'I'm Crazy 'Bout My Baby' (with Alexander Hill). In 1932 he toured Europe in the company of fellow composer, Spencer Williams, and played prestige venues such as London's Kit Kat Club and the Moulin Rouge in Paris. Worldwide fame followed with the formation of Fats Waller And His Rhythm in 1934. The all-star group featured musicians such as Al Casey (guitar), Herman Autrey (b. 4 December 1904, Evergreen, Alabama, USA, d. 14 June 1980, New York, USA; trumpet), Gene Sedric (b. 17 June 1907, St. Louis, Missouri, USA, d. 3 April 1963, New York, USA; reeds), Billy Taylor or Charles Turner (string bass), drummers Harry Dial (b. 17 February 1907, Birmingham, Alabama, USA) or Yank Porter (b. c.1895, Norfolk, Virginia, USA, d. 22 March 1944, New York, USA) and Rudy Powell (clarinet). Signed for Victor, the ensemble made over 150 78 rpm records between May 1934 and January 1943, in addition to Waller's output of piano and organ solos, and some big band tracks. The Rhythm records were a revelation. High-class musicianship accompanied Waller's exuberant vocals, sometimes spiced with sly, irreverent asides on popular titles such as 'Don't Let It Bother You', 'Sweetie Pie', 'Lulu's Back In Town', 'Truckin'', 'A Little Bit Independent', 'It's A Sin To Tell A Lie', 'You're Not That Kind', 'Until The Real Thing Comes Along', 'The Curse Of An Aching Heart', 'Dinah', 'S'posin', 'Smarty', 'The Sheik Of Araby', 'Hold Tight' and 'I Love To Whistle'.

Waller had massive hits with specialities such as 'I'm Gonna Sit Right Down And Write Myself A Letter', 'When Somebody Thinks You're Wonderful', 'My Very Good Friend The Milkman' and 'Your Feet's Too Big'. He recorded ballads like 'Two Sleepy

Fats Waller

People' and 'Then I'll Be Tired Of You', and several of his own compositions, including 'Honeysuckle Rose' and 'The Joint Is Jumpin'' (written with Razaf and J.C. Johnson). In 1935, Waller appeared in the first of his three feature films, *Hooray For Love* which also featured Bill 'Bojangles' Robinson. In the following year he received excellent reviews for his rendering of 'I've Got My Fingers Crossed' in *King Of Burlesque*. In 1938, he toured Europe again for several months, this time as a big star. Besides performing concerts in several cities, including a performance at the London Palladium, he appeared in an early television broadcast from Alexandra Palace, and became the first, and probably the only jazz musician, to play the organ of the Notre Dame de Paris. He returned to England and Scotland the following year. Back in the USA, Waller toured with a combo for a while, and during the early 40s performed with his own big band, before again working as a solo artist. In 1942 he tried to play serious jazz in concert at Carnegie Hall - but was poorly received. In 1943, he returned to Broadway to write the score, with George Marion, for the bawdy musical *Early To Bed*. The comedy high-spot proved to be 'The Ladies Who Sing With The Band'.

Waller teamed with 'Bojangles' Robinson again, in 1943, for the film of *Stormy Weather*, which included a version of 'Ain't Misbehavin''. He stayed in California for an engagement at the Zanzibar Club in Los Angeles. On his way back to New York on the Santa Fe Chief railway express, he died of pneumonia as it was pulling into Kansas City. His life had been one of excess. Enormous amounts of food and liquor meant that his weight varied between 285 and 310 lbs - 'a girthful of blues'. Days of carousing were followed by equal amounts of sleeping, not necessarily alone. Jazz continually influenced his work, even when he was cajoled into recording inferior material. He worked and recorded with leading artists such as Fletcher Henderson, Ted Lewis, Alberta Hunter, Jack Teagarden, Gene Austin and Lee Wiley. Waller felt strongly that he did not receive his fair share of the songwriting royalties. He was known to visit the Brill Building, which housed New York's prominent music publishers, and obtained advances from several publishers for the same tune. Each, however, had a different lyric. He sold many numbers outright, and never received credit for them. Two which are rumoured to be his, but always attributed to Jimmy McHugh, 'I Can't Give You Anything But Love' and 'On The Sunny Side Of The Street', were included in the 1978 Broadway show *Ain't Misbehavin'*. Most of the numbers were genuine Waller, with a few others like 'Mean To Me', 'It's A Sin To Tell A Lie', 'Fat And Greasy' and 'Cash For Your Trash' which, in performance, he had made his own. The majority of his recordings have been reissued and appear on a variety of labels such as RCA, Saville, Halcyon, Living Era, President, Swaggie (Australia) and Vogue (France).

Selected albums: *Ain't Misbehavin'* (1980, released on CD in 1989), *Fats At The Organ* (1981, released on CD in 1988), *20 Golden Pieces* (1982), *Piano Solos (1929-41)* (1983), *African Ripples* (1984), *Live At The Yacht Club* (1984), *Fats Waller In London* (1985), *My Very Good Friend The Milkman* (1986), *Armful O'Sweetness* (1987), *Dust Off That Old Pianna* (1987), *Complete Early Band Works 1927-9* (1987), *Take It Easy* (1988), *Fats Waller And His Rhythm 1934-36 (Classic Years In Digital Stereo)* (1988), *Spreadin' Rhythm Around* (1989), *Ragtime Piano Entertainer* (1989), *Loungin' At The Waldorf* (1990), *1939/40 - Private Acetates And Film Soundtracks* (1993).

Further reading: *The Music Of Fats Waller*, John R.T. Davies. *Fats Waller*, Charles Fox. *Fats Waller*, Maurice Waller and Anthony Calabrese. *Ain't Misbehavin'': The Story Of Fats Waller*, E.W Kirkeby, D.P. Schiedt and S. Traill. *Stride: The Music Of Fats Waller*, P. Machlin. *Fats Waller: His Life And Times*, Alyn Shipton.

Watch Your Step

After interpolating songs into other people's shows for several years, this 'syncopated musical' containing Irving Berlin's first complete Broadway score, was presented at the New Amsterdam Theatre in New York on 8 December 1914. The slight book, by Harry B. Smith, was based on Augustin Daly's play *Round The Clock*, which is said to have been adapted from a French farce. Audiences probably believed that fact when faced with a story in which a character dies leaving a a great deal of money to anyone who can claim they have never been in love. The stars were the world's premier ballroom dancers Vernon and Irene Castle who were making their final professional appearance together. Shortly after this show closed Vernon left to join the Canadian Air Force and was killed in an air crash in 1918. Berlin's score for *Watch Your Step* introduced some of the elements and rhythms from Tin Pan Alley to the hallowed halls of the legitimate musical theatre. The mostly happy, singable songs included 'Play A Simple Melody', 'They Always Follow Me Around', 'Show Us How To Do The Fox-Trot', 'The Minstrel Parade', 'When I Discovered You', 'Settle Down In A One-Horse Town', 'When It's Night Time In Dixieland', 'Lock Me In Your Harem And Throw Away The Key', and 'I've Got To Go Back To Texas'. The New York run of 175 performances was followed by a further 275 in London, where the cast included Joseph Coyne, Ethel Levey, and the versatile Lupino Lane in his first West End show.

Waters, Ethel

b. 31 October 1896, Chester, Pennsylvania, USA, d.

1 September 1977. One of the most influential of popular singers, Waters' early career found her working in vaudeville. As a consequence, her repertoire was more widely based and popularly angled than those of many of her contemporaries. It is reputed that she was the first singer to perform W.C. Handy's 'St Louis Blues' in public, and she later popularized blues and jazz-influenced songs such as 'Stormy Weather' and 'Travellin' All Alone', also scoring a major success with 'Dinah'. She first recorded in 1921 and on her early dates she was accompanied by artists such as Fletcher Henderson, Coleman Hawkins, James P. Johnson and Duke Ellington. Significantly, for her acceptance in white circles, she also recorded with Jack Teagarden, Benny Goodman and Tommy Dorsey.

From the late 20s, Waters appeared in several Broadway musicals, including *Africana*, *Blackbirds Of 1930*, *Rhapsody In Black*, *As Thousands Cheer*, *At Home Abroad*, and *Cabin In The Sky*, in which she introduced several diverting songs such as 'I'm Coming Virginia', 'Baby Mine', 'My Handy Man Ain't Handy No More', 'Till The Real Thing Comes Along', 'Suppertime', 'Harlem On My Mind', 'Heat Wave', 'Got A Bran' New Suit' (with Eleanor Powell), 'Hottentot Potentate', and 'Cabin In The Sky'. In the 30s she stopped the show regularly at the Cotton Club in Harlem with 'Stormy Weather', and appeared at Carnegie Hall in 1938. She played a few dramatic roles in the theatre, and appeared in several films, including *On With The Show*, *Check And Double Check*, *Gift Of The Gab*, *Tales Of Manhattan*, *Cairo*, *Cabin In The Sky*, *Stage Door Canteen*, *Pinky*, *Member Of The Wedding*, and *The Sound And The Fury* (1959). In the 50s she was also in the US television series *Beulah* for a while, and had her own Broadway show *An Evening With Ethel Waters* (1957).

Throughout the 60s and on into the mid-70s she sang as a member of the organization which accompanied evangelist Billy Graham. Although less highly regarded in blues and jazz circles than either Bessie Smith or Louis Armstrong, in the 30s Waters transcended the boundaries of these musical forms to far greater effect than either of these artists and spread her influence throughout popular music. Countless young hopefuls emulated her sophisticated, lilting vocal style and her legacy lived on in the work of outstanding and, ironically, frequently better-known successors, such as Connee Boswell, Ruth Etting, Adelaide Hall, Mildred Bailey, Lee Wiley, Lena Horne and Ella Fitzgerald. Even Billie Holiday (with whom Waters was less than impressed, commenting, 'She sings as though her shoes are too tight'), acknowledged her influence. A buoyant, high-spirited singer with a light, engaging voice that frequently sounds 'whiter' than most of her contemporaries, Waters' career was an object lesson in determination and inner drive. Her appalling childhood problems and troubled early life, recounted in the first part of her autobiography, *His Eye Is On The Sparrow*, were overcome through grit and the application of her great talent.

Selected albums: *His Eye Is On The Sparrow* (c.1963), *Ethel Waters Reminisces* (c.1963). Compilations: *Ethel Waters* (1979), *The Complete Bluebird Sessions (1938-39)* (1986), *On The Air (1941-51)* (1986), *Ethel Waters On Stage And Screen (1925-40)* (1989), *Who Said Blackbirds Are Blue?* (1989), *Classics 1926-29* (1993).

Further reading: *His Eye Is On The Sparrow*, Ethel Waters. *To Me It's Wonderful*, Ethel Waters.

Webb, Marti
b. 1944, Cricklewood, London, England. In 1963, at the age of 19, singer Marti Webb was 'plucked from the chorus' of the London production of Leslie Bricusse and Anthony Newley's hit musical, *Stop the World - I Want To Get Off*, to star opposite Tommy Steele, in *Half A Sixpence*. In the subsequent 1967 film version she dubbed the singing voice of her replacement, actress Julia Foster. In 1965 Webb played Nancy in a national tour of Lionel Bart's *Oliver!*, and re-created the role in a major West End revival in 1967. In the early 70s, Webb appeared in one of the in vogue 'biblical' musicals, *Godspell*, with a superior cast which included Jeremy Irons, David Essex and Julie Covington. She also featured in a musical adaptation of J.B. Priestley's *The Good Companions*, with a score by André Previn and Johnny Mercer. Much better all round, was *The Card*, with songs by Tony Hatch and Jackie Trent, in which Webb impressed with her duet with Jim Dale on 'Opposite Your Smile', and the solo, 'I Could Be The One'. It was in the 80s, however, that she came to prominence after successfully replacing Elaine Page in *Evita*. In 1980 she appeared in an invited concert and a television broadcast of a 'song cycle', *Tell Me On A Sunday*, with a score by Andrew Lloyd Webber and lyricist Don Black. This spawned both a studio and television soundtrack album, and Webb took one of the show's songs, 'Take That Look Off Your Face' into the UK Top 10. Two years later, when an expanded version of *Tell Me On A Sunday* was joined with *Variations* to form the two part 'theatrical concert', *Song And Dance*, Webb's 50 minute solo performance was hailed as a 'remarkable *tour de force*'. She also took over various roles in other Lloyd Webber productions, including his longest-running British musical, *Cats*. Webb's singles included 'Didn't Mean To Fall In Love', 'Ready For Roses Now', 'Ben' (UK Top 5), and three popular television themes: 'Always There' from *Howard's Way* (UK Top 20); 'Someday Soon' from *The Onedin Line* and a duet with Paul Jones on 'I Could Be So Good For You' from *Minder*. In 1991 Webb toured the UK and the

Channel Islands with *The Magic Of The Musicals*, co-starring with television's *Opportunity Knocks* winner Mark Rattray.

Selected albums: *Tell Me On A Sunday* (1980), *Won't Change Places* (1981), *I'm Not That Kind Of Girl* (1983), *Encore* (1985), *Always There* (1986), *Gershwin* (1987), *Marti Webb - The Album* (1993), *Performance* (1993).

Weill, Kurt

b. 2 March 1900, Dessau, Germany, d. 3 April 1950, New York City, New York, USA. After studying piano and composition as a child, Weill pursued his studies into adulthood and at the age of 20 was conducting opera with local companies. By the mid-20s Weill had established a reputation as a leading composer in the modern idiom. He was eager to make opera a popular form, accessible to the widest audience. He was also politically aware and wanted his work to have social significance. In collaboration with Bertolt Brecht he wrote *Little Mahagonny* (later expanded to become *The Rise And Fall Of The City Of Mahagonny*) and then gained success with *The Threepenny Opera* (1928). Although a massive success in Germany, the show failed in the USA in 1933, but was a hit when it was revived in 1954. The show's best-known song, 'Mack The Knife', was a hit for several singers. Weill and his wife, singer Lotte Lenya, emigrated to the USA in 1935 where he formed a working association with Group Theatre, the influential left-wing drama company which was home to such rising talents as Lee J. Cobb, John Garfield, Clifford Odets, Frances Farmer and Elia Kazan. He also wrote for the popular theatre and attracted attention with *Knickerbocker Holiday* (1938). The show was written to star Walter Huston, an actor with no singing voice. Weill was equal to the task and, with lyrics by Maxwell Anderson, he fashioned a song which worked just as well, whether sung or spoken. This was 'September Song', one of Weill's most enduring compositions. In 1941 he wrote the show *Lady In The Dark* (with lyricist Ira Gershwin), from which came 'My Ship', 'The Saga Of Jenny' and 'One Life To Live'. In 1943 he wrote *One Touch Of Venus* with Ogden Nash, with a major song in 'Speak Low'. Another 40s stage show, *Street Scene*, later became a success in Germany, where it was staged by the Dusseldorf Opera in 1955. Four years later an unusual circle was completed when the New York City Opera performed it to critical acclaim. Towards the end of the 40s Weill wrote two more Broadway shows, *Love Life* and *Lost In The Stars*. The latter was an adaptation of Alan Paton's novel, *Cry The Beloved Country*, one of the first works by a South African to attract international attention with its plea for tolerance and an end to discrimination. Weill was working on *Huckleberry Finn*, an adaptation of Mark

Twain's celebrated novel, when he died in April 1950.

Further reading: *The Days Grow Short: The Life And Music Of Kurt Weill*, Ronald Saunders.

Welch, Elisabeth

b. 27 February 1908, New York City, New York, USA. After working in obscurity as a singer and dancer in various New York nightspots, Welch attracted considerable attention with her appearance in the 1923 show *Runnin' Wild*, in which she introduced a new dance to the new tune, 'Charleston'. She appeared in several all-black revues on and off Broadway during the next few years, including *Chocolate Dandies* (1924) and Lew Leslie's *Blackbirds Of 1928*. It was with the latter show that she first visited Europe, appearing at the Moulin Rouge in Paris in 1929. She was a great success and returned to the city the following year. By 1933 she had decided that she preferred life away from the USA and settled in London. During the 30s she established herself as a star of London's nightlife and continued to appear in revues, musicals and plays throughout the next few decades. Several of the songs with which she is associated, such as 'As Time Goes By', 'Love for Sale', 'Stormy Weather', 'LaVie En Rose', and her signature tune 'Solomon', have since become standards. In 1976 she appeared with Linda Lewis in the Caryl Brahms/Ned Sherrin London stage show, *I Gotta Shoe*. A remarkable survivor, she continued to appear on radio and television and to make records. She also played a cameo role, singing 'Stormy Weather', in Derek Jarman's 1980 film *The Tempest*. In 1985, while returning home from the London theatre where she was appearing in *Jerome Kern Goes To Hollyood*, she was battered unconscious by a mugger, but was back on stage less than 24 hours later. A year after that she was in New York, performing her one-woman show *Time To Start Living*, and in 1989 she starred in a one night concert revival of *Nymph Errant*, a show in which she had first appeared in 1933. Fifty years on, the cream of British showbusiness gathered at the Lyric Theatre in London to pay tribute to Elisabeth Welch, and give her an unprecedented (as far as anyone there could remember) five standing ovations.

Selected albums: *Elisabeth Welch Sings The Irving Berlin Songbook* (1958), *Elisabeth Welch In Concert* (1986), *Where Have You Been* (1987), *This Thing Called Love* (1989). Compilation: *Miss Elisabeth Welch (1933-40)* (1979).

West Side Story

Opening at the Winter Garden Theatre in New York on 26 September 1957, the stage musical *West Side Story* shook audiences with its powerful, even aggressive score, dancing and storyline. Transposing

Steve Lawrence (*What Makes Sammy Run?*)

the *Romeo And Juliet* story to contemporary New York, the plot traced the doomed love affair between a member of one of the incoming Puerto Rican families and a native-born American. Maria, the Puerto Rican girl, and Tony, her lover, are denied happiness through the conflict between the two sides in the urban gang war. In a fight, Tony kills Maria's brother, Bernardo. Later, Tony, believing that Maria has been killed by Bernardo's friend, Chino, is himself killed. This death stuns the rival gangs, the Puerto Rican 'Sharks' and the American 'Jets'. With music by Leonard Bernstein, lyrics by Stephen Sondheim, a book by Arthur Laurents, and the exciting and dynamic Tony-winning choreography of Jerome Robbins (who had also conceived the idea for the show), *West Side Story* blasted many preconceptions about form and content of American musical comedy. The first song, 'America', cynically contrasted the difference between the expectations of immigrants and the reality they found in their new homeland (although some later recordings managed to turn it into a paean of praise for the USA). 'Gee, Officer Krupke!' was wickedly funny and realistically disrespectful of authority. Amongst the songs that had a lighter mood than those which dominated much of the show were 'I Feel Pretty', sung by Carol Lawrence as Maria, 'Maria' sung by Larry Kert as Tony, and 'Tonight', a duet for Maria and Tony. The other songs included 'Something's Coming', 'One Hand, One Heart', 'Cool', 'Somewhere', and 'A Boy Like That' which was sung by Chita Rivera as Anita. Rivera also led the ensemble in 'America'. Critical reaction was good, and word of mouth reports ecstatic. The show ran for 732 perormances on Broadway and a 1,039 in London. There were major New York revivals in 1968 and 1980, and West End audiences saw the show again in 1973, 1984 and 1992. The 1961 screen version starred Natalie Wood, Richard Beymer, Rita Moreno, Russ Tamblyn, and George Chakiris. Leonard Bernstein conducted the original full-length score for the first time in 1984 for a recording with opera stars, Kiri Te Kanawa and José Carreras. The event, which was filmed and televised, ensured the album's substantial sales. *West Side Story* has also spawned many hit singles in radically different interpretations from artists as diverse as P.J. Proby ('Somewhere' and 'Maria') and the Nice ('America').

What Makes Sammy Run?

Many years before director Robert Altman took the lid off the Hollywood screenwriters' power game in his 1992 film *The Player*, this show, with its theme of greed and corruption in the movie business, opened at the 54th Street Theatre in New York on 27 February 1964. Budd and Stuart Schulberg's libretto was based on the former's novel, and told of the all-time, first class American heel - Sammy Glick (Steve

Lawrence). By consistently stealing his colleagues' ideas and projects, (particularly those of his friend Al Manheim (Robert Alda), Glick graduates from his job as a copy boy on the New York *Record* to a position as a screenwriter at World Wide Pictures in Hollywood (he comes up with a vehicle for the studio's latest star, entitled *Monsoon*, having lifted the plot from the 1932 classic *Rain!*). Regarded as the studio's new genius, he becomes first a producer, and then, eventually, head of the studio. The price he has had to pay is the loss of a good woman, a fellow-writer from his early days, Kit Sargent (Sally Ann Howes), the burden of an unfaithful nymphomanic wife, Laurette Harrington (Bernice Massi), and causing the the suicide of Sidney Fineman (Arny Freeman), his mentor at the studio. Surely he must feel guilty about that? Not Sammy, he just keeps on running. Ervin Drake's score contained no hits for the popular singer Steve Lawrence to make his own, but 'A Room Without Windows' and 'My Home Town' did achieve some modest popularity. The rest of the numbers included 'The Friendliest Thing', 'A Tender Spot', 'Something To Live For', 'A New Pair Of Shoes', 'Lights! Camera! Platitude!', 'Maybe Some Other Time', 'You Can Trust Me', 'Kiss Me No Kisses', 'I Feel Humble', and 'Some Days Everything Goes Wrong'. Abe Burrows directed what became a popular attraction which ran for over a year, a total of 540 performances. Steve Lawrence made one other appearance in a Broadway book musical when he starred with his wife Eydie Gormé in *Golden Rainbow* (1968), which was based on Arnold Schulmans' play *A Hole In The Head*, and ran for nearly a year.

Where's Charley?

Frank Loesser's first Broadway book musical was based on the much-loved English farce, *Charley's Aunt*, by Brandon Thomas, which was first performed in London in 1892. *Where's Charley?* opened at the St. James Theatre in New York on 11 October 1948 with a book by George Abbott which was set at Oxford University in England. Undergraduates Jack Chesney (Byron Palmer) and Charley Wykeham (Ray Bolger) have invited two young ladies, Amy Spettigue (Allyn Ann McLerie) and Kitty Verdun (Doretta Morrow), to lunch on the understanding that they are to be chaperoned by Charley's rich widowed Aunt Donna Lucia D'Alvadorez. Her train is late, so Charley, who is appearing in drag in the University show, substitutes for her, and sparks off a sequence of hilarious events which ends with Charley being found out when his skirt falls down, and the real Aunt Donna marrying Jack's impoverished father, Sir Francis Chesney (Paul England). Ray Bolger was outstanding and his version of the show's hit song, 'Once In Love With Amy', is one of the golden moments in the history of the musical theatre.

Loesser's score also contained another number which attained some popularity, 'My Darling, My Darling', along with other equally engaging items such as the rousing 'New Ashmolean Marching Society And Students' Conservatory Band', 'Make A Miracle', 'Lovelier Than Ever', 'The Woman In His Room', and 'At The Red Rose Cotillion'. *Where's Charley* was a charming, thoroughly likeable show, and audiences continued to flock to see it for 792 performances. After touring on the road in the USA, it was revived briefly on Broadway, with Bolger, in 1951. He also starred in the 1952 movie version. In 1991 Loesser's wife, Jo Sullivan, and their daughter Emily Loesser, were in an acclaimed production of the show which was presented at the North Shore Music Theatre in Massachussetts. Although Bolger's distinctive recording of 'Once In Love With Amy' has appeared in many forms and was virtually copied word for word by Barry Manilow on his 1991 album, *Showstoppers*, no full-length recording of the original Broadway cast of *Where's Charley?* was issued. However, an album was released from the 1958 London production which starred Norman Wisdom and ran for 380 performances. In 1993 it was reissued on CD - in stereo for the first time.

Which Witch

Billed as the 'Norwegian Operamusical', *Which Witch* was originally commissioned as a concert piece for the Bergen International Festival in May 1987. While in that form it toured Scandanavia, North America, and Europe and was the subject of a best-selling album, before being transformed into the full-blown musical which opened at the Piccadilly Theatre in London on 22 October 1992. The show was the brainchild of Benedicte Adrian and Ingrid Bjornov, members of the highly successful Norwegian pop group, Dollie Deluxe. They composed the music together, and Adrian, a coloratura soprano, played the leading role while Bjornov served as musical director. The librettist and director was Piers Haggard, and the lyrics were written by Kit Hesketh, one half of the satirical comedy team of Kit And The Widow. The 'historically authenticated' 16th century story concerns an Italian girl, Maria Vittoria (Adrian), who spurns an arranged marriage to the German banker Anton Fugger (Stig Rosen), and declares her love for the Catholic Bishop Daniel (Graham Bickley). However, his sister, Anna Regina (Vivien Parry), spreads the word that Maria is a witch and she is burned at the stake. Audiences were taken aback by some of the special effects - one scene included 'several male demons with flapping gentitals exposed - rutting with witches'. The score, 'a pastiche of 19th century composers', contained in excess of 30 numbers, including items such as 'The Blessing', 'Bad Omens', 'Maria's Curse', 'Black Mass', 'The

Exorcism', and 'Almighty God'. One song which caught the attention was entitled '2,665,866,746,664 Little Devils'. The show was savaged by the critics in 'some of the worst reviews since Pearl Harbor'. Scandanavian package tours supplemented the few local patrons for a time, and King Harald and Queen Sonja of Norway visited the 'most heavily-panned London stage musical in a generation', but, after a run of 10 weeks, *Which Witch* was withdrawn with losses estimated at around £2 million. Theatre watchers were quick to point out that other recent 'disasters' at the Piccadilly included *Moby Dick*, *King*, and *Metropolis*.

White, George

b. George Wietz, 1890, New York, USA, d. 11 October 1968, Hollywood, California, USA. A producer, director, author, dancer, and actor, White's first taste of show business came in his teens when he formed a burlesque dancing team with Ben (or Benny) Ryan. Later, he had generally modest solo roles in shows such as *The Echo* (1910), *Ziegfeld Follies*, *The Whirl Of Society*, *The Pleasure Seekers*, *The Midnight Girl*, and *Miss 1917* which had music mainly by the young Jerome Kern. In 1919, he produced and directed the first of a series of revues, *George White's Scandals*, which combined the best of America's own burgeoning popular music (as opposed to the imported European variety) with fast-moving sketches and glamorous women. The shows were similar to, although perhaps not quite so lavish as, the undisputed leader of the genre, the *Ziegfeld Follies*. The *Scandals* appeared annually until 1926, and that edition, the longest runner of them all with 424 performances, was particularly notable for its score by De Sylva, Brown And Henderson, which introduced several enduring numbers such as 'Lucky Day', 'Black Bottom', and 'Birth Of The Blues'. There was no *George White Scandals* in 1927, but there *was* a show *about* the *Scandals* entitled *Manhattan Mary* which ran for a decent 264 peformances. White produced it and also co-write the book with Billy K. Wells. It too, had songs by De Sylva, Brown And Henderson which included 'The Five-Step' and 'It Won't Be Long Now', and starred White himself and the highly popular zany comedian Ed Wynn. The *Scandals* proper resumed in 1928, and there were further editions in 1929 and 1931. In the latter show, the future movie star Alice Faye appeared in the chorus, and this time the songs were by Lew Brown and Ray Henderson (De Sylva had gone off to Hollywood). Ethel Merman introduced the lovely 'Life Is Just A Bowl Of Cherries' and 'Ladies And Gentlemen, That's Love', as well as duetting with Rudy Vallee on 'My Song'. Vallee also sang 'The Thrill Is Gone' (with Everett Marshall) and 'This Is The Missus' (with Peggy Moseley). *George White's Music Hall Varieties*

The Who (*The Who's Tommy*)

replaced the *Scandals* in 1932, and in the cast was another Hollywood star of the future, tap-dancer supreme Eleanor Powell, and the likeable song-and dance man (among other things) Harry Richman, who introduced Herman Hupfield's delightful ballad 'Let's Put Out The Lights And Go To Sleep'. There were two more stage presentations of *George White's Scandals* - in 1936 and 1939 - but fashions had changed - and they ran for only just over 100 performances each. *George White's Scandals* of 1934, 1935, and 1945 were filmed, and the first two launched Alice Faye on her way to a glittering movie career. Over the years, the stage productions and the films showcased some of America's most talented artists such as Bert Lahr, Gracie Barrie, Cliff Edwards, Willie and Eugene Howard, Ann Miller, Ray Middleton, Ella Logan, Ann Pennington, Lou Holtz, W.C Fields, Dolores Costello, Ray Bolger, and Ethel Barrymore. The other songwriters involved included Irving Caesar, George Gershwin (five scores), Jack Yellen, Harold Arlen, Sammy Stept, Herb Magidson, and several more.

Who's Tommy, The

The Who made rock 'n' roll history in 1969 when they released the album of *Tommy*, a rock opera containing a medley of songs telling the story of a young boy who is struck deaf, dumb and blind when his war-hero father is murdered by his mother's lover, and who goes on to become a wizard of the pinball machines. It was filmed in 1975 by the flamboyant director Ken Russell, and several live concert versions were presented during the 70s. Pete Townshend, its principal composer, refused to participate in the 1979 West End stage production which ran at the Queen's Theatre for 118 performances. Fourteen years later, *Tommy* became the surprise hit of the Broadway season when it opened at the St. James Theatre in New York on 22 April 1993 to ecstatic reviews. Townshend collaborated with director Des McAnuff on a revised book, which up-dates the story to World War II, and the role of the grown Tommy, so often played by Roger Daltrey, is taken this time by Michael Cerveris. The by now familiar score is enhanced by a staggering array of psychedelic lighting and audio effects, kaleidosopic projections, banks of videos screens, with at one point, during 'Pinball Wizard', the whole theatre itself being transformed into a huge, glittering pinball machine. One stunning scene in which several paratroopers descend into an aircraft cockpit equals the *Miss Saigon* helicopter sequence, and makes sense of the US television ads for the show which claimed that it 'stimulates senses you never knew you had'. All this was noted by the Tony Awards committee, and *Tommy* won outright for director, scenic design, choreography, and lighting design, and tied with *Kiss Of The Spider Woman* for best score. General opinion seemed to be that the show was 'going to pack them in for some time, as for sheer rock 'n' roll fun *Tommy* is hard to beat'.

Will Rogers

Further reading: *The Who's Tommy: The Musical*

Whoopee

This lavish Florenz Ziegfeld production, which was a vehicle for the zany talents of the energetic 'eye-popping' comedian Eddie Cantor, opened at the New Amsterdam Theatre in New York on 4 December 1948. It had a score by Walter Donaldson (music) and Gus Kahn (lyrics), two writers who were more at home in Tin Pan Alley than on Broadway. True to form, two of the their songs for this show became huge all-time hits. William Anthony McGuire's book, which was based on Owen Davis's 1923 play *The Nervous Wreck*, concerns Henry Williams (Cantor), a timid hypochondriac, who has been sent to a health farm in California. He helps the lovely Sally Morgan (Frances Upton) to escape from the amorous clutches of the local Sheriff Bob Wells (Jack Rutherford). They take refuge in the local Indian reservation, the home of Sally's heart's desire, Wanenis (Paul Gregory), who, in the end, turns out to be as milky-white as she is. The situation gave Cantor a good excuse to wear his trade-mark blackface for a time, and race around like a man possessed. He also introduced 'Makin' Whoopee', with its salutory lesson on life and love: 'Picture a little love nest, down where the roses cling/Picture that same sweet love nest, think what a year can bring/He's washing dishes, and baby clothes/He's so ambitious, he even sews/But don't forget folks, that's what you get folks/For makin' whoopee'. The other enduring number in the show, 'Love Me Or Leave Me', was sung by Ruth Etting. It became forever associated with her, and titled the 1955 film biography in which she was portrayed by Doris Day. The rest of the score included 'I'm Bringing You A Red, Red Rose', which also became popular through Etting's recording, and 'Come West, Little Girl, Come West', 'Until You Get Somebody Else', 'The Song Of The Setting Sun', 'Here's To The Girl Of My Heart!', and 'Gypsy Joe'. Buddy Ebsen, the lanky dancer who seemed able to twist his body into every conceivable shape, made his Broadway debut in this show, and George Olsen's Orchestra, purveyors of the sweetest sounds around, were also on board for most of the time, except for a couple of months when it was replaced by Paul Whiteman and his men. Ziegfeld's glamour and Cantor's antics ensured that *Whoopee* had a decent run of 379 performances, and the comedian also starred in the 1930 film version. The show was revived on Broadway in 1979 with Charles Repole, and stayed for nearly six months.

Wild Rose

(see **Sally**)

Will Rogers Follies, The

This lavish production, which had music by Cy Coleman and a book and lyrics by Broadway veterans Betty Comden and Adolph Green, was sub-titled 'A Life In Revue'. It was summed up neatly by one critic thus: 'The time is the present, and Gregory Peck's recorded voice as impresario Florenz Ziegfeld instructs the theatrically resurrected Rogers, 16 showgirls, 16 other actors and six dogs on how to stage the life story of America's favourite humorist in the style of the Ziegfeld Follies.' The Will Rogers Follies opened at the Palace Theatre in New York on 1 May 1991 with television and film actor Keith Carradine in the central role of the folksy philosopher Rogers surrounded by a production which was guaranteed to dazzle owing to the presence of the master of flash and panache, director and choreographer Tommy Tune. Just a few of the evening's highlights featured a chorus line of girls dressed as steers, a pink powder-puff ballet, and an amazing stagewide staircase which changed colours throughout. With appearances in the real Ziegfeld Follies and his newspaper columns and radio programmes, Rogers is generally accepted as being America's first multimedia superstar, but one who despite his fame stayed in touch with the people until his death in an air crash in 1935. Comden and Green attempted to sum up this facet of his character in the lyric of 'Never Met A Man I Didn't Like', the only really memorable number in a score which also included 'Let's Go Flying', 'Will-A-Mania', 'Give A Man Enough Rope', 'My Big Mistake', 'No Man Left For Me', and 'Without You'. Singer-songwriter Mac Davies and Larry Gatlin were two of the replacements for Carradine during the show's highly successful run of 1,420 performances. Just before it closed in September 1993, old-stager Mickey Rooney played the role of Rogers's father Clem for a time. The show won a Grammy for best original cast album, along with Drama Desk and Drama Critics Awards, and Tonys for best musical, score, director, choreographer, lighting, and costumes. One unpleasant aspect of the production occurred when Tommy Tune was accused of sexism and racism with regard to a billboard which showed three half-naked women, and the fact that the large cast did not contain one non-white performer.

Williams, Bert

b. 1877, New Providence, Nassau, Bahamas, d. 5 March 1922. After moving to the USA, Williams worked in vaudeville with moderate success. In 1898 he teamed up with George Walker and the two song and dance men became a success in New York City in the show *In Dahomey*, and also toured overseas. When Walker died in 1907, Williams continued on his own. In 1913 he met impresario Florenz Ziegfeld, who saw his act at the Lafayette in Harlem and was so impressed that he brought Williams into his *Follies* show. Williams appeared in every *Follies* until 1920, featuring such songs as 'You Ain't So Warm!' and 'Nobody', a song with which he became synonymous. Despite his great popularity in these shows, Williams was still subjected to severe racial discrimination; on a mundane if wounding level, he could not buy a drink in the bar of the theatre he helped to fill every night. In March 1922, Williams was onstage at the Shubert-Garrick Theatre in Detroit, in a performance of *Under The Bamboo Tree*, when he collapsed and died as a result of pneumonia.

Willson, Meredith

b. Robert Meredith Reiniger, 18 May 1902, Mason City, Iowa, USA, d. 15 June 1984, Santa Monica, California, USA. An instrumentalist and musical director; then a composer-lyricist-librettist, Willson was 55-years-old when he hit the Broadway big-time. Educated at the Damrosch Institute of Musical Art in New York, Willson was a flute and piccolo soloist with John Philip Sousa's concert band from 1921-23, and with the New York Philharmonic 1924-29, playing under Arturo Toscanini. During the 30s and early 40s he worked extensively on radio as musical director on shows such as *Ship Of Joy*, *Carefree Carnival*, *Good News Of 1938*, *Maxwell House Coffee Time*, *Fanny Brice* and *John Nesbitt*. When he was in his late 30s, he composed the symphony, 'The Missions Of California', and scored movies such as Charles Chaplin's *The Great Dictator* (1940) and Lillian Hellman's *The Little Foxes* (1941). During World War II, Willson was a major in the Armed Forces Radio Service. On release, he had his own radio show from 1946 into the early 50s, and also hosted *The Big Show* with actress Tallulah Bankhead, and composed its closing theme, 'May The Good Lord Bless And Keep You'. In December 1957, *The Music Man*, for which Willson wrote the book, music and lyrics, opened on Broadway to unanimously favourable reviews. The show which was set in Willson's home state of Iowa, c.1912, starred Robert Preston, in his first musical, as Professor Harold Hill, and Barbara Cook as Marion, the librarian. The songs, set in a variety of musical styles, included 'Rock Island', 'Trouble', 'Goodnight My Someone', 'The Sadder-But-Wiser Girl', 'Marion The Librarian', 'My White Knight', 'Wells Fargo Wagon', 'Shi-poopi', 'Lida Rose', 'Will I Ever Tell You?', 'Gary, Indiana' and 'Till There Was You'. The show ran for 1,375 performances, and was filmed in 1962, with Preston; Cook being replaced by Shirley Jones. Apart from the original cast and film soundtrack records, Willson and his wife Rini performed the score on their own album, with their individual comments. Willson's next musical, *The Unsinkable Molly Brown* (1960), with Tammy Grimes

in the title role, included the songs 'I Ain't Down Yet', 'Belly Up To The Bar Boys', 'Keep A-Hoppin'' and 'Are You Sure?'. The film version, with Grimes replaced by Debbie Reynolds, was made in 1964. Willson's final Broadway musical, for which he also wrote the book, was *Here's Love* (1963). Adapted from George Seaton's 1947 comedy-fantasy movie about a department store's Santa Claus, starred Janis Paige and Craig Stevens, and ran for 334 performances. The songs included 'The Big Clown Balloons', 'Arm In Arm', 'You Don't Know' and 'Pine Cones And Holly Berries'. Willson's Broadway career had been comparatively brief, but significant.
Further reading: *And There I Stood With My Piccolo*, Meredith Willson. *But He Doesn't Know The Territory*, Meredith Willson.

Wilson, Sandy

b. Alexander Galbraith Wilson, 19 May 1924, Sale, Cheshire, England. A composer, lyricist and author. After studying at Harrow, and Oxford University where he wrote and appeared in many undergraduate productions, Wilson began to make his mark in the West End by contributing songs to revues such as *Slings And Arrows* (1948) and *Oranges And Lemons* (1949). In 1950 he provided the lyrics for a provincial production of Michael Pertwee's musical play, *Caprice*, and then was the author and composer of *See You Later* (1951) and *See You Again* (1952). His big break came in 1953 when he was asked to write the book, music and lyrics for *The Boy Friend*, a lighthearted, but entirely accurate spoof of the musical comedies of the 20s - flappers, and all that. After starting its life as an hour-long entertainment at the tiny Player's Theatre, *The Boy Friend* moved first to the Embassy and was expanded before finally transferring to Wyndhams's Theatre in the West End on 14 January 1954 where it ran for over five years. Later that year, the Broadway production, in which Julie Andrews made her New York stage debut, opened at the Royale Theatre for a run of 485 performances. The show has subsequently been produced in many countries throughout the world, and enjoyed revivals in New York (1958) and London (1967). The 1971 film version was directed by Ken Russell and starred Twiggy, Christopher Gable, Moyra Fraser, and Tommy Tune. Sandy Wilson's other stage work, generally as a composer and/or author and lyricist, includes shows such as *The Buccaneer* (1955), *Valmouth* (1958), *Pieces Of Eight* (1959), *Call It Love* (1960), *Divorce Me, Darling!* (1965), *As Dorothy Parker Once Said* (1966), *Sandy Wilson Thanks The Ladies* (in which he also appeared, 1971), *His Monkey Wife* (1971), *The Clapham Wonder* (1978), and *Aladdin* (1979). In 1993 he announced that another London revival of *The Boy Friend* would open in 1994 at its original birthplace, the Player's

Norman Wisdom

Theatre, before moving to the West End.
Further reading: all by Sandy Wilson *This Is Sylvia. The Boy Friend. I Could Be Happy: His Autobiography. Ivor* (a biography of Ivor Novello). *The Roaring Twenties.*

Wisdom, Norman

b. 4 February 1918, Paddington, London, England. A slapstick comedian, singer and straight actor, Wisdom has been a much-loved entertainer for four decades in the UK, not to mention such unlikely places as Russia and China. He broke into films in 1953 with *Trouble In Store,* and in the 50s had a string of box office smashes with *One Good Turn, Man Of The Moment, Up In The World, Just My Luck, The Square Peg* and *Follow A Star.* Dressed in his famous tight-fitting Gump suit, he was usually accompanied by straight man Jerry Desmonde, and, more often than not, portrayed the little man battling against the odds, to win justice and his sweetheart. He nearly always sang in his films and his theme song 'Don't Laugh At Me', which he co-wrote, was a number 3 hit in 1954 on EMI/Columbia. He also made the Top 20 in 1957 with a version of the Five Keys' 'Wisdom Of A Fool'. In 1958, Wisdom appeared in the West End musical, *Where's Charley?*, based on Brandon Thomas's classic farce, *Charley's Aunt.* Frank Loesser's score included 'Once In Love With Amy' and 'My Darling, My Darling', and the show ran for 18 months. In 1965, Wisdom played the lead in Bricusse and Newley's musical *The Roar Of The Greasepaint - The Smell Of The Crowd,* which toured UK provincial theatres. He wasn't considered sufficiently well known in the US to play the part on Broadway, but did make his New York debut the following year when he starred in *Walking Happy,* a musical version of *Hobson's Choice* with a score by Cahn and Van Heusen. He also appeared on US television in the role of Androcles, with Noël Coward as Julius Caesar, in Richard Rodgers' musical adaptation of Bernard Shaw's *Androcles And The Lion.* His feature films during the 60s included *On the Beat, A Stitch In Time* and *The Night They Raided Minsky's* with Jason Robards and Britt Ekland. Thanks to television re-runs of his films he is regarded with warm affection by many sections of the British public, and can still pack theatres, although, like many show business veterans, he is not called on to appear much on television. In his heyday, he made two celebrated 'live', one-hour appearances on *Sunday Night At The London Palladium,* in the company of Bruce Forsyth, that are considered to be classics of their kind. In 1992, with the UK rapidly running out traditional funny men (Benny Hill and Frankie Howerd both died in that year), Wisdom experienced something of a renaissance when he played the role of a gangster in the movie *Double X,* starred in a radio series, *Robbing Hood,* released an album, *A World Of Wisdom,* completed a sell-out tour of the UK, and published his autobiography.
Selected albums: *I Would Like To Put On Record* (1956), *Where's Charley?* (1958, London Cast), *Walking Happy* (1966, Broadway Cast), *Androcles And The Lion* (1967, television soundtrack), *A World Of Wisdom* (1992).
Further reading: *Trouble In Store,* Richard Dacre. *Don't Laugh At Me,* Norman Wisdom.

Wish You Were Here

In the early 50s when Broadway audiences were enjoying such lavish musicals as *Call Me Madam, The King And I, Can-Can,* and *Kismet, Wish You Were Here* went one better than all of them, and splashed out on a real swimming pool which was built into the stage. Perhaps the show's director, producer, choreographer, and co-librettist Joshua Logan still had fond watery memories of his association with the enormously successful *South Pacific* a few years earlier. In any event, the pool attracted a good deal of early publicity, as did a record of the title song by Eddie Fisher which soared to the top of the US chart just three weeks after the show opened at the Imperial Theatre on 25 June 1952. The story, which was adapted by Joshua Logan and Arthur Kober from Kober's 1937 play, *Having A Wonderful Time,* is set in Camp Karefree, a Jewish adult summer vacation resort in the Catskill Mountains. Teddy Stern (Patricia Marand) loses interest in her mature boyfirend, Herbert Fabricant (Harry Clark), when the young, suave and slinky waiter-cum-dancer, Chick Miller (Jack Cassidy), sweeps her off her feet. It's all perfectly legal because - back home in New York - he is a law student. Besides the title number, which also became a hit for Jane Froman and Guy Lombardo, Harold Rome's amusing and tuneful score contained another appealing ballad, 'Where Did The Night Go', along with 'Tripping The Light Fantastic', 'Goodbye Love', 'Could Be', 'Ballad Of A Social Director', 'Mix And Mingle', 'Camp Kare-Free', 'Summer Afternoon', 'Don José Of Far Rockaway', and 'Flattery'. *Wish You Were Here* was a warm and friendly show so it was not surprising that it ran for nearly a year a half, a total of 598 performances. The 1953 London production, with Bruce Trent, Shani Wallis, Elizabeth Larner, and Dickie Henderson, stayed at the Casino Theatre for eight months (complete with swimming pool). The 1987 British film of the same name which starred Emily Lloyd and Tom Bell, bears no resemblance to this musical production.

Wiz, The

Unlike the 1903 Broadway version of *The Wizard Of Oz*, this highly contemporary reworking of L. Frank Baum's novel stayed closely to the original and much-loved story in spite of an all-black cast and a high-level sound system which dispensed a brand new rock score. In William F. Brown's book, Dorothy (Stephanie Mills), is once again whisked off to the Land Of Oz on a whirlwind so that she can skip along the Yellow Brick Road with familiar characters such as the Scarecrow (Hinton Battle), the Tinman (Tiger Haynes), the Lion (Ted Ross), the extremely wicked witch (Mabel King), and wonderful Wizard (Andre De Shields). Charlie Smalls' powerful score was skilfully integrated into the plot, and contained the insinuating 'Ease On Down The Road', which became a soul-music favourite, along with 'He's The Wizard', 'Slide Some Oil On Me', 'Be A Lion', 'Don't Nobody Bring Me No Bad News', and 'If You Believe'. After surviving some predictably poor reviews (this was not a typical Broadway show) enthusiastic word-of-mouth boosted the show's appeal, and resulted in a remarkable four-year run of 1,672 performances. Tony Awards went to Geoffrey Holder for his brilliant costumes and direction, and *The Wiz* also won for best musical, score, supporting actress (Dee Dee Bridgewater), supporting actor (Ted Ross), and choreographer (George Faison). The show toured the US, and was presented in London in 1984, where it starred Elaine Delmar, Celena Duncan, and Clarke Peters. The 1978 film starred Diana Ross, Michael Jackson, Lena Horne, Ted Ross, and Richard Pryor.

Wizard Of Oz, The

Although it was adapted by L. Frank Baum from his own 1900 novel for children, *The Wonderful World Of Oz*, this stage show differed in several respects from the story that is so familiar to millions via the 1939 classic film which starred Judy Garland. It is probably true to say that it blew into the Majestic Theatre in New York on 20 January 1903, because the opening scene contains a spectacular hurricane effect which transports the young and shy Dorothy Gale (Anna Laughlin) and Imogene the Cow from their home in Kansas to the Land Of Oz. She becomes involved in some exciting adventures with most of the customary characters, including the Tin Woodman and the Scarecrow who were played by two star comedians from vaudeville, David Montgomery and Fred Stone, and the Cowardly Lion (Arthur Hill), before eventually being confronted by the formidable Wizard (Bobby Gaylor) himself. Unlike the film with its wonderful score by Harold Arlen and E.Y. 'Yip' Harburg, the songs for this show were a kind of a hotch-potch cobbled together from a variety of composers and lyricists, mainly L. Frank Baum (lyrics) with Paul Tietjens and A. Baldwin Stone (music), along with others such as Theodore Morse, Vincent Bryan, Edward Hutchinson, James O'Dea, and Glen MacDonough. They included 'Hurrah For Baffins Bay', 'Sammy', 'In Michigan', 'Niccolo's Piccolo',

'Alas For A Man Without Brains', and 'When You Love Love Love'. *The Wizard Of Oz* ran for 293 performances which meant that in a Broadway season when 26 other musicals made their debut, it was a big hit.

Wodehouse, P.G.

b. Pelham Grenville Wodehouse, 15 October 1881, Guildford, Surrey, England, d. 14 February 1975, Southampton, Long Island, New York, USA. A lyricist, and librettist, and the author of a series of more than 90 humorous novels, mostly dealing with an 'hilarious, light-hearted satire on life among the British gentry, notably the inane Bertie Wooster and his impeccable valet, Jeeves'. His father was a British judge, based in Hong Kong, and Wodehouse lived in the colony with his parents until he was four, and then, for the next four years, was entrusted to a family in London, along with his three brothers. After elementary education at various boarding schools, he attended Dulwich College in the outskirts of London, and excelled at Latin and Greek. He graduated in 1900, and worked for a time at the Hong Kong & Shanghai Bank in London. A year later, he joined *The Globe* newspaper, eventually becoming the editor of the humorous column, 'By The Way'. In 1904, he wrote the lyric for 'Put Me In My Cell', for a new show, *Sergeant Brue*, which opened in December at the Strand Theatre. Two years later, the renowned actor-manager, Seymour Hicks, offered him the job of writing song lyrics for the Aldwych shows. It was at the Aldwych Theatre that Wodehouse met the young American composer, Jerome Kern, who was just beginning to make a name for himself. Together, they wrote the song, 'Mr. Chamberlain', a satire on the British politician, Joseph Chamberlain, for *The Beauty Of Bath*. It stopped the show each night, and became a country-wide hit. During the next few years, in between his prolific literary output which involved several trips to the USA, Wodehouse contributed sketches and lyrics to three more London shows, *The Gay Gordons*, *The Bandit's Daughter*, and *Nuts And Wine*. In September 1914, he married an English widow, Ethel Rowley, in New York, and finally settled in the USA. Three months later, in his capacity as the drama critic of *Vanity Fair*, he attended the first night of the musical, *Very Good Eddie*, which had music by Jerome Kern, and a libretto by Philip Bartholomae and Guy Bolton (b. 23 November 1884, Broxbourne, Hertfordshire, England, d. 6 September 1979). When Kern introduced Wodehouse and Bolton, it marked the beginning of collaboration during which the trio (two Englishmen and one New Yorker), contributed books, music and lyrics to a number of witty, entertaining, and highly successful Broadway musicals. Firstly though, there were two false starts: Wodehouse was called in to assist the

P.G. Wodehouse

lyricist-librettist, Anne Caldwell, on *Pom-Pom* (1916), and then the new team was asked to 'Americanize', and provide a new book and some additional songs for a Viennese operetta called *Miss Springtime*. The show was a hit, and included some charming Wodehouse lyrics in numbers such as 'Throw Me A Rose', 'My Castle In The Air', and the risqué 'A Very Good Girl On Sunday'. The trio's first original musical comedy, *Have A Heart* (1917), had music by Kern, and lyrics by Wodehouse, who also collaborated with Bolton on the book. Although critically acclaimed, the show ran for less than a 100 performances, despite an outstanding score which included 'You Said Something', 'And I Am All Alone', 'They All Look Alike', 'Honeymoon Inn', 'I See You There', and 'Napoleon'. The young team's initial impact was made in February 1917 with *Oh, Boy!*, the first, and more successful of their two famous 'Princess Theatre Shows'. Kern and Bolton had already worked together at the Princess in 1915, with lyricist Schuyler Greene. The tiny theatre had a capacity of only 299, and so was not able to handle the large operetta-style productions that were currently in vogue, or afford to employ established performers and writers. Kern, Wodehouse, and Bolton were interested in writing more intimate shows anyway, with songs that were integrated into plots that, sometimes bordered on farce with their tales of misidentity and suchlike, but came as a welcome relief from the stodginess of the European imports. *Oh, Boy!* was a prime example of what they were aiming for, and was a smash hit from the start, eventually running for over 450 performances. One of the show's stars, Anna Wheaton, helped to promote the production with her successful record of one of the hit numbers, 'Till The Clouds Roll By', and some of the other songs (nearly 20 of them) included 'Ain't It A Grand And Glorious Feeling', 'A Package Of Seeds', 'Flubby Dub', 'The Cave Man', 'Nesting Time In Flatbush', 'Words Are Not Needed', 'An Old Fashioned Waltz', and the delightfully rueful duet, 'You Never Knew About Me'. The production transferred to London two years later, where it was re-titled *Oh, Joy!*, and gave Beatrice Lillie her first role in a book musical.

While *Oh, Boy!* was resident at the Princess Theatre, Wodehouse was involved with four other New York shows in 1917. Firstly, he collaborated again with Kern and Bolton for *Leave It To Jane*, a musical adaptation of George Ade's comedy, *The College Widow*, and similar in style to *Oh, Boy!*, which included 'The Siren's Song', 'The Crickets Are Calling', 'Leave It To Jane', 'The Sun Shines Brighter', 'Wait Till Tomorrow', 'Cleopatterer' (an amusing piece of Egyptian hokum), and several more. The show was revived Off-Broadway more than 40 years later, in 1959, and ran for over two years. For Wodehouse, *Leave It To Jane* was followed by *Kitty Darlin'* (music by Rudolph Friml), *The Riviera Girl* (music by Emmerich Kalman and Kern), and *Miss 1917* (music by Victor Herbert and Kern). The young rehearsal pianist for *Miss 1917* was George Gershwin, in his first professional job in the theatre. In February 1918, Wodehouse, Bolton, and Kern completed their final Princess Theatre show together, *Oh, Lady!, Lady!!*. The all-star cast included Vivienne Segal, who sang 'Not Yet', 'Do Look At Him', 'It's A Hard, Hard World for A Man', and 'When The Ships Come Home', amongst others. It is sometimes said that disagreements over financial affairs between Kern and Wodehouse caused them to part, at least temporarily. In any event, although the three men were to work in pairs during the next few years, the brief spell when they combined to contribute to the dawn of a joyous revolution of the American musical theatre, was over, except for *Sitting Pretty* (1924), which proved to be a 95 performance disappointment.

During the next two years Wodehouse contributed book and/or lyrics to productions such as *See You Later*, *The Girl Behind The Gun*, *The Canary*, *Oh, My Dear!*, *The Rose Of China*, and *The Golden Moth*, with a variety of composer, lyricists and librettists, such as Jean Schwartz, Joseph Szulc, Ivan Caryll, George Barr, Louis Verneuill, Anne Caldwell, Louis Hirsch, and Jerome Kern, with whom he wrote 'The Church Around The Corner' and 'You Can't Keep A Good Girl Down' for *Sally* (1920). In the early 20s, he collaborated with Kern again on two successful London shows, *The Cabaret Girl* and *The Beauty Prize*. Two years later, Bolton and Wodehouse wrote the book for George and Ira Gershwin's hit, *Oh, Kay!*, and they were both involved again in *The Nightingale* (1927) ('Breakfast In Bed', 'May Moon', 'Two Little Ships'), with music by Armand Vecsey. In 1927, Jerome Kern staged his masterpiece, *Show Boat*, with lyrics by Oscar Hammerstein. Interpolated into their score, was 'Bill', a song which was written by Kern and Wodehouse nearly 10 years previously, and cut from the original scores of *Oh, Lady! Lady!!* (1918) and *Zip Goes A Million* (1919). It was sung in *Show Boat* by Helen Morgan, and provided Wodehouse with the biggest song hit of his career. In the following year, he collaborated with lyricist Ira Gershwin, his brother George, and Sigmund Romberg, for the popular *Rosalie*, starring Marilyn Miller ('Hussars March', 'Oh Gee! Oh Joy!', 'Say So', 'West Point Song', 'Why Must We Always Be Dreaming?'). Ironically, for someone who had been at the forefront of the radical changes in American show music for the past 10 years, Wodehouse's final set of Broadway lyrics were for an operetta. With lyricist Clifford Grey, and composer Rudolph Friml, he contributed numbers such as 'March Of The

Musketeers' and 'Your Eyes' to Florenz Ziegfeld's music adaptation of Alexander Dumas' *The Three Musketeers* (1928), which starred Vivienne Segal and Dennis King, and ran for over 300 performances. With a final flourish, Wodehouse's Broadway career ended with a smash hit, when he and Bolton provided the book for Cole Porter's *Anything Goes* (1934). In that same year, Bertie Wooster and Jeeves appeared together in a novel for first time, and Wodehouse, who had been balancing several balls in the air for most of his working life, at last allowed the musical one to drop to earth. During the 30s he spent some time in Hollywood, adapting his novel, *A Damsel In Distress,* for the screen. In July 1940, while at his villa in Le Touquet on the French Riviera, he was taken into custody by the German invading forces, charged with being an enemy alien, and interned in the local lunatic asylum at Tost in Upper Silesia. In June 1941, he was moved to Berlin, and subsequently broadcast a series of humorous talks about his experiences as a prisoner of war, which were transmitted to America. In Britain, where the population was constantly under siege from German aircraft, Wodehouse was reviled in the press and on radio, and there was talk of him being tried for treason - although most of the British population had not heard what turned out to be fairly innocuous broadcasts. Still in custody, he was transferred to Paris, and eventually liberated in August 1944. He returned to the USA in 1947, and became an American citizen in 1955. He continued to write constantly, and in 1971, on his 90th birthday, his 93rd volume was published. Four years later, perhaps in a belated national gesture of reconciliation, Wodehouse, was created a Knight Commander of the British Empire in the UK New Year honours list, just two months before he had a heart attack, and died in a Long Island hospital on the 14 February 1975.

Woman Of The Year

A vehicle for the celebrated film actress Lauren Bacall, who had enjoyed a great deal of success in the 1970 Broadway musical *Applause. Woman Of The Year* opened at the Palace Theatre in New York on 29 March 1981, with music and lyrics by John Kander and Fred Ebb, and a book by Peter Stone which was based on the 1942 film starring Spencer Tracy and Katherine Hepburn. Stone changed the characters of the two principals from a seen-it-all sportswriter who falls for an extremely versatile sportswoman, to a satirical cartoonist Sam Craig (Harry Guardino), who is permanently feuding with the high-powered, hard-bitten television personality Tess Harding (Bacall). The arguments continue to rage (only more so) after they are married. According to the critics, it would have been nothing without Lauren Bacall, but the score was entertaining without being brilliant, and

included 'Woman Of the Year', 'When You're Right, You're Right', 'So What Else Is New?', 'One Of The Boys', 'Sometimes A Day Goes By', and 'We're Gonna Work It Out'. The highspot of the show comes towards the end of the second act when the super-successful Tess and Marilyn Cooper, as a downtrodden, disillusioned housewife, argue that 'The Grass Is Always Greener' (Cooper: 'You're always in the magazines, that's wonderful'/Tess: 'What's so wonderful? You can hold a husband, that's wonderful'/Cooper: 'What's so wonderful? There's more to life than husbands'/Tess: 'I could use a husband'/Cooper: 'You can have *my* husband'/Tess: 'I've already *had* your husband . . .'). During the show's run of 770 performances, two of the actresses who succeeded Lauren Bacall were also stars of the big screen - Raquel Welch and Debbie Reynolds. Miss Bacall and Marilyn Cooper won Tony Awards for their strong, amusing performances, and there were additional Tonys for the show's score and book.

Wonderful Town

Given that the score for this show was the work of the *On The Town* team of Leonard Bernstein (music) and Betty Comden and Adolph Green (lyrics), it does not take a great deal of imagination to realise that the wonderful, friendly, and generally too-good-to-be-true city in question is New York. This musical advertisement for the 'Big Apple', which opened at the Winter Garden in New York on 25 February 1953, had a book by Joseph Fields and Jerome Chodorov based on their play, *My Sister Eileen*, which was adapted from stories by Ruth McKinney. It concerns two young ladies, Ruth Sherwood (Rosalind Russell) and, of course, her sister Eileen (Edie Adams) who have travelled from Ohio to the big city in an effort to find fame and fortune. Ruth is a writer who cannot seem to get a man, while Eileen the actress has difficulty holding them off. During their subsequent hilarious adventures, Eileen goes to jail for assaulting a policeman, and the editor of the classy *Manhattan* magazine, Robert Baker (George Gaynes), makes it clear that he hates Ruth's stories, but then falls in love with their writer. No hits emerged from the lively, tuneful and amusing score, which included 'Christopher Street', 'Ohio', 'One Hundred Easy Ways', 'What A Waste', 'A Little Bit In Love', 'A Quiet Girl', 'Conga!', 'Swing!', 'It's Love', and 'Wrong Note Rag'. Rosalind Russell, who had starred in the non-musical 1942 film of *My Sister Eileen*, was outstanding in this rare Broadway appearance. *Wonderful Town* ran for 559 performances in New York, and a further 207 in London with Pat Kirkwood and Shani Wallis. Over 30 years later, in 1986, a major West End revival starred one of Britain's favourite comedy actresses, Maureen Lipman. The 1955 musical film, with Betty Garrett,

Mark Wynter

Janet Leigh, and Jack Lemmon, reverted to the original title of the play, *My Sister Eileen*.

Words And Music

By the early 30s Noël Coward was at the peak of his creativity. This is clear from the material he wrote for the revue *Words And Music*, which opened at the Adelphi Theatre in London on 16 September 1932. There were normally at least one or two particularly memorable songs in any Coward show, but in *Words And Music* he really excelled himself. The score included the classic 'Mad About The Boy', 'Mad Dogs And Englishmen' the author's most famous comedy number, and 'The Party's Over Now' which Coward subsequently used to close his cabaret act, as well as lesser-known items such as 'Let's Say Goodbye', 'Something To Do With Spring', and 'Three White Feathers'. Given the privilege and pleasure of introducing those songs were cast members John Mills, Romney Brent, Doris Hare, Norah Howard, Joyce Barbour, and Ivy St Helier. Ironically the show failed to last for more than five months, which meant that it was the first collaboration between Coward and impresario C.B. Cochran to lose money. Much of the material formed the basis of *Set To Music*, a revue which starred Beatrice Lillie, and ran for 129 performances on Broadway early in 1939.

Wynter, Mark

b. Terence Lewis, 29 January 1943, Woking, Surrey, England. Wynter was one of several UK heart-throbs in the early 60s who took their lightweight cue from the USA. Once the extrovert champion of many a school sports day, he was serving in a general store by day and singing with the Hank Fryer Band in Peckham Co-op Hall, London in the evening when his well-scrubbed, good looks betrayed star potential to Ray Mackender, a Lloyds underwriter who dabbled in pop management. As 'Mark Wynter', the boy was readied for his new career with vocal exercises, tips on stage demeanour from a RADA coach and advice about a middle-of-the-road repertoire from Lionel Bart. After exploratory intermission spots in metropolitan palais, he was signed to Decca Records who he rewarded with UK hit parade entries until 1964 - beginning with 'Image Of A Girl' (1960) at number 11. At the height of his fame two years later, he breached the Top 10 with covers of Jimmy Clanton' 'Venus In Blue Jeans' and Steve Lawrence's 'Go Away Little Girl' before subsequent singles hovered - as they had previously - mostly between 20 and 40. He resorted to a-side revivals of such 50s chestnuts as 'It's Almost Tomorrow' and 'Only You' but, with the levelling blow of the beat boom, he continued to perform in venues where current chart standing had no meaning.

Wynter turned his attention to the theatre, both straight and musical. After playing the leading role in *Conduct Unbecoming* for more than a year at the Queen's Theatre in London and then for six months in Australia, he appeared with Evelyn Laye and Stanley Baxter in *Phil The Fluter*, with Julia McKenzie in *On The Twentieth Century*, and in *Charley's Aunt*. He also starred in *Side By Side By Sondheim* in Toronto, Chichester, and on the UK tour. In the 1982 Chichester Festival season he acted in several plays including *On The Rocks* and *Henry V*, and also sang in *Valmouth*. Wynter played the male lead in Sheridan Morley's *Noël And Gertie* in London, Hong Kong, and New York. His other work in musicals during 80s included the role of the King in a revival of *The King And I*, the title roles in *Hans Andersen* and *Barnum*, the 1986 revival of *Charlie Girl* with Cyd Charisse and Paul Nicholas in London, and Robert Browning in *Robert And Elizabeth*. From 1990-92, most of Wynter's working life was spent on the famous rubbish dump in the New London Theatre which is inhabited by Andrew Lloyd Webber's *Cats*. His many television appearances have included a series with Dora Bryan, *According To Dora*, *Tale Of Two Rivers* with Petula Clark, and his own series *Call In On Wynter*.

Y

Yellen, Jack

b. 6 July 1892, Razcki, Poland, d. 17 April 1991. Growing up in the USA after his family emigrated there in 1897, Yellen began writing songs while still at school. At first he wrote music and lyrics but after a short while specialized in lyrics, working with several different collaborators. Yellen had some early successes with 'All Aboard For Dixie', 'Are You From Dixie?' (both with music by George L. Cobb) and 'How's Ev'ry Little Thing In Dixie?' (with Albert Gumble). After World War I, Yellen worked with Gumble again, writing 'Peaches', and produced with Abe Olman, 'Down By The O-H-I-O'. Many of his songs of this period were used in Broadway revues and shows such as *What's In A Name?*, *Bombo*, *Rain Or Shine*, *John Murray Anderson's Almanac*, and *George White's Scandals*. In 1920 Yellen was introduced to composer Milton Ager and they began a fruitful collaboration which included 'A Young Man's

Fancy', 'Who Cares?', 'Hard-Hearted Hannah, The Vamp Of Savannah', 'Crazy Words, Crazy Tune' and 'Ain't She Sweet?' In 1928 Yellen and Ager went to Hollywood, where they collaborated on such songs as 'I'm The Last Of The Red Hot Mommas', 'Happy Feet', 'A Bench In The Park' and 'Happy Days Are Here Again', which became the theme song of the Democratic Party and was virtually synonymous with President Franklin D. Roosevelt's New Deal. Unusually, Yellen wrote words and music for one song, written to record his emotions on the death of his mother. Sung by Sophie Tucker, 'My Yiddishe Momme' became a huge success with audiences of all races and creeds. In the 30s Yellen worked with Harold Arlen and Ray Henderson and also wrote lyrics and screenplays for several musical films. In 1939 and into the early 40s Yellen took another fling at Broadway, working with Sammy Fain, Henderson and others, on shows such as a further edition of *George White's Scandals*, *Boys And Girls Together*, *Son O'Fun*, and *Ziegfeld Follies Of 1943*. Among the best songs from this period was 'Are You Havin' Any Fun?' (with Fain). In the 50s and 60s Yellen was a director of ASCAP, occasionally writing material for Sophie Tucker with whom he had formed a special musical bond.

You're A Good Man, Charlie Brown

Sometimes known as the 'Peanuts' musical, this show, which was based on Charles Schultz's enormously successful American comic strip of that name, opened Off Broadway at Theatre 80 St. Marks on 7 March 1967. Music, book and lyrics were by Clark Gesner and told of a day in the life of the strip's familiar young characters who include the sensitive but bemused Charlie Brown (Gary Burghoff), Lucy (Reva Rose), Patty (Karen Johnson), Schroeder (Skip Hinnant), Linus (Bob Balaban), and, of course, the lovable pooch Snoopy (Bill Hinnant), who, in his imaginary persona as a World World I pilot, is constantly in pursuit of his opposite number, the deadly German flying ace, the Red Baron. They all get involved in numbers such as 'My Blanket And Me', 'Little Known Facts', 'T.E.A.M.' 'Suppertime', 'You're A Good Man, Charlie Brown', 'Book Report', 'Happiness', and 'Queen Lucy'. To the surprise of many, Charlie and his friends continued to appeal for a total of 1,597 performances in New York, while road companies carried the message throughout the USA. The concept was unfamiliar to British audiences, and the London production folded after nearly three months.

Youmans, Vincent

b. Vincent Miller (Millie) Youmans, 27 September 1898, New York, USA, d. 5 April 1946, Denver, Colorado, USA. Youmans was an important composer and producer for the stage during the 20s and 30s, whose career was cut short by a long illness. He worked for a Wall Street finance company before enlisting in the US Navy during World War I, and co-producing musicals at Great Lakes Naval Training Station. On leaving the navy he worked as a song-plugger for Harms Music, and as a rehearsal pianist for shows with music by influential composer, Victor Herbert. Youmans wrote his first Broadway score in 1921 for *Two Little Girls In Blue*, with lyrics by Ira Gershwin. One of the show's songs, 'Oh Me, Oh My, Oh You', was a hit for novelty singer, Frank Crumit. Youmans' next show, *Wildflower* (1923), with book and lyrics by Otto Harbach and Oscar Hammerstein II, ran for a creditable 477 performances, and included 'April Blossoms', and 'Bambalina', recorded by Paul Whiteman and Ray Miller. *Mary Jane McKane* ('Toodle-oo', 'You're Never Too Old To Learn') and *Lollipop* ('Take A Little One-Step') both reached the Broadway stage in 1924, and in the following year Youmans, in collaboration with lyricist Irving Caesar, wrote a quintessential 20s score for *No, No, Nanette*, one of the decade's most successful musicals. The show contained several hits including 'Too Many Rings Around Rosie', 'You Can Dance With Any Girl At All', and the much-recorded standards, 'I Want To Be Happy' and 'Tea For Two'. The show was filmed, with modifications to its score, in 1930, 1940, and in 1950 as *Tea For Two*, starring Doris Day and Gordon MacRae.

In contrast, Youman's 1926 show, *Oh, Please*, with songs such as 'I Know That You Know', and 'Like He Loves Me', with lyrics by Anne Caldwell, was a relative failure, despite the presence of Beatrice Lillie in the cast. For *Hit The Deck* (1927), Youmans assumed the role of producer in partnership with Lew Fields. The show was a substantial success, running for 352 performances, and featuring 'Sometimes I'm Happy' (lyric by Clifford Grey and Irving Caesar) and 'Halleluja' (lyric by Clifford Grey and Leo Robin). The show was filmed in 1930, and in 1955, with an all-star cast including Tony Martin, Vic Damone, Debbie Reynolds, Jane Powell, and Ann Miller, and contained a new Youmans song, 'Keepin' Myself For You', with a lyric by Sidney Clare. Despite containing some of his best songs, Youmans' next few shows were flops. *Rainbow*, ran for only 29 performances; *Great Day*, with the title song, 'More Than You Know' and 'Without A Song' (lyrics by Billy Rose and Edward Eliscu) ran for 36 performances; *Smiles*, starring Marilyn Miller, and Adele and Fred Astaire, and featuring 'Time On My Hands' (lyric by Mack Gordon and Harold Adamson), 63 performances; and *Through The Years*, with the title song, 'Kinda Like You'; and 'Drums In My Heart', with lyrics by Edward Heyman, 20 performances.

Youmans' last Broadway show, *Take A Chance*, did much better. It starred Jack Haley and Ethel Merman and ran for 243 performances. Youmans contributed three songs, with lyrics by Buddy De Sylva: 'Should I Be Sweet?', 'Oh, How I Long To Belong To You', and Miss Merman's 'show-stopper', 'Rise 'N' Shine', which was also a hit for Paul Whiteman. Apparently disenchanted with Broadway, Youmans moved to Hollywood and wrote his only major film score, *Flying Down To Rio* (1933). Celebrated as the film that brought Fred Astaire and Ginger Rogers together as a dance team, the musical numbers, with lyrics by Gus Kahn and Edward Eliscu, included 'The Carioca', 'Orchids In the Moonlight' and 'Music Makes Me'. Shortly afterwards, Youmans contracted tuberculosis, and spent much of the rest of his life in sanitoria. In 1934 his publishing company collapsed, and in 1935 he was declared bankrupt for over half a million dollars. In 1943 he seemed well enough to return to New York to plan his most ambitious project, an extravaganza entitled, *The Vincent Youmans Ballet Revue*, a combination of Latin-American music, classical music, including Ravel's 'Daphnis And Chloe', with choreography by Leonide Massine. It was a critical and commercial disaster, losing over four million dollars. Youmans retired to New York, then to Denver, Colorado, where he died in 1946. Despite his relatively small catalogue of songs, and his penchant for rarely using the same collaborator, Youmans is rated among the elite composers of his generation. In 1971, *No, No, Nanette* was revived on Broadway, running for 861 performances.
Compilations: *Through The Years With Vincent Youmans* (1972), *Wildflower/Gershwin's Tiptoes'* (1979).

Your Arms Too Short To Box With God
(see *Dont Bother Me I Cant Cope*)

Your Own Thing
By the late 60s, rock music had become the dominant force in the world of popular entertainment generally, but its first big impact on Broadway was still to come in April 1968 with *Hair*. Some three months before that, on 13 January, this modern conception of William Shakespeares's *Twelfth Night* complete with a rock score by Hal Hester and Danny Apolinar, arrived at the Off Broadway Orpheum Theatre. Donald Driver's book takes a sly dig at men's fashionably long hair in a story which involves brother and sister Viola (Leland Palmer) and Sebastian (Rusty Thatcher), who, unbeknown to each other, are chasing the same singing job with a rock group based at a fashionable discotheque operated by Olivia (Marian Mercer). Orson (Tom Ligon), the manager of The Four Apocalypse, needs a male vocalist so Viola adopts an effective disguise. Too effective, as it turns out, because Olivia decides that she fancies him/her and the complications begin. After some delicate negotiations, Olivia transfers her affections to the far more suitable (and manly) Sebastian, Viola gets the job - and Orson too. The songs, some of which had fairly predictable titles, included 'The Now Generation', 'I'm On My Way To The Top', 'The Flowers', 'I'm Me!', 'Come Away Death' (lyric-Shakespeare), and 'The Middle Years', but none of the them threatened to break into the US charts which were being headed at time by artists such as the Beatles, Aretha Frankin, and the Lemon Pipers. One innovation in *Your Own Thing* was the clever use of film and slide projectors to mix traditional aspects of the piece with this contemporary treatment. The show enjoyed an impressive run of 933 performances in New York, but failed to impress in London and was withdrawn after six weeks.

Z

Ziegfeld
Good old British ballyhoo claimed that this was Britain's most expensive musical ever when it opened at the London Palladium on 26 April 1988. With a £3.2 million budget and a 60-strong cast, the 'opulent and gaudy' show was the brainchild of veteran impresario Harold Fielding and director and choreographer Joe Layton, and purported to be a celebration of the Ziegfeld Follies whilst also telling the life story of Florenz Ziegfeld himself. Ned Sherrin and Alistair Beaton wrote the book in which the legendary 'girl glorifier', played by Len Cariou, is portrayed as a shifty, egotistical manipulator, and an incorrigible womanizer. One critic pointed out that 'it was dedicated to a man with no heart', and that may well have been the reason why, in spite of some great old songs, the 450 costumes, 27 sets, and plenty of girls sited on revolving staircases, roulette wheels and most other places, by August the show was in trouble. Fielding brought in his old friend Tommy Steele to revamp the production, and Topol, who had enjoyed a personal triumph in London with *Fiddler On The Roof* in 1967, replaced Cariou, but it was all to no avail and *Ziegfeld* crashed in October after a run of just over five months. It recouped hardly any of its original investment, and Harold Fielding faced reported personal losses of £2.5 million.

Ziegfeld Follies

This series of high-class, spectacular, and elaborate revues, each one containing a mixture of skits, dances, songs, variety acts, and at least 50 beautiful women, was inaugurated in 1907 by Florenz Ziegfeld, 'the greatest showman in theatrical history'. From 1907-10 the shows were known as the *Follies*, and presented at the Jardin de Paris in New York. One of the first of the stars to emerge from the *Follies* was Nora Bayes, who also wrote and introduced the enormously popular 'Shine On Harvest Moon' with her second husband Jack Norworth in the 1908 edition. Yet another 'moon' song, 'By The Light Of The Silvery Moon', written by Edward Madden and Gus Edwards, turned up in the Follies of 1909. Other artists making one or more appearances in that first quartet of shows included Grace La Rue, Bickell And Watson, Helen Broderick, Mae Murray, Sophie Tucker, Lillian Lorraine, the black comedian Bert Williams, and 'funny girl' Fanny Brice, who appeared in nine editions of the Follies through until 1936. Also featured were the Ann Held Girls, named for Ziegfeld's first 'wife'. From 1911 onwards the name up in lights became the *Ziegfeld Follies* (one of Ziegfeld's signs, 'the largest electric light sign in American history', measured 80 feet long and 45 feet high, with 32,000 square feet of glass, and weighed eight tons), and was presented annually under that title until 1927, with the exception of 1926, when, owing to contractual wrangles, it was called *No Foolin'* and then *Ziegfeld's American Revue*. During those 17 years a host of the most beautiful showgirls, along with the cream of America's vaudeville performers and popular songwriters, contributed to what was billed as 'A National Institution Glorifying The American Girl'. Unlike a book show where the score is usually written mainly by one team of songwriters (with the odd interpolation), the musical items for each edition of the *Follies* were the work of several hands, including Dave Stamper, Gene Buck, Victor Herbert, Raymond Hubbell, Harry Smith, Gus Edwards, Joseph McCarthy, and Rudolph Friml. Some of the many enduring numbers that first saw the light of day in the *Ziegfeld Follies* include 'Woodman, Woodman, Spare That Tree' (1911, Irving Berlin), 'Row, Row, Row' (1912, Jimmy Monaco and William Jerome), 'The Darktown Poker Club' (1914, Jean Havaz, Will Vodery and Bert Williams), 'Hold Me In Your Loving Arms' and 'Hello, Frisco!' (1915, Louis A. Hirsch and Gene Buck), 'A Pretty Girl Is Like A Melody', 'Mandy' and 'You'd Be Surprised' (1919, Irving Berlin), 'Tell Me, Little Gypsy' and 'The Girls Of My Dreams' (1920, Irving Berlin), 'Second Hand Rose' (1921, Grant Clarke and James F. Hanley), 'My Man' (1921, Channing Pollock and Maurice Yvain), 'Mr. Gallagher And Mr. Sheen' (1922, Ed Gallagher and Al Shean), and 'Shaking The Blues Away' (1927, Irving Berlin). After a break, during which Ziegfeld lost a fortune in the Wall Street Crash, the impresario mounted the last *Follies* of his lifetime in 1931, but the score consisted mainly of old numbers, such 'Half Caste Woman', 'You Made Me Love You', and the first *Ziegfeld Follies* hit, 'Shine On Harvest Moon'. After he died in July 1932, the rights to the shows' title was bought by the Shubert Brothers, who, in collaboration with Ziegfeld's widow, Billie Burke, presented further editions, notably in 1934 and 1936. Both starred the late producer's brightest star, Fanny Brice, and, somewhat ironically, introduced better songs than were in the last few 'genuine' editions, such as 'I Like The Likes Of You' and 'What Is There To Say?' (1934, Vernon Duke and E.Y. 'Yip' Harburg), and 'Island In The West Indies' and 'I Can't Get Started' (1936, Vernon Duke and Ira Gershwin). None of the last three *Follies*, in 1943, 1956, and 1957, were critically well received, although the 1943 show ran for 553 performances - more than any of the others in the long series. The 1957 Golden Jubilee edition was down to eight girls, but had a genuine star in Beatrice Lillie. She was the last in a glittering line of performers, most of whom owed their start to the *Ziegfeld Follies*, including Fanny Brice, Bert Williams, Ann Pennington, W.C. Fields, Eddie Cantor, Will Rogers, Lillian Lorraine, Leon Erroll, Ray Dooley, Nora Bayes, Vivienne Segal, Helen Morgan, Marilyn Miller, Ed Wynn, Ruth Etting, and Eddie Dowling. The vast array of brilliant directors, choreographers, set and costume designers, who combined to create what are remembered as the most dazzling and extravagant shows ever seen on Broadway are too numerous to name: and the live elephants which appeared on stage in the 1915 edition were not credited individually.

Further reading: *The Ziegfeld Follies*, M. Farnsworth. *Stars Of The Ziegfeld Follies*, J. Phillips.

Ziegfeld, Florenz

b. 21 March 1867, Chicago, Illinois, USA, d. 22 July 1932, New York, USA. The most important and influential producer in the history of the Broadway musical. It is said that Ziegfeld was involved in his first real-life, but accidental, 'spectacular' at the age of four when he and his family were forced to seek shelter under a bridge in Lake Park during the great Chicago fire of 1871. While in his teens he was constantly running a variety of shows, and, in 1893, his father, who was the founder of the Chicago Music College, sent him to Europe to find classical musicians and orchestras. Florenz returned with the Von Bulow Military Band - and Eugene Sandow, 'the world's strongest man'. The actress Anna Held, with whom Ziegfeld went through a form of marriage in 1897, (they were 'divorced' in 1913) also came from

Europe, and she made her US stage debut in Ziegfeld's first Broadway production, *A Parlor Match*, in 1896. He followed that with *Papa's Wife*, *The Little Duchess*, The *Red Feather*, *Mam'selle Napoleon*, and *Higgledy Piggledy* (1904). Two years later, Held gave an appealing performance in Ziegfeld's *The Parisian Model*, and introduced two songs that are always identified with her, 'It's Delightful To Be Married' and 'I Just Can't Make My Eyes Behave'. Her success in this show, combined with her obvious star quality and potential, is said to have been one of the major factors in the impresario's decision to launch a series of lavish revues in 1907 which came to be known as the *Ziegfeld Follies*. These spectacular extravaganzas, full of beautiful women, talented performers, and the best popular songs of the time, continued annually for most of the 20s. In addition, Ziegfeld brought his talents as America's master showman to other (mostly) hit productions such as *The Soul Kiss* (1908), *Miss Innocence*, *Over The River*, *A Winsome Widow*, *The Century Girl*, *Miss 1917*, *Sally*, *Kid Boots*, *Annie Dear*, *Louie The 14th*, *Ziegfeld's American Revue*, later retitled *No Foolin'*, and *Betsy* (1926). After breaking up with Anna Held, Ziegfeld married the glamorous actress Billie Burke. He opened his own newly-built Ziegfeld Theatre in 1927 with *Rio Rita* which ran for nearly 500 performances, and the hits continued to flow with *Show Boat* (1927), *Rosalie*, *The Three Musketeers*, and *Whoopee* (1928). In 1929, with the Depression beginning to bite, he was not so fortunate with *Show Girl*, which only managed 111 performances, and to compound the failure, he suffered massive losses in the Wall Street Crash of the same year. *Bitter Sweet* (1929) was a bitter disapointment, and potential hits such as *Simple Simon* with its score by Richard Rodgers and Lorenz Hart, *Smiles* with Fred Astaire and his sister Adele, the last *Follies* of his lifetime (1931), and *Hot-Cha* (1932) with Bert Lahr, simply failed to take off. It is said that he would have been forced into bankrupcy if his revival of *Show Boat*, which opened at the Casino on 12 May 1932, had not been a substantial hit. Ironically, Ziegfeld, whose health had been failing for some time, died of pleurisy in July, two months into the run. His flamboyant career, coupled with a reputation as a notorious womaniser, has been the subject of at least four films: *The Great Ziegfeld* (1936) with William Powell which won two Oscars; *Ziegfeld Girl* (1941) with Judy Garland, Lana Turner, and Hedy Lamarr; *Ziegfeld Follies*, William Powell again, with Fred Astaire; and a television movie *Ziegfeld: The Man And His Women* (1978).

Further reading: *Ziegfeld, The Great Glorifier*, E. Cantor and D Freedman. *Ziegfeld*, C. Higham. *The World Of Flo Ziegfeld*, R. Carter. *The Ziegfeld Touch*, Richard and Paulette Ziegfeld.

Zorba

Two years after their great success with *Cabaret*, composer John Kander and lyricist Fred Ebb reunited first for *The Happy Time*, and then for this musical, which, like *Cabaret*, had an unusual and sometimes sinister theme. *Zorba* opened a the Imperial theatre in New York on 17 November 1968, with a book by Joseph Stein which was set in Crete and based on the novel *Zorba The Greek* by Nikos Kazantzakis. It told of the earthy and larger-than-life Zorba (Herschel Bernardi) and his young friend Nikos (John Cunningham), who has inherited a disused mine on the island. In spite of financial failures, and tragedies involving the deaths of those close to him, including the French prostitute Hortense (Maria Karnilova), who was in love with him, Zorba rises above it all, secure in the passionate belief that life is for living - right to the very end. Kander and Ebbs's score caught the style and mood of the piece perfectly with songs such as 'Y'assou', 'The First Time', "Life Is', 'The Top Of The Hill', 'No Boom Boom', 'The Butterfly'. 'Only Love', 'Happy Birthday', and 'I Am Free'. Boris Aronson won a Tony Award for his imaginative and colourful sets, and *Zorba* ran for 305 performances. In October 1983 the show was revived on Broadway with Anthony Quinn and Lila Kedrova who had won such acclaim for their performances in the 1964 film, *Zorba The Greek*. Kedrova won a Tony Award, and the production ran for longer than the original, a total of 362 performances.